Soft Power and Diplomatic Strategies in Asia and the Middle East

Mohamad Zreik
School of International Studies, Sun Yat-sen University, China

IGI Global
PUBLISHER of TIMELY KNOWLEDGE

A volume in the Advances in Public Policy and Administration (APPA) Book Series

Published in the United States of America by
IGI Global
Information Science Reference (an imprint of IGI Global)
701 E. Chocolate Avenue
Hershey PA, USA 17033
Tel: 717-533-8845
Fax: 717-533-8661
E-mail: cust@igi-global.com
Web site: http://www.igi-global.com

Library of Congress Cataloging-in-Publication Data

Names: Zreik, Mohamad, 1992- editor.
Title: Soft power and diplomatic strategies in Asia and the Middle East /
  edited by Mohamad Zreik.
Description: Hershey, PA : Information Science Reference, 2024. | Includes
  bibliographical references and index. | Summary: "This book provides an
  in-depth, comparative analysis of China's application of soft power in
  two distinct geopolitical contexts"-- Provided by publisher.
Identifiers: LCCN 2024014789 (print) | LCCN 2024014790 (ebook) | ISBN
  9798369324448 (hardcover) | ISBN 9798369347836 (paperback) | ISBN
  9798369324455 (ebook)
Subjects: LCSH: China--Foreign relations--21st century. | Asia--Foreign
  relations--China. | China--Foreign relations--Asia. | Middle
  East--Foreign relations--China. | China--Foreign relations--Middle East.
Classification: LCC JZ1734 .S639 2024 (print) | LCC JZ1734 (ebook) | DDC
  327.5105--dc23/eng/20240418
LC record available at https://lccn.loc.gov/2024014789
LC ebook record available at https://lccn.loc.gov/2024014790

This book is published in the IGI Global book series Advances in Public Policy and Administration (APPA) (ISSN: 2475-6644; eISSN: 2475-6652)

British Cataloguing in Publication Data
A Cataloguing in Publication record for this book is available from the British Library.

All work contributed to this book is new, previously-unpublished material. The views expressed in this book are those of the authors, but not necessarily of the publisher.

For electronic access to this publication, please contact: eresources@igi-global.com.

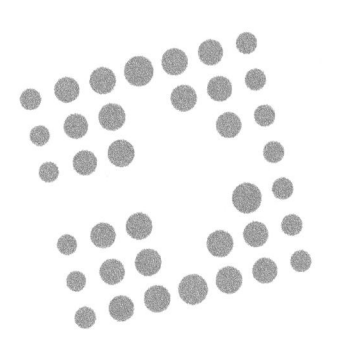

Advances in Public Policy and Administration (APPA) Book Series

ISSN:2475-6644
EISSN:2475-6652

Editor-in-Chief: Mohamad Zreik, Sun Yat-sen University, China

MISSION

Proper management of the public sphere is necessary in order to maintain order in modern society. Research developments in the field of public policy and administration can assist in uncovering the latest tools, practices, and methodologies for governing societies around the world.

The **Advances in Public Policy and Administration (APPA) Book Series** aims to publish scholarly publications focused on topics pertaining to the governance of the public domain. APPA's focus on timely topics relating to government, public funding, politics, public safety, policy, and law enforcement is particularly relevant to academicians, government officials, and upper-level students seeking the most up-to-date research in their field.

COVERAGE

- Government
- Law Enforcement
- Political Economy
- Politics
- Public Administration
- Public Funding
- Public Policy
- Resource allocation
- Urban Planning

> IGI Global is currently accepting manuscripts for publication within this series. To submit a proposal for a volume in this series, please contact our Acquisition Editors at Acquisitions@igi-global.com or visit: http://www.igi-global.com/publish/.

Titles in this Series

For a list of additional titles in this series, please visit:
http://www.igi-global.com/book-series/advances-public-policy-administration/97862

Economic and Societal Impact of Organized Crime Policy and Law Enforcement Interventions
Alicia Danielsson (University of Bolton, UK & Hume Institute for Postgraduate Studies, Switzerland)
Information Science Reference • © 2024 • 350pp • H/C (ISBN: 9798369303276) • US $240.00

The Convergence of Traditionalism and Populism in American Politics From Bannon to Trump
Adrian David Cheok (Nanjing University of Information Science and Technology, China)
Information Science Reference • © 2024 • 288pp • H/C (ISBN: 9781668492901) • US $235.00

Regulating Fair Competition Toward Sustainable Development Goals
Siti Fazilah Abdul Shukor (University of Tunku Abdul Rahman, Malaysia) Farahdilah Ghazali (University of Malaysia Terengganu, Malaysia) Nur Yuhanis Ismon (University of Tun Hussien Onn, Malaysia) and Aerni Isa (Taylor's University, Malaysia)
Information Science Reference • © 2024 • 285pp • H/C (ISBN: 9798369303900) • US $275.00

Analyzing Energy Crises and the Impact of Country Policies on the World
Merve Suna Özel Özcan (Kirikkale University, Turkey)
Engineering Science Reference • © 2024 • 283pp • H/C (ISBN: 9798369304402) • US $240.00

Using Crises and Disasters as Opportunities for Innovation and Improvement
Saeed Siyal (School of Economics and Management, Beijing University of Chemical Technology, China)
Information Science Reference • © 2024 • 323pp • H/C (ISBN: 9781668495223) • US $240.00

Cognitive Governance and the Historical Distortion of the Norm of Modern Development A Theory of Political Asymmetry
Renny Rueda (American University in the Emirates, UAE)
Information Science Reference • © 2024 • 254pp • H/C (ISBN: 9781668497944) • US $215.00

Financial Evaluation and Risk Management of Infrastructure Projects
Kleopatra Petroutsatou (Aristotle University of Thessaloniki, Greece) and Constantin Zopounidis (Technical University of Crete, Greece & Audencia Business School, France)
Information Science Reference • © 2024 • 248pp • H/C (ISBN: 9781668477861) • US $225.00

701 East Chocolate Avenue, Hershey, PA 17033, USA
Tel: 717-533-8845 x100 • Fax: 717-533-8661
E-Mail: cust@igi-global.com • www.igi-global.com

Table of Contents

Detailed Table of Contents

Chapter 1
    Ali Omidi, University of Isfahan, Iran
    Asma Emami, University of Isfahan, Iran

Soft power as one manifestation of power allows countries to gain influence through means such as political values, cultural diplomacy, and foreign policy attitudes. Iraq has become a venue for influential players such as Iran and the US to exert their soft power after 2003. Iran employs shared religious ties with the Shiite population in Iraq, promotes its independent anti-imperialist foreign policy as a value, highlights the shared geography and historical memories between the two countries, and applies other similar elements to enhance its soft power. On the other hand, the United States employs cultural attractions and promotes values such as freedom, democracy, and human rights. The United States presents itself as an idealistic democratic archetype and encourages Iraq to emulate its model in the post-Saddam era. The aim of this chapter is to provide a comparison of soft power status of Iran and the US in the post-Saddam Iraq.

Chapter 2
    Reema Roy, Asutosh College, India
    Piyush Kumar, Accenture, Kolkata, India
    Moumita Chatterjee, Aliah University, India
    Dhrubasish Sarkar, Supreme Institute of Management and Technology, India

Online social media platforms enable an individual or agency to communicate interactively and exchange of opinion. Twitter is a very popular platform worldwide for the exchange of opinions. The chapter tries to identify the effectiveness of social media diplomacy and effectiveness of the communication made on Twitter. The study wants to identify the role of Twitter in maintaining the international relations between India and China. There are three key factors that can be identified as the basis of the relationship. Those are business, boarder tension, and the cultural exchange. The study has taken two Twitter handles of Sun Weindong, Chinese Ambassador to India, @China_Amb_India, and India in China, Embassy of India Beijing, @EOIBeijing, for the analysis. The discourse analysis method and content analysis have been adopted by accessing Twitter data and news contents of the study. The study also investigates the impact on the users presenting the word cloud. This study shows a new path in the area of open diplomacy.

Chapter 3

China's Soft Power Diplomacy in Vietnam: Assessing the Dynamics and Efficacy of Belt and
Road Architecture 36

Mohor Chakraborty, South Calcutta Girls' College, India

China's economic rise, coupled with its military heft and soft power acculturation, stimulates a sense of enigma in international relations. The "Chinese dream" theorizes the realization of great national rejuvenation and comprehensive national power, and the BRI is ample evidence to this effect. This is discernible in the Southeast Asian region, demonstrated by China's credence and acceptability, notwithstanding the fact that many of these states share contested sovereignty claims with China in the disputed South China Sea. Vietnam's inclusion in the BRI offers a unique case study, as it endeavors to strike a harmonious balance between realism and neoliberal considerations of national interests. The BRI, in synergy with Vietnam's "Two Corridors, One Economic Circle" framework, offers the pedestal for bilateral cooperation. Given this backdrop, this chapter analyzes the dynamics, principal areas of cooperation within the BRI framework, and its social, political, and economic ramifications for Vietnam as well as on China's international image as facilitator of soft power.

Chapter 4

China's Soft Power Diplomatic Cooperation in Africa and the Middle East: Towards a Win-Win
Multilateral Cooperation? 59

Ndzalama Mathebula, University of Johannesburg, South Africa
Mohamad Zreik, Sun Yat-sen University, China

In the new global order foreign policy, bilateral and multilateral cooperation has come to be better understood and practiced through soft power as compared to coercive means (hard power). Many states globally have achieved their foreign policy through soft power diplomacy such as China. In this chapter, the authors aim to examine China's soft power through their infrastructure investment in the Middle East and the African continent. The crux of the study is not to review China's soft power and if their cooperation's yield a win-win outcome for all involved actors. Rather, the study is set to assess the value of China's soft power cooperation. The idea lies in quantifying the true value of China's soft power in a bilateral and multilateral settings and determining how much of a win each actor procures through the cooperation. This research adopts a qualitative method explored in a thematic and comparative research design. The comparative approach applied between the Middle East and Africa enable for China's soft power to be a dependent variable that can be applied in different regions simultaneously. Herein, the comparison enables the authors to compare China's foreign policy behavior in two distinct regions and settings and to further assess how these outcomes either reflect China's soft power or the state behavior in many of the Africa and the Middle East states.

Chapter 5

Chinese Discursive Strategies During the Syrian Civil War: Communicating Opposition to
Western Understanding of Human Rights and R2P 75

Matthieu Grandpierron, ICES, France
Eric Pomès, ICES, France

The Syrian situation crystallises all the questions related to the issue of the application of the responsibility to protect to sovereign states. It illustrates the delicate balance between the protection of human rights and international security. By contrast to the Russian position, China's has been more discreet and became more and more present in conjunction with the development of its geopolitical project Belt and Road Initiative. This chapter investigates all of these questions from the perspective of official Chinese discourses related to Syrian civil war. Beginning with the key assumption that what matters more to understanding how the Chinese view the international order is not what they say but how they say it, this chapter uses critical discourse analysis in order to unpack the implicit meanings of official Chinese narratives and views on the international order.

In the chapter, the defining characteristics of the national identity of the Chinese nation are explored, arguing that it directly affects the formation of the Chinese worldview in international relations. To discuss China at a qualitatively new level, the chapter examines the hidden correlations between Chinese state identity and Chinese history and political philosophy. There are also discussed several religious directions in China, which have played the significant role in the formation of Chinese identity and Statehood of China.

This chapter delves into the strategies employed by the Dominican Order in their missionary activities within the Ming and Qing dynasties of China. It underscores their initiatives to weave Western religious doctrines into the Chinese spiritual landscape, representing an early form of religious and cultural diplomacy. The engagement of the Order with local communities, their linguistic accomplishment, and their active involvement in the socio-political spheres of the region are explored in depth. Furthermore, the chapter scrutinized the social initiatives undertaken by the Order, particularly in relation to child welfare, and evaluates their impact on the social fabric of the era. Through a comprehensive investigation of the influence exerted by the Dominican Order in China, this study unveils the multifaceted nature of cultural exchange, shedding light on the lasting effects of these historical interactions on Sino-Iberian relations and the evolution of soft power dynamics.

The current study aims to investigate the role of media in fostering the Belt and Road Initiative (BRI) and serving Chinese foreign policy in the Arab region. The BRI, also known as the One Belt One Road initiative, is a Chinese government-led development strategy that aims to connect Asia, Europe, and Africa through a network of infrastructure projects, trade, and investment. The Arab region is a significant part of the BRI, and China's engagement in the region has been increasing in recent years. However, little is known about how media in China and the Arab region present and shape the public perception of BRI and its implications on Chinese foreign policy in the region. The research question of this study is: "How do Chinese and Arab media present and shape the public perception of BRI in the Arab region and its implications on Chinese foreign policy?" The results of this study will provide a comprehensive understanding of the role of media in shaping the public perception of BRI and its impact on Chinese foreign policy in the Arab region.

Chapter 9

This research seeks a strategic framework for Iran-China relations through the analytical method and using the theoretical model of interdependence. The main question of this research is to examine the variables of these strategic relations. The research hypothesis is that the three variables of transportation, energy, and security exist as platforms for cooperation between the two countries based on the "interdependence" model. Due to rapid industrial growth, China has an increasing demand for fossil energy. Iran's three relative advantages include the provision of a stable energy supply, secure transit access to Central Asia and the Eastern Mediterranean, and the establishment of security in the Middle East. This study first analyzes the nature of bilateral relations between Iran and China. The nature of Iran's objectives in bilateral relations with China comprises two levels: "economic" and "political". The nature of China's objectives in bilateral relations with Iran includes two levels: "geographical areas of China's soft power objectives" and "energy security". It then examines Iran's position in three situations based on China's soft power harmony under the Belt and Road project. Finally, the interdependence variables of Iran and China under the Belt and Road Initiative are analyzed.

Chapter 10

This chapter delves into China's soft power strategy through South-South Cooperation (SSC) in Asia, focusing on how its economic growth and cultural outreach enhance its regional influence. It examines China's self-identification as a developing country and its principle of non-intervention, which bolster its appeal among its SSC partners. The analysis identifies the Belt and Road Initiative (BRI) and the Global Development Initiative (GDI) as key to China's soft power in Asia, with both initiatives serving infrastructural development and cultural promotion without imposing political conditions. These efforts resonate in the Middle East and developing Asian countries, aligning with China's preference for engaging state actors to ensure regional stability. However, the chapter also highlights the limitations of China's quest for regional influence, particularly in the realm of public diplomacy.

Chapter 11

Soft power is a term coined by Joseph Nye whereby, in addition to command and obedience, power is primarily shown in the ability to influence the behaviour and goals of the other side through non-military means. These means of getting other states to share one's own goals and values range from negotiating skills to the seductive power of economic success models to cultural offerings between the production of dreams and ideology. Nye defines it as when a state can get others to admire its ideals and want what they want, but it does not have to spend as much on rewards or threats to move them in their direction. Therefore, seduction is seen as more effective than coercion, and many values, such as democracy, human rights, and individual opportunities, become deeply seductive. This chapter explores the development of the notion of soft power in international politics.

Chapter 12

Aileen Joy Adion Pactao, Palawan State University, Philippines

The era of globalization, which is characterized by intensified borderless exchanges and increased interconnectedness, pressures countries to reassess their use of 'hard power' in realizing nation's objectives as well as dealing with the global community. China has been recognizing the importance of 'soft power' – the need to enhance its global image. Primarily, this strategy is called 'charm offensive' which projects a "benign national image" to secure strong alliances and demonstrate itself as an epitome of social and economic success. This matter is another interesting subject of various discourses and not yet exhausted by existing knowledge production efforts and hence, the focus of this chapter. Specifically, through the use of secondary literature and scrutinization of policy statements and landmark speeches of officials, diplomats, and cultural agents of soft power, this chapter examines China's charm offensive in Southeast Asia – focusing on its sources, limits, and implications to the stability of the region.

Chapter 13

Md. Obaidullah, Daffodil International University, Bangladesh
Md. Showkat Raihan, University of Barishal, Bangladesh

In the current multipolar world, China has emerged as a formidable competitor to the United States, employing soft power strategies to expand its influence, particularly in South Asia—a region of strategic importance for both nations. This study utilizes Joseph Nye's soft power theory to comparatively analyze the approaches of China and the US. Employing case study analysis, including document research and content analysis, the research reveals that China strategically utilizes soft power by promoting its culture in educational institutions and leveraging the Belt and Road Initiative (BRI) for trade infrastructure development in South Asia. Conversely, the US relies on its renowned education system, attracting students from the region, and implements soft power through foreign aid, trade, investment, and security cooperation. As the global order undergoes transformations, comprehending these soft power dynamics is crucial for deciphering the intricacies of contemporary international relations.

Chapter 14

Habib Badawi, Lebanese University, Lebanon
Karim Wattar, Lebanese American University, Lebanon

In an epoch defined by China's staggering economic ascent, the global panorama witnesses an expansive sprawl of Beijing's interests, notably in regions as diverse as the Middle East and North Africa. Central to this burgeoning influence is China's deft and strategic employment of "soft power" strategies, fostering calculated and symbiotic "strategic partnerships" with Arab states. This diplomatic approach, characterized by nuanced elements such as non-interventionism, cultural dissemination, and collaborative economic ventures, stands as a linchpin in China's diplomatic toolkit. In the face of Western portrayals casting shadows of a "Chinese menace," Beijing finds itself compelled to vehemently defend its peaceful policy objectives. Beyond mere economic gains, China's motives are laced with geopolitical and geostrategic considerations, adding layers of depth to its engagements. This meticulously orchestrated outreach encapsulates a significant facet of China's broader recalibration towards the Western sphere. This chapter undertakes a comprehensive exploration of the intricate and manifold facets of China's soft power diplomacy, offering a panoramic view of its profound influence extending across the intricate landscapes of Asia and the Middle East. Through a nuanced lens, it illuminates the mosaic of strategies, motivations, and implications that underpin China's burgeoning presence in these pivotal regions, painting a vivid tapestry of its ever-evolving global entrenchment. Various sources are used as support for the chapter. Press conferences, readings, academic journals, and scholarly articles are just some of the references found in the chapter. Additionally, expert opinions from well-renowned scholars were taken into consideration about China's growing influence in Asia and the Middle East in the fields of trade, technology, and politics. Furthermore, visual representations, such as images and graphs, are placed to facilitate selected aspects for the readers.

Chapter 15

Mohamad Al Mokdad, CEDS, Paris, France
Weam Karkout, Lebanese University, Lebanon

This research deals with the study of the soft power and its effects on one of the most important regions in the world, which is the Middle East region, and it was found that through soft power, a country can penetrate other countries through a variety of tools without resorting to hard power. Three components of soft power were found—culture, political values, and foreign policy—as soft power does not mean concern for national interests only and ignoring the interests of others. By getting to know the components of American and Chinese soft power that have been identified in research and the continuous growth that is happening rapidly, both United States of America and China have been able to build soft power in areas that include political, economic, social, and technological. They have played the tools of soft power. Culture, foreign policy, and political values have an important role in establishing the principle of peace and international and regional cooperation. The study found that there are effects of the soft power of both countries in the Middle East, especially the Arab region, especially since the Chinese economic rise has made the Arab states the first supplier of oil, and that China's investments in the Arab Gulf region in various fields have contributed to the impact of its economic tools in the region. On the other hand, Chinese and American exports, including the military industries, increased to the Arab states, and they occupied advanced ranks in the import table. In addition, China and USA seek to find an important role for it in the future in protecting international shipping lines in the region to protect its growing economic interests. The study showed the difference regarding the way each of the two countries deal with soft power and its impact on the Middle East region.

Chapter 16

Enkhzul Buyandlai, Mandakh University, Mongolia
Ariunaa Lkhagvajav, University of Finance and Economics, Mongolia
Myadagmaa Bayartsogt, Dornod University, Mongolia

The study examines the effectiveness of investing in higher education, specifically providing scholarships for Mongolian students, in the context of China's soft power in higher education. A combination of quantitative and qualitative data analysis techniques was employed to identify China's influence on

Mongolian education. The questionnaire was used for gathering quantitative data. The satisfaction survey included eight variables including reliability, correlation, regression, and crosstabulation. During the interview, participants were asked seven questions about their study experience in China. Additionally, the case study evaluated the advantages and disadvantages of studying in China based on the personal experiences of the participants. The study concluded with a SWOT and TOWS analysis. This level of satisfaction can be determined by various factors such as education outcomes, economic efficiency, cultural and social improvement, comparison of education quality with other countries, personal needs or development, and overall satisfaction with education in China.

In the era of globalization, the problem of national image becomes more prominent, and international brand marketing becomes one of the powerful ways for a country to enhance its national image. National branding is an active process aimed at enhancing the reputation of a country, while national image is something that exists in the perception of the audience. Since the reform and opening-up, China's comprehensive national strength has continuously increased, and the world's perception of China has become stronger. Chinese enterprises and brands have gradually overcome the stereotypical impression of being low-quality and cheap. However, in the increasingly fierce competition among major powers, it is urgent to construct China's national image through national brand marketing. China should implement a nation brand plan from a top-level design, involve the entire society, strengthen open communication with the international community, and further promote Chinese enterprises and brands to go global.

In the context of increasing strategic competition between the United States (US) and China in the Indo-Pacific region, soft power has become an important tool in implementing foreign policy, enhancing the overall national power, especially for emerging superpowers like China. To achieve the goal of becoming a global superpower comparable to the US, China has focused on increasing its soft power in countries with important geopolitical positions on the regional and global map. Accordingly, Vietnam is China's neighboring country with a strategic position for China's process of expanding its power in Southeast Asia. Therefore, Vietnam is one of the countries most strongly affected by China's strategy to increase its soft power in strategic competition with the US. This chapter aims to analyze the opportunities and challenges that China's strategy to increase its soft power brings to Vietnam through political-diplomatic, economic-commercial, cultural educational fields.

Preface

Soft power has emerged as a defining feature of contemporary international relations, reshaping the dynamics of diplomacy and global influence. In the midst of this evolving landscape, the ascendancy of China stands out as one of the most profound geopolitical shifts of the 21st century. As China expands its presence and asserts its influence across diverse regions, it strategically harnesses the elements of soft power alongside conventional diplomatic tools.

This edited volume, *Soft Power and Diplomatic Strategies in Asia and the Middle East*, delves into the complexities of China's soft power diplomacy, focusing on its engagements in two contrasting geopolitical landscapes: the Middle East and East Asia. Through a comparative lens, this book offers a nuanced exploration of how China navigates its foreign policy objectives in these distinct contexts.

The contributors to this volume represent a diverse array of expertise, spanning disciplines such as international relations, Asian studies, and political science. Their contributions collectively provide a comprehensive analysis of the strategies, mechanisms, and channels through which China fosters relationships and projects its influence in the Middle East and East Asia.

The primary objective in compiling this volume is to fill a noticeable gap in the existing scholarship. While numerous studies have examined China's foreign policy, there remains a dearth of focused, comparative analyses on its soft power application in these specific regions. By addressing this gap, it aims to offer fresh insights, provoke further academic inquiry, and contribute to a deeper understanding of China's evolving role in global affairs.

This book is intended to be a resource not only for academics and researchers but also for policymakers, diplomats, and practitioners involved in shaping international relations. By offering a blend of theoretical frameworks, empirical analyses, and case studies, it is hoped to provide practical insights that inform informed decision-making and strategic planning.

The topics covered in this volume range from cultural exchanges and economic collaborations to religious engagements and digital diplomacy. Each chapter offers a unique perspective on different facets of China's soft power strategies, shedding light on its adaptability, complexities, and implications for global geopolitics.

As editor, I am immensely grateful to the contributors for their scholarly contributions and dedication to this project. I believe that their expertise and insights will enrich the academic discourse surrounding China's soft power diplomacy and contribute to a more nuanced understanding of contemporary international relations.

In conclusion, I hope that this edited volume serves as a catalyst for further research, dialogue, and collaboration in the field of soft power diplomacy. By examining China's diplomatic strategies in Asia and the Middle East, I aim to contribute to a broader conversation on the evolving dynamics of global power and the role of soft power in shaping international relations.

Chapter 1: A Comparative Analysis of the Soft Power of Iran and US in the Post-Saddam Iraq: Soft Power

Ali Omidi and Asma Emami from the University of Isfahan, Iran, meticulously compare the soft power strategies employed by Iran and the United States in post-Saddam Iraq. By highlighting elements such as religion, foreign policy stance, geography, and historical narratives, the authors dissect how both nations seek to influence Iraqi perceptions. Through a descriptive-analytical approach, they assess the reactions of the Iraqi populace towards these soft power dynamics.

Chapter 2: A Discourse Analysis of Twitter Communication to Foster Digital Diplomacy Between India and China

Reema Roy, Piyush Kumar, Moumita Chatterjee, and Dhrubasish Sarkar from various Indian institutions delve into the role of Twitter in facilitating digital diplomacy between India and China. Through discourse and content analysis, they examine the effectiveness of Twitter communication in maintaining international relations, focusing on factors such as business, border tensions, and cultural exchanges.

Chapter 3: China's Soft Power Diplomacy in Vietnam: Assessing the Dynamics and Efficacy of Belt and Road Architecture

Mohor Chakraborty from South Calcutta Girls' College, India, scrutinizes China's soft power diplomacy in Vietnam within the Belt and Road Initiative (BRI) framework. By analyzing areas of cooperation and their socio-political and economic ramifications, the chapter sheds light on China's influence in Vietnam and its broader international image as a soft power facilitator.

Chapter 4: China's Soft Power Diplomatic Cooperation in Africa and the Middle East: Towards a Win-Win Multilateral Cooperation?

Ndzalama Mathebula from the University of Johannesburg, South Africa, and Mohamad Zreik from Sun Yat-sen University, China, explore China's soft power diplomacy through infrastructure investments in Africa and the Middle East. Employing qualitative methods, they aim to assess the value and outcomes of China's soft power cooperation in these regions, emphasizing win-win outcomes for all involved parties.

Chapter 5: Chinese Discursive Strategies During the Syrian Civil War: Communicating Opposition to Western Understanding of Human Rights and R2P

Matthieu Grandpierron and Eric Pomès from ICES, France, investigate China's discursive strategies during the Syrian civil war, focusing on its opposition to Western narratives on human rights and Responsibility to Protect (R2P). Through critical discourse analysis, they uncover implicit meanings in official Chinese narratives, shedding light on China's views on the international order.

Chapter 6: Chinese State Identity and Its Place in the International System

Nika Chitadze from International Black Sea University, Georgia, explores the correlation between Chinese state identity and its worldview in international relations. By delving into Chinese history, political philosophy, and religious directions, the chapter elucidates how state identity shapes China's international engagements.

Chapter 7: Dominican Missionary Strategies in Ming and Qing China

Zhicang Huang from Sun Yat-sen University, China, delves into the missionary strategies employed by the Dominican Order during the Ming and Qing dynasties in China. Through an exploration of their cultural and religious initiatives, linguistic proficiency, and social engagement, the chapter illuminates the early forms of religious and cultural diplomacy, shedding light on their lasting impact on Sino-Iberian relations.

Chapter 8: Media's Role in Fostering the Belt and Road Initiative and Chinese Foreign Policy in the Arab Region

Tianzhe Qi and Wei Hou from various Chinese institutions investigate the role of media in promoting the Belt and Road Initiative (BRI) and shaping Chinese foreign policy in the Arab region. By analyzing media portrayal and public perception of the BRI, the chapter provides insights into how media influences regional dynamics and perceptions of Chinese initiatives.

Chapter 9: Reflections on the Development of Strategic Relations Between Iran and China

Jamal Mokhtari from Ferdowsi University of Mashhad, Iran, presents a strategic framework for examining Iran-China relations through the lens of interdependence theory. By assessing variables such as transportation, energy, and security, the chapter evaluates the potential for strategic cooperation between the two nations, offering insights into their evolving relationship dynamics.

Chapter 10: Silk Roads of Influence: China's Soft Power and South-South Cooperation in Asia

Inayat Kalim and Asad Hyatt from COMSATS University, Islamabad, Pakistan, delve into China's soft power strategy through South-South Cooperation in Asia. By analyzing the Belt and Road Initiative (BRI) and the Global Development Initiative (GDI), the chapter examines how China's economic and cultural outreach shapes its regional influence, while also highlighting the limitations of its soft power efforts.

Chapter 11: Soft Power: An Enduring Notion in Contemporary International Politics

Sureyya Yigit from New Vision University, Georgia, provides a comprehensive overview of the concept of soft power in contemporary international politics. By exploring Joseph Nye's framework and its applications, the chapter examines the dynamics of influence and persuasion in global affairs, emphasizing the importance of non-coercive means in achieving foreign policy objectives.

Chapter 12: Soft Power and Power Contest: Great Power Contest in Southeast Asia: Sources and Limits of China's Charm Offensive

Aileen Joy Pactao from Palawan State University, Philippines, analyzes China's charm offensive in Southeast Asia amid intensifying strategic competition with the United States. By examining the sources, limits, and implications of China's soft power strategy, the chapter provides insights into its impact on regional stability and geopolitics.

Chapter 13: Soft Power Competition: A Comparative Analysis of China and the US in South Asia

Md. Obaidullah from Daffodil International University, Bangladesh, and Md. Raihan from the University of Barishal, Bangladesh, conduct a comparative analysis of soft power strategies employed by China and the US in South Asia. Through case studies and content analysis, the chapter examines the approaches of both nations, highlighting their respective strengths and weaknesses in the region.

Chapter 14: Soft Power Diplomacy: China's Influence in Asia and the Middle East

Habib Badawi from Lebanese University, Lebanon, and Karim Wattar from Lebanese American University, Lebanon, explore China's soft power diplomacy in Asia and the Middle East. By examining strategic partnerships and economic engagements, the chapter assesses China's efforts to cultivate influence and counter Western narratives, offering insights into its evolving role in the region.

Chapter 15: Soft Power Dynamics: Analyzing Chinese and American Influence in the Middle East

Mohamad Al Mokdad from CEDS-Paris, France, and Weam Karkout from Lebanese University, Lebanon, investigate the soft power dynamics of China and the US in the Middle East. Through an examination of cultural, political, and foreign policy influences, the chapter elucidates the differing approaches of both nations and their impact on the region.

Chapter 16: The Impact of China's Soft Power on the Educational Development of Young Mongolians

Enkhzul Buyandlai from Mandakh University, Mongolia, Ariunaa Lkhagvajav from the University of Finance and Economics, Mongolia, and Myadagmaa Bayartsogt from Dornod University, Mongolia, evaluate the impact of China's soft power on the educational development of young Mongolians. Through a combination of quantitative and qualitative analysis, the chapter assesses the effectiveness of Chinese educational initiatives in Mongolia, providing insights into their outcomes and implications.

Chapter 17: The Interconstruction of China's National Brand and National Image

Jiaxi Zhou from Shanghai Academy of Social Sciences, China, explores the interplay between China's national brand and national image in the era of globalization. By examining national branding strategies and international perceptions, the chapter elucidates how China constructs and enhances its global image through branding initiatives.

Chapter 18: The Soft Power Impact of China in Strategic Competition with the United States in Vietnam

Kiet Le Hoang, Hiep Tran, Minh Nguyen Anh, and Phúc Nguyễn from various Vietnamese institutions examine China's soft power impact in Vietnam amid strategic competition with the United States. By analyzing China's charm offensive and its implications for regional stability, the chapter offers insights into the dynamics of great power rivalry in Southeast Asia.

These chapters collectively offer a comprehensive exploration of soft power dynamics in diverse geopolitical contexts, providing valuable insights into China's evolving role in international affairs.

In closing, the chapters compiled in this volume offer a multifaceted examination of China's soft power diplomacy in the complex geopolitical landscapes of Asia and the Middle East. Soft power, as elucidated by Joseph Nye, has become increasingly instrumental in shaping international relations, often serving as a more effective tool than traditional forms of coercion or military might.

The ascendancy of China as a global power has been accompanied by a strategic deployment of soft power tactics, aimed at enhancing its influence, promoting its interests, and shaping international perceptions. Through initiatives such as the Belt and Road Initiative (BRI), cultural exchanges, media campaigns, and economic partnerships, China seeks to cultivate relationships and project its image as a responsible global actor.

The diverse array of perspectives presented in this volume underscores the complexity of China's soft power strategies and their varied implications across different regions. From the comparative analysis of China's soft power in South Asia and the Middle East to the examination of its impact on educational development in Mongolia, each chapter offers unique insights into the mechanisms and dynamics of China's diplomatic engagement.

Furthermore, the chapters shed light on the interplay between China's soft power and other key players in the international arena, such as the United States and regional actors like India and Vietnam. This interplay highlights the intricate dynamics of great power competition and cooperation, as well as the evolving nature of diplomacy in a multipolar world.

As editor, I believe that this volume makes a significant contribution to the scholarly discourse on soft power diplomacy and China's role in global affairs. By providing a comprehensive analysis of China's soft power strategies in diverse contexts, we aim to deepen our understanding of the complexities of contemporary international relations and offer valuable insights for policymakers, academics, and practitioners alike.

I extend my heartfelt gratitude to the contributors for their invaluable contributions and dedication to this project. Their expertise and scholarly rigor have enriched this volume and enhanced our understanding of the complex dynamics of soft power diplomacy in the 21st century.

In conclusion, I hope that this volume serves as a catalyst for further research, dialogue, and collaboration in the field of soft power diplomacy. By fostering a deeper understanding of China's diplomatic strategies and their implications, we aspire to contribute to a more informed and nuanced approach to global governance and cooperation in the years to come.

Mohamad Zreik
School of International Studies, Sun Yat-sen University, China

Chapter 1
A Comparative Analysis of the Soft Power of Iran and US in Post–Saddam Iraq

Ali Omidi
https://orcid.org/0000-0003-1882-0456
University of Isfahan, Iran

Asma Emami
University of Isfahan, Iran

ABSTRACT

Soft power as one manifestation of power allows countries to gain influence through means such as political values, cultural diplomacy, and foreign policy attitudes. Iraq has become a venue for influential players such as Iran and the US to exert their soft power after 2003. Iran employs shared religious ties with the Shiite population in Iraq, promotes its independent anti-imperialist foreign policy as a value, highlights the shared geography and historical memories between the two countries, and applies other similar elements to enhance its soft power. On the other hand, the United States employs cultural attractions and promotes values such as freedom, democracy, and human rights. The United States presents itself as an idealistic democratic archetype and encourages Iraq to emulate its model in the post-Saddam era. The aim of this chapter is to provide a comparison of soft power status of Iran and the US in the post-Saddam Iraq.

INTRODUCTION

Soft power can be defined as the ability to influence others and achieve desired outcomes through attraction rather than coercion or inducement. It is based on shaping the beliefs and desires of others in a way that leads to obedience and compliance. Soft power is distinct from hard power, which relies on economic and military strength. Joseph Nye, a prominent scholar on soft power, identifies culture, values, and foreign policy as sources of soft power. Culture becomes a source of soft power when it is attractive

DOI: 10.4018/979-8-3693-2444-8.ch001

to others, values are influential when they are upheld domestically and internationally, and foreign policy gains soft power when it is perceived to have moral authority. Soft power is cost-effective, persuasive, and can produce desired results in international relations, making it a focus for politicians and foreign policy decision-makers (Nye, 2010).

The United States has recognized the importance of soft power in its foreign policy, particularly during the presidency of Barack Obama. After the military invasion of Iraq and the fall of the Baath regime, the United States faced growing resentment among the Iraqi people. Asymmetric armed resistance groups posed challenges to American security interests. In response, the United States shifted its strategy in Iraq and focused on soft power, emphasizing cultural dimensions and promoting values such as freedom, democracy, and human rights.

The Islamic Republic of Iran, as a regional power with geographical proximity to Iraq and a shared religious and ethnic identity with Iraq's Shiite and Kurdish populations, actively sought to maximize its interests in Iraq following Saddam Hussein's fall. Iran emphasized the shared Shia geopolitical context, highlighted common identity and similarities, and employed its anti-Zionist and anti-occupation foreign policy as soft power tools.

Considering that both Iran and the United States have utilized soft leverages, as well as hard power to exert influence in post-Saddam Iraq, this research provide a comparison of Iran and the US soft power's ingredients in post-Saddam Iraq, and examine the attitudes of the Iraqi people towards these two states.

Iran's Soft Power in Iraq

Iran's cultural power and influence in Iraq have significant dimensions, particularly when it comes to the role of Shia religion. The proximity of Iran to the Persian Gulf region, where the majority of Shiites in the Middle East reside, gives Iran a central position of influence. Iran itself is home to a large portion of the Shiite population in the region, making it a significant center of religious and cultural influence (Dorj and Hedayati Shahidani, 2021: 87). Religion holds a vital place in the relations between Iraq and Iran, given that Iraq has the second-largest Shiite population in the world. Iraqi Shiites comprise around 60% of the country's population, primarily consisting of Arabic speakers and including smaller numbers of Kurds and Turkmen (Jafari and Nikravesh, 2015). This makes Iraq a strategic country for Iran, as most other countries in the region are predominantly Sunni and aligned with Saudi Arabia and other influential Sunni nations.

The existence of sacred sites in both countries and religious tourism also serve as capacities for the Islamic Republic of Iran to exercise soft power in Iraq. Iran possesses Shiite holy places like the Holy Shrine of Imam Reza, Hazrat Masoumeh, and the Jamkaran Mosque, attracting numerous tourists from all over the world, particularly from neighboring Iraq. Every year, hundreds of thousands of Iraqis travel to Iran to visit these holy places, with Mashhad and Qom being their primary destinations. During their stay, these pilgrims can be influenced by Iranian culture, subsequently acting as promoters of Iranian culture upon their return to Iraq. Additionally, Iraq is home to the shrines of several prophets (including Adam, Noah, Seth Wasi, Yunus, and Shoaib Nabi) and the holy shrine of Hazrat Abul Fazl Abbas, along with the holy shrines of six Shia imams in Najaf and Karbala. These sites hold special importance and attraction, and they receive approximately 40,000 Iranian pilgrims each month (Jadidi et al., 2022: 44).

Another significant cultural event that showcases the two countries' cultural affinity is the commemoration and observance of the Muharram days (Tasu'a and Ashura ceremonies). Every year, a large number of Iranian Muslims participate in the Arbaeen walking ceremony, gathering on the 40th day after the martyrdom of Imam Hussein. It is estimated that three to four million religious tourists, mainly from Iran, visit the holy cities of Iraq during the commemoration of Ashura Husayn in Arbaeen (Jadidi et al., 2022: 44). This event, which is the world's largest annual religious gathering, effectively transfers Iranian culture to Iraq. The Arbaeen March serves as a cross-border activity that facilitates cultural, social, executive, and economic interactions between Iran and Iraq, thereby bolstering Iran's influence in Iraq through soft power. The Arbaeen March plays a pivotal role in promoting and perpetuating these shared values between Iran and Iraq, serving as a foundation for a long-term strategy to enhance cultural interactions between the two nations. The involvement of elites and policymakers can further deepen and solidify the impact of the Arbaeen March on Iran-Iraq relations. In summary, the Arbaeen March has six key effects on Iran's soft power in Iraq: it strengthens public diplomacy efforts in Iran, fosters citizen diplomacy, establishes social connections between Iran and Iraq, mitigates tensions between Arab and Persian communities, facilitates joint operations rooms, and establishes an Arbaeen headquarters. Consequently, the religious practice of the Arbaeen March has a positive influence on Iran's soft power in Iraq, supporting the claims made by practice theorists in the field of International Relations that practices possess ontological significance in shaping international phenomena independently (Masoudi & Nourian, 2023).

The seminaries and religious authorities in Iran, particularly in the city of Qom, and Iraq, particularly in Najaf, hold significant influence and serve as sources of Iran's soft power in post-Saddam Iraq. The continuous interaction between these centers of religious education and knowledge has allowed Iranians to exert considerable influence on the people of Iraq. Often, protest movements against foreign presence or the government in Iraq are led by religious authorities with the support of the Islamic Republic of Iran. The religious scholars and students from both Iran and Iraq form a crucial source of soft power for Iran in Iraq (Amjadian et al., 2022: 2544).

The institution of religious authority or Marja, being trans-territorial in nature, plays a substantial role in Iran's influence in Iraq due to the trans-territorial nature of Shiism. At times throughout history, there has been a single Shia authority for followers of this religion, as seen in the tobacco embargo and the influence of a single authority. Ayatollah Sistani, one of the most influential references for taqlid (religious emulation) in Iraq, has played a prominent role in shaping Iraq's constitution and legal framework. His close ties with Iran, as well as his meetings with Iranian officials, further solidified Iran's soft power in Iraq (Amjadian et al., 2022).

Additionally, Iran has established various educational institutions and universities, both scientific and religious that attract foreign students, particularly Shiite students from Iraq. Institutions such as Al-Mustafa International University, the University of Religions and Denominations, the University of Islamic Denominations, the Ahl al-Bayt Institute of Higher Education, and the Imam Khomeini Educational and Research Institute have provided education to thousands of Iraqi students in Iran. These educational facilities have contributed to Iran's soft power in Iraq (Mehr News Agency, 2023; Iran's Student Affairs Organization, 2023). Overall, the religious and cultural ties between Iran and Iraq, facilitated by pilgrimages, religious institutions, and educational exchanges, have significantly enhanced Iran's soft power in Iraq, shaping perceptions, and fostering a sense of common identity and civilization.

Iranian films and series are known as family and moral films without sexual scenes and vulgar language throughout Iraq, especially in Kurdistan, and have opened their place in the hearts of the viewers of this region. According to statistics, nearly 70% of the people of Iraqi Kurdistan watch Iranian serials. So far, several Iranian historical series with a large audience, including Hazrat Yusuf, Imam Ali, Men of Angels, Mukhtar, etc., have been aired on Iraqi channels and have met with wide welcome. One of the reasons why Iraqis like Iranian series and cartoons is the cultural commonality and religious and religious adjacencies and the traditions and beliefs of the nations of the two countries (iribnews, 2018).

Al-Alam Network was established in February 2003 by Iran in order to inform and cover daily news for Arabic-speaking people. This network has news offices in Tehran, Baghdad, and Beirut and airs programs to approximately 300 million Arabic-speaking viewers, who are mainly present in the Persian Gulf and the Mediterranean. The latest poll conducted in the field of news media is proof of the claim that this network is the fifth most popular news network that has been able to overtake other networks such as BBC Arabic and Al-Hura (ISNA, 2009). Attracting this number of audiences in Arab countries is largely due to the fact that this network has been able to reflect the desires of Arab audiences in the region. The channel al-Mayadeen, based in Beirut and established in 2012, is widely believed to receive funding from the Iranian government. It extensively covers Iraqi affairs and seems to have attracted some viewership previously associated with Al-Alam. Al-Kawthar, launched in 2006 by IRIB and headquartered in Tehran, is a religious channel owned by the state. Within Iraq, there are several channels that align with Iran's ideology. The actual number of viewers is a subject of debate, as Facebook 'likes' (although not a completely reliable indicator) suggest that the most popular channels have a viewership ranging from 2 to 5 million (Watkins, 2020).

One of the primary tenets of Iranian foreign policy is opposition to occupation and domination. Iran's independent stance and its resistance against the United States are regarded as valuable, attracting numerous individuals and groups who oppose imperialism and criticize the unjust structure of international politics. This attitude serves as a platform for Iran's soft power. As a result, Iran has provided both spiritual and material support to liberation movements in the Middle East, particularly in occupied Palestine. The Islamic Republic's backing of militant groups and liberation movements in countries like Lebanon, Palestine, Yemen, and Iraq has bolstered Iran's positive image. Many people regard Iran as a role model and often follow the guidance of Iranian leaders and authorities.

The Islamic Republic of Iran's efforts in combating ISIS and terrorism have effectively enhanced its favorable perception among the Iraqi people. When ISIS emerged in Iraq, Iran promptly dispatched its military and civilian forces to provide assistance without hesitation. This unwavering support contributed to the development of a positive perception of Iran among Iraqis. According to the Guardian newspaper, Iran has exerted the greatest influence in the fight against ISIS in Iraq and has consequently garnered significant popularity among the local population (The Guardian, 2015). Iran sent more than 1,000 advisers from the Quds branch of the Islamic Revolutionary Guard Corps to help the Iraqi security forces. The role of the Quds Force has been to reactivate, arm, and train the Shiite military forces established in Iraq against terrorism (Kirkpatrik, 2020). According to the statements of Brigadier General Masoud Jazayeri, Iran was able to help Iraq in the best way by mobilizing the masses of all ethnic groups against ISIS (Daily Telegraph, 2014). After ISIS attacked several Kurdish cities, including Shingal, and when the capital of the Kurdistan Region (Erbil) was endangered, Iran was the first country to provide weapons to the Kurdistan Regional Government to fight ISIS (Geranmayeh, 2017). Furthermore, Iran's important role in protecting the territorial integrity of Iraq during the issue of Kurdistan's claim for independence in 2020, not only strengthened the political forces friendly to Iran in the political arena of this country, but also made Iran a strategic and reliable ally for the Baghdad government. With the support of the Iraqi military and paramilitary forces, Iranian forces guarded the Shiite religious centers and the cities around them and pushed the terrorists back from important cities such as Tikrit in 2015 (Wood, 2015) and Mosul in 2017. Therefore, Iran's anti-terrorism policies in Iraq have significantly had an enormous level of influence in this country.

Economically, Iran's economic influence in Iraq has also led to the expansion of its soft power in this country. In the meantime, after the 2003 US-led attacks on Iraq, Iran became Iraq's largest trading partner; so this bilateral trade reached 4 billion dollars (Katzman, 2008: 4). Furthermore, the Iranian government and state-owned companies have made significant investments in the reconstruction of Iraq. Particularly, Iraq's two holy cities, Najaf and Karbala, which are the holiest Shiite sites and attract hundreds of thousands of Iranian pilgrims each year, are receiving substantial investments from Iranian state-owned companies. The governor of Najaf province has reported that the Iranian government allocates an annual budget of 20 million dollars for construction projects aimed at enhancing the tourism infrastructure of the city. (Wong, 2007: 4-5).

Iran's involvement in the reconstruction of Iraq extends beyond the restoration of shrines. It actively engages in various other sectors, including the development of Iraq's electricity network. In recent years, Iraq has entered into agreements to import electricity and natural gas from Iran, offering a convenient and cost-effective solution to address its persistent electricity shortages. In 2013, Iraq signed a contract to directly purchase up to 1,200 megawatts of electricity from Iran (Oktav, 2018). Cooperation in the field of rail transportation, bank transfers and insurance coverage, railways, and cancellation of visa fees are also among the agreements made between the two countries. Dozens of large Iranian companies are active in Iraqi construction projects in the fields of road construction, power plants, bridges, stadiums, and water and sewage treatment plants. Examining Iran customs data shows that Iran's export of non-oil goods to Iraq increased from 6 billion dollars in 2013 to 10 billion in 2022 (Financial Tribune, 2023).

While Iran's soft power elements possess strength in Iraq, its fluctuating political landscape has led to significant variations in its popularity among the Iraqi people. Mediating variables strongly influence Iraqi public sentiment towards Iran. Following the emergence of ISIS in 2014, Iran provided assistance to Iraq in repelling jihadist attacks, and Iranian-affiliated armed groups fought against ISIS as part of the Popular Mobilization Forces (Hashd al-Shaabi). This factor substantially bolstered trust in the Islamic Republic of Iran and fostered the belief that Iran is a reliable partner in Iraq, particularly among the Shiite population. In 2014, 86% of Shiites expressed trust in Iran (Figure 1). As per, a public opinion poll conducted in 2017 revealed that nearly 70% of Iraqis viewed Iran positively. However, the same poll conducted in 2020 indicated a significant decline in Iran's popularity. In fact, the percentage of Iraqi Shiites with a favorable attitude towards the Islamic Republic of Iran decreased from 88% in 2015 to 15% in 2020 (Bardakci, 2023:2).

This negative view has continued in 2023 (Figure 2), possibly because Iraqi people perceive Iran as a hindrance to their nation's cohesion. During the Davos Summit, Iraqi Foreign Minister Fawad Hossein stated that the people of his country are bearing the consequences of the tension between Washington and Tehran. He also criticized Tehran's attack on Erbil (2024), deeming it a violation of international law, and mentioned that Iraq intends to file a complaint with the Security Council. Hossein further asserted, "It is unfortunate that there is tension between Washington and Tehran. Typically, when there is tension between these two countries, Iraqis pay the price, and conflict erupts on Iraqi soil. Now, with the tension between Israel and Iran, the situation remains the same" (The Cradel, 2024). Sometimes Iraqis scapegoat Iran for their economic hardships, national unity and political problems.

The US Soft Power in Iraq

The presence of the US military in Iraq has contributed to an increase in anti-American sentiments among certain segments of the Iraqi population. For many Iraqis, the US military presence represents

Figure 1. Iraqis who believe that Iran is a reliable ally number (percent)
Source: IIACSS (2019: 21)

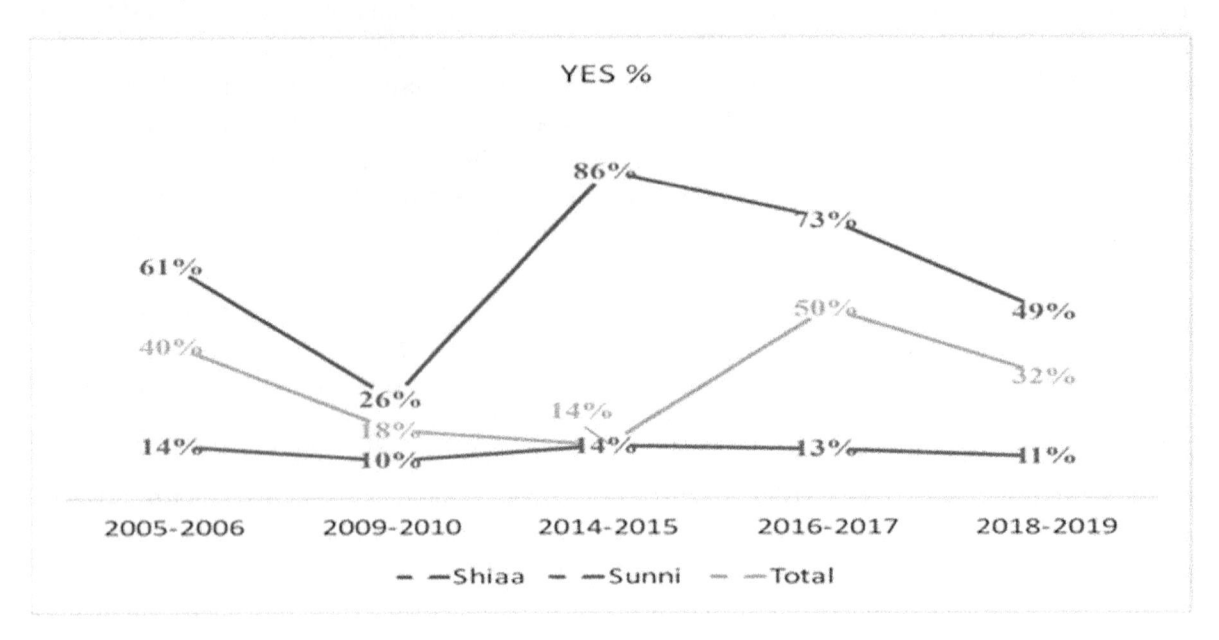

humiliation and occupation, with the Abu Ghraib prison scandal severely damaging the image of the United States (Nye, 2004). In response, the United States has employed soft power strategies to bolster its influence and rebuild its reputation in Iraq. It has sought to promote values and ideals such as freedom, democracy, and human rights as a model for post-war Iraq. The United States has actively advocated

Figure 2. Iran in Iraqi public opinion
Source: Bardakci (2023: 2-3

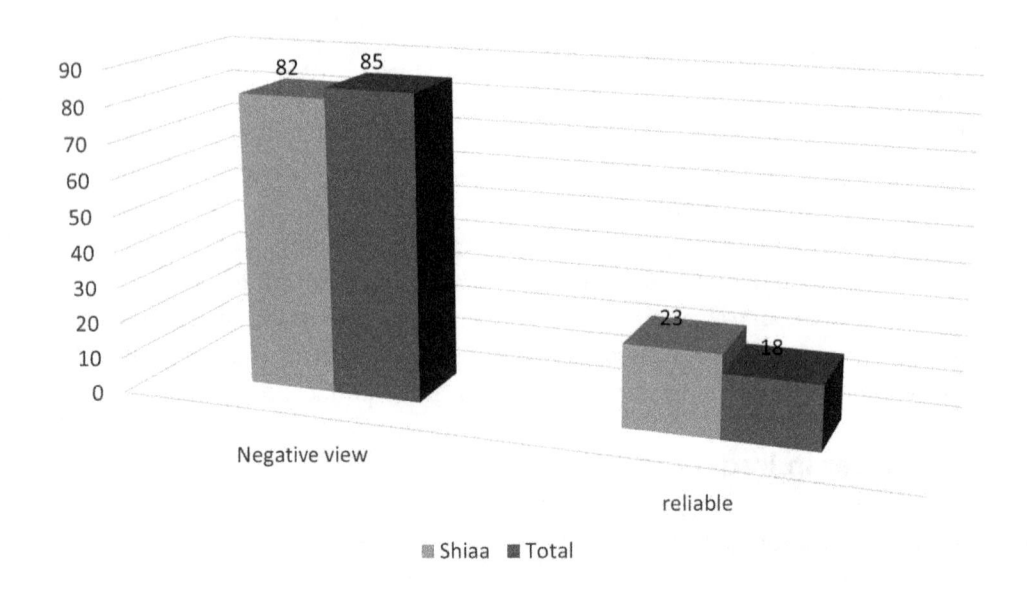

for democratic values and institutions in Iraq, particularly following the overthrow of Saddam Hussein's regime. Efforts to establish a democratic government, hold elections, and uphold the rule of law have been seen as manifestations of American values and principles. The concept of democracy as a model for political governance has influenced and shaped discussions on governance in Iraq. Through the promotion of democratic values and processes, the US aimed to demonstrate the benefits of democratic governance and foster a sense of empowerment among the Iraqi people. Many Iraqis believe that their new and progressive constitution was drafted and implemented with the influence and assistance of the United States.

In line with Iraq's transition towards democracy following Saddam's regime, the Iraqi constitution declares the country's political system to be a parliamentary republic. Article 2, paragraph (c) prohibits the formulation of laws that contradict democracy, while principle 6 emphasizes the peaceful and democratic transfer of power. Additionally, Article 45 of the Iraqi constitution, found in the third part, recognizes the principle of separation of powers as a foundation of democracy in the country's political structure. The constitution gives priority to the parliament and advocates for a parliamentary government system, highlighting the parliament's role in overseeing the executive branch's performance and the election of the president by the parliament (Article 58). Article 47 recognizes the election of Iraqi parliament representatives by the people as a means of democratic representation.

In line with the implementation of constitutional articles, the holding of elections, and the rotation of power among political elites, Iraq held its first parliamentary elections in 2005. Subsequent rounds of parliamentary elections took place in 2010, 2014, and 2018. The existence of a vibrant civil society in the United States, the freedom of information circulation, and the overall political atmosphere characterized by political values such as democracy, as well as political activities like political parties, civil society organizations, and information dissemination, are aspects that can appeal to the Iraqi people. These capabilities are particularly significant given the living conditions during Saddam's era, characterized by one-party dictatorship and non-compliance with democratic standards and rules of political engagement. The United States supported Kurdish autonomy after the First Persian Gulf War (1991) and is still very popular among Kurds. The United States emphasized the importance of protecting individual liberties, promoting gender equality, and ensuring justice for all Iraqis as part of its efforts to protect human rights in Iraq. The United States sought to present itself as a defender of human rights and a promoter of justice and equality in the country. So the new constitution of Iraq, in paragraph (c) of Article 1, does not allow the development of laws contrary to fundamental rights and freedoms, and Article 5, mentions the people as the source of authority and legitimacy. In the second part of the Iraqi constitution, article 14, the equality of the Iraqi people before the law, regardless of the existence of discrimination in terms of color, race, religion, and religion, in the fifteenth article, the right of every person to enjoy freedom, and in the sixteenth principle, the enjoyment of equal opportunities for It guarantees all Iraqi people. Also, the 17th principle recognizes the privacy of individuals by stating that every person's privacy is protected unless it conflicts with the rights of others and public customs and manners. Articles 35, 39, 40, and 41 of the Constitution of Iraq recognize the freedom of expression, thought, and freedom to choose the individual characteristics of each person according to their religion and religion and guarantee the freedom to perform religious acts. Also, Article 19 of the Iraqi Constitution reserves the right to sue for all people. The twenty-third article in the Iraqi constitution declares that the private property of individuals is reserved, and Article 23 does not allow the expropriation of property except in circumstances such as public interest and fair compensation (The Iraqi Constitution).

The United States also worked to promote gender equality in Iraq. The country's efforts included supporting women's rights and empowerment, supporting initiatives to combat gender-based violence, and promoting women's participation in political and economic arenas. The goal of the United States was to highlight the importance of gender equality as a fundamental principle of human rights and inclusive development. The United States encouraged and supported women's participation in political processes in Iraq. In this regard, provide training and capacity-building programs for women in leadership roles, support women's organizations and political networks, and support women's representation in decision-making institutions. The United States sought to have women's voices heard and their views included in policy-making (Marques, 2023). The United States introduced initiatives to promote women's economic empowerment in Iraq, including providing training and resources for women entrepreneurs, supporting access to credit and financial services, and promoting women's participation in the labor market. The United States did this with the goal of increasing economic opportunities for women and contributing to their overall empowerment and independence. The United States also supported awareness-raising campaigns to promote gender equality in Iraq. It sought a cultural shift towards greater gender equality and women's rights through partnerships with local organizations, civil society groups, and government institutions to promote gender mainstreaming and challenge gender stereotypes and discrimination (Marques, 2023).

Another initiative undertaken by the United States to enhance its soft power in Iraq is its assistance in the country's reconstruction efforts. This assistance takes the form of an economic development aid program overseen by the United States Agency for International Development (USAID). The USAID began its operations in Iraq in 2003. Between 2003 and 2009, the United States allocated a total of 49 billion dollars to the reconstruction of Iraq through this program (everycrsreport, 2010). As part of the development and reconstruction programs implemented after the occupation of Iraq, approximately 3,000 schools were reconstructed and restored, and over 20 million textbooks were printed and distributed. Moreover, tens of thousands of teachers at various levels benefited from the educational and technical assistance provided by the United States Agency for International Development (USAID) development program (Hosseinpour, 2018). In its report on its activities in Iraq, the USAID mentions the allocation of over 300 million dollars in the fiscal year 2017-2018 for humanitarian aid. These assistance efforts encompass providing shelter, ensuring access to safe water and food security, and delivering health services (USAID, 2018).

American culture, encompassing music, film, fashion, and technology, has exerted a significant influence on Iraqi society. American movies and TV shows enjoy popularity, and genres like hip-hop and pop music are widely embraced. American brands and products are also prevalent, highlighting the impact of American consumer culture. American technology companies and their products, including smartphones, social media platforms, and apps, have made a substantial impact on Iraqi society. The widespread use of platforms like Facebook, Instagram, and YouTube has facilitated the dissemination of American cultural content and trends. American technological innovations and digital culture have shaped communication patterns, online behavior, and lifestyle habits in Iraq.

The United States has implemented various educational and cultural exchange programs in Iraq, including the Fulbright Program, the Fulbright Visiting Professor Program, the Iraqi Young Leaders Exchange, and the Information Technology Exchange Program. These initiatives aim to foster mutual understanding, academic cooperation, and cultural exchange between Iraqis and Americans. As part of its cultural influence in Iraq, the United States has utilized the Fulbright program to award scholarships to Iraqi students, providing support for their education, accommodation, and healthcare. Additionally, the

"Fulbright Professors Visit" program has been designed for Iraqi professors and scientists to engage in scientific activities in the United States, with the goal of equipping and enhancing Iraqi universities with new scientific tools. The program spans 10 weeks, during which participating professors and scientists conduct research, engage in discussions, and exchange ideas with American counterparts. At the conclusion of the program and upon their return to Iraq, participants are expected to present a report on their scientific accomplishments for the benefit of their fellow countrymen. By acquainting Iraqi professors with new scientific methods and elevating the standard of education and teaching in Iraqi universities, these initiatives strengthen the capacities of universities in the country and facilitate scientific and educational cooperation between Iraqi and American professors. (Hosseinpour, 2018). The "Exchange of Young Iraqi Leaders" program is another educational and cultural initiative implemented by the United States of America in Iraq. This program, overseen by the educational and cultural affairs department of the U.S. Department of State, primarily targets exceptional Iraqi undergraduate students between the ages of 18 and 24. With a duration of six weeks, the program aims to cultivate future leaders for Iraq and strengthen the relationship between the people of the United States and Iraq. It seeks to establish a cohort of young individuals in both countries who possess a strong sense of social responsibility and are committed to fostering relationships with individuals from diverse ethnic and religious backgrounds. The program focuses on social development, familiarization with global issues, the acquisition of individual leadership skills, and fostering collaboration and mutual understanding between American and Iraqi societies and cultures. By participating in this program, Iraqi students not only gain essential skills to effect positive change in their society but also become acquainted with American cultural norms, democratic principles, values, and the Western way of life (World Learning, 2019).

Another cultural program implemented by the United States of America in Iraq is the "Information Technology Exchange Program." Recognizing the significance of human capital and the need to enhance the skills of the federal IT workforce, Congress established the IT Exchange Program in 2002. The program aims to improve federal information technology skills through personnel exchanges between the government and the private sector (GAO, 2005). The Department of Educational and Cultural Affairs of the U.S. Department of State proposed and implemented this program specifically for Iraq. Under this program, six Iraqi communication technology experts travel to the United States for a 12-week period to engage in studies and research. Alongside their educational activities, these experts also benefit from various educational programs and have the opportunity to meet and engage in discussions with technology companies, universities, and leading firms in the communications field (such as Google and Twitter). Equipping program participants with the necessary skills and capabilities for the development of Iraq's technology industry stands as one of the primary objectives of this program (Bastami, 2011: 137).

The establishment of the American University of Baghdad, often referred to as the "American," on March 14, 2019, represents the most recent endeavor of the American government to exert influence in Iraq's educational sphere. The university's president, Michael Mullenix, an American national, remarked, "This University is extensive, and I feel more like the mayor of a city than the president of a university!" The academic focus of the institution encompasses political science and management (academicpositions, 2021). While the United States had previously established universities in Sulaymaniyah, Erbil, Salah al-Din, and Dohuk, the decision to construct a university in the capital city of Iraq dedicated to management and humanities is regarded as noteworthy.

Although the United States offered numerous exchange programs and financial assistance to Iraqi citizens. However, between 2016 and 2023, the number of Iraqi students studying at US universities declined sharply, from 1,900 to about 500 (Figure 3).

Figure 3. Iraqi students in the US universities
Source: IIE (2023)

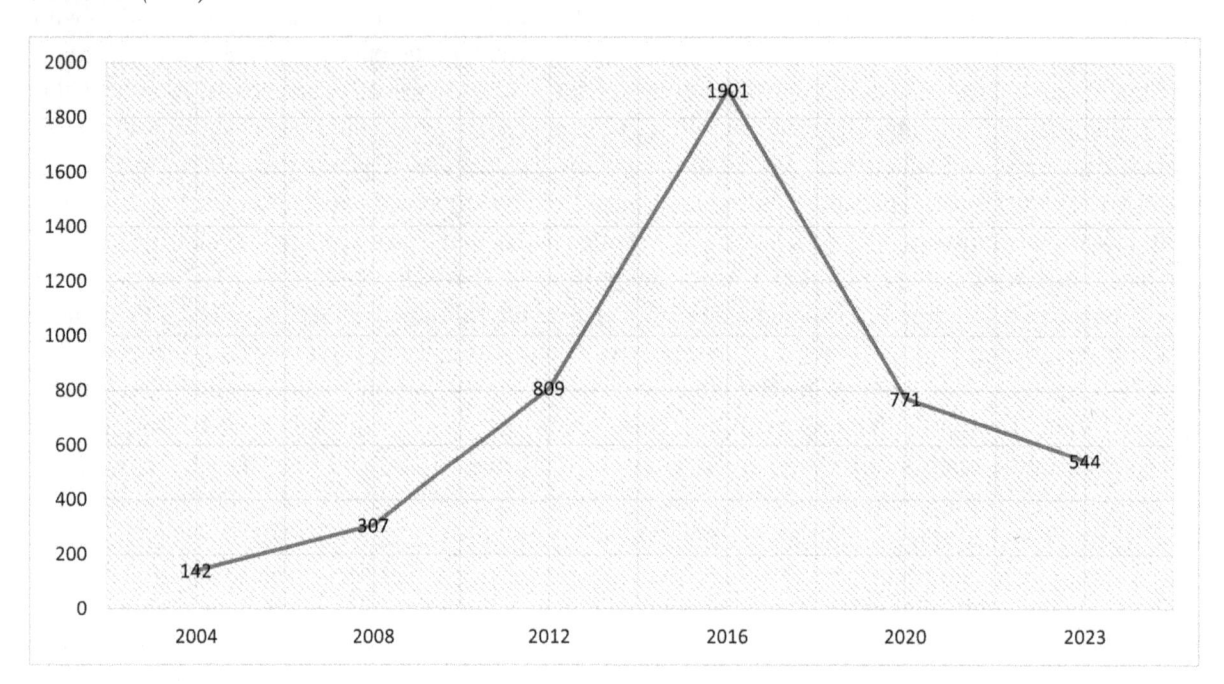

American media outlets, such as CNN and Voice of America, have a substantial presence in Iraq. These media organizations deliver news and information that influence public opinion and facilitate the exchange of ideas. The accessibility of American media and the Internet has granted Iraqis access to a diverse range of information and perspectives, including those originating from the United States.

One of the most influential audio and visual media from the United States is Hollywood cinema. Following the American military invasion of Iraq in March 2003, Hollywood cinema focused its efforts on producing films that aimed to justify the military intervention and present a favorable and acceptable image of American militarism to the Iraqi public opinion. Films produced by Hollywood since 2003 explicitly address this issue. Some notable examples include "The Devil's Double," "The Hurt Locker," and "Green Zone." In these films, the intention is to rationalize the United States' attack on Iraq and portray the actions of American soldiers in Iraq as legitimate. The films are crafted in a manner that portrays Iraq as a chaotic state, with the United States portrayed as a savior coming to rescue Iraq.

According to published statistics, approximately 93% of Iraqis who use the internet are members of Facebook, and around 40% of Iraqis actively engage in social networks. On average, Iraqi users spend about 8 hours per day on social media platforms. There are approximately 400,000 Arabic-speaking Twitter users and 100,000 Instagram users in Iraq. Additionally, many ministries, official government institutions, and organizations in Iraq have official pages on YouTube, making it the second most popular social network in the country after Facebook. According to IRNA, Iraq ranks fifth in terms of internet usage, with 14 million users, and fourth in terms of Facebook usage among Arab countries (IRNA, 2017).

Radio and television networks are also used to influence the minds of the Iraqi people. Radio Seva and Al-Hura TV are two media that the United States has benefited from. Radio Seva is a product of the Broadcasting Board of Governors, which was launched with an initial budget of $35 million and is funded by Congress. Radio Seva broadcasts international news daily for 7 hours and its main goal is to influence the audience under 35 years old in the Middle East. This radio is available on the FM wave all days of the week and broadcasts news and specialized programs to its audience along with popular Western and Arabic music. Also, this radio network, in addition to finding and attracting an audience among Arab youth, also seeks to communicate and talk with them. For this reason, in his radio talk show, he deals with social issues, including the issue of marriage. Nevertheless, music plays a key role in this station (Gedda, 2002).

Al-Hura is an Arabic-language satellite television channel launched by the United States government in 2004. This program is more dedicated to broadcasting news programs and is similar to Arabic satellite channels in terms of format (Fahmy, Wanta & Nisbet, 2012). Al-Hura TV channel, like Radio Seva, avoids broadcasting sharp and provocative images and language. This network offers a range of educational, news, and entertainment programs, including; The morning talk show broadcasts educational and entertainment programs for children, shows for women, cooking shows, documentaries, technology programs, soap operas, sitcoms, movies, and nightly news shows (Baylouny, 2006). This network does not have its own foreign office and uses other news agencies such as the Associated Press television news agency, which provides facilities for foreign journalists based in the Middle East (Kothari, 2018).

One of the actions of the United States of America in order to conquer the hearts of the Iraqi people was to include the name of "Umm Qasi" in the list of 10 brave women of the world, which was announced by the US State Department. Am-Qusi is an Iraqi woman who sheltered 15 Iraqi students in her home to be safe from ISIS. This Iraqi woman received an award for her bravery from Melania Trump, the first lady of the United States. The impact of this event increased when Alhurra network covered this news (Alhurra, 24 March 2018).

However, mediating variables sometimes overshadow the soft power of the United States. Findings from public opinion polls indicate that the United States of America had limited popularity among Iraqi Shiites and Sunni citizens between 2005 and 2014. However, there has been a significant increase in the popularity of the United States among Iraqi Shiites, reaching 47% in 2014. This suggests a notable rise in the percentage of Shiites who view the United States as a reliable partner during this period. Survey data consistently reflects this popularity in subsequent years, with a favorable opinion among Shia citizens standing at 42% in 2018. Similarly, a similar trend can be observed among Sunni citizens, although the popularity of the United States among Sunnis has experienced fewer fluctuations, following a relatively stable and balanced trajectory from 2005 to 2017. However, in 2019, there was a significant increase, with the percentage reaching approximately 40%. On the other hand, the level of popularity of the United States among Iraqi Kurdish-speaking citizens has remained consistently high throughout the mentioned time period, standing at 75%. According to the data in Figure 4, the popularity of the United States among Kurdish-speaking citizens has remained on a steady trend until the present, with the rate reaching 72% in 2019, showing little change compared to 16 years ago. (Figure 4).

Since the Gaza war in October 2023 and the United States' strong support for Israel, American trust and influence in Iraq have reached an all-time low. Currently, only 7% of the Iraqi population believes that the United States plays a positive role in the Middle East region. (Dagher & Kaltenthaler, 2023).

Comparing the Soft Power Components of the Islamic Republic of Iran and the United States

The research results reveal that both the Islamic Republic of Iran and the United States possess potential sources of soft power in Iraq. While there are similarities and differences in their application of soft

Figure 4. Iraqis who believe that the United States is a reliable ally number (percent)
Source: IIACSS (2019: 21)

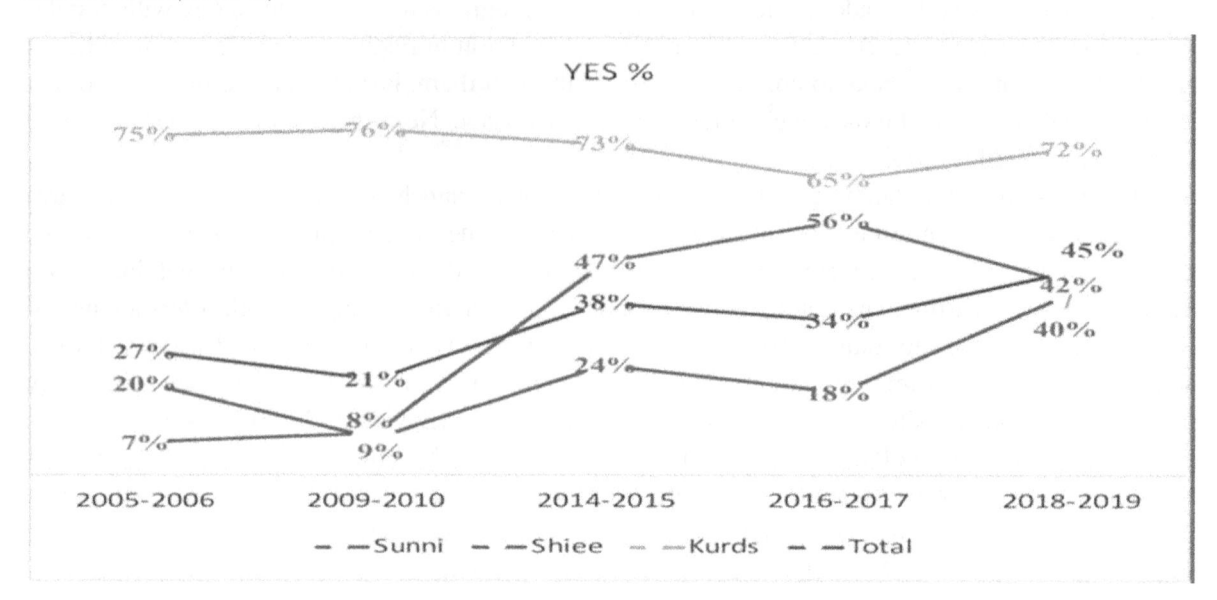

power in Iraq, each country has distinct sources of soft power. The Islamic Republic of Iran primarily derives its soft power from cultural values and shared political beliefs. It utilizes soft power to elevate the Islamic world and counter foreign dominance. By adhering to religious and moral values, Iran aims to create attractiveness and influence in the public opinion of Iraqi society. On the other hand, the United States relies predominantly on liberal and secular values as the basis of its soft power. The country harnesses substantial material resources, combined with media, cultural, political, and economic tools, to promote its political and cultural values.

The different aspects of the soft power of the Islamic Republic of Iran and the United States can be observed in various areas. The Islamic Republic of Iran places emphasis on political Islam, while the United States emphasizes liberalism and secularism. Iran employs its soft power to highlight democracy and combat colonialism, Zionism, and imperialism. In contrast, the United States accentuates the liberation of Iraq from Saddam's regime and its own role in this process. The cultural dimension of soft power stands out as the primary strength of the Islamic Republic of Iran, whereas the United States relies on media tools, scientific diplomacy, and economic interactions as its key soft power instruments in Iraq.

Despite the differing political values and attitudes of the Islamic Republic of Iran and the United States, there are some similarities in their soft power approaches in Iraq. Both countries prioritize the promotion of democracy and countering terrorism in Iraq, which has generated appeal among the Iraqi population. Both countries apply a lot of public and cultural diplomacy sources in exerting soft power.

Given Iraq's pluralistic population and its ethnic and religious diversity, the soft power of both Iran and the United States has been able to influence specific segments of the Iraqi people. Iran's religious affinity with Iraqi Shiites and its use of religion as a primary tool of soft power has made the Shiite population in Iraq particularly receptive to Iran's soft power components. However, it is important to note that the Shiite population in Iraq is not homogeneous in terms of political and ethnic inclinations but rather diverse, resulting in fluctuating levels of influence for Iran even within the Shiite community.

Table 1. Comparison of Iran and US soft power in Iraq

Similarities	Differences	Sources
The emphasis of the two countries on democracy in Iraq and protecting the rights of minorities	The US emphasis on political liberalism and secularism and Iran's emphasis on political Islam	Political values
Two countries' use of media, scientific diplomacy and public diplomacy	The US emphasis on liberal and non-religious values. Iran's emphasis on religious values.	Cultural Values
Countering terrorism and ISIS	The US emphasis on military presence in Iraq, America's opposition to militia groups and Washington's support for Israel. Iran's emphasis on the end of US military presence, Iran's support for Shia militias and Iran's support for the rights of the Palestinian people	Foreign Policy

Despite the cultural and historical similarities between Iran and the Kurds, Iraqi Kurds have shown a greater inclination towards the United States. This shift can be attributed to factors such as the death of Jalal Talabani as Iran's staunch supporter and Iran's focus on Shiite elements in Iraq, which led to a decline in Iran's popularity among Iraqi Kurds. However, during the emergence of the ISIS threat in Iraq, Iran's support for Iraqi Kurds temporarily increased its soft power among this population. Nevertheless, in subsequent years, with the Kurdish independence referendum and Iran's opposition to it, Tehran's soft power among the Kurds diminished once again. Iran's occasional military attacks on Kurdish groups opposed to Iran and Israeli intelligence bases within Iraqi Kurdistan have further undermined its soft power among Iraqi Kurds. Additionally, the political competition between Shiites and Sunnis in Iraq, Iran's support for Shiites, and the tendency of Iraqi Sunnis to align with Saudi Arabia and Turkey have contributed to Iran's relatively low soft power among Iraqi Sunnis. However, it's worth noting that the soft power of the United States is also not particularly high among Sunni Arabs in Iraq, as Iraqi Sunnis view Washington as the main cause of their political decline in Iraq following the fall of Saddam Hussein.

Indeed, the evolving political landscape in Iraq has resulted in varying attitudes towards the United States and Iran among Shiites, with both positive and negative perspectives emerging. The continuous support provided by the United States to the Kurds has made them the most receptive group among the majority population in Iraq in terms of soft power. Furthermore, the United States' efforts in the fight against ISIS have garnered support within the Iraqi public opinion. However, the imperialist policies pursued by the United States in the Middle East region, particularly its unwavering support of the Israeli regime, have led to a decrease in Washington's soft power in the eyes of the Iraqi people, especially after October 2023. These policies have generated negative sentiments and diminished the attractiveness of the United States' soft power in Iraq (Table 1).

CONCLUSION

The ethnic and religious diversity in Iraq has indeed influenced the soft power of both the Islamic Republic of Iran and the United States, with each country appealing to specific segments of the population. Iran's cultural affinity with Iraqi Shiites have contributed to Iran's significant soft power influence in Iraq. Iran's anti-imperialist and anti-Israel policies also find support among certain segments of the Iraqi population. However, the instability in Iraq and negative propaganda against Iran have sometimes led to

Iran being scapegoated for Iraq's problems, and some Iraqis hold Iran responsible for their challenges. This perception is reflected in polls and affects Iran's soft power.

Following the fall of the Baath regime by the United States, the shadow of Saddam Hussein's dictatorship was lifted from Iraqi society. Iraqi Shiites and Kurds view the United States as the liberator from Saddam's rule and the catalyst for the establishment of a democratic government in Iraq. The U.S. leadership in the fight against ISIS has also garnered support among many Iraqis. The U.S. cultural diplomacy has had a positive effect in attracting Iraqi elites. However, the continued U.S. military presence in Iraq is seen by Iraqis as a symbol of occupation and humiliation. Furthermore, America's strong support for Israel has had a negative impact on its image among Arabs and the Iraqi people. As a result, the United States is not highly popular in opinion polls among Iraqi Arab people.

The main findings suggest that both Iran and the United States wield different forms of soft power in Iraq. The U.S. soft power primarily targets the Kurds, Iraqi liberals, and elites. Iran's soft power, on the other hand, primarily resonates with ordinary Iraqis, particularly the Shiite population. Recent polls indicate that both Iran and the United States do not enjoy high favorability among the Iraqi people. One of the main reasons for this sentiment is the perception among Iraqis that the ongoing conflict between these two countries is a significant factor contributing to the continuing instability in Iraq.

REFERENCES:

Academicpositions. (2021). *American University of Iraq – Baghdad.* https://academicpositions.com/employer/american-university-of-iraq-baghdad

Alhurra. (2018). *Iraqi and Mauritanian women among the 'bravest' women in the world.* https://www.alhurra.com/a/courage-award/426536.html

Aljazeera. (2018). *Iraq elections final results: Sadr's bloc wins parliamentary poll.* https://www.aljazeera.com/news/2018/5/20/iraq-elections-final-results-sadrs-bloc-wins-parliamentary-poll

Amjadian, F., Sanai, A., & Jalali, R. (2022). Characteristics of Iran-US soft power in modern Iraq in the years (2016 to 2020). *Iranian Journal of Political Sociology*, 5(8), 2535–2554.

Bardakci, M. (2023). *Iran and the Iraqi Shiites: A Cyclical Relationship.* https://www.uikpanorama.com/blog/2023/02/23/mb/

Bastami, M. (2011). *American Public Diplomacy in the Middle East.* Imam Sadegh Publishing House.

Baylouny, A. M. (2006). Al-Manar and Alhurra: Competing satellite stations and ideologies. *European Center for Security Studies*, (2), 1–27.

Customs of the Islamic Republic of Iran. (2023). *Annual Statistics.* Available at: http://www.irica.ir/web-directiry/55335-html

Dagher, M. & Kaltenthaler, K. (2023). *The United States Is Rapidly Losing Arab Hearts and Minds Through Gaza War.* While Competitors Benefit. https://www.washingtoninstitute.org/policy-analysis/united-states-rapidly-losing-arab-hearts-and-minds-through-gaza-war-while

Daily Telegraph. (2014). *Iraq crisis: Iran pledges military help against ISIL as battle for Tikrit escalates.* https://www.telegraph.co.uk/news/worldnews/middleeast/iraq/10933934/Iraq-crisis-Iran-pledges-military-help-against-Isis-as-battle-for-Tikritescalates.ht

Dorj, H., & Shahidani, M. H. (2021). The Soft Impact of the Islamic Republic of Iran on Strengthening Shiite Power in the Iraqi Political Equation (2003-2020). *Soft Power*, *11*(25), 81–103.

Everycrsreport. (2010). *Iraq: Reconstruction Assistance.* https://www.everycrsreport.com/reports/RL31833.html

Fahmy, S. H., Wanta, W., & Nisbet, E. C. (2012). Mediated public diplomacy: Satellite TV in the Arab world and perception effects. *The International Communication Gazette*, *74*(8), 728–749. doi:10.1177/1748048512459144

Financial Tribune. (2023). *Exports to Iraq Hit Record High of $10b in FY 2022-23.* https://financial-tribune.com/articles/domestic-economy/117826/exports-to-iraq-hit-record-high-of-10b-in-fy-2022-23

GAO. (2005). *Information Technology Exchange Program.* Retrieved from: https://www.gao.gov/products/GAO-07-216

Gedda, G. (2002). Radio Sawa: Music as a Tool. *Foreign Service Journal*, 53-56.

Geranmayeh, E. (2017). Iran's strategy against the Islamic State. *ECFR Council.* https://www.ecfr.eu/article/commentary_irans_strategy_against_the_islamic_state320

Hosseinpour, M. B. (2018). The public diplomacy of the United States of America in Iraq during the George D. Bush. *International Journal of Nations Research.*, *4*(40), 48–68.

IIACSS. (2019). *Iraq Recent Protests. Were they Unexpected.* https://iiacss.org/wpcontent/uploads/2019/10/October_protests_2019.pdf

IIE. (2023), Open Doors, at: https://www.iie.org/research-initiatives/open-doors/

Iran's Student Affairs Organization. (2023). *62 Iranian universities were recognized as accredited by the country of Iraq for the study of Iraqi students.* Available at: https://saorg.ir/portal/home/?news/235224/248672/285020/

IRIBNEWS. (2015). *Iran Series' popularity among Iraqi Kurdish people.* https://www.iribnews.ir/fa/news/2960040

IRNA. (2017). *Statistics of Iraqi Virtual users.* Available at: https://www.irna.ir/news/82786210/93

ISNA News Agency. (2009). *Al-Alam ranking among Arab news channels.* https://www.isna.ir/news/8806-00002.101886/%

Jadidi, A., Nasiri, S., & Barzin, S. (2022). Sources of soft power of the Islamic Republic of Iran in Iraq (2020-2010). Soft power. *Studies*, *11*(4), 29–54.

Jafari, A. A., & Nikravesh, M. (2015). Iran's cultural soft power resources in the Iraq. *Soft Power*, *5*(12), 29.

Katzman, K. (2008). *Iran's Activities and Influence in Iraq.* https://www.files.ethz.ch/isn/118352/2007-12-26_Iran_Influence-Iraq.pdf

Kothari, M. (2018). Rereading the Media War Case in Iraq: America and the Rapid Media Response Team. *Middle East Studies Quarterly, 16*(1), 33-54.

Marques, A. C. (2023). *Women's economic empowerment in Iraq: a double-edged sword?* https://cfri-irak.com/en/article/womens-economic-empowerment-in-iraq-a-double-edged-sword-2023-11-08

Masoudi, H., & Nourian, A. (2023). Arbaeen March and Its Effect on Iran's Soft Power in Iraq:Practice Theory. *Contemporary Researches on Islamic Revolution, 5*(15), 1–18.

Mehr news agency. (2023). *More than 50 thousand Iraqi students study in Iran.* Available at: https://www.mehrnews.com/news/5900848

Nye, J. S. (2004). *Can America Regain Its Soft Power After Abu Ghraib?* https://archive-yaleglobal.yale.edu/content/can-america-regain-its-soft-power-after-abu-ghraib

Nye, J. S. (2010). The Future of Soft Power in US Foreign Policy. In I. Parmar & M. Cox (Eds.), *Soft Power and US Foreign Policy: Theoretical, Historical and Contemporary Perspectives.* Routledge.

Oktav, O. Z. (2018). Understanding Iran's Approach to Violent Non-state Actors: The ISIS and YPG Cases. *Violent Non-state Actors and the Syrian Civil War, 16*(2), 193–210. doi:10.1007/978-3-319-67528-2_10

Statista. (2023). *Languages most frequently used for web content as of January 2023, by share of websites.* https://www.statista.com/statistics/262946/most-common-languages-on-the-internet/

The Cradel. (2024). *Iraq mulls suspension of border security deal with Iran.* https://thecradle.co/articles-id/19283

The Guardian. (2015). *What do Iraqis think of Iran?* Retrieved from: https://www.theguardian.com/world/iran-blog/2015/mor/17/iran-viewed-from-iraq-fight-against-isis

US Department of State. (2004). *U.S. Commitment to Women in Iraq.* https://2001-2009.state.gov/g/wi/rls/36751.htm

US Department of State. (2019). *The Fulbright Program.* Retrieved from: https://www.stste.gov/fulbright-program-univeils-updated-indentity

USAID. (2018). *Iraq: Sophisticated emergency,* Retrieved from: https://www.usaid.gov/sites/default /files/ documents/1866/iraq_arabic_fs05_03-09-2018.pdf

Watkins, J. (2020). *Iran in Iraq: The limits of 'smart power' amidst public protest.* http://eprints.lse.ac.uk/105768/

Wong, E. (2007). *Iran Is Playing a Growing Role in Iraq Economy.* https://www.nytimes.com/2007/03/17/world/middleeast/17iran.html

Wood, C. (2015). *Iran-Iraq Relations Cooling.* Available at: https:// www.thetrumpet.com/article/13106.2.0.0/middle-east/iran/iran-iraq-relations-cooling

World Learning. (2019). *Iraqi Young Leaders Exchange Program.* Retrieved from: https://www.world-learning.org/program/iraqi-young-leaders-exchange-program

Chapter 2
A Discourse Analysis of Twitter Communication to Foster Digital Diplomacy Between India and China

Reema Roy
Asutosh College, India

Piyush Kumar
https://orcid.org/0000-0003-0006-8868
Accenture, Kolkata, India

Moumita Chatterjee
https://orcid.org/0000-0002-1497-0388
Aliah University, India

Dhrubasish Sarkar
https://orcid.org/0000-0002-7418-2922
Supreme Institute of Management and Technology, India

ABSTRACT

Online social media platforms enable an individual or agency to communicate interactively and exchange of opinion. Twitter is a very popular platform worldwide for the exchange of opinions. The chapter tries to identify the effectiveness of social media diplomacy and effectiveness of the communication made on Twitter. The study wants to identify the role of Twitter in maintaining the international relations between India and China. There are three key factors that can be identified as the basis of the relationship. Those are business, boarder tension, and the cultural exchange. The study has taken two Twitter handles of Sun Weindong, Chinese Ambassador to India, @China_Amb_India, and India in China, Embassy of India Beijing, @EOIBeijing, for the analysis. The discourse analysis method and content analysis have been adopted by accessing Twitter data and news contents of the study. The study also investigates the impact on the users presenting the word cloud. This study shows a new path in the area of open diplomacy.

DOI: 10.4018/979-8-3693-2444-8.ch002

1. INTRODUCTION: SINO-INDIAN DIPLOMACY AT A CROSSROAD

India and China are rising giants of Asia. Both are the world's most populous countries and fastest-growing major economies. The far-reaching growth in China and India's global diplomatic and economic influence has also enhanced the significance of their bilateral relationship. China and Asia's growing superpowers are China and India (Halmstad, 2012). These are the two most populated countries in the world with the fastest-growing major economies. The significance of China and India's bilateral relationship has been further heightened by the far-reaching rise of their worldwide political and economic power. For thousands of years, China and India, two of the oldest civilizations on Earth, have coexisted peacefully. The attempts by both nations to rekindle diplomatic, cultural, and economic relations have been successful. China has become India's top commercial partner, and both nations have made an effort to deepen their military and strategic ties. In the current state of the world economy, the economic link between two countries is regarded as one of the most important bilateral relationships. The diplomatic relations between India and China reached their 70th anniversary in the year 2020. But the relationship between the two has become weaker rather than stronger in the mentioned year. This happened firstly, for COVID- 19 pandemic and secondly, after the death of 20 Indian Army personnel in Galwan (Rao, 2020) when the Indian and Chinese armies confront each other after 45 years.

In the mid of April 2020; Indian satellite and human intelligence respectively inform the Indian Government about the existence of near about 2500 army personnel rehearsing war at the Line of Actual Control (LAC). On 5 May 2020; the Indo – Chinese troops first near Pyongyang Lake and on 9 May 2020; the first clash between the Indo –Chinese army took place at Nakula Pass and several Indian and Chinese soldiers were injured. Since then, military tensions on Indo – China border have been rising till August of the same year. Talks with the National Security Advisor, Foreign Minister S. Jayshankar and The Indian Ambassador to Beijing began with the Chinese Government. When asked by India about China's aggression policy, China said that India is adopting an aggression policy as mentioned by Indian Home Minister Amit Shah said in 2019 in his speech. Wang Xianfeng who has been found as a press officer at the Chinese mission in Islamabad tweeted that China and Pakistan's sovereignty has been questioned by India's activities, which include altering the status quo of Kashmir unilaterally and escalating regional tensions. These acts have also complicated relations between China and India and between India and Pakistan (Laskar, 2020).

It is noteworthy that despite all this, the government of India (GOI) is promoting through its various social media and television that everything is calm at LAC. 'Global Times' a leading English daily of China wrote Indian Prime Minister Narendra Modi once again demonstrated the great importance he places on diplomacy through social media accounts by wishing Chinese Premier Li Keqiang a happy 60th birthday on his SinaWeibo account.

From Social to Digital: A Paradigm Shift?

Freedom of the internet and the online media, digital world has changed the facets of public diplomacy over the years. It is more open and transparent now as Tom Fletcher, retired British foreign diplomat describes it as 'Naked diplomat' (Fletcher, 2016). Foreign Diplomacy in the age of social media is leaving its protected past, to become much more interactive, totally networked and more people centric. In the time of ongoing conflict between India and China, these nations are becoming global examples of employing social media in fostering communication. Even western counterparts of global powers like the

United States are also using their social media diplomacies to make a new international stature. Digital Diplomacy, the most modern iteration of diplomacy has further enhanced the speed and extended the reach of public diplomacy. The ability to engage in a two-way conversation on a real-time basis has brought diplomacy out of the closed doors right onto the streets. India, the world's largest democracy, has been quick to understand and appreciate the potential of social media as a tool to pursue foreign policy goals. The recent election of Mr. Modi as the Prime Minister has given a huge fillip to the social media engagement by the Indian diplomats. Consular and cultural diplomacy quite evidently benefits from this surge in digital interactions but if used prudently, social media promises to bring substantive long-term foreign policy benefits.

The Backdrop

The China-India border standoff, which started in May 2020, is still going on today at several flashpoints in the Himalayan region of Ladakh's rocky terrain. The issue has come to be defined by a bloody battle between Indian and Chinese troops in the Galwan Valley in June 2020. It was the bloodiest combat in more than 40 years and resulted in losses on both sides. The standoff's primary cause is still not entirely clear even two years later (indiatoday.com, 2022). A large portion of the discourse currently in existence is unable to give a complete picture of or explanation for the development. However, a closer examination of China's domestic debates and conversations on India in the years leading up to and following the Galwan incident reveals a clear and thorough explanation of the factors that may have caused the border crisis and also provides hints as to how to proceed. The current border conflict is placed within the larger context of Chinese foreign policy and global strategy.

Confidence-Building Measures in the Military Field along the Line of Actual Control in the India-China Border Areas Agreement was signed in 1996. "*Intending to prevent risky military activity along the line of real control in the India-China border areas*," reads Article VI (1) of the 1996 agreement. Within two kilometers of the line of actual control, neither side may open fire, produce biodegradation, use hazardous chemicals, perform blast operations, or engage in firearms or explosives hunting. For routine fire at small-arms ranges, this prohibition shall not apply (peacemaker.un.org, 1996). However, Article VI (4) is more relevant in this situation because it states that if border personnel from the two sides come into contact because of disagreements over the alignment of the *Line of Actual Control* (LAC) or for any other reason; they must exercise restraint and take all necessary precautions to prevent a worsening of the situation. To assess the situation and avoid any tension building up, all parties must immediately consult through diplomatic and/or other channels.

The 2005 Agreement says that the two sides will settle the boundary dispute through amicable and peaceful negotiations, according to Article 1. Aside from verbal threats, neither party may use physical force against the other (mea.gov.in, 2005). Both sides agreed not to use their military resources against one another in the 2013 Agreement on Border Defense Cooperation. These practices of not firing have been instilled into the soldiers because no round has been shot on the Sino-Indian border in Ladakh since 1962 to prevent any escalation.

India has been enhancing the LAC portion of its border infrastructure. The Chinese might have been enraged by the improvement of the Darbuk-Shyok-Daulat Beg Oldi road. The Chinese demand in the ongoing negotiations also assumes that India will halt the construction of its infrastructure (Subramanian, 2020). One common defense is that China's action is motivated by regional issues, like India's choice to alter Jammu and Kashmir's and Ladakh's status.

The two nations' ties have been slowly getting worse. India has opposed both the *China-Pakistan Economic Corridor* (CPEC) and *China's Belt and Road Initiative* (BRI) (CPEC). India's claims about Gilgit-Baltistan are additionally seen by China as an implicit criticism of the CPEC. Foreign direct investment from China is now subject to limits and regulations from India (mea.gov.in, 2017). Chinese behavior is also being influenced by the internal pressures that have been created within China, which have been brought on in part by the COVID-19 pandemic. Since the People's Republic of China was established in 1949, the COVID-19 pandemic has been the country's most catastrophic health catastrophe. The decline of the Chinese economy is a factor in the rising political pressure on the government of the nation.

Pressures on the Chinese leadership have become significantly harsher as a result of the coupling of political and economic problems, and the swelling tide of anti-China sentiment around the world has made matters even worse. Along the LAC and in the South China Sea, Chinese aggressiveness has been seen (Roy Chaudhury, 2021). This could be an intentional attempt by the Chinese authorities to draw attention away from local problems. Although India claims to be non-aligned, there is a growing perception that it has sided with the United States. The area of U.S.-China relations is possibly where India's tilt toward the United States is most obvious. Recent events are frequently cited to support the belief that anytime there is a conflict of interest between China and the United States, India prefers to support the United States (Tomar, 2002).

In the Indo-Pacific, the United States and India have converged on geopolitical positions against China. India is a part of the Quad, which includes the United States, Japan, Australia, and India and has a clear anti-China undertone. China is once again left out of the U.S. President's proposal to restructure the G-7, which would include nations like India (India has expressed its willingness) but exclude China. India is being portrayed more and more as a Chinese rival and is being incorporated into a larger anti-Chinese alliance, which offends China. India's forces are kept busy in the border regions by the intense tensions with Pakistan.

Nepal brought up border disputes with India. China is significantly expanding its influence in that region, while Sri Lanka is diversifying its foreign policy. The Citizenship Amendment Act infuriated Bangladesh greatly. India is excluded from the transition process in Afghanistan even though Pakistan, China, Russia, and the United States are all involved.

The remainder of the chapter is organized as follows. Section 2 focusses on the literature review. Section 3 discussed the objectives of the study. The methodology of the research and data presentation & analysis are described in Section 3 and 4 respectively. Section 5 describes the experimental results and analysis. The last two sections focus on findings followed by conclusion and future work.

2. EVOLUTION OF DIPLOMACY: THROUGH THE LENS OF LITERATURE

Sarvjeet (2016) has stated that 'diplomacy' means the conduct of official relations between sovereign states, but like any other art or science, it evolved significantly in its methods and practices. The two world wars were the greatest experiments in the conduct of multilateral diplomacy in modern times. Public diplomacy got a shot in the arm with the invention of the radio, but a real watershed moment came with mainstreaming of the internet. Over the last couple of years, digital diplomacy has become one of the fascinating areas of research in the field of Social Science and Communication as well. New media and Information Communication Technology have opened up a new arena for governments, individuals, and organizations to interact with overseas audiences. Melissen (2005) has described the idea of 'public democracy'. According to him 'public democracy' is related to nation-branding, propaganda, and international cultural interactions. Propaganda and nation-branding, like public diplomacy, focus on informing and persuading foreign audiences to have a favorable attitude toward the source nation or to affirm preexisting opinions. Melissen describes the importance of technology in the field of open diplomacy and called the evolution 'cyber diplomacy. He includes that smart civil society requires soft power in the understanding of the parts of validity and self-criticism in the current global economic landscape, and this tendency is projected to continue in the coming years.

Owen (2017) has opined that the new media environment is way more dynamic and tries to develop unanticipated ways that have serious consequences for diplomatic governance and foreign relations. Dijck (2012) has said that Twitter was first described as the 'SMS of the Internet in 2006. Jack Dorsey said he wanted Twitter to be like electricity, e-mail, SMS, or phone. Twitter's capacity to deliver messages to various hardware platforms has been essential to its success. When Twitter was launched, it was not the only or even the first microblogging service. Other stand-alone microblogging services such as Tumblr had already appeared on the scene. During the first years after its emergence, Twitter was often called a service in search of a user application. Twitter's motto of Twitter's home page now reads, 'Share and discover what's happening right now, anywhere in the world. In November 2009, Twitter changed its guidance posting from 'What are you doing?' to 'What's happening?'. This subtle but meaningful change in Twitter's interface indicates a strategy that emphasizes (global, public, public) news and information over the (personal, private) conversation. Peña-Araya et al. (2017) have observed that the massive growth of the social web generated vast amounts of user data easy and publicly available, opening a whole new spectrum for social research and behavioral science. Khan et al. (2021) have analyzed the public engagement strategies for diplomacy used by a German ambassador on Twitter. By analyzing the Twitter content, they presented a Public Engagement Model (PEM) for social media communication and also highlighted three main factors that promote online public engagement. Duncombe (2017) has shown the important role of Twitter in the negotiation strategy and how online social media can shape the struggle for recognition, and thereby legitimize political possibilities for change in the limelight of Iran–US relations. Sobel et al. (2016) have shown the use of Twitter by US embassies and their study reveals inconsistencies among embassies in Twitter use and Twitter content. They have suggested the possibility of viewing such Twitter activity as public diplomacy. Chhabra (2020) has discussed how Twitter has played a significant role in the realm of diplomacy in the recent past and coined the term 'Twiplomacy'. Palit (2018) has identified that social media diplomacy has great significance in policymaking for foreign affairs and strategic communication building for countries like India-China-USA and many more global powers. The ever-expanding economies are using social media to communicate with the global audience purposefully to create a better image and enhance goodwill. Ratha et al. (2014) have observed that China has surpassed India as India's top commercial partner, and the two countries have attempted to strengthen their strategic and military ties. The economic relationship between two countries is regarded as one of the most important bilateral relationships.

3. EXCAVATING THE ISSUE

In terms of the diplomatic relationship between India and China during the period of the emergence of social media like Twitter, the study wants to enquire about the effective role of Twitter as a medium of

Table 1. Tweet statistics

Node	Number of Tweets Retrieved
Sun Weindong	278
India in China	200

open diplomacy between India and China. This study also wants to identify the characteristics of social media diplomacy and the effectiveness of the communication made on Twitter. With this, it wants to find the impact of open diplomacy on the users of Twitter. In the end, the study is interested to observe the kind of spatial distribution among the participants in the conversation in terms of their national identity.

The researchers took mixed method to reach the aim of the study. The two methods are – discourse analysis and content analysis. As the study has focused on the Twitter handle analysis, two Twitter handle are being taken as sample and discourse analysis has been done with the help of statistical software named Python. As the study has been done during the period of December17, 2021 to May 17, 2022; the news (e-contents) ware selected through Google search tool and the relevant news were taken for the content analysis.

Node Selection as Sample

The study will undertake a sentiment analysis method using statistical software by selecting total 2 Nodes or Vertexes as sample. For the current observations, we have utilized two nodes: Sun Weindong, Chinese Ambassador to India, @China_Amb_India and India in China, Embassy of India Beijing, @EOIBeijing

As, the current Indian Ambassador to China, Pradeep Kumar Rawat doesn't have twitter presence, we have considered the official embassy twitter handle as the replacement node for the study.

Data Extraction

We have extracted all tweets for the nodes between the periods of December17, 2021 to May 17, 2022. The total statistics on tweets collected is represented in table 1.

Pre-Processing

Before proceeding with the sentiment analysis, we need to clean the extracted tweets, for that process we have utilized the steps like, hyperlink removal, removal of Non-ASCII characters, stop words removal, tokenization, stemming, POS tagging.

After cleaning, we are storing the clean text in the data files, for further analysis. An example of cleaned tweet is displayed in table 2.

4. WHAT THE CONVENTIONAL MEDIA REFLECTS

The authors enjoyed searching through traditional media for the material that was highlighted before delving into the Twitter data. It appeared that conducting a content analysis beforehand would aid in comprehending Twitter activity more clearly, and this is easily justified.

Table 2. Example of pre-processing

Tweet	Cleaned Tweet
From IP Man to The Grandmaster, Wing Chun, with its flowing martial arts style and philosophy, has been portrayed on the big screen numerous times. Watch the Wing Chun episode of @cgtn_inheritors here: https://t.co/ZKrJgoHAID#wingchun #martialarts #KungFu	ip man grandmaster wing chun flowing martial arts style philosophy portrayed big screen numerous times watch wing chun episode cgtn inheritors wingchunmartialartskungfu
Countries around the world are like passengers aboard the same ship who share the same destiny. https://t.co/GhWmTbG4Uu	countries around world like passengers aboard ship share destiny

In December 2021: India faced the issues like *"Delhi records 1,313 fresh COVID-19 cases, highest since May 26; India's Omicron tally crosses 1,000-mark"* (The Economic Times, 2017), PM Modi shouted suggestions for improving business in India. *"Sensex ends 800 points lower"* (Livemint, 2021) etc. In Indian media, we find one common issue like *"Chinese City of 13 Million Locked Down Amid COVID-19 Scare"* (Krishnan, 2021). As the World was discussing COVID and the laymen named the virus a Chinese virus. So it has a possibility that the main tweets at that time were related to COVID and China was not active on this topic in December 2021.

In January 2022: the scenario changed as we explore that in 2021, commerce between China and India reached USD 125.66 billion, rising 43.3% from 2020, according to data from the General Administration of Customs, which was reported by the state-run Global Times (Economic Times, 2022). For more than ten years, India has emphasized its concerns about the expanding trade deficit with China and urged Beijing to open its markets to Indian IT and pharmaceutical companies. According to observers, a significant portion of China's increase in exports to India this year can be attributed to the import of medical supplies and raw materials for India's booming pharmaceutical industry as a result of the country's widespread COVID-19 second wave and recurrent outbreaks of the virus (Economic Times, 2022). At this time the subjectivity curve is more active than in India. India has shown a stable action concerning Tweet (Zreik, 2023b).

In February 2022: the media did not show any serious issues between India and China but In March 2022 one of the important elements of international relations was published in the media, *"India is Snapping up Cheap Russian Oil, and China Could Be Next" (Tan, 2022).* Significant oil-importing nations like China and India had been struggling with rising crude costs since last year. Even though oil prices had been erratic lately, fluctuating between gains and losses, they were still over 80% higher than they were a year ago. This would be in sharp contrast to the rhetoric used by leading global organizations and governments that were shunning Russian oil. The U.S. had imposed energy sanctions on Russia as a response to its aggressive and unjustifiable assault on Ukraine, and the U.K. wanted to do the same by the end of the year. The European Union is debating whether to follow suit as well *(Tan, 2022).*

In March 2022: besides COVID Omicron updates, Russian oil (fuel) was at the base of the news between India and China. Here a triangle of relationships was seen. One of the main factors behind the Indo-China relationship is the diplomatic approach of America towards India and China. On 29th March 2022, India Today reported that India's fuel costs are updated every day. However, from November 2021 until last Tuesday, when they were increased, the rates were left unaltered for 137 days. Since then, there has been a practically daily increase in the rates. Both gasoline and diesel prices have jumped by roughly INR 5 per litre in the past week. So it was an important deal for India to buy Russian oil at a decreased price (India Today, 2022).

India, the third-largest oil importer in the world after China and the US, has agreed to buy 3 million barrels of Russian oil at a significant discount, a government official in India said. Given Russian supply and Indian demand, the purchase, which was first reported by the Wall Street Journal, is rather modest. But if the United States and its allies pressure governments around the world to isolate Russia, the volume could rise in the months ahead, adding to the notion that India is steadfastly preserving its extensive trade and military links with Moscow. According to the Washington Post, since it consistently refrained from condemning Russia at the UN, India has come under fire from certain U.S. legislators in recent weeks. But representatives of the Biden administration have frequently refrained from condemning an Asian power that is viewed as an essential component of its plan to confront China (Shih, 2022).

Another very crucial indent happened in March 2022. Chinese Foreign Minister Wang Yi met with National Security Advisor Ajit Doval and External Affairs Minister of India Dr S. Jaishankar twice after unexpectedly arriving that evening on March 19, 2022. According to Prof. Rajan Kumar of the JNU School of International Studies, 'Beijing is attempting to make contact with New Delhi to prevent a worsening of the current circumstances at the Ladakh border. Despite numerous rounds of military and political talks, there hasn't been any movement toward de-escalation in Ladakh' (Siddiqui, 2022; Zreik, 2023a). Jaishankar stayed away from the press conference. Only a brief statement outlining the topics discussed during the conversation between the two foreign ministers was released by the Ministry of External Affairs. The two ambassadors also spoke about how recent events would affect trade and economic connections, according to the statement.

Additionally, it noted that India continues to press for dialogue and an end to hostilities while Russia provided its views on Ukraine, including current negotiations. A statement from the PMO also listed the conversations the prime minister held with Lavrov. Lavrov was given more flexibility and consideration than Wang Yi, demonstrating the value India places on friendly nations. India exhibited its foreign policy throughout both trips. It expressed to China that bilateral ties would stay damaged if the LAC is not resolved and refused to give in to Chinese pressure. It enabled the expansion of commerce and diplomatic relations while refuting the Chinese demand to put the border issue on ice. China should have recognized India's intentions, one hope. India demanded a truce and negotiations and did not support Russia's activities in Ukraine. It also made a mediation offer. The prime minister would have projected disparities between relations by sending a personal message to Putin via Lavrov, something he never did with Wang Yi.

In April 2022: the news of Chinese Foreign Minister Wang Yi's visit to India and the outcome was hot cake along with the COVID issues. At the end of April 2022, on the website of CARNEGIE, it was found that in response to the worrying escalations and expansions of China's authoritarian and repressive practices made possible by technology, American politicians tightened tech prohibitions. Washington has two primary interests. Though the new is not directly related to India. But the news has an indirect connection to the triangle relationship between India-America-China (Carnegie, 2022).

In May 2022: there a headline was found on the Asian edition of Bloomberg *"China, US Are Racing to Make Billions from Mining the Moon's Mineral"*. In an era when the cosmos is getting more crowded, the absence of cooperation between the US and China on space research is particularly risky. To close the digital divide and investigate the business potential, billionaires like Elon Musk and Jeff Bezos are launching an increasing number of satellites alongside developing nations like Rwanda and the Philippines. As ideological divides over the pandemic, political persecution, and now Vladimir Putin's war widen, the stakes are even higher when it comes to the US and China, which are building economic barriers in the name of national security. If they can't work together in space, it might lead to an arms race

Figure 1. Subjectivity curve

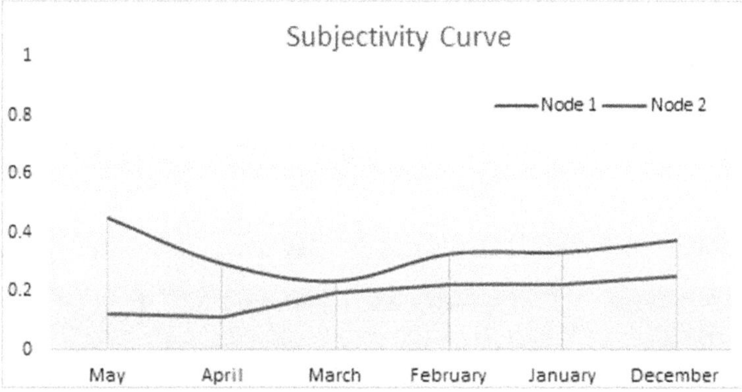

as well as conflicts over the extraction of resources that could be worth hundreds of billions of dollars on the moon and elsewhere (Einhorn, 2022). The news was based on the power conflict between U.S and China but the news has another side of interest. India is also an upcoming power in space. So if U.S and China want to challenge each other India is obviously in the queue.

5. POLITICS OF DIPLOMACY: DOES DIGITAL SUBSTITUTE THE REAL?

The researchers utilized the cleaned tweets to perform sentiment analysis and extract subjectivity and polarity from the tweets. Using that we created sentiment curve for the time period.

Subjectivity Curve: Subjectivity refers to the degree to which a person is personally involved in an object. What matters the most here are personal connections and individual experiences with that object, which may or may not differ from someone else's point of view?

The subjectivity curve for node 1 and 2 is shown in Figure 1.

The study's Subjectivity Curve shows that node-1 corresponds to Sun Weindong's Tweets, whereas node-2 reflects the Indian Embassy in Beijing (figure 1). Figure 1 illustrates the degree to which more active and individualized Sun Weindong, the Chinese Ambassador to India (Node 1) is compared to the Indian Embassy at the starting point of the curve. However, both Nodes 1 and 2 are extremely subject-oriented in February and March. When Russia began its invasion of Ukraine in February, the price of Russian oil dropped. China and India both desired to purchase Russian oil at a steep discount at that time. Due to this, Chinese Foreign Minister Wang Yi was unexpectedly visiting India at that time. Indian media later brought it to light. So it was a big deal and the staff of discussion. In May 2022; the power conflict between China and America became the headlines of the news. The subjective figure is also showing a higher degree of subjectivity during May 2022.

Polarity Curve: Polarity refers to the strength of an opinion. It could be positive or negative. If something has a strong positive feeling or emotion associated with it, such as admiration, trust, love; this will indeed have a certain orientation towards all other aspects of that object's existence. The same goes for negative polarities.

In our study, we are utilizing the polarity of the extracted tweets to get a polarity curve. The polarity curve for node 1 and node 2 is shown in Figure 2.

Figure 2. Polarity curve

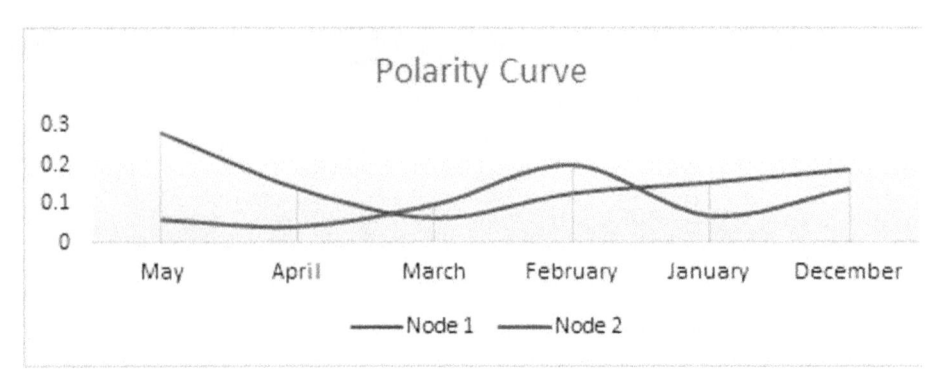

In the study, researchers found that most of the Tweets from both of the nodes are positive. In March, 2022; there are a few negligible negative Tweets are found. It can be based on the Chinese Minister's visit.

Post Frequency: The authors studied the number of posts by the nodes categorized by month. While Node 1's tweet volume is little high compared to Node 2, but it was noted that during the month of February, the difference in tweets frequency between the nodes was higher. Post frequency for the nodes is shown in Figure 3. The frequency of Tweets also reflected the sudden visit of Wang Yi to India.

Word cloud: A tag cloud (also known as a word cloud, wordle or weighted list in visual design) is a visual representation of text data, which is often used to depict keyword metadata on websites, or to visualize free form text. Tags are usually single words, and the importance of each tag is shown with font size or color. When used as website navigation aids, the terms are hyperlinked to items associated with the tag.

Using the processed tweets, we extracted the top 80 keywords used in the extracted data's time period. The word clouds for Node 1 and Node 2 are shown in Figure 4 and 5 respectively.

The word cloud of Node 1 reflects the internal affairs of China like the "President", "Jinping", "China" etc. There is a word, that is, Foreign Minister. It can be said that the agenda of the India visit by the Foreign Minister was a crucial issue for that time. On the other hand, the word cloud of Node 2 reflects "eoibeijing" (means Embassy of India in Beijing, China), "beijing", "brics" (Brazil, Russia, India, China, and South Africa) etc.

Figure 3. Tweet frequency

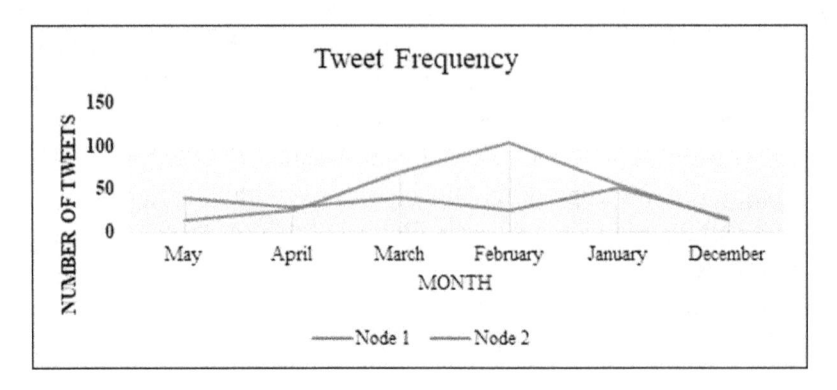

Figure 4. Word cloud for Node 1

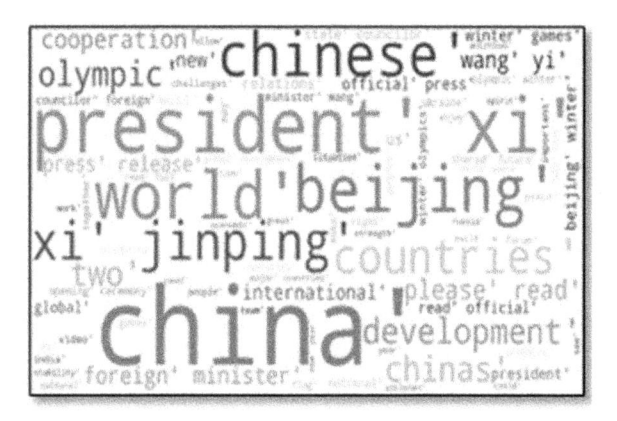

Top Keywords: From the word cloud, we can see the top keywords for both the nodes. The larger the size of the word, the more frequent it is used. We tried to continue this further by extracting top 10 keywords for every month for both the nodes. Figure 6(a-f) and Figure 7(a-f) shows the top 10 keywords for both the nodes.

In figure 6, the researchers have found a few specific words which are seed relevant to the study, like "world", "global", "cooperation", "new relations", "development", "ukrain", "us",, and "china". The words which are retrieved from the Node 1 are very common for any internal or external affairs of any country. The word "Olympic" is commonly applied to China as China always has kept a strong focus in Olympic Games. But Russia's storming of Ukraine has been spotted as an important issue for China (Zreik, 2024a).

Important terms like "eoibeijing," "ambassador," "ninaad," (Indian dance representation in China), "vikrammistri," (the previous Indian ambassador to China who was highly active on Twitter), and "china community" can be seen in figure 7. Ukraine is not in the list, same to Node 1. Internal matters pertaining to India, such as "amritmahotsav" and "yoga," are included. The Chinese holiday known as "World Yoga Day" has been observed, according to the Indian Embassy in China's website.

Figure 5. Word cloud for Node 2

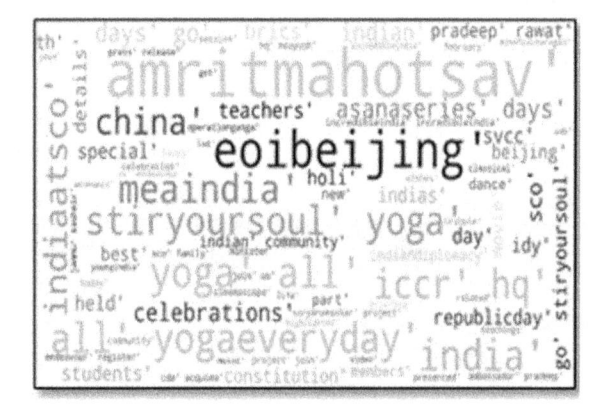

Figure 6. Node 1 word cloud (Dec - May)

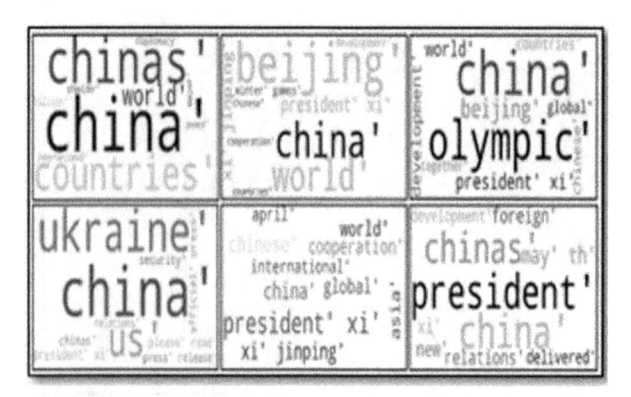

Positive and Negative Keywords: After processing sentiment analysis, we extracted top 80 keywords from both positive and negative tweets for both nodes. Figure 8 and Figure 9 show the top 80 keywords from negative and positive tweets for Node 1 respectively.

Remarkably, the negative Tweets from Node 1 include the terms "councilor," "state," "foreign minister," "wang," "official," "security," and "press." China's current foreign minister, Wang Yi, has been identified as one of the negative tweeters. The list additionally includes terms like "state," "press," and "councilor." These remarks can be in reference to the Chinese media and the internal operations of authorities. It known to all that Chinese Press is run according to the 'Authoritarian Theory'[1].

The Figure 10 and the Figure 11 are presenting the Word Cloud for negative Tweets and positive Tweets respectively. The Node 2, shows the words "vaccine", "cooperation", "brics" and "joint" as the negative words. Only the word "brics" seems associated to International affairs of India.

The positive words "meaindia" (Ministry of External Affairs of India), "china", "chinese", "xi", "eoibeijing", "development" are being observed by the researchers.

The word "eoibeijing" is common in both of Nodes. In the website of Indian Embassy to China, we will find updated newsletters where the cultural activities are describing vividly. Both the countries have a goal of development which is also noticeable.

Figure 7. Node 2 word cloud (Dec - May)

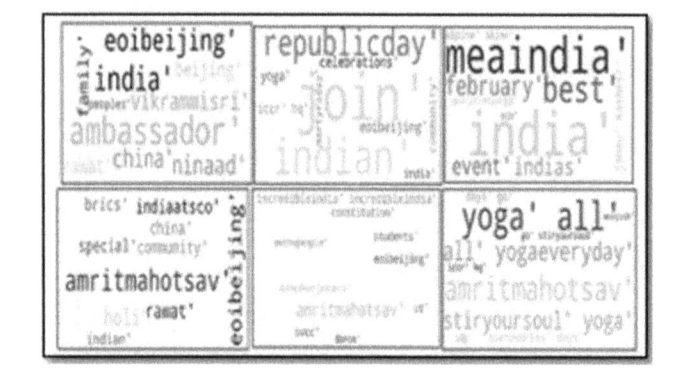

Figure 8. Word cloud for negative tweets (Node 1)

Figure 9. Word cloud for positive tweets (Node 1)

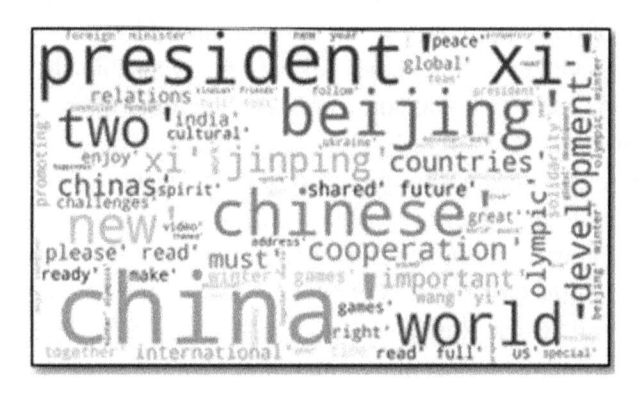

Figure 10. Word cloud for negative tweets (Node 2)

Figure 11. Word cloud for positive tweets (Node 2)

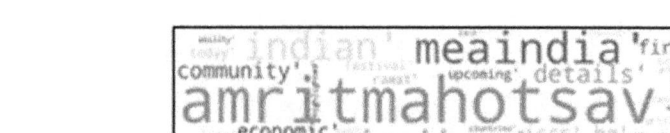

6. CONCLUSION: CAN DIPLOMATIC ISSUES BE RESOLVED DIGITALLY OR IS THIS AN ALIBI?

From the above analysis (both of the News Content analysis and the Sentiment analysis) the authors have discovered a line-up of open diplomacy between India and China through Twitter and its impact.

Both the Chinese ambassador to India and the Indian embassy to China have upheld a commendable position. The study supports the notion that commercial and cultural interchange form the cornerstone of the two nations' foreign ties.

The visit of China's foreign minister to India is a significant event during the study period. Nothing previous could be discovered on Twitter or conventional media. It was an unexpected guest. Foreign Minister Wang Yi visited Pakistan during the final week of March 2022 as part of a tour of South Asia in order to attend a summit of the Organization of Islamic Cooperation. He visited Nepal as well. China and India have not spoken out against Russia's invasion of Ukraine. Since the Cold War era, Russia has developed diplomatic and economic connections with both China and India, and it refers to its operations as a "special military operation." When 20 Indian and four Chinese soldiers were killed in a high-altitude battle in a contested region of the western Himalayas in June 2020, relations between China and India turned tense. Since then, India has placed restrictions on the entry of numerous Chinese businesses. At an annual press conference held in Beijing in March 2022; Wang argued that rather than "sucking each other's energies," Asia's two largest countries should cooperate to achieve common objectives (Das, 2022). During the said visit, the researchers found the frequency of Twit was very high, especially on Node 1 (Chinese Ambassador's Node). In the word cloud of the study, the word "cooperation" has been found in both of the nodes.

Even though the Ukraine problem was not discussed during China's Foreign Minister's visit to India, the study portrays a different picture. The low cost of Russian oil is of great concern to both nations, and America has significant influence over the matter.

The importance of the BRICS Summit is recognized by both nations. At present, it seems that the G7 is dedicated to preserving the existing international system, which China and Russia specifically perceive as "unipolar," meaning that it is centered around the US and dictated by US foreign, global, and domestic policies that are in force at the moment. Both countries (and others) want to play a more inclusive role in international affairs, as befits their status. China is the second-largest economy in the world, with India coming in at number five. Nevertheless, neither of them has the desired level of influence in global financial institutions like the World Bank and IMF. For this reason, alternative policy banks like the Asian Infrastructure Investment Bank and the BRICS own New Development Bank have been created. There are also claims that Washington's policies have started to have a bigger influence on international organizations like the United Nations, which is situated in New York. Reform-related demands are getting louder and louder. Understanding the shifting global dynamics and where pressures may start to build, challenges that need to be solved, and possibilities that exist requires understanding how the BRICS states view these changes. Because of this, Chinese President Xi Jinping has referred to the BRICS 2022 Summit Declaration as a significant document that has to be thoroughly examined (Devonshire-Ellis, 2022). In the Summit of 2022, the BRICS leaders discussed topics such as counterterrorism, trade, health, traditional medicine, environment, science, technology, and innovation in agriculture, as well as technical and vocational education and training. They also discussed important global issues like the COVID-19 pandemic, global economic recovery, and the multilateral system's reform (Zreik, 2024b). The Prime Minister of India Narendra Modi urged for the BRICS Identity to be strengthened and recommended creating an online database for BRICS papers, a BRICS Railways Research Network, and fostering MSMEs' collaboration. This year, India will host the BRICS Startup event to improve ties between startups in the BRICS nations. The Prime Minister further stated that as BRICS members, we should be aware of one another's security concerns, support one another in the identification of terrorists, and avoid politicizing this delicate subject. The "Beijing Declaration" was adopted by the BRICS leaders (PIB, 2022).

The diplomatic relations between both nations is depended on the cultural exchange too. The Government of India has launched the Azadi Ka Amrit Mahotsav to commemorate and celebrate 75 years of independence as well as the illustrious past of its people, culture, and accomplishments (amritmahotsav. nic.in, 2022). The word cloud shows the words like "meaindia", "ninaad", "azadi ka amrit mahotsav". After checking the "meaindia" which is the Website of the Ministry of External Affairs of India to China, it can be seen that the Indian Embassy has taken different cultural activities like "Ninaad" – the Kathak dance programme, Tabla playing class, Bollywood movie showing, Yoga class and many more. So from these activities, one inference can be drawn that India has a keen interest in a cultural exchange programme and India is walking accordingly.

This study reveals that traditional diplomacy is necessary for open diplomacy via Twitter. Both nations make internal diplomatic decisions, which are subsequently made public via the Twitter account. China and India communicate with one other via their Twitter handles. The elements underlying both open diplomatic contacts and traditional diplomatic interactions are depicted in Figure 12. Open diplomacy is an emerging rival connection path, while traditional diplomacy remains the mainstream one. A number of important variables are at play between the two countries, including the role of America, security, the G-7, and BRICS. Another element that contributes to maintaining a decent, steady condition of external relations is culture. We have to wait for its young stage.

Social Media Diplomacy and Its Impact

In this study, Twitter has been taken as the social media. The writers examine here how social media diplomacy is far more formal than conventional diplomacy. Twitter is one of the communication channels in both nations. Users can be seen using Twitter when any fresh information is released by contemporary media. Therefore, modern media is the primary information source for the people. However, a lot of contemporary media, including TV networks and newspapers, are keeping an eye on Twitter accounts

Figure 12. Formal factors behind the traditional diplomacy and open diplomacy between India and China

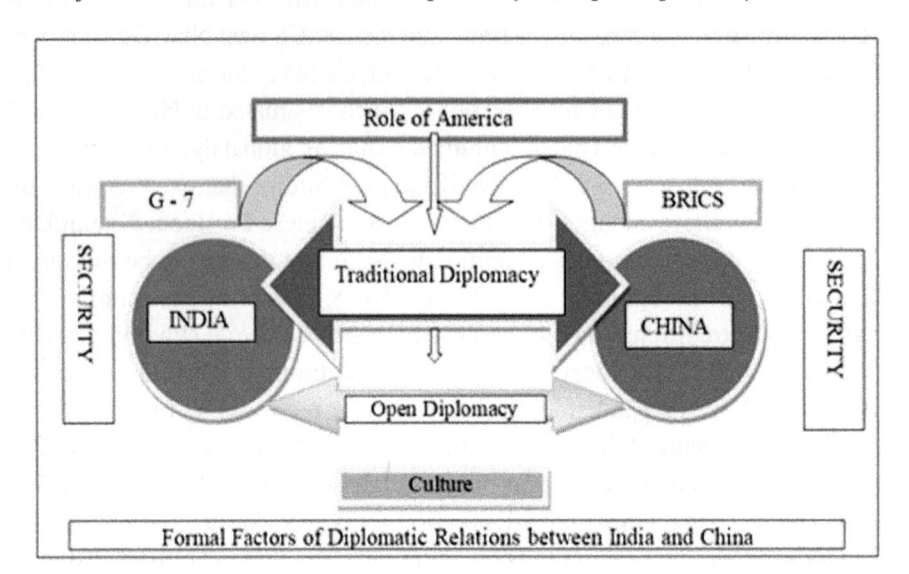

and waiting for news, or sometimes they are even waiting for confirmation of any breaking news. After announcing the Foreign Minister's visit to India on Twitter, PIB received confirmation. So, it can be inferred that the interdependency between contemporary media and social media has grown up.

The users of Twitter are micro-bloggers. According to the research, users start to participate once the news has been released or shown. They respond to diplomatic concerns with Twits. There has been no hate speech discovered from either of the nodes. Words like "councilor," "joint," "security," "vaccine," and so forth have been identified as unfavorable terms from both Nodes. The COVID vaccination may not be widely accepted, hence the word may be interpreted negatively. However, perhaps in light of the incident in Galwan, the two countries' lack of collaboration and border tension are not in a favorable place. The consumers have seen negative effects from these issues. After the word cloud analysis, it has been explored that the users of both nations show positive attitudes to their internal issues.

The words like President, and Olympic are positive words for the users of China. The Indian users use "Amrit Mahotsav", "eoibeijing" which are significantly major positive words. In 2022, India is celebrating 75 years of independence and the Government of India has taken the project "Swadhinata Ka Amrit Mahotsav" to celebrate Independence Day. Both the countries are looking forward to the "joint" "cooperation" for "development". It is a positive sign for both. The visit of Wang Yi can be identified as the key factor for the users. Because after Galwan attack, both the countries were waiting for the betterment of the relationship which is crucial for the business and security for both. During the period of visit, the users of Twitter twit the most. In this study, we found that social media showcase only the surface level diplomacy.

Twitter is becoming an open forum for expressing an opinion to users. In near future, Twitter may become an essential tool of digital diplomacy. The conscious use of Twitter may help the policy maker to develop positive relations between the nations. With this, social media literacy for the common people is also important.

The study has taken for a limited period, so it is hard to generalize any conclusion. With this, the study has explored only two Nodes for the analysis. The media which are the source of official declarations or notifications had to be added to this study. A few public forums also can be taken for further study.

On behalf of all authors, the corresponding author states that there is no conflict of interest.

The datasets generated by the survey research during and/or analyzed during the current study are available in the Dataverse repository, https://github.com/debris69/Ind-China-Discourse-Analysis-Data

REFERENCES

Carnegie. (2022, April 25). https://carnegieendowment.org/2022/04/25/denying-support-for-chinese-and-china-enabled-authoritarianism-and-repression-pub-86924

Communication Theory. (n.d.). https://www.communicationtheory.org/authoritarian-theory/

DasK. N. (2022, March 23). https://www.reuters.com/world/chinese-foreign-minister-visit-india-friday-bloomberg-quint-2022-03-23/

Devonshire-Ellis, C. (2022, June 28). *silkroadbriefing*. https://www.silkroadbriefing.com/news/2022/06/28/china-has-urged-the-west-to-read-the-new-14th-brics-summit-declaration-carefully-this-is-what-it-says/

Dijck, J. v. (2012). Tracing Twitter: The Rise of a Microblogging. *International Journal of Media and Cultural Politics*, 333–348.

Economic Times. (2022, January 14). conomictimes.indiatimes.com/news/economy/foreign-trade/india-china-trade-grows-to-record-125-billion-in-2021-despite-tensions-in-eastern-ladakh/article-show/88900383.cms

EinhornB. (2022). *Bloomberg*. https://www.bloomberg.com/news/features/2022-05-17/china-us-are-in-a-space-race-to-make-billions-from-mining-the-moon-s-minerals

Fletcher, T. (2016). The Naked Diplomat: Understanding Power and Politics in the Digital Age. HarperCollins UK.

Halmstad, H. I. (2012). *Sino-Indian Relations:Complex Challenges in a Complex Relationship*. https://www.diva-portal.org/smash/get/diva2:543006/FULLTEXT01.pdf

India Today. (2022, March 29). https://www.indiatoday.in/business/story/petrol-diesel-price-per-litre-hiked-century-delhi-fuel-rates-cities-1930720-2022-03-29

indiatoday.com. (2022, February 3). https://www.indiatoday.in/india/story/chinese-soldiers-drowned-river-galwan-clash-2020-austrialian-report-1908119-2022-02-03

Krishnan, A. (2021, December 22). *The Hindu*. https://www.thehindu.com/

Laskar, R. H. (2020, June 13). *India: Hidustan Times*. https://www.hindustantimes.com/india-news/chinese-diplomat-links-ladakh-standoff-to-scrapped-art-370-creates-a-flutter/story-Jn0zkpbBFql6pcs-dfKe82K.html

Livemint. (2021, December 17). https://www.livemint.com

Melissen, J. (2005). *The New Public Diplomacy.* Palgrave Macmillan.

Owen, D. (2017). The new media's role in politics. In The age of perplexity: Rethink the world we knew. Penguin Random House Grupo Editorial.

Palit, P. S. (2018). *India's Use of social media in public diplomacy. Rising Power Quarterly, 3.*

Peña-Araya, V., Quezada, M., Poblete, B., & Parra, D. (2017). Gaining Historical and International Relations Insights from Social Media: Spatio-Temporal Real-World News Analysis using Twitter. *EPJ Data Science.*

PIB. (2022, June 24). https://pib.gov.in/PressReleaseIframePage.aspx?PRID=1836853

RaoN. (2020, July 7). https://thewire.in/diplomacy/india-china-70-years-diplomatic-relations

Ratha, K. C., & Mahapatra, S. K. (2014). *India-China Bilateral Relations: Confrontation and Conciliation. In Vision 2020: Sustainable Growth.* Economic Development, and Global Competitiveness.

Roy ChaudhuryD. (2021, October 29). https://economictimes.indiatimes.com/news/defence/chinas-aggression-in-south-china-sea-faces-strong-global-pushback/articleshow/87351835.cms?from=mdr

Sarvjeet, S. (2016). *Digital Diplomacy in India: Virtual networks, Real gains.* Communication des Institutions Publiques.

Shih, G. (2022, March 22). *World: The Washington Post.* https://www.washingtonpost.com/world/2022/03/17/india-russia-oil/

Siddiqui, H. (2022, March 25). *Financial Express.* https://www.financialexpress.com/defence/why-did-chinese-foreign-minister-wang-yi-come-unannounced-here-is-what-experts-say/2472016/

Subramanian, N. (2020, June 16). *indianexpress.com.* https://indianexpress.com/article/explained/lac-stand-off-india-china-darbuk-shyok-daulat-beg-oldie-dsdbo-road-6452997/

TanW. (2022, March 27). *CNBC.* https://www.cnbc.com/2022/03/28/russia-india-india-buys-cheap-russian-oil-china-could-be-next.html

The Economic Times. (2017, December 17). https://economictimes.indiatimes.com

TomarR. (2002, June 25). https://www.aph.gov.au/About_Parliament/Parliamentary_Departments/Parliamentary_Library/pubs/rp/rp0102/02RP20

Zreik, M. (2023a). The Sacred Paths: A Case Study of Pilgrimage Routes in Southeast Asia With a Special Focus on Thailand. In V. Martinho, J. Nunes, M. Pato, & L. Castilho (Eds.), *Experiences, Advantages, and Economic Dimensions of Pilgrimage Routes* (pp. 226–240). IGI Global. doi:10.4018/978-1-6684-9923-8.ch011

Zreik, M. (2023b). Sustainable and Smart Supply Chains in China: A Multidimensional Approach. In B. Bentalha, A. Hmioui, & L. Alla (Eds.), *Integrating Intelligence and Sustainability in Supply Chains* (pp. 179–197). IGI Global.

Zreik, M. (2024a). China's Energy Conundrum: Navigating Through Crises, Policy Responses, and Global Impact. In M. Ozel Ozcan (Ed.), *Analyzing Energy Crises and the Impact of Country Policies on the World* (pp. 139–159). IGI Global. doi:10.4018/979-8-3693-0440-2.ch008

Zreik, M., & Zhu, R. (2024b). Riding the Dragon: The Emergence and Impact of Over-the-Top Media in China. In N. Kalorth (Ed.), *Exploring the Impact of OTT Media on Global Societies* (pp. 75–90). IGI Global. doi:10.4018/979-8-3693-3526-0.ch005

ENDNOTE

[1] According to authoritarian theory, the ruling class, authorities, or powerful bureaucrats dominate all sources of communication (Communication Theory, n.d.).

Chapter 3
China's Soft Power Diplomacy in Vietnam:
Assessing the Dynamics and Efficacy of Belt and Road Architecture

Mohor Chakraborty

https://orcid.org/0000-0003-2082-5088

South Calcutta Girls' College, India

ABSTRACT

China's economic rise, coupled with its military heft and soft power acculturation, stimulates a sense of enigma in international relations. The "Chinese dream" theorizes the realization of great national rejuvenation and comprehensive national power, and the BRI is ample evidence to this effect. This is discernible in the Southeast Asian region, demonstrated by China's credence and acceptability, notwithstanding the fact that many of these states share contested sovereignty claims with China in the disputed South China Sea. Vietnam's inclusion in the BRI offers a unique case study, as it endeavors to strike a harmonious balance between realism and neoliberal considerations of national interests. The BRI, in synergy with Vietnam's "Two Corridors, One Economic Circle" framework, offers the pedestal for bilateral cooperation. Given this backdrop, this chapter analyzes the dynamics, principal areas of cooperation within the BRI framework, and its social, political, and economic ramifications for Vietnam as well as on China's international image as facilitator of soft power.

China's economic rise, coupled with its military heft and soft power acculturation, stimulates a sense of enigma in international relations. Its employment of a blend of hard and soft power, which is either a source of trepidation or enticement, contributes significantly to the country's global status. The "Chinese dream" theorizes the realization of great national rejuvenation and comprehensive national power and the Belt and Road Initiative (BRI) architecture is ample evidence to this effect. The BRI, though an instrument of burgeoning soft power diplomacy, supplements China's economic and military status. As the largest trading partner of more than 140 countries (Ministry of Foreign Affairs of the People's

DOI: 10.4018/979-8-3693-2444-8.ch003

Republic of China [FMPRC], 2023, para. 15) and holding the distinction of the largest manufacturer, the largest foreign exchange reserves, the second-largest spender on Research and Development, top bilateral creditor, second-leading destination of foreign capital and third-largest outbound investor in the world (FMPRC, 2022, para. 2) its position of strength can hardly be exaggerated. The combination of military prowess as a source of hard power on the one hand and soft power indicators like the network of overseas Chinese and the allure of development initiatives of the ilk of BRI, Global Development Initiative (GDI), Global Security Initiative (GSI) and Global Cultural Initiative (GCI) on the other, has cemented its legitimacy to a considerable extent. This is demonstrated by China's credence and acceptability among the Association of Southeast Asian Nations (ASEAN) member-states, notwithstanding the extrapolation of the contested and overlapping territorial and maritime claims to sovereignty shared by many of the ASEAN members vis-à-vis China. As the ASEAN states seek the advantages of the partnership of BRI's emphasis on building a "community of common destiny", conditioned by the imperatives of national interest and pragmatic realism, they pursue policies of cooperation, mutual trust and synergy-building with China, thereby facilitating its conduct of soft power diplomacy.

Among the Southeast Asia/ASEAN countries, Vietnam's inclusion as a beneficiary of the BRI projects, presents a unique case study, premised on the considerations of pragmatic national interest, given its discordant ties with Beijing pertaining to contradictory sovereignty claims in the South China Sea. Their differences are further compounded by grey zone tactics followed by China, its challenges to Vietnam's oil exploration ventures, fishing activities, etc. in the disputed littoral zone. Encompassed and represented by the "nine-dash line", China has declared the South China Sea as an integral part of its "core interest" of sovereignty, extending exclusive jurisdiction rights to fishing, navigation and "terra-claims" on the islands, underwater reefs, seafloor geographical entities and adjacent waters. In response, ASEAN, as a collective entity, has generally been more accommodative, evading a direct confrontational posture, while emphasizing a stance of conciliation and cooperative security with Beijing. However, the organizational stance, has, at times, evoked contradictory responses from aggrieved member-states like Vietnam, bringing ASEAN's institutional role in addressing and mediating the conundrum to the center of debate and scrutiny.

In spite of the trepidation in Sino-Vietnam relations, bilateral trade, investment and people-to-people/tourism interactions have demonstrated a positive trend, providing impetus to their soft power-based association. In this regard, the BRI, in synergy with Vietnam's Two Corridors, One Economic Circle framework, offers the pedestal for bilateral cooperation in the spheres of connectivity, human resources, infrastructure, investments, trade, among others. Since the primary focus of the Two Corridors, One Economic Circle-BRI synergy is the acceleration of transport infrastructure, especially in road and railways, the two countries have signed a Memorandum of Understanding (MoU) to jointly promote economic corridor collaboration. Cooperation among five provinces and cities, viz. Hanoi, Hai Phong, Quang Ninh and Lao Cai of Vietnam and Yunnan province of China (Ministry of Planning and Investment of the Socialist Republic of Vietnam, 2023, para. 6) constitutes one of the two economic corridors within the Two Corridors, One Economic Circle framework, aimed not only at connecting major economic centers of the two countries, but also facilitating transport infrastructure connectivity at the border areas, as a conduit of trade and tourism interaction.

In this backdrop, the chapter acknowledges the inherent dilemma in Vietnam's China policy as the former seeks to balance realist considerations with pragmatic national interests. It situates the dynamics of Sino-Vietnam relations within the theoretical framework of realism and neoliberalism, while highlighting the correlation between power and asymmetrical interdependence, providing a political-economic rationale for bargaining, hedging and heuristics. The purpose of the chapter is as follows: to situate the theoretical framework of the study, employing the realist, neoliberal interdependence and heuristic paradigms; analyze the impulses of Sino-Vietnam dichotomy, taking cognizance of the cooperative and discordant factors; analyze the dynamics, principal areas of cooperation within the BRI framework and its social, political and economic ramifications for Vietnam as well as on China's international image as facilitator of soft power; assess the efficacy, relevance and impact of China's soft power strategy in Vietnam; and identify the challenges, prospects and opportunities, as the two countries follow specific directions, measures and strategies to enhance political trust, deepen and elevate partnership in future, for which the BRI serves as a facilitator.

BRI IN SINO-VIETNAM MATRIX: SITUATING THE DEVELOPMENTAL POTENTIAL

Developed in juxtaposition to the "Clash of Civilizations" thesis, the doctrine of "Peaceful Rise-Peaceful Development" embodies the crux of China's soft power theory and praxis. Constituting the theoretical core of national rejuvenation, the President of China, Xi Jinping's "Peaceful Rise-Peaceful Development" thesis, acknowledges the imperative of balancing domestic reforms and development with a peaceful and stable external environment, pursuing the path of independent, open, peaceful and scientific cooperation and common development. China has launched a triad of development initiatives, viz. GDI, GSI and GCI as an adjunct to the "Peaceful Rise-Peaceful Development" thesis, to widen its soft power strategy, outreach and influence. These initiatives not only buttress comprehensive national power, but also bind and engage beneficiary states with it, through aid, trade, investments and prospects of development. The BRI, as a grandiose project announced by China in 2013, has generated a high degree of optimism and willingness of several countries to embark on the geo-economic architecture, that principally aspires to revive the ancient Chinese trade routes, known as "Silk Road". Since its inception, China has hailed the BRI as the "project of the century", envisioning it as a geo-economic and geo-strategic blueprint to promote and strengthen connectivity and influence across the "…Asian, European and African continents and their adjacent seas, connecting the vibrant East Asian and European economic circles at its two ends." Served by a network of roads, high-speed railways, fiber-optical lines, transcontinental submarine optical cable projects and satellite information passageways, the initiative is poised to shift the center of geo-economic power towards Eurasia.

At the time of its launch, China projected the mega-trade volumes among the BRI countries would reach a tune of US$ 2.5 trillion over the next decade (2013-2023). (FMPRC, 2015, p. 1) Since the launch of BRI, China has endeavored to build a "…global network of connectivity consisting of economic corridors, international transportation routes and information highway as well as railways, roads, airports, ports, pipelines and power grids" (FMPRC, 2023, para. 7) facilitating the transport of goods, capital, technologies and human resources across its beneficiary networks. According to the BRI Investment Report, 2023, "Cumulative BRI engagement in the full 10 years since the announcement of the BRI in 2013 breached the USD 1 trillion mark to reach USD 1.053 trillion", with future growth expected in sectors like "…manufacturing in new technologies (e.g., batteries), renewable energy, trade-enabling infrastructure (including pipelines, roads), Information and Communication Technology (ICT; e.g., data centers), resource-backed deals (e.g., mining, oil, gas), high visibility or strategic projects (e.g., railway)." (Nedopil, 2024, p. 7) The geographical stretch of BRI member-states, from the Eurasian continent to

Africa and Latin America and the participation of countries and international organizations, with more than 150 countries and over 30 international organizations that have signed BRI cooperation documents, testify to its burgeoning significance.

Vietnam's inclusion in BRI in 2017 demonstrates its classical hedging posture towards China, while maintaining a cautious distance and limited alignment with it, taking cognizance of their asymmetry in the levels of economic and military development and capability. With the end of the cold war in 1991, the normalization of Sino-Vietnam relations was ushered in, following 13 years of hostility. Since then, Vietnam has pursued a hedging strategy as the most rational and viable option in its policy towards China.

Rationale and Theoretical Framework of Analysis

Vietnam's objectives of safeguarding supreme national interests, sovereignty, territorial integrity and political autonomy vis-à-vis the threat of China's expansionist overtures have been balanced by political pragmatism, stimulating the pursuit of economic, trade and cultural cooperation for national development. In this broad ambit, Sino-Vietnam relations may be situated within the theoretical framework of realism/ hedging, neoliberal interdependence and heuristics. First, in the post-normalization period, Vietnam has pursued hedging as a strategy towards China to produce mutually advantageous effects under situations of high uncertainties, while emphasizing internal/hard balancing by embarking on military augmentation and modernization drive and external/soft balancing mechanisms by promoting multilateral engagement with like-minded partners. (Hiep, 2013, p. 335) Hedging has emerged as an effective strategy for addressing the security dilemma, as Jervis (1978, p. 78) explains, introduced by an actor's (China, in this case) offensive realist rationale of a power-maximizer, aspiring regional hegemony, as opposed to maintaining a balance or equality. By contrast, following the realist logic of security maximization through deterrence, Vietnam has sought to maintain the status quo and the region's balance of power. As China continues its grey-zone tactics of intimidating states like the Philippines and Vietnam, which have commercial stakes and disputes over territorial claims in the South China Sea littorals, international opinion against this unilateral infringement of a state's sovereign rights and jurisdiction, bolstered by voices of like-minded partners like India, United States (US) etc., have a deterrent effect on Beijing. Deterrence is a significant guarantee to maintaining the status quo and respect to the tenets of a peaceful and stable maritime order.

Second, the neoliberal theory of interdependence, particularly the interrelation between power and asymmetrical interdependence as a power resource, provides a political-economic explanation, characterized by "bargaining", as rational actors pursue their respective national interests by responding to incentives. (Chakraborty, 2023, p. 45) Vietnam takes cognizance of the imperative of interdependence in a globalized world order, given the cost-benefit computations and advantages yielded by aligning with or accommodating China. This has been demonstrated by the steady rise in Sino-Vietnam trade and investment ties, exploring their structural complementarity, natural geographic advantage in logistics, transportation, etc. in various spheres including agricultural products, infrastructure construction and raw materials. (Yang, 2023) Thus, in the context of the interdependent, liberal, global order, Sino-Vietnam relations are driven by economic pragmatism through the expansion and deepening of bilateral economic cooperation, facilitating domestic development on the one hand, and focusing on direct engagement by fostering bilateral mechanisms to build mutual trust and nurture cooperation, on the other.

Third, heuristic policies provide a bridge between the cognitive and rationalist policies, by envisaging their integration as a means of seeking realistic and productive assessments of foreign policy decision making. Effective heuristic strategies, marked by "non-compensatory" decision rule, when combined with cognitive approaches, simplify the problems, if any, by eliminating unacceptable alternatives and reducing the decision matrix. Besides, it corresponds to rational choice decision-making, as actors switch to a compensatory mode of decision-making, opting for the most rational choice among the alternatives, while attempting to minimize risks and maximize benefits. Therefore, as Opperman (2014, p. 23) argues, by prioritizing diplomacy to military force in the conduct of foreign relations, heuristics places a premium on conflict resolution and dispute settlement mechanisms for confidence-building and understanding. The principle of conflict resolution is thus premised on achieving understanding on key issues in conflict, a political agreement or consensual decision on future interactions or resource distribution, the pursuit of which has been reflected in Vietnam's acceptance and inclusion in the BRI as well as deliberations on solving outstanding strategic issues with China, both at the bilateral and organizational levels, through ASEAN platform.

A blend of the three theoretical premises discussed above serves as the vantage point of perceiving China's soft power diplomacy in Vietnam, with reference to the BRI. The realist perception is tempered with strains of the tangible, critical geopolitical and geoeconomic imperatives and the constructivist logic of intangibles, represented by images and perceptions in conditioning Sino-Vietnam interactions. For instance, the vestiges of the Sino-Vietnam War (1979) and the threat perception generated by China's hegemonic overtures in the South China Sea have resulted in a "security dilemma" in Vietnam's psyche. The Sino-Vietnam binary reflects a classic case synergizing the shards of history with defensive realism, implying that the means employed by China to enhance its security interests have a disproportionate impact on Vietnam, thereby setting in a security dilemma, sparking apprehension regarding the power asymmetry and future intentions of China. On the other hand, Vietnam's defensive realist logic of security maximization seeks to maintain the regional balance of power by adhering to both internal and external balancing mechanisms. Taking cue from this realist premise, the neoliberal explanation of Sino-Vietnam interactions follows seamlessly, within the framework of the interrelation between power and asymmetrical interdependence as a power resource, including both its hard and soft elements. The primacy of securing Vietnam's national interests and developmental logic, particularly in the context of interdependent globalization, has facilitated its "limited alignment" with China, preparing the ground for employing both hard power strategies like its uncompromising posture towards issues pertaining to "core interests" of sovereignty and soft power strategies (facilitated by the BRI, for instance), in favor of infusing mutual trust and benefit, interdependence and shared development. In this context, Acharya's (Acharya, 2003-2004, p. 150) explanation may be extrapolated to argue that, while adhering to the theory of interdependence, characterized by "bargaining" and "accommodation" of China in pragmatic pursuit of national interests, on the one hand, Vietnam's resort to "bamboo diplomacy" or external balancing strategy of forging cooperative engagements with "like-minded" partners, on the other, entails a deterrent effect on China. In conjunction with China's willingness to pursue greater cooperation and interdependence, acting "…in the spirit of building a community with a shared future", the heuristic principles of issue-based cooperation and conflict resolution, primarily anchored on rational-choice decision-making, by maximizing benefits and minimizing risks, have opened the vistas of cooperation between China and Vietnam. This has, in effect, paved the way for confidence-building, preventive diplomacy, development-based cooperation and soft-power interactions, with the BRI acting as a conduit.

SAGA OF DICHOTOMY IN SINO-VIETNAM RELATIONS: COOPERATION AND DISCORD

Sino-Vietnam relations have been a saga of oscillation from one end of "comradeship plus brotherhood" to the other end representing discord and conflict. For centuries, parts of Vietnam existed under the suzerainty of Chinese dynasties. Subsequently, by the mid-20th century, as Vietnam was engaged in a struggle to overthrow the French colonial yoke, it received military and moral support from Beijing. However, relations took an awkward turn following the conclusion of the Vietnam War in 1975, when Vietnam showed allegiance towards the Soviet camp, thereby antagonizing China. The January 1974 clash between Chinese and South Vietnamese forces over the Paracel Islands in the South China Sea, during which dozens of Vietnamese sailors and soldiers were killed, left a bitter after-taste in bilateral ties. (Chakraborti, 1985, p. 5) Although until its reunification (1975), Vietnam recognized Chinese sovereignty over the Paracel and Spratly Islands, in the post-reunification period, it claimed both the islands, based on historical claims of discovery and occupation rights. Besides, China has embarked on a spree of land reclamation for military and strategic purposes, raising the sensitivity of the South China Sea as a hotbed of rivalry and one-upmanship with Vietnam. The existence of dichotomous strains of cooperation and conflict in bilateral relations has been discussed below.

Dynamics of Discord: Sino-Vietnam Relations in Perspective

Connecting the Indian Ocean through the Malacca Strait to the southwest and commanding access to the East China Sea to the northeast, the strategic location and bounty of natural resources have catapulted the South China Sea to the core of global geo-political and geo-economic computations. The South China Sea forms the cockpit of protracted conflict stemming from overlapping claims to sovereignty over disputed islets, island regimes and its impact on maritime demarcation among China, Brunei, Malaysia, the Philippines, Taiwan and Vietnam. China's insinuations range from dedicated "terra-claims", land reclamation and artificial island-building activities, positioning/installing navy and air force units, surface-to-surface and surface-to-air missiles, enhancing military surveillance to communication and logistics infrastructure-building in the form of port facilities and airstrips. It has not only expanded anti-access area-denial capabilities in the Paracel and Spratly Islands, thus challenging overflight, freedom of navigation and Intelligence Surveillance and Reconnaissance exercises by regional and extra-regional states, but also has been interfering/protesting in oil and gas exploration activities in the contested domain. Its rejection of the verdict of the Permanent Court of International Arbitration (2016) and acknowledgement of construction activities in the South China Sea reef and islands as among the country's top accomplishments under Xi Jinping's leadership (Chakraborti & Chakraborty, 2020, p. 4) while voicing support for a peaceful resolution of the territorial disputes through the conclusion of a Code of Conduct (COC) and negotiations with stakeholders involved, underlines Beijing's duality in this respect.

The conflict between China and Vietnam pertains to overlapping sovereignty claims in the Paracel and Spratly Islands, compounded by China's assertiveness in the region. Chinese vessels, including civilian, Coast Guard and research ships, sail through sensitive locations into Vietnamese waters, thereby posing a direct challenge to its freedom of navigation, sovereignty and territorial integrity. During the 1970s-1980s, incidents like the Sino-Vietnam War (1979), China's intensified naval activities in the Spratly Islands (1986) and its seizure of Gac Ma and Subi reefs (1988) resulted in bilateral relations reaching a nadir. In the post-normalization phase (since 1991), though relations have not deteriorated to the level of a full-scale war, China's hegemonic forays have bolstered the distrust of its intentions in the Vietnamese psyche, alluding to the General Secretary of the Chinese Communist Party (and later President of China), Jiang Zemin's candid observation, "It is abnormal for China and Vietnam to be in a state of confrontation, but it is also unrealistic for their relations to return to the status of the 1950s and 1960s." (as cited in Wilhelm, 1991) Sino-Vietnam territorial competition encompasses various dimensions, including surface and undersea areas, the seabed, airspace, outer space and even the virtual realm and has expanded in scope and intensity. Additionally, China's harassment of Vietnam's oil exploration activities in the South China Sea, with instances of snapping the cables of survey vessels, intercepting fishing boats and resorting to "grey zone" tactics like harassing Vietnamese fishermen with water cannons by Chinese Coast Guard ships, etc. have not only vitiated the regional scenario, but also fueled a rapid rise in Vietnam's defense spending, skepticism and risky incidents. (Mai, 2023)

China's harassment of Vietnam's oil exploration ships (2011) in the South China Sea for developing hydrocarbon assets in collaboration with companies like Exxon Mobil, Chevron etc. and joint ventures with countries like India and Russia, Vietnam's dispatch of naval vessels to prevent China's establishment of oil rigs in the Paracel Islands (2014), China's attempts at preventing Vietnam's drilling activities in Vietnamese Exclusive Economic Zone (EEZ) (2019), China's installation of research stations including defense silos and military grade runways on the Fiery Cross and Subi Reefs and establishment of two administrative districts covering the Paracel and Spratly Islands (2020) are some of the instances that have exacerbated the volatility in bilateral relations. In its most-heavy-handed intrusion in recent years, the month-long standoff between the Coast Guards of China and Vietnam following the operation of Chinese Coast Guard contingent and survey vessel around Vanguard Bank (2019) and the month-long intrusion of a Chinese research vessel in Vietnamese EEZ (June 2023), flanked by ships, operating around Vietnam's joint oil and gas ventures (in collaboration with Russian firms) are noteworthy. (Council on Foreign Relations in New York, 2023) Between 2014-2022, at least 98 Vietnamese boats have been reportedly destroyed by Chinese vessels. (Snell, 2023) These incidents have led to deterioration of bilateral diplomatic ties, prompting Vietnam to enhance its web of alliance relations with "like-minded" partners as a deterrent move vis-s-vis China.

Finally, the inclusion of an extra "dash" to the "nine-dash line" map, depicting Taiwan and most of the Paracel and Spratly Islands as Chinese territory in the "Standard National Map" released by the Chinese Ministry of Natural Resources (2023), is allegedly in violation of the United Nations Convention on the Law of the Sea (UNCLOS) norms. Rejecting the map as "baseless", the spokesperson of Vietnam's Ministry of Foreign Affairs, Pham Thu Hang, reiterated a consistent stance on the sovereignty of the Spratly and Paracel Islands, resolutely "…opposing all of China's claims on the South China Sea based on the dotted line", regarding it as a violation of Vietnam's sovereign rights and jurisdiction over the waters as stipulated in the UNCLOS (as cited in Le, 2023). Summarily then, since the establishment of diplomatic relations between China and Vietnam spanning 74 years, bilateral ties have been interspersed with a fair share of conflict, as enumerated above.

Dynamics of Concord: Sino-Vietnam Relations in Perspective

Although relational strains persist in the dynamics of Sino-Vietnam relations, the conduct of economic, trade, investment and people-to-people/tourism interactions has demonstrated a positive trend, primarily driven by the imperatives of globalization and interdependence, thereby expanding the scope for China's soft power influence in Vietnam. Since the end of the cold war, economic interactions between China and

Vietnam have developed on a solid foundation, with the resumption and expansion of border trade. The establishment of the "Comprehensive Strategic Partnership" (2008), the highest official designation for a diplomatic relationship, has been a hallmark. Facilitated by diplomatic, high-level exchanges between the two countries, China's acceptance of the three working groups to discuss solutions to the disputes over the land border, the maritime boundary in the Gulf of Tonkin and maritime issues in the South China Sea on the one hand and Vietnam's acceptance of the "One-China" principle, on the other, led to the initial warming of ties in the post-cold war period. The two sides sustained diplomatic exchanges through high-level meetings at ministerial, vice-ministerial and expert (working group) levels, as well as exchange mechanisms between Party committees at the Central level to expand cooperation and address unresolved issues, thus attempting to bolster trust and confidence. (Hai, 2021, p. 170)

Pending the South China Sea issue, diplomatic negotiations have erected the pedestal to bolster bilateral, and by extension, regional peace, stability and development through the signing of the Land Border Treaty (1999), Agreement on the Delimitation of the Tonkin Gulf and the Vietnam-China Fisheries Cooperation Agreement (2000), Land Border Demarcation and Marker Planting (2008) and three documents on land border management (2009). A milestone in Sino-Vietnam ties was marked by the visit of the then Secretary General of the Communist Party of Vietnam (CPV), Le Kha Phieu to Beijing in 1999, which laid the foundation for holistic bilateral cooperation and signing of the "Joint Statement on Comprehensive Cooperation" (2000), incorporating the "16 golden words" towards strengthening "… friendly neighborliness, comprehensive cooperation, long-term stability, and future-oriented thinking", envisaging a transformation of relations based on the "Spirt of Four Good", viz. "good neighbors, good friends, good comrades, good partners." (Son & Phong, 2023) Marking a milestone in Sino-Vietnam cooperation, Xi Jinping's momentous state visit to Vietnam in December 2023, after a hiatus of six years, envisaged to "…deepen and further elevate the Vietnam-China Comprehensive Strategic Cooperative Partnership" and "…build a Vietnam-China Community with a shared future having strategic significance." (Joint Statement between Vietnam and China, 2023, para. 6-7, as cited in VN Express, 2023) In addition to bilateral cooperation, the two countries have embarked on strengthening multilateral coordination, within international and regional frameworks and agreements, like ASEAN Regional Forum (ARF), Asia-Pacific Economic Cooperation (APEC), East Asia Summit (EAS), World Trade Organization (WTO) and Regional Comprehensive Economic Partnership (RCEP) agreement.

Within the ambit of ASEAN-led negotiations, there has been a marked advance in negotiations in the South China Sea, towards streamlining the framework and essential elements of the COC. Following the lull induced by COVID-19, ASEAN-China negotiations on an "effective, substantive and actionable COC" resumed in March 2023, envisaging the incorporation of the Declaration on the Conduct of Parties in the South China Sea (DOC) principles into a binding framework for dispute resolution. The negotiation and subsequent follow-up of Joint Working Group meetings and Senior Officials Meetings on Implementation of DOC, held in 2023 have called for full and effective implementation of DOC, practical maritime cooperation, consultations on COC, strengthening dialogue and exercising restraint to enhance mutual trust, deepen cooperation in environmental protection, scientific research etc. in order to transform the South China Sea into an area of peace, friendship and cooperation. (FMPRC, 2023a, para. 2) These cooperative endeavors not only pave the way for confidence-building, but also for enhancing China's legitimacy, essentially underlining its soft power-based access in Vietnam.

The impact of the South China Sea issue on the tenuous diplomatic balance between China and Vietnam, in general, and the interplay of hard power-soft power relations, in particular, with its axiomatic implications for the BRI, can hardly be exaggerated. In this context, Xi Jinping's emphasis on linking China's maritime strategy to interim and long-term national goals, with the ultimate motivation of achieving "…the great rejuvenation of the Chinese people" ("national rejuvenation") by 2049, the centenary of the founding of the People's Republic of China serves as the sine qua non. China's policy and imperatives in the South China Sea may be situated within the wider maritime strategic ambit which envisions its "end state" of assuming "maritime great power" (MGP) status and its aspirations for national rejuvenation, the oft-quoted "Chinese dream." (National Ethnic Affairs Commission, 2012) An analysis of China's *Five-Year Plan (FYP)* documents, particularly its 12th (2011-2015), 13th (2018-2023) and 14th (2021-2025) editions, in conjunction with *China's Vision for Maritime Cooperation under the BRI (2017)* establishes the holistic architecture of China's pursuit of the wide gamut of security interests, including the role of the People's Liberation Army-Navy (PLA-N), Coast Guard, maritime militia and military facilities on reclaimed South China Sea features, as well as for addressing economic, diplomatic, environmental, cultural, legal and scientific issues. On this ambitious pathway, Beijing promotes the BRI as a policy initiative serving its "…national maritime development strategy focused on building China into a maritime great power" in addition to rejuvenating its days of halcyon, reminiscent of a "resplendent maritime civilization." (Tobin, 2018, pp. 8-9) The geostrategic, geoeconomic and soft power vision contained in the mutually reinforcing impulses of the BRI and MGP strategies seek to tether BRI patrons in a connecting and overarching web of alliances, thus stimulating China's external outreach, development-based aspirations, heralding "common prosperity through mutually beneficial cooperation." Based on the above analysis, the "multidisciplinary" aspirations of the BRI, in tandem with its MGP strategy advance and fortify China's comprehensive national and maritime security, economic returns on investments, marine governance and resource management, scientific and technological innovation and escalating influence on BRI patrons like Vietnam (Zreik, 2024). In addition to reiterating the developmental prospects of the BRI for Vietnam, the imperatives of enhancing maritime security, including both traditional and non-traditional components, collaborative governance and joint resources management through prioritized policy coordination and dialogue mechanisms, provide the pedestal for BRI's efficacy for both partners. Simultaneously, Vietnam's discretion and strategic autonomy, while maintaining a "cautious" and "limited" scale of engagement, would not only facilitate a balanced and nuanced posture vis-a-vis China, but also act as the panacea for addressing the inherent dilemma in bilateral ties, accentuated by domestic national sensitivities.

BRI as Conduit for Sino-Vietnam Cooperation: Situating the Rationale, Sectors of Collaboration, and Ramifications

The introduction of "Doi Moi" or economic reforms policy in 1986 has facilitated Vietnam's transformation from a centrally planned to a market economy as well as its ascent to a middle-income country from its status as one of the poorest countries in the world. The World Bank acknowledges Vietnam as not only "…one of the most dynamic emerging countries in the East Asia region," but also as a resilient development success story, inducing aspirations for further progress and growth in terms of connectivity, infrastructure, trade and investment, aimed at improving the standard of living of its people. According to World Bank estimates, between 2002 and 2022, Vietnam's per capita Gross Domestic Product (GDP) increased 3.6 times, reaching almost US\$ 3700, with poverty rates declining from 14% in 2010 to 3.8% in 2020. Vietnam's economy has been projected to grow at 4.7%, 5.5% and 6% in 2023, 2024 and 2025 respectively. (World Bank, 2023) Fueled by the imperative of rapid economic and industrial development and modernization drive in the era of globalization and interdependence, the basic rationale behind

Vietnam's involvement within the BRI framework is to synergize it with Two Corridors, One Economic Circle, which constitutes one of the basic pillars for establishing a China-Vietnam community with a shared future. The development-based initiatives rationalizing its aspirations call for huge investments, particularly in the spheres of transport and infrastructure, telecommunication, electricity and other energy sources, water security, digital economy, science and technology etc., for which BRI investments are viable. It would contribute to the promotion of connectivity, green transition, digital transformation, whilst bolstering "...friendship and mutual understanding among peoples" (FMPRC, 2023, para. 7) of the two countries. The achievements of the BRI since a decade of initiation, in the formation of economic corridors, road and railway networks, clean energy development, information infrastructure, Human Resource Development, environmental and ecosystem protection, business connectivity and the soft spheres like art and cultural exchanges, fostering people-to-people connectivity, find synergy with beneficiaries like Vietnam, for mobilizing resources for national development. Riding on the wave of cautious optimism towards a development-induced future, Vietnam underscores the importance of harnessing Beijing's infrastructure program to enhance mutual connectivity and trade linkages.

BRI projects in Vietnam primarily pertain to connectivity of transport infrastructure, especially railway and road connectivity and energy. In 2017, Vietnam and China signed an MoU on linking the Two Corridors and One Economic Circle framework with BRI, to facilitate cooperation in connecting transport infrastructure and trade among China's southwestern provinces with Vietnam's northern cities and provinces via the corridors of Hai Phong-Hanoi-Lao Cai-Kunming and Hai Phong-Hanoi-Lang Son-Nanning and the Beibu Gulf economic belt. Vietnam hailed the positive effects of the linkage, envisaging to boost industrialization and modernization, while widening avenues of bilateral convergence in connectivity, finance, infrastructure, investments, trade, etc. in addition to providing opportunities to small and medium enterprises to participate in regional and global value chains, contribute to knowledge-based economy and sustainable and inclusive development. Acknowledging the BRI as a significant conduit to "...enhance cooperation and deepen international integration for peace, stability, security, prosperity and sustainable development", the then President of Vietnam, Tran Dai Quang, attended the Inaugural BRI Forum at Beijing (2017) and supported the "...initiatives and efforts to foster economic links and regional connectivity for shared benefit of nations." He welcomed the economic, infrastructure and connectivity-based opportunities offered by the BRI, ensuing "...inter-continental transport infrastructure, favorable trade and investment conditions, forging linkages among enterprises, broadening and deepening people-to people bonds." (Jun & Yanna, 2017)

Vietnam aspires the status of modernity-oriented, industrialized, developing country, graduating from the lower-middle income group to the upper-middle income group by 2030 and finally leap to the status of a developed and a high-income country by 2045, the centenary of the nation's founding. Towards this end, the CPV's leadership, following its 13th National Congress in 2021, reaffirmed "three strategic breakthroughs" identified by its two preceding sessions - fostering a socialist-oriented market economy, investing in human resources and building an integrated and modern infrastructure system in accordance with the new development phase. Besides, the CPV is committed to "...advance Doi Moi process across the board, and actively increase Vietnam's international integration in service of building and defending the nation" together with multilateralization and diversification of external relations. (Press Release on opening session of 13th National Party Congress, 2021, as cited in Vietnam Plus, 2021) The BRI is an important source of funding that Vietnam could tap to finance its burgeoning demands for infrastructure projects, growing exponentially. This is substantiated by the fact that, between 2016 and 2020, Vietnam's need for infrastructure investment in the transport sector doubled from the period 2011-2015 (Zreik, 2023). Factors like decreased inflow of Official Direct Assistance, following its attainment of the middle-income country status in 2011, difficulties in promoting Public Private Partnership projects arising from tightening financial and legal regulations and limited state-funded investment due to budgetary constraints were major challenges towards securing investments from diverse sources. Since projections for 2016-2040 period pegged investment needs for infrastructure at US$ 605 billion (United Nations Economic and Social Commission for Asia and the Pacific, 2017, p. 14) the enhanced demand for investments may have acted as a precursor to its endorsing the BRI as a "catalyst" for regional development.

Impact of BRI in Vietnam: China's Exemplar of Soft Power Diplomacy?

Economic, trade and investment cooperation between China and Vietnam has yielded fruitful results, exploring their structural complementarity, geographical proximity and natural geographical advantage, further augmented by the development and upgradation of connectivity infrastructure as part of BRI projects. In the post-normalization period, Sino-Vietnam trade relations exhibited a growing trend, rising from US$ 179 million in 1992, US$ 1 billion in 1995 to 2.46 billion in 2000. The value of bilateral trade has grown rapidly in the period following Vietnam's BRI inclusion, with China maintaining its position as its largest trading partner and Vietnam as China's fourth-largest trading partner in the world and the largest among ASEAN countries. In 2018, a year after Vietnam joined BRI, bilateral trade turnover reached US$ 100 billion. (Vietnam Chamber of Commerce and Industry-Center for WTO and International Trade, 2023) Between 2018 and 2022, Sino-Vietnam trade increased by 19.7% to a record value of US$ 230.2 billion, surpassing US$ 200 billion mark for the first time in the history of their trade relations. Furthermore, in the first 10 months of 2023, bilateral trade reached US$ 185.1 billion. Vietnam accounted for 25% of China's total trade with ASEAN in the first 11 months of 2023. (The State Council Information Office of the People's Republic of China, 2023) The impact of the enhanced profile of bilateral trade and economic relations is reflected in the promotion of investment and industrial cooperation, including in sectors like agricultural products, electronics, energy, infrastructure, machinery, manufacturing, textiles, among others, thereby unveiling the future roadmap for collaboration in the fields of new energy and digital economy. Chinese investors rank sixth among foreign investors in Vietnam, running 3949 active projects in Vietnam with a total registered capital exceeding US$ 25.8 billion (as of November 2023). This demonstrates a marked rise since 2000, when Chinese investment in Vietnam accounted for US$ 180 million, running about 80 projects, or even in 2012, when investments accounted for US$ 349 million. Between 2018 and 2021, Chinese investment in Vietnam has risen, accounting for US$ 1.15 billion, US$ 1.64 billion, US$ 1.87 billion and US$ 2.2 billion for four successive years. It accounted for US$ 1.7 billion in 2022 and US$ 2.92 billion between January-September 2023 (Textor, 2023; Zerik, 2024).

The rise in China's investment profile in Vietnam is directly proportional to the upgradation of infrastructure and connectivity initiatives, stimulated by BRI projects, since investors in both countries, whether at the level of the government or private enterprise, are enthused by prospects of promoting cross-border investments, particularly through ports, highways, railway networks and their planned extension. Above all, as a conduit of soft power propagation, the complex and multifaceted set of social and structural components mediating border trade not only include state policies or guidelines and specific geographical variables, but are also conditioned by ethnically embedded relations (Nguyen & Wu, 2023, pp. 4-5), encouraging interactions and exchange of cultural, social, financial and physical capital across borders.

In this context, the present section discusses the following BRI projects in Vietnam and their overall socio-economic impact. First, Hanoi Metro-operated 13 km long Cat Linh-Ha Dong metro railway line (operational in November 2021), covering three districts in Hanoi. Built by the China Railway Sixth Group, with total investment value of US$ 886 million, the metro project is an important component of the BRI-Two Corridors and One Economic Circle synergy, marking the first urban metro railway line to be constructed in Vietnam. This citizen-centric and environment-friendly project is aimed at phased reduction of people's dependence on private transport, minimizing congestion and reducing pollution in Hanoi. (Nguyen, 2023)

Second, coal-fired 1200 MW Vinh Tan Thermal Power Complex: the power plant consists of five thermal power plants, with a whopping Chinese investment of US$ 1.75 billion, proposed to generate 1200 MW, on completion. A joint investment venture of China's Southern Power Grid Company (55% stake), China Power International Development Company (40% stake) and local Vincomin Electricity accounting for the remainder, the project is listed as a key for Sino-Vietnamese cooperation, addressing electricity shortage in South and Southeastern Vietnam's economic zones. The project, as part of the Sino-Vietnam development plan, is an important component of BRI. Of the four plants, Vin Tan-1 (operational in 2018), is not only the biggest project invested by Chinese companies in Vietnam under BRI, but also the maiden project under Build-Operate-Transfer (BOT) scheme in Vietnam. (Belt and Road Portal - BRI Official Website, 2017)

Third, Soc Son waste-to-energy plant, located in Nam Son Waste Treatment Complex in Hanoi, exemplifies green development cooperation and is the largest waste-to-energy plant in Vietnam. With a capacity of handling 4,000 tons of solid waste and 1,740 tons of wastewater daily, the project became operational in 2022, with a total investment of US$ 303 million. It has made important contributions to improving the city's appearance and environment. (Kiet, 2022)

The immediate outcome of the BRI projects operational in Vietnam has been positive, with beneficial economic and social impact. For instance, the Cat Linh-Ha Dong metro railway project received soaring popularity as a mode of easy, regular transport, recording 262% increase in commuters in the first three months of 2023, as compared to 2022, catering to 2.65 million passengers. As attested to by a representative of Hanoi Metro, its positive impact on enhancing urban transportation, regional economic and urban spatial development is noteworthy, in addition to acting as an encouragement for other Vietnamese cities to emulate and invest more in urban rail transit systems. (as cited in Dong, 2023) The Vinh Tan power plant is expected to reduce carbon dioxide emissions by about 20,000 tons annually, relative to subcritical units of the same size and meet the power demand of 1.25 million residents, by providing more than 7.2 billion KWH power, thereby addressing the urgent power imbalance between the northern and southern parts of Vietnam. (Chunting, 2018) Besides, Saigon proposes to transform the region into a power generation hub and promote local social and economic development, in tandem with boosting energy security of the people. The Soc Son waste-to-energy plant envisages reduced pollution levels, by processing 4,000 metric tons of daily urban waste, which accounts for more than 60% of Hanoi's daily generated waste. The project promises to revolutionize urban waste management by converting wastes into green energy as it is expected to generate 75 MW power per hour. (Yan, 2023)

Besides, Chinese investments in Vietnam have provided employment options for the local populace, accounting for labor restructuring, improved local industrial support mechanism and driven the growth of local exports, as demonstrated, for instance, by the increase in Chinese investments in the Vietnam textile industry, as a result of which, several large-scale modern textile enterprises have formed a relatively complete industrial chain locally (Dongri, 2023), with prospects of extending to the global industrial and supply chains. The introduction of new and advanced technologies and management models has acted as a boost for local business firms to enhance and upgrade management skills and productivity. Thus, as China claims, by integrating resources for technological innovation, it is paving the way for introducing "new productive forces" (Dan & Zhou, 2024) through overseas investments, premised on the twin drivers of digital technology and green transformation, envisaged as the harbinger of high quality and futuristic economic development.

In the matrix of hard power-soft power interplay guiding bilateral ties between China and Vietnam, four underlying factors come into play: First, the constructivist, perception-based analysis pertaining to domestic legitimization and acceptance of Chinese investments and soft power insinuation in Vietnam, of which BRI is a conduit. Second, Vietnam government's/CPV's urgency and interest in facilitating this legitimization in the public eye, wherein two divergent dynamics need balancing. While on the one hand, Vietnamese national sentiments vis-à-vis China have been marred by a history of conflict and the latter's hegemonic ambitions, the twin strains of securing its development-based national interests and strengthening the pedestal for heuristic understanding, which may pave the way for addressing unresolved bilateral issues, like the South China Sea, on the other, demand judicious governmental responses. Third, an outcome-based assessment in terms of the socio-economic, political and environmental impact of the BRI projects, also shape Vietnam's domestic perceptions vis-à-vis China. Finally, China's balancing act as it seeks to legitimize soft power influence in Vietnam as a means to negotiate hard power projection gains significance.

Thus, in the case of Vietnam, domestic political dynamics drive performance and nationalistic legitimation of external investment fundings through China's BRI. The concerns and trepidations of Vietnamese public sentiments regarding China's hegemonism, evident, for instance in the wake of the Oil Rig Crisis (2014), fueling public discourse concerning Vietnam's "overdependence" on China have provided a push for the CPV to pursue the policy of economic hedging, while maintaining what Goh (Goh, 2007-2008, p. 116) and Laksmana (Laksmana, 2017, p. 114) refer to as "limited alignment" or "pragmatic equidistance" from China's strategy of "omni-enmeshment." Thus, CPV elites attach primary importance to nationalistic legitimation of their perception of China in general and Chinese investments in particular, providing performance legitimation of projects and investment-driven ventures a secondary importance. (Dung & Ho, 2022, p. 11) This brings to the fore the delicate balance of optimizing performance with power diffusion, forming the framework of the domestic justification of the degree of acceptance of BRI.

Adding to the legitimacy of BRI projects, while augmenting China's credentials as a facilitator of soft power, the United Nations (UN) has envisaged specific measures to help BRI beneficiary states strengthen their National Policy Capacity (NPC) to implement the projects more efficiently, providing for their approval by the Development Policy and Analysis Division (DPAP) and funding by the UN Peace and Development Trust Fund. Within this framework, China and the UN have allotted US$ 200 million (of US$ 1 billion Fund value) under the UN Peace and Development Trust Fund, to assist countries to build modern, green cities, advance scientific and technological innovation, support people-to-people exchanges, promote communication, transportation and power systems (Zhenqiu, 2017) towards fortifying the heuristic policy of maintaining peace, stability and economic development.

It may not be implausible to argue that the BRI can facilitate both hard power and soft power interactions in the context of China-Vietnam relations. In terms of facilitating hard power, BRI's efficacy has been demonstrated, for instance, in the sphere of enhancing maritime security, with the signing of two cooperation agreements for joint patrols in the Gulf of Tonkin in South China Sea and the establishment of a hotline to handle fisheries incidents (Nguyen, 2023b), thus generating confidence and consensus-building. Secondly and closely related to the above is the facilitation of practical maritime cooperation, not only in the ambit of Sino-Vietnam binary, but also within the extended domain of Vietnam's energy security endeavors/joint ventures for oil exploration with India, Russia and other multi-national/corporate stakeholders in its EEZ. The success of these endeavors would act as an image-booster for ASEAN as well, since the unresolved South China Sea issue considerably debilitates the realization of the ASEAN Political-Security Community, posing a challenge to the notion of ASEAN centrality (Zreik, 2021). Third, BRI's success may further the cause of Vietnam's defense diplomacy with China, allaying concerns vis-à-vis the former's dependence on Russia for arms import, exacerbated in the context of the Ukraine conflict. This is significant as Vietnam embarks on the strategy of internal balancing by reducing dependence on Russian arms supply, diversifying its sources of arms imports and promoting indigenous development. (Storey, 2024, p. 6) Finally, in the backdrop of the calls for UN-Security Council reforms and a more democratized and eclectic representation of the Council by expanding its membership, much to China's chagrin, the BRI architecture may be used to its leverage (Narasimhan, 2024) to influence the voices of its BRI partners.

In the overarching aspirational framework of "building a community with shared future", towards achieving common, comprehensive, cooperative and sustainable security, the tapestry of Chinese "initiatives" of the ilk of BRI, GSI, GDI and GCI, may be viewed in the matrix of hard power-soft power continuum. Resolute on building an "indivisible" regional security architecture, China's emphasis on expanding international consensus on common security, forging an effective paradigm of international security cooperation, exploring peaceful solutions to "hotspot" issues and promoting the reform of global security governance, while being antipodal to the tenets of liberal institutionalism in practice, theorizes "…respect for the diversity of civilizations", thus allaying the "China threat" thesis and supplementing it with the "Peaceful Rise-Peaceful Development" doctrine. This forms the fulcrum of the soft power matrix of both BRI and GCI, which "…inject fresh and strong energy into the common development and progress of human society" (The State Council Information Office of the People's Republic of China, 2023a, para. 1).

Sino-Vietnam Cooperation and BRI: Weighing the Challenges, Opportunities, and Charting the Future

The BRI's principal rationale of leveraging China's economic, geo-strategic and soft power clout converges with the imperative of ensuring the security of Sea Lanes of Communication and freedom of navigation of the littorals through which it passes or proposes to pass. Securing Beijing's geo-strategic and geo-economic interests calls for expanding its web of alliances and associates of the BRI on the one hand, while cementing and enhancing its legitimacy and acceptance as a facilitator of soft power, on the other. China has been successful to a considerable extent in terms of the former, with BRI membership extending "…from the Eurasian continent to Africa and Latin America", and "…more than 150 countries and over 30 international organizations" signing the BRI cooperation documents, in addition to establishing "…over 20 specialized multilateral cooperation platforms." (FMPRC, 2023, para. 4) Through the crafting of the "community of shared destiny", China promotes high quality development of BRI, and proposes to proactively open up the eastern coastal areas, central, western and northeast regions, expediting construction of the New International Land-Sea Trade Corridor in the western region, Hainan Free Trade Port, upgrading pilot free trade zones and expanding globalization-oriented network of high-standard Free Trade Agreements. These aspirations are buttressed by infrastructure miracles like the building of the world's largest networks of high-speed highways, expressways, airports, ports etc. Beijing projects BRI as a conduit of economic diplomacy and for furthering world peace and development. It translates to fostering a geo-economic cooperative design, as opposed to a geopolitical or geo-strategic one, based on the five pillars of policy coordination, connectivity facilitation, unimpeded trade, financial integration and forging of people-to-people bonds. (FMPRC, 2022a, pp. 27-28) Thus, China is building, brick by brick, an alternative international system, with Chinese characteristics and unveiling the opportunities of BRI to script a "community with a shared future" in pursuit of a "modernization drive." This initiative, as acknowledged by Nguyen Vinh Quang, Vice President of Vietnam-China Friendship Association, acts as an inspiration for "…Vietnam's social and economic development" (as cited in Aixin, 2023) while upholding the spirit of "camaraderie plus brotherhood" with Vietnam.

Within the scaffold of this ambitious geo-strategic architecture, China's aspirations of a "benevolent" entry into the Indo-Pacific region through its spree of building infrastructure, ports, deep water ports and container terminals, proposed to connect with the mainland through a string of road and railway corridors, logistical stations, storage facilities and free-trade zones, is translating into a reality. Simultaneously, BRI's emphasis on building a modernized economy and new pattern of development encapsulates the "spirit" of human progress, world harmony and people-centric development, serving the cause of "common prosperity through mutually beneficial cooperation." (FMPRC, 2022a, pp. 54-55) Herein lies the potential of BRI to situate China as a facilitator of soft power.

In spite of Vietnam's acknowledgement and expression of support for BRI, it is aware of the public distrust of China following certain incidents like the 2014 Oil Rig incident, public protests against a bill on Special Economic Zone that proposed to allow foreign business to lease land for up to 99 years, granting preferential treatment to occupying Vietnamese land (2018) (Do, 2019, p. 213) in addition to public concerns about toxic Chinese products, disregard for local employment laws, environmentally unsustainable projects, poor quality products, etc. by Chinese investors. Concerns in Vietnamese investor circles abound regarding the potential competition to the domestic market from the influx of Chinese investors. It may be added in this context, that the agreement on strengthening bilateral cooperation in economic zones, trade and investment, among other areas, thereby providing opportunities for greater flow of Chinese Foreign Direct Investments (FDI) and access to supporting-investment firms supplying raw materials and components to manufacturers in Vietnam, signed in course of Xi Jinping's visit to Hanoi in December 2023, may further fuel the unease among Vietnamese investors. (Nguyen, 2023a)

As a consequence of the US-China trade standoff and burdens of tariffs and higher costs, the relocation of Chinese firms to countries like Vietnam, which have a large working population and easier access to developed markets, is a cause for domestic trepidation as well and calls for more stringent legal provisions by Hanoi towards protecting the interests of the domestic market, workers and investors. It would not be a misplaced caveat for Vietnam to be mindful of the terms and conditions entailing Chinese investments and issues of openness, transparency, principles of financial responsibility to avoid projects that create unsustainable debt burden, adherence to balanced ecological and environmental protection and preservation standards, transparent assessment of project costs and skill and technology transfer to help long-term maintenance of the assets. In addition, it would be pragmatic for Hanoi to draw lessons from the experiences of its BRI counterparts, mired in ballooning deficits and the vicious debt-trap that some have inevitably become a part of (Zreik, 2022). This is demonstrated in the cases of Argentina, Ethiopia, Montenegro, Pakistan, Sri Lanka, Zambia etc., with costly projects pushing debt-to-GDP ratios to unsustainable levels, resulting in balance of payments crises. (Bennon & Fukuyama, 2023) Vietnam's ASEAN neighbors like Indonesia, Malaysia and Thailand, while acknowledging the positive impact of

BRI, are also concerned about issues of financial viability of projects, terms of loan, transparency, accountability, local workers' safety, risk management, compliance with social, environmental and governance standards and the like. (Busbarat, Camba et al., 2023) Finally, it is imperative for Vietnam to calculate the costs of environmental degradation and development-induced displacement that BRI projects may entail. For instance, public demonstrations against the environmental impact of the Vinh Tan complex, not only emitting cinders and ash from both construction and operation sites, but also contamination of water resources and its impact on the flora and crops in the surroundings, is a case in point. (Vietnam Plus, 2018) Summarily then, though China's enhanced geo-economic and geo-strategic leverage in the region facilitated by the BRI may be an acceptable and welcome initiative for Vietnam, it would be judicious on its part to weigh the options and pragmatically calibrate its interests, priorities and stakes.

China and Vietnam have embarked upon specific "directions, measures and strategies" to enhance political trust, deepen and elevate partnership in future, for which the BRI would definitely serve as a facilitator. As Hanoi prioritizes the development of bilateral relations, welcoming infrastructure and connectivity projects within the BRI framework, Beijing's reciprocation and emphasis on "…jointly building a community with a shared future for mankind" (Xinhua, 2023) reflects a cooperative future, with the BRI acting as the fulcrum. As envisaged by the Vietnamese Prime Minister, Pham Minh Chinh, attracting greater and unimpeded trade and investments from China is contingent on implementing judicious policies, creating favorable investment conditions through a combination of factors "…including the regulatory framework, infrastructure and political determination." These measures are aimed at encouraging border trade, formation of appropriate border trade zones, developing logistics systems, connecting supply chains, promoting e-commerce, enforcing strict anti-smuggling and anti-trade fraud laws, improving the legal framework, addressing corruption, simplifying administrative procedures and business conditions (as cited in Vietnam Plus, 2023) while prioritizing transparency, convenience and international competitiveness, socio-economic development, green transition and environmentally sustainable ventures. This futuristic blueprint synergizes with China's efforts to promote trade and investment cooperation, emphasizing the need for favorable conditions for competent enterprises to invest in Vietnam.

The impact of China's soft power diplomacy through BRI and its efficacy for Vietnam is not only analyzed and balanced in terms of serving the realist-based logic of mutual national interest and development, but also the constructivist understanding of popular perception and acceptance. While the present dispensation in Vietnam acknowledges and welcomes China's involvement in the nation in lieu of BRI investments and its soft power insinuation, Xi Jinping's aspirations of prioritizing neighborhood diplomacy and emphasis on "…steadily promoting the building of a China-Vietnam community with a shared future that carries strategic significance" (Xinhua, 2023) would not culminate, pending the moderation or reversal of skepticism about China among the common people of Vietnam. In addition to the existing projects, greater cooperation in infrastructure and connectivity, notably Lao Cai-Hanoi-Hai Phong route linking Kunming-Hanoi-Hai Phong economic corridor, high speed Hanoi-Ho Chi Minh City etc.; coastal road from Quang Ninh to Ca Mau and other breakthrough priority areas like road connectivity; customs efficiency through "smart border gate" model; port cooperation; economic, trade and investment; education, training and people-to-people programs are in the offing. (Dong, 2023a) Simultaneously, it must be mindful of facilitating avenues of people-to-people contacts between the two countries as a means of confidence-building and public participation. Since the degree and extent of the success of soft power diplomacy is primarily guided by perception, China's emphasis on more people-centric projects and exchanges, whether based on tourism/cross-border travel or through the dissemination of aesthetic and cultural channels of exchange like music, films, theatres, language training, sports, student and youth exchanges and Track-II diplomacy with Vietnam would widen the ambit of cooperation. Such initiatives would serve as further channels of heuristic management of political consensus-building at the bilateral level, thereby upholding peace, stability and inclusiveness. In this context, the efficacy of China's BRI projects may be demonstrated in terms of the signing of two cooperation agreements for joint patrols in the Gulf of Tonkin in South China Sea and the establishment of a hotline to handle fisheries incidents (Nguyen, 2023b) thus generating confidence-building and consensus building on a couple of contentious issues.

Notwithstanding the negative impact of the BRI experienced by different beneficiary states, the last decade has exhibited significant development entailed by the BRI, within the broad framework of enhancing connectivity, infrastructure, trade, financial and people-to-people connectivity, thus injecting "…new impetus into the global economy, creating new opportunities for global development, and building a new platform for international economic cooperation." Expanding from physical connectivity to institutional connectivity, envisaging the principles of "…planning together, building together, and benefiting together" (FMPRC, 2023, para. 2, 6) the BRI has focused on specific areas of cooperation in economic corridors, international transportation routes and information highways as well as railways, roads, airports, ports, pipelines and power grids. Besides, BRI's encouragement of art festivals, expos, exhibitions and programs engaging people-to-people exchanges like the Silk Road Community Building Initiative and the Brightness Action program, in addition to fostering interactions between non-governmental organizations, think tanks, media organizations and the youth, has further facilitated its soft power diplomacy.

The dynamics of Sino-Vietnam relations are influenced by hard power-soft power interactions, explained through the perspective lens of the triad of realism, neoliberal interdependence and heuristics. The imperative of balancing the hard power-soft power interactions, given the asymmetry in power, resource endowment and capabilities between China and Vietnam, is facilitated by the BRI, serving the purposes of addressing challenges to maritime and energy security, while providing the architecture for shared development and progress. As China proclaims, the BRI has "…delivered fruitful outcomes and won widespread support and participation", fostering "tangible benefits to people of participating countries", pressing ahead with "…construction of transborder thoroughfares between China and neighbouring countries and thoroughfares along the Belt and Road routes", improved infrastructure, trade and investment, sustainable and green development, people-to-people exchanges and cultural interactions. (Central Committee of the Communist Party of China, 2016, p. 82) Xi Jinping's emphasis on coordinating the hard and soft elements of security, implicit in his acknowledgement of security as the "precondition for development" (The State Council Information Office of the People's Republic of China, 2023a, para. 11) - the moniker guiding China's repertoire of "initiatives" like BRI, GDI, GSI and GSI - forms the fulcrum for the realization of its status as a maritime great power, guided by the polestar of "great national rejuvenation" by 2049. The BRI provides opportunities to fulfil Vietnam's aspirations of the status of modernity-oriented, industrialized, developing country, graduating from the lower-middle income group to the upper-middle income group by 2030 and finally leap to the status of a developed and a high-income country by 2045, the centenary of the nation's founding. Simultaneously, China's emphasis on exploring peaceful solutions to contentious issues and promoting the reform of global security governance extends the space for policy coordination and dialogue mechanisms on dispute resolution and confidence-building, which may be explored further in terms of mitigating the South China Sea issue. However, BRI's efficacy would impinge on the actual outcome of promoting "cultural exchanges to transcend estrangement, mutual learning to transcend clashes and coexistence to transcend feelings of superiority" (The State Council Information Office of the People's Republic of China, 2023a, para. 7) rather than limiting these aspirations to diplomatic vocabulary. As a responsible regional actor, endowed with resources, both physical and human, motivated by a developmental drive, while maintaining strategic autonomy in decision-making, it would be judicious for Vietnam to leverage and utilize the opportunities unfolded by the BRI to its best advantage and navigate the challenges, seeking to maintain the desired equilibrium in bilateral relations. In the context of the interdependent world order, countries would be diplomatically well-informed to weigh the costs of being pulled into bilateral "mind-games" (Indian Minister of External Affairs, Jaishankar S., as cited in Hindustan Times, 2024) and supplement it with diversified interactions at multilateral, regional and even sub-regional levels as the underlying principle of deterrence and balancing against active or potential hegemons.

China envisages eight major "steps" for bolstering the future strategy and viability of the BRI, viz. building a multidimensional Belt and Road connectivity network; supporting an open world economy; promoting both signature projects and "small yet smart" livelihood programs; promoting green development through green infrastructure, green energy and green transportation; advancing scientific and technological innovation; supporting people-to-people exchanges and facilitate dialogue on civilizations with BRI partner countries; promoting integrity-based Belt and Road cooperation by working with international organizations to carry out research and training; and strengthening institutional building for international Belt and Road cooperation. (State Council of the People's Republic of China, 2023) These initiatives propose to assist in the development-induced, sustainable modernization drive of beneficiary nations in general and Vietnam, in particular, thus expanding the avenues of cooperation with and through accepting China's position, image and potential as a soft power facilitator and complementing the comprehensive strategic cooperative partnership substantially with political trust, goodwill and confidence-building.

CONCLUSION

The interaction of hard power-soft power dynamics in Sino-Vietnam relations, premised on the theoretical matrix of realism, neoliberal interdependence and heuristics, is manifested in bilateral cooperation within the BRI framework. The advantages accruing from Vietnam's partnership of BRI seek to balance the asymmetry in power, resource endowment and capabilities between China and Vietnam, not only serving the purposes of addressing challenges to maritime and energy security, but also providing the architecture for shared development and progress through improved infrastructure, trade and investment, people-to-people exchanges and cultural interactions. While leveraging the opportunities and advantages of BRI in various spheres judiciously, it is an imperative for Vietnam to address its challenges in a pragmatic manner, mindful of securing and safeguarding national interests and strategic autonomy, adeptly balanced with its quest for peace and sustainable development towards a progressive future.

REFERENCES

Acharya, A. (2003-2004). Will Asia's past be its future? *International Security*, *28*(3), 149–164. https://www.jstor.org/stable/4137480. doi:10.1162/016228803773100101

Aixin, L. (2023, December 23). Vietnam chooses justice and national interest that can prevent itself from becoming a pawn: Former Vietnamese official. *Global Times*. https://www.globaltimes.cn/page/202312/1303569.shtml

Belt and Road Portal - BRI Official Website. (2017, July 17). *Vinh Tan 1 power plant largest Chinese investment in Vietnam.* https://eng.yidaiyilu.gov.cn/p/20048.html

Bennon, M., & Fukuyama, F. (2023, August 22). China's road to ruin: The real toll of Beijing's Belt and Road. *Foreign Affairs.* https://www.foreignaffairs.com/china/belt-road-initiative-xi-imf

Busbarat, P., & Camba, A. (2023, December 5). *How has China's Belt and Road Initiative impacted Southeast Asian countries?* https://carnegieendowment.org/2023/12/05/how-has-china-s-belt-and-road-initiative-impacted-southeast-asian-countries-pub-91170

Central Committee of the Communist Party of China. (2016). *13th Five-Year Plan for Economic and Social Development of the People's Republic of China, 2016-2020.* https://en.ndrc.gov.cn/policies/202105/P020210527785800103339.pdf

Chakraborti, T. (1985). *India and Kampuchea: A phase in their relations, 1978-1981.* Minerva Associates Pvt. Ltd.

Chakraborti, T., & Chakraborty, M. (2020). *India's strategy in the South Chia Sea.* Routledge.

Chakraborty, M. (2023, November). ASEAN's tryst with community-building: Towards comprehensive dispute settlement. In *Special Report: ASEAN's Critical Assessment and Practical Reforms*, (pp. 22-34). Asian Vision Institute & Konrad Adenauer Stiftung-Asian Vision Institute. https://www.kas.de/documents/264850/29101139/Special+Report+ASEAN%27s+Critical+Assessment+and+Practical+Reforms.pdf/

Chunting, L. (2018, July 30). *Chinese-funded Vinh Tan Plant kicks off to boost power supply in Vietnam.* https://www.yicaiglobal.com/news/chinese-funded-vinh-tan-plant-kicks-off-to-boost-power-supply-in-vietnam

Council on Foreign Relations in New York. (2023). *China's maritime disputes: 1895-2023.* https://www.cfr.org/timeline/chinas-maritime-disputes

Dan, S., & Zhou, D. (2024, February 6). New productive forces need new industrialization. *China Daily.* https://global.chinadaily.com.cn/a/202402/06/WS65c17539a3104efcbdae9d5d.html#:~:text=Recently%2C%20%22new%20productive%20forces%22,advancing%20high%2Dquality%20economic%20development

Do, T. H. (2019). *Vietnam and the South China Sea: Politics, security and legality.* Routledge.

Dong, H. (2023a, September 17). *Chinese conglomerates eye railway expansion in Vietnam.* https://theinvestor.vn/chinese-conglomerates-eye-railway-expansion-in-vietnam-d6651.html#:~:text=He%20suggested%20that%20Power%20China,Hanoi%2DHai%20Phong%20rail%20lines

Dong, K. (2023, August 10). *China's infrastructure projects improving the Vietnamese life quality greatly.* https://www.ichongqing.info/2023/08/10/chinas-infrastructure-projects-improving-the-vietnamese-life-quality-greetly-insights/

Dongri, H. (2023, December 10). Enormous potential in economic and trade cooperation between China and Vietnam. *Global Times.* https://www.globaltimes.cn/page/202312/1303346.shtml

Dung, P. X., & Ho, B. T. E. (2022, September 13). How regime legitimation influences Vietnam's strategy toward US-China strategic rivalry. *International Journal of Asian Studies*, 1–20. doi:10.1017/ S1479591422000286

Environment at Vinh Tan power complex under Scrutiny. (2018, February 26). *Vietnam Plus*. https://en.vietnamplus.vn/environment-at-vinh-tan-power-complex-under-scrutiny/126980. vnp#:~:text=Locals%20once%20blockaded%20the%20National,many%20perennial%20trees%20and%20 crops

Goh, E. (2007-2008). Great powers and hierarchical order in Southeast Asia: Analyzing regional security strategies. *International Security*, *32*(3), 113–157. doi:10.1162/isec.2008.32.3.113

Hai, D. T. (2021, May 26). Vietnam and China: Ideological bedfellows, strange dreamers. *Journal of Contemporary East Asia Studies*, *10*(2), 162–182. doi:10.1080/24761028.2021.1932018

Hiep, L. H. (2013, December). Vietnam's hedging strategy against China since normalization. *Contemporary Southeast Asia*, *35*(3), 333–368. doi:10.1355/cs35-3b

Hindustan Times. (2024, February 23). Jaishankar cautions against this 'mind game' by China: Raisina Dialogue 2024. https://www.hindustantimes.com/india-news/jaishankar-cautions-against-this-mind-game-by-china-i-dont-think-we-should-play-it-101708666270969.html

Jervis, R. (1978, January). Cooperation under the security dilemma. *World Politics*, *30*(2), 167–214. doi:10.2307/2009958

Joint Statement between Vietnam and China. (2023, December 13). *VN Express*. https://www.vietnam. vn/en/tuyen-bo-chung-viet-nam-trung-quoc/

Jun, T., & Yanna, L. (2017, May 11). Interview: Vietnamese President looks forward to Belt and Road Forum in China. *Xinhua*. http://www.xinhuanet.com/english/2017-05/11/c_136273962.htm

Kiet, A. (2022, January 19). Vietnam's largest waste-to-power plant to begin operation from January 20. *Hanoi Times*. https://hanoitimes.vn/vietnams-largest-waste-to-power-plant-goes-into-operation-from-jan-20-319806.html

Laksmana, E. A. (2017). Pragmatic equidistance – how Indonesia manages its great power relations. In D. B. H. Denoon (Ed.), *The United States and the future of Southeast Asia* (pp. 113–135). New York University Press.

Le, H. (2023, August 31). Vietnam opposes China's new national map. *VN Express*. https://e.vnexpress. net/news/news/vietnam-opposes-china-s-new-national-map-4648426.html

Mai, N. (2023, October 27). "Grey zone" activities cast a shadow over cooperation and peaceful prospects in East Sea. *Hanoi Times*. https://hanoitimes.vn/grey-zone-activities-cast-a-shadow-over-cooperation-and-peaceful-prospects-in-east-sea-325164.html

Ministry of Foreign Affairs of the People's Republic of China (FMPRC). (2015, March 28). *Vision and actions on jointly building Silk Road Economic Belt and 21st-Century Maritime Silk Road*. https:// en.ndrc.gov.cn/newsrelease/201503/t20150330_669367.html

Ministry of Foreign Affairs of the People's Republic of China (FMPRC). (2022, October 20). *Foreign Ministry Spokesperson Wang Wenbin's Regular Press Conference*. https://www.fmprc.gov.cn/mfa_eng/xwfw_665399/s2510_665401/2511_665403/202210/t20221020_10788936.html

Ministry of Foreign Affairs of the People's Republic of China (FMPRC). (2022a, October 25). *Full Text of the Report to the 20th National Congress of the Communist Party of China.* https://www.fmprc.gov.cn/eng/zxxx_662805/202210/t20221025_10791908.html

Ministry of Foreign Affairs of the People's Republic of China (FMPRC). (2023, October 18). *Building an open, inclusive and interconnected world for common development.* Keynote Speech by H. E. Xi Jinping, President of the People's Republic of China at the opening ceremony of the Third Belt and Road Forum for International Cooperation. http://www.beltandroadforum.org/english/n101/2023/1018/c124-1175.html

Ministry of Foreign Affairs of the People's Republic of China (FMPRC). (2023a, October 26). *The 21st Senior Officials' Meeting on the Implementation of the Declaration on the Conduct of Parties in the South China Sea Held in Beijing.* https://www.mfa.gov.cn/mfa_eng/wjbxw/202310/t20231027_11169603.html

Ministry of Planning and Investment of the Socialist Republic of Vietnam. (2023, November 13). *Vietnam, China enjoy stronger partnership.* https://www.mpi.gov.vn/en/Pages/2023-11-23/Vietnam-China-enjoy-stronger-partnershiptnvm4e.aspx

Narasimhan, S. L. (2024, February 20). India must be wary of China's global security plan. *The Tribune.* https://www.tribuneindia.com/news/comment/india-must-be-wary-of-chinas-global-security-plan-592477

National Ethnic Affairs Commission. (2012, November 29). *Achieving rejuvenation is the dream of the Chinese people.* https://www.neac.gov.cn/seac/c103372/202201/1156514.shtml

Nedopil, C. (2024). *China Belt and Road Initiative investment report 2023.* Griffith Asia Institute, Griffith University & Green Finance & Development Center. https://greenfdc.org/china-belt-and-road-initiative-bri-investment-report-2023/#:~:text=Of%20the%202023%20engagement%2C%20about,the%20onset%20of%20COVID%2D19

Nguyen, H. (2023a, December 28). Vietnam wary of China's swift, large-scale investment. *Voice of America.* https://www.voanews.com/a/vietnam-wary-of-china-s-swift-large-Scale-investment/7416324.html

Nguyen, M. (2023b, December 12). Vietnam, China sign 36 agreements in Xi's visit. *Hanoi Times.* https://hanoitimes.vn/vietnam-china-sign-36-agreements-in-xis-visit-325615.html

Nguyen, S., & Wu, Y. (2023, June 15). Cat Linh-Ha Dong urban rail becomes popular means of transport. *Hanoi Times.* https://hanoitimes.vn/cat-linh-ha-dong-urban-rail-becomes-popular-means-of-transport-323957.html#:~:text=The%20Cat%20Linh%2DHa%20Dong%20elevated%20railway%20has%20brought%20great,urban%20railway%20line%20in%20Hanoi

Nguyen, S. T., & Wu, Y. (2023, April 26). Vietnam's bilateral trade intensity: The role of China. *Journal of Chinese Economic and Business Studies*, 1–22. doi:10.1080/14765284.2023.2206785

Oppermann, K. (2014, January). Delineating the scope conditions of the poliheuristic theory of decision making: The noncompensatory principle and the domestic salience of Foreign Policy. *Foreign Policy Analysis, 10*(1), 23–41. doi:10.1111/j.1743-8594.2012.00182.x

Press Release on opening session of 13th National Party Congress. (2021, January 26). *Vietnam Plus* https://en.vietnamplus.vn/press-release-on-opening-session-of-13th-national-party-congress/195396.vnp

Snell, G. (2023, June 17). Tensions high as Chinese vessels shadow Vietnam's oil, gas operations. *Voice of America.* https://www.voanews.com/a/tensions-high-as-chinese-vessels-shadow-vietnam-s-oil-and-gas-operations-/7141273.html

Son, N., & Phong, V. (2023, December 12). New stature in Vietnam-China relations. *Nhandan.* https://special.nhandan.vn/vietnam-trungquoc_en/index.html

State Council of the People's Republic of China. (2023, October 18). *Xi announces major steps to support high-quality Belt and Road cooperation.* https://english.www.gov.cn/news/202310/18/content_WS-652f65e6c6d0868f4e8e05bd.html

Storey, I. (2024, February 16). Vietnam and the Russia-Ukraine War: Hanoi's 'bamboo diplomacy' pays off but challenges remain. *ISEAS Perspective, 2024*(13), 1-9. https://www.iseas.edu.sg/articles-commentaries/iseas-perspective/2024-13-vietnam-and-the-russia-ukraine-war-hanois-bamboo-diplomacy-pays-off-but-challenges-remain-in-ian-storey/

Textor, C. (2023, November 11). *Annual FDI flows from China to Vietnam, 2012-2022.* https://www.statista.com/statistics/720408/china-outward-fdi-flows-to-vietnam/

The State Council Information Office of the People's Republic of China. (2023, December 13). *Bilateral trade between China, Vietnam hits monthly record high.* http://english.scio.gov.cn/pressroom/2023-12/13/content_116876643.htm#:~:text=Vietnam%20has%20since%202016%20remained,first%2011%20months%20of%202023

The State Council Information Office of the People's Republic of China. (2023a, March 19). *Global Civilization Initiative injects fresh energy into human development.* http://english.scio.gov.cn/topnews/2023-03/19/content_85177312.htm

Tobin, L. (2018). Underway-Beijing's strategy to build China into a maritime great power. *Naval War College Review, 71*(2), 1–32. https://digital-commons.usnwc.edu/nwc-review/vol71/iss2/5/

United Nations Economic and Social Commission for Asia and the Pacific. (2017, September 15). *Infrastructure financing strategies for sustainable development in Vietnam.* https://www.unescap.org/sites/default/files/20170915%20National%20Study%20-%20Infrastructure%20Financing%20-%20Viet%20%20Nam.pdf

Vietnam Chamber of Commerce and Industry- Center for WTO and International Trade. (2023, July 5). *China – Vietnam's largest trading partner.* https://wtocenter.vn/chuyen-de/22257-china--vietnams-largest-trading-partner

Vietnam Plus. (2023, June 28). PM calls for more Chinese investments. https://en.vietnamplus.vn/pm-calls-for-more-chinese-investments/255398.vnp

Wilhelm, K. (1991, November 6). China and Vietnam normalize relations. *The Washington Post.* https://www.washingtonpost.com/archive/politics/1991/11/06/china-and-vietnam-normalize-relations/8b90e568-cb51-44a3-9a84-90a515e29129/

World Bank. (2023, April 14). *The World Bank in Vietnam.* https://www.worldbank.org/en/country/vietnam/overview

Xinhua. (2023, December 12). Xi Kicks off Vietnam visit, calling for China-Vietnam community with a shared future. https://english.news.cn/20231213/c6bb337d3a454a468ad426793ea4f0cb/c.html

Yan, L. (2023, November 22). China aids Hanoi with waste to power plant. *China News.* http://www.ecns.cn/business/2023-11-22/detail-ihcvcsuf3225468.shtml

Yang, L. (2023, December 12). China-Vietnam trade soars amid complementary economic cooperation. *Global Times.* https://www.globaltimes.cn/page/202312/1303497.shtml

Zhenqiu, G. (2017, May 11). UN to help Belt and Road countries improve National Policy Capacity: Senior official. *Xinhua.* http://www.xinhuanet.com//english/2017-05/11/c_136272667.htm

Zreik, M. (2021). China and Europe in Africa: Competition or Cooperation? *Malaysian Journal of International Relations, 9*, 51-67. no1.3 doi:10.22452/ mjir.vol.9

Zreik, M. (2022). Chinese Soft Power: A Case Study of Panda Diplomacy. *Global Politics and Current Diplomacy, 10*(1), 19–37.

Zreik, M. (2023). USA–Myanmar relations: democratization and beyond. *Southeast Asia: A Multidisciplinary Journal, 23*(3), 162-174. doi:10.1108/SEAMJ-02-2023-0018

Zreik, M. (2024). Soft Power and China-Taiwan Competition for Influence in Latin America. In *China and Taiwan in Latin America and the Caribbean: History, Power Rivalry, and Regional Implications* (pp. 115–141). Springer Nature Switzerland. doi:10.1007/978-3-031-45166-9_6

Chapter 4
China's Soft Power Diplomatic Cooperation in Africa and the Middle East:
Towards a Win–Win Multilateral Cooperation?

Ndzalama Mathebula
(iD) https://orcid.org/0000-0003-4313-8555
University of Johannesburg, South Africa

Mohamad Zreik
(iD) https://orcid.org/0000-0002-6812-6529
Sun Yat-sen University, China

ABSTRACT

In the new global order foreign policy, bilateral and multilateral cooperation has come to be better understood and practiced through soft power as compared to coercive means (hard power). Many states globally have achieved their foreign policy through soft power diplomacy such as China. In this chapter, the authors aim to examine China's soft power through their infrastructure investment in the Middle East and the African continent. The crux of the study is not to review China's soft power and if their cooperation's yield a win-win outcome for all involved actors. Rather, the study is set to assess the value of China's soft power cooperation. The idea lies in quantifying the true value of China's soft power in a bilateral and multilateral settings and determining how much of a win each actor procures through the cooperation. This research adopts a qualitative method explored in a thematic and comparative research design. The comparative approach applied between the Middle East and Africa enable for China's soft power to be a dependent variable that can be applied in different regions simultaneously. Herein, the comparison enables the authors to compare China's foreign policy behavior in two distinct regions and settings and to further assess how these outcomes either reflect China's soft power or the state behavior in many of the Africa and the Middle East states.

DOI: 10.4018/979-8-3693-2444-8.ch004

INTRODUCTION

The concept of soft power in international relations has garnered significant attention in recent years, particularly as a contrast to the more traditional notion of hard power. Soft power, a term coined by Joseph Nye in the late 20th century, encapsulates the ability of a country to persuade or attract others to do what it wants, without force or coercion (Nye, 1990). This form of power is rooted in the appeal and attractiveness of a nation's culture, political ideals, and policies. Soft power operates through different channels compared to hard power, which relies on military and economic means. It is exercised through cultural influence, educational exchanges, diplomacy, and foreign aid, amongst other methods (Nye, 2008). The strength of soft power lies in its subtlety and the way it shapes the preferences and opinions of other nations through appeal and attraction, rather than intimidation or coercion.

In the realm of international relations, soft power has become an increasingly valuable tool for states to achieve their foreign policy objectives. This shift is partially due to the global environment's changing nature, where military might alone be insufficient to ensure influence and the growing interconnectedness of states necessitates more nuanced approaches. Countries that effectively wield soft power are often able to create a positive image globally, attract foreign investments, and influence global opinion and policies in a way that aligns with their own interests (Zreik, 2021a).

In this context, the significance of soft power lies not only in its ability to accomplish what hard power does, but also in its capacity to achieve results that are unattainable through force alone. It promotes a more cooperative and interdependent world, where nations are influenced by the attractive power of culture, values, and policies, rather than the threat of force (Nye, 2004). Understanding and harnessing soft power has thus become a crucial aspect of contemporary international relations and diplomacy.

China's foreign policy and its approach to soft power are multidimensional and have evolved significantly over the past few decades (Zreik, 2023a). Historically, China's foreign policy was characterized by a relatively insular approach, prioritizing domestic concerns and non-interference in the affairs of other nations (Zheng, 2016). However, with its economic rise and increasing global integration, China has adopted a more assertive and proactive stance in international relations (Liu, 2020). Central to China's soft power approach is its emphasis on economic development as a tool for diplomacy. This is exemplified in its extensive investment in infrastructure projects across the globe, particularly in developing countries. Through initiatives like the Belt and Road Initiative (BRI), China seeks to build a network of trade routes and strengthen economic ties with countries in Asia, Europe, Africa, and beyond (Zreik, 2022). These projects are not only a means of economic expansion but also serve as a vehicle for China to exert its presence and spread its developmental model.

Cultural diplomacy is another key aspect of China's soft power strategy. The country has made significant efforts to promote Chinese culture and language internationally, through means such as Confucius Institutes, cultural exchange programs, and media expansion (Li & Xiaohong, 2016). These endeavors aim to enhance China's global image, foster cultural understanding, and create a favorable environment for its foreign policy goals. Additionally, China employs its soft power through international aid and development assistance. This approach, often termed as 'checkbook diplomacy,' involves providing financial assistance, loans, and aid to other countries (Okano-Heijmans & Asano, 2018). This strategy not only aids the recipient countries but also helps in creating a positive image of China as a benevolent and responsible global power. However, China's soft power approach also faces challenges and criticisms. Issues such as human rights concerns, lack of political freedoms, and territorial disputes in regions like the South China Sea have sometimes negatively impacted its global image (Morton,

2016; Wu, 2016; Nathan & Scobell, 2015). Moreover, skepticism about the intentions behind China's economic investments and aid can also limit the effectiveness of its soft power (Nye, 2019; Barr, 2011; Xu, Wang, & Song, 2020).

The Middle East and Africa hold significant positions in global geopolitics, largely due to their strategic locations, vast natural resources, and the dynamic socio-political landscapes. The Middle East, in particular, has been a focal point of international attention for decades, primarily because of its vast oil reserves (Snow, 2016). This region's energy resources are crucial for the global economy, making it a hotbed of geopolitical competition and alliances. The Middle East's geopolitical importance is further amplified by its geographic location, serving as a crossroads between Europe, Asia, and Africa, and its proximity to major sea routes (Zreik, 2021b).

Africa's significance in global geopolitics, on the other hand, has been rising steadily, driven by its rich natural resources, including minerals, oil, and arable land. The continent's demographic trends, with a rapidly growing young population, also add to its global geopolitical importance, offering a vast market for goods and services and potential for economic growth (D'Alessandro & Zulu, 2017). Africa's political landscape, with its mix of emerging democracies, authoritarian regimes, and conflict zones, presents both challenges and opportunities for international engagement and influence.

Both regions are arenas for influence by major powers, including the United States, China, Russia, and European countries. The competition for influence in these regions is not only about direct control over resources but also about securing political alliances, market access, and strategic military bases. China, for instance, has been increasing its presence in both the Middle East and Africa through investments, trade, and infrastructure projects, as part of its broader strategy to expand its global presence (Tiboris, 2019). Furthermore, the Middle East and Africa are critical in terms of security concerns. The Middle East has been central to global security dynamics due to ongoing conflicts, terrorism, and the complex interplay of regional powers like Saudi Arabia, Iran, and Turkey (Zreik, 2023b). Africa's security issues, including conflicts, terrorism, and piracy, have international implications, affecting global security and posing challenges to international peacekeeping and humanitarian efforts (Taylor, 2018).

The primary objective of the chapter is to provide a comprehensive analysis of China's soft power approach within the context of its diplomatic relations in Africa and the Middle East. The chapter aims to explore how China leverages its soft power, particularly through infrastructure investments, to cultivate and enhance its bilateral and multilateral relationships in these strategically significant regions. Rather than merely assessing whether China's engagements result in a win-win scenario for all involved parties, the focus is on evaluating the true value and impact of China's soft power initiatives. By employing a comparative research design, the chapter seeks to understand the nuances of China's foreign policy behavior and the varying outcomes in these two distinct geographical areas. This approach enables a deeper understanding of how China's soft power is manifested and perceived differently across diverse regional landscapes, thereby providing insights into the effectiveness and implications of China's expanding global influence.

THEORETICAL FRAMEWORK

The conceptualization of soft power in international relations is a nuanced and evolving topic. Soft power, as initially articulated by Joseph Nye, refers to the ability of a country to persuade or attract others to follow its lead through appeal and attraction, as opposed to coercion or payment (Nye, 1990). This form of power is derived from the attractiveness of a nation's culture, political ideals, and policies. It represents a persuasive approach to international relations, engaging with and influencing others through cultural appeal, ideological alignment, and normative means.

Soft power contrasts sharply with hard power, which is exercised through military and economic means. While hard power compels others to act in ways that they might not otherwise choose, soft power is about co-opting them, shaping their preferences through appeal and attraction. This includes aspects like cultural diplomacy, where a country's culture, values, and institutions inspire others, educational exchanges that foster goodwill and understanding, and foreign policies perceived as legitimate and morally authoritative (Mogensen, 2015). Furthermore, soft power is not just about the resources a country possesses but how those resources are translated into influence. For instance, the global appeal of a country's culture, the legitimacy of its political values, and the perceived moral authority of its foreign policy can all contribute to its soft power (Keating & Kaczmarska, 2019). This conceptualization acknowledges that the real power of a nation is not just in its ability to change what others do, but also to shape what others want.

In the contemporary global landscape, the relevance of soft power has grown. In a world where borders are increasingly porous and the information flow is instant and ubiquitous, the ability to win hearts and minds is often as important as economic or military strength. As such, soft power has become a crucial component of national strategy, with countries investing in public diplomacy, cultural initiatives, and international broadcasting to improve their image and influence abroad.

The distinction between soft power and hard power is a fundamental concept in international relations, encapsulating two distinct methods by which states exert influence and pursue foreign policy objectives. Hard power refers to the use of military and economic means to influence the behavior or interests of other political bodies (Cohen, 2017). This form of power is coercive, relying on the ability to use force or provide or withhold financial resources as a means of persuasion. Military interventions, economic sanctions, and financial incentives are typical instruments of hard power (Cohen, 2017). It is tangible, often directly measurable, and has immediate and forceful impacts.

Soft power, in contrast, operates through attraction and persuasion rather than coercion or payment. Coined by Joseph Nye, this concept revolves around the ability of a country to shape the preferences of others through appeal and attraction, deriving from elements like cultural influence, political values, and foreign policies (Nye, 1990). Soft power is exercised through means such as cultural diplomacy, international aid, and the promotion of political ideals that resonate with others (Nye, 2008). Unlike hard power, it is not about directly altering states' actions but about shaping the underlying preferences, attitudes, and perceived legitimacy of a nation's actions and policies. The effectiveness of soft power lies in its subtlety and indirect approach. It operates over a longer term and is often less visible than the direct methods of hard power. However, its impacts can be profound, shaping global opinions, creating favorable international norms, and establishing a country as a global leader in a certain domain. A country with high soft power attracts others to follow its lead without the need for coercion.

In practice, states often use a combination of soft and hard power, a strategy known as "smart power." This approach understands the limitations of both forms of power when used in isolation and seeks a balance that optimizes influence and results (Gallarotti, 2015). For instance, while economic sanctions (hard power) can compel immediate action, cultural exchange programs (soft power) can build long-term diplomatic relationships.

Soft power plays a pivotal role in both bilateral and multilateral cooperation, shaping international relations in subtle yet profound ways. In bilateral settings, soft power is often manifested through cultural diplomacy, educational exchanges, and collaborative initiatives that align with the mutual interests and values of the involved nations (Zreik, 2021a). For instance, when a country promotes its culture, language, and educational opportunities, it not only fosters a positive image but also builds bridges of understanding and trust, which are crucial for sustaining long-term cooperative relationships. This form of influence is particularly effective in creating a favorable environment for negotiations, enhancing communication, and resolving conflicts.

In multilateral cooperation, the role of soft power is equally significant but operates on a more complex level due to the involvement of multiple actors with diverse interests and cultural backgrounds. Here, soft power is instrumental in shaping global narratives and norms, influencing the agenda and outcomes of international organizations and forums. Countries that successfully employ soft power in multilateral settings are often seen as leaders or consensus builders, capable of uniting different nations around common goals and values (Atkinson, 2014). This can be seen in international climate change discussions, where soft power is used to build consensus on global environmental policies, or in global health initiatives, where collaboration is key to addressing worldwide health crises.

Soft power in these contexts also involves the projection of a nation's model of governance, development, and societal values as a template for others to emulate (Nye, 2019). By showcasing successful policies, social systems, or economic models, countries can indirectly influence the internal dynamics of other nations, steering them towards similar paths. This aspect of soft power is particularly evident in the way nations like China or the Scandinavian countries promote their development models as alternatives to the Western paradigm (Zhang, Wasserman, & Mano, 2016). Moreover, soft power is crucial for building alliances and coalitions. In a globalized world where challenges are increasingly transnational, such as terrorism, climate change, or pandemics, the ability to attract and co-opt becomes as important as the ability to coerce. Nations that can leverage their cultural and ideological appeal are more effective in forging strong, resilient alliances that can act collectively in the international arena.

The relevance of soft power in contemporary foreign policy has become increasingly pronounced in the complex and interconnected world of international relations. In an era where the sheer might of military or economic power is insufficient to fully address global challenges or to secure lasting influence, soft power emerges as a crucial component in the strategic toolkit of nations. Soft power, with its focus on attraction and persuasion, offers an alternative or complementary approach to the traditional hard power tactics of coercion and payment. In a globalized world, the ability of a nation to shape preferences and influence others through cultural appeal, political values, and foreign policies can yield substantial dividends. This is particularly evident in areas such as international diplomacy, where the power to persuade and build coalitions is critical for achieving objectives without resorting to force.

Moreover, in the age of information and digital connectivity, the role of media, culture, and narratives in shaping public opinion and international perceptions is heightened. Countries that can effectively communicate their values and policies, and present a positive and attractive image to the world, find it easier to gain international support and legitimacy for their actions (Snow, 2020). Soft power is thus an essential tool in managing international image and reputation, an aspect increasingly vital in the 21st-century diplomatic landscape. Furthermore, soft power is instrumental in building and maintaining alliances and partnerships. In addressing global challenges such as climate change, terrorism, or pandemics, the ability to attract allies and form international coalitions based on shared values and goals is more effective and sustainable than attempting to coerce support. Nations that wield soft power effectively often find themselves at the center of these coalitions, leading and influencing the global agenda. The relevance of soft power is also evident in its ability to impact long-term relationships and perceptions.

While the effects of soft power are not always immediately visible or quantifiable like those of hard power, its impacts are often more enduring (Nye, 2019). Cultural exchanges, educational programs, and other soft power tools help in building deep-rooted connections and mutual understanding between nations, laying the foundation for long-term cooperation and influence (Zreik, 2023a).

METHODOLOGY

The justification for employing a qualitative research method in the study of China's soft power in Africa and the Middle East is rooted in the nature of the subject matter, which is inherently complex and multifaceted. Qualitative research, with its emphasis on understanding human behavior, perceptions, and social contexts, is particularly well-suited for exploring the nuanced aspects of soft power. Unlike quantitative methods, which focus on numerical data and statistical analysis, qualitative research allows for an in-depth exploration of attitudes, opinions, and motivations. This is essential for comprehensively understanding the dynamics of soft power, which involve subjective elements such as cultural influence, political values, and the effectiveness of diplomatic relations.

Furthermore, qualitative research is flexible and adaptive, enabling researchers to delve deeply into specific case studies, historical contexts, and cultural nuances that define China's interactions with African and Middle Eastern nations. This method allows for a more holistic understanding of the phenomena, capturing the richness and complexity of international relations and the subtleties of diplomatic engagements. In the context of China's soft power, qualitative research can uncover the layers of strategy, perception, and influence at play, offering insights that might be overlooked by more quantitative approaches.

Additionally, qualitative research is conducive to a thematic and comparative research design, as it facilitates the analysis of patterns, themes, and narratives across different case studies. By employing this method, the study can draw meaningful comparisons between China's soft power strategies in Africa and the Middle East, identifying similarities and differences in approaches and outcomes. Such a comparative analysis is crucial for understanding the variable impacts of soft power in different geopolitical contexts.

The thematic and comparative research design employed in the study of China's soft power in Africa and the Middle East is a strategic approach that allows for a nuanced analysis of complex international relations dynamics. This design is particularly effective in dissecting and understanding the intricate layers of soft power, as it facilitates the identification of themes and patterns across different geopolitical contexts. By comparing China's diplomatic strategies and their impacts in two distinct regions, the research can uncover how regional specificities influence the effectiveness and perception of soft power. This comparative approach not only highlights the similarities and differences in China's foreign policy but also provides insights into the broader implications of its global influence.

When it comes to data sources and selection criteria for this study, a diverse range of materials is essential to gain a comprehensive understanding of the subject. Primary sources such as government documents, policy statements, and official speeches provide firsthand insights into the strategies and intentions behind China's foreign policy. Secondary sources, including scholarly articles, books, and expert analyses, offer critical perspectives and contextual information. The selection criteria for these sources prioritize credibility, relevance, and diversity, ensuring a balanced and in-depth understanding of China's soft power initiatives. However, the study's thematic and comparative design, along with its data sources, inherently come with limitations and scope considerations. One key limitation is the rapidly evolving nature of international relations and foreign policy may mean that some data becomes outdated quickly. Moreover, focusing primarily on China's initiatives might limit the understanding of the reciprocal nature of international relations, where the policies and attitudes of African and Middle Eastern countries also play a crucial role.

The scope of the study, therefore, should be defined with these limitations in mind. While it aims to provide a comprehensive analysis of China's soft power in these regions, it is not exhaustive and should be seen as a contribution to the ongoing discourse on global diplomacy and international relations. The study's findings should be interpreted as part of a broader, evolving understanding of soft power in the context of China's rising global influence.

LITERATURE REVIEW

The concept of soft power, coined by Joseph Nye in the early 1990s, plays a pivotal role in understanding China's foreign policy strategies. Soft power refers to the ability of a country to persuade others to do what it wants without force or coercion. Nye's theory (2004) emphasizes culture, political values, and foreign policies as primary sources of soft power. In the context of China, soft power is intertwined with the idea of cultural diplomacy and economic incentives. Kurlantzick (2007) and Wang (2011) explore how China has adapted the soft power concept, incorporating traditional Chinese cultural values and leveraging economic growth as a model for developing countries.

China's engagement in Africa is a significant part of its soft power strategy, mainly through infrastructure investments and economic partnerships. Zreik (2021c) and Brautigam (2009) provide comprehensive analyses of China's investment strategies, focusing on how these investments are portrayed as mutual economic cooperation rather than neo-colonial exploitation. Mohan and Power (2008) discuss the principle of non-interference in domestic affairs, a cornerstone of China's policy in Africa, which appeals to many African leaders.

In the Middle East, China's soft power is characterized by a cautious balancing act, navigating the complex political landscape. Scobell and Nader (2016) and Olimat (2023) analyze China's non-interventionist policy, contrasting it with the more interventionist approaches of Western powers. China's focus on economic partnerships, particularly in the energy sector, is a vital component of its Middle East policy. The Belt and Road Initiative (BRI) also features prominently in this context, as noted by Blanchard (2021).

A comparative analysis of China's soft power in Africa and the Middle East reveals both similarities and differences in strategies and outcomes. While both regions are part of the BRI, the political, economic, and cultural contexts differ significantly. In Africa, China's approach is often seen as a development partner, while in the Middle East, it is more of a strategic player in energy security and political stability. This section should draw on comparative studies, such as those by Murphy (2022), to highlight these differences. The review critically assesses the 'win-win' rhetoric often associated with China's foreign policy. This involves analyzing whether the cooperation truly yields mutual benefits or favors China's interests. Studies by Shambaugh (2013) and Callahan (2015) argue that while China's soft power initiatives are often successful in creating a positive image, there are underlying strategic interests that guide these initiatives. The sustainability of Chinese investments and their long-term impact on local economies and political autonomy are key considerations in this analysis.

China's Soft Power in the Middle East

Sharma (2023) notes that Belt and Road Initiative remains the most significant form of soft power in the Middle East, an initiative that continues to expand China's influence in the Middle East. Such a strategy, cooperation and diplomacy has proven to be an ideal partner for both regions through the improvement and advancement of developmental instruments such as infrastructure, energy, and information technology in the Middle East. Rafizaden (2023) maintains that China's engagement with the Middle East has been efficient and successful due to that employment of the multidimensional policy focusing of the application soft power, peacemaker, and mediator approach along with long-term investments.

Yildirimcakar and Han (2022) flag the significance of the Middle East's energy deposits to China's economy. It was until early 1990s that China lost its oil self-sufficiency and simultaneously gained interest in forming cooperation with the Middle East (Alterman, 2009). Since the inception of this multilateral cooperation key findings point towards an increasing pattern of cross boarder-investments. While China's entrenchments in the Middle East region have been surmised to foster disengagement and dissatisfaction between the Middle East and the United State of America while deeming China as a more strategic partner for the region (Alterman, 2009). To illustrate through two distinct occasions, an Arab public opinion survey conducted by Shibley Telhami and Zogby International in 2006 contended that 78% of respondents expressed a very unfavorable attitude towards USA (Alterman, 2009). On the same note a polling carried out by the Tony Blair Institute for Global Change revealed that numerous Middle East states find some Western nations as favorable partners. However, China still gains the epitome of a more preferred partner for the region (Talabany et al. 2022).

China's multidimensional diplomatic approach has a positive contemporaneous effect in the Middle East region while it simultaneously addresses countable hurdles known to the region (Osman, 2017). In three categories of soft power China has succeeded in enhancing its image and legitimacy in the Middle East. These include economic soft power, comprising of energy, infrastructure, checkbook diplomacy and manufacturing. Cultural soft power is disseminated through educational outreach, arts, and media while political soft power includes the nuclear deal with Iran, the post Arab spring and involvement in peace processes (Osman, 2017). Such as the South Sudan peace process which was coined by some analysts as China's 'testing ground' for a more involvement towards political intervention and becoming a responsible global actor (Osman, 2017).

Such diplomacy has procured the Middle East region a positive impact from trade, scholarships to China, development funding, Chinese goods at affordable prices, vaccine provision during the pandemic and improved quality of education in the region. China has further enhanced its image in the region through charity means in some underdeveloped Middle East countries such as Yemen. In which China has provided substantial health aid and medical assistance in return for a market access and energy supplies. Moreover about 163 Chinese medical personnel's now serve at Yemen through this initiative (Alterman, 2009). Equally so, China's soft power in the Middle East continues to have a much positive effect China in one way or another. It places China in a geostrategic position beyond the Asian region, enhances its legitimacy through involvement in the peace processes, sufficient oil deposits through trade, an improved image through CIs and most importantly stability over the region which is crucial to the acceleration of the Belt and Road Initiative which is a vital tool for China's foreign policy. The Middle East region is vital for the maritime component of the BRI due to China's dependency on energy exports (Eslami and Papageorgios, 2023). Undoubtably China has maintained a role of being perceived as a responsible power and partner in the Middle East. Since 2022 expanded cooperation between Middle

East and China resulted in the Middle East region receiving an estimated 23% of the BRI engagement up from 16.5% in 2021.

China's Soft Power in Africa

Cooke (2009) argues that Africa generally perceives China to have a positive impact on Africa through their soft power in the continent. A survey by the Britain-based YouGov-Cambridge Globalism Project conducted in 2022 still maintains this image of China in Africa (Bartlett, 2022). The survey argues that irrespective of Wuhan, China being the epicentre of the corona virus outbreak, many of the African states still discern China as a better ally, multilateral and bilateral partner. China remains a large partner in Africa with states like South Africa, Nigeria and Kenya which have maintained that China has a positive impact on Africa. The latter concurs to the effectiveness of China's soft power in the African continent. Cloke (2020) posits that within the African region China's soft power diplomacy is mirrored through what would generally be referred to as China's Infrastructure Footprint in Africa. This footprint is further amplified through trade, grants, loans, long-term investments and debt relief initiatives. It is for this reason that Cloke (2020) argues that China has intricately fused soft power and economic hard power from an African context. As one reviews the form of soft power applied by China in Africa one is greeted by numerous form that range from education, investments, infrastructure, grants, cultural and health to name a few. Considering the multifactored nature of China's soft power in Africa, it is safe to define it within the realms of a multidimensional and pliable soft power diplomacy. An approach that is designed to narrow the identified aperture.

A purposive employment of China's soft power in Africa is traced back to the beginning of the 2000s, precipitated by the objective of maximising economic clout and ensuring energy resource sufficiency for China. Bassan (2021) notes the since the inception of the twenty-first century, China has not only used its soft power in the African region to foster its economic interests but it further projected towards promoting alternative views on global issues coined as the Afro-Asian rhetoric.

Irrespective of Africa's mineral deposits China is further attracted by Africa's ability to influence and configure global consensus considering that Africa provides the biggest single bloc of votes at the United Nations General Assembly. Furthermore, members of its regional organisations have membership in a variety of global institutions which China sought to influence in advancing its international narrative (Nantulya, 2018). Of equal importance, numerous African leaders have praised Beijing's treatment of African counterparts as equals (Nantulya, 2018). Nantualya (2018) contends that China has used a central idea in Chinese culture known as *guanxi,* referring to a system of social networks and influential relations that facilitate business and political dealings through personal ties, and favours. For this reason engagements between China and Africa have peaked at $282 billion and in the first quarter of 2022 China's new direct investment in Africa was estimated at $1.38 billion (Forum on China-Africa Cooperation, 2023).

Kamal and Haroon (2019) posit that in order to determine the real effectiveness of China's investment and cooperation in Africa it is essential to assess the success of long-term and short-term investment while bilateral relations further compound the effectiveness. Kamal and Haroon (2019) further note that China's diplomacy to Africa is distinguished from the Western front in two ways firstly, China strictly adheres to a political non-interference policy propelled by the nuances of African sovereignty, China avoids being caught up in a position of being criticised of undermining the sovereignty of African states through their cooperation's. Secondly, China emphasis on aid that has no conditionalities.

Nonetheless, China's impact on Africa has been said to note yield a win-win cooperation, rather numerous African states such as Zimbabwe, DRC, and Kenya contend to China being very exploitative and gaining more from these partnerships (Ronning, 2016). Much of the exploitation is understood through debt diplomacy and China's ownership of mines across the continent (Mathebula and Segkololo, 2023).

In three country case studies Kamal and Haroon (2019) paint the effectiveness and impact of China's presents and soft power in Africa in three states namely, Botswana, Kenya and Nigeria. One common factor in three of these cases is the strategic partnerships fostered between these states and China. However, the effectiveness tends to be impeded by the unique challenges already known to each states which then tends to undermine the efficiency of the cooperation.

In the case of Botswana there has been considerable debates regarding China's interventions in Africa and whether they resonate with conventional colonialist structures and therefore, exploitative (Kamal and Haroon, 2019). In the case of Kenya, regulatory weakness and the loose application of laws on property rights by the Kenyan government has been flagged as the main impediment towards mutual economic beneficiation between China and Kenya. Lastly, in Nigeria, the risk of extreme interdependence emerges with Nigeria being on the far depended end (Kamal and Haroon, 2019). The argument is underpinned by the fact that China having a large market of complete goods in Nigeria such as automobiles, auto parts, textiles and garments, electronic appliances and chemical products. Which has simultaneously undermined local production in Nigeria (Kamal and Haroon, 2019).

Comparative Analysis and Discussion

When curating the finding and evidence for the Middle East and Africa there are numerous points of contrast and similarity in both regions. Evidence presented strongly suggests that the configuration of China's soft power diplomacy in both regions is always informed by the existing challenges in the region or specific country. This is to say China's soft power can be compared to molding clay which is molded according to the respective partner as a panacea that can solve a challenge to the envisioned cooperation itself. This is evident in the multidimensional approach applied by China in both regions. Thus, China has distinguished itself by not fixating on a blanket approach strategy in their foreign policy, but rather strongly investing in studying and understating the exact nature and landscape of their cooperative partners before even establishing partnerships. This argument is underpinned by the type and degree of soft power applied by China that is carefully tailored to address the challenges or reduce gaps in numerous forms.

To illustrate, in the Middle East China has invested in positioning itself as a responsible power through its involvement in peace process which can be considered as a priority for many of the warring parties in the Middle East and considering the regions history and trail of conflict. In Africa on the other hand, China has strategically invested in ensuring that they counter many of the Western outcry's that have been expressed by African states. They have achieved this in numerous ways, firstly by adhering to a political non-interference bearing in mind Africa's colonial history, promoting the Afro narrative on the global stage, and treating African leaders with respect and equal counterparts. Thus, it can be argued that China strives to enhance its legitimacy and image to its partners and on the global stage as a way of promoting its global agenda.

Therefore, it is safe to assert that China does not necessarily employ the same form of soft power in both regions. Thus, given this predicament the effectiveness and outcomes of China's soft power are bound to vary across both regions. This, however, does not dismiss the fact that China employs a multidimensional approach in both regions and the fact that its cooperation's does concur to a win-win cooperation in both regions.

The contrasting point of departure in both these regional cases is the effectiveness and value of cooperation's contending towards determining how much of a win there is for these regions and their cooperation with China. In the case of the Middle East region, we can contend to a ratio of 1:2 between the Middle East and China. Where 1 represents the Middle East and 2 represents China's value of the win. Meaning that every deal closed between China and the Middle East scores a win for the Middle East and has a double effect win for China. For instances, China's involvement in peace process in the Middle East brings stability for the Middle East but for China it ensures the acceleration and stability of the BRI while also enhancing China's legitimacy in the region and global stage. Thus, contending to a 1:2 ratio. This is mainly rooted in the Middle East perceiving China as a better partner and a good replacement for the United States, thus, deeming every cooperation with China efficient and life changing for the region.

On another hand China's cooperation with Africa have yielded good development for the continent in terms of CIs, educational programs, infrastructure, foreign direct investment, and trade. However, in terms of the effectiveness and value of the win-win cooperation's Africa does not share the same sentiments with that Middle East region. Rather evidence from Africa strongly regards China's presents in Africa as unequal in terms of the win-win cooperation and suggesting that China gains more than Africa. Thus, summing up the ratio at 1:3 thus, all deals closed between China and the African region have a single score for Africa while having a triple effect for China. To illustrate infrastructure investments by China in Africa have scored China minerals, market for their goods while also relieving China of its unemployed workforce as Chinese personals are the once who work on these infrastructure projects (Mathebula and Segkololo, 2023). The effectiveness of China's cooperation in Africa is mainly impeded by Africa's quality of governance in individual states and existing debt. The challenges known to mining and property laws in selected African states make China's investment come across as exploitative and not effective as witnessed in the case of the DRC, Kenya, and Angola to name a few.

CONCLUSION

In a nutshell this research has achieved all the objectives set out in the introduction. Firstly, by conceptualizing the idea of China's soft power in its various forms in the Middle East and African continent. The main idea this research set out to explore was to compare China's soft power diplomacy in two different regions to determine its effectiveness and value. Key findings gathered from the study suggest that China applies a very flexible soft power approach that is shaped by the regions needs and solutions to existing challenges. With this approach China has won these regions and have proved to be a preferred partner in these regions as compared to its USA counterpart. Nonetheless, through this study it was further determined that the effectiveness and value of cooperation of China's soft power is not only determined by China's approach solely. Rather, unique regional and country condition also contribute towards the effectiveness of the cooperation and how much of a win it yields for each actor involved in the cooperation. Hence this study proposes that there should be greater investment towards unpacking how country conditions in terms of its economy and politics tend to shape the outcomes of bilateral and multilateral cooperation.

REFERENCES

Alterman, J. B. (2009). China's Soft Power in the Middle East. In Chinese Soft Power and its implications for United States, Competition and Cooperation in the Developing World. Centre for Strategic and International Studies.

Atkinson, C. (2014). *Military soft power: Public diplomacy through military educational exchanges.* Rowman & Littlefield.

Barr, D. M. (2011). *Who's afraid of China? The challenge of Chinese soft power.* Bloomsbury Publishing. doi:10.5040/9781350223967

Bartlett, K. (2022). *Survey: Africans See China as Positive Force.* VOA. https://www.voanews.com/a/survey-africans-see-china-as-positive-force/6813313.html

Bassan, M. (2021). VII China's Soft Power in Africa: Promoting Alternative Perspectives. In B. Baykurt & V. de Grazia (Eds.), *Soft-Power Internationalism: Competing for Cultural Influence in the 21st-Century Global Order* (pp. 181–207). Columbia University Press. doi:10.7312/bayk19544-009

Blanchard, J. M. F. (2021). Belt and Road Initiative (BRI) blues: Powering BRI research back on track to avoid choppy seas. *Journal of Chinese Political Science, 26*(1), 235–255. doi:10.1007/s11366-020-09717-0

Brautigam, D. (2011). *The dragon's gift: the real story of China in Africa.* Oxford University Press.

Callahan, W. A. (2015). Identity and security in China: The negative soft power of the China dream. *Politics, 35*(3-4), 216–229. doi:10.1111/1467-9256.12088

Chaziza, M. (2023). *China's Soft Power Projection Strategy: Confucius Institutes in the MENA Region.* BESA Centre Perspectives Paper No. 2,209.

Cloke, F. (2020). Soft Power Diplomacy on the African Continent: The Rise of China. *Journal of Social and Political Sciences, 3*(1). https://ssrn.com/abstract=3563515 doi:10.31014/aior.1991.03.01.165

Cohen, E. A. (2017). The big stick: the limits of soft power and the necessity of military force. Academic Press.

Cooke, J. G. (2009). China's Soft Power in Africa. In Chinese Soft Power and its implications for United States, Competition and Cooperation in the Developing World. Centre for Strategic and International Studies.

D'Alessandro, C., & Zulu, L. C. (2017). From the Millennium Development Goals (MDGs) to the Sustainable Development Goals (SDGs): Africa in the post-2015 development agenda. A geographical perspective. *African Geographical Review, 36*(1), 1–18. doi:10.1080/19376812.2016.1253490

Eslami, M., & Papageorgiou, M. (2023). China's Increasing Role in the Middle East: Implications for Regional and International Dynamics. *Georgetown Journal of International Affairs, 24*(1).

Gallarotti, G. M. (2015). Smart power: Definitions, importance, and effectiveness. *The Journal of Strategic Studies, 38*(3), 245–281. doi:10.1080/01402390.2014.1002912

Godwin, M., Talabany, S., Shelley, J., Verelst-Way, T., & El-Badawy. (2022). How to not lose friends and influence in the Middle East: The narratives advancing Russia and China's soft power. Tony Blair Institute of Global Change.

Karim, M., Kamal, R., & Haroon, O. (2019). China in Africa. In J. Syed & Y. H. Ying (Eds.), *China's Belt and Road Initiative in a Global Context*. Palgrave Macmillan Asian Business Series. Palgrave Macmillan. doi:10.1007/978-3-030-14722-8_10

Keating, V. C., & Kaczmarska, K. (2019). Conservative soft power: Liberal soft power bias and the 'hidden' attraction of Russia. *Journal of International Relations and Development, 22*(1), 1–27. doi:10.1057/s41268-017-0100-6

Kurlantzick, J. (2007). *Charm offensive: How China's soft power is transforming the world*. Yale University Press.

Li, J., & Xiaohong, T. (2016). A global experiment in the internationalization of Chinese universities: Models, experiences, policies, and prospects of the Confucius Institutes' first decade. *Chinese Education & Society, 49*(6), 411–424. doi:10.1080/10611932.2016.1262682

Liu, F. (2020). The recalibration of Chinese assertiveness: China's responses to the Indo-Pacific challenge. *International Affairs, 96*(1), 9–27. doi:10.1093/ia/iiz226

Mathebula, N. C., & Sekgololo, M. J. (2023). Africa-China Relations: A Case of Foreign Direct Investment and the Democratic Republic of Congo's Mining Sector. *African Review (Dar Es Salaam, Tanzania),* (Special Issue), 1–15. doi:10.1163/1821889x-bja10083

Mogensen, K. (2015). International trust and public diplomacy. *The International Communication Gazette, 77*(4), 315–336. doi:10.1177/1748048514568764

Mohan, G., & Power, M. (2008). New African choices? The politics of Chinese engagement. *Review of African Political Economy, 35*(115), 23–42. doi:10.1080/03056240802011394

Morton, K. (2016). China's ambition in the South China Sea: Is a legitimate maritime order possible? *International Affairs, 92*(4), 909–940. doi:10.1111/1468-2346.12658

Murphy, D. C. (2022). *China's Rise in the Global South: The Middle East, Africa, and Beijing's Alternative World Order*. Stanford University Press.

Nantulya, P. (2018). Grand Strategy and China's Soft Power Push in Africa. *Africa Centre for Strategic Studies.* https://africacenter.org/spotlight/grand-strategy-and-chinas-soft-power-push-in-africa/

Nathan, A. J., & Scobell, A. (2015). *China's Search for Security*. Columbia University Press.

Nye, J. S. (1990). Soft power. *Foreign Policy,* (80), 153–171. doi:10.2307/1148580

Nye, J. S. Jr. (2004). Soft power and American foreign policy. *Political Science Quarterly, 119*(2), 255–270. doi:10.2307/20202345

Nye, J. S. Jr. (2008). Public diplomacy and soft power. *The Annals of the American Academy of Political and Social Science, 616*(1), 94–109. doi:10.1177/0002716207311699

Nye, J. S. (2019). Soft power and public diplomacy revisited. *The Hague Journal of Diplomacy*, *14*(1-2), 7–20. doi:10.1163/1871191X-14101013

Okano-Heijmans, M., & Asano, T. (2018). Economic diplomacy. In *Routledge Handbook of Japanese Foreign Policy* (pp. 251–266). Routledge. doi:10.4324/9781315643076-17

Olimat, M. S. (2023). China and the Middle East: An Overview. *Routledge Companion to China and the Middle East and North Africa*, 9-24.

Osman, R. (2017). *China's soft power: An assessment of positive image building in the Middle East.* Masters Dissertation.

Rafizadeh, M. 2023 (23 July). How China became an ideal partner in the Middle East. *Arad News*. https://arab.news/9peht

Rønning, H. (2016). How Much Soft Power Does China Have in Africa? In X. Zhang, H. Wasserman, & W. Mano (Eds.), *China's Media and Soft Power in Africa*. Palgrave Series in Asia and Pacific Studies. doi:10.1057/9781137539670_5

Scobell, A., & Nader, A. (2016). *China in the Middle East: the wary dragon*. RAND Corporation.

Shambaugh, D. (2013). Assessing the US "pivot" to Asia. *Strategic Studies Quarterly*, *7*(2), 10–19.

Sharma, A. (2023). China's Soft Power in the Middle East. In China's Engagement with the Islamic Nations. Understanding China. Springer. doi:10.1007/978-3-031-31042-3_2

Snow, D. M. (2016). *The Middle East, Oil, and the US National Security Policy: Intractable Conflicts, Impossible Solutions*. Rowman & Littlefield.

Snow, N. (2020). Rethinking public diplomacy in the 2020s. In *Routledge handbook of public diplomacy* (pp. 3–12). Routledge. doi:10.4324/9780429465543-2

Taylor, W. A. (2018). *Contemporary security issues in Africa*. Bloomsbury Publishing USA. doi:10.5040/9798400631450

Tiboris, M. (2019). *Addressing China's Rising Influence in Africa*. Chicago Council on Global Affairs.

Wang, J. (Ed.). (2011). *Soft power in China: Public diplomacy through communication*. Springer. doi:10.1057/9780230116375

Wu, S. (2016). *Maritime security in the South China Sea: regional implications and international cooperation*. Routledge.

Xu, H., Wang, K., & Song, Y. M. (2020). Chinese outbound tourism and soft power. *Journal of Policy Research in Tourism, Leisure & Events*, *12*(1), 34–49. doi:10.1080/19407963.2018.1505105

Yildirimcakar, E., & Han, Z. (2022). China's soft power strategy in the Middle East. *Israel Affairs*, *28*(2), 199–207. doi:10.1080/13537121.2022.2041309

Zhang, X., Wasserman, H., & Mano, W. (Eds.). (2016). *China's media and soft power in Africa: promotion and perceptions*. Springer.

Zheng, C. (2016). China debates the non-interference principle. *The Chinese Journal of International Politics*, *9*(3), 349–374. doi:10.1093/cjip/pow010

Zreik, M. (2021a). Academic Exchange Programs between China and the Arab Region: A Means of Cultural Harmony or Indirect Chinese Influence? *Arab Studies Quarterly*, *43*(2), 172–188. doi:10.13169/arabstudquar.43.2.0172

Zreik, M. (2021b). The Potential of a Sino-Lebanese Partnership through the Belt and Road Initiative (BRI). *Contemporary Arab Affairs*, *14*(3), 125–145. doi:10.1525/caa.2021.14.3.125

Zreik, M. (2021c). China and Europe in Africa: Competition or Cooperation? *Malaysian Journal of International Relations, 9*(1), 51-67.

Zreik, M. (2022). The Chinese presence in the Arab region: Lebanon at the heart of the Belt and Road Initiative. *International Journal of Business and Systems Research*, *16*(5-6), 644–662. doi:10.1504/IJBSR.2022.125477

Zreik, M. (2023a). Stirring Up Soft Power: The Role of Chinese Cuisine in China's Cultural Diplomacy. In K. Kankaew (Ed.), *Global Perspectives on Soft Power Management in Business* (pp. 292–306). IGI Global. doi:10.4018/979-8-3693-0250-7.ch015

Zreik, M. (2023b). Uncovering the Methods of Operation and Funding of Armed Groups in the MENA Region: A Special Focus on Libya and Yemen. *Asian Journal of Political Science*, *1*(1), 100–119.

KEY TERMS AND DEFINITIONS

Africa: Africa is a continent comprising multiple countries with diverse cultures, languages, and economic conditions. It is rich in natural resources and has become an arena for global competition and cooperation.

Bilateral Cooperation: Bilateral cooperation involves interactions and agreements between two countries or parties, often with specific goals and interests in mind.

Checkbook Diplomacy: Checkbook diplomacy is a strategy where a country provides financial assistance, loans, or aid to other nations as a means of promoting its interests and influence in international relations.

Comparative Research Design: Comparative research design involves analyzing and comparing different cases or contexts to gain insights into similarities, differences, and relationships between them.

Diplomacy: Diplomacy is the practice of conducting negotiations and maintaining relationships between countries through peaceful means, often involving dialogue, negotiation, and the exchange of information.

Infrastructure: Infrastructure refers to the fundamental physical and organizational structures and facilities needed for the operation of a society, including transportation, energy, communication, and public services.

Middle East: The Middle East is a region located in Western Asia and parts of North Africa, known for its geopolitical significance, rich energy resources, and complex socio-political dynamics.

Multilateral Cooperation: Multilateral cooperation refers to interactions and agreements involving multiple countries or parties, typically aimed at addressing shared challenges, promoting mutual benefits, and fostering international cooperation.

Soft Power: Soft power, as defined by Joseph Nye, refers to a country's ability to influence and persuade others through attraction, culture, political ideals, and policies rather than coercion or force.

Thematic Research Design: Thematic research design is an approach to research that focuses on identifying and analyzing recurring themes, patterns, or concepts within a specific field or subject matter.

Chapter 5
Chinese Discursive Strategies During the Syrian Civil War:
Communicating Opposition to Western Understanding of Human Rights and R2P

Matthieu Grandpierron
ICES, France

Eric Pomès
ICES, France

ABSTRACT

The Syrian situation crystallises all the questions related to the issue of the application of the responsibility to protect to sovereign states. It illustrates the delicate balance between the protection of human rights and international security. By contrast to the Russian position, China's has been more discreet and became more and more present in conjunction with the development of its geopolitical project Belt and Road Initiative. This chapter investigates all of these questions from the perspective of official Chinese discourses related to Syrian civil war. Beginning with the key assumption that what matters more to understanding how the Chinese view the international order is not what they say but how they say it, this chapter uses critical discourse analysis in order to unpack the implicit meanings of official Chinese narratives and views on the international order.

INTRODUCTION

Since the end of the Cold War, a new exception to the ban on the use of armed force has been debated: humanitarian intervention. This situation has given rise to a concept, the responsibility to protect, which is in turn the subject of much criticism. The Western air strikes against Syria in April 2018 highlighted all the tensions contained in this idea. *Never again! Something must be done!* These are the phrases trotted out to describe the human tragedies that punctuate international life and to call for humanitarian action. It is therefore worth trying to investigate what lies behind this debate and what is at stake. This

DOI: 10.4018/979-8-3693-2444-8.ch005

endeavor shows that the interpretation given in this area refers to several pairs of contradictory principles: sovereignty versus protection (of individuals, of the international community), use of force versus jus contra bellum, justice versus security (Badescu, 2011; Bohm, 2013; Gray, 2015).

This reflection on humanitarian action highlights the question of how the international order, and therefore international law, is changing under the influence of the rise of the individual and the international community. Is the international order evolving towards humanist values? Or are these merely a way of imposing a new form of domination? What is at stake here is the long-standing and almost insoluble question of the purpose of international law. Humanitarian action makes it possible to study the tensions within international law, which shows that any interpretation is ultimately based on the choice made in favour of one of these aims. Why should a state spend money and take risks to protect people with whom it has no connection? Why should the principle of non-interference and non-intervention yield to this need for protection? These questions reveal the confrontation between two dimensions of political liberalism. On the one hand, there is macro-liberalism, which implies freedom of political and economic preference for states, protection of their independence and integrity, and the neutrality of international law. On the other hand, there is a micro-liberalism applied to individuals, which entails their protection by the State whose raison d'être it is, the neutrality of the State in relation to their choices, and resistance to oppression by their government. There is a clear contradiction between these two liberalisms. How can they be reconciled in international law? Does humanitarian intervention make this reconciliation possible?

The Syrian example crystallizes all the questions raised by the delicate balance between the protection of human rights and international security. Syria has been at war since 2011. From peaceful demonstrations calling for more democracy, the situation has evolved into a non-international armed conflict, which began as an inter-Syrian conflict and escalated with the territorial conquest of Daesh from Iraq, Russian intervention, Turkish operations against the Kurds and Western military operations, first against Daech and then against the government in power.

At the beginning of 2011, Syria appeared to be stable in comparison with the "Arab Spring" revolts that led to the departure of Tunisian President Zine al-Abidine Ben Ali and Egyptian President Hosni Mubarak, and the growing popular unrest in Libya. In Damascus, the population failed to mobilize in a demonstration planned for early February (Baron, 2019).

By early March, however, there were growing calls for political reform, a new constitution and an end to the state of emergency. On 15 March, the first demonstration was held in Damascus to demand the abolition of the emergency law and the emergency courts. The movement spread to other cities and arrests increased. The shift from peaceful demands to open confrontation with the regime took place in Deraa, in the south of the country, near the Jordanian border. Several teenagers accused of painting anti-regime graffiti were arrested and tortured, and the protests were sparked by brutal repression by the security services. From there, the movement spread across Syria.

To avoid a revolution that could sweep away the regime, as in other Arab countries, the government cracked down on the demonstrations. This repression in turn provoked new demonstrations. A cycle of violence began in medium-sized cities such as Homs and Hama.

On 21 April, responding to the growing protests, Bashar al-Assad announced to lift the state of emergency, abolish the State Security Court and allow certain peaceful demonstrations under certain conditions. These announcements were too late to calm the protests; the demonstrators now wanted the fall of the regime, not just a few reforms. The conditions for prolonged conflict were now in place (Bellamy, 2022).

Despite the upsurge in violence, it was only in the summer of 2011 that Arab and Western countries had a real grasp of the Syrian issue, although there was no agreement on a course of action. In August, Western leaders called for Bashar al-Assad to step down, arguing that the Syrian president had lost all legitimacy. But this Western position was the subject of hostility on the part of Russia and China. That disagreement is one of the essential and enduring elements of the conflict. Russia and China will veto any Security Council resolution against the Assad regime (Szekely, 2023).

Throughout this conflict, the United Nations remained relatively aloof due to the opposition of both the Russians and the Chinese, who, scalded by the Libyan adventure, were not prepared to let the West establish itself in a new Middle Eastern country at the risk of destabilizing the entire region, and the West, which rejected the Russian draft resolutions on the grounds that they were allies of the Syrian government. As soon as the Syrian crisis was raised at the Security Council in April 2011, a rift emerged between the United States and some European Union countries, which condemned the excessive use of force against demonstrators, and Russia, which maintained that it was the government's responsibility to maintain order and therefore denounced and opposed external interference, particularly by Qatar and Saudi Arabia.[1] The use of force in Syria and against Syria continues, as illustrated by the Western strikes on 13 and 14 April 2018 in response to an alleged use of chemical weapons by the Syrian regime on the grounds of deterring the regime from any further use. These strikes came after the rejection - with a Russian veto - of draft resolution 2018/321 condemning the use of chemical weapons.[2] However, these strikes do not meet any of the exceptions set out in Article 2(4), which is why Russia called for an emergency meeting of the Security Council on 14 April 201 in order to obtain a resolution condemning the aggression against a sovereign state. Russia, Bolivia and China voted in favor of the text, eight countries voted against and four abstained. For his part, the UN Secretary-General called on the international community to avoid actions that "could aggravate the crisis in Syria and the suffering of its people" (Kolb, 2018, p.485).

By contrast to the Russian position, China's has been more discreet and became more and more present in conjunction with the development of its geopolitical project Belt and Road Initiative. This chapter investigates all of these questions from the perspective of official Chinese discourses related to Syrian civil war. Beginning with the key assumption that what matters more to understanding how the Chinese view the international order is not *what* they say but *how* they say it (e.g., the narratives used, the emotions and analogies mobilized, etc.), this chapter uses critical discourse analysis in order to unpack the implicit meanings of official Chinese narratives and views on the international order. This chapter therefore unpacks a first set of questions: How does China communicate and publicly engage with the concepts of human rights and of sanctions applied by Western powers to Syria? How do the Chinese use the Syrian civil war to support their project of an alternative world order? This chapter then continues by investigating discursive strategies used by Chinese officials to reject the application of Western understandings of international law and propose an alternative.

To achieve its research objectives, this chapter relies on the systematic study of Chinese public discourses related to the Syrian civil war from 2011 using a critical discourse analysis approach. As such, it enables to unpack implicit meanings and to offer an understanding of how discourses are constructed.

In order to do this, the article will first be an explanation of our research method. Then we will show that for China, Western sanctions against Syria are evidence that international law is a tool of Western neo-colonialism. To counter this neo-colonial enterprise, China has adopted a discursive strategy. Its aim is to show that human rights are not political rights, but economic rights. Finally, this article argues that human rights are a battleground for great power status and competing visions of world order.

Research Method and Operationalization of the Literature About Human Rights and Responsibility to Protect

Studying official public documents raise some methodological questions and difficulties. The most important one is what credit can be given to such documents whose purpose is often to publicly justify foreign policies, and therefore can't be taken as the truth, as the motives and real understanding of state officials. In other words, public documents often display what State officials want us to think, instead of what they really think. To avoid these difficulties, we adopted a rigorous and systematic critical discourse analysis approach (Klotz & Prakash, 2008; Fairclough, 2010; Wodak & Meyer, 2016). This well-established methodology is grounded in the belief that it is not only what we say that matters, but also that how we say it matters (Tully, 1988). It therefore holds that an analysis of rhetorical strategies used by State officials would allow us to create a plausible reconstruction of the key understandings of a given situation. Importantly, these include not only the explicit arguments we usually associate with debates and decision-making, but also the much more 'implicit' strategies of persuasion and rhetorical patterns. To ensure the rigor of our study, we constructed a 'coding dictionary' operationalizing the existing literature as well as our intuitions that allowed us to search for evidence that would support our analysis of our dataset. Once we had developed, piloted, revised and finalized the coding dictionary, we then carefully read each document several times, manually coded it using QDA Miners (a mixed-methods analysis software program).

Our coding dictionary was constructed to incorporate the major debates found in the literature and is articulated around several categories and questions. The first one asks the question if human rights issues are a subject of a global contestation? This section attempts to identify whether Chinese officials want to challenge the roots of the liberal international order and thus replace it, using human rights issues as a pretext (Ginsburg, 2020; Kwak, 2021). Most studies on China haven't sufficiently engaged with the question of why they would promote a change (Buzan & Lawson, 2014). Furthermore, do Chinese and Syrian officials resort to legal and security arguments to contest the international order or do they build a more profound challenge by linking it to their specific history (Wang & Cheng, 2022) and philosophy (Ford, 2015)

The second section is how the understanding of international law. This category of codes aims to investigate how Chinese officials understand international law and principles and what kind of ideas they put behind them. More precisely, this section aims at investigating whether Chinese officials accept the western meaning (as universal) of international norms and human rights but oppose the way Western countries apply them; or if they contest their meaning and make the argument they need to be culturally adapted. (Heilmann & Schmidt, 2014). Said differently, this section aims at measuring if China engages into what the literature called "rhetorical adaptation" (Dixon, 2017; Fung, 2019; Foot, 2020). This series of codes also aim to measure to what extent are the following ideas present in Chinese and Syrian discourses about Human rights and coercive sanctions: (A) the use by western countries of international law as a disguise for their geopolitical interests (Hurd, 2017; Wang & Cheng, 2022) and thus is not truly international (Roberts, 2017; Rühlig, 2018; Jorgensen, 2018).

The third section aims to investigate if Chinese officials indirectly or directly define what should be the core of the international world order? Scholars have outlined that there are two opposing positions in the definition of the world order: one that defends the idea of an order based on economic, cultural and political globalization under the leadership of the Western world, while the other defends the multipolar order based on a particularistic approach based on "the balance of interests, the multiplicity of political-cultural forms and the multiplicity of centres of international influence" (Chebankova, 2017, p. 217).

Chinese Understanding of the Application of Western Sanctions to Syria: International Law as a Tool of Western Neo-Colonialism

The core element constituting Chinese critic to the Western approach to the Syrian civil war is that Western countries use the internal political situation of Syria to engage in neo-colonial foreign policies. This neo-colonial approach is embedded, according to Chinese officials, in the understanding that international law and more particularly the concepts of human rights and responsibility to protect are power tools. This idea has been extensively studied by critical approaches and recall the works of Antonio Gramsci (2021), Robert Cox (1983), Michel Foucault (1995) and Steven Lukes (2004) about how social norms contribute to reproduce power hierarchies. To this, according to Chinese officials, Western powers don't hesitate to manipulate the meaning of "international community" to pretend their practices are supported and even encouraged by the other countries.[3] The justification for all coercive measures is found in the defense of the "values" of the Community. In doing so, the discourse on "sanctions" cleverly mixes and confuses the register of legality and legitimacy. This use of international law through the term "sanctions" demonstrates the need to consider law as a discourse, as an instrument of legitimization, in other words as an instrument of power (Anghie, 2004; Koskenniemi, 2004; Chimni, 2017).

"Sanctioning" a country for its lack of respect of norms erected as universal moral principles can be traced back to the First World War, at the very moment when liberal democracy was asserting itself as the only "legitimate" model to act on the international scene. The economic sanction in its current conception originates from the practice of the economic blockade which reached its climax between 1914 and 1917 against the German empire (Osborne, 2004). Woodrow Wilson called it "something more formidable than war" (Mulder, 2022, p.1). The aim was to bring about the total isolation of the target state and then its asphyxiation in order to make it aware of the right behavior to adopt on the international scene. Article 16 of the Covenant of the League of Nations, adopted at the end of the First World War, contributed to transforming the military policy of the economic blockade into a peacetime policy. This transformation marked a turning point by opening the possibility of resorting to coercive action in peacetime. The aim was to bring about the total isolation of the target state and then its asphyxiation in order to make it aware of the right behavior to adopt on the international scene.

This idea has been present in Chinese discourses since the beginning and is associated with the implicit discourse that the West, especially the United States, use international law as a power tool (Ronzitti, 2016). This understanding that international law is a tool of power explains the apparently ambivalent Chinese positions about the question of Human Rights protection. If China supported taking coercive measures against Iraq after its invasion of Koweit (Dittmer & Kim; 1993), this position has been abandoned after Western countries used human rights issues as pretext to implement regime changes. When the concept "responsibility to protect" was created in 2001, China was already against it. The opposition to it has been clarified since then to explicitly put forward the risk the concept of responsibility to protect would put on the roots of international law and of the UN system (as understood by China): State's sovereignty. This element constitutes now the basic structure of Chinese discourses: Humanitarian interventions or sanctions should be opposed because they constitute the first step of a process leading to regime change.[4]

More precisely, Chinese discourses articulate a narrative describing a fight between national sovereignty, as guaranteed by the UN charter, against western political inference with a second narrative according to which Western countries manipulate meanings of concepts such as "international community" in an attempt to gain legitimacy for their policies of sanctioning countries not in line with Western understanding of human rights.[5] In the case of Syria, the Chinese veto at the UN Security Council has been also justified by the precedent created by Western countries in Libya. In the case of Libya, the use of the concept of responsibility to protect was used to justify the need to implement a no-fly zone over Libya, which was later used by Western countries to engage in regime change. Hence a repetitive argument in Chinese discourses: the situation in Syria can only be solved pacifically and in the respect of the Syrian state's sovereignty.[6] The consequence of this is that Western approach worsen the situation instead of improving it.[7] However, the Chinese opposition to regime change does not mean that Chinese officials are giving a blank cheque to Damas, as shows the fact that China voted in favour of the UN resolutions restricting Syria's use of chemical weapons. This is an example of Chinese will to appear as a responsible great power (Gegout & Suzuki, 2020), that is able to manage the international system better than the United States, as section three will investigate.

Chinese Discursive Strategy to Oppose the Application of Sanctions to Syria: Human Rights Are Not Political Rights but Economic Rights

In their discourses, Chinese officials argue that rights are not individual and linked to the person but are defined as being collective and belong to the social group and are linked to the issue of economic development (Odgaard, 2020). The idea is that economic development is the necessary conditions for human rights. Without a strong economic development, human rights can't be developed. As such, the priority should be the economy. At first this idea was just found in Chinese discourses addressing Chinese domestic situations[8], to then be found in Chinese discourses addressing situations in other countries after 2014.[9] In the case of Syria; the solution advocated by China put the emphasis on economic development[10], and more specifically put forward the importance of the Belt and Road Initiative as a key factor.[11]

The presence of economic narratives linked to the idea of human rights is a reference of Ancient Chinese political thought when the main duty of a responsible government under the mandate of Heaven was to provide security against starvation. Applied to contemporary China, the emphasis is put on providing economic growth and protecting the population against economic insecurity. Human rights, in their western understanding, are not a priority and cannot be achieved without a strong economic development (deLisle, 2013).

The phrasing of human rights in economic terms has two advantages in Chinese diplomatic strategy. The first one is related to Chinese soft power and consists in proposing a different path to development to other countries than the Western path. The argument is that human rights can be protected and can be improved only when the economy is improving. In other words, it is the economic growth that enables human rights and no the opposite. In that situation, China can offer a legitimate model because of its domestic success: "China's economic success is a manifestation of China's provision of democratic rights because placing priority on economic development reflects the will of the people" (Yu, 2013, p.111). [12] And also because the Chinese path, contrary to the Western liberal model, does not discriminate nor creates hierarchy between the various types of regimes and cultures.[13] Chinese officials support this narrative by an orthodox reading and understanding of the UN Charter, and especially of the idea of State equality: the type of regime and the nature of political institutions is not an international concern but a domestic issue only (Xiao Yang, 2012).[14]

The second consequence of lining human rights to economic development is that it contributes to make human rights issues a purely domestic question, and not an international one. As such, Human rights are by no mean an international matter, and concerns about human rights expressed by other countries are illegitimate. Therefore, Chinese officials link the question of human rights to a much broader issue expressed in the dichotomic terms of "sovereignty against inference".[15]

To block any Western attempt to geopolitically instrumentalize the issue of Human rights, Chinese officials develop the realist argument that relevant international actors are States, and States only.[16] This argument thus rejects NGOs and individuals as being the subject of international law, which does not apply to them as a consequence. There is the clear qualification of Human rights issues as being domestic political affairs that can only be managed by the State in question.

The combination of the argument that rights are constrained and enable by law with the ideas that human rights are a domestic affair and with the other idea that only States are subject to international law is an implicit critic of the existing international order.[17] Instead of doing like the West and promote values in a universal definition, values need to be culturally adapted to regional and local contexts (Chan, 2006; Li, 2010; Heilman & Schmidt, 2014). This consists of an alternative view of the international system as it opens the door to its regionalization. It is *de facto* a way to illustrate Chinese international ambitions and bid for great power status on its own terms and not on those of the West, as the next section will show.

Human Rights as Battleground for Great Power Status and Competing Visions of the World Order

The issue of human rights offers another illustration of the Sino American rivalry about the future of the international order. At the heart of the rivalry are the criteria associated to great power status, such as the ability to solve regional and international problems (Brown, 2004; Cai, 2013; Forsberg et al., 2014), the prevention (and punishment) of physical aggression (Morris, 2011) that violates international law (Jackson, 2000), to the prevention of potential human rights violations embodied in the recent concept of the responsibility to protect (R2P) (Evans & Sahnoun, 2002). The international order is therefore not neutral. It must certainly maintain the stability of the international scene, but it is above all a tool for the dominant great power (or the dominant alliance) to maintain its domination (Schweller & Pu, 2011). International rules can therefore be rewritten according to the interests of the dominant power (Dunne, 2003).

Since 2008, the issue of human rights has taken a global dimension related to the international status of China. In their discourses, Chinese officials often criticize the West, and more particularly the US to have double standards against China with the objective to prevent a power transition in the favor of Beijing from happening (Peerenboom, 2005). In this battle for international respectability, China first had a defensive position which consisted in violently responding to those arguing rule of law did not exist in China. Then and following its economic and geopolitical growth, China used the issue of human rights to criticize the legitimacy of the US and of its allies to manage the international system. This started by a casting the US in the role of the villain driven by personal interests and unable to respect international rules[18], at heart of the criticism is the argument that US allies are biased when they use the notion of Human rights.[19] The objective is to delegitimize the western interpretation of the international world order to pave the way for a Chinese alternative interpretation.

With time, Chinese officials have developed the argument that China would be better than the United States at providing solutions to international issues because China is a more mature country that does not practice double standards[20]; while the United States and its allies are compared to immature children.[21] As such, there can be only one "true" guarantor of international law (as written in the UN Charter): China and not the US.

The analysis of official Chinese discourses about the situation in Syria shows the presence of what scholars working on Chinese discourses and legal strategies at the UN evolution (Fung, 2019; Foot, 2020) call, following Jennifer Dixon (2017), "rhetorical adaptation". It is a strategy that simultaneously modifies norm content while reducing critiques of obstructionism. In terms of posture related to human rights, Chinese position follows the evolution identified by Rosemary Foot about the more specific question of responsibility to protect (2020). From 2000 to 2008, Chinese posture consisted in "norm disregard" (ignoring or rejecting a relevant norm), then adopted a "norm avoidance" posture until 2009 (arguing that action falls outside norm perimeter). These defensive postures started to be replaced by more offensive postures after 2009-2010 and included "norm interpretation" (tweaking norm defini-tion, limitation, or application)[22] to include, since 2011, "norm signaling" (expressing support for norm practices or suggesting what norm should be applied)[23]. One particular example is the initiative taken by China to create, in the UN Human Rights Commission, a non-western caucus of states that made sure that western-sponsored resolutions against China and other Third world states never come to a vote (Béja, 2010).

This rhetorical adaptation of human rights by Chinese officials lead to a final element that is implicitly mentioned in Chinese discourses about human rights after 2020: an alternative vision of the international order. Chinese officials develop a view of new organizing principles for the international order that differ from the US and Occidental interpretation. The argument is that international law, and more broadly, the Occidental order needs to be decolonized and that China is a legitimate actor to offer an alternative (Heritage & Lee, 2020). What hides behind the Chinese alternative of international order is an idea of revenge against the West, which deprived it of its rights by imposing compliance with international law and forced it to behave according to rules China did not participate in creating (Lowenheim & Heimann, 2008; Anghie, 2014; Coicaud, 2016; Xuetong, 2019). The alternative proposed by China is a revenge over centuries of perceived humiliations, because it is based on principles opposite to those sustaining the Occidental order: regionalism of crisis management instead of its internationalization and the need for countries to practice the idea of "harmony".[14]

The vision of a harmonious international order was officially incorporated into Chinese diplomacy and geopolitics by Xi Jinping at the 19th Communist Party Congress. On that occasion, Xi Jinping explained that the causes of wars and conflicts lay in the violation of the rule of State sovereignty guaranteed by the United Nations Charter, the failure to comply with UN decisions, and the failure of dialogue and consul-tation in conflict resolution. This serves as a platform for the ideological construction of an alternative to the Western international order. International institutions are to be assessed on their ability to bring peace (preventing imperialism), prosperity (not making development aid conditional on liberal political reforms) and harmony to the world. What would result from this model is a regionalized international order that would be based on a fusion of the ideology of the mandate of Heaven (as opposed to the will of the People) that recalls the Ming ontology (Ford, 2015; Brook, 2019; Zarakol, 2022). Because the US is a destabilizing factor of regional harmony, and therefore, should be expelled from the management of regional affairs in which they have no legitimacy.

REFERENCES

Anghie, A. (2004). Imperialism, Sovereignty and the Making of International Law. Cambridge University Press.

Baron, X. (2019). *Histoire de la Syrie: de 1918 à nos jours*. Tallandier.

Béja, J.-P. (2010). *The Impact of China's Tiananmen Massacre*. Taylor and Francis.

Bellamy, A. J. (2022). *Syria Betrayed: Atrocities, War, and the Failure of International Diplomacy*. Columbia University Press. doi:10.7312/bell19296

Bohm, A. (2013). Responding to Crises: The Problematic Relationship between Security and Justice in The Responsibility to Protect. *Global Policy*, *4*(3), 247–257. doi:10.1111/1758-5899.12030

Brook, T. (2019). *Great state: China and the World*. Profile Books.

Brown, C. (2004). Do Great Powers have Great Responsibilties? Great Powers and Moral Agency. *Global Society*, *18*(1), 5–19. doi:10.1080/1360082032000173545

Buzan, B., & Lawson, G. (2014). Capitalism and the emergent world order. *International Affairs*, *90*(1), 71–91. doi:10.1111/1468-2346.12096

Cai, C. (2013). New great powers and international law in the 21st century. *European Journal of International Law*, *24*(3), 755–795. doi:10.1093/ejil/cht050

Chan, G. (2006). *China's Compliance in Global Affairs: Trade, Arms Control, Environmental ` Protection, Human Rights*. World Scientific Publishing Company.

Chebankova, E. (2017). Russia's idea of the multipolar world order: Origins and main dimensions. *Post-Soviet Affairs*, *33*(3), 217–234. doi:10.1080/1060586X.2017.1293394

Chimni, B. S. (2017). *International Law and World Order: A Critique of Contemporary Approaches* (2nd ed.). Cambridge University Press. doi:10.1017/9781107588196

Coicaud, J.-M. (2016). The question of emotions and passions in mainstream international relations, and beyond. In Y. Ariffin, J.-M. Coicaud, & V. Popovski (Eds.), *Emotions in International Politics: Beyond Mainstream International Relations* (pp. 23–47). Cambridge University Press. doi:10.1017/CBO9781316286838.003

Cox, R. W. (1983). Gramsci, Hegemony and International Relations: An Essay in Method. *Millennium*, *12*(2), 162–175. doi:10.1177/03058298830120020701

deLisle, J. (2013). From economic development to what and why? China's evolving legal and political engagement between law and economic development. In *Rethinking Law and Development, Rethinking Law and Development: The Chinese Experience*. Taylor and Francis.

Dittmer, L., & Kim, S. (Eds.). (1993). *China's Quest for National Identity*. Cornell University Press. doi:10.7591/9781501723773

Dixon, J. M. (2017). Rhetorical adaptation and resistance to international norms. *Perspectives on Politics*, *15*(1), 83–99. doi:10.1017/S153759271600414X

Dunne, T. (2003). Society and Hierarchy in International Relations. *International Relations*, *17*(3), 303–320. doi:10.1177/00471178030173004

Evans, G., & Sahnoun, M. (2002). The Responsibility to Protect. *Foreign Affairs*, *81*(6), 99–110. doi:10.2307/20033347

Fairclough, N. (2010). *Critical Discourse Analysis*. Routledge.

Foot, R. (2020). *China, the UN, and Human Protection: Beliefs, Power, Image*. Oxford University Press. doi:10.1093/oso/9780198843733.001.0001

Ford, C.A., (2015). *The mind of empire: China's History and Modern Foreign Relations*. Academic Press.

Forsberg, T., Heller, R., & Wolf, R. (2014). Introduction: Russia and the Quest for Status. *Communist and Post-Communist Studies*, *47*(3–4), 261–268. doi:10.1016/j.postcomstud.2014.09.007

Foucault, M. (1995). *Discipline and Punish: The Birth of the Prison* (2nd ed.). Vintage Books.

Fung, C. (2019). *China and Intervention at the UN Security Council. Reconciling Status*. Oxford University Press. doi:10.1093/oso/9780198842743.001.0001

Gegout, C., & Suzuki, S. (2020). China, Responsibility to Protect, and the Case of Syria: From Sovereignty Protection to Pragmatism. *Global Governance*, *26*(3), 379–402. doi:10.1163/19426720-02603002

Ginsburg, T. (2020). Authoritarian International Law? *The American Journal of International Law*, *114*(2), 221–260. doi:10.1017/ajil.2020.3

Gramsci, A. (2021). Cahiers de Prison: Anthologie. Gallimard.

Gray, C. (2015). *The Limits of Force. In RCADI* (Vol. 376). Brill.

Heilman, S., & Schmidt, D. (2014). *China's Foreign Political and Economic Relations: An Unconventional Global Power*. Rowman & Littlefield Publishers.

Heritage, A., & Lee, P. K. (2020). *Order, Contestation and Ontological Security-sSeeking in the South China Sea*. Palgrave Macmillan. doi:10.1007/978-3-030-34807-6

Hurd, I. (2019). *How to do Things with International Law*. Princeton University Press. doi:10.23943/princeton/9780691196503.001.0001

Klotz, A., & Prakash, D. (Eds.). (2008). *Qualitative Methods in International Relations: 1 Pluralist Guide*. Palgrave Macmillan. doi:10.1057/9780230584129

Kolb, A. (2018). *The UN Security Council Members' Responsibility to Protect. A Legal Analysis*. Springer. doi:10.1007/978-3-662-55644-3

Koskenniemi, M. (2004). International law and hegemony: A reconfiguration. *Cambridge Review of International Affairs*, *17*(2), 197–218. doi:10.1080/0955757042000245852

Kwak, J.-H. (2021). Global justice without self-centrism: Tianxia in dialogue on mount Uisan. *Dao*, *20*(2), 289–307. doi:10.1007/s11712-021-09777-w

Li, X. (2010). *Civil Liberties in China*. ABC-CLIO.

Lowenheim, O., & Heimann, G. (2008). Revenge in international politics. *Security Studies*, *17*(4), 685–724. doi:10.1080/09636410802508055

Lukes, S. (2004). *Power: A Radical View* (2nd ed.). Palgrave Macmillan.

Morris, J. (2011). "How Great is Britain?" Powers, Responsibility and Britain Future Global Role. *British Journal of Politics and International Relations*, *13*(3), 326–347. doi:10.1111/j.1467-856X.2011.00450.x

Mulder, N. (2022). *The Economic Weapon: The Rise of Sanctions as a Tool of Modern War*. Yale University Press.

Odgaard, L. (2020). Responsibility to Protect goes to China: An interpretivist analysis of how China's coexistence policy made it a Responsibility to Protect insider. *Journal of International Political Theory*, *16*(2), 231–248. doi:10.1177/1755088219899416

Osborne, E. W. (2004). *Britain's Economic Blockade of Germany: 1914 - 1919*. Cass. doi:10.4324/9780203495230

Peerenboom, R. (2005). Assessing human rights in China: Why the double standard. *Cornell International Law Journal*, *38*(1), 71–172.

Roberts, A. (2017). *Is International Law International?* Oxford University Press. doi:10.1093/oso/9780190696412.001.0001

Ronzitti, N. (2016). *Coercive Diplomacy. Sanctions and International Law*. Brill. doi:10.1163/9789004299894

Rühlig, T. (2018). *How China Approaches International Law: Implications for Europe*. Jorgensen.

Schweller, R. L., & Pu, X. (2011). After Unipolarity: China's Visions of International Order in an Era of U.S. Decline. *International Security*, *36*(1), 41–72. doi:10.1162/ISEC_a_00044

Szekely, O. (2023). *Syria Divided: Patterns of Violence in a Complex Civil War*. Columbia University Press. doi:10.7312/szek20538

Tully, J. (Ed.). (1988). *Meaning and context: Quentin Skinner and his critics*. Princeton University Press.

Wang, J., & Cheng, H. (2022). China's approach to international law: From traditional westphalianism to aggressive instrumentalization in the Xi Jinping Era. *Chinese Journal of Comparative Law*, *10*(1), 140–153. doi:10.1093/cjcl/cxac020

Wodak, R., & Meyer, M. (Eds.). (2016). *Methods of Critical Discourse Studies* (3rd ed.). Sage.

Xiaoyang, S. (2012). *China in UN Security Council Decision-Making on Iraq: Conflicting Understandings, Competing Preferences*. Taylor & Francis. doi:10.4324/9780203113615

Xuetong, Y. (2019). *Leadership and the Rise of Great Powers*. Princeton University Press. doi:10.2307/j.ctvc77dc8

Yu, G. (2013). *Rethinking Law and Development: The Chinese Experience*. Taylor and Francis. doi:10.4324/9780203583104

Zarakol, A. (2022). *Before the West: The Rise and Fall of Eastern World Orders*. Cambridge University Press. doi:10.1017/9781108975377

ENDNOTES

[1] For an overview, please refer to: S/PV.6520, 21 avril 2011.

[2] For the debates, please refer to: S/PV.8228.

[3] See for example: Yang Jiechi, President of the Central Commission of Foreign Affairs of the Chinese Communist Party, interview, 15 July 2016.

[4] See for example: Foreign minister Wang Yi statement, March 2021: "China supports Syria's sovereignty, independence, and territorial integrity, opposes external intervention and the so-called 'regime change'."

[5] A representative example can be found in: Visiting Chinese State Councillor and Foreign Minister Wang Yi meets with Syrian Foreign Minister Faisal Mekdad, 17 July 2021: "China calls upon the international community to respect the choices of the Syrian people, to properly resolve differences through peaceful means, and opposes any external military intervention".

[6] A representative example can be found in the Joint Statement by Representatives of Iran, Russia and Türkiye on Outcomes of the 21st International Meeting on Syria in the Astana Format, Astana, 24-25 January 2024

[7] See for example: Ambassador Liu Jieyi, China's Permanent Representative to the UN: "Sanctions will further deteriorate the humanitarian situation in Syria and are not conductive to the political resolution of the Syrian issue", 28 February 2017 (United Nations Security Council, S/PV.7893).

[8] See for example: Ministry of Foreign Affairs Spokesperson Qin Gong speech on the publication by the US State department of a report on the human rights in China, 12 March 2008.

[9] A representative example can be found in the Ministry of Foreign Affairs Spokesperson about the joint declaration of the friendly countries supporting China in the 47th session of the Human Rights Council, 22 June 2021.

[10] See for example: Statement from the Syria Recovery Trust Fund meeting, 2018: "China will support Syria's post-war reconstruction, focusing on economic development and infrastructure, as a pathway to peace".

[11] See for example: Belt and Road Imitative Summit, 2021: "Syria is invited to participate in the Belt and Road Initiative as a strategic partner to contribute to regional connectivity and development". See also: Ministry of Foreign Affairs of the People's Republic of China RRI forum speech, 2019: "The reconstruction of Syria aligns with the goals of the 'Belt and Road' initiative, and the ways for Syria to participate can be explored".

[12] See for example: President Xi Jinping discourse "Staying committed to and jointly promoting development to bring Asia-Pacific cooperation to new heights", 17 December 2022: "As an ancient Chinese historian observed: 'Governance is all about enriching the people'. China has won the battle against poverty and finished building a moderately prosperous society in all respect".

[13] See for example: Chinese Ministry of Culture and Tourism, 2019: "Through cultural diplomacy, China seeks to enhance its relationship with Syria, building on the shared history and mutual respect between our civilizations.

[14] See for example: Li Baodong's statement at the Security Council, 12 march 2012: China opposes any external forces interfering in. Syria's internal affairs and supports the Syrian people in independently choosing their own development path."

[15] See for example: Ministry of Foreign Affairs Spokesperson declaration on the Summit for democracy organized by the United States, 5 December 2022: "While the US and the EU say they will focus on protecting the centrality of the UN Charter, it is the US and some European countries that have ignored principles of the UN Charter (…) and have interfered in China's internal affairs and even waged war against sovereign countries like Iraq and Syria in the name of human rights".

[16] See for example: Xi Jinping's speech at the Arab League, 2016: "We should work together to prmote the early realization of peace in Syria and support the reconstruction of the Syrian state".

[17] See for example: Ministry of Foreign Affairs Spokesperson comments about the joint declaration of friendly countries supporting China in the 47th session of the UN Human Rights Council, 22 June 2021.

[18] See for example: Ministry of Foreign Affairs Spokesperson Wang Wenbin regular press conference, 15 December 2022.

[19] See for example: Ministry of Foreign Affairs Spokesperson Mao Ning's regular press conference, 12 Mai 2022.

[20] President Xi Jinping speech at the G20 Summit, 15 November 2022

[21] A representative example can be found in: the transcript of Foreign Minister Wang Yi discussion with US Secretary of State Antony Blinken, 31 October 2022.

[22] See: Ministry of Foreign Affairs Spokesperson Hua Chunging comments on the joint declaration of friendly countries to support China in the 3rd Commission in the UN General Assembly, 7 October 2020.

[23] See for example: Ministry of Foreign Affairs Spokesperson Mao Ning's regular press conference, 12 Mai 2022.

Chapter 6
Chinese State Identity and Its Place in the International System

Nika Chitadze
International Black Sea University, Georgia

ABSTRACT

In the chapter, the defining characteristics of the national identity of the Chinese nation are explored, arguing that it directly affects the formation of the Chinese worldview in international relations. To discuss China at a qualitatively new level, the chapter examines the hidden correlations between Chinese state identity and Chinese history and political philosophy. There are also discussed several religious directions in China, which have played the significant role in the formation of Chinese identity and Statehood of China.

INTRODUCTION

In the XXI century, the world scientific community studies China's rise and role in the international system with great interest. A large number of scientists and researchers believe that China will become an even stronger international entity in the future, and therefore, its formation as a hegemon will become inevitable.

A certain group of Western scientists are very skeptical of the possibility of the formation of a Chinese world order (Sinocentric order) and believe that the rise of the Chinese state is only a temporary phenomenon. These scientists, based on several data, predict that in a few years, China's political and economic progress will stop, which will hinder its formation as a hegemon.

The above position is opposed mainly by scientists of Chinese origin. According to their belief, China does not aspire to monomodal hegemony, but it wants to form a type of multipolar world order where the voices of all nations, regardless of their strength or status, will be heard equally in the international community.

DOI: 10.4018/979-8-3693-2444-8.ch006

China being in favor of multipolarism is not new, but it is important to know that the roots of the Chinese multipolarism narrative are rooted in ancient Chinese political philosophy, where the main concepts were: law, mutual respect, duty, division, humanism, ethics and the supremacy of morality.

The growing scientific interest in the rise of China in the 21st century has raised the need for a scientific justification of its state identity, although, despite the significant amount of scientific literature surrounding the problem, it can be said that the issue is still unsystematized.

Therefore, for an objective, deep, and comprehensive analysis of the Chinese state identity, it is appropriate to consider the research topic from multidisciplinary positions.

Research Methods

The work is based on the method of narrative and historical-descriptive analysis of literature, which involves the description of the main content of the selected sources and their meaningful interpretation.

The method of narrative and historical-descriptive analysis of the research topic provides an opportunity to evaluate the existing scientific literature around China's state identity relatively easily, systematically and at the same time, in depth. In addition, with the selected methods, we will be able to determine - qualitatively, at what level the research topic is studied in world science.

Both primary and secondary sources are used in the study of the literature surrounding the topic. Primary sources include statements by top officials of the Communist Party of the People's Republic of China, official documents, and political doctrines, including English translations of ancient Chinese texts.

Findings

The scientific novelty of the paper is due to the following:

- For the first time, taking into account the multicomponent nature of the research topic, using the methods of historical-descriptive and narrative analysis of literature, the Chinese state identity and its influence on the formation of China's vision towards international relations (processes) are shown;
- For the first time, by studying the theoretical-conceptual aspects of the Chinese state identity, in particular, by comparing the views of the legalist, Confucian and other schools, their role in determining the Chinese state identity is investigated. Also, the level of treatment of the topic of Chinese state identity in world science;
- By analyzing the concept of "heavenly kingdom" and the historical periods related to it, it was revealed that it represents an alternative to the liberal international order.

UNDERSTANDING THE CHINESE NATION AND ITS VISION OF INTERNATIONAL RELATIONS

Theoretical-Methodological and Historical Characteristics of Chinese Statehood

There are many mythological, but few historiographical references to the signs of the early Chinese state identity. The reason lies in the antiquity of the issue because the early Chinese state formation process dates back to BC. With the period of the 20th century, the collection of information about which is related to various difficulties.

The existence of the ancient state identity of the Chinese is indicated by the word "Huaxia" (Chinese: 華夏; pinyin: huáxià), which was the name of the proto-Chinese tribes living around the Yellow River (Huanghe), the cradle of Chinese civilization. The name "Huasia" is connected with the establishment of the first Chinese mythologized dynasty - "Xia" (XX-XVI centuries BC), after which dynasties with already historically proven state symbols - "Shan" (XV BC) were created -XX centuries) and "Zhou" (X-II centuries BC) (China, Lu, 2022).

For some scholars, the characteristic features of the modern Chinese state originate from the period of early Chinese dynasties and kingdoms (before 221 BC). Moreover, in the last period in the field of political sciences and international relations, the position that the system of relations of the early Chinese kingdoms was analogous to the modern anarchic international order is becoming stronger (Hui, 2010).

Chinese national identity is reflected in the word - "China" (中国 - Zhōngguó). Based on various historical sources, the origin of "Chungkuo" dates back to BC. It covers the 10th century, however, unlike "Huasia", it did not refer to a specific ethnicity or geography, because etymologically "Chungkuo" refers to the central state or states, although for the Chinese the word had the meaning of the middle kingdom (Zhao, 2016).

In researching the nature of Chinese state identity, it is important to note that in the centuries-old history of China's development, "Chungkuo" has always referred to more than a state emerging around a single dominant ethnic group. Along with the word "chungkuo" is also a concept that expresses the metaphysical center of the universe.

It should be noted that the Chinese state identity was strongly influenced by the ancient Chinese political philosophy, namely, two powerful schools - Legism and Confucianism, whose further analysis from the point of view of researching the Chinese state identity is necessary.

The political-administrative model of united China was first laid in BC. year In 221, when the first Chinese imperial dynasty - Qin (221-207 BC) was founded.

The prerequisites for the formation of the first Chinese empire were created in the V-III centuries BC, known as the "Warring States" or "Seven Mighty Kingdoms" period. At that time, seven independent states/kingdoms were represented in the territory of modern China: Qin, Chu, Qi, Khan, Zhao, Wei, and Yan (Peremolov, 2017). According to many scholars, this period was a turning point in Chinese history, as the Chinese kingdoms, under constant threat from each other, were forced to engage in high-level politics, diplomacy, and warfare.

The independent Chinese kingdoms were subdued by the Qin kingdom through military and political means, after which the era of the Chinese Empire began.

Under the conditions of the Qin Empire, colossal steps were taken in the formation of the Chinese state identity: the art of state management, legislative and administrative arrangements, technologies, the model of selection of officials, etc. were developed. According to many scientists, the structure of the centralized state organization created during the Qin Empire continues to exist today.

Despite the strong influence of Confucianism in Chinese societies, the political-philosophical guide of the First Empire was represented by "legalism" - the so-called school of jurists, under the conditions of which Confucianism turned into a conflicting worldview of state interests.

The philosophy of Legism favored a strong and despotic form of government. According to him, the rule of law was the cornerstone of the functioning of the state, which could be protected and enforced even by harsh punitive mechanisms. Unlike Confucianism, legalists had a low view of human innate qualities and thought that human nature needed to be suppressed by strict legal mechanisms.

Legalism also had a great impact on the establishment of heightened collective responsibilities in Chinese society, as it introduced a model of collective punishment, implying that "one person's crime spreads to the whole family or community (Garishvili, 2010)."

The basic content and conceptual aspects of Legism are presented in the political-philosophical treatise - "The Book of the Ruler of the Shan District" (4th century BC). The author of this work is Gun Sun Yan (390-338 BC), under the pseudonym Shan Yan (Mkurnalidze, Khamkhadze, 2000).

In the Qin Empire, Shan Yan's book was the most widely read and widely read, and the imperial court took responsibility for the practical implementation of the concepts conveyed in the book.

Using Shan Yan's knowledge, a political and organizational-legal model of the art of strong centralized management was successfully created in the newly-born empire.

The success of the principle of centralism in the Qin Empire was also related to the fact that patronymics were a widespread form of Chinese public organization from ancient times. Patronymy was a space of coexistence of hundreds or thousands of people connected by family and clan relations. As a rule, Chinese patronymics were divided into two age groups: "fathers-elder brothers" and "sons-younger brothers". The first group of patronymics - "fathers-elder brothers" was obeyed by the second group - "sons-younger brothers", which can be considered one of the foundations of the tradition of Chinese state paternalism and social hierarchy (Peremolov, 2017).

Naturally, legalism would also play a major role in the development of the Chinese centralized economy. Legalist Shan Yan thought that one of the main factors of the functioning of a strong state is participation in economic processes. Thus, Legism favored state monopoly in such strategic and important areas as salt and iron production (Peremolov, 2017). In addition, Shan Yan considered military strength and developed agriculture as the main components of the state's strength. He was saying:

A state can gain stability through [successful] agriculture and warfare, and a ruler will also be appreciated through [successful] agriculture and warfare. (Peremolov, 2017)

Because Shan Yan advocated rigid methods of state administration, he opposed moralism and humanism in state administration, which were highly valued in Confucian philosophy. Shan Yan thought that the "humane ruler" of the Confucian worldview would not be able to ensure social order in the state.

It should be noted that one of the characteristic features of the Chinese state identity was formed by Shan Yan's model of selecting officials. His political treatise talks about how the aristocracy was an obstacle for China. The point is that for a certain period in China, it was the representatives of the aristocracy who held high political and public positions. The said tradition gave the aristocrats a great incentive to carry out political activities tailored to the individual. Consequently, the role of the emperor as the overseer of public order was under serious attack.

According to Shan Yan's model, an egalitarian system of appointment and ranking in political and public positions was established. The purpose of this model was the formation of such an apparatus of political and civil servants that could function only under the authority of the emperor (Peremolov, 2017). Under the Qin Empire, the Shan Yan model established a new political culture that involved the selection of officials based on the results of qualifying examinations.

It should also be taken into account that the knowledge that emerged within the framework of legalism made it possible for the Chinese to allow the revision of one of the most sensitive issues - old customs and traditions. On this issue, legalists thought that a strong ruler should be able to instantly transform the priorities of the state, taking into account the changing environmental factors, and therefore, as necessary, change customs and traditions (Garishvili, 2019).

For a certain group of scholars, China's state identity was most strengthened not during the First Qin Empire, but during the Manchu Dynasty (1644-1911 AD), the last dynasty of Qin. The geographical-ethnic and socio-political heritage of the late Qin Empire and the internal policies pursued greatly influenced the formation of China as an assimilated multi-ethnic state (Zhao, 2006).

As noted, the word "Chung Kuo" (China) meant the Central Kingdom but was not associated with any specific ethnicity or geographic location. "Chung Kuo," as understood, was (and still is to a large extent) a metaphysical category for many centuries, linking together the 56 ethnic groups in modern China through historical memory. This was confirmed by many episodes of Chinese history when the reins of centralized management were held by representatives of non-dominant ethnic groups: Kidan - Liao Dynasty (907-1125); Jurjeni - Dzini dynasty (1115-1234); Tanguts - Si-Sia dynasty (982-1227); Mongols - Yuan Dynasty (1206-1368); Manchus Qin Dynasty (1644-1911) (Biran, 2017).

Under the conditions of the last Qin Dynasty, the word "Chung Kuo" itself already meant the Chinese Empire. In the Qin imperial court, there was a belief that the identification of the "Chung Kuo" with the empire, on the one hand, did not conflict with the preservation of the identity of the Manchurian people, and on the other hand, this move would lead to their support by the most widespread ethnic group in China - the Khans. Based on this political context, the Qin Dynasty from the early period of its rule actively used the word "Chungkuo" in international relations, in particular, in diplomatic correspondence with other states/kingdoms.

In international relations, one of the clear illustrations of defining the Qin Empire as "Chungkuo" was the 1656 decree of the Qin court regarding the territorial dispute with Mongolia. In the document, Qin is represented as "Chungkuo" (Zhao, 2006). The same is confirmed by the 1689 "Peace Agreement of Nerchinsk" between the Qin Empire and the Russian Kingdom. In the agreement, the international subject - Qin is fixed - as "Chungkuo" (Vostlit, 2022).

The Manchu Qin dynasty further established China as a space of effective centralized rule that united many ethnic groups into one structure. A vivid illustration of this passage is the following excerpt from the 1907 Joint Memorial of the Manchurian and Khanate People:

The Manchus, Mongols, and Khanals are different branches of the same tree; They have one ancestor and will find development together in the future. (Zhao, 2006)

Choushiang Lu, associate professor of the School of Modern Languages, Literature, and Culture of the University of Maynooth, Ireland, offers interesting essays on the topic of Chinese state identity. In 2020 Ch. Lu edited and co-authored the book "Chinese National Identity in the Era of Globalization", which includes a compilation of works on Chinese state identity.

According to the book, the study of China within the framework of the word - nationalism established in world science is problematic, because the terms - nation-state, national identity, and nationalism - are products of the Western worldview, which appeared in the 18th-19th century.

The term - nationalism - was imported to China from the West, which complicated the task of defining Chinese-specific nationalism. Based on the search for Chinese nationalism and state identity, the book presents the opinion of the famous Chinese philosopher Lin Yutang (1895-1976), who believed that Chinese nationalism and the Chinese state identity were related to the ancient philosophical concept -

"Tianxia" (Chin. 天下;), and the very word "Chungkuo" (China) stood above the understanding of the nation-state for the philosopher (Zhouxiang, 2020).

The ancient Chinese philosophical category "Tianxia" literally meant everything under the sky. The exact dates of the origin of the word are still unknown, as "Tianxia" underwent significant conceptual and structural changes during the rule of different dynasties. According to one of the versions, "Tianxia" was created during the "Spring-Autumn Period" (Chinese: 春秋时. 771 – 403 BC) (Wang, 2017). It is worth noting that for many centuries, Chinese philosophers used "Tianxia" as a kind of transcendental order.

The "Tianxia" category has been widely studied in the project of the famous Chinese research group - "Tsinghua School". Within this school, it was determined that in the pre-Qin period (before 220 BC) "Tianxia" conceptually and geographically meant not only China, but the whole world, because the Chinese philosophers of antiquity did not have adequate scientific knowledge about the shape and area of the earth, and they could not Imagine that there were other peoples living in distant areas, developed like them. According to the definition of the "Tsinghua School", "Tianxia" was a combination of physical areas and a social dimension, the same as the social sphere, which in itself meant the interaction between people (Xuetong, 2013).

It is worth noting that "Tianxia" is still relevant in modern China and is reflected in the actions of the ruling Communist Party of the People's Republic of China. One of the goals of the party in recent years is to ensure a foreign policy with Chinese characteristics and at the same time compatible with modern challenges. The relevance of "Tianxia" was also indicated by President Hu Jintao's (2003-2013) heightened interest in the re-actualization of the ancient Chinese worldview. Moreover, according to a certain group of researchers, the modern Chinese concept of "harmonious world" is related to the philosophical category of "Tianxia" (Government of China, 2022). The etymology of "Tianxia" gives the reason to use the word "sky" as its Georgian equivalent.

According to Sinologists, the Chinese "heaven" represented the concept of a civilized society and included intangible aspects such as culture, morality, and values (Levenson, 1958).

The term "sky" was actively used even before the formation of Chinese kingdoms. Chinese researchers Junfeng Liu and Deyuan Huang concluded that in ancient Chinese societies (the authors mean large human settlements before the formation of large cities and kingdoms or earlier) "heaven" was associated with the metaphysical order and included the categories of ethics and morality. Analyzing the ancient Chinese materials, the authors came up with the following formulation of "country under heaven":

Only the worthy and intelligent were appointed as rulers in "heaven" (persons who possessed the mandate of heaven - Chinese 天命 - t'ien ming); The society (under the heaven) was sincere and friendly - the villages coexisted peacefully with each other." (Liu, 2006)

J. Liu and D. According to Huang's research, the concept of "heaven" had to change three times in Chinese history. In the early Chinese dynasties - Xia, Shan, and Zhou - "heaven" was equated with the metaphysical category as well as the city-state. In the later periods, in particular, during the "Autumn-Spring" and "Warring Kingdoms", the "sky" was loaded with the content of a federal kingdom, and during the Qin and Khan empires (206 BC - 220 AD), "Heavenly" was enriched with political aspects. During the rule of the Sun (960-1279) and Min (1368-1644) dynasties, the "sky" already embodied the socio-ethical order (Liu, 2006).

Although during the "Autumn-Spring" and "Warring States" "sky" was used with the connotation of a federal kingdom, its definition was still ambiguous. The reason for this was that there were many conflicting philosophical schools in China during the mentioned periods. For example, according to philosophers Modze and Hanfei, "Tsiskvesheti" embodied the highest form of world order and thus stood at the top of the pyramid of the hierarchy of social organizations. According to the philosophers Mencius, Confucius, and Sundzi, the "heaven" was one dimension of moral power, included many kingdoms, and belonged to all mankind (Xuetong, 2013).

Yuri Pine, a visiting professor from the Department of Asian Studies of the "Hebrew University of Jerusalem" and various universities in China, offered the scientific community a different perception of "Heaven". According to the professor, in the 4th century BC and later periods, the "heaven" was already loaded with the idea of a multi-ethnic imperial space, to consolidate the Kingdom of Zhou (Chinese: 周朝 1046-256 BC) with its neighboring peoples (Pines, 2017).

The dominant opinion among Chinese researchers is that "heaven" was a kind of systematic combination of governance, which was based on culture and values; Everything was above the racial, ethnic, or geographical border, among them, it had the character of political and international order. We can use cosmopolitanism, social internationalism, and transnationalism as modern equivalents of "underworld" (Wang, 2017).

The international dimension of "Heavenly" is very interesting. According to researchers Lei Zhang and Zhengron Hu, China has always imagined itself as the "center of heaven" and the epitome of the best culture (Zhang, 2017). Some Sinologists do not agree with this position. According to them, "under the sky" unequivocally indicated the international order of Chinese characteristics, although it did not mean the international relations formed a priori around China, but expressed the harmonious relationship of peoples devoid of national sentiments (Por, 2022).

It will be found a very interesting observation about the Chinese "sky" and the international order from the life of the Italian Jesuit priest and cartographer Matteo Ricci (1552-1610).

M. Ritchie was the first European to enter the Forbidden City in 1601 at the invitation of the 14th Ming Emperor. By order of the emperor, he was tasked with creating a world map.

M. Ritchie approached the task assigned by the emperor with special responsibility. Unlike other European cartographers, he did not deliberately place China in the Far East on the map. The Jesuit priest seems to have been well informed about Chinese philosophy, especially the concept of "mandate of heaven" and "heaven". In his "Notes on China," he talks about the Chinese people's view that the earth was flat and square, and China was the center of the square. All this M. Ritchie took note, and he placed China at the center of the world on his "Ten Thousand Countries Great Map" (Liu, 2006).

Prof. Salvatore Babone's definition of the Chinese "sky" M. It is a kind of continuation of Richie's spirit. In his opinion, the Chinese "underworld" represented "a combination of Chinese state centralism and a universal moral code." According to the professor's observation, "under the heaven" was not cosmopolitan, but represented the system of administration of the international order, which was based on the supremacy of one specific state (China) (Babones, 2017).

According to the researchers of the political dimension of "Heaven", the concept was loaded with politically important aspects during the powerful Han dynasty, when one of the defining narratives of the Chinese state identity - one country ruled by one people - appeared during the Han period (Lewis, 2017).

From the point of view of the search for China's state identity, the period of the Khan dynasty is particularly important. Under the conditions of the Khan Empire, Chinese state administration, agriculture, and other fields developed, however, the rapid rise of the empire during this period was seriously threatened by the constant invasions of tribes living in the north.

According to the "Records of the Grand Historian" (eg Shiji) and the "Book of Khan", the Khan dynasty was defeated in one of the skirmishes with the northern tribes, after which the empire faced a desperate situation; the emperor needed to recognize the leader of the tribes of the northern peoples - Chan-yu as the regional representative of the empire (Lewis, 2017).

After the emperor's recognition of Chan-Yu, relations between the Khan's China and the northern peoples gradually began to diversify. 100-80 BC The Khan dynasty succeeded in partially integrating the population of the northern people into its imperial structure. According to scientists, it was the integration of the northern people into the imperial structure that made Khan's China a multi-ethnic, multicultural, and highly developed empire. with that

It turned out that the integration of the northern tribes into Khan's China had a military-political calculation - the northerners were famous warriors, which provided an opportunity to reform Khan's military forces and increase their effectiveness. Khan got stronger from a military point of view. According to widespread reports, the Imperial Court of the Khan skillfully used northern warriors against their opponents, to suppress internal rebellions and to fight against such nomadic tribes (Wang, 2017).

The researchers of the Khan dynasty evaluate the period of the empire as a variant of the Chinese hegemony because the structure of the hegemony of the empire was analogous to the traditional model of relations between the center and the periphery. It should be emphasized that in this imperial structure, the inhabitants of the peripheral areas, that is, "uncivilized," were referred to as "barbarians."

According to a certain group of researchers, the existence of the center-periphery hegemonic model in the Khan dynasty was confirmed by the effective use of the northern peoples for the military-political purposes of the empire, and at the same time, limiting the possibility of their promotion to the imperial court for a certain period. However, on the mentioned issue, in the second part of the scientists-researchers, we will meet an opposite position:

In traditional China, the difference between the barbarians [(not the people of the Khan)] and the Chinese was not racial. The differences were cultural, which at the same time provided an opportunity for transformation [of ethnicities] and [diversification of communication channels]. (Jilin, 2018)

It seems that for a certain period in the Khan's empire, society was divided on the one hand, ethnic-political, and on the other hand, only on cultural grounds. Despite this ambiguity, it is Khan's empire that is attributed to the so-called concept of a timeless, multi-ethnic China, which meant the harmonious coexistence of different peoples under Chinese civilization (Chu, 2022). It is with this concept that the mystery of the longevity of Chinese civilization can be explained (Jilin, 2018).

The Essence of the Confucian Civilizational State and the Features of Its International Order

The Western political elite, science, media and society are particularly interested in China's rapid development in the 21st century. This is evidenced by the attention of world politics on China, the increased number of conferences, studies and publications on the subject of China at the international level. Alongside this growing interest, there is growing sentiment in the West that China will soon pose a threat to the liberal international order.

Two factors mainly affect the formation of such an attitude towards China in the West: 1) the ambiguity of China's expected actions, which is caused by the unsystematic knowledge of the Chinese state identity in science; 2) ontological and epistemological incompatibility between Western and Chinese worldviews.

The book "The China Wave: Rise of a Civilizational State" by Zhang Weiwei, professor of Fudan University and Geneva School of Diplomacy, is a rare exception that offers the scientific community a scientific definition of the Chinese state.

According to the author, the West studies the issue of Chinese state identity only from its worldview prism. As an example, J. Weiwei highlighted the existence of non-objective, pro-propagandistic narratives in the West regarding China's state model: "The Chinese Communist Party will soon lose power," "China will collapse like the Soviet Union and Yugoslavia," "After Deng Xiaoping's death, China will descend into chaos," "2008 The financial crisis will eventually destroy the Chinese economy," "Democratic processes will soon begin in China," according to the author. None of the above-mentioned "predictions" have been justified yet, but skepticism about China's development "path" is still relevant in the West (Weiwei, 2012).

As a counterweight to the constant skepticism towards the Chinese state model in the West, Zh. Weiwei formulated his own vision of China's national identity. According to the author, China is absolutely different from the Western understanding of the nation-state, and the so-called represents a civilized state. According to the author, China is the single longest and "continuous" civilization in the world since ancient times, which naturally puts it above the nation-state category. J. Weiwei supported his thesis with the following 8 arguments:

1. A large population: China is the product of the assimilation of hundreds of states (kingdoms), which manifested itself as the entirety of Chinese civilization. Although India, like China, is numerous, it cannot be called homogeneous like the Chinese nation;

2. Vast territories: Russia and Canada are ahead of China by this criterion. However, China is distinguished from them by the fact that many states (kingdoms) were assimilated into one nation on its vast territory. China's assimilation scenario failed in the Soviet Union, and Canada is characterized by a small population and a short history;

3. Long traditions: Chinese traditions are based on cosmopolitanism. In China, you will meet various achievements of humanity, a unique synthesis of wisdom, knowledge, type of political government, economic model, education, art, music and literature. It is believed that the secret of the success of the Chinese development model lies in the reformation and modernization of these traditions - this is especially manifested by the outstanding ability of the population to adapt ancient Chinese knowledge to modern challenges. This is indicated by the terminology often used in the vocabulary of China's ruling elites. For example, the word "harmony" or "harmonious Chinese society" is actually a modernized version of the ancient Chinese concept of "taihe" (common harmony). The political, economic and social life of China is also greatly influenced by the worldviews formed by the philosophical schools of the "Spring-Autumn Period" and the "Warring States Era" before the United China: Confucianism, Daoism, Legism, Mohism, etc.;

4. Rich culture: China has one of the richest cultural heritages in the world. In China, 56 ethnic groups coexist, although they may differ more than conventionally, German from French;

5. A unique language: Chinese characters were developed as early as the Shan Dynasty (16th century BC). Over the course of a long history, the Chinese language has undergone successful reforms - the language was simplified and a romanized phonetic transliteration system of the Chinese literary language was created on the basis of the Latin alphabet, the same as Pīnyīn, which greatly simplified the process of learning the Chinese language for foreigners;

6. Distinctive Politics: "Communist Party of China" (CCP) (Chin: 中國共産黨|中国共产党) Conceptually different from the Western understanding of "party". The CCP is focused on expressing the interests of the Chinese nation as a whole, while "parties" in the West serve the interests of certain groups. Historical practice has proven that the "party" of the Western model cannot be justified in China. A good example of this is China's 1911 "Xinhai", aka bourgeois revolution, as a result of which China was declared a republic for a short time. The transfer of the Western political model to China has led to chaos and disintegration;

7. Distinctive Society: Chinese society is largely dominated by the Confucian philosophical worldview. In Confucianism, the family occupies a central place. He is responsible for the formation of the mentioned public hierarchy. The unconditional centrality of the family in China is also manifested in writing. For example, "nation" in Chinese consists of two characters- 1) „Th State" (国) and 2) „Family" (家);

8. Distinctive economy: Historically, China was based on a "humanistic" economic model rather than a market one. Chinese researchers call the "humanistic" economy a type of socialist economy with Chinese characteristics, which is not aimed at maximizing profits, but at meeting the needs of the entire society. The state and the economy were intertwined in China. It can be said that the modern Chinese economic model (according to the definition of some Chinese researchers - a socialist market economy) is a synthesis of the traditional Chinese "humanistic" and Western market economy. This hybrid model of the Chinese economy fully expresses the historical peculiarity of the Chinese nation (Weiwei, 2012).

Based on the above arguments, J. Weiwei also concluded that the Chinese "civilized state" possesses all the necessary resources to produce its characteristic values, political models, and moral-ethical standards (Weiwei, 2012).

It can be found interesting opinions regarding the peculiarity of the Chinese model of development in the monograph of the Georgian scientist, Doctor of Economic Sciences, Professor Nodar Chitanava - "Global Challenges in a Unipolar World." According to the professor, three main approaches to the formation of economic systems in the modern world are distinguished: American, European, and East Asian. The American system is characterized by the objective pursuit of profit maximization, where the basic principle of the system - competition - is considered as an aggressive way of economic development.

The European system "is based on the Protestant ethic based on the principle of corporatism, and the management system is based on the consensus of the interests of large groups of society, which means that the protection of the interests of business, society, and the state is realized in advance. Appropriate mechanisms (institute of social partnership) are created for socio-economic stabilization. In this system, competition is seen as a guarantee of equal opportunities." The main essence of the East-Asian system ("Confucian capitalism") is that man is a member of a collective. Although the public welfare is above the interests of the individual, Confucian capitalism recognizes that "without a strong desire to make a profit, it is impossible to raise the welfare of the people. If entrepreneurship is not developed, we will never achieve national prosperity. National prosperity will not last long unless it rests on the moral principles of goodness and justice. Competition is considered as coexistence - taking care of one's benefit means taking care of the partner's benefit as well" (Chitanava, 2021).

The concept of China as a different nation-state is shared by some Western researchers. One such person is the British Marxist, former editor-in-chief of the famous magazine of the Communist Party of Great Britain (CPGB) - "Marxism Today" - Martin Jacques. In his book "When China Ruled the

World", it is repeatedly noted that China is significantly different from other nation-states. According to the author, "China is not a nation-state, but a civilization and a continent, which includes a long history, dynasties, Confucius, distinctive thinking, traditions, a system of ethical codes of social relations. (Chin, 系, guānxi), Respect for family, ancestors, parents and older generations, values and philosophy with a different worldview." (Jacques, 2012).

Although the concept of the Chinese state is multidimensional, M. In Jacques's book, special attention is focused on the role of Confucianism in the historical processes of the formation of the "civilized state".

Confucius - proverb. Kundze (551-479 AD) was one of the most influential thinkers in the history of mankind. His birthplace is believed to be Lu Kingdom (modern Shandong Province). Like Socrates, Buddha, and Jesus, Confucius is not proven to have authored any of the texts on his teachings, although Confucian historians often credit him with the Chronicles, the "Annals of Spring and Summer." The "Annals" are the most common and important texts about Confucian philosophy. (Chin. 論語, *Lúnyǔ*) The same - "Selected Writings" of Confucius, which was compiled by his disciples and to some extent evokes in the reader the association of the style of the structure of Plato's dialogues.

During the work of Confucius, when China was represented as many Daxa kingdoms, the Chinese philosophy and approaches to state management developed quite strongly. At that time dozens of philosophical schools developed based on mutual differences. In terms of the philosophy of state management, Daoism, Confucianism, and Legalism were considered to be the biggest schools.

Before the establishment of the first Chinese empire (Qin Dynasty), Confucianism was a widespread doctrine, which, in addition to organizing the ethical-social dimension of Chinese society, also influenced the principles of internal and external management of the kingdoms.

Confucianism was declared a state ideology only during the reign of the Second Chinese Empire (Khan Dynasty). It was under the conditions of the Second Empire that deliberate work was carried out in the direction of collecting, creating, and archiving existing literature on Confucianism.

Under the conditions of the same empire, Confucianism was approved as an examination subject for the selection of officials at the imperial court. The mentioned fact proved that without a thorough knowledge of Confucius, the imperial court did not accept the existence of any other alternative to mastering the art of the civil servant profession.

Despite the establishment of Confucianism as the state ideology during the Han Empire, there were many occasions in China's later history when Confucianism weakened and went into a long period of decline. For example, during the rule of different Chinese dynasties, Buddhism and later Christianity were thought of as a counterweight to Confucianism. This was accompanied by many centuries of competition between schools of Chinese philosophy in China. Confucianism faced its most real threat of destruction when the first leader of the People's Republic of China, Mao Zedong, identified it as an obstacle to state development and launched the "anti-Confucian campaign" (ie Pikong; 1966-1976) (Roger, 1998).

Despite the existence of ascending and descending phases of Confucianism in the history of Chinese development, this philosophical school was able to deal with the paradigms prevalent in different periods and to have a great influence on the Chinese state identity.

In this context, it is of great interest to highlight the five most important words/concepts of Confucian philosophy. These are: 1) humanity; 2) justice/propriety; 3) fertility; 4) intelligence; 5) Reliability.

Under the influence of Confucianism, the philosophical category of "filial piety" is still relevant in China. In the Chinese nation, familiality and the responsibilities associated with it play a major role in Chinese national identity.

The topic of familiality is detailed in content in one of the chapters of the "Annals" of Confucius - "Xiaojing", where there is a dialogue between Confucius and his disciple Zengzi (Zengzi, Zeng Shen) about the obligations of a person towards parents, family, and ruler. In this chapter, Confucius says:

Since we received our body, skin, and hair from our parents, it is completely unacceptable to abuse them. This is the main duty of the family. This duty is fulfilled only when we can establish ourselves in the world, find our "dao" (path) in life, preserve a worthy name for our descendants, and bring glory to our parents. Therefore, filial piety begins with dependence on parents, continues in the service of the ruler (state), and ends with finding one's place in the world - becoming an exemplary person. If these family relationships are not preserved, from the Son of Heaven (the ruler) to the common people, trouble (chaos) will set in. (Columbia University, 1999)

This excerpt proves the close correlation between Chinese state paternalism, social collectivism, and familism.

It should be noted that China also attaches special importance to its past. It is no coincidence that Confucianism, as the moral compass of the Chinese nation, has not lost its relevance to this day (Jacques, 2012). For the Chinese, the past is an important factor in binding society, and therefore, in Chinese society, great attention is paid to the importance of preserving old concepts. The reason is that China itself expresses a living history - every member of Chinese society, whether a researcher, civil servant, entrepreneur, or ordinary citizen, has a strong sense of history (past) (Huang, 2012).

According to some Chinese scholars, Confucianism also greatly influenced Chinese foreign policy, because the starting point of Confucianism is humanity, and during the rule of many dynasties, Chinese international relations were based on this pacifist idea. According to this position, in contrast to the expansionist nature of Western empires, imperial China's foreign policy was aimed at spreading the principles of humanism, harmonious order, and peaceful neighborhood in East Asia (Zhang, 2015).

The second part of scientists opposes the mentioned opinion. In their estimation, the history of imperial China is full of historical facts of expansionism and conquest:

- Creation of Qin (221-206 AD) empire by military conquest of various kingdoms;
- The expansion of the Khan Empire (206 BC-220 AD) to its west and the Korean Peninsula;
- Expansion of the Tan Empire (AD 618-907) in the direction of Central Asia;
- Return of the northern territories by the Min Empire (1368-1644), which were seized by the Jurgens during the Sun Dynasty (960-1279);
- Expansion of the Manchu Qin Empire (1644-1911) from Manchuria-Mongolia to Tibet-Xinjiang (Zhang, 2015).

Scholars skeptical of China's pacifist foreign policy have further researched that from the first Qin Empire to the last Manchu Qin Dynasty, China had about 3,131 wars, which equated to an average of 1.5 wars per year (Zhongguo Junshishi Bianxiezu, 2015).

It seems that those scholars who believe in the existence of a pacifist foreign policy in Chinese history may be implying that warfare in China was mainly conducted within the framework of Chinese civilization, as distinct from the practice of conquering foreign nations.

It is very interesting what position Confucius himself had regarding the conduct of the war. In the chronicles - "Annals of Spring and Summer" - the 241-year history of China (722-481 AD) is presented, where the moral-ethical aspects of warfare are discussed. Based on the analysis of this text, scholars have determined that Confucius opposed war because it involves the taking of human life, which is incompatible with Confucian humanistic ideals.

However, in Confucianism, one can identify a narrative of justification for waging war, known as the so-called In the name of a just war. Since Confucius considered the "world" of his time to be non-ideal, from this point of view, he considered it permissible to wage war only if it was just, served high ethical ideals, and aimed at restoring lost dignity (Kam-por, 2010). Accordingly, in Confucianism, it was also permissible to wage a punitive war against the "uncivilized" (barbarians) to protect Chinese culture.

In China, before the advent of Western empires, the threat of destruction of Chinese culture most often came from the northern nomadic tribes, against whom punitive operations appeared to be compatible with Confucian logic.

The issue of the difference between the civilized and the uncivilized (barbarians) in China was studied in depth by the outstanding professor of historical sciences, Nicola Di Cosmo. In his book - "Ancient China and its Enemies: The Rise of Nomadic Powers in the History of East Asia" - it is noted that the civilized included people who shared Confucian ideals, and the uncivilized were those who did not know these ideals. According to Di Cosmo's formulation, the mentioned cultural dichotomy in Chinese society did not mean the non-acceptance of the uncivilized by the civilized or their oppression, because in Confucianism, the "civilized" was obliged to act as an example to win the hearts of the uncivilized (Di Cosmo, 2022).

The ambiguity of attitude to various issues in Confucianism (peace - by winning the heart or peace - by force) made scientists think about the dualism of this philosophical school - pacifist or forced Confucianism, around which discussions in the world academy are still active.

Despite the lack of broad consensus on several issues of Confucianism in scientific circles, it appears that Confucianism represented the philosophical, religious-spiritualistic, and political guide of the Chinese nation throughout the centuries-old history of China. These influences proved so powerful that interest in the intellectual heritage of Confucianism in China is still strong today.

At the end of the 20th century, Confucianism again became an object of political and scientific contemplation in the CCP and the Chinese Academy. The idea of creating a theory of Chinese international relations is also related to the same period, which remains relevant in China to this day and is, to some extent, nourished by the Confucian political philosophy.

Significantly greater interest in Confucianism has been shown during the administration of the President of the People's Republic of China, Xi Jinping (2013-present). The Chinese president has repeatedly stated his position on the role of Confucianism in the development of humanity. This is evidenced by the scientific symposium dedicated to the 2565th anniversary of Confucius organized in China in 2014 with the participation of Xi Jinping, where the CCP elites paid special attention to the importance of Confucian pacifism in modern international relations (Quansheng, 2018). At the symposium, Xi Jinping said that the Chinese nation especially loves and appreciates peace; Such an attitude towards peace on the part of the Chinese derives from Confucian values, which is confirmed by ancient Chinese phrases: "The health of a country is to have friendly and good neighbors," "Distant relatives are not as good as your near neighbors" and "Do not wish for others what you would not wish for yourself." myself". According to Xi Jinping, "The idea of mutual respect is deeply rooted in the spirituality of the Chinese people, which continues to be the basic philosophy of China's foreign policy." (Library CHINA US Focus, 2022).

Regarding the actualization of Confucianism, the Chinese Academy of Sciences sees opportunities for modernization in Confucian philosophy, which would become a prerequisite for the creation of the discipline of Chinese international relations (Quansheng, 2018).

Along with the study of the correlation between Legism, "Heaven", Confucianism, Chinese state identity, and Chinese foreign policy, there is also interest in the world scientific circles - about the historical varieties of Chinese international orders.

On this topic, Prasenjit Duara, professor of historical sciences at Duke University, discussed the essence of the Chinese international order in his article - "The Chinese World Order in Historical Perspective". According to the author, the international order established by the Chinese imperial dynasties was very different from the international orders of the Westphalian and Cold War periods, because it did not even formally represent a system of relations between equal states. The Chinese international order was very paternalistic and hierarchical, which is referred to in science as the "tribute system" (the same as "Tsefeng"). It should be noted that Western history does not know the analogy of the tribute system (Duara, 2019).

It is interesting, how exactly the Chinese tribute system differs from the Western-type international order.

Mark Menkal, professor of historical sciences and emeritus at Stanford University, tried to answer this question. In his article - "The Qin Tribute System: An Interpretive Essay" - he pointed out that understanding the model of the Chinese imperial tribute system is associated with epistemological complexity and it is impossible to understand this model within the existing Western paradigms (Mancall, 2013).

M. According to Menkal, in the Chinese international order, China was the administrator of the civilized society, and the emperor represented the mediator between heaven and earth; Along with the biological aspects, the Chinese emperor also had non-biological (divine) characteristics: on the one hand, he was a "son of heaven", holding the "mandate of heaven", and on the other hand, a man who stood at the head of civilization (Mancall, 2013).

It will be found interesting information about the peculiarities of the Chinese international order in the book - "USA, China and the Struggle for world order". The paper mentions that the Chinese international order was based not only on Confucianism but also on an equally strong Chinese philosophical school - Legism. The author concludes that the Chinese international order is not a product of a single philosophical school, but a synthesis of several (Ikenberry, 2015). Within the framework of the work, the period of the end of the Chinese international order was also determined - the beginning of the XX century, when the Western Westphalian system reached the highest form of expansion and, accordingly, completely absorbed the Chinese international order (Ikenberry, 2015).

According to some scholars, the Chinese international order was more associated with the space where China was presented as a metaphysical and ethical-cultural category, and not as a hegemonic nation-state in the traditional sense. This opinion is supported by the fact that during the rule of the Mongol and Manchu dynasties over the Chinese space, the centuries-old experience of Chinese state administration and culture could not be ignored, because even for the said dynasties, Chinese state management skills and culture were so strong and comprehensive that they were forced to submit to it (Suisheng, 2015).

The issue of the geographical component of the Chinese international order is also very interesting. It is a fact that the coverage area of the Chinese international order extended to a large part of the kingdoms of East Asia, which was indicated by the level of spread of Chinese writing, products, bureaucratic administration tradition, and culture in the region.

A good example of understanding the scale of the Chinese international order was also the history of the development of Vietnam and Korea because the governance structure of both kingdoms was derived from the Chinese state administration model. Along with the influence of the Chinese language on their writing and language, the Confucian system of selecting officials was established. Over the centuries, the Chinese international order extended to Japan, whose development was greatly influenced by Chinese worldview, culture, and writing (Suisheng, 2015).

Sinologists believe that the fundamental research of the Chinese imperial international order can reveal the future features of the international order model with modern Chinese characteristics. In the circles of sinologists, there are two positions on this issue:

Group of Researchers No. 1: Unlike the Western post-Westphalian order, in the Chinese international order, power was not a determining factor in the establishment of hegemony. The post-Westphalian order was characterized by a power-oriented colonial foreign policy on the part of imperialist states, with the ultimate goal of capturing resources in the peripheries and influencing the natives. In this sense, the Chinese international order was very different. Chinese civilization, without the use of force, was the center of attraction for neighboring nations - more than a hegemon in the classical sense. This is confirmed by the rule of China by the Mongols (Yuan Dynasty, 1271-1368) and North-Eastern Manchurians (Qin Dynasty, 1644-1911). Both dynasties came under the influence of Chinese worldview traditions without force.

Research group N2: The Chinese international order was a reflection of the Chinese model - legalism, analogous to Western classical realism, in which hard power and the strategy of seizing subsistence resources were considered as the determining factors of power. In the historical Chinese international order, "China" was presented as a highly developed civilization to which the neighboring nations and peoples had to show obedience. Naturally, the mentioned dichotomy between the "cultural" center and the "uncultured" periphery in the region would lead to inequality, which is far from the worldview principles declared by the Chinese pacifist philosophical schools (Suisheng, 2015).

The above-mentioned scientific discussions about the system of international relations with Chinese characteristics have further highlighted the need to study the structural analysis of China as an international entity.

Examples of the Chinese Soft Power Policy

China's Belt and Road Initiative (BRI)

China's Belt and Road Initiative also called "One Belt One Road" (OBOR) was launched in 2013 to boost economic integration connectivity. (such as infrastructure, trade and investment) with its neighbors and trading partners in Africa, Asia, Europe and beyond). At the APEC summit in November 2017, president Xi said the following:

The Belt and Road Initiative will boost interconnected development. This initiative is from China, but belongs to the world. It is rooted in history, but it is oriented toward the future. It focuses on the Asian, European, African continents, but it is open to all partners. I am confident that the launch of the Belt and Road initiative will create a broader and more dynamic platform for Asia-Pacific cooperation. (Belt and Road Initiative, 2022)

Many U.S. analysts view the BRI differently than how Chinese leaders describe. For example, Nadege Rolland, senior fellow with the National Bureau of Asian Research state the following:

The Belt and Road Initiative is generally understood as China's plan to finance and build infrastructure projects across Eurasia. Infrastructure development is in fact the only one BRI's five components which include strengthened regional political cooperation, unimpeded trade, financial integration and people to people exchanges. It is top-level design for which the central government has mobilized the country's political, diplomatic, intellectual, economic and financial resources. (Belt and Road Initiative, 2022)

The Belt and Road Initiative can provide a big boost for China's economy and soft power image. China hopes to create overseas opportunities for Chinese firms, create the new markets and stimulate economic development for poorer regions of China.

As the most scholars consider the Belt and Road Initiative is the "New Era of Globalization and puts a major focus on countries in Asia, Eastern Africa, Eastern Europe, and Middle East." According to the Belt and Road Portal, currently 145 countries are taking part in the Initiative, together representing more than a third of the world's GDP and two thirds of the world's population.

The Belt and Road Initiative combines three initiatives:

1. The (land based) Silk Road Economic Belt comprising six development corridors.
2. The 21st Century Maritime Silk Road.
3. The Polar Silk Road.

The Silk Road Economic Belt is a long-term vision for the infrastructural development, connectivity, economic cooperation of Eurasia comprising six corridors:

1. New Eurasian Land Bridge Economic Corridor (NELBEC).
2. China-Mongolia-Russia Economic Corridor (CMREC)
3. China-Central Asia-West Asia Economic Corridor (CCWAEC)
4. China-Indochina Peninsula Economic Corridor (CICPEC)
5. Bangladesh-China-India-Myanmar Economic Corridor (BCIMEC)
6. China-Pakistan Economic Corridor. (CPEC)

The 21st Century Maritime Silk Road connects China to Southeast Asia, Indonesia, India, the Arabian Peninsula, Somalia, Egypt and Europe encompassing the South China Sea, Strait of Malacca, Indian Ocean, Gulf of Bengal, Arabian Sea, Persian Gulf and the Red Sea.

The fully fund of the Belt and Road Initiative project is USD 4 to 8 trillion (Belt and Road Initiative 2022).

The Polar Silk Road

On January 26, 2018 the Peoples Council of China published a white paper titled "China's Arctic Policy." A document is China's Arctic strategy to develop "Polar Silk Road" under the "Belt and road Initiative."

Figure 1. Great silk road and polar silk road
Source: Chanukvadze, 2024

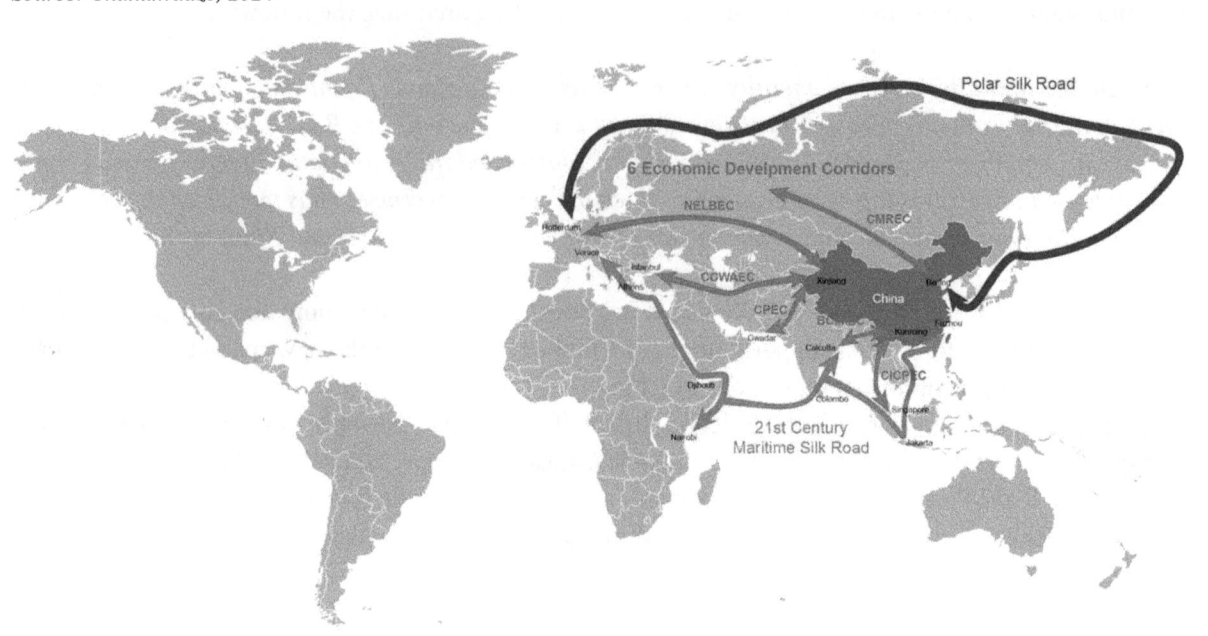

The Arctic is situated at a special geographical location. The Arctic Circle is about 21 million square kilometers belonging to Canada, Denmark, Finland, Iceland, Norway, Russia, Sweden and The United States. States from outside of the Arctic region do not have territorial sovereignty in the Arctic, but they do have rights of scientific research, navigation, overflight, fishing and resource exploration.

China is an important stakeholder in Arctic affairs. Geographically, China has defined itself as a "Near Arctic State" (Grieger, 2022).

According to European Parliamentary research Service (EPRS) China's Arctic research interests are strategic, going far beyond efforts to, gain a better understanding of the impact of climate change on the region, on the China and for the better forecasting. Scientific information is needed to foster China's geostrategic ambitions related to shipping, resource extraction.

There are concerns about China's Arctic strategy internationally, and it is often perceived alongside Russian militarization of the Arctic as a dual threat to the establishing of international order.

As Chinese officials announced China will construct Polar Silk Road in between 2021-2025 year (Five-year plan).

The Polar Silk Road refers to Arctic shipping routes connecting three major economic centers: North America, East Asia and Western Europe. (see map)

If the global temperatures continue to rise in line with current trends by 2030 the Arctic may be free from the ice during the summer. This opens up new routes for shipping and that is a main reason of the Arctic Silk Road project.

There are three potential routes across the Arctic: the northeast passage around Eurasia, the Northwest passage around North America and the central arctic ocean route.

For China they offer a shorter and cheaper alternative to current shipping routes, which reach major markets in Europe via the Indian Ocean and the Suez Canal (Chanukvadze, 2024).

Considering all of the facts, China's rapid economic development strategies and initiatives such as the Belt and Road Initiative, Made in China 2025 and the Polar Silk Road are China's effort to develop and grow its economic and political power internationally.

CONCLUSION

In the study, with the methods of historical-descriptive and narrative analysis of literature, we tried to determine the Chinese state identity and the impact of this identity on China's vision of international relations. It was also analyzed at what level the issue of Chinese state identity has been processed in world science.

At the same time, the multi-component nature of the research topic was a big challenge. This circumstance made us decide to choose a research strategy that would help us to present the Chinese state identity as a whole and the attitudes of the bearer of such behavior towards international processes. Thus, we considered it logical to start our search with the word "China". Society made sure that the category "China" is not only a word but a set of philosophical concepts.

It should be noted that the philosophical definitions of the Chinese state identity highlighted the expediency of studying the ancient Chinese "underworld" concept. Due to the heterogeneity of "Under heaven", it was an attempt to analyze the prerequisites, development stages, and content aspects of the concept from different historical periods. Based on the study of the materials found around this issue, we concluded that the "heaven" is an internal and, at the same time, international order, which is loaded with different views of Chinese philosophical schools. The opinion is that "heavenly" is a Chinese alternative to the liberal international order.

REFERENCES

Babones, S. (2017). Taking China Seriously: Relationality, Tianxia, and the 'Chinese School' of International Relations. Oxford Research Encyclopedia of Politics, 1. doi:10.1093/acrefore/9780190228637.013.602

Belt and Road Initiative. (2022). *Belt and Road Initiative*. Retrieved from: https://www.beltroad-initiative.com/belt-and-road/

Biran, M. (2017). Periods of Non-Han Rule. In M. Szonyim (Ed.), *A Companion to Chinese History*. Wiley Blackwell. doi:10.1002/9781118624593.ch11

Chanukvadze, S. (2024). *China: As an Emerging Superpower*. Georgian-American University.

China, C. (2022). *Chronology of Chinese Dynasties*. Retrieved from: https://china.lu/en/our-history-26

Chitanava, N. (2021). *Global Challenges in the Unipolar World*. Iverioni.

Chu, S. (2022). Whither Chinese IR? The Sinocentric Subject and the Paradox of Tianxia-Ism. *International Theory, 14*(1), 19. doi:10.1017/S1752971920000214

Di Cosmo, N. (2002). *Ancient China and Its Enemies: The Rise of Nomadic Power in East Asian History*. Cambridge University Press. doi:10.1017/CBO9780511511967

Duara, P. (2019). The Chinese World Order in Historical Perspective. *China and the World*, *02*(04), 2019. doi:10.1142/S2591729319500238

Garishvili, M. (2019). *Introduction to the Philosophy of Law. Course of Lectures.* TSU.

Grieger, G. (2018). EPRS-European Parliamentary Research Service. *China's Arctic Policy.* European Union. Retrieved from: https://www.europarl.europa.eu/RegData/etudes/BRIE/2018/620231/EPRS_BRI(2018)620231_EN.pdf

Huang, P. (2021). Beijing Consensus, or Chinese Experiences, or What? In *When China rules the world: the end of the western world and the birth of a new global order.* Penguin Books.

Hui, V. (2010). *War and State Formation in Ancient China and Early Modern Europe.* Cambridge University Press. doi:10.1017/CBO9780511614545

Ikenberry, G. J., Wang, J. & Zhu, F. (2015). China, and the struggle for world order: ideas, traditions, historical legacies, and global visions. Palgrave Macmillan.

Jacques, M. (2012). *When China rules the world: the end of the western world and the birth of a new global order.* Penguin Books.

Jilin, X., & Ownby, D. (2018). *Rethinking China's Rise: A Liberal Critique.* Cambridge University Press.

Kam-por, Y. (2010.) Confucian Views on War as Seen in the Gongyan Commentary on the Spring and Autumn Annals. *Dao, 9,* 97–111. https://doi.org/DOI 10.1007/s11712-009-9145

Levenson, R. J. (1958). *Confucian China and Its Modern Fate: the problem of intellectual continuity.* Routledge.

Lewis, M. E., & Hsieh, M. (2017). Tianxia and the Invention of Empire in East Asia. In *Wang Bang Chinese Visions of World Order: Tianxia, Culture, and World Politics.* Duke University Press. doi:10.1215/9780822372448-002

Library, China-US Focus. (2022). *Xi Jinping's Speech in Commemoration of the 2,565th Anniversary of Confucius' Birth - Library CHINA US Focus.* Retrieved from: http://library.chinausfocus.com/article-1534.html

Liu, J. (2006). The Evolution of Tianxia Cosmology and Its Philosophical Implications. *Frontiers of Philosophy in China*, *1*(4), 517–538. Advance online publication. doi:10.1007/s11466-006-0023-6

Liu, J., & Deyuan, H. (2006). The Evolution of Tianxia Cosmology and Its Philosophical Implications. *Frontiers of Philosophy in China*, *1*(4), 533. doi:10.1007/s11466-006-0023-6

Mancall, M. (2013). The Ch'ing Tribute System: An Interpretive Essay. In J. K. Fairbank (Ed.), *The Chinese World Order: Traditional China's Foreign Relations.* Harvard University Press.

MFA of China. (2022). *Harmonious World: China's Ancient Philosophy for New International Order.* Retrieved from: https://www.mfa.gov.cn/ce/cena//eng/xwdt/t410254.htm

Perelomov, L. (2017). *Yang Shang: Book of the Ruler of the Shang Region Librarium.* Ripol-Classic.

Pines, Y. (2009). *Envisioning Eternal Empire: Chinese Political Thought of the Warring States Era.* University of Hawaii.

Por, S. S. (2020). *Tianxia: China's Concept of International Order.* Global Asia. Retrieved from: https://www.globalasia.org/v15no2/cover/tianxia-chinas-concept-of-international-order_shiu-sin-por

Quansheng, Z. (2018). *The influence of Confucianism on Chinese politics and foreign policy.* Asian Education and Development Studies.

Roger, T. A., & Rosemont, H. (1998). *The Analects of Confucius: A Philosophical Translation, trans.* Ballantine Books.

Suisheng, Z. (2015). Rethinking the Chinese World Order: The imperial cycle and the rise of China. *Journal of Contemporary China*, 2–22.

Vostlit. (2022). *Treaty of Nerchinsk August 28, 1689.* Retrieved from: https://www.vostlit.info/Texts/Dokumenty/China/XVII/1680-1700/Russ_kit_otn_17_v_II/pril1.htm

Wang, B. (2017). *Chinese Visions of World Order: Tianxia, Culture, and World Politics.* Duke University Press. doi:10.1515/9780822372448

Weiwei, Z. (2012). *The China Wave: Rise of a Civilizational State.* World Century Publishing Corporation.

Xiaojing. (1999). *Selections from the Classic of Filiality (Xiaojing), Asia for Educators.* Columbia University.

Xuetong, Y. (2013). *Ancient Chinese thought, modern Chinese power.* Princeton University Press. doi:10.1515/9781400848959

Zhang, F. (2015). Confucian Foreign Policy Traditions in Chinese History. *The Chinese Journal of International Politics*, 8(2), 197–218. doi:10.1093/cjip/pov004

Zhang, L., & Zhengrong, H. (2017). Empire, Tianxia and Great Unity: A Historical Examination and Future Vision of China's International Communication. *Global Media and China*, 2(2), 202. doi:10.1177/2059436417725213

Zhao, G. (2016). Reinventing China: Imperial Qing Ideology and the Rise of Modern Chinese National Identity in the Early Twentieth Century. *Modern China*, 32(1), 6. https://www.jstor.org/stable/20062627

Zhongguo Junshishi Bianxiezu. (2015). *The Compilation Team of 'China's Military History'. Zhongguolidai zhanzheng nianbiao* (Vol. I). II A Chronology of Wars in Chinese History.

Zhouxiang, L. (2020). *Introduction: Constructing and Negotiating Chineseness in the Age of Globalisation. In Chinese National Identity in the Age of Globalisation.* Palgrave Macmillan.

Chapter 7
Dominican Missionary Strategies in Ming and Qing China

Zhicang Huang

https://orcid.org/0000-0003-2905-083X

Sun Yat-sen University, China

ABSTRACT

This chapter delves into the strategies employed by the Dominican Order in their missionary activities within the Ming and Qing dynasties of China. It underscores their initiatives to weave Western religious doctrines into the Chinese spiritual landscape, representing an early form of religious and cultural diplomacy. The engagement of the Order with local communities, their linguistic accomplishment, and their active involvement in the socio-political spheres of the region are explored in depth. Furthermore, the chapter scrutinized the social initiatives undertaken by the Order, particularly in relation to child welfare, and evaluates their impact on the social fabric of the era. Through a comprehensive investigation of the influence exerted by the Dominican Order in China, this study unveils the multifaceted nature of cultural exchange, shedding light on the lasting effects of these historical interactions on Sino-Iberian relations and the evolution of soft power dynamics.

1. THE VOYAGE OF IBERIAN INFLUENCE ACROSS THE SEAS

The turn of the 16th century represented a pivotal period in the annals of world and maritime history, underscored by the expanding influence of Iberian empires in commerce and imperialism. Guided by Prince Henry, the Navigator (1394-1460), Portuguese explorers navigated to Cape Verde, the westernmost point of the African continent, by 1448, setting up a profitable series of trading stations throughout their voyage. By the mid-15th century, the Christian conquest had subsumed vast tracts of Nasrid dominions, culminating in 1492 with the fall of Granada to the Catholic Monarchs. This event extinguished nearly eight centuries of Islamic tenure in Iberia. With the conquest of the last Moorish stronghold in Granada and the expulsion of the Jews, the King and the Queen of Spain, Ferdinand II of Aragon (1452-1516)

DOI: 10.4018/979-8-3693-2444-8.ch007

and Isabella I of Castile (1451-1504) shifted their focus to the Atlantic. Following the momentous expeditions led by Christopher Columbus (1451-1506), a new maritime world emerged, transforming the Atlantic Ocean into a second Mediterranean, initially for the Iberian monarchies and subsequently for other Western European powers, especially the Dutch and the English. Spanish military extended their dominion over substantial territories in the Americas, encompassing the realms of the Aztec and Inca civilizations, integrating these lands into the colonial framework of the empire. The creation of the viceroyalties in New Spain, with Mexico established in 1521 and Peru in 1542, coupled with the consolidation of a permanent strategic presence in Asia by 1565, stood for the peak of Spanish territorial expansion abroad. However, this expansion also hinted at upcoming financial difficulties. Castilian authorities faced the challenge of reconciling the demands of colonial expansion with European geopolitical objectives, ultimately deciding to allocate the wealth derived from American silver to support conflicts motivated by religious convictions and dynastic ambitions (Tremml-Werner, 2015, p. 45). In pursuit of his ambitious vision to elevate Spain to global prominence, Philip II (1527-1598) built upon the legacy of his predecessors, the Catholic Monarchs and Charles V (1500-1558). The dynastic union with Portugal from 1580 to 1640, provided critical momentum for Philip II's strategy.

Spanish and Portuguese vessels then embarked on voyages in search of spices, gold, potential Christian allies, and new converts across the Atlantic and further into the Indian Ocean and, eventually, the Pacific. This period of exploration, which lasted for two centuries, was characterized by armed merchant ships reinforced by formal naval forces. The globalization of maritime activities connected economic systems globally and ignited a rivalry for naval dominance. After the demise of King Philip II, significant socio-economic tensions complicated Spanish imperial policy and weakened royal authority.[1] Instead, the Dutch dominated trade during the 17th century, the British asserted naval dominance by the end of the 18th century, a position the Americans would inherit in the 20th century. The narrative of Spanish evolution during these epochs attracts diverse interpretations from historians. John Elliott, whose work has shaped the prevailing narrative of Spain's decline post-Philip II, argues that the 16th century witnessed unification, social harmony, and economic growth due to the influx of wealth from the Americas. However, he posits that the subsequent century was plagued by revolts, weakened central governance, and rampant inflation (Elliott, 2002). In contrast, Carla Rahn Phillips challenges the idea of decline by underscoring the diversity within the Iberian empires. She highlights how these empires spanned global territories and cultures, each contributing to the overall success in terms of enduring presence and cultural integration. Building upon this notion, the concept of soft power as articulated by Joseph Nye suggests that influence extends beyond military might, about the ability to shape preferences through cultural and ideological appeal—a strategy evident in the Iberian empire's promotion of its religious and cultural values (Nye, 2004). Furthermore, the relatively stable performance of the Iberians overseas and the manner in which the Spaniards engaged with the Manila system serve as a counterpoint to the Habsburgs' downfall, precipitated by an absolutist, interventionist, and excessively bureaucratic government (Phillips, 2007, pp. 71-86).

The Manila Galleon undeniably constituted the preeminent trans-Pacific route between the 16th to the 19th centuries. Despite their arrival on the new American shores, the Spaniards continued to conquer the wealthy lands of the mythical Cathay and the Spice Islands, renowned for producing the most sought-after spices in European commerce. As a result, several Castilian expeditions to East Asia were carried out in the 16th century. The inaugural journeys were spearheaded by Ferdinand Magellan and Juan Sebastián Elcano in 1519, followed by García Jofre de Loaisa in 1525. The expedition conducted by Miguel López de Legazpi departed from the Viceroyalty of New Spain in 1564, aiming to forge a lasting Spanish presence in the Philippine Islands as a strategic precursor to broader ambitions (Cervera Jiménez, 2020, p. 70). A series of subsequent events indicated that the Spaniards redirected their focus towards the Chinese Empire.

Prior to the relaxation of maritime restrictions in Fujian province, the Ming dynasty had maintained a cautious approach to foreign trade, often enforcing strict sea bans to control piracy and influence over regional commerce. The Ming relaxed trade regulations for Fujian in 1567, allowing Chinese vessels to sail freely. This policy coincided with the first European landings on China's southern coasts. The Spaniards, arriving in the Philippines, found themselves well-positioned to trade with China during this period of liberalized maritime commerce. The easing of previous trade constraints corresponded to a major demand for silver, abundantly produced in the Americas and consequently overvalued. Additionally, the Spaniards quickly realized that silver was the primary commodity they could offer in exchange for Chinese goods.[2] Trading silver with China became a profitable venture. This trade arrangement was sustained from the 16th into the 17th century, with little variation over the following hundred years. Spain dispatched iron and military supplies to the Philippines via the Cadiz-Manila passage, reciprocally importing spices, silk textiles, indigo, musk, and camphor. This maritime path, traversing the Cape of Good Hope, was active from 1765 to 1834. Despite receiving comparatively less scholarly focus than the Manila Galleon route, it was instrumental in unlocking the trade doors of Asia for Spain and initiating the first stages of globalization.[3]

Since Miguel López de Legazpi led the Spaniards to the Philippines and settled there in 1571, Spanish officials commenced trade relations with China, capitalizing on Manila's advantageous location. This development gave rise to an acknowledged trading circuit connecting China, the Philippines, Mexico, and Spain. The city of Xiamen, located on the south-eastern coast of Fujian province, functioned as a maritime gateway, meeting point, and vital centre for the entire maritime trade network in the province. In 1585, Juan González de Mendoza, a Spanish bishop, authored *Historia del Gran Reino de la China* [The History of the Great and Mighty Kingdom of China and the Situation Thereof], a comprehensive and detailed work on China's natural environment, politics, history, culture, religion, and economy during the 16th century. This work generated considerable intrigue within European circles and became the leading source of knowledge on China in Europe before the publication of Nicolas Trigault's *On the Christian Expedition to China*. The first Spanish reference to Xiamen is located in a narrative that describes the voyage of Augustinians Martín de Rada and Jerónimo Marín, who landed there on 15th July 1575:

This Tansuso is a very fresh and pleasant town of four thousand inhabitants, garrisoned by a thousand soldiers and surrounded by a strong and well-fortified wall with iron-clad gates. The houses are built on fine stonework foundations, with walls of whitewashed adobe, and some of brick. The houses are well-crafted, with fine and elegant courtyards, and the streets are wide and beautiful, all paved. (González de Mendoza, 2008, pp. 190-191)[4]

Tansuso in the quotation, or transcribed as Zhongzuosuo, referred to the city of Xiamen during the Ming dynasty (1368-1644).[5] Dominican missionary Albino Andrés noted that the city was fortified with a wall and the island itself came to be known as Hsia Men, meaning "gate of the great house." This name was colloquially abbreviated to Emng, leading some foreigners to refer to it as Emuy, which has become its commonly recognized name today (Andrés, 1952, p. 39). Further observations in the area can be found in the religious reports. Before becoming a modern city, Xiamen was marked by a transitory and socially complex population, with few permanent settlers and a majority dependent on fishing as their primary source of income. The city underwent expansion in the 17th century:

All fifteen kingdoms of China, which they call provinces, were there, and consequently all the vices, and at the same time different languages could be heard, and different customs could be observed; new maliciousness could be seen, the bustle and noise being so remarkable, and the speech of the multitude so crowded, that sometimes I felt shaken by the earth rather than by the men. (Riccio, 1667, Chapter VIII, Section 2)[6]

Other industries emerged with societal development, such as salt production, described as "another industry that provided considerable profit" (Andrés, 1952, p. 49). According to records by Albino Andrés (1952), "other important industries included preserved food, various noodles, medicinal wines, paper umbrellas, ice factories, tanneries, and other small businesses yielding various objects of common use" (pp. 49-50).[7] The location facilitated trade among most towns and villages in Fujian.

The detailed observations recorded by Albino Andrés and other Dominican missionaries, along with those of early European explorers, form an indispensable corpus of Western literature on China during its early interactions with the West. Their works serve as a window into the multifaceted nature of Chinese society, from intricate city defences to the nuances of local life. These meticulous records not only enhanced their missionary endeavours but also enriched the European understanding of the East, laying the groundwork for the academic field of sinology and the study of East Asian cultures.

In 1626, the Spanish Governor of Manila seized control of northern Taiwan, viewing it as a crucial trade conduit with China while also seeking avenues for missionaries to enter China, thereby bypassing the Portuguese dominion in Macao. In 1630, the authority dispatched Ángel Cochi and Tomás Sierra, Dominican friars based in Taiwan, to Fujian as ambassadors to foster trade relations between the two regions, presenting a noteworthy opportunity for the Order to breach China. Following their settlement in Fu'an in north-eastern Fujian, issues related to cultural and religious exchanges between Chinese and Western spheres gained prominence. Initially, the matter revolved around a debate among Roman Catholic missionaries concerning the religious nature of Confucianism, Chinese rites, and their potential integration into Catholic rituals to facilitate Christianization. The debate over integrating Christian teachings with Chinese traditions can be seen as an early exploration into what we now understand as soft power. This discussion aimed to identify ways to contextualize Christian ideas within Chinese cultural norms, suggesting an early recognition of the need to bridge cultural divides for effective communication of new beliefs. However, it eventually escalated into a political conflict between China and the Roman Curia, known as the Chinese Rites controversy. The 1650s denoted a period of steady Catholic advancement in China, with the Dominican Victorio Riccio turning Xiamen into an important mission hub for Fujian during this phase, aided by other missionaries.

2. THE DOMINICAN ORDER IN CHINA: FROM ARRIVAL TO INTEGRATION

The traditional religions in Xiamen were derived from the same roots as the religious beliefs prevalent among the people of Fujian, with Taoism, Confucianism, and Buddhism being the primary faiths. It is noteworthy that Buddhism, the first "foreign" religion to influence China during the first century of the Han dynasty, underwent a lengthy process of adaptation and transformation of indigenous religions, such as Taoism and Confucian thought, throughout the history of China. Between the 16th and 17th centuries, prior to the fall of the Ming dynasty, the emergence of the "Unity of the Three Teachings," which advocated for a synthesis of aspects and practices from the spiritual cultures of these three religions, achieved a convergence between scholarly and popular culture. This tradition ultimately culminated in the establishment of Buddhist culture in China (Cheng, 2006, pp. 469-470). In the 17th century, these three beliefs were coexisted by the Chinese people, who exhibited a notable inclination towards animism, placing significant emphasis on ancestor worship and family traditions.

The introduction of the first Western religions, such as Islam in the 7th century, gained a substantial following in the north-eastern region of China. Specifically, the city of Quanzhou in Fujian province, from the late 8th to the 15th century, served as the commercial port where Muslim traders conducted business with China, due to the commercial influence of the Maritime Silk Road that connected the south-eastern coast of China with Southeast Asia. Christianity of the same period was introduced by the Nestorians but left no visible trace. The Franciscan missions appeared in the 14th century, followed by a strengthening presence of the Jesuits in the 16th century and later the Dominicans and other religious orders in the 17th century. Figures such as Martín de Rada, Bernardino Escalante, and Juan González Mendoza were notable for their writings, through which Europeans began to form their perception and outlook on China (Serna Arnaiz, 2019, pp. 249-264).

Traditional Chinese culture was widespread in Fujian, yet due to its coastal location, it unavoidably absorbed influences from foreign civilizations. For the Dominican Order, Fujian and Taiwan were exceptional regions; regarded as central hubs for their activities in China, and by the 17th century, great progress had been made in spreading Catholicism. Following Ángel Cochi's arrival in Fujian in 1632 and the establishment of the first missionary district there, missionaries from Hispanic territories began to arrive in the province. This led to the creation of several Dominican martyrs in China, such as Francisco Fernández de Capillas (1607-1648), who arrived in Fujian in 1642 and then undertook numerous apostolic tasks in the region. Pedro Sanz (1680-1747) was in Xiamen in 1715 and moved to Fu'an shortly thereafter to disseminate the faith, undeterred by the challenges he would face.[8] Joaquín Royo (1691-1748), accompanying Pedro Sanz on the journey to the Philippines, did not stay in Xiamen but travelled through neighbouring areas. Other friars, including Juan Alcober (1694-1748), Francisco Serrano (1695-1748), Francisco Díaz (1713-1748), and others, also devoted themselves to missions in Fujian and promoted the growth of Christianity in China.

The missionaries' interest in establishing missions in new territories compelled them to develop varying strategies based on local circumstances. In some cases, they were forced to play roles beyond their religious responsibilities. A notable figure related to Catholicism in Xiamen in the mid-17th century, the Italian Dominican Victorio Riccio, represents a special case that exemplifies such task. Two particularly relevant sources provide information to analyse the missionary contributions of Riccio to the city of Xiamen, where, in addition to his roles as interpreter and negotiator, he also acted as a diplomat in trade between southern Fujian and Manila. One is the manuscript *Hechos de la Orden de Predicadores en el Imperio de China*, written in 1667, which serves as a history of Dominican missions in China and recounts Riccio's personal experiences in the Philippines and China, as well as historical events of that time. The other source, written by José María González and titled *Un misionero diplomático: vida del padre Victorio Riccio en el tercer centenario de su primera entrada en China (1655-1955)* covers Riccio's entire religious life. Additionally, the manuscript titled *Discurso y parecer en que se demuestra que no combiene que la nación de China (que llaman sangleyes) habite ni viva de asiento en las Islas Philipinas* contains further descriptions of Riccio's involvement in Chinese politics and diplomacy.

Victorio Riccio was among the missionaries who benefited from the groundwork laid by Ángel Cochi and his companions. Born on January 18, 1621, in Santa María de Cintoia, a suburb of Florence, Italy, Riccio descended from the noble Ricci family. However, wishing to Hispanize his name, he chose to modify his surname by adding an "o" at the end, which is why his name often appears in documents as Victorio Riccio (Busquets Alemany, 2006, p. 394). Riccio took his vows at the Santo Domingo convent in Fiesole, Tuscany, Italy, and then completed his ecclesiastical career at the Minerva in Rome, serving as a Lector. Later, Riccio became a Philosophy professor at his original convent in Fiesole. The turning point came when Father Friar Juan Bautista de Morales received approval from the Master of the Order, which allowed for the recruitment of forty religious members from Europe to the Philippines. Motivated by the desire to convert non-believers, Riccio seized this opportunity and got enlisted to this primarily missionary division of the Dominican Order at the earliest opportunity.

In 1646, Riccio boarded on the fleet of General Don Lorenzo Fernández de Córdova at the port of Cádiz and arrived in Mexico with all his dispatches on September 13 of the same year. On April 8, 1648, Riccio, along with other religious members, arrived at Casiguran in Baler, Philippines, and disembarked at the port of Lampón. From there, they trekked to the city of Manila for twelve days, facing many challenges due to bad weather, "having no place to rest but the bare ground, and nothing to change into," in Riccio's own words (González, 1955, p. 13). Despite the hardships endured on the journey to Manila, his life improved significantly upon arrival. Moreover, the evangelical experiences gained in this city would aid him throughout his time in China, as he not only worked at the San Gabriel Hospital for Chinese in Manila from April 20, 1652, but also served as the General Procurator of the Province in San Gabriel de Binondoc, a position he was assigned by the Provincial Congregation on April 25, 1654. Furthermore, he held the roles of Province Secretary and Master of Novices during the same period. However, due to the pressures arising from the controversy over Chinese rites among missionaries, Riccio stayed in Manila to learn the Fujian Chinese dialect, which he mastered perfectly afterwards. Thus, he was able to preach fluently in this language and also wrote books on Chinese calligraphy and vocabularies during his stay in the region.

Seizing a brief period of peace in 1655, the superiors selected five missionaries to preach in China (Riccio, 1667, Book III, Chapter II, Section 1). The chosen ones were the Dominicans Gregorio López, Domingo Coronado, Diego Rodríguez, Raimundo del Valle, and the protagonist, Victorio Riccio. In July of the same year, they arrived at the port of Xiamen and set foot on land, accompanied by Catholic soldiers to ensure their safety.

During the journey to Xiamen, Riccio's health deteriorated due to an illness he had contracted in Manila. As Riccio himself wrote in his memoir, he could barely stand. He was carried in a sedan chair to the city, where "he was given rest in a Christian's bed, and all the religious men commended his soul, for the illness was so severe they thought he would die" (Riccio, 1667, Book III, Chapter II, Section 6). Riccio eventually overcame the illness and survived, so while he stayed in the city to recover, his four companions continued their journey to Fu'an, the final destination of their mission.

While Riccio was in Xiamen, the island served as the base for Zheng Chenggong, known in the West as the Pirate-Emperor Koxinga, who had established his power on the island of Xiamen and then took control of the coastlines of Fujian and Zhejiang provinces. The Zheng family maintained a close relationship with the Catholic faith, which allowed Riccio to freely propagate the faith in this area. The first thing Riccio did was to build a chapel in front of Zheng's palace. According to records, "when Riccio arrived in this land, there were only two churches in ruins located in what is now called the diocese of Xiamen, one in the city of Hing-hoa [Xinghua, the ancient name of Putian] and the other in the city of Choanchiu

[Quanzhou]. These two churches had been built by the Jesuit Fathers" (Andrés, 1952, p. 369). Riccio later transformed what was a small chapel into a temple, which he solemnly blessed the following year.

On August 5, 1655, the first mass was celebrated in Riccio's house. By then, Riccio converted and baptized a considerable number of people, most of whom were not from the island, as he noted; "many were baptized, including some prominent individuals, but almost all from other places, and not from Xiamen itself" (Ferrando & Fonseca, 1871, Vol. III, Book V, Chapter I). His residence served as more than just a home in the literal sense; it functioned as a dispensary or orphanage. He founded the first Holy Childhood in the Xiamen Mission, as the island's excessive population and the lack of hygiene, typical of a fishing port, led to contagious epidemics like smallpox, which resulted in a significant loss of lives, particularly among the most vulnerable age groups like infants. Riccio baptized several infants and cared for many sick individuals. The economic strain led many local parents to abandon their sickly children. In response, Riccio had posters hung on street walls and city gates, imploring residents not to harm these vulnerable youths and assuring care for any child they could not support. Nonetheless, as the number of orphaned children swelled, the capacity of his modest dwelling was stretched to its limits. As the initiator of child welfare programs in China, Riccio's founding of the Holy Childhood in Xiamen marked a pioneering step. In the beginning, this initiative was solely intended for the rescue and salvation of Chinese children, but it later expanded to include other countries. In the locations where the Holy Childhoods were established, the most robust Christian communities also took root.

While the actions observed in Xiamen during that era might not have been explicitly framed as soft power, the underlying principles of these historical efforts are in line with contemporary scholarly analyses. Jeffrey Haynes has investigated how individuals throughout history, irrespective of their secular or religious affiliations, have harnessed the influence of religion to achieve strategic objectives. His research proposes that when religious leaders share beliefs with main policymakers, they can influence policy outcomes through what is now understood as religious soft power. This concept reflects the subtle yet major function that religion-based initiatives have performed in community development and policy shaping, even before the term "soft power" was coined (Haynes, 2008, p. 143).

Based on Haynes' observations about religious soft power, it becomes clear that the geography of a place like Xiamen significantly influences the spread and impact of these religious activities. Through geopolitics, which explores how the Earth's landscapes and societies shape political interactions, we gain insights into how religion operates within these confines. The unique location and population dynamics have been key in determining the flow of religious and cultural exchange, thus affecting political and global relations. This link between the physical world and religious influence showcases the intricate ways geography acts as both a backdrop and a force in advancing the agendas of religious leaders and communities.

3. VICTORIO RICCIO (1621-1685): THE MISSIONARY AMBASSADOR BETWEEN EMPIRES

Between 1661 and 1665, Victorio Riccio became well-known for his role as an intermediary in maritime conflicts in China. Within this setting, the varied roles of religious figures such as Riccio become clear, especially when we look at their impact outside of formal religious ceremonies. Similar to how preachers might carry their parts and values into daily life, Riccio and others like him continued to embody and spread their institution's core principles in everyday situations. Their influence was expressed through simple yet meaningful elements such as dress, speech patterns, and body language, which helped convey the shared identities and standards of their communities (Cook, 2013). Drawing on Riccio's diplomatic image, Anna Busquets Alemany highlights in her research the significance of the friars' roles as interpreters and cultural mediators, both for the Christian communities in China and to ensure the commercial relations between Fujian and Manila. Moreover, Chinese sources also provide descriptions of this Dominican missionary. Although these details are seldom mentioned, they are considered valuable for further research on Riccio's character. According to the *General History of Taiwan*, "initially, the Roman Catholic priest Li Keluo [Riccio's Chinese name] preached in Xiamen. Zheng Chenggong welcomed him with respect and invited him to be an advisor to his power" (Lian, 2006, p. 20). Zheng was deeply influenced by his Christian father, which justifies his kind treatment of Riccio. It is important to note that during this period of turmoil between the Ming to Qing dynasties, the most powerful groups in China felt an urgent need to consolidate their influence. Over time, many Western missionaries had acquired advanced scientific and cultural knowledge, which was crucial for gaining influence. German Jesuit Johann Adam and Belgian Ferdinand Verbiest secured influential positions at the Qing court. Other foreigners like Jesuit Francesco Sambiasi or Michał Boym were court invitees. Thus, the close relationship between Zheng and Riccio surprised no one.

In 1661, Zheng Chenggong defeated the Dutch in Taiwan. Around this time, news reached that about one hundred thousand Chinese residents on the island of Luzon, Philippines, had endured prolonged mistreatment by the Spanish, especially under the ruthless administration of Governor-General Diego Fajardo Chacón. Zheng's generals suggested he annex Luzon as a foreign base, leading Zheng to send Riccio to Manila to demand tribute payments from the Spanish Governor-General while secretly planning a revolt with the Chinese locals, who would be supported by Zheng's warships and soldiers (Lian, 2006, p. 20). However, this plan, meant to be secret, was exposed. As a result, the Spanish strengthened their defences and sent soldiers from the island of Mindanao to defend Manila and prevent Zheng from coming to power. At that time, the Chinese in Manila incited an uprising that lasted several days but ultimately failed. Tens of thousands were killed, and some fled in small boats to Taiwan, though most drowned en route. The Spanish were also uneasy about the prospect of a counterattack from Zheng, so they sent Riccio along with an emissary to Taiwan to negotiate peace. Zheng was enraged upon hearing about the massacre of Chinese by the Spanish, and his generals also advised punitive actions. However, before any retaliation could take place, Zheng died on July 23, 1662.

In his diplomatic capacity, Victorio Riccio bridged the cultural divide, skilfully navigating the complex world of international diplomacy during a period filled with tension and conflict. His communication led to discussions that could change the relationships between these nations. This is shown in a letter from Zheng Chenggong to Governor-General Manrique de Lara of Manila, written on April 21, 1662, but wrongly dated as March 7. The letter reads:

You [the Spaniards] are no different from the Dutch, another small state, who harass our merchant ships and provoke incidents. To this day, I have subdued Taiwan, commanding hundreds of thousands of excellent soldiers and a thousand warships. I was on the verge of invading Manila myself in person. You are well aware that we are very close, from Taiwan to your area, easily reached by sea; setting out tomorrow, we could arrive by the afternoon. However, considering that your envoy has come to plead for trade agreements, a conduct unlike the Dutch, I decide to pardon your offenses and for now, remain in Taiwan with my armed forces. Therefore, I am authorizing Father Riccio to demand that you submit to my rule and pay annual tributes. Should there be any deceit on your part, my ships will immediately arrive and utterly destroy your city and treasures, just as I have done with the Dutch. By then, it will be too late. Consider and decide carefully, but do not delay, the decision is yours. (Zheng, Zheng, & Zheng, 2012)

Amidst these high-stakes negotiations, Riccio's journey to Manila as a delegate from Xiamen was a key diplomatic mission. His entry into the city was met with considerable attention:

Father Ambassador entered the city adorned with the magnificent insignias of a high mandarin, mounted on a richly harnessed horse, to the rhythm of the army's drums and bugles, and the roar of the salute fired from the city's bastions. He was accompanied by the cavalry and infantry of the garrison, and amidst the general rejoicing and applause of the residents, he reached the royal hall, where he presented his credentials and delivered the embassy. (Ferrando & Fonseca, 1871, p. 11)

On April 4, 1663, Riccio returned to Manila, this time bearing a letter from Zheng Chenggong's son, Zheng Jing. The Governor-General of the Philippines received him with great hospitality. Riccio would then deliver the response in the form of a letter back in Xiamen. In 1664, all missionaries in the empire were summoned to Beijing. Six of the ten Dominican missionaries residing in the provinces of Fujian and Zhejiang remained in Fu'an, and the other four, who went to Beijing, were later relocated to Guangzhou. Instead of going to Beijing, Riccio moved to Fuzhou, "where he stayed hidden for ten months and then moved to the Dutch factory near Fo-cheu, where he publicly ministered, dressed as a Fleming" (Archives of the Province of the Holy Rosary, Section 34 China, Tome 4, Document 4). That same year, the alliance formed by the Qing dynasty and the Dutch East India Company took Xiamen, and Riccio was sent to Jilong, Taiwan, to evangelize the soldiers and locals. A few months after the Dutch left Taiwan, Riccio returned to the Philippines on March 19, 1666, and would live there for nineteen more years in Manila.

Religion is known as one of the oldest parts of human culture. It can bring people together or push them apart and is often seen as a way to influence others without using force. This soft power attribute of religion is not confined solely to nations with established religious institutions but extends to secular states and non-state religious entities as well (Ozturk, 2023). Joseph Nye's framework of soft power, characterized by the capacity to influence others through attraction rather than coercion, offers a pertinent lens through which to examine Victorio Riccio's engagements in China (Nye, 2004). Riccio introduced Western religious and cultural values to the local socio-political context, exemplifying soft power in action. The practice of cultural diplomacy, as Milton Cummings outlines it—the exchange of cultural elements to foster mutual understanding between nations (Cummings, 2003)—is evident in Riccio's experience of local customs and dialogues. While Robert Woodberry's analysis of missionary activities as precursors to the spread of liberal democratic values (Woodberry, 2012) provides a long-term view, it is essential to contextualize Riccio's contributions within his historical period. His actions might not have directly laid the foundation for immediate socio-political transformations. Still, they were part of interactions that gradually shaped the region's cultural and political dynamics.

4. SHAPING THE SPIRITUAL LANDSCAPE IN MING AND QING

In the mid-16th century, the coastal towns of southeast China, notably Xiamen and Haicheng, ushered in a transformative period as non-governmental overseas trade gained legalization. This newfound legitimacy catalysed a vibrant maritime commerce, with an estimated 30 to 40 merchant vessels departing annually from Xiamen and Haicheng to the Philippines between 1571 and 1580. These ships bore an extensive array of exports, encompassing porcelain, iron, silk, ceramics, agricultural commodities, traditional Chinese medicinal ingredients, fruit, sugar, gunpowder, and mercury, among others. Predominantly, these goods were destined for Manila, barring a select portion appropriated for consumption by the Spanish colonizers in the Philippines and the members of the upper classes, which was subsequently transported to Mexico (Xiamen Chorography Compilation Committee, 1993, p. 22). This flourishing trade facilitated the arrival of missionaries seeking to evangelize during the Spanish colonization process.

Evangelisation had been an important theme during the Spanish colonisation process. Prior to Legazpi's arrival in the Philippines, the aspiration of "creating a utopian Christian community in a New World" was prevalent among colonizers, but it was not easy to realize it in real life (Cervera, 2015, p. 39). In 1574, when a Chinese official from Fujian visited Manila to express gratitude for Spanish assistance against pirate Lin Feng, he proposed bringing a Spanish delegation to China. As a result, Martín de Rada and Jerónimo Marín arrived in Xiamen that same year. This first Spanish expedition had set several objectives: firstly, to request permission for the propagation of Christianity in China; secondly, to establish a stable economic tie with Fujian, similar to the Portuguese arrangement with Guangdong; and thirdly, to gather more information about China to help the Spaniards plan strategically for the future (Ollé, 2002, pp. 58-59). Despite their inability to achieve these goals, they gained crucial understanding of China and collected over a hundred Chinese books to transport back to Manila (Folch Fornesa, 2008, p. 54). They visited numerous locations in Fujian, using Xiamen as their starting point. Xiamen was "the first port where they landed when they came from the Islands to the mainland" (González de Mendoza, 2008, p. 234). The missionaries travelled along the coast to the north, reaching Quanzhou before journeying to the provincial capital, Fuzhou. Upon completing their expeditions, they returned to their initial departure point. From that time forward, Xiamen has been regarded as a critical entry point for friars.

In the early years, the Augustinians were the sole religious order established in the Philippines. Later, other orders, such as the Order of Friars Minor Franciscans and the Order of Preachers Dominicans, utilized Manila as a base for visiting China. Interestingly, it was the Dominicans who forged enduring connections, especially with Fujian and Taiwan. Before the first Dominican arrived, the Jesuits had evangelized the mission territory of China for nearly half a century (Núñez Fernández, 2010, p. 4). The Dominican Victorio Riccio initiated the propagation in Xiamen in 1655, at the end of the Ming dynasty. Like most missionaries, Riccio was trained in the Xiamen dialect in Manila before starting on his mission. He was the first missionary to reside in this port city for a prolonged period and became the founder of the Xiamen mission. To effectively spread the gospel, Riccio oversaw the construction of churches and celebrated masses to garner public attention. He expanded the missionary work to the surrounding areas of Xiamen during his stay (González, 1955).

Despite Victorio Riccio's efforts, missionaries encountered numerous challenges, primarily due to the growing distrust of Chinese authorities. The Chinese authorities' scepticism towards foreign religious figures was mirrored by a wariness among the general population, fuelled by cultural and religious differences. This distrust was exacerbated by the missionaries' association with colonial powers, casting them in the light of foreign intruders rather than benevolent religious guides. Officials, concerned about the potential for social unrest and the undermining of Confucian values, were inclined to restrict missionary activities, leading to increased scrutiny and, in some cases, outright prohibition. The local people, influenced by their leaders and protective of their traditions, were often hesitant to embrace the foreign concepts introduced by the missionaries, adding another layer of complexity to the challenges faced by Riccio and his successors in their evangelical mission. He left Xiamen in 1663, passing the mantle to his companion, Gregorio Lopez. Lopez remained in Xiamen only briefly, as he was soon sent by the Provincial of the Philippines to visit all the empire missions. Few Spanish or Chinese records document the progress of the Xiamen missions in the succeeding years, possibly due to the onset of resistance against missionaries in 1664, which temporarily halted missionary activities in Xiamen. Arcadio del Rosario's arrival between 1676 and 1686 signified the restoration of the Xiamen missions, as he constructed a church in Xiamen and preached in the prefectures of Quanzhou, Zhangzhou, and Xinghua.

Magín Ventallol, a missionary who arrived in Xiamen in 1682 and worked there for 45 years. Beyond church building, he founded a beguinage, which served as an inspiration for future missionaries. In 1706, Ventallol became the first Apostolic Administrator of the Dominican Order in Fujian and the Vicar Apostolic of the province in 1718 (Andrés, 1952, p. 65). Shortly after his arrival, he hosted Francisco Pallú, the first Vicar Apostolic of China, in Xiamen and accompanied him in visiting neighbouring missions for several months. Ventallol's highly regarded undertaking significantly influenced the evangelical development in the area at the time.

Nonetheless, the diffusion of Christianity in Xiamen from 1655 to 1852 was hindered primarily due to an unfavourable local political environment and inadequate communication. While the Jesuits evangelized in Zhangzhou, they seldom visited the port of Xiamen. Dominicans perceived the island as a centre for revolutionaries and a haven for pirates, with a highly mobile population frequenting the area for political, military, or commercial purposes. It was not until 1842, when Xiamen opened to foreign trade, that missionaries were able to experience a modicum of religious freedom. In other words, they were finally able to build schools, churches, holy infancies, and hospitals with fewer restrictions. Additionally, they could travel and preach in various parts of China (Andrés, 1952, p. 68). The history of missionary activities in Xiamen illustrates the challenges and opportunities faced by religious orders in their attempts to spread Christianity in China. The Dominican Order, in particular, were instrumental in linking the Philippines with Fujian and Taiwan, despite the daunting political and communicational hurdles they faced.

5. CONCLUSION

In reflecting upon the Dominican missionary strategies in Ming and Qing China, it is imperative to consider the subtle, yet profound, influence these activities had on the soft power interplay between the Iberian empire and the East. The Dominicans, perhaps unwittingly, established what could be regarded as a precursor to religious and cultural diplomacy in the region. Their in-depth engagement with local communities, commitment to linguistic excellence, and their active involvement in the socio-political tapestries of Fujian and Taiwan, highlight a nuanced approach to evangelism that transcended mere proselytization. The interweaving of Western religious ideologies with the Chinese spiritual framework marked a dynamic intercultural dialogue, an illustrative of the Dominican approach to exert influence. Their activities extended beyond the realm of spiritual conversion to include engagement in cultural exchanges, setting a foundation for a deeper and more elaborate mutual comprehension among diverse civilizations. The sustained scholarly interest in China within Spanish and European academic discourse can be partially attributed to the historical precedents set by these missionary interactions, though the full spectrum of their impact remains a subject of contemplative analysis.

The Dominican Order's participation in social outreach, such as caring for children, highlights their extensive social involvement during their mission. While these actions align with what are now recognized as soft power practices, where humanitarian actions strengthen diplomatic ties, it is crucial to assess their broader implications. Historical accounts indicate that although some of these activities were beneficial, they were also intertwined with the Order's religious objectives, including the potential religious indoctrination of youth in institutions like the Holy Childhood. The narrative of Xiamen's missionary history provides a multifaceted perspective on the evolution of soft power, revealing how spiritual missions can be both conduits for cultural exchange and instruments of religious influence. These undertakings reveal the complex relationship between humanitarian aid and the spread of belief systems, a dynamic that continues to shape the discourse on diplomatic relations and cultural interactions.

As the global community continues to grapple with the complexities of intercultural diplomacy and the strategic deployment of soft power, the experiences of Dominican missionaries in Ming and Qing China present a rich historical narrative for examination. These strategies highlight a formative period of cultural and religious engagement, characterized by a blend of cooperation and conflict. This history invites contemplation on the dual potential of such interactions to cultivate enduring connections and to assert specific cultural agendas. Thus, the Dominican legacy in China serves not merely as a singular lesson but rather as a case study, where the lines between humanitarian action, cultural exchange, and religious expansion are often interlaced and subject to interpretation.

REFERENCES

Alemany, A. B. (2006). Los frailes de Koxinga. In P. S. Aguilar (Ed.), *La Investigación sobre Asia Pacífico en España* (pp. 393–422). Universidad de Granada.

Alfonso Mola, M. (2021). La ruta directa entre Cádiz y Manila (1765-1834): Tres alternativas al Galeón de Manila. *Andalucía en la Historia*, (73), 24–29.

Andrés, A. (1952). *Historia de las Misiones Dominicanas en Amoy*. Unpublished manuscript, Archives of the Province of the Holy Rosary, Spain.

Cervera Jiménez, J. A. (2020). El Galeón de Manila: Mercancías, personas e ideas viajando a través del Pacífico (1565-1815). *México y la Cuenca del Pacífico*, 9(26), 69–90. doi:10.32870/mycp.v9i26.677

Cheng, A. (2006). *Historia del Pensamiento Chino*. Bellaterra Edicions.

Cook, H. (2013). *Performing Identity: Descriptive and Symbolic Representation in New Zealand and the United Kingdom* [Doctoral dissertation, University of Exeter]. University of Exeter Repository.

Cummings, M. C. (2003). *Cultural Diplomacy and the United States Government: A Survey*. Center for Arts and Culture.

Elliott, J. H. (2002). *Imperial Spain, 1469-1716*. Penguin Books.

Ferrando, J., & Fonseca, J. (1871). *Historia de los PP. Dominicos en las islas Filipinas y en sus Misiones del Japón, China, Tung-king y Formosa, que comprende los sucesos principales de la historia general de este archipiélago, desde el descubrimiento y conquista de estas islas hasta el año de 1840* (Vol. III). Imprenta y Estereotipia de Manuel Rivadeneyra.

Folch Fornesa, D. (2008). Biografía de Fray Martín de Rada. *Revista Huarte de San Juan. Geografía e Historia, 15*, 33–63.

González, J. M. (1955). *Un Misionero Diplomático. Vida del padre Victorio Riccio en el tercer centenario de su primera entrada en China (1655-1955)*. Studium.

González de Mendoza, J. (2008). *Historia del Gran Reino de la China*. Editorial Miraguano.

Haynes, J. (Ed.). (2008). *Routledge Handbook of Religion and Politics*. Routledge. doi:10.4324/9780203890547

Hernández, B. (Ed.). (2019). Transocéanos. Viajes culturales en los mundos conocidos (siglos XVI-XVIII). Centro para la Edición de los Clásicos Españoles.

Lian, H. (2006). *Taiwan Tongshi* [General History of Taiwan]. Huadong Shifan Daxue Chubanshe.

Martínez-Sicluna y Sepúlveda, C. (Ed.). (2020). *Autoridad, Poder y Jurisdicción en la Monarquía Hispánica*. Dykinson. doi:10.2307/j.ctv153k3z8

Núñez Fernández, A. (2010). Jesuitas. *Inforsi, 106*, 4.

Nye, J. S. (2004). *Soft Power: The Means to Success in World Politics*. Public Affairs.

Ollé, M. (2002). *La Empresa de China. De la Armada Invencible al Galeón de Manila*. Acantilado.

Ozturk, A. E. (2023). Religious Soft Power: Definition(s), Limits and Usage. *Religions, 14*(2), 135. doi:10.3390/rel14020135

Phillips, C. R. (2007). The Organization of Oceanic Empires: The Iberian World in the Habsburg Period. In J. H. Bentley, R. Bridenthal, & K. Wigen (Eds.), *Seascapes: Maritime Histories, Littoral Cultures, and Transoceanic Exchanges* (pp. 71–86). University of Hawaii Press. doi:10.2307/j.ctt6wr35q.8

Riccio, V. (1667). Hechos de la orden de Predicadores en el imperio de China [Unpublished manuscripts]. Archives of the Province of the Holy Rosary, Section 34 China, Volume 31, Books I, II, III.

Ruiz Ortiz, M. Á. (2012). La monarquía española de los Austrias en los siglos XVI y XVII. *Revista de Claseshistoria*, (336), 1–12.

Serna Arnaiz, M. (2019). Modos y modas. Primeros retratos occidentales de los reinos de China y de los indios de América. In B. Hernández (Ed.), Transocéanos. Viajes culturales en los mundos conocidos (siglos XVI-XVIII) (pp. 249-264). Centro para la Edición de los Clásicos Españoles.

Tremml-Werner, B. (2015). Spain, China and Japan in Manila, 1571-1644: Local Comparisons and Global Connections. Amsterdam University Press.

Woodberry, R. D. (2012). The Missionary Roots of Liberal Democracy. *The American Political Science Review, 106*(2), 244–274. doi:10.1017/S0003055412000093

Xiamen Chorography Compilation Committee. (1993). *Xiamen Gangshi* [History of Xiamen Port]. Renmin Jiaotong Chubanshe.

Zheng, C., Zheng, J., & Zheng, H. (2012). *Yanping Erwang Yiji* [The collection of works of the two Yanping sovereigns]. Shanghai Cishu Chubanshe.

ENDNOTES

1.   The political and economic expansion in the 16th century corresponded to the reigns of Charles V and Philip II, known as Habsburg Spain. Further information on the Spanish Empire governed by the House of Habsburg can be found at: Ruiz Ortiz, M. Á. (2012). La monarquía española de los Austrias en los siglos XVI y XVII. *Revista de Claseshistoria*, (336), 1-12; Rodríguez de la Peña, M. A. (2020). La idea de Monarquía universal y los primeros Habsburgo. In C. Martínez-Sicluna y Sepúlveda (Ed.), *Autoridad, Poder y Jurisdicción en la Monarquía Hispánica* (pp. 49-68). Dykinson.

2.   In December 1573, the viceroy of New Spain, Martín Enríquez, reported to King Philip II on the burgeoning trade with the Chinese and highlighted the importance of the silver as a medium of exchange: "the difficulties of this trade and commerce is that neither this land nor the Spain, as far as we now understand, can bring them anything that they do not have, because they have an abundance of silk and linen... it can be seen that the trading with the Chinese must be through silver, which is what they value most." See the letter in Cervera Jiménez, J. A. (2020). El Galeón de Manila: Mercancías, personas e ideas viajando a través del Pacífico (1565-1815). *México y la Cuenca del Pacífico*, 9, 77.

3.   For research on the route between Cádiz and Manila, see Alfonso Mola, M. (2021). La ruta directa entre Cádiz y Manila (1765-1834): Tres alternativas al Galeón de Manila. *Andalucía en la Historia*, 73, 24-29.

4.   Source text: "Este Tansuso es un pueblo muy fresco y de cuatro mil vecinos, y tiene de guarnición mil soldados y muy buena y fuerte cerca y las puertas con chapas de hierro fortificadas; las casas tienen los cimientos de buena cantería, y las paredes de tapia encalada, y algunas de ladrillos, con los aposentos muy bien labrados, y buenos y galanos patios, anchas y lindas calles, todas enlosadas."

5.   Throughout Chinese history, town names changed to conform to new civil administrative systems introduced by successive rulers or conquerors. For an overview of Chinese dynastic succession, see Beja, F. B. (1984). *China: Su Historia y Cultura Hasta 1800*. El Colegio de México.

6.   Source text: "Hallábase pues en ella todas las naciones de los quince reinos de China, que llaman ellos provincias, y consiguientemente todos los vicios y al paso que se oían diversas lenguas, y se veían diferentes costumbres; se aprecian nuevas maldades, siendo el tráfago, y bullicio tan notable, y el discurso del gentío tan apiñado, que a veces se me ofreció menearse la tierra, y no los hombres."

7.   Source text: "Otras industrias importantes son las conservas, los fideos de toda clase, vinos medicinales, sombrillas de papel, factorías de hielo, de curtidos y otras pequeñas industrias que producen varios objetos de uso común."

8.   Pedro Sanz was born in Ascó, Tarragona, and was baptized in the parish church on September 3, 1680. He arrived in the Philippines in 1713. Two years later, he and Father Matéu arrived in Xiamen.

Chapter 8
Media's Role in Fostering the Belt and Road Initiative and Chinese Foreign Policy in the Arab Region

Tianzhe Qi
School of Journalism and Communication, Northwest Minzu University, Lanzhou, China

Wei Hou
iD https://orcid.org/0000-0003-2041-6356
Institute of Culture, China

ABSTRACT

The current study aims to investigate the role of media in fostering the Belt and Road Initiative (BRI) and serving Chinese foreign policy in the Arab region. The BRI, also known as the One Belt One Road initiative, is a Chinese government-led development strategy that aims to connect Asia, Europe, and Africa through a network of infrastructure projects, trade, and investment. The Arab region is a significant part of the BRI, and China's engagement in the region has been increasing in recent years. However, little is known about how media in China and the Arab region present and shape the public perception of BRI and its implications on Chinese foreign policy in the region. The research question of this study is: "How do Chinese and Arab media present and shape the public perception of BRI in the Arab region and its implications on Chinese foreign policy?" The results of this study will provide a comprehensive understanding of the role of media in shaping the public perception of BRI and its impact on Chinese foreign policy in the Arab region.

1. INTRODUCTION

An economic and trade strategy aimed at connecting Asia, Europe, and Africa, the Belt and Road Initiative (BRI) is being led by the Chinese government. It is also known as the One Belt One Road Initiative (OBOR). Since its introduction by Chinese President Xi Jinping in 2013, this initiative has played a pivotal role in China's diplomatic endeavours (Huang, 2016; Cheng, 2016; Dunford & Liu, 2019; Zreik,

DOI: 10.4018/979-8-3693-2444-8.ch008

2023a). By collaborating with participating countries to build a network of roads, railroads, ports, and other infrastructure projects, the BRI hopes to achieve its goals. China's presence in the Middle East has increased in recent years (Zreik, 2022) because of the region's significance in the Belt and Road Initiative.

The media has a crucial role in shaping public opinion and determining the effectiveness of government programs and initiatives. The media has the power to mould the public's perception of the BRI and the impact it will have on Chinese foreign policy in the Arab region. The Chinese government has actively promoted the BRI in all forms of media, from state-run newspapers and television to social media. The BRI has been portrayed in Chinese media as an effort that benefits all parties involved, fostering regional economic growth and collaboration (Zhang & Wu, 2017; Yang & Van Gorp, 2021).

The BRI has also received substantial coverage among the Arab media, but with varying degrees of enthusiasm and scepticism (Zreik, 2024). The BRI is seen by some Arab media as a chance for economic growth and progress, while others voice concern about the potential negative repercussions on local economies, environmental degradation, and debt problems (Kamel, 2018). Public opinion, policy decisions, and the growth of support or resistance to the BRI are all profoundly impacted by media coverage of the program, particularly as it pertains to the BRI's ramifications for Chinese foreign policy in the Arab area (Xuming, 2018; Zreik & Zhu, 2024).

Little is known about how Chinese and Arab media communicate and affect public perception of the BRI and its repercussions on Chinese foreign policy in the Arab area, despite the importance of media in moulding public opinion and influencing governmental decisions. Therefore, the purpose of this research is to examine the function of the media in advancing the BRI and advancing Chinese foreign policy in the Arab world. This research will add to the existing literature on media, Chinese foreign policy, and the Arab area by analysing how the media portrays the BRI and the impact it has on Chinese foreign policy in the region.

To understand the BRI and its impact on Chinese foreign policy in the region, it is important to understand how the public and the media see it. But data on how the Chinese and Arab media portray BRI and its effects on China's foreign policy is scarce. Policymakers, academics, and the general public all need to know how the media influences public opinion of the BRI and its effects on Chinese foreign policy in the Arab region, but there is a knowledge deficit in this area. This research aims to address this information gap by investigating how the media advocate for the BRI and support Chinese foreign policy in the Arab world. This study aims to fill that knowledge gap by examining the relationship between the media, Chinese foreign policy, and the Arab region.

Study authors ask, "How do Chinese and Arab media present and shape public perception of the Belt and Road Initiative (BRI) in the Arab region, and its implications on Chinese foreign policy?" The media has such a large influence on public opinion and policymaking that the answer to this question is crucial. This research seeks to learn how the media has helped promote the BRI and the Chinese government's foreign policy goals in the Arab world. Questions like, "How do Chinese and Arab media cover the BRI in the Arab region?" or "What are the key themes and narratives used by the media to frame the BRI?" or "How does the media's portrayal of the BRI affect public perception of Chinese foreign policy in the region?" or "What are the potential implications of media coverage of the BRI on Chinese foreign policy in the Arab region?" will help researchers delve deeper into the research question. Findings from this study will provide light on how the media has influenced popular opinion of the BRI and how it has affected China's foreign policy in the Arab area.

This research is important because it could provide light on how the media affects public opinion of the Belt and Road Initiative and how it affects Chinese foreign policy in the Arab area. Understanding the role of media in promoting the BRI is vital since it is a major development program with the goal of connecting Asia, Europe, and Africa through a network of infrastructure projects, trade, and investment. Possible effects of media coverage of the BRI on Chinese foreign policy toward the Arab world will also be illuminated by this research. The findings of this study will help policymakers, academics, and the general public appreciate how the media affects popular perceptions of the Belt and Road Initiative and Chinese foreign policy in the Arab world. Little is known at the moment about how media in China and the Arab region communicate and affect popular view of the BRI and its repercussions on Chinese foreign policy, therefore our research will help fill that void. Ultimately, this research has important implications for figuring out how the media affects public opinion and how that affects policy decisions about the BRI and Chinese foreign policy in the Arab region.

The small sample size is the primary caveat of this study. The sample may not be typical of the community at large despite efforts to interview a wide range of people (journalists, academics, government officials, business leaders, and locals). The study also overlooked the viewpoints of people outside the Arab region who may be affected by BRI in addition to the region's residents.

2. LITERATURE REVIEW

The Belt and Road Initiative has been the subject of extensive research from a wide range of academic disciplines. Due to the extensive media coverage of the BRI, especially in nations either participating in or opposed to the initiative, this study focuses on analysing the Arab and Chinese media coverage of the BRI. As a result, the offered literature and analysis are set within this context.

Lasswell's investigation of political propaganda in 1927 is considered the literary forerunner to the modern practice of analysing news texts. Lasswell's goal was to extract key messages from politicians' speeches and other written materials by analysing their rhetoric. The framework and methodology used in media content analysis are comparable.

The BRI has been the subject of more and more media content analysis studies in recent years. Xiao, Li, & Hu (2019), for instance, looked at how this initiative was reported on in China's state-run media (China Daily) and in the media of the United States (The New York Times), which views China as an adversary. According to the research, Chinese media outlets covered the project's nuts and bolts in greater depth than their American counterparts did. The Chinese media painted a good picture, whereas their American counterparts painted a darker one.

Zhang and Wu (2017) did a similar thing, comparing how the BRI was portrayed in Chinese and Western media by analysing articles from China Daily and the Financial Times. The Financial Times painted China as an authoritarian and geopolitical danger, whereas Chinese media focused on the initiative's peaceful nature and the expansion of international cooperation.

Hu (2019) looked at how the BRI was covered in Chinese and American media outlets such China Daily, CNN, and CNBC. The investigation concluded that the BRI had not garnered enough support in the West and that there were issues with the project's communication, details, and reporting.

Xin and Matheson (2018) looked into how the English-speaking media have described the BRI through metaphor. News reports from the United Kingdom, India, Pakistan, Australia, the United States, and Africa were analysed. War, slogan, campaign, game, and strategy were commonplace in the English-speaking countries, while rejuvenation, golden luck, and historical cooperation were highlighted in Pakistan and Africa.

Hatef and Luqiu, in their 2018 analysis, zeroed exclusively on Afghanistan because of its significance to China's BRI project. They looked at articles from the People's Daily and the Global Times and concluded that the politically unstable countries such as Afghanistan may benefit from the endeavour.

Huang (2018) looked at two major countries that will be affected by China's project: Pakistan and India. He discovered that Pakistan was optimistic about the venture, albeit sceptical, while India saw China as an adversary. By comparing the coverage of the China-Pakistan Economic Corridor in the Pakistani and Chinese newspapers, Afzaal et al. (2019) found generally positive and friendly discourses about China, suggesting that Pakistan had a favourable attitude toward the project.

Ravitsky (2018) looked at how the project was covered in Russia, an integral part of China's project. The article highlighted the mutual benefits that will come from the strategic cooperation between Russia and China.

Media coverage from European outlets like Le Monde (France), The Guardian (United Kingdom), Sueddeutsche Zeitung (Germany), and El Pais (Spain) as well as Chinese outlets like Global Times, Xinhua News, and People's Daily were analysed by Arifon et al. (2019) to determine how different countries in Europe approached the initiative. The Chinese media, meanwhile, emphasized teamwork and mutual benefit. The project was mostly disregarded by European media, who expressed scepticism and saw it as the work of a single individual (Zreik, 2023b).

Using the Global Database of Events, Language, and Tone (GDELT), Herrero and Xu (2019) examined the BRI and its reputation in all nations. They looked at content released about the BRI in 2017 and 2018 and found that the vast majority of it had a favourable tone and focused on trade and investments. Some nations saw the project as a chance to boost their economies, while others saw it as a potential threat to their governments.

3. METHODOLOGY

This investigation made use of a qualitative approach to research. Exploring complex phenomena and learning about people's unique perspectives and experiences calls for a qualitative research approach. The purpose of this research was to examine how media coverage of the Arab world has helped advance China's Belt and Road Initiative. Qualitative research was judged acceptable as it enables for an in-depth investigation of the experiences and perceptions of those involved in media coverage of the BRI in the Arab area.

Journalists, media analysts, and experts in the Arab world and China were interviewed semi-structured for this study. Experts and participants in Arab media's coverage of the BRI were sought out for the interviews. The interviews were taped with the participants' permission and were conducted in both English and Arabic. The semi-structured interviews provided both freedom of inquiry into material pertinent to the study and uniformity of information gathered. Due to the widespread nature of the COVID-19 outbreak and the locations of the respondents, the discussions were place virtually through the use of video conferencing software.

In this investigation, interviews served as the major means of gathering information. Experts in the Arab world and China were interviewed, as well as journalists and media analysts. To fully understand the perspectives of those who have contributed to media coverage of the Belt and Road Initiative in the Arab area, interviews were chosen as the technique of data gathering. Experts and participants in Arab media's coverage of the BRI were sought out for these interviews, which were done in both English and Arabic.

Data from interviews with Chinese and Arab journalists, academics, government officials, business executives, and local citizens involved in Belt and Road Initiative projects in the Arab region were analysed. The identified topics concerned the influence of BRI on Chinese foreign policy in the Arab region, public perceptions of BRI's benefits, and the role of the media in moulding such perceptions.

The respondents' comments were then organized into groups according to the recurring themes that emerged. This made it possible to compare and contrast the interviewers' points of view. The data was interpreted by looking for commonalities among interviewee responses in order to grasp how they felt about BRI and how it would affect Chinese foreign policy in the Arab world.

Interpretation of the data and corroboration from the interviews formed the basis for the findings drawn from the analysis. The findings illuminated how the media has contributed to the promotion of BRI and the advancement of Chinese foreign policy in the Arab area. Finally, officials and researchers interested in BRI and Chinese foreign policy in the Arab region were given suggestions based on the findings.

4. FINDINGS AND DISCUSSION

4.1. Presentation of Findings

The results of this research highlight the many ways in which the Belt and Road Initiative coverage in Chinese and Arab media diverges. The economic benefits of BRI are often emphasized in Chinese media, with the implication being that all parties engaged will benefit. Chinese media frequently highlight the good aspects of BRI, such as job creation and infrastructure development, according to one Chinese journalist who covers BRI in the Arab region. They believe it will boost China's economy and international standing. However, not all Arab media outlets share this optimistic view of BRI.

The Arab media's coverage of BRI has been more sceptical as issues about the sustainability of debt and the consequences of Chinese investments have been raised. A journalist from an Arab country who covers BRI in the region has said, "Arab media often question the motives behind BRI and are concerned about the long-term implications of Chinese investment." Corruption fears and a lack of transparency surrounding some activities are top concerns.

According to the research, BRI is generally portrayed in Chinese media as a grand strategy to expand Chinese presence and soft power in the region. In the words of a Chinese specialist on media and foreign policy, "Chinese media often frame BRI as a way to enhance China's image as a responsible global actor and promote its role as a leader in international development." When it comes to regional geopolitics and the quest for power among regional nations, however, BRI is often defined by Arab media. One Arab government official involved in BRI policies has remarked, "Arab media often see BRI as part of a broader competition for influence in the region, with China competing against other powers such as the United States and Russia."

One of the main concerns of the study was the relevance of the Arab world's viewpoint on BRI. A wide range of opinions was revealed through the interviews, with some participants being in favour of BRI and others expressing serious concerns. An Arab journalist covering BRI in the region has observed that since the United States and Europe failed to address the demands of the region, "many Arab countries are seeing China as an alternative partner to the West." The potential benefits of BRI for economic growth and job creation in the region have been emphasized by several government officials and business leaders who share this view. An official in the government with decision-making authority on the

BRI said, "We see BRI as a key driver of economic growth in the region and an opportunity to enhance our cooperation with China."

Others, however, who were also interviewed, voiced worries about the hazards and difficulties that could be encountered when using BRI. According to a scholar who focuses on China's foreign policy toward the Arab world, "there are concerns that BRI projects may be used as a tool for China to expand its influence in the region and advance its strategic interests." Some locals have voiced worries about the potential environmental and social impacts of BRI projects.

The interviews done here provide insight into how the media in the Arab area has influenced popular opinion of the BRI. Some interviewees even claimed that the media was essential in fostering favourable opinions of BRI initiatives, demonstrating the central role that media plays in moulding public opinion. Quite well, the Chinese media has been promoting BRI throughout the Arab region, as one Arab journalist put it. They have promoted the positive effects of BRI projects, such as more jobs, improved infrastructure, and expanded commerce and investment, through a number of channels. Similarly, a Chinese journalist has said, "The media has played a critical role in promoting BRI and increasing public awareness of China's efforts in the Arab region. We've pointed out how advantageous BRI projects are for both China and the Arab world.

Several interviewees have pointed out that the media's influence on public opinion is not always for the better. A scholar who studies the relationship between the media and Chinese foreign policy has found that coverage of the Belt and Road Initiative is frequently biased and incomplete. It highlights the benefits of BRI projects while downplaying or omitting their downsides. In addition, an Arab media expert has said, "The media has a tendency to exaggerate the benefits of BRI and overlook the potential risks and challenges."

4.2. Discussion of Findings

This study found that media outlets in the Arab world are essential in raising awareness and shaping attitudes about the Belt and Road Initiative. The Belt and Road Initiative has received widespread public support in both China and the Arab world. Articles praising the initiative have appeared in both China and the Arab world's media, which have focused on the economic benefits of BRI projects and the possibility for stronger ties between China and the Arab world. According to one Chinese journalist who focuses on the Belt and Road Initiative and Chinese foreign policy toward the Arab world, the initiative has been portrayed as a win-win situation for all parties. According to an Arab academician, "BRI is a way to enhance mutual understanding and cooperation and has been highlighting the economic benefits it can bring to the region."

The Arab media has, like the Chinese media, portrayed BRI in a positive light, stressing the importance of China's investment in the area and its potential for economic expansion. A journalist from the Arab world who covers BRI said, "the Arab media has been generally positive towards the Belt and Road Initiative, emphasizing the importance of Chinese investment in the region and the potential for economic growth." The positive presentation of BRI in Chinese and Arab media has likely contributed to the warm reception it has received in the Arab world.

However, several of those interviewed expressed concerns about the hazards and difficulties presented by BRI projects, particularly with respect to the potential impact on the environment and the maintainability of debt loads. An expert on Chinese foreign policy in the Middle East has said, "there are concerns that BRI projects could have negative environmental impacts, particularly in countries with weak environmental regulations." There was also concern among several Arab states that BRI projects might raise their debt to China. Among those involved in making decisions about the Belt and Road Initiative, one Arab official official said, "we need to be cautious in accepting Chinese investment and loans, as we do not want to become overly indebted to China and risk our economic stability."

The media's promotion of the Belt and Road Initiative and China's foreign policy in the Arab region has been shown to present challenges and opportunities by this study. One of the most often mentioned challenges by those we interviewed was the potential for media bias and manipulation. If we take the example of a Chinese journalist covering BRI in the Arab region, we find that they say things like, "Chinese media emphasizes the potential benefits of the Belt and Road Initiative and strives to minimize any negative impacts, in order to provide a more optimistic and balanced portrayal of this important initiative." As with any large-scale development project, transparency and accountability are crucial. To that end, the Chinese government has taken significant measures, such as creating the multilateral Asian Infrastructure Investment Bank (AIIB) and encouraging more communication and collaboration with its Arab partners.

They did, however, highlight a number of potential beneficial contributions the media may make to BRI and Chinese foreign policy in the Arab region. "Media can help to bridge the cultural and linguistic gap between China and the Arab world, and provide a platform for dialogue and understanding," said an Arab professor who specializes in Chinese foreign affairs. As mutual understanding and cooperation between China and the Arab world are crucial to the execution of BRI projects, this could help foster that.

Respondents also saw an opening for the media to play a role in advocating for sustainable development and social responsibility within BRI initiatives. According to an Arab business executive involved in BRI projects, "media can help to raise awareness about environmental and social issues related to BRI projects and hold businesses and governments accountable for their actions." This can ensure that local populations and the environment benefit from BRI initiatives, while also promoting sustainable development.

In light of the results of this study, further investigation of the media's coverage of the Belt and Road Initiative and Chinese foreign policy in the Arab area could yield useful insights. Examining how public opinion toward BRI projects has changed as a result of media coverage is one avenue to pursue. It will be fascinating to know if the positive image of BRI in Chinese and Arab media is reflected in the sentiments of local communities towards BRI projects, said one scholar questioned for this study. What is their opinion on Chinese investment in these initiatives, and do they think they will benefit their countries?

The influence of social media on public opinion of BRI is another potential avenue for further study. The importance of social media sites like Twitter and Facebook is growing rapidly throughout the Arab world, particularly among the region's youth, as one journalist interviewed for this study put it. It would be interesting to observe the effect of social media advocacy for and criticism of BRI projects on public opinion.

Further study should also look into how the media affects China's foreign policy toward the Arab world. China's foreign policy toward the Arab world is influenced by a number of elements, not only media coverage, according to one government source quoted in this report. Whether or not the media coverage is aiding China's efforts to strengthen ties with Arab countries would be an intriguing study.

5. CONCLUSION

The research looked into how the media has helped publicize the Belt and Road Initiative and Chinese foreign policy in the Arab world. According to interviews with Chinese and Arab journalists, academics, government officials, business executives, and local people, media coverage of BRI in the region is mostly positive, with a focus on economic development and collaboration. However, linguistic barriers and cultural differences make it difficult for people to effectively communicate.

Media coverage of BRI and Chinese foreign policy in the Arab region was found to have a significant impact on public opinion. Reporters and academics have emphasized the need for balanced reporting, while political and economic leaders have praised the media for its ability to promote cross-cultural understanding and dialogue.

The study identified a number of advantages and disadvantages for media coverage of BRI and Chinese foreign policy in the Arab region. It's important for media outlets, government agencies, and corporate partners to better communicate and coordinate in order to achieve their goals, such as increasing cultural and language interchange and facilitating people-to-people diplomacy.

The study concludes with a number of suggestions for future research, including the importance of analysing media coverage of BRI in particular Arab countries, the role of social media in shaping public opinion on BRI, and the role of the media in shaping China's image and soft power in the Arab area. The study finds that the media may play an important role in promoting the Belt and Road Initiative and Chinese foreign policy in the Arab region, but it also proposes areas for improvement and more study.

By analysing how the media has shaped public opinion and perspectives on the BRI in the Arab region, this study contributes to the current literature on Chinese foreign policy and the BRI. The study sheds light on how BRI has been covered in Chinese and Arab media, as well as the possible impact of media coverage on public opinion. The paper also gives recommendations for future research and policymaking, as well as an analysis of the benefits and drawbacks of the media's position in BRI and Chinese foreign policy.

This research shows that media has a significant impact on Arab public opinion and perceptions of the Belt and Road Initiative. The media in China and the Arab world approach and prioritize BRI coverage in various ways, and these differences can shape how the public perceives the initiative. The study also underlines the potential for media to facilitate mutual understanding and collaboration between China and the Arab area by reporting on the BRI in a way that stresses the advantages for both sides and answers complaints.

This research provides important policy insights for those involved in the Belt and Road Initiative and Chinese foreign policy toward the Arab world. The study shows how the media has a major impact on how people think about and talk about the BRI. Therefore, government officials and business leaders working in BRI projects in the Arab area should pay attention to how their projects are depicted in the media and endeavour to better convey their goals and benefits to the public. "We need to make sure that our message is getting over to the people," said one respondent, involved in BRI decision-making in Arab region. "We have to be more forthright about our plans and objectives."

Based on the findings, the media in China and the Arab world need to communicate and collaborate more. This may help dispel stereotypes and pave the way for more productive dialogue between the two regions. "We need to work more closely with our Chinese colleagues to ensure that our coverage is fair and balanced, " said one Arab journalist who covers BRI and Chinese foreign policy in the Arab region. "Isolation will get us nowhere; we need to build bridges."

The paper concludes that more research is needed into how the BRI would affect the Arab world. One expert in media, Chinese foreign policy, and the Arab region remarked, "There is still so much we don't know about the BRI and its impact. More research is needed to properly understand the benefits and drawbacks it presents."

Potentially more can be learned if the study's sample size and breadth are increased. Quantitative information could be gleaned from a combination of internet surveys and focus groups with in-depth interviews with people living in different parts of the world. Non-Arab viewpoints, such as those in the other BRI countries, could be explored in subsequent research.

Future research may also look into how social media affects public view of BRI. Although this research primarily examined conventional news outlets, it is clear that social media like Twitter, Facebook, and WeChat are having an ever-greater impact on shaping public opinion and discourse. Future research into the impact of online discussion forums dedicated to the topic of BRI on public opinion will be very intriguing.

Finally, long-term political, social, and economic impacts of the BRI could be studied in future research. Although the results of this study were examined, the impact of BRI projects on local economy and communities was not. A deeper dive into the long-term implications of BRI would be beneficial for policymakers and stakeholders.

REFERENCES

Afzaal, M., Hu, K., Ilyas Chishti, M., & Khan, Z. (2019). Examining Pakistani news media discourses about China–Pakistan Economic Corridor: A corpus-based critical discourse analysis. *Cogent Social Sciences*, *5*(1), 1683940. doi:10.1080/23311886.2019.1683940

Arifon, O., Huang, Z. A., Zheng, Y., & Zyw Melo, A. (2019). Comparing Chinese and European Discourses regarding the "Belt and Road Initiative". *Revue française des sciences de l'information et de la communication*, (17).

Cheng, L. K. (2016). Three questions on China's "belt and road initiative". *China Economic Review*, *40*, 309–313. doi:10.1016/j.chieco.2016.07.008

Dunford, M., & Liu, W. (2019). Chinese perspectives on the Belt and Road Initiative. *Cambridge Journal of Regions, Economy and Society*, *12*(1), 145–167. doi:10.1093/cjres/rsy032

Hatef, A., & Luqiu, L. R. (2018). Where does Afghanistan fit in China's grand project? A content analysis of Afghan and Chinese news coverage of the One Belt, One Road initiative. *The International Communication Gazette*, *80*(6), 551–569. doi:10.1177/1748048517747495

Herrero, A. G., & Xu, J. (2019). *Countries' perceptions of China's Belt and Road Initiative: A big data analysis* (No. 2019-59). HKUST IEMS Working Paper.

Hu, L. (2019, October). External Communication Research of the Belt and Road Initiative——Comparative analysis of the relevant reports on the Belt and Road Initiative in China daily, CNN and CNBC. In *4th International Conference on Modern Management, Education Technology and Social Science (MMETSS 2019)* (pp. 615-623). Atlantis Press. 10.2991/mmetss-19.2019.125

Huang, H. (2018). *China's image in the Belt and Road Initiative: case study of Pakistan and India*. Academic Press.

Huang, Y. (2016). Understanding China's Belt & Road initiative: Motivation, framework and assessment. *China Economic Review*, *40*, 314–321. doi:10.1016/j.chieco.2016.07.007

Kamel, M. S. (2018). China's belt and road initiative: Implications for the Middle East. *Cambridge Review of International Affairs*, *31*(1), 76–95. doi:10.1080/09557571.2018.1480592

Lasswell, H. (1927). *Propaganda technique in the world war/Harold D. Lasswell*. Kegan Paul, Trench, Trubner & Co.

Ravitsky, M. (2018). Jumping onto the train? How Russian media cover China's Belt and Road Initiative. *Asian Politics & Policy*, *10*(3), 564–570. doi:10.1111/aspp.12403

Xiao, Y., Li, Y., & Hu, J. (2019). Construction of the Belt and Road Initiative in Chinese and American media: A critical discourse analysis based on self-built corpora. *International Journal of English Linguistics*, *9*(3), 68–77. doi:10.5539/ijel.v9n3p68

Xin, J., & Matheson, D. (2018). One Belt, competing metaphors: The struggle over strategic narrative in English-language news media. *International Journal of Communication*, *12*, 21.

Xuming, Q. I. A. N. (2018). "One Belt One Road" Initiative and China and the Middle East Media Exchanges. *Journalism*, *8*(5), 239–245.

Yang, H., & Van Gorp, B. (2021). A frame analysis of political-media discourse on the Belt and Road Initiative: Evidence from China, Australia, India, Japan, the United Kingdom, and the United States. *Cambridge Review of International Affairs*, 1–27.

Zhang, L., & Wu, D. (2017). Media representations of China: A comparison of China daily and financial times in reporting on the belt and road initiative. *Critical Arts*, *31*(6), 29–43. doi:10.1080/02560046.2017.1408132

Zreik, M. (2022). The Chinese presence in the Arab region: Lebanon at the heart of the Belt and Road Initiative. *International Journal of Business and Systems Research*, *16*(5-6), 644–662. doi:10.1504/IJBSR.2022.125477

Zreik, M. (2023a). The Sacred Paths: A Case Study of Pilgrimage Routes in Southeast Asia With a Special Focus on Thailand. In V. Martinho, J. Nunes, M. Pato, & L. Castilho (Eds.), *Experiences, Advantages, and Economic Dimensions of Pilgrimage Routes* (pp. 226–240). IGI Global. doi:10.4018/978-1-6684-9923-8.ch011

Zreik, M. (2023b). Managing Diversity: A Study of Multicultural Workplaces in Arab and Chinese Societies Post Pandemic. In R. Diab-Bahman & A. Al-Enzi (Eds.), *Global Citizenship and Its Impact on Multiculturalism in the Workplace* (pp. 250–273). IGI Global. doi:10.4018/978-1-6684-5436-7.ch011

Zreik, M. (2024). Soft Power and China-Taiwan Competition for Influence in Latin America. In C. R. Veney & S. O. Abidde (Eds.), *China and Taiwan in Latin America and the Caribbean. Studies of the Americas* (pp. 151–141). Palgrave Macmillan. doi:10.1007/978-3-031-45166-9_6

Zreik, M., & Zhu, R. (2024). Riding the Dragon: The Emergence and Impact of Over-the-Top Media in China. In N. Kalorth (Ed.), *Exploring the Impact of OTT Media on Global Societies* (pp. 75–90). IGI Global. doi:10.4018/979-8-3693-3526-0.ch005

Chapter 9
Reflections on the Development of Strategic Relations Between Iran and China

Jamal Mokhtari

🆔 https://orcid.org/0009-0009-8826-453X

Ferdowsi University of Mashhad, Iran

ABSTRACT

This research seeks a strategic framework for Iran-China relations through the analytical method and using the theoretical model of interdependence. The main question of this research is to examine the variables of these strategic relations. The research hypothesis is that the three variables of transportation, energy, and security exist as platforms for cooperation between the two countries based on the "interdependence" model. Due to rapid industrial growth, China has an increasing demand for fossil energy. Iran's three relative advantages include the provision of a stable energy supply, secure transit access to Central Asia and the Eastern Mediterranean, and the establishment of security in the Middle East. This study first analyzes the nature of bilateral relations between Iran and China. The nature of Iran's objectives in bilateral relations with China comprises two levels: "economic" and "political". The nature of China's objectives in bilateral relations with Iran includes two levels: "geographical areas of China's soft power objectives" and "energy security". It then examines Iran's position in three situations based on China's soft power harmony under the Belt and Road project. Finally, the interdependence variables of Iran and China under the Belt and Road Initiative are analyzed.

1. INTRODUCTION

Civilizational relations between Iran and China have a long history of more than 2600 years, centered on the Silk Road between the two countries. The two countries, China and Iran, are interdependent due to their prominent position in the regional and global geopolitical structure. As the world's second-largest economy and a permanent member of the UN Security Council, China plays an important role in Iran's strategic relations. China's power structure in the international system is constantly growing. Based on

DOI: 10.4018/979-8-3693-2444-8.ch009

its economic power, China is striving for more power and changing the shape of international relations. The indicators of the superiority of Chinese power in various economic dimensions as well as political and military influence have expanded and are of interest to Iran's diplomatic apparatus. China's policy of balancing and de-escalation is always of interest to Iran. China has been actively involved in the Iranian nuclear issue (Djallil, 2011: 236). As a result of Western sanctions, Chinese companies entered the Iranian gas industry after Western companies had left the country. Both Iran and China have not accepted the order desired by the United States and are trying to change this order, and this issue has significant implications for the creation of a strategic alliance with China, leading to the emergence of new powers in the international arena, Asia and the Middle East. Will China believes that America's plan to contain this country involves making the environment in East and Southeast Asia unsafe, creating differences with neighbors, making the main route of energy transmission unsafe, and conflicts with neighboring and American protectorate countries. In this regard, some overlaps in the two countries' foreign policies, economic and military exchanges and energy cooperation are the factors for the development of relations between the two countries. In order to counter America-centered actions of the West, China has taken extensive measures in partnership with the emerging countries of the world economy in the form of BRICS, the Eurasian Bank and also the "Belt and Road Initiative", the latter being a geo-economic mechanism that attracts the attention of the world. . This megaproject has annexes in the form of bilateral and multilateral cooperation agreements. One example is the comprehensive cooperation agreement (25 years) between Iran and China. In 2020, the 25-year comprehensive cooperation agreement between Iran and China was signed by both sides as part of the Belt and Road Initiative. This document also pursues geopolitical goals (geo-economics', geo-strategic and geo-cultural). However, relations between Iran and China are not yet institutionalized and are far from ideal. Despite Iran and China's common interest in addressing regional and international threats, strategic and stable relations between the two parties have not developed. By analyzing the nature of relations between Iran and China, this research concludes that these two countries have different goals in their relations with each other, which are not contradictory at the same time, but challenges may arise. China wants to expand its soft power through the Belt and Road project, and Iran wants to improve its economic and political conditions by following China's development model.

2. THEORETICAL FRAMEWORK (INTERDEPENDENCE)

In international relations, the existence of common interests in various fields forms the basis for cooperation between countries, and the growth of such cooperation leads to interdependence over time. In this research, the theory of interdependence was used to explain the strategic relations between Iran and China. The interdependence theory smooths out the strategic relations between countries by increasing the cost of military actions and aligning the economic interests of countries, creating the basis for long-term economic and political relations. This theory expresses the intersection of economics and politics in international relations. The two political and economic systems interact closely, and the ideas that focus on the superiority of one over the other are trapped in a form of reductionism (Gill & David, 1988: 77). Robert Cohen and Joseph Nye are the most important and original creators of the theory of interdependence, who see the influence of military power and force as a useful and effective instrument in the field of international relations as diminishing day by day. With the publication of the book "Power and Interdependence: World Politics in Transition" in 1977, Cohen and Nye delivered the most important work in the field of interdependence theory. Under these conditions of voluntary cooperation, economic interests take the place of conflict and antagonism between countries (Nye & Keohan, 1971:5-35). Fred Halliday believes that the theory of interdependence is rooted in internationalist thinking. According to it, we are part of a wider society of nation states, which reduces political differences (Pevehouse, 2004:250-253). Interdependence is definitely not a guarantee against war, but it is seen as an important force for peace (Cooper, 2015: 57). Roach also believes that interdependence increases the costs of war for all parties (Roach, 2014: 437).

2.1. The Basic Concepts of Interdependence Theory

1- Power: In the interdependence system, power is still the most important influencing factor in political negotiations. Cohen and Nye adopted the concept of power from Weber. According to Weber, power is the probability that a social actor will succeed in achieving its goals despite the resistance of other actors, regardless of the means used by the powerful actor to this end. Cohen and Nye also considered power as "the ability to control resources that stand in the way of achieving one's goals".

2- Symmetry and asymmetry: although there is no military threat in the world of interdependence, there is an asymmetry in interdependence, i.e. the degree of dependence of countries on each other is not the same, which is due to the position of countries in the world arena (Nye & Keohan, 1977:11). Symmetry and asymmetry in the theory of interdependence refer to the degree of dependence of two parties on each other.

3- Vulnerability and susceptibility: interdependence is basically a theory defined on the basis of mutual vulnerability. A relationship that has a high cost for both parties in case of failure. Cohen and Nye also agree with this view: "We should abandon the simplistic notion that interdependence opens up new horizons for us and eliminates all international conflicts". According to Cohen and Nye, interdependence imposes numerous costs on countries in various areas. As a result, interdependence leads to countries' sensitivity and vulnerability (Keohane & Nye, 1987: 270).

3. ANALYSIS OF THE NATURE OF BILATERAL RELATIONS BETWEEN IRAN AND CHINA

The nature and level of relations between countries are measured by various indicators such as coordination, cooperation, alliance, alliance and convergence. There are different levels from coordination to convergence. When it is said that two countries have united with each other, they have actually created two similar political and socio-economic systems. In such a situation, two countries have a common destiny and cannot act without consensus. In the face of such an alliance, the interests of the two countries are linked. To achieve important goals, countries need alliances with each other. An alliance is an important degree of rapprochement that can bring two or more countries to achieve strategic goals. China is a suitable alternative for Iran in this area. In forming a strategic alliance, the role of each player depends on its power.

3.1. Analysis of Iran's Objectives in Bilateral Relations With China

The nature of Iran's objectives in its relations with China encompasses the two levels of "economics" and "politics", both of which are influenced by China's "soft power". On the economic level, Iran's goal is to create an alliance with China as a business partner and strategic ally in international institutions and to disrupt the order of American unilateralism, which it desperately needs in the context of international sanctions. Since Iran has severed its strategic ties with America, its foreign policy approach is to look eastward, which is a geopolitical concept. The components of China's economic power are very compatible with the indicators Iran is considering. For this reason, Iran seeks a strategic alliance with China, as China seeks economic development, self-restraint, and compromise with its neighbors and trans-regional allies while fighting American hegemony. On this basis, China's foreign policy approach is based on peaceful relations with the countries of the region and the world (Pollack, 2003:617-627). This sentence by Zakaria shows well the role and position of China in the world economy: the fastest growing economy, the largest producer, the second largest consumer, the largest saver and the second largest military spender (Zakaria: 2009: 92). Iran also needs communication with China and Chinese investment in its infrastructure sectors to achieve the goals of its 20-year vision document and 5-year development plans. Iran's current account balance also reached 4,7% in 2022. Iran's share of international trade has declined over the past 40 years and will only amount to 0.24% in 2022; at its peak in 1974, it was 1.1%. Oil sanctions remove 50 billion dollars of oil revenue from Iran's economy every year. Financial sanctions (such as SWIFT and banking sector sanctions) were also imposed against Iran since 2012.

At the "political" level, the use of China's veto power in the UN Security Council and China's support for the Iranian nuclear negotiations (5+1) are among the most important goals that make up the essence of Iran's relations with China. Countering US unilateralism is the most important common ground in Iran-China relations. Iran and Jain have no history of conflict and serious disputes with each other. The most important goal that Iran pursues in bilateral relations with China is to reach the level of strategic relations with China. China, as a superior power in the international system whose power matrix is ever increasing and which has improved its indicators of power superiority in various economic dimensions, political and military influence, has been perceived by Iran's diplomatic apparatus to develop cooperation with this country. The center of international wealth and power is part of Iran's national goals at regional and international levels. China's cooperation with international organizations and active participation in UN peacekeeping missions. The country's policy of attracting tourism and creating ideological incentives are also the foundations of the country's soft power in the field of politics. Perhaps the greatest contemporary source of China's soft power in the realm of political values is the development model of the People's Republic of China, which is attractive to Iran and which Iran is trying to implement in its own country.

3.2. Analysis of the Nature of China's Objectives in Bilateral Relations With Iran

The nature of China's objectives in its relations with Iran can be analyzed on two levels: "the geographical areas of China's soft power objectives" and "energy security". The Chinese leadership believes that China should not only seek to expand and enhance its power in the economic, military and technological dimensions, but also pay special attention to the soft dimensions of its power. To this end, the Middle East region and the oil-rich countries of the Persian Gulf, including Iran, are important. China's influence in the Persian Gulf region and Iran poses a challenge to the influence of the United States in this region. Through soft power, China seeks to expand its influence in key regions of the world, including the Persian Gulf and Iran, to eventually become a hegemon. To this end, China must challenge America, and Iran is one of the countries that has always challenged America's power. China's goals in bilateral relations with Iran are to expand its sphere of influence through soft power, which in the current situation is facilitated by the Belt and Road project. Therefore, for China, Iran is a region that offers energy security, trade markets and a region in line with China's power expansion strategies in the Middle East. According to some researchers, soft power consists of five key elements: Culture, ideas, development model, international institutions and international image (Yu, 2008:122). The Belt-Road Project is an idea that aims to expand China's soft power, which encompasses many geographical areas, including Iran. In the age of global communication, sources of soft power such as culture, political values and diplomacy are part of what makes a country strong. It seems that the first belief that has helped the Chinese achieve a high position in the world is their understanding of the concept of difference. Confucius says that along with differences, there should also be harmony (Sari al-Qalam, 2010: 59). At the level of "energy security", the Persian Gulf region and Iran as the center of the world energy hub have always been the focus of international powers (Hays Gries, 2005: 401-412). Therefore, for China, Iran is a region that offers energy security, trade and regional markets in line with China's power expansion strategies in the Middle East. China is now very active in a variety of global issues such as the environment, energy security, stability of the international monetary system, counter-terrorism, health issues and prevention of nuclear proliferation.

4. ANALYZING IRAN'S POSITION ON THE APPLICATION OF CHINA'S SOFT POWER HARMONY IN THE BELT AND ROAD PROJECT

Since the Belt and Road Iran's position on the application of Project involves 147 countries according to the US think tank Council on Foreign Relations" (CFR) and Iran is one of them, we will analyze three Chinese strategies with regard to Iran's position in the implementation of this project. By implementing these three strategies, China shows its ability of soft power harmony in the implementation of the Belt Road project so that the countries involved in this project can have the necessary flexibility in different situations while protecting their interests. Therefore, in these three strategies of China, Iran is placed in three different situations: subsidiary, central and joint, which we will analyze below;

4.1. The Strategy of Expanding Economic Cooperation (Reference to Iran's Secondary Position in the Belt and Road Initiative)

Before and after the collapse of the bipolar system, China has focused its foreign policy on strengthening solidarity and cooperation with other advanced countries to prepare the ground for multipolarization. Therefore, in the grand strategy of Chinese foreign policy, expanding relations with major powers and establishing a certain degree of coordination with the international system are among the fundamental priorities of this country, priorities that limit its relations with countries such as Iran. Of course, the Middle East in general and Iran in particular is one of the most important issues that China needs to cooperate with to some extent (Alami, April 4, 2011). China views Iran only as part of a larger strategy of global interaction and economic development and does not put all its eggs in one basket (Figueroa, January 17, 2022). In line with its grand strategy, China considers stability and cooperation in relations with America and the major powers as the best option and tries to show itself as a "responsible share-holder" in the international system. It is in the nature of things that a responsible shareholder in the Western-oriented order cannot establish special relations with the countries that the West regards as a threat. Therefore, China's cooperative relations with major powers, especially the United States, have limitations on Iran-China relations. Creates. This strategy was pursued by China until 2013.

4.2. Defeat Strategy (Iran's Position in the Belt-Road Initiative Program)

The strategy to defeat the Chinese government is inspired by one of the most important principles of Leninism (the theory of the weakest links of international capitalism). According to Lenin, the international forces of anti-communism form a complete chain of capitalist countries and regions since the beginning of the 20th century. Some links of this chain are stronger, such as the United States, and others are weaker, such as the less developed countries. According to the theory of failure, communists should focus on breaking the weakest links first. The most recent implementation of the Chinese government's Leninist failure solutions is an ambitious initiative called the "Belt and Road Initiative". This initiative was designed by Communist Party General Secretary Xi Jinping in 2013 to put the least influential of the leading anti-China powers out of control (Maochun Yu, June 15, 2021).This plan aims to connect Asia with Africa and Europe through land and sea links to improve regional integration, increase trade and boost economic growth. It defines 5 main priorities: policy coordination, infrastructure connectivity, barrier-free trade, financial integration, people-to-people communication. China's plan was accompanied by investments in infrastructure development for ports, roads, railroads, airports, power plants and telecommunication networks. This plan covers 138 countries. China's goal of this plan goes beyond infrastructural development. In fact, the country wants to develop a broad and dependent market for China, expand its political and economic power and create suitable conditions for building a high-tech economy (Chatzky & McBride, January 28, 2020). According to some information, between 50 and 60 companies are involved in this project.

Three factors played a role in the development of this plan: First, the competition between China and America. The second factor is the legacy of the 2008 financial crisis for China, during which the country's market was saturated, and this plan provided an alternative market for large Chinese state-owned enterprises outside the country's borders. The third factor was to support businesses and the dynamism and mobility of the economy in the country's central provinces, which had lagged behind the coastal areas (Jie & Wallace, September 13, 2021). The Belt and Road Initiative has many strategic implications as China seeks to link its economic, geostrategic and security interests. Nowhere is this more evident than in the country's relations with Iran, as it helps China expand its interests and connect the Middle East, Central Asia and South Asia. This plan has placed Iran at the center of China's global plans. Iran's natural geography is a bridge between the world's oceans and the landlocked countries of Central Asia (a market of about 65 million people) and the South Caucasus region (Armenia, Azerbaijan, Georgia). Iran is a very good guarantee for China's dominance in Central Asia. Central Asia currently has three exits to the world markets: to the east through China, to the south through Iran and to the west through Russia. In December 2014, a 925 km long railroad line was opened from Kazakhstan to Turkmenistan and towards Iran. Iran occupies a crucial position in this plan, as it is the only major country linking the Belt and Road. In general, China is pursuing the following goals with the Belt and Road Initiative: 1) Securing access to Asian and European markets 2) China's dependence on the sea by land, as the seas (Taiwan Strait, Malaga Strait, Strait of Hormuz, Indian Ocean) are largely under American domination. 3- Diversification of energy supply routes (roads, railroads, oil and gas pipelines). 4- Bypassing the traditional rival India. 5- Creating a strategic balance with Russia and preventing NATO's eastward expansion (Verdi Nezhad, March 16, 2020).

4.3. Deviation Strategy (Reference to Iran's Participation in the Belt and Road Initiative)

The diversionary strategy involves supporting all regimes that are dissatisfied with the US or that are staunch enemies of the US and its allies in order to divert US strategic resources and political focus. China has been using this strategy for decades. The main countries to which this strategy applies are Iran, North Korea, Venezuela, Cuba and North Vietnam. China's support for the Comprehensive Joint Plan of Action under the 2015 nuclear deal (5+1) is one of Beijing's measures that correspond to the diversionary strategy.

5. INTERDEPENDENCE VARIABLES OF IRAN AND CHINA IN THE CONTEXT OF THE BELT-ROAD INITIATIVE

5.1. Overlaps in the Two Countries' Foreign Policies

The rejection of unilateralism and the non-acceptance of the Western order have led to different foreign policy stances. For example, Iran's and China's attitudes towards the crisis in Sudan, Libya and Syria and the West's intervention in these countries are similar. By vetoing two resolutions, China caused the West's attempt to intervene in the Syrian crisis to fail. China's support for Iran on the nuclear issue and the cooperation between the two countries in the Middle East crisis are further overlaps in the foreign policy of these two countries. Both Iran and China are under Western sanctions to a certain extent, China is still under Western sanctions in the military and technological fields, Iran is also under Western nuclear, economic and military sanctions, dealing with sanctions and finding ways to circumvent sanctions is one of the overlaps in China's and Iran's foreign policies. Despite many ups and downs in the history of Iran and China, maintaining and developing bilateral relations is one of the inviolable principles of the two countries' foreign policies. Some of the characteristics, including the leadership of two civilization areas in East and West Asia, the fundamental bases of the foreign policy of the two countries, including respect for the territorial integrity of the countries, non-interference in the internal affairs of the countries, belief in the principles of peaceful coexistence in the world community, and the positions of the Islamic Republic of Iran. Non-dependence on political blocs and rejection of the discriminatory behavior of Western powers is one of the other overlaps in the foreign policy of the two countries.

5.2. Energy, Iran, and Ensuring China's Energy Security

Relations between Iran and China are primarily based on economic interests, in particular the growing demand for energy. The level of energy consumption is closely related to the countries' level of development. China is a country whose economic growth and development has been accompanied by a rapid pace in recent decades, with the result that energy consumption in this country increased by 60% between 2000 and 2005. The demand for energy in this country is rising sharply due to its economic growth and development, and the issue of "energy security" has become an important issue for this country. The high economic growth of China and the vastness of this country, which is known as the third largest country in the world after Russia and Canada and the most populous country in the world, have increased the demand for energy, and due to the limited and insufficient energy resources in China, Iran has become an important partner in this field of "energy security". Energy diplomacy is part of the country's foreign policy to obtain reliable, cheap and abundant energy. Dialogue and building relationships with the major energy-producing countries in the Middle East and regional organizations, as well as building strategic relationships with these countries, are at the forefront of Chinese policies (Yusheng Goa, 2008: 257). China's energy security strategy is based on a strong coordination between geopolitical interests and energy-related interests in the country. Today, China consumes about 25% of the world's energy and is the world's largest importer of crude oil. The upward trend of China's crude oil consumption in recent years shows a growth in consumption of about 85% between 2007 and 2018. In 2019, China's oil import reached more than 10 million barrels per day, and in the first half of 2020, it reached an average of 10.95 million barrels per day. This level of Chinese oil demand is seen as an opportunity for Iran. Among Asian countries, Saudi Arabia is responsible for the largest share of energy exports to China. Iran, as the second largest holder of gas reserves and the fourth largest holder of oil reserves, plays an important role in this area. As one of the major players in the energy sector, Iran plays a crucial role. In general, 69% of China's energy needs are covered by coal, 24% by oil, 4% by gas and 1% by nuclear energy (Medeiros, 2016: 10). The Comprehensive Strategic Agreement is instrumental in ensuring China's energy security, as the Persian Gulf can supply more than half of China's energy needs and energy security is the main element of China's interests in the Persian Gulf (Leverett & Bader, 2005).China has been an importer since 1993, despite being the fifth largest oil producer in the world. In 2011, China was the most important buyer of Iranian oil, importing 10% of its oil imports via Iran. The West's long-term sanctions against Iran have removed the possibility of Western companies having a presence in the energy sector in Iran, and China can become active in this area.

Among the Chinese companies investing in the Iranian energy industry are the following: December 2008 agreement with Sinopec to develop Yadavaran oilfield, June 2009 agreement between China National Oil Company and National Iranian Oil Company to develop Phase 11 of Iran's South Pars gas field, August 2009 agreement with China National Oil Company to develop Azadegan South oilfield, July 2009 agreement with China National Oil Company to develop North Azadegan oilfield and... Iran ranks first in the world in combined oil and gas reserves, holding about 340 billion barrels of oil equivalent, and these valuable reserves will require upstream and downstream investments of about USD 250 billion over the next 10 years. A look at crude oil consumption statistics in China shows that annual growth in Chinese crude oil consumption amounted to around 6% in the 30-year period to 2019, while this growth fell to 3.7% in the decade to 2019. Chinese oil production in 2019 and 2020 was just over 4 million barrels and the country's imports were around 11 million barrels per day. China's demand horizon in various patterns for 2030 to 2040 has a limited increase and has been predicted to be less than one million barrels per day, so although China's crude oil consumption has always been increasing, the acceleration of this trend has been and will be decreasing. Crude oil consumption in China will decline after 2030. When analyzing the reasons for this trend, it should be noted that the share of transportation in crude oil consumption in China will increase from 80% in 2020 to 52% in 2050 according to the existing plan. The situation is completely different for gas: the annual growth of demand in the Chinese gas market was more than 3.1% from 1990 to 2000, and the average annual growth between 2000 and 2019 was 13%. Gas consumption in China amounted to about 300 billion cubic meters in 2019, half of which was imported, and this is a large capacity for Iran to convert crude oil into products and transport it to China. Iran can be connected to China's large consumption market in three ways: direct energy supply, energy transit from other countries, and supplying the needs of Chinese companies on the way to the energy belt. There are two ideas in this area: First, Iran can transport Persian Gulf oil from the western regions to the eastern regions on the coast of Oman, reducing transportation costs and downplaying the role of one of the vital straits threatening China's energy security (Strait of Hormuz). The Gore-Jask pipeline is the first step in this endeavor. The importance of this pipeline lies in the fact that it can transport not only Iranian oil but also Iraqi oil. Secondly, the focus should be on the Makran area near Gwadar-Chabahar and from there, with the help and participation of China, the crude oil should be converted into products and transported to China or other countries.

5.3. Security: Iran's Important Role in Countering Terrorism and Securing China's Security Outsourcing

Following its economic success, China has built its strategy on countering its rivals and enemies and transferring this capability outside its borders. In this regard, mastering the seas beyond its borders has become one of the country's priorities. As part of this strategy to deal with external threats, China has put strengthening the country's economic foundations on the agenda and has established extensive exchanges and relations with various regions of the world, especially the Persian Gulf and the Middle East. China's policy of "externalism" in the field of security and attempt to enter the realm of regional rule-making encourages the country more than ever to have strategic allies, including Iran. Beijing views Iran and Central Asia not only from an economic perspective, but also from a security perspective. Central Asia is an unstable region, and establishing stability in this region requires cooperation between the actors involved. An important institutional infrastructure that supports security cooperation between Iran and China is the Shanghai Cooperation Organization. Recently, Saudi Arabia and China discussed the fight against terrorism for the first time, but Iran has also held several security and defense talks with China (Vatanka, April 26, 2021). The global and regional ambitions of Iran and China, as well as confrontational relations with the United States, have lent security to the Iran-China Strategic Community Agreement. In recent years, China has consistently cited the hegemony of some powers as one of the threats to its national security in its national security documents (State Council, 2009). Iran is one of the most important buyers of military weapons from China. According to statistics from the Stockholm Institute for International Peace Studies, Iran was the second largest buyer of Chinese weapons after Pakistan between 2005 and 2009 (Swaine, 2010).

Iran's role in ensuring regional security has changed the paradigm of West Asia. The recent normalization of Iranian-Saudi relations mediated by China is just the tip of the iceberg in terms of a larger paradigm shift in West Asia. Russia, Iran and China have a key role to play in shaping this change, which could render Anglo-American interventions in the region obsolete. There are currently more than 60 Western military bases or facilities and around 50,000 American troops stationed in West Asia. While Russia and Iran have played a more decisive military and security role in this development, China has sought to use its economic power to underscore this regional paradigm shift. Existing security concerns include sensitive sea lanes, including the Straits of Malacca, Hormuz and Bab al-Mandeb, which could be used to cut off energy supplies and trade between China and the Persian Gulf region. To counter these threats, Russia, Iran and China have been conducting regular naval exercises. The various diplomatic and security initiatives of Iran, Russia and China finally came to maturity with the outbreak of the Ukraine war, when international relations fundamentally changed and the inherent vulnerabilities of the West's unipolar power became apparent. According to most prominent international relations theorists, including Steven Walt and John Mearsheimer, the international system is in a state of transition - from a unipolar situation to a multipolar structure; however, this new (multipolar) system is not yet institutionalized. One of the key components for stabilizing the multipolar order is the organization of the security structure of the different regions of the world. In this context, one of the controversial and very crucial regions for stabilizing the structure of the multipolar order is the West Asian region. In recent years, changes have taken place in this region in the area of extra-regional actors and the behavior of intra-regional actors. In the area of extra-regional actors, the presence of the United States has decreased and the role of China and the troika of Europe, India and Russia has increased. As for the approach of regional actors, the members of the Persian Gulf Cooperation Council, especially Block A, which includes Saudi Arabia, the United Arab Emirates and Bahrain, are on the way to changing the normative and behavioral characteristics of the past decades, from Arab-Zionist conflict to Arab-Iranian conflict. What makes relations with China attractive to Middle Eastern countries, including Iran, is China's non-interference in the political affairs of Middle Eastern countries. This characteristic of China is very different from its dealings with Western countries, especially the United States of America, which is associated with military interventions in Middle Eastern countries. What is now important for China in the Middle East and is considered one of the country's strategic goals is maritime and commercial security. Maritime and commercial security will help China to safely export its goods to the Middle East and ensure the safety of importing energy resources and raw materials from the Middle East.

Iran and China have cooperated on regional institutional issues, multilateral issues and security. The Shanghai Cooperation Organization is a clear example in this field, and China, as one of its founding members, has played an important role in Iran's accession to this organization. The importance of the issue arises from the fact that the Shanghai Cooperation Organization is of fundamental importance to Iran in several respects. On the one hand, Central Asia, as an unstable and fragile region in the north of Iran, needs security management. On the other hand, the most important centers of terrorism and security crisis in the east and southeast of Iran (Afghanistan and Pakistan) are also part of the Shanghai Cooperation Organization. What is important in this context is that America is present in all these regions, and this presence is in no way desirable for Iran, China or Russia. These areas pose a common security threat to Iran and China and can only be addressed through multilateral institutional cooperation. One of the major security concerns of both Iran and China is extremism and terrorism, which affect and threaten each country in one way or another. Iran, which is geographically located in the immediate vicinity of military and terrorist movements and groups, has placed the fight against extremists such as ISIS at the forefront of its security policy. China's strategy is along the same lines, as it has opted to fight terrorism due to its proximity to countries and regions that are prone to the spread of terrorism. In addition, 40% of China's energy needs flow through the Strait of Hormuz and there is a possibility that this important strait could be threatened. This danger also exists in the event of military conflicts. Therefore, the Chinese have launched the One Belt One Road initiative to address the above challenges.

5.4. Transportation: Iran, Four Transit Routes of the World, and Its Role in Connecting China to Europe

It is "the issue of transit and especially east-west transit" that connects China to Europe. Iran's natural geography has played an important role in transportation and transit throughout history and is an important factor in strengthening China's economic interests in West Asia and facilitating economic access to a large part of Iran's western and northern neighbors. The possibility of safe access to the western countries up to the Mediterranean Sea and to the northern neighbors, including Central Asia, is an important advantage for increasing the volume of maritime trade between China and Iran's western and northern countries. Indeed, Iran's geographical location makes it incompatible with isolation and it is considered the center of relations between the countries of the Middle East and the world. Another aspect of Iran's importance as a transit country is China's presence in the Persian Gulf, which is the most important energy supply area from a Chinese perspective. Iran is the shortest link between the Caspian Sea and the Persian Gulf. It is very necessary to pay special attention to the transportation, transit and logistics sector of Iran, China and the countries in the region, and it is necessary to pay special attention to it in the MOU between Iran and China, in any case, Iran is at the crossroads of the world's four transit routes and its capacity should be utilized as much as possible. Therefore, China can utilize Iran's ports and railroad lines to develop its exports in the Middle East and gain long-term benefits. The completed rail links between Bandar Abbas and Azerbaijan, Bandar Abbas and Turkey, as well as the currently completed Chabahar-Sarkh, Chabahar-Afghanistan and Kermanshah-Iraq rail links can lead to a strengthening of China's presence in West Asia and Central Asia. The need to connect Iran-Iraq-Syria with the Mediterranean, the need to attract Chinese capital for the completion of the Rasht-Astara railroad to Azerbaijan and Russia, the use of China's capacity to build the Kermanshah-Khosravi-Khanqin-Baghdad-Latakia railroad and the unification of Pakistan's railways To complete the East-West corridor, there are some projects that must be seen in the understanding between Iran and China. Pakistan is one of China's biggest allies in the Belt and Road Initiative and China has invested around 67 billion dollars in Pakistan. In the agreement between Iran and China, Iran should now emphasize the CPEC plan, among others, and establish a rail link between China and Pakistan as soon as possible so that Iran can reach China through Pakistan. Of course, it should be mentioned that one of the problems of the Iran-Pakistan-China rail link is Pakistan's railroad standard. The rail meets the world standard (14-35 rails), but the India-Pakistan rail (16-76 rails) is not standardized and the Battle Rail is famous. One of the initiatives that Iran has proposed to China in the field of transit is the "Iran Road" initiative, which was presented to the 10 member countries of this pact at the 12th ECO Summit. On this basis, all of Central Asia is considered Iran's transit neighbors to connect them with the Azad Sea to facilitate the passage of transit goods from Iran in less time and the goods can easily pass through Iran. The next capacity that Iran can utilize under the agreement with China and activate through Chinese investment is the discussion of the "Tehran-Mediterranean" corridor, which is one of the most strategic transit corridors. This corridor complements the East-West corridor that connects China with Europe. China is one of the most important exporters to Europe. Strategically located in West Asia, Iran shares borders with 15 countries and has a sea channel on its north and southwest coasts, which plays an important role in connecting East Asia to Europe. Iran's advantage is that it can transfer goods from China across several borders. Iran currently has 2 active rail borders through which China can export to Europe. Chinese goods can enter Iran via Kazakhstan-Uzbekistan-Turkmenistan-Sarkhes and be transported by rail to the Razi border and from there to Turkey. This route is completely covered by rail from Sarkhes to Razi Border. This was a route proposed by Iran for the transit of Chinese goods. The second railroad route that Iran has proposed for the transportation of goods to China is the Kazakhstan-Turkmenistan-Inchebron-Razi railroad corridor. These two routes are pure rail and single cargo transportation that China can use to export its goods to Europe.

CONCLUSION

The common denominator of the strategic framework of Iran-China relations is the dissatisfaction with the existing international order and the unilateralism of the United States in the field of the international system, which has led to the overlapping of the foreign policy of these two countries. With its Belt Road Initiative and corridor diplomacy, China is trying to create a discourse and new poles in the international arena with its own center of gravity. With its Belt Road Initiative and corridor diplomacy, China is trying to create a discourse and new poles in the international arena with its own center of gravity. Iran, with proper understanding of the conditions and developing its strategic relations with China in the three areas of ensuring China's energy security, assisting in outsourcing China's security and countering extremism in the region, and connecting China to Europe through its transit position based on the model of interdependence, can have a significant impact on the formation of a new international order and meet its needs of the other party by utilizing its internal capabilities. As the world's four transit routes, Iran is the link between East Asia and Europe and the Persian Gulf. The quality of China's political structure also guarantees the possibility of building a long-term strategic relationship. In the meantime, however, challenges may arise.

Challenges

1- Although China has been Iran's largest trading partner since 2009, Iran remains a small partner for China. Even in the Middle East, Saudi Arabia and the United Arab Emirates have a superior position in trade with China. In 2020, the value of China's trade balance with each of Saudi Arabia, the United Arab Emirates, Turkey and Israel surpassed the country's trade with Iran. With a total trade volume of 14.9 billion dollars, Iran was China's 43rd trading partner in terms of sales of export items (Ziabari, December 3, 2021). It seems that China's view of Iran is still far from reaching a strategic level, and Iran-China relations in the current situation are just one of the relationships Beijing has to manage in the region.

2- One of Iran's biggest infrastructure projects in the last ten years has been the expansion of the port of Chabahar on the Indian Ocean coast, while China has invested heavily in the realisation of its rival project, namely Pakistan's Gwadar port, and India is also a competitor of China. It has invested the most in the port of Chabahar, which leads to a kind of conflict of interests and priorities.

3- One of the fundamental tasks of Chinese foreign policy is to establish a certain degree of harmony with the international order in order to advance the process of the country's peaceful rise as a great power on the international stage. China's cooperative relations with Western powers and China's acceptance of the most important norms of the international community in recent years have led to China-Iran relations being subject to constraints. Some important deals between Iran and China have been canceled due to pressure from the United States and the withdrawal of the Chinese side. For example, since the early 1990s, the United States exerted great pressure on China to prevent it from engaging in nuclear cooperation with Iran, which it finally succeeded in doing in 1992. Its thwarted Iran's attempt to buy a 20 MW research reactor from China. in 1995, he prevented the implementation of the Iran-China agreement on the transfer of 2 300 MW reactors. China also voted in favor of 4 resolutions against Iran in the Iranian nuclear case process in the Security Council. China does not seek to destroy the existing order and revolutionary behavior; the goal of this country is to take maximum advantage of the existing order.

4- The reluctance of both Iran and China to publicize the details of the agreements means that, on the one hand, experts in this field are not working properly and, on the other hand, public opinion is not optimistic about it.

5- The strategic agreement between China and Saudi Arabia in 2022 and China's statement in support of Saudi Arabia's anti-Iranian positions on Iran.

6- The strengthening of China's military presence and arms sales to the Persian Gulf Cooperation Council members, especially Saudi Arabia and the United Arab Emirates, means interfering in the regional security structure and balance of power in favor of the Saudi-oriented order and aligning with the Arab anti-Iranian bloc. On this basis, the Chinese security model can be opposed to the security model of the Islamic Republic of Iran (intra-regional balance).

7- China has slowly and deliberately set foot in the Middle East. But due to its lack of historical, political, economic, technological and cultural presence in the region, it still seems unlikely that China will be able to take the place of the United States of America and Europe in the Middle East and become a strategic player in the Middle East in the short and medium term.

8- The share of Iran's trade with China is at a much lower level compared to Saudi Arabia. Iran's imports from China in 2022 amount to 890 million dollars and its exports to China to 350 million dollars.

REFERENCES:

al-Qalam, S. M. (2010). The concept of power and the performance of foreign policy: comparing China and Iran. Foreign Relations Quarterly, 8(5).

Alemi, A. (2021). Iran and China; Necessities and Realities of Mutual Cooperation in New Global Confrontations. *Iranian diplomacy*. http://irdiplomacy.ir/fa/news/2001428

Chatzky, A., & McBride, J. (2020). China's Massive Belt and Road Initiative. *Council on Foreign Relations*. https://www.cfr.org/backgrounder/chinas-massive-belt-android-initiative

Figueroa, W. (2022). *China and Iran Since the 25-Year Agreement: The Limits of Cooperation*. Diplomat Media Inc. https://thediplomat.com

Gill, S., & David, L. (1988). *The Global Economy: Perspectives, Problems and Policies*. Harwester Wheatsheaf.

Jie, Y., & Wallace, J. (2021). What is China's Belt and Road Initiative (BRI)? *Chatham House*. https://www.chathamhouse.org

Keohane & Nye, Jr. (1987). Power and interdependence revisited. *International Organisation, 41*(4).

Leverett, F., & Bader, J. (2005). Managing China-U.S. energy competition in the Middle East. *The Washington Quarterly, 29*(1), 187–201. doi:10.1162/016366005774859643

Medeiros, E. S. (2016). *Chinese Foreign Policy: The Africa Dimension*. ChinaAfrica.

Pollack, J. D. (2003). *China and the United States Post-9/11*. Foreign Policy Research Institute.

Roach, S. (2014). Unbalanced: The Codependency of America and China. Yale University Press.

State Council. (2009, Jan. 12). *China White paper on National Defence 2008*. Retrieved 12 01, 2009, from www.china.org.cn

Swaine, M. D. (2010). Beijing's Tightrope Walk on Iran. *China Leadership Monitor*, 3.

Vatanka, A. (2021). Making Sense of the Iran-China Strategic Agreement. *Middle East Institute*. https://www.mei.edu

Verdinejad, D. (2020). *The Importance of Iran for China, Donya-e-Eqtesad newspaper*. Retrieved on 1 Bahman 1400, No. 3748878. https://donya-e-eqtesad.com

Yu, M. (2021). *Iran in China's Grand Strategy*. Stanford University Hoover Institution. https://www.hoover.org

Yu, X. (2008). *The Role of Soft Power in China's Foreign Strategy. In China International Studies: Guoji Wenti* (Vol. 11). Yanjiu.

Yusheng Goa, H.E. (2008). *China, India and the United States Competition for Energy Resources*. The Emirates Center for Strategic Studies and Research (ECSSR).

Zakaria, F. (2009). *The Post American World*. Allen Lane.

Ziabari, K. (2021). Iran's New Asia-Focused Foreign Policy Is a Fantasy. *Foreign Policy*. https://foreignpolicy.com

Chapter 10
Silk Roads of Influence:
China's Soft Power and South–South Cooperation in Asia

Inayat Kalim
COMSATS University, Islamabad, Pakistan

Asad Hyatt
https://orcid.org/0009-0005-1474-6203
COMSATS University, Islamabad, Pakistan

ABSTRACT

This chapter delves into China's soft power strategy through South-South Cooperation (SSC) in Asia, focusing on how its economic growth and cultural outreach enhance its regional influence. It examines China's self-identification as a developing country and its principle of non-intervention, which bolster its appeal among its SSC partners. The analysis identifies the Belt and Road Initiative (BRI) and the Global Development Initiative (GDI) as key to China's soft power in Asia, with both initiatives serving infrastructural development and cultural promotion without imposing political conditions. These efforts resonate in the Middle East and developing Asian countries, aligning with China's preference for engaging state actors to ensure regional stability. However, the chapter also highlights the limitations of China's quest for regional influence, particularly in the realm of public diplomacy.

INTRODUCTION

The world's ongoing drift toward multipolarity is the hallmark of the present global order. It has introduced new actors in interstate relations who are playing a multitude of roles. The spirit of South-South Cooperation (SSC) has existed for a considerable time but new actors are introducing new cooperative modalities in this concept of international collaboration where states from the Global South assist each other in political, economic, social, cultural, environmental, and technical domains. Meanwhile, the debate over whether SSC is a mere replication of the traditional North-South cooperation model reproducing global dependency patterns is still not settled. Today, SSC participants are not only interested in its practice but are also finding it pertinent to measure the impact of their development cooperation activities.

DOI: 10.4018/979-8-3693-2444-8.ch010

In international relations, numerous schools of thought have studied SSC from their standpoints. When seen from a functionalist lens, SSC is considered a technical concept, aimed at the transfer of best-practice projects in the facilitation of expected results without any political interests. Functionalists also play up the themes of international solidarity observed among SSC participants. Meanwhile, dependency theorists pin the motivations of the Global South on the desire to circumvent core states in meeting developmental needs and to discourage expropriation at the hands of the latter (Jules & Silva, 2008). Neoliberals emphasize interest-driven activities in SSC, based on open border policies for multinational organizations, non-governmental organizations, and international institutions, to effectuate cooperation mechanisms initiated by states of the Global South (Diko & Sempijja, 2021).

What the authors of this chapter find most interesting is the realist element of SSC that came to scholarly attention after Joseph S. Nye shaped the concept of soft power (Nye, 1990, 2011). In Nye's perspective, traditional realists ignore soft power at their own peril, since the balance of hard power overlooks the power of transnational ideas. He distinguishes soft power from military or hard power wherein culture, political values, and public diplomacy, among other resources, play an undeniable part in influencing the behaviors of targets. SSC enters the soft power domain when it creates a strong attraction among participating states by way of exchange and assistance programs. Nye highlights the importance of recipients as much as that of the agents themselves. In SSC, too, the participants in a reciprocal relationship are both agents and recipients thus invoking the notion of soft power. A growing literature is highlighting the rising realist tendencies in the practice of SSC. On one hand, nationalistic fervor coupled with pragmatic approaches gaining ground in the dispensation of SSC is eroding the concept of non-interference in partner countries (Mawdsley, 2019), whereas on the other hand, in contrast with the functionalist reading of the concept, the re-politicization of SSC is challenging the conventional views of development (De Moraes Achcar, 2022).

The majority of the literature that has reviewed SSC from the perspective of soft power has taken up the example of Brazil while conceptualizing the country's development cooperation discourse and highlighting the strategic motivations of its foreign aid (Bry, 2017; Sasongkojati & Subono, 2023). China's SSC activities have been present in scholarly discourse but not to the extent that matches those of Brazil. What is more prevalent about China's SSC practices is the study of the country's involvement in development and aid activities in Latin America and Africa (Amanor & Chichava, 2016; Cheru, 2016; DeHart, 2012). Its development efforts in Asia, which are continually enhancing its influence — and its soft power — are still an understudied area. This chapter thus attempts to fill the gap in evaluating China's SSC practices from the prism of soft power and focuses on the region of Asia and the Middle East. It is pertinent to note that China considers itself a part of the Global South and many inter-governmental organizations and international financial institutions place it under the category of a developing economy. This classifies China's collaborative projects in the developing world under the ambit of SSC and makes the developmental behavior of the country suitable for study under the soft power concept.

CONCEPTUALIZATION

South-South Cooperation

SSC has its roots in the Bandung Conference of 1955 where the Third World raised its collective case of neutralism and non-alignment (Herrera, 2005). Over time, the Third World has come to be known as the Global South, yet its spirit of solidarity has continued to prevail. Today, SSC has the endorsement of the United Nations Office for South-South Cooperation (UNOSSC) which considers it a developmental process among two or more developing countries through exchanges and collective actions (UNOSSC, n.d.). At the same time, the proverbial boundaries of the Global South are becoming blurred after the advent of developing countries' large-scale Foreign Direct Investment (FDI) not only in countries of the South but also in those of the North (Mawdsley, 2012a). The practice of SSC itself has moved from its initial stage of not being considered a geostrategic tool until the early 2000s, to gaining visible ideational legitimacy up until about 2015, to its present stage where the ideational and operational distinction of the Global South from the traditional donors is weakening and muscular narratives are making it difficult to limit the principles of non-interference (Mawdsley, 2019). One such rising donor from the Global South is China, whose policymakers talk about the sovereignty of the nation-state but have nevertheless stirred the debate about whether the Chinese model is antithetical to free-market democracy. It is for this reason that the export of the Chinese model to the Global South through SSC has been extensively discussed (Qi & Dauvergne, 2022).

Soft Power

To provide a lens through which SSC can be viewed, this chapter draws on Joseph S. Nye's contribution to the conceptualization of soft power (Nye, 1990, 2011). The idea of soft power, as presented by Nye, rests on the premise that a state will face less resistance to the fulfillment of its intentions if its power is considered legitimate by others. Soft power emanates from three basic resources which include the attraction to a country's culture, the upholding of its political values, and the legitimacy of its foreign policies in the eyes of others. There are also cases when resources are shaped for projecting soft power. These include exchange, assistance and training programs, information agencies, and public diplomacy, among others. Public diplomacy is a notable aspect of soft power because of the two-way communication that it allows through exchange and relation-building programs and mass media approaches ranging from daily information dissemination activities to strategic communications. Wielding soft power, countries depict behaviors that are typical of the exercise of power. This starts from agenda-setting, where a country uses its influence in the system of international governance to restrict or encourage the actions of others. The second soft power behavior is positive attraction which is generated by a country's benignity, i.e., its respectful and supportive relations with others; brilliance, i.e., its exemplary capabilities and domestic affairs; and beauty, i.e., its values and ideals that others find attractive (Vuving, 2009). Attraction not only depends on the qualities of the agent but also on others' perception of those qualities. Likewise, the third soft power behavior is persuasion through the use of arguments and narratives to expand a country's influence.

SSC and Soft Power

While SSC has been viewed from a range of theoretical frameworks in international relations, soft power provides an interesting perspective. The resources of soft power often align with the essence of SSC, especially, as observed earlier, after the increase in politicization of the latter. One of the basic resources of soft power is culture which transmits knowledge and values within individual groups and across different groups. Direct cultural contacts, describes Nye, also provide a way of realizing alternative models of development. In SSC, the different cultures that come into contact with each other experience the same phenomenon. In numerous cases, culture has brought nations naturally together during their engagement in SSC. In like manner, political attractiveness grows among SSC partners when their individual political values and foreign policies reflect universal values. When SSC reflects common political values among participating countries, the practice has been termed Social Justice-oriented South-South Cooperation (SJSSC) where equitable engagement and local agenda-setting take precedence (Birn et al., 2017). The shaped resources of soft power mentioned earlier also lead to the manifestation of soft power when taken up under the ambit of SSC. While exchange, assistance, and training programs play a major role in this regard, information organizations and the form of public diplomacy that is exercised through the exchange of personnel equally contribute to the enhancement of the soft power of participating countries.

China as Part of the Global South

China's Gross Domestic Product (GDP) is presently the highest in the world in Purchasing Power Parity (PPP) terms and the second highest in nominal terms (World Bank, n.d.). But for the country's developmental initiatives to be considered as SSC, it must be a part of the Global South. If we look at this side of the picture, 200 million people in the country lived below the poverty line in 2021, according to the World Bank's representative in China (Ruwitch, 2021). The UN and the International Monetary Fund (IMF) term China a developing economy, whereas China classifies itself at the World Trade Organization (WTO) and elsewhere as a developing country. This official assertion by China is a clear indication of its intent to be identified with the Global South. The South and SSC are defined by China from the perspective of its political and regional initiatives and the logic of connectivity (Kohlenberg & Godehardt, 2021). It is, meanwhile, pertinent to note that China officially declares its development aid as SSC but defines the concept broadly at international forums (Gülseven, 2023; Haug & Kamwengo, 2023). Since China officially considers itself a developing country having commonalities with the Global South, and the same recognition is given by international bodies, there is a valid premise to regard China's collaborative projects with other developing countries as SSC.

CHINA'S SOFT POWER RESOURCES AT PLAY IN SSC

A look at China's resources of soft power in the context of SSC reveals that the Belt and Road Initiative (BRI) is the primary channel of influence in Asia and beyond. The political and economic model that the country has adopted while rising as the world's second-largest economy is also proving to be a main factor in enhancing its soft power during its international interactions under SSC. Its extensive efforts in the public diplomacy domain are, however, striving to reach a level on par with those of the West.

Culture

China is one of the world's oldest civilizations. With its history, the country brings a rich culture, and, consequently, the tools for advancing its soft power. The antiquity of Chinese culture possesses an evident economic flair as well. The ancient Silk Road has for centuries served as a conduit of cultural exchanges with the nations it passed through. Even today, economic benefits motivate China, and other countries of Asia, to engage in cultural collaborations. While China might be cautious in liberalizing its cultural trade, it is much more open to cultural cooperation (Zhao, 2023). Even as culture has come to be a vehicle for its soft power, the country has yet to match the cultural reputation that other major powers of the world enjoy.

The most prominent galvanizer of China's soft power and SSC in modern times is the BRI which has played a two-pronged role in the cultural domain. Cultural cooperation between China and some Asian countries before the BRI was driven by disparate agendas and lacked a coherent strategy. The BRI, as a means of facilitating integration, first streamlined these cultural interactions and secondly, its numerous cultural exchange and training programs helped alleviate skill and expertise shortages (Jianming, 2020; UNDESA, n.d.). Among these programs, some have been launched solely under the auspices of the BRI, for example, the Silk Road (Dunhuang) International Culture Expo, Silk Road International Film Festival, and Silk Road International Book Fair. Meanwhile, many have been launched through collaboration between various UN agencies and BRI projects. The UN is primarily engaging in BRI's cultural endeavors to implement Sustainable Development Goals (SDGs) and is providing research, analysis, and capability-building support (UNDESA, n.d.). Even the state-owned and partially state-owned companies involved in BRI projects have been engaging in cultural collaborations in their host countries. Senior managers of these companies learn the customs and languages of the host countries to interact with locals without the use of interpreters, Chinese employees participate in cultural and sports events to build rapport, and non-Chinese employees are introduced to Chinese technologies and culture (Yao et al., 2020). In South Asia, owing to vast political differences among countries, impediments to regional development have been a persistent issue but the BRI, with its potential to spur cooperation, can be expected to encourage the integration of cultures and commerce.

One of the several facilitators of the BRI and a resource of China's soft power is the network of Confucius Institutes, operating on the lines of Western institutions like the British Council, Alliance Française, and the Goethe Institute and, through a range of activities, primarily serving China's cultural goals. The degree and non-degree programs offered by the institutes provide opportunities for students (especially from the Global South) to gain a first-hand understanding of Chinese culture, all the while satiating the desire of students in these institutes to visit China (Xiantang & Nascimento, 2020). Some governments and scholarly circles, however, emphasize the political (and economic) imperatives emanating from the cultural goals of these institutes. In the regions where there is a greater presence of Confucius Institutes, the trade volume of China depicts a positive correlation. This is more pronounced in Southeast Asia, along with Eastern Europe (Li et al., 2021). In addition to that, the institutes have also been contributing to the increase in China's foreign direct funding to the countries of the Global South (Lien et al., 2012), thus serving as a key element in the external activism that is increasingly visible in China's foreign policy (Parepa, 2020). The hundreds of Confucius Institutes operating across the world have contributed to the debate on the efficacy of SSC by being considered instruments of both soft power and SSC. The Western world is consequently taking steps to limit its cooperation with these institutes but the Global South is welcoming them for their offers of free training and education.

Political Values

China's political and diplomatic exchanges that influence its SSC practices emanate from its traditional values. A set of values that are often termed "Chinese characteristics" are ingrained in the country's political engagements with other countries. The concept of harmony, emphasizing well-being in relations with others, plays a major part in how China deals with its partners when it comes to both diplomacy and development cooperation. Additionally, mutual respect, mutual benefits, and win-win principles are a regular feature in China's narratives related to foreign assistance. China has also insisted that Common but Differentiated Responsibility (CBDR) is an important international consensus on international development cooperation and recipients of aid need to have a controlling voice in the programs they participate in (Permanent Mission of China to the UN, 2013).

Development strategies that have not followed the Western models have resulted in the economic rise of China and several others in Southeast Asia. In China specifically, good governance, not the Western concept of democracy, is the ultimate aim of the political journey (Wang & Guo, 2015). This allows China's SSC partners to look up to an alternative model of development and funding, offered in infrastructure, energy, and communication sectors. Chinese scholars often frame SSC as an antithesis of imperialism, colonialism, and hegemonism while the country distances itself from hierarchical interstate relations that have a legacy of colonialism and post-colonialism (Mawdsley, 2012b). China also distances itself from Western norms and values when responding to the Global South's value preferences. Yet, China's political ambition of becoming a greater power drives its participation in aid programs in the Global South.

Chinese development cooperation in the form of aid offers another benefit to Asian countries that are struggling to put their financial situation in order: the absence of political strings. Chinese investment offers come with attractive terms and in sums not comparable with what traditional donors have been offering — not to mention the debate of debt traps that China is accused of laying in the Global South. At the same time, China's stated principle of non-interference when dealing with its development partners echoes well with state actors (Shipton & Dauvergne, 2021). Its advocacy of the principle stems from the intent of promoting non-interference in global governance systems and presenting sovereignty and territorial integrity as infallible. Needless to say, the principle is in contrast with that of Western financial institutions like the IMF and the World Bank which ask for governance and macroeconomic reforms of recipients. China's principle of non-interference also helps it build economic partnerships in the Global South while at the same time giving it some protection against Western criticism.

China's economic interests are another factor in its funding of projects in Asia. This has led the country to prioritize cooperation in low-politics rather than in high-politics. Many of the initiatives in this domain are China's alternative institutions which allow greater control over their protocols and governance structures in order to offer engagements with the Global South in a manner that China desires. The Washington Consensus might have made the Global South reliant on the IMF and the World Bank but the so-called Beijing Consensus offers alternative policy prescriptions in the form of the Asian Infrastructure Investment Bank (AIIB), the New Development Bank (NDB), and, of course, the BRI (Yağcı, 2016). These institutions allow China to have a greater sway in the global governance system while increasing the visibility of its values and interests. China's strategy of direct financial assistance has also leaned more toward sharing of the country's development experience. The Special Economic Zones (SEZs) that China has established in other developing countries are another instrument for expanding its political relationships while enhancing its soft power. Ultimately, these initiatives, with their outreach in the Global South, provide China with the economic means to expand its political and security relations. The view from the Global South related to China is not free of concerns but it still considers that China has the potential to build a more balanced world order with greater political and economic opportunities (Baumann et al., 2022).

Foreign Policy

When it comes to its relations with the Global South, soft power instruments are gaining ground in China's foreign policy. One of the labels assigned to its foreign policy is "deep pluralism", where power and political authority, among other things, are diffused across a range of interacting and interdependent actors (F. Zhang & Buzan, 2022). A global society that allows various nations to meet their ends requires a strong level of collaboration among all the actors involved. With Chinese culture's emphasis on collaboration, rather than individualism, official narratives in China's foreign policy have called for greater cooperation among countries. SSC has been a part of China's priorities ever since the founding of the People's Republic, even when this practice was not known as such. The Communist regime, in its early days, had extended economic and technical assistance to other countries of the South which helped it gain political support (Ness, 2018). With time, cooperation with developing countries has become a major foreign policy goal of China.

China's foreign policy in recent times has undertaken proactive efforts in the immediate regions around the country. For this purpose, China has devised a number of strategies that preserve its security and maintain regional stability; one being the prioritization of multilateral regional blocks, like the Shanghai Cooperation Organization (SCO), Asia-Pacific Economic Cooperation (APEC), ASEAN Plus Three (APT), and Boao Forum for Asia, to name a few. In this regional contextualization, China has attempted to weave its foreign policy, too, around the principle of non-interference in the internal matters of other countries. With the launch of the BRI in 2013, the mega project was also envisioned to uphold the principle of non-interference as it undertook numerous developmental projects in countries of the Global South, causing it to be seen favorably across Eastern, Central, and Western Asia as well as other regions where it had its outreach. The BRI has become one of the top foreign policy priorities of the Chinese government and provides China with a set of structures to collaborate with its partners from the Global South. These include cooperation forums, financing of projects running under the BRI, foreign aid, free trade agreements, SEZs, and technology centers (Murphy, 2022).

China's foreign policy has also been termed "infrastructural" where transportation and communication networks have led the cooperation agendas with partner countries (Mikko Huotari et al., 2014). Under this foreign policy, China's infrastructure projects play a central part in building the image that the country intends to portray on the international stage. These are areas that remained neglected by traditional actors of development cooperation and, with the enhancement of China's soft power emanating from investment in these areas, a challenge to Western hegemony in development and governance has become evident. Even among the rising powers of Asia, it is China's foreign economic policy that is the most coherently tied to its development agenda (Parlar Dal et al., 2021). Many Asian countries where China has initiated development projects under SSC have had pervasive instability and poor governance. Since Western aid providers had not made significant inroads into such regions, even under North-South cooperation mechanisms, China has successfully been able to maximize its soft power. China's State-Owned Enterprises (SOEs), not deterred from investing in these regions, have proved themselves as valuable entities in China's foreign policy quiver. They have received special focus from the Chinese government and have been at the forefront of internationalizing China's image. They forge alliances and build professional relationships with multinational companies in projects that are both under the ambit of the BRI or are separate from the Initiative. This plays out well in the SSC domain since developing countries are in dire need of investments and infrastructure, and Chinese SOEs are available to meet these demands.

At the ideational level too, China has been benefiting from its development cooperation in Asia. As Chinese investments provide material benefits to Asian countries, China's foreign policy discourse invokes an image of benevolence in contrast with the major powers of the West. This narrative has also been termed "benevolent developmentalism" under which China considers it a responsibility to develop the Global South in a manner that can be seen as the strong taking care of the weak (Smith, 2021). It is because of this growing soft power of China that in the second decade of the twenty-first century more leaders from the global South visited China than the United States (Thomas, 2021).

A Successful Economy

Economic influence is a unique resource of soft power that has elements of both hard power and soft power. Its conceptualization as a continuum better explains how it pervades the blurred lines between the two types of power (Blair et al., 2022). Toward the gradient of soft power, governments' economic actions to create attraction become more pronounced. After opening up to the world in the late 1970s, China demonstrated an unmatchable economic growth rate while lifting millions of people out of poverty (Zreik, 2021). Later in the twenty-first century, China remained unfazed by events like the 2008 Global Financial Crisis, and as the Western liberal economies struggled, China was investing in the Global South, establishing its financial dependability. This was an exceptional opportunity for Chinese soft power as the country's economic model started to become popular in the developing world. Numerous Western scholars have suggested that China and other middle-income regions can provide new ideas of economic development that are different from those originating from the West (Bruton et al., 2021). The Global South, with its problems of sustaining democracy and stability, finds this model easier to adopt as it looks up to alternative economic and governance values to raise the lives of citizens. One solution offered by China is the linking of sustainable security to sustainable development (Goh, 2019). This allows countries to bank upon economic growth and regional cooperation to offset their security issues. At the same time, with accusations against China for weaponizing its trade, the ability of an economic power to force a change in the behavior of others' security choices is not a given (Zreik, 2022). This is why the extent to which China's trade partners in Asia would adjust their security policies in light of the ongoing U.S.-China competition in the Asia-Pacific remains to be seen.

Using its strong economic prowess, China has been engaging extensively in the SSC domain with Asian countries in infrastructure, education, and agriculture. When building economic alliances in Asia, it focuses on SSC to engender win-win results along with peaceful settlement of regional issues. China's rapidly growing economy has been a determining factor in building a positive image of the country as it brings income incentives, especially for people in underdeveloped regions. Such regions are in greater need of economic development rather than political development, making the Chinese form of governance a non-factor for many (Xi & Primiano, 2020). Apart from the role of SOEs in enhancing China's soft power which has already been discussed, China' Privately-Owned Enterprises (POEs) are also active in Asia, oftentimes supported and subsidized by the Chinese government, to build BRI-related projects and arrange the supply of natural resources back to China. These POEs prefer to invest in the developing economies of Asia because of the presence of populated but unsaturated markets where competition is low and incomes are rising (Oh & No, 2020).

China's engagements, however, have not been one-sided. It has been exporting its products and services during its conduct of SSC which has raised questions regarding the commercial aspect of this cooperation. Since reciprocity and mutual benefit form the backbone of SSC, the argument of China's dichotomy has been disregarded over the provision of infrastructure and development support in return for its exports (Besharati, 2019). Productive engagement with countries in its geographic periphery and assurance of supply of resources for its economic growth are understandable goals of the expansion of China's soft power in the region. South-South trade has consequently come to be intra-Asian where China is playing the major part (UNCTAD, 2019).

With the launch of the BRI, China's soft power rose exponentially as the project provided avenues of economic exchange that were previously unheard of. Lack of adequate infrastructure was one of the major obstacles in Asian nations' economic growth and Chinese investments under the BRI provided the right answers. The BRI has thus combined the elements of hard power and soft power to present a narrative of regional development that appears more inclusive to the Global South.

Assistance and Exchange Programs

Unlike the basic resources of soft power, some resources are required to be shaped for the purpose. In the case of China, they range from aid and assistance programs to an ambitious framework of growth principles named the Global Development Initiative (GDI). China's soft power capabilities in this domain start with the opening up and internationalization of its educational sector. As a result of heavy government investment, the attractiveness of China's educational opportunities has significantly improved. Ever since education became a part of China's policy of international cooperation under the "Medium and Long-Term Education Reform and Development Plan 2011–2020," it has been serving the foreign policy goals of the country through the enhancement of soft power.

China, from time to time, releases white papers highlighting the aims and elements of its foreign aid program. Key features of the last white paper, issued in 2021, were the BRI and a "global community of shared future (D. Zhang, 2021)." The paper also revealed that Asia and Africa received the largest portion of Chinese aid, amounting to over 80 percent of the total. Other sources corroborate this claim, specifically highlighting Southeast Asia as the biggest recipient of China's foreign assistance (Copper, 2016).

China repeatedly makes it a point that it does not intend to utilize its foreign aid programs to interfere in the internal affairs of the recipient countries and that the Western form of democracy is not a prerequisite for their disbursement. This makes China's aid programs particularly appealing to countries that are not full democracies (Zreik, 2024). There have been accusations that Chinese aid has led to inefficiencies and corruption among such recipients, though empirical studies have shown that it has, along with the aid from the United States and Organization for Economic Co-operation and Development - Development Assistance Committee (OECD-DAC), in fact, spurred economic growth in recipient countries (Dreher et al., 2017). When investing in nations of the Global South whose capability of capitalizing on aid is debated, China appears to be taking a long-term approach to reaping its returns. In contrast with neoliberal actors who are looking for shorter-term interests, China demonstrates a greater "patient capital" where it may be willing to let its investments sink for a considerable time before the bearing of results (Lin & Wang, 2017). This Chinese approach and its increasing acceptability in the Global South is challenging the U.S.-led system of development finance and forcing traditional donors to review their models.

China's aid programs have not only generated positive economic effects in the recipient countries but they have also allowed China to reap the benefits of its soft power. Ever since the founding of the

People's Republic, returns on Chinese aid programs have helped the country from being recognized at the United Nations to the expansion of its diplomatic relations and resolution of its border disputes. The developing countries to which China has over time provided aid have come to view China favorably and, in some cases, this aspect of China's soft power has augmented its security policy by competing with American and Indian influence in the region (Copper, 2016).

The latest addition to China's soft power toolkit is the GDI, launched in 2021 to support international development through financial commitments, capacity building, and collaboration. Under this initiative, China is upgrading and replenishing its SSC Assistance Fund with the United Nations and embedding it in the cooperation mechanisms of the BRICS grouping. The GDI is taking the narrative of China's concept of development off from where the BRI left, prioritizing international development over the country's political and economic liberalization. Since China has linked this initiative with the UN and the Sustainable Development Goals, the GDI is gaining greater global acceptance as compared to the BRI after being seen as a UN-centered effort focused on multilateralism (Mitić, 2023). The GDI has found several backers in Asia too, owing to its state-centric nature that relates well with their approaches to development.

Public Diplomacy

Public diplomacy plays out in the soft power domain when states employ it to pursue economic interests and influence political attitudes. In 2015 when China released its first public diplomacy report, it termed the practice as a way of building bilateral exchanges beyond the state level (Liu, 2018). Since then, public diplomacy has become one of the key channels of China's soft power. With the country consolidating its economic and political position at the global level, its confidence is now reflected in its public diplomacy with investments amounting to tens of billions of dollars (Nye, 2019). In conformity with the mainstream scholarship on public diplomacy, Nye believes that public diplomacy is a two-way communication process. However, Chinese public diplomacy has so far been functional and upfront. The vehicles for its one-way communication have been its various information agencies (including the state media) and cultural initiatives, whereas those for its two-way communication have been its exchange programs, financing activities, and elite-to-elite interactions. Nye endorses the three dimensions of public diplomacy proposed by Leonard et al. (2002) which include communication of domestic and foreign policies on a daily basis, strategic communication over months and years, and the building of relationships over years and decades.

Daily Communication. In the structure of the Chinese government, the state has a central role in building the country's image and the Communist Party of China (CPC) leads the efforts for public diplomacy. With the advent of social media, Twitter provided a unique opportunity for officials and diplomats to undertake daily communications and tell the China story to the world while legitimizing China's overseas projects. Apart from the "Wolf Warrior" diplomacy that Chinese diplomats have come to be known for in their social media interactions, when it comes to SSC, the diplomats' messages related to China's aid programs have produced positive results. This was surprisingly evident in a study in India where, in addition to the ineffectiveness of critical messaging, and despite a recent violent conflict, Chinese diplomats' messages of aid improved China's perceptions (Mattingly & Sundquist, 2023). In a manner that has largely been self-referencing, the daily communications of China's public diplomacy work in collaboration with the state media. The Xinhua news agency has been leading the daily information dissemination efforts of the state media in promoting the BRI while acting as an extension of the government's communication network and contributing to the promotion of China's foreign policy. Notwithstanding the effectiveness of China's public diplomacy through this medium, the narratives offered by Chinese diplomats and news outlets face strong competition from entities critical of China's aid and development programs owing to the open nature of digital media (Vila Seoane, 2023).

Strategic Communication. The BRI, despite being an infrastructure project, has been the most prominent element of China's strategic communication related to SSC. The primary narrative of this mega project relates to its cooperative nature which has been extended both to the developed and the developing countries. China also relates the BRI with the historical injustices of colonialism that affected China, as well as other countries of the present-day South. The narrative presented in this regard is that China understands the challenges faced by formerly colonized countries and has no intentions of dominating or exploiting them or interfering in their internal affairs (Ohnesorge & Owen, 2023). The BRI, thus, is presented as much larger than an infrastructure project. The state media has been the main vehicle for advancing China's strategic communication over the BRI and other SSC projects launched or supported by the country, whereas its ambassadors have been active in meeting the goals of public diplomacy through strategic communications facilitated by their increased visibility, local connections, and counternarratives to Western countries' criticism of China. At the same time, Confucius Institutes are playing a due part in China's strategic communications arsenal by constantly adapting to the resistance and criticism from the West. Since symbolic events also contribute to a country's soft power potential under the ambit of strategic communications, China regularly hosts and supports events related to SSC independently as well as under the auspices of the UN (Zreik, 2023). To mention just a recent few, China International Fair for Trade in Services (CIFTIS), a major annual event, incorporated a special SSC component in 2021 to promote the digital economy for SSC, and later in 2022, China hosted a dedicated international forum on SSC and trade in services. While collaborating with the UN, various departments of the Chinese government frequently organize joint SSC events with the UNOSSC, and the latter acknowledged at the Belt and Road Forum of 2023 that the BRI aligns with the principles of SSC while facilitating consultations and joint contributions (UNOSSC, 2023).

Building Relationships. The third and the most long-term approach to public diplomacy is the building of lasting relationships. The activities involved in this dimension are unique in the sense that they are focused on key individuals. Educational scholarships are a main instrument in this dimension which China has been effectively using in Asia, and the world over, after internationalizing its higher education through Confucius Institutes, student exchange programs, and scientific collaborations. In addition to that, China has also been providing aid to countries of the Global South in the higher education sector. This helps China in a twofold manner. On one hand, it supports the improvement of educational standards in China through the principles of complementarity and mutual promotion, whereas, on the other, high-quality talent attracted through scholarships contributes to the high-quality development of the BRI (Song, 2021). Two notable projects, the Asian Universities Alliance (AUA) and the University Alliance of the Silk Road (UASR) working out of Tsinghua University and Xi'an Jiaotong University respectively, have the potential to mold the international order and make China a leader in the knowledge domain. Likewise, exchange and training programs that have existed since the founding of the People's Republic are another part of China's toolbox through which it strengthens relationships with key individuals in Asia and beyond. In recent times, the BRI has expanded these programs' canvas and the COVID-19 pandemic has allowed China to share its experience of combating the pandemic. China's training programs strengthening its soft power mainly bank upon its educational sector, research institutes, and think tanks; all of which function while being directly connected with the goals of China's policies (Yuhan et al., 2022).

Mass Media Approach to Public Diplomacy

China's public diplomacy efforts in the media domain have a greater focus on media outlets and journalists from the Global South. The country is taking up joint ventures both in traditional and digital media, and buying and investing in media outlets to extend its influence. At the level of exchange of personnel, frequent — and popular —training programs that last from two weeks to ten months mainly encourage the participation of journalists from Asia-Pacific (Lim & Bergin, 2020). All China Journalists Association (ACJA) is a body that is active in arranging such visits and training programs for journalists from Asia, and needless to say, its affiliation with the CPC provides it the government's tutelage. A major benefit of these programs that China has accrued is that the participants, especially from the Global South, gain a favorable view of the country and often become advocates of its foreign policy vision. Similarly, the Belt and Road News Network (BRNN) and the Belt and Road News Alliance (BRNA), with their extensive partnership networks, are not only promoting content related to the BRI but are also effectively utilizing their news distribution services, training programs, and joint projects. In addition to that, China has bilateral content-sharing agreements that provide convenient and ready-made content to "hard-pressed" editors in the Global South, invariably favoring China (Marsh et al., 2023). However, despite all these extensive measures, the influence of Chinese media remains far lesser, at least in Asia, than that of the United States where the latter has gained a significant outreach.

CONCLUSION

China has lifted millions of people out of poverty in a matter of decades, its GDP ranks at the top of the world in PPP terms, and it is the largest trading partner of over a hundred countries. Yet it prefers to call itself a developing country. When China's successful development model is presented to its SSC partners, including those that are not liberal democracies, the recipients often find it appealing, adding to China's soft power. The basic and shaped resources of soft power that China employs in its SSC practice point to its ability to increase its attractiveness on the basis of its economic prowess and its stated principle of non-interference in the internal affairs of its partners. Scholars meanwhile suggest being open to learning from the Chinese experience. This is even more pertinent for the Global South which started off disadvantaged under the Bretton Woods system and is still stuck in a catch-up phase.

China's rich cultural tradition has also had an economic dimension. While the Silk Road permeated Chinese culture across the Eurasian landmass, it was primarily a trade route enabling Chinese businessmen to sell their products and bring resources back into China. In the Silk Road's legacy, the BRI is also diffusing Chinese culture through carefully crafted programs, but at its core, it is an economic project that plugs infrastructure, energy, and communication gaps of participating countries while facilitating the flow of resources and materials back into China. Now the GDI is consolidating the soft power strategy of the BRI. Having been launched at the UN, the GDI is getting greater global acceptance and presenting China as a responsible state that is at the center stage of international developmental efforts. For any of these mega projects, China claims that it does not attach political strings to its offers. This further increases its soft power appeal in Arab and many developing Asian nations where the state has a greater sway over the society. China's preference to deal with state actors also directly adds credence to the claim.

The immediate regions around China are much higher on the country's list of foreign policy priorities since China's territorial integrity hinges on the stability of its geographical periphery. As achieving regional stability is contingent on economic stability, the success of the BRI and other developmental projects, in a self-perpetuating cycle, is paramount for showcasing China's dependability in the region. Engaging in public diplomacy is a useful way of such image building in the region and China is leaving no stone unturned to dominate in this domain. Its diplomats and state media are aggressively active on social media, the BRI is invoking historical similes to the formerly colonized nations of the Global South, and a range of programs are building relations with media organizations and key individuals in Asia. In the face of all these efforts, China's public diplomacy so far has not come up to par with that of the United States. Since this is not true in many other spheres of soft power, other contenders of influence in Asia and the Middle East might prefer to take a leaf out of China's book.

REFERENCES

Amanor, K. S., & Chichava, S. (2016). South–South Cooperation, Agribusiness, and African Agricultural Development: Brazil and China in Ghana and Mozambique. *World Development, 81*, 13–23. doi:10.1016/j.worlddev.2015.11.021

Baumann, M.-O., Haug, S., & Weinlich, S. (2022). *China's expanding engagement with the United Nations development pillar: The selective long-term approach of a programme country superpower.* Friedrich-Ebert-Stifung.

Besharati, N. A. (2019). *Measuring Effectiveness of South-South Cooperation* (52; Occasional Paper Series). Southern Voice. https://www.ssc-globalthinkers.org/sites/default/files/2019-10/191010-Ocassional-Paper-Series-No.-52_final-1.pdf

Birn, A.-E., Muntaner, C., & Afzal, Z. (2017). South-South cooperation in health: Bringing in theory, politics, history, and social justice. *Cadernos de Saude Publica, 33*(2, suppl 2). Advance online publication. doi:10.1590/0102-311x00194616 PMID:28977125

Blair, R. A., Marty, R., & Roessler, P. (2022). Foreign Aid and Soft Power: Great Power Competition in Africa in the Early Twenty-first Century. *British Journal of Political Science, 52*(3), 1355–1376. doi:10.1017/S0007123421000193

Bruton, G. D., Ahlstrom, D., & Chen, J. (2021). China has emerged as an aspirant economy. *Asia Pacific Journal of Management, 38*(1), 1–15. doi:10.1007/s10490-018-9638-0

Bry, S. (2017). Brazil's Soft-Power Strategy: The Political Aspirations of South–South Development Cooperation. *Foreign Policy Analysis, 13*(2), 297–316. doi:10.1093/fpa/orw015

Cheru, F. (2016). Emerging Southern powers and new forms of South–South cooperation: Ethiopia's strategic engagement with China and India. *Third World Quarterly, 37*(4), 592–610. doi:10.1080/0143 6597.2015.1116368

Copper, J. F. (2016). China's Foreign Aid and Investment Diplomacy in South Asia. In China's Foreign Aid and Investment Diplomacy, Volume II (pp. 49–91). Palgrave Macmillan US. doi:10.1057/9781137532725_2

De Moraes Achcar, H. (2022). South-South cooperation and the re-politicization of development in health. *World Development*, *149*, 105679. doi:10.1016/j.worlddev.2021.105679

DeHart, M. (2012). Remodelling the Global Development Landscape: The China Model and South–South cooperation in Latin America. *Third World Quarterly*, *33*(7), 1359–1375. doi:10.1080/0143659 7.2012.691835

Diko, N., & Sempijja, N. (2021). Does participation in BRICS foster South-South cooperation? Brazil, South Africa, and the Global South. *Journal of Contemporary African Studies*, *39*(1), 151–167. doi:10 .1080/02589001.2020.1837746

Dreher, A., Fuchs, A., Parks, B., Strange, A. M., & Tierney, M. J. (2017). Aid, China, and Growth: Evidence from a New Global Development Finance Dataset. SSRN *Electronic Journal*. doi:10.2139/ssrn.3051044

Goh, E. (2019). Contesting Hegemonic Order: China in East Asia. *Security Studies*, *28*(3), 614–644. do i:10.1080/09636412.2019.1604989

Gülseven, Y. (2023). China's Belt and Road Initiative and South-South Cooperation. *Journal of Balkan & Near Eastern Studies*, *25*(1), 102–117. doi:10.1080/19448953.2022.2129321

Haug, S., & Kamwengo, C. M. (2023). Africa beyond 'South-South cooperation': A frame with limited resonance. *Journal of International Development*, *35*(4), 549–565. doi:10.1002/jid.3690

Herrera, R. (2005). Fifty years after the Bandung conference: Towards a revival of the solidarity between the peoples of the South? Interview with Samir Amin. *Inter-Asia Cultural Studies*, *6*(4), 546–556. doi:10.1080/14649370500316844

Huotari, M., Heilmann, S., Rudolf, M., & Buckow, J. (2014). China's Shadow. https://merics.org/en/report/chinas-shadow-foreign-policy

Jianming, Z. (2020). China and BRI: From Business to Geopolitics? In V. Talbot & U. Tramballi (Eds.), *Looking West*. Ledizioni. doi:10.14672/55262996

Jules, T. D., & Silva, M. M. de sá e. (2008). How Different Disciplines have Approached South-South Cooperation and Transfer. *Society for International Education Journal*, *5*(1), 45–64.

Kohlenberg, P. J., & Godehardt, N. (2021). Locating the 'South' in China's connectivity politics. *Third World Quarterly*, *42*(9), 1963–1981. doi:10.1080/01436597.2020.1780909

Leonard, M., Stead, C., & Smewing, C. (2002). *Public diplomacy*. Foreign Policy Centre.

Li, Q., Han, Y., Li, Z., Wei, D., & Zhang, F. (2021). The influence of cultural exchange on international trade: An empirical test of Confucius Institutes based on China and the 'Belt and Road' areas. *Ekonomska Istrazivanja*, *34*(1), 1033–1059. doi:10.1080/1331677X.2020.1819849

Lien, D., Oh, C. H., & Selmier, W. T. (2012). Confucius institute effects on China's trade and FDI: Isn't it delightful when folks afar study Hanyu? *International Review of Economics & Finance*, *21*(1), 147–155. doi:10.1016/j.iref.2011.05.010

Lim, L., & Bergin, J. (2020). *The China Story: Reshaping the World's Media*. International Federation of Journalists. https://findanexpert.unimelb.edu.au/scholarlywork/1460412-the-china-story--reshaping-the-world's-media

Lin, J. Y., & Wang, Y. (2017). Development beyond aid: Utilizing comparative advantage in the belt and road initiative to achieve win-win. *Journal of Infrastructure. Policy and Development*, *1*(2), 149. doi:10.24294/jipd.v1i2.68

Liu, T. (2018). *Public Diplomacy: China's Newest Charm Offensive*. https://www.e-ir.info/2018/12/30/public-diplomacy-chinas-newest-charm-offensive/

Marsh, V., Madrid-Morales, D., & Paterson, C. (2023). Global Chinese media and a decade of change. *The International Communication Gazette*, *85*(1), 3–14. doi:10.1177/17480485221139459

Mattingly, D. C., & Sundquist, J. (2023). When does public diplomacy work? Evidence from China's "wolf warrior" diplomats. *Political Science Research and Methods*, *11*(4), 921–929. doi:10.1017/psrm.2022.41

Mawdsley, E. (2012a). *From recipients to donors: Emerging powers and the changing development landscape*. Zed Books. doi:10.5040/9781350220270

Mawdsley, E. (2012b). The changing geographies of foreign aid and development cooperation: Contributions from gift theory. *Transactions of the Institute of British Geographers*, *37*(2), 256–272. doi:10.1111/j.1475-5661.2011.00467.x

Mawdsley, E. (2019). South–South Cooperation 3.0? Managing the consequences of success in the decade ahead. *Oxford Development Studies*, *47*(3), 259–274. doi:10.1080/13600818.2019.1585792

Mitić, A. (2023). China's New Initiatives and the Shaping of Eurasia's Strategic Environment. In D. Proroković & E. Entina (Eds.), Eurasian Security After NATO (pp. 113–139). Institute of International Politics; Economics; Institute of Europe of the Russian Academy of Sciences. doi:10.18485/iipe_eas-nato.2023.ch6

Murphy, D. C. (2022). *China's rise in the Global South: The Middle East, Africa, and Beijing's alternative world order*. Stanford University Press.

Nye, J. S. (1990). Soft Power. *Foreign Policy*, *80*(80), 153–171. doi:10.2307/1148580

Nye, J. S. (2011). *The Future of Power* (1st ed.). Public Affairs.

Nye, J. S. (2019). Soft Power and Public Diplomacy Revisited. *The Hague Journal of Diplomacy*, *14*(1–2), 7–20. doi:10.1163/1871191X-14101013

Oh, Y. A., & No, S. (2020). The patterns of state-firm coordination in China's private sector internationalization: China's mergers and acquisitions in Southeast Asia. *The Pacific Review*, *33*(6), 873–899. doi:10.1080/09512748.2019.1599410

Ohnesorge, H. W., & Owen, J. M. (2023). Mnemonic Soft Power: The Role of Memory in China's Quest for Global Power. *Journal of Current Chinese Affairs*, *52*(2), 287–310. doi:10.1177/18681026231193035

Parepa, L.-A. (2020). The Belt and Road Initiative as continuity in Chinese foreign policy. *Journal of Contemporary East Asia Studies*, *9*(2), 175–201. doi:10.1080/24761028.2020.1848370

Parlar Dal, E., Dipama, S., Çaytaş, Ş., & Sezgin, A. (2021). Assessing the Development–Foreign Policy Nexus of the Asian Rising Powers: South Korea, China, Japan and Indonesia. *Global Policy*, *12*(5), 653–662. doi:10.1111/1758-5899.13008

Permanent Mission of China to the UN. (2013). *China's Position Paper on the Development Agenda beyond 2015* (Meetings and Statements). http://un.china-mission.gov.cn/eng/hyyfy/201309/t20130925_8399922.htm

Qi, J. J., & Dauvergne, P. (2022). China's rising influence on climate governance: Forging a path for the global South. *Global Environmental Change*, *73*, 102484. doi:10.1016/j.gloenvcha.2022.102484

Ruwitch, J. (2021, March 5). What China's 'Total Victory' Over Extreme Poverty Looks Like in Actuality. *NPR*. https://www.npr.org/2021/03/05/974173482/what-chinas-total-victory-over-extreme-poverty-looks-like-in-actuality

Sasongkojati, R. M. H. D., & Subono, N. I. (2023). Strategic Culture, South-South Cooperation, and Soft Power Politics: Explaining Brazilian Foreign Aid. *Jurnal Ilmu Sosial Dan Ilmu Politik*, *27*(2), 176. doi:10.22146/jsp.81267

Shipton, L., & Dauvergne, P. (2021). The Politics of Transnational Advocacy Against Chinese, Indian, and Brazilian Extractive Projects in the Global South. *Journal of Environment & Development*, *30*(3), 240–264. doi:10.1177/10704965211019083 PMID:34393471

Smith, S. N. (2021). China's 'Major Country Diplomacy': Legitimation and Foreign Policy Change. *Foreign Policy Analysis*, *17*(2), orab002. Advance online publication. doi:10.1093/fpa/orab002

Song, L. (2021). Deepening Cooperation in Running Schools Between China and Southeast Asia to Promote the Development of "the Belt and Road Initiative". *2nd International Conference on Management, Economy and Law (ICMEL 2021)*, 291–296. 10.2991/aebmr.k.210909.043

Thomas, N. (2021, July 28). *Far more world leaders visit China than America*. Lowy Institute. https://www.lowyinstitute.org/the-interpreter/far-more-world-leaders-visit-china-america

UNCTAD. (2019). *Energizing South-South trade: The global system of trade preferences among developing countries* (Policy Brief 74). https://unctad.org/system/files/official-document/presspb2019d3_en.pdf

UNDESA. (n.d.). *Partnering for a better future*. https://www.un.org/sites/un2.un.org/files/progress_report_bri-sdgs_english-final.pdf

UNOSSC. (2023). *Belt and Road Forum Seeks to Strengthen South-South Cooperation*. https://unsouthsouth.org/2023/10/22/belt-and-road-forum-seeks-to-strengthen-south-south-cooperation/

UNOSSC. (n.d.). *About South-South and Triangular Cooperation*. https://unsouthsouth.org/about/about-sstc/

van Ness, P. (2018). China and the Third World: Patterns of Engagement and Indifference. In S. S. Kim (Ed.), *China and the World: Chinese Foreign Policy Faces the New Millennium* (4th ed.). Routledge. doi:10.4324/9780429501708-7

Vila Seoane, M. F. (2023). China's digital diplomacy on Twitter: The multiple reactions to the Belt and Road Initiative. *Global Media and Communication, 19*(2), 161–183. doi:10.1177/17427665231185697

Vuving, A. (2009). How Soft Power Works. SSRN *Electronic Journal.* doi:10.2139/ssrn.1466220

Wang, Q., & Guo, G. (2015). Yu Keping and Chinese Intellectual Discourse on Good Governance. *The China Quarterly, 224*, 985–1005. doi:10.1017/S0305741015000855

World Bank. (n.d.). *GDP, PPP Data.* World Bank Open Data. Retrieved 5 February 2024, from https://data.worldbank.org

Xi, J., & Primiano, C. (2020). China's Influence in Asia: How Do Individual Perceptions Matter? *East Asia (Piscataway, N.J.), 37*(3), 181–202. doi:10.1007/s12140-020-09334-x PMID:32837181

Xiantang, P., & Nascimento, A. (2020). Research on the Selecting Model of Confucius Institute Scholarships. *Boletim Do Tempo Presente, 9*(1), 2–12.

Yağcı, M. (2016). *A Beijing Consensus in the Making: The Rise of Chinese Initiatives in the International Political Economy and Implications for Developing Countries* (SSRN Scholarly Paper 2910831). https://papers.ssrn.com/abstract=2910831

Yao, W., Hu, S., Chu, Z., & Zhang, B. (2020). The Status of University-Industry Collaboration Participating in the People-to-People and Cultural Exchanges in Engineering Technology Among the Belt and Road Initiative Participants. *2020 ASEE Virtual Annual Conference Content Access Proceedings*, 35375. 10.18260/1-2--35375

Yuhan, P. S., Zakharova, S., & Fedorova, G. (2022). China's strategy to strengthen soft power in the Asia-Pacific region: 016. *Dela Press Conference Series: Economics, Business and Management, 1.*

Zhang, D. (2021). *China's Third White Paper on Foreign Aid—A Comparative Analysis* (2021/3; Brief). Department of Pacific Affairs, Australian National University.

Zhang, F., & Buzan, B. (2022). The Relevance of Deep Pluralism for China's Foreign Policy. *The Chinese Journal of International Politics, 15*(3), 246–271. doi:10.1093/cjip/poac014

Zhao, S. (2023). Culture and trade: Chinese practices and perspectives. *International Journal of Cultural Policy, 29*(2), 135–151. doi:10.1080/10286632.2021.2009820

Zreik, M. (2021, September 1). The Potential of a Sino-Lebanese Partnership through the Belt and Road Initiative (BRI). *Contemporary Arab Affairs, 14*(3), 125–145. doi:10.1525/caa.2021.14.3.125

Zreik, M. (2023). Governance in Post-COVID-19 China: Challenges, Responses, and Opportunities. In C. Negrão, I. Maia, & J. Brito (Eds.), *Multidisciplinary Approaches to Organizational Governance During Health Crises* (pp. 214–235). IGI Global. doi:10.4018/978-1-7998-9213-7.ch011

Zreik, M., Iqbal, B., & Rahman, M. N. (2022). Outward FDI: Determinants and Flows in Emerging Economies: Evidence from China. *China and WTO Review, 8*(2), 385-402. doi:10.14330/cwr.2022.8.2.07

Zreik, M., & Zhu, R. (2024). Riding the Dragon: The Emergence and Impact of Over-the-Top Media in China. In N. Kalorth (Ed.), *Exploring the Impact of OTT Media on Global Societies* (pp. 75–90). IGI Global. doi:10.4018/979-8-3693-3526-0.ch005

Chapter 11
Soft Power:
An Enduring Notion in Contemporary International Politics

Sureyya Yigit

ⓘ https://orcid.org/0000-0002-8025-5147

New Vision University, Georgia

ABSTRACT

Soft power is a term coined by Joseph Nye whereby, in addition to command and obedience, power is primarily shown in the ability to influence the behaviour and goals of the other side through non-military means. These means of getting other states to share one's own goals and values range from negotiating skills to the seductive power of economic success models to cultural offerings between the production of dreams and ideology. Nye defines it as when a state can get others to admire its ideals and want what they want, but it does not have to spend as much on rewards or threats to move them in their direction. Therefore, seduction is seen as more effective than coercion, and many values, such as democracy, human rights, and individual opportunities, become deeply seductive. This chapter explores the development of the notion of soft power in international politics.

"What is soft power? It is the ability to get what you want through attraction rather than coercion or payments. It arises from the attractiveness of a country's culture, political ideals, and policies." -Joseph S. Nye Jr.

"In a power hungry, power worshipping society, men label themselves atheist." - Ernest Hemingway

INTRODUCTION

Definitions of power in political science are usually based on various power theories and concepts of power found in other traditions related to the humanities. The study of power in political science is fundamentally based on this scientific discipline to make its concepts useful for studying interstate

DOI: 10.4018/979-8-3693-2444-8.ch011

conflicts (Pietrzak, 2023). Power can mean something different in other scientific disciplines, independent of international politics; hence, power processes between states should be examined as structurally analogous to power processes between people.

Formative definitions of power in the past can be attributed to Max Weber's sociological definition. For Weber, power is every opportunity to assert one's own will within a social relationship, even against resistance, regardless of what this opportunity is based on (Mucha, 2007). Weber understands power as arising from a social relationship between at least two actors. The basis for power is diverse, as is the nature of its effect. For Foucault, too, power represents a relationship that cannot be reduced to a pure understanding of power as coercive power.

Hence, it is less about power than a means of repression, as described by Habermas, when he applies power to the systemic structures of society. This is an understanding of power that also appears somewhat in Machiavelli. He writes about securing success through power, equating this with violence, i.e., coercive power, and serves primarily to ensure the survival of a state and the unrestricted accumulation of power (Clarke, 2022). Realist theories were later founded on this basis. Therefore, with Thucydides and Hobbes, Machiavelli truly represents historical realism. Machiavelli's negative view of humanity, the great importance attributed to the military in maintaining and acquiring power, and the renunciation of moral inhibitions by the end justifying all means are principles that can be applied either way and found similarly in the more recent political theories of realism.

Foucault is more concerned with power as an object of relationships between actors, as he expressed in his nominalist formula that power is the name given to a complex strategic situation held in society (Bevir, 1999). This is reminiscent of Arendt and her understanding of power not as a property of a person, a class or an institution but as a relational phenomenon in the interaction between actors (Penta, 1996). According to Elias, power only arises through the interaction between individuals, first designating power as a social relationship because no one can have power or be powerful alone (Newton, 1999). However, Elias views power as a structural characteristic of human relationships. Therefore, social interaction, the imminent contextuality, and the relationships between actors and themselves constitute power production. Accordingly, no resource located only in one actor can be described as power. A state can have hard power, i.e. military capacity, but conceptually, this is not permitted. The logical consequence of this understanding of power is that it is equated with power; similarly, an individual can certainly have power or strength. However, he can only produce power with others.

This basic assumption of power as a social relationship between actors or individuals shapes global understanding as power between states is understood as structurally analogous to power between people. If an actor wants to assert his/her interests, s/he can utilise the resources. This can occur in coercive power – hard power – or the form of attractiveness and likeability – Soft Power. However, the power that s/he can exercise is only expressed in the asymmetrical confrontation with the resistance of at least one further actor. This premise, which seems logical concerning the relationship between two individuals, can also be transferred to states. The reason this transfer is possible is because individuals control the state. Understanding states as unitary actors, as in realism, appears in the context of this approach. Against the background, the polymorphic forms of being international actors are no longer current. When a state enters into relationships with other states, it does so not as a static actor but as a collective of people or institutions with diverse interests.

Hence, when the origin of power is discussed, most political scientists speak in quite an undifferentiated manner about sources and means of power. One is replaced by the other almost at will. Clear conceptual distinctions are rarely made and hardly discussed. The distinction based on the diversity of sources and means fluctuates among researchers. According to Nye, the analogous terms are sources and resources, which are much closer to one another regarding sound and etymology than their respective translations and are used synonymously in Nye's works (Nye, 1990).

METHODOLOGY

Motivation and historical relevance issues must be considered to develop a methodological approach that best fits a research project such as this. One of psychology's oldest, most fundamental, and most difficult questions is why actors do something and why exactly that and not something else. The numerous methods used to fathom it go back just as far. Science is formulated and understood as the attempt to systematically and methodically generate knowledge from human experience and protect it from error. This method is regarded as an instrument for gaining knowledge to address theoretical questions in all aspects and phases - such as discovery, organisation of data collection and preparation, and analysis.

In the pedagogical school regarding motivation research, various methods may be distinguished between hermeneutics, phenomenology, and dialectics. One option is to recognise a Tripartism with traditional pedagogy aligned within the areas of educational theory and theory of pedagogy (Walder, 2015). Whilst some consider a division between spiritual science and behaviourism, Weiner recognises a division between a reinforced hermeneutic or empirical approach (Howarth, 2004). Others foresee a heuristic process which offers the spiral of knowledge (Adelman & Riedel, 2012). It describes a symmetrical cycle of expectations, induction, synthesis, deduction, analysis/reduction and experience, in which the genesis of problems/case studies and their generalisation and examination and, if necessary, of their correction, new findings arise. Weiner's distinction arises as central theory is singled out due to its relationship to psychological motivation research and identifies a basic problem of psychological research that has long existed (Graham, & Weiner, 1996). The main idea is the preference of a twofold structure. The dichotomy described can be partially put into perspective by combining both approaches with suitable proceedings and integration. Discussing the distinction between hermeneutics and empiricism is important for the knowledge gained in this work because both methods are based on a fundamentally different view of humanity.

The methodological distinction between empirical social science and hermeneutic humanities becomes a partial dichotomy with sharpened comparisons concerning the modern against the old pedagogy. The rapid development of empirical educational research in the last decades has significantly contributed to this, as for thousands of years, educational science has been guided by a philosophical-argumentative approach.

Hermeneutics is also called the art of interpretation, which strives with the help of a hermeneutical circle or spiral, indicating a higher understanding. Existing prior knowledge or understanding as a starting point becomes a hermeneutical experience made by a text read and interpreted based on prior knowledge. Understanding the text now leads to this pre-understanding being corrected, deepened and refined. Included is a possible goal of understanding the author better than he has understood himself. The interpretation leads, in the ideal case, to further creativeness. This systematic scientific approach to things and phenomena was developed over the centuries to gain better insight into reality. The hermeneutical method as a science emerged in the 16th century and was promoted by Kant, Schleiermacher, Dilthey and Heidegger (Pietrzak, 2021).

To conclude, in the 6th century BC, when critical thinking and a factual interest towards things, matters, and how they originated, man increasingly came to the realisation that one can find truth through critical thinking and within the humanities, the argumentative method has been around for a very long time. In the field of educational sciences developed in the 4th century BC, Socrates used questioning-developing classroom discussions, the Socratic method of eliciting innovative ideas from another called Maieutic, with a strong disposition towards dialogue and reasoning (Westfall, 2009). Later, during the Roman Empire, great emphasis was placed on grammar and rhetoric, with teachers specifically educating young minds, including notable personalities such as perhaps the greatest orator, Cicero (Yiğit, 2022). The basic educational understanding at that time differs radically from today's pedagogy. Nevertheless, it becomes clear that the Romans' methodical principles, such as model learning or rewarding positive student behaviour, are still used today and are rooted in Greco-Roman antiquity. The first structural approaches and approaches to the sciences emerged at this time through Aristotle, the objects of investigation, and different historical contexts. This again demonstrates the complexity of discussion, in which a research method enables the best access to pedagogy and, in this case, of power and research focused on motivation.

LITERATURE REVIEW

Distinguishing himself from the neo-realist school and their understanding of power as a resource, Baldwin and Dahl developed and coined a relational concept of power, among others (Dahl, 1957); Baldwin, 2013). Baldwin defines power not as the property of a state but rather as a social relationship between actors (Baldwin, 1978). Power is not static and prescribed to an actor but is created during negotiation processes between educated actors. This aspect is emphasised by Barnett and Duvall, who assert that more than the pure neo-realist view of power, the ability of an actor to assert his interests in the actions of another actor is needed to satisfy the analysis of international phenomena (Barnett & Duvall, 2005). Instead, what is needed is a definition of power that integrates social structures and processes into consideration.

This understanding of power not as a possessed resource but as a relationally conditioned and negotiated power corresponds to a predominantly liberal conception of power. This follows Weber's definition of power that has already been introduced, in which social interaction is also a constitutive component of the appearance and effectiveness of power. Despite his criticism of the neo-realist concept of power from power as resources, Baldwin acknowledges the advantage of the reductionist tendencies of this approach. He emphasises that resources should be distinct from power but can be useful in operationalising and measuring it.

Since 1945, the US and its European allies should have learned that hard and soft power are important in a successful foreign policy (Pietrzak, 2022). Instead, the United States and Europe have worked diligently to take responsibility for using hard and soft power rather than pooling their resources to have a greater impact on international peace and security (Pietrzak, 2009). According to Ruggie, the most important aspect of the international order after World War II was not the hegemony of the United States but rather the fact that the hegemon was American (Ruggie, 1982). This meant that the United States had decided to cooperate with its allies rather than dominate them, that Washington had agreed to curb its power through involvement in multilateral organisations, and that its political system had tolerated the interference of allies so that they had the opportunity to influence the decision-making of the USA.

On the contrary, as Burns states, leadership must be distinct from the needs and goals of followers (Burns, 1996). Leadership is an interactive process in which the leader is followed and accomplished because he can convince his followers. The United States has convinced its followers to base a normative consensus on soft power by listening to its allies and taking their opinions seriously. However, suppose the leading power fails to bring its soft power to support military actions. In that case, the supposed followers may use their first opportunity to avoid it. This is exactly what happened in recent years, leading to the transatlantic Iraq crisis and the tense relationship with the Trump administration (Yigit, 2021).

Tensions over US leadership and uncertainty throughout its future foreign policy have brought the European Union's soft power - and, to a lesser extent, hard power - capabilities into sharper focus (Yigit, 2022a). The EU's soft power approach is based on the assumption that the strength of the law can successfully replace the law of the strongest. Thanks partly to US security precautions, Europe prefers sovereignty transfer and holds on to soft power instead of building hard power skills. Europe's preference for regulations-based politics is not, as Kagan claims, simply due to its lack of hard power (Kagan, 2002). Rather, it results from its history and its political complexity. Wallace states that Europe's tendency towards highly regulated politics can be explained by its large population density, the vulnerability of its environment and the permeability of its borders (Wallace, 1999). The more light-hearted approach to governance in the United States is due to its vast spaces and continental expansion.

The United Nations (UN) remains the most important platform for discussing all issues relevant to establishing a new world order. Significantly, the UN has recently identified promising ways to strengthen world domestic policy through narrower cooperation with non-state actors and multinational companies. Opening the international stage to civil society is one of the strongest instruments for the sustainable promotion of soft power.

Since the end of the Cold War, cultural diplomacy has become less important as one of the most important instruments for socialisation and building a shared memory. The value of culture as a means of building trust has recently been demonstrated in the form of hearts and minds, primarily aimed at the developing world, which has been rediscovered. However, more is needed to launch these campaigns after the fact, for example, to convince the population that the negative consequences of globalisation were not aimed at them. When dealing with countries that have not yet benefited from the "Western model" and therefore tend to reject it, cultural issues and expertise are essential to understanding these societies' complexity. Compared to other policy instruments, cultural exchange programs, education and training, and other forms of cultural diplomacy are extremely inexpensive (Pietrzak & Grębowiec, 2023). However, in the long term, they are extremely productive in expanding our understanding and creating personal connections. For this reason, the members of security communities should develop a soft power cultural strategy that shows ways to open their culture to others and to enter into a sustainable dialogue with them.

A soft power solution cannot be a substitute for convincing military options. However, if US and European soft power resources could be effectively combined they could prevent some difficulties from transforming into military disputes. It could also increase the ability of the international community to deal with post-conflict situations in a way that promotes stability. Transatlantic cooperation in the future will need an effective combination of soft and hard power resources from each side of the Atlantic. The unresolved query that the West faces today relates to the United States desiring to continue on a unilateral track which is heavily based on hard power or finding a balance between using soft and hard power that reinforces alliances and is able to pacify potential opponents.

The world we live in has changed fundamentally after the end of the Cold War and once more after the COVID-19 pandemic (Roman, Roman, Grzegorzewska, Pietrzak & Roman, 2022). Profound upheavals have taken place, making it difficult to think about coherently. While the story has so far more or less appeared predictable and flowed from a certain point, world events today have become so complex that its course can hardly be predicted. In a world characterised by an extraordinary multiplicity of actors and contradictory trends - from regional integration to retreat into identity - traditional realities such as war and peace alongside threats are changing, while new developments are giving rise to concern. Problems and phenomena such as ethical responsibility, security, the environment, sustainable development and the fight against poverty affect today's world. An ever-increasing number of political and social actors are mobilising in the "Global Village" (Knippa, 2016).

Today, world politics is no longer just the sum of intergovernmental relationships and no longer exclusively the concern of diplomats and high government officials. With the rapid development of means of communication and the dissemination of information, a large number of actors such as NGOs, civil society, large companies, and foundations, but also intellectual currents and behaviours such as those that resulted in the attack on September 11, 2001, are now involved in world events. The political boundaries are permeable, making traditional state regulation methods difficult and making world politics an extremely complex, transnational process.

Today, people often talk about the need for so-called global governance (Yigit, 2022b). While this is not a clear-cut concept, it is becoming increasingly important. When one talks about global governance, one is referring to the idea, which is important, that the general interest is no longer clear and no longer coincides with a specific geographical area. On the contrary, it is changeable and mobile and can be temporarily assigned to diverse groups. People are talking today at all levels, from companies to government policy to the UN governance as a network of control, which is always carried out by a limited number of international actors, the emergence of specific and global problem areas and the increasing interdependence of states. Nevertheless, global governance should not be imagined as a new institutional structure, a counterpart to the UN, but rather as an interplay of political, economic, social and cultural forces that can today be summarised under the term soft governance, which can embrace globalisation rather than endure it.

Among the numerous methods, procedures and agreements that underlie international relations, one term, in particular, has become increasingly important in recent years, symbolising new approaches to controlling and directing world events: the term soft governance, which is related to the term soft power, which was first coined by Joseph Nye in 1990 in his work Bound to Lead (Nye, 1991). His later book, Soft Power: The Means to Success in World Politics, further developed this concept (Nye, 2004). The concept of soft governance has used soft power as the main instrument for controlling and directing international events.

With the reflections on soft governance that will be explored in this chapter, an attempt will be made to define the concept of Nye in a comprehensive entirety in terms of the governance of international affairs, in particular by incorporating one of the wide ranges of working methods and frameworks used by the various actors. The approach is to expand to a more comprehensive perspective, incorporating methods still being developed. Therefore, there is a particular focus on the initiatives and experiences in implementing this new type of governance as guidelines and actual events. This terminological shift, replacing the word power with governance, may permit the researcher to only look at the actual power struggles, not focus entirely on hard power, and be concerned with the game's emerging rules. One must, however, retain the importance of the traditional balance of power. Although one should not underestimate the control of global political events, there is a need to describe the emerging forms of relationships in greater detail. However, one must briefly discuss the definition of soft power. Afterwards, in the second step, try to use the concept of soft governance as openly as possible to identify a new practice in today's international relations.

Soft Power: Definition and Development

The term motivation and the concepts that underlie it take time to grasp (Pietrzak, 2022b). Both interest and motivation are used in many contexts, and there are often quite different concepts behind the terms used. Just as numerous are the research approaches and individual aspects of motivation that are examined, these aspects, in turn, are partly interconnected but sometimes have nothing to do with each other. In rare cases, they do not have anything to do with motivation. Therefore, researchers today largely agree that motivation as a collective term is similar to an umbrella above a dense braid out of interwoven concepts that deal with individual aspects of motivation. At the same time, various terms and concepts are used synonymously, although they mean something different.

Soft power is a much-discussed concept that is not scientifically uniformly defined. One may delimit it from violence - Hard Power - and describe it as a non-violent interference strategy. Nye points out that many people do not understand power (Nye, 2016). According to his definition, it is essentially about getting the behaviour from others you want. There are diverse ways to do this: one could use direct force (hard power) and give orders. These are followed because those who wield the power are stronger than the recipients. However, it is called soft power as it is perhaps a second dimension of might as it enables others to want what you want them to do without using violence.

Although Nye sees soft power as the future of power, they are hardly found in current psychology or education textbooks. One may consider soft power as influence strategies that are usually considered offensive and represent forms of manipulation. Such influence techniques can be particularly effective because of the imperceptible steering of behaviour, with no reactance generated. The expression here is negative due to being compared to manipulation. The decisive factor is the effect of soft power: behaviour becomes so controlled that it imperceptibly happens, and – different from hard power – no resistance is caused. It is imperceptible, meaning that soft power runs below people's natural perception threshold and works on a deeper level. This fact is the first indication of the fundamental mechanisms of the human psyche, which are structured and illustrated using an iceberg model. These forms of influence can be seen as weapons of influence.

Psychological research is the core element that researches and provides such techniques. Lynd recognised many decades ago that this should not be viewed uncritically, though which psychological research has dedicated itself to this one specific area? There is no direct reference to this in psychological textbooks. Accepting the definition of Soft Power as people acting below their threshold of perception in their thoughts and feelings to influence, it recognises the person acting as quite similar to the holistic definition of motivation. Motivating other people means getting them to do something they want. This comprehensive definition of motivation is also used for Soft Power. Soft power and motivation become congruent: Soft Power is the superior construct, and motivation covers a greater sub-area that explains and provides a variety of techniques that soft power can use.

Soft power can be derived from many other research fields, which is not only relevant for motivating researchers. To illustrate, public relations consulting is now part and parcel of everyday political business. Nye's research on soft power also focuses on powerful American institutions such as the US

State Department. Soft Power is described in this instance as cultural diplomacy. There are numerous historical examples of the targeted use of soft power combined with Hard Power. The military was, therefore – perhaps more than any other institution – the closest to developing and encouraging psychological research. The list becomes exceedingly long when identifying institutions that need soft power.

Political Science Conceptions of Power

In principle, explaining what power means in other scientific disciplines, independent of international politics, and why power processes between states should be examined as structurally analogous to power processes between people is necessary. However, the power one can exercise is only expressed in the asymmetrical confrontation with resistance to at least one further actor. This premise, which seems logical concerning the relationship between two individuals, can also be transferred to states. The reason this transfer is possible is because individuals control a state. Understanding states as unitary actors, as in realism, appears in the context of this work. Against the background, the polymorphic forms of being of international actors are no longer current. When a state enters into relationships with other states, it does so not as a static actor but as a collective of people or institutions with diverse interests.

Having outlined how power is viewed and justified in the humanities, the following section will provide an overview of its political science concepts, their operationalisation of political science schools of thought, and the definitions of the respective taxonomies. The evolutionary change from understanding power as a resource to power as relational to an initial concept of structural power is described. The main part of this work should be theoretically justified. This then attempts to expand and supplement the existing concept of structural power.

When discussing the origin of power, most political scientists need to speak more about sources and means of power. One is replaced by the other almost at will. Clear conceptual distinctions are rarely made and hardly discussed. The distinction is based on the diversity of words, such as source and means. Nye uses sources and resources that are much closer to one another in sound and etymological terms than other words, such as means and are used synonymously in Nye's works.

Nye is credited with having invented 1990 the concept of Soft Power to designate the capacity of states to obtain what they want through attraction rather than coercion. One can identify three approaches. A first definition bases Soft Power on the notion of influence and can be summarised as follows: capacity for a political actor, a State, a multinational firm, an NGO, an international institution (UN or the IMF) or even a network of citizens (the globalist movement) to indirectly influence the behaviour of another actor through non-coercive, structural, cultural or ideological means.

A second definition is based on the notion of seduction. Soft power would be the ability to seduce and persuade other states without using force or threat to make the other want the same thing as you. It is based on a state's positive image or reputation, its prestige - often its economic or military performance - its communication capabilities, and the degree of openness of its society. It considers the exemplary nature of its behaviour (of its domestic policies, the substance and style of its foreign policy), the attractiveness of its culture, its ideas - religious, political, economic, philosophical - and its scientific and technological influence. It appreciates its place within international institutions, its capacity to control the agenda of debates, to decide what is legitimate, to discuss or not and thus to freeze power relations when they are most favourable to it.

A third definition synthesises the two previous ones quite well by affirming that Soft Power designates a state's capacity to influence another state's behaviour to lead it to adopt the same point of view through cultural and ideological means. It mobilises resources based on the attractiveness and seduction embodied by its cultural model. Soft Power complements Hard Power, which designates the traditional means of any foreign policy: the army and diplomatic and economic pressures.

Soft Power, therefore, combines diplomatic initiative, image seduction, and the propagation of values in the service of a global foreign policy of influence whose objective is to benefit in return from favourable economic benefits and factors of growth and development. This raises the question of whether it is a new concept or just the formalisation of the influence strategy that each state has adopted since the dawn of time.

Without a doubt, this is what it is. However, if this concept is clearly explained to the point that we are talking about its return to the international scene, it is because the planet is globalised. Against the backdrop of a global energy and financial crisis and even a water crisis, each nation has directly competed with the entire world. Each of them has acquired the conviction that its civilisational sustainability, sometimes its survival, required the maximum mobilisation of its forces. Very few have warlike power; when this power exists, it is annihilated by a symmetrical power among competitors. All that remains to finalise the objectives is the attractive powers of the economy, culture and religion. In short, the detour of analysis, inventive strategy, and diplomacy, in a word, intelligence. However, is there an optimal combination between membership and coercion that would guarantee harmonious development for each society? Finally, Soft Power's strategies are all the more interesting today as with the appearance of modern technologies; they are supported by diffusion vectors unlike those we knew barely three decades ago.

Soft Power Approaches: A Typology

The first typology, represented among others by the United States and Russia, combines Hard and Soft Power. If these nations have an economic and cultural capacity to influence the behaviour of other nations, they occasionally activate military means to achieve their objectives. It should be noted that if this combination varies in degrees depending on the political powers in place, it has always been consistent. We should add a variant of a combination of Soft Power with purely verbal and incantatory Hard Power to this first typology. For example, Iran is an interesting example in this regard.

The second typology concerns economic Soft Power countries. Germany, Brazil, Japan, and India are convincing examples of Soft Power serving successful economic interests. For this typology, one will note a variant here: that of China, which, after initially operating on an essentially economic Soft Power, has added to this dimension over the last decade of cultural expansionism.

The third typology, first cultural and civilisational, concerns old Western Europe: France, Spain, and the United Kingdom. However, if driven by the history of ideas and religions, the cultural domain in the broad sense of the term dominates this typology; we cannot reduce it to pure intellectual and moral attractiveness. Indeed, this Soft Power is combined with real economic power, centred in particular on the export of sophisticated technologies.

The list of countries cited according to these three typologies must be completed. However, the analysis would only be complete if it was limited to considering the countries taken separately. Suppose each of the major countries on the planet can implement Soft Power strategies independently. In that case, this is different for most countries whose economic and political weight, considered individually, is too limited. These countries must position themselves within large groups (European Union, MERCOSUR, FTAA and NAFTA). These are flourishing in the four corners of the planet, either on transstate constructions with an economic vocation, with a political vocation, or both. These systems allow a majority of countries to preserve their interests, either by placing themselves in the sphere of influence of a country of recognised weight, by grouping by adding forces to create their sphere, or by playing the North-South opposition in order to counterbalance American unilateralism with the multilateralism of emerging countries.

These spheres of influence, intersections, overlaps, shifts, and clashes should lead to a more pragmatic vision of the cards that France and the EU have to play in what sometimes resembles an imbroglio. The return of soft power in international relations is familiar, except perhaps the theorisation of a concept that all countries have appropriated in their power strategies. Rather than talking about a return, it would probably be appropriate to talk about significant developments. The new technological communication media's capacity to cover the entire planet is incommensurable with the classic economic and cultural diffusion vectors. Very few states, if any, have succeeded in putting in place watertight filters – perhaps except North Korea - to escape this progressive envelopment.

However, while essentially Anglo-Saxon culture operates through contamination, globalisation and the crisis have led to the paradox that a State must both tighten in on itself, implement inventive strategies, and simultaneously join sharing groups to resist better. France and its link with the EU fall into this scenario. Apart from a few delimited centres of tension, the era is no longer one of Hard Power. For states with the means to assert their global or regional power, the time has come for Smart power, a subtle blend of targeted shows of force and consensual diplomacy. As for the other States, the majority, each according to its values and pragmatism, contributes its share to a military defence system under the security umbrella of a more capable actor. At the same time, this allows it to devote itself to soft power actions on its own behalf. France in Europe, and as a whole in NATO, correspond to this pattern. The era is all the less about hard power than about the primary philosophy of Trump's Make America Great Again or the Obama Administration, which substituted far more intellectually sophisticated and thoughtful strategies.

However, one perceives that this development could ultimately generate the constitution of three large blocs with competing interests and distant civilisational values: the Anglo-Saxon world, to which all or part of Europe, Russia, and China will be added. One must add two major regional powers in terms of demographics and economic power to these blocks: India and Brazil. The rest of the planetary space is then shared between these blocks according to the smart or soft power that each has the means to develop. Thus, concerning the major questions to come, such as energy, water, and global warming complicated by ethnic-religious oppositions and population movements linked to large economic disparities, the point of balance between these large blocks will not only be a fragile parenthesis of history. Because if soft power is as old as time, hard power is even older.

The question arises as to what extent this distinction can lead to distortions in one's theoretical landscape (Pietrzak, 2022). This assumes that more than certain concepts implicit in the most realistic power theories must be explicated or problematised. Thus, this results in a theoretical indifference that affects the structure of the entire investigation in its comprehensibility and logic mechanisms. Namely, it is the logical separation from sources of power, which per se is to produce power and power resources that actors in given contexts can become tools to assert power interests.

When power resources are described as power sources, one is forced to refer to them to understand some bumps along the way on content-related contradictions, where the alleged sources of power do not allow them to bubble up. This is the case, for example, when a political power uses a resource relevant to it in the context of interstate competition with another power, which it cannot produce itself but can obtain from a third actor. In this way, it could undermine a prior power position of the competing actor, regardless of the pre-trial disposition of power resources. In various political science theories, power resources per se make an actor in whose hands they are powerful - this is the tenor of the power as resource approach. This view is shortened because political power is fundamentally developed in negotiation processes between actors and does not remain static and unchangeable over time and space with one actor. The resulting aporias lead realist theorists to an unhelpful expansion of the related theoretical structure. In a sense, one is on the wrong floor if one gives such importance to the abundance of available power resources named and classified in the literature.

The misunderstanding lies where the origins of power and questions about its production should be positively determined from the actors' perspective and their material characteristics. One arrives at many empty categories of power, which cannot stand independently and only have an impact when considering their contextual embedding. The alternative is to understand resources as a means of achieving goals and not artificially as something whose outflow is a priori. A form of power is to exaggerate what has been discussed in this chapter. At the same time, the origins of power should be examined on a different ontological level.

That only particular phenomenological resources as sources of power are considered is a consequence of the reductionist tendencies of the realist theoretical tradition. Reality should not be captured in its complexity and entirety. The problem is that the generalizability of these theories is limited to problem cases that already fall within the framework of one's theory. All other options are hidden. This approach has advantages and can cover certain areas of international relations extremely specific and concretely. This creates a tautology since only cases with known and defined characteristics can be considered. Therefore, the content of realist theories for explaining international relations or conflicts is limited. Understanding power as resources is akin to a theory of gravity that can describe the fall of an apple but must deny that the fall of an orange follows the same mechanism (namely gravity) that only occurs through other media (namely an orange). To explain why he is so narrow, Waltz sharply distinguishes his statements about theory from his findings about laws (Waltz, 1997). A theory should be obtained through speculative processes that explain laws that can, in turn, be derived from observations. The law of gravity, which applies to both oranges and apples, would therefore be completely compatible with a theory for Waltz in which the focus lies exclusively on the case of apples and, through the limitation of their premises, excludes any other fruit from consideration per se. The problem here is that in the intellectual successor to Waltz, the boundaries between theory and law became blurred, and the terms needed to be separated enough. This is due to the attempt of most political scientists - following Waltz - to grasp and describe the complexity of the entire political reality and to derive potential from these descriptions for predicting future, similar situations. In order to meet this goal, the core of Waltz's theory has been expanded in recent decades, and analytical categories have been added using empirical induction to such an extent that its theoretical character has been diluted.

This understanding of power not as a possessed resource but as relationally conditioned and negotiated power corresponds to a predominantly liberal conception of power. This follows Weber's definition of power that has already been noted, in which social interaction is also a constitutive component of the appearance and effectiveness of power. Despite his criticism levelled at the neo-realist concept of power from power as resources, Baldwin acknowledges the advantage of the reductionist tendencies of this approach (Baldwin, 2014). He emphasises that resources should be distinct from power but can be useful in operationalising and measuring it.

Relational power is used to analyse international phenomena and power shifts, though the spatial and temporal are subject to limitations. Relational power only works if there is an interaction between two or more actors. Thus, relational power advances the understanding of power as a resource and integrates social relationships as a definitional component. However, simultaneously, the spectrum of emergence and impact of relational power is limited to very specific interactions. Therefore, It is taken from other simultaneous interactions and relationships. The concept of relational power cannot offer an understanding independent of specific interactions of a limited number of actors. In addition to this temporal limitation, relational power also suffers from spatial limitations. Any connection between the actors in the relationship is considered a constitutive element for the emergence of power during an interaction; if this is not present, no power arises. Therefore, a complete analysis of what is to be described or discovered as effective power is not possible or should not have any claim to completeness. This creates the need to expand the concept of relational power and shift the focus towards the impact of structures.

CONCLUSION

Soft-power and hard-power politics and their respective resources are most effective when combined. Soft power can help legitimise Hard Power. Although hard power is essential to winning wars and often lending credibility to strategic decisions, soft power is even more important to achieving and maintaining peace. Soft Power is the new requirement for trust between people and states. Soft and hard power are not considered interchangeable. Europe is extremely hesitant to use military power - of which it has little - and rely very much on soft power - which it is well equipped with. However, Europe's hard power deficit undermines its diplomatic clout, particularly when dealing with its ally, the unipolar USA. This fact creates tension which leads onto issues regarding the United States' soft power politics in their reactions to international challenges being often neglected.

Defined by Nye 1990 as the ability to seduce and attract, soft power puts power into perspective in an unconventional framework. The geopolitical tradition distinguishes two types of relations between nations within interstate relations. The first is based on traditional power, a symmetrical relationship of rivalry and negotiation - hard power. In a traditional geopolitical economy, war measures forces; as for diplomacy, it seeks compromises and agreements. Finally, the economy and trade between nations, in turn, presuppose exchange. The second interstate relations are based on influence (soft power). They, therefore, relate to an asymmetrical relationship between an influenced and an influential person, who, by his prestige, by the links he has created outside his borders with elites and foreign populations, by the attraction of his cultural model or political, through the favourable prejudices it enjoys, can influence other nations, to obtain, through co-optation, strategic results in its favour, to define the political agenda internationally. Within international relations, obtaining the neutrality of governments initially unfavourable to their cause at the first level is not negligible. Disarming the hostility of others and other nations is strategically important. At a higher stage, the influence strategy is set in motion to obtain control of areas and networks to generate favourable behaviours. Trade and obtaining political support in international organisations is possible at this level. This privileged relationship makes it possible to create allies and, therefore, multilateral support for the causes defended by the influential nation. At the last stage, when the methods of persuasion and seduction aim to produce total mimicry and absolute adhesion, the values of the influential nation and its world vision are shared by the Other, who comes to behave according to its model. The consent of the "influenced" is explained neither by threat nor explicit reward. The strategy is indirect, although it can be deliberate.

Nye attempts to identify the determinants of power, and therefore influence, in the post-Cold War international system. For him, power is represented by the capacity for a State to influence other States so that the latter adopts behaviour consistent with the interests of the first. To achieve this, countries can use two main methods: Hard Power and Soft Power. Hard power refers to using traditional tools, either coercion through the threat of military reprisals or incitement by dangling economic and financial interests. In contrast, Soft Power refers to the ability of a state to obtain what it desires through the power of attraction of its culture, ideas, domestic policies and diplomacy. When these are perceived as legitimate in the eyes of other states, the Soft Power of the country in question increases. Soft Power, whose importance has increased with the development of new information and communications technologies, therefore has the effect of co-opting the interests of other actors in the international system or at least the perception of their interests.

Despite a demonstrated defence of universal values, there is an ambiguity relating to Soft Power. The defence of universal values constitutes one of its classic and essential foundations. Display is vital because how they are perceived from the outside matters. It is universal because each civilisation puts concepts that are not identical behind words with different priorities. Thus, the family, the clan, and the tribe are notions sometimes foreign to the West, for example, which reduces the family unit to those close to it. Furthermore, if the term values are often used as an argument for persuasion, it is rarely detailed and hierarchical, and the fundamental ideals are rarely highlighted. One can draw a parallel between the vital needs of the individual, defined according to Maslow's pyramid, and those of a nation as a collective being (Maslow & Lewis, 1987).

Without falling into eccentricity, one can imagine that soft power serves a noble cause through honest means. Conversely, it would be utopian to ignore that this non-material power, which aims to seduce others, does not presuppose strategies of influence exercised through information, manipulation, and a complete range of diversified means, including information such as disinformation, economic aid, propaganda and corruption. One can find oneself on the dark side of seduction, even of a bluff based on illusion. This reminds us of a classic pragmatism concisely summarised by Deng Xiaoping when he declared that it does not matter whether a cat is black or white as long as it catches mice. Thus, Soft Power is diplomacy adapted to the moment. It takes multiple forms, but with common features determining the typologies one may observe across countries which are global, continental or regional powers.

REFERENCES

Adelman, L., & Riedel, S. L. (2012). *Handbook for evaluating knowledge-based systems: Conceptual framework and compendium of methods*. Springer Science & Business Media.

Baldwin, D. A. (1978). Power and social exchange. *The American Political Science Review*, 72(4), 1229–1242. doi:10.2307/1954536

Baldwin, D. A. (2013). Power and international relations. Handbook of International Relations, 2, 273-297.

Baldwin, D. A. (2014). Neoliberalism, neorealism, and world politics. In *The Realism Reader* (pp. 313–319). Routledge.

Barnett, M., & Duvall, R. (2005). Power in international politics. *International Organization*, 59(1), 39–75. doi:10.1017/S0020818305050010

Bevir, M. (1999). Foucault, power, and institutions. *Political Studies*, *47*(2), 345–359. doi:10.1111/1467-9248.00204

Burns, J. S. (1996). Defining leadership: Can we see the forest for the trees? *The Journal of Leadership Studies*, *3*(2), 148–157. doi:10.1177/107179199600300212

Clarke, M. T. (2022). Machiavelli's Virtuous Princes: Rhetoric, Power, and the Politics of Ironic Historiography. *The Journal of Politics*, *84*(1), 483–495. doi:10.1086/715596

Dahl, R. A. (1957). The concept of power. *Behavioral Science*, *2*(3), 201–215. doi:10.1002/bs.3830020303

Graham, S., & Weiner, B. (1996). Theories and principles of motivation. Handbook of Educational Psychology, 4(1), 63-84.

Howarth, D. (2004). Towards a Heideggerian social science: Heidegger, Kisiel and Weiner on the limits of anthropological discourse. *Anthropological Theory*, *4*(2), 229–247. doi:10.1177/1463499604042817

Kagan, R. (2002). *Power and weakness* (Vol. 113). Hoover Institution.

Knippa, M. (2016). Features of Human Anatomy: Marshall McLuhan on Technology in the Global Village. *Lutheran Mission Matters*, *24*(3), 371–384.

Maslow, A., & Lewis, K. J. (1987). Maslow's hierarchy of needs. *Salenger Incorporated*, *14*(17), 987–990.

Mucha, J. (2007). The concept of "social relations" in classic analytical interpretative sociology: Weber and Znaniecki. In Essays in Logic and Ontology (pp. 119-142). Brill.

Newton, T. (1999). Power, subjectivity and British industrial and organisational sociology: The relevance of the work of Norbert Elias. *Sociology*, *33*(2), 411–440. doi:10.1177/S0038038599000243

Nye, J. S. Jr. (1990). The changing nature of world power. *Political Science Quarterly*, *105*(2), 177–192. doi:10.2307/2151022

Nye, J. S. (1991). *Bound to lead: the changing nature of American power*. Basic books.

Nye, J. S. (2004*). Soft power: The means to success in world politics*. Public Affairs.

Nye, J. S. Jr. (2016). Limits of American power. *Political Science Quarterly*, *131*(2), 267–283. doi:10.1002/polq.12478

Penta, L. J. (1996). Hannah Arendt: On power. *The Journal of Speculative Philosophy*, 210–229.

Pietrzak, P. (2021). Immanuel Kant and Niccolò Machiavelli's Traditions and the Limits of Approaching Contemporary Conflicts—The Case Study of the Syrian Conflict (2011–Present). *Statu Nascendi Journal of Political Philosophy and International Relations*, *2*, 53–84.

Pietrzak, P. (2022). How Did Bashar Al-Assad Get Away With the Ghouta Chemical Attack? The Promise of Relinquishing Syria's Chemical Weapons Arsenal That Was Never Fully Fulfilled. In Regulating Human Rights, Social Security, and Socio-Economic Structures in a Global Perspective (pp. 125-141). IGI Global.

Pietrzak, P. (2022b). Introducing the idea of Ontology in statu nascendi to the broader International Relations Theory. In *International Conference Proceeding Series-International Conference on Economics and Social Sciences in Serik* (pp. 570-585). Academic Press.

Pietrzak, P. (2023). Approaching Regional Conflicts through the Prism of Ontology in statu nascendi—The New Compartmentalization of the IR Theory. *Statu Nascendi*, *6*(1), 97–154.

Pietrzak, P., & Grębowiec, M. (2023). Building trust on social media as part of higher education institutions' marketing strategy. In Privacy, Trust and Social Media (pp. 242-252). Routledge.

Pietrzak, P. W. (2009). American "Soft Power" after George W. Bush's Presidency. In A. Mania & Ł. Wordliczek (Eds.), The United States and the World: From Imitation to Challenge (pp. 187–194). Jagiellonian University Press.

Roman, M., Roman, M., Grzegorzewska, E., Pietrzak, P., & Roman, K. (2022). Influence of the COVID-19 Pandemic on Tourism in European Countries: Cluster Analysis Findings. *Sustainability (Basel)*, *14*(3), 1602. doi:10.3390/su14031602

Ruggie, J. G. (1982). International regimes, transactions, and change: Embedded liberalism in the postwar economic order. *International Organization*, *36*(2), 379–415. doi:10.1017/S0020818300018993

Walder, A. M. (2015). A theoretical model for pedagogical innovation: A tripartite construction of pedagogical innovation focusing on reasons for and means of innovating. *Journal of Studies in Social Sciences*, *12*(1).

Wallace, W. (1999). The sharing of sovereignty: The European paradox. *Political Studies*, *47*(3), 503–521. doi:10.1111/1467-9248.00214

Waltz, K. N. (1997). Evaluating theories. *The American Political Science Review*, *91*(4), 913–917. doi:10.2307/2952173

Westfall, J. (2009). Ironic midwives: Socratic maieutics in Nietzsche and Kierkegaard. *Philosophy and Social Criticism*, *35*(6), 627–648. doi:10.1177/0191453709104450

Yiğit, S. (2021). Trump vs China. *The Trade Wars of the USA, China, and the EU: The Global Economy in the Age of Populism*, 67.

Yiğit, S. (2022). "Cicero and the Art of Rhetoric", 5. Media Literacy Forum, Social Sciences in the Age of Digital Transformation Proceedings Book, Eds: ADILBEKOVA, OZEL, TURKER, COSAN & SAHIN, Iksad Publications 25 December 2022, ISBN: 978-625-8254-04-4, pp. 557-574.

Yigit, S. (2022a). European Union's Strategy in the Far North: Arctic Rivalry. In Global Agenda in Social Sciences (vol. 9). IJOPEC Publication.

Yigit, S. (2022b). Digital Transformation: The Challenges Facing SMEs. In Digital Transformation and New Approaches in Trade, Economics, Finance and Banking. Rowman & Littlefield.

KEY TERMS AND DEFINITIONS

Attraction: The action or power of evoking interest in or liking for someone or something.

Foreign Policy: The collection of strategies a country uses to guide its relationships with other countries.

Incentive: An external influence such as an expected reward inciting to action.

International Politics: International Politics is about the world we live in, the challenges we face, power and struggles, and the opportunities – as well as obstacles – for peaceful relations among peoples, societies, states, organisations.

Leader: The person who leads or commands a group, organization, or country.

Motivation: A process of inducing and stimulating an individual to act in certain manner.

Power: The right or ability to govern, rule, or strongly influence people or situations.

Sphere of Influence: The claim by a state to exclusive or predominant control over a foreign area or territory.

States: A nation or territory considered as an organized political community under one government.

Chapter 12
Great Power Contest in Southeast Asia:
Sources and Limits of China's Charm Offensive

Aileen Joy Adion Pactao

https://orcid.org/0009-0007-7276-042X

Palawan State University, Philippines

ABSTRACT

The era of globalization, which is characterized by intensified borderless exchanges and increased interconnectedness, pressures countries to reassess their use of 'hard power' in realizing nation's objectives as well as dealing with the global community. China has been recognizing the importance of 'soft power' – the need to enhance its global image. Primarily, this strategy is called 'charm offensive' which projects a "benign national image" to secure strong alliances and demonstrate itself as an epitome of social and economic success. This matter is another interesting subject of various discourses and not yet exhausted by existing knowledge production efforts and hence, the focus of this chapter. Specifically, through the use of secondary literature and scrutinization of policy statements and landmark speeches of officials, diplomats, and cultural agents of soft power, this chapter examines China's charm offensive in Southeast Asia – focusing on its sources, limits, and implications to the stability of the region.

INTRODUCTION

The growing presence and impact of China in Southeast Asia and other parts of the world is often attributed by scholars (Lum, Morrison, & Vaughn, 2008; Kurlantzick, 2007; Hoey, 2007) to its soft power labeled as a *charm offensive*[1] – foreign assistance, trade, investment, diplomacy, and vast market potential. This 'charm' is utilized by China to project a "benign national image", secure strong alliances, and demonstrate itself as an epitome of social and economic success (Kurlantzick, 2007). Specifically, this

DOI: 10.4018/979-8-3693-2444-8.ch012

soft power works in Southeast Asia because of the benefits it accrues to the member states and the inconsistent behaviors and actions of the United States (US) in the region (Lum, Morrison, & Vaughn, 2008).

The concept of soft power can be traced back as early as the works of Hans Morgenthau and, more recently, by Harvard Professor Joseph Nye, Jr. which created a debate among policymakers and pundits to consider another source of influence, instead of focusing heavily on military and economic might (Ullah, 2015). This kind of power capitalizes on the utilization of the tools of public diplomacy and culture to shape foreign policies hence, it refers to the ability of the state to realize its goals and objectives through attraction, rather than coercion or payments. Moreover, Nye asserted that soft power is not only about 'ephemeral popularity' but, a means of getting things done by affecting a country's behavior without commanding it and is often a result of the country's cultural attractiveness, its policies, and ideals.

In a post-Cold War system that reflects intensified economic interconnectedness and multidimensional dynamics, soft power is argued as a crucial resource due to power diffusion and transition. Particularly, it has led to a declining relevance of hard power as diplomacy has evolved to be more implied through means of persuasion and attraction hence an increase in soft power (Chang & Kim, 2016). This argument can be situated in the context of China as it promotes its visibility and influence in Southeast Asia. Most of the available accounts (e.g., Jia, 2010; Jain & Chakrabarti, 2023) pertaining to the rise of China are centered on the military and economic aspects of its growing dominance in this region as well as in the world. Yet "soft power" resources have been increasingly recognized as a crucial component of Great Power status (Gill & Huang, 2006). Specifically, in this age of globalization, hard power is now perceived as insufficient for achieving foreign policy objectives by policymakers and academics (Nye, 2004; Gates, 2007 in Heng, 2009). Hence, various ways on how to best project "soft power" are gaining momentum in the existing body of knowledge (Gill & Huang, 2006; Nye, 2005; Kurlantzick, 2007). Nye (2004) emphasized that this type of power is usually generated by countries whose [existing and prevailing] values and ideas reflect the current [ruling] ideas and/or values of pluralism, self-determination, individualism, and liberalism, those who have multiple access to various channels of information and communication, and those that commonly consider the utilization of soft power as credible and legitimate. While Nye's theory of soft power is apparently America-centric, it can be considered as a "general framework" that applies to all countries, groups, and individuals. However, it must be noted that there might be an individuality in 'soft' power strategies as Asian powers [continuously] engage in power competition.

This paper aims to examine China's charm offensive in Southeast Asia by analyzing the available secondary literature and studies (or body of knowledge), buttressed with the scrutinization of policy statements or landmark speeches of government officials, diplomats, and cultural agents of 'soft' power. Specifically, the exploration centers on the sources, limits, and implications of this soft power in Southeast Asia. This includes the assessment of the effects of the West Philippine Sea on China's soft power in the region as well as the realities of great power contest. By taking these matters into account, useful policy lessons can be drawn that may facilitate the promotion and enhancement of regional stability in Southeast Asia despite the seemingly endless power competition between the so-called great powers (China, the United States, and Japan including India in South Asia).

Conceptualizing China's Charm Offensive in the Twenty-First Century

Power is an important concept in strategic studies as well as in international relations. While almost everyone talks about this, only a few completely understand it (Nye, 2004) because it is demonstrated in different ways ranging from subtle diplomatic schemes to a certain amount of state resources that can trigger or facilitate a total war. It is measured by how a state can alter and channel the behavior of other states (Freeman, 1997). Additionally, it reflects the ability of the state to achieve its goals and objectives as well as the capacity to control events, including the decisions and actions of other states. While military capability is commonly argued as the measure of power, despite its destructive capacity, it is only one of the elements of statecraft (Zreik, 2023a). This is mainly because power can be exercised in different ways, working within the spectrum between hard power and soft power (De Castro, 2007). In this sense, soft power is argued to be an effective tool for enhancing an image and dominance thus, complementing a country's hard power.

The concept of power, which was recently furthered in the works of Harvard Professor Joseph Nye, Jr., has been enthusiastically taken into account by scholars, policymakers, and other think tanks in the People's Republic of China (PRC). Over the past decade, China has become more confident in demonstrating to the global stage the advantage of having sheer economic prowess, population size, and political potential (Hwang, 2008); it essentially focused on enhancing its image in the world by using its soft power resources. As this country's influence consistently expands in terms of economic, military, and political power, other states are becoming more and more aware of its relevance and influence. Specifically, by joining multilateral institutions, supporting peacekeeping engagements, assisting with nonproliferation issues, fighting narcotics and human trafficking, facilitating and driving economic growth in Latin America and Africa, and developing nations [with emerging markets], Beijing is sending a message that it wants only a peaceful rise – a manifestation of its growing soft power strategy (Lee & Hao, 2018; Ullah, 2015; Hwang, 2008; Hoey, 2007).

In 2009, during the 11th Conference of Chinese Diplomatic Envoys Stationed Abroad, the importance of public diplomacy in Chinese foreign policy was emphasized by Chinese President Hu Jintao. In his words,

[China] should strengthen public diplomacy and humanities diplomacy and commence various kinds of cultural exchange activities in order to disseminate China's great culture. (President Hu Jintao, 2009 in Tai-Ting Liu, 2018)

This statement significantly affirmed the inclusion of public diplomacy as a tool of its nation's policy and signified the country's belief in the greatness of its culture hence, must be furthered, expanded, and disseminated to the world. Since then, it gradually became a notable priority of the next leadership. Moreover, in 2012, in the party report of the 18th National Congress of the CCP, China explicitly specified the guidelines of 'making good efforts to advance public diplomacy' (Xinhua 2012 as cited by Tai-Ting Liu, 2018). After this event, President Xi Jinping introduced the concept of 'telling a good story of China and disseminating the voice of China.' President Xi further outlined the China Dream as the country's grand ideological principle which becomes the framework for China's continued development while public diplomacy is one of the ways for the realization of this Xi's vision. These are the central tenets of China's public diplomacy which clearly reflect its desire to enhance its global image (Tai-Ting Liu, 2018). These diplomatic tools and approaches were furthered as the country established various offices and engaged different sectors (e.g., public, private, and academic institutions and organizations).

China is indeed charming the world with its economic and cultural resources to enhance its status and image through soft means. It is primarily invested in projecting a positive, accommodating, and likable existence that may involve showcasing potential, relatability, reliability, friendliness, and charisma. Further, in this sense, China uses its soft power resources (e.g., diplomatic approaches, taking international responsibilities) to ease foreign perception of its presence in the region as a threat. Instead of aggressive rhetoric and positioning, it apparently tries to design the regional agenda and influence the preferences and interests of member-states in Southeast Asia by boosting its image in the region. It portrays itself as an emerging, benevolent, and responsible power that advocates a pluralistic, multipolar, and distributive global order in which states respect each other's affairs, work for common interests, and conflicts are resolved diplomatically, while seemingly downplaying any desire to strategically dominate the region. Thus, as initially reflected by the data, China is outwardly focused on political consolidation, economic growth, and modernization. These strategies are all set toward one ultimate objective that is, to expand China's presence and impact in the twenty-first century.

In this specific section, to further the discussion above, the sources, limits, and implications of China's charm offensive were explored by including the effects of the West Philippine Sea on China's soft power in the region as well as the realities of great power contest.

Sources and Limits of China's Charm Offensive

China's charm offensive is derived from different channels of resources (foreign policy and engagement in multilateral institutions, domestic policy and values, and culture) and, at the same time, constraints by various factors such as foreign policy incoherence, aggressive approach, and domestic issues and challenges. While various circumstances display its success, some issues highlight its limitations.

Sources of China's Charm Offensive

The most common sources of soft power by a country are its culture, membership in various international organizations, and foreign policy as well as its domestic politics and values (Nye, 2004; Gill & Huang, 2006). These sources are evident in the context of China.

The 'Great' Culture of China

Soft power is usually derived from the cultural realities of a state (Gill & Huang, 2006). In a statement by former Prime Minister Lee Kuan Yew of Singapore "Soft power is achieved only when other nations admire and want to emulate aspects of that nation's civilization" (Chang & Kim, 2016) which connotes that soft power is cemented by the recognition and appreciation of the rest of the world to a country's culture as a model hence, must be followed and adopted.

Particularly, with globalization, 'culture' plays an increasingly important role in international relations. It has become one of the most uncertain yet inevitable critical elements on the global stage (Ørmen et al., 2021) since it has direct effects on the beliefs and values of national leaders (Lane & Ersson, 2016). However, it must be noted that culture is a double-edged sword – it can facilitate both harmony and conflict. Because of the increasing number of online platforms for cultural diffusion, this element uniquely connects differences around the world and ultimately forming them into a shared reality (Ørmen et al., 2021). China, as a dominant power, capitalizes on its culture to maintain, assert, and expand its dominance not just in the region but, on the global stage (Zreik, 2024a).

In the past thirty years, China's influence has increased as globalization continues to intensify various exchanges including cultural exchange. Its civilization has always been known for its inclusivity, openness, diversity, and continuously invigorates itself through interacting with other cultures. Specifically, history revealed that as early as the ancient Silk Road, China facilitated various exchanges with the world (206BC-AD25) and during the Tang Dynasty (618-906 AD), the country drew significant attention from scholars, traders, emissaries, and holy men in quest of wealth, inspiration, guidance, and power (Gill & Huang, 2006). As a result, the spread of its civilization is evident in its neighboring countries like Vietnam, Japan, and Korea. This implies that its culture has always had a decisive influence in neighboring East and Southeast Asian countries.

Further, the status of this country as classic Asia's dominant power led to abundant reserves of soft power that are now being utilized in various engagements (Gill & Huang, 2006). These reserves rely more on the country's think tanks, an increasing number of universities that teach Chinese language and culture (known as Confucius Institutes or CIs)[2], Chinese academic scholarships, increasing foreign students' enrollment (mostly from Southeast Asian countries), hosting major cultural engagements (e.g., Beijing Olympics), and a significant number of traditional and digital platforms (Xinhua News Agency, China Central Television (CCTV), China Radio International (CRI), and China Daily/Global Times with increasing number of international offices and thousands of correspondents and locally recruited employees, publications in eight languages - Chinese, English, French, Russian, Spanish, Arabic, Portuguese, and Japanese) that store and disseminate information about Chinese culture across the world (Dai & Cheng, 2022; Gill & Huang, 2006). Essentially, the political and economic system of the country has always acknowledged that information must be controlled and managed, people must be indoctrinated (Shambaugh, 2015), and there must be a strong and established "going out" strategy that advocates for media presence overseas to challenge, if not balance, what is considered 'Western media monopoly'. In other words, the available information platforms allow the continuous dissemination of Chinese cultural elements which, on the other hand, imposes 'power anxiety' to the West.

Also, Chinese [people] share one belief and that is 'their culture is fundamentally a world culture'. Particularly, in 2014, President Xi Jinping announced:

We should increase China's soft power, give a good Chinese narrative, and better communicate China's messages to the world. (Shambaugh, 2015, page 99)

This statement reflects the country's commitment to forward its soft power and enhance its image. As its power increases, it also believes that enhancing its 'image' is important. During this year, the country has revealed to the world different initiatives such as "the Twenty-First-Century Maritime Silk Road," "the Chinese dream," and "the Asia-Pacific dream." These are different yet interconnected messages that tell the world about China's projection of a 'good and responsible image' that is characterized by working collaboratively and diplomatically with different countries thereby addressing or debunking the "China threat theory" (Lai, 2012).

Recently, in October 2023, President Xi Jinping issued instructions about forwarding Chinese culture during a national meeting in Beijing. He specifically outlined a new cultural mission for the entire nation – "to further advance cultural prosperity, build a leading country in culture, and foster modern Chinese civilization at a new starting point" and this is known as "Xi Jinping Thought on Culture" (Zheng, 2023). Furthermore, he stated that,

It is important to carry forward Chinese cultural heritage, promote the creative transformation and innovative development of fine traditional Chinese culture, and promote the prosperity of the cultural sector. (Xi Jinping, 2023 in Wei, 2023)

President Xi emphasized the importance of enhancing the nation's image in global discourse, advocating for mutual learning and exchanges between civilizations, and fully cultivating the potential and available resources of the entire nation in the cultural sector. This call aligns with the intention of enhancing China's soft power and further the influence of Chinese culture. Moreover, this introduction is perceived as a great timing as China already has a strong and abundant "hard power" which permits the nation to solidify its historical cultural wealth and enhance its confidence while furthering its "soft power" on the global stage.

Significantly, China wields soft power through societal and cultural channels, including educational linkages, international media platforms, literature, art, film, music, scholars, and sports figures. The abovementioned data emphasized that 'culture' is viewed as the heart and soul of China's soft power (Kong, 2015; Glaser & Murphy, 2009). It is considered by China as a valuable tool to increase its soft power and forward the idea that 'China is a civilized, responsible, and reliable nation". The country's cultural story is argued to be appealing hence a key to soft power development.

To summarize these key insights about culture as the primary source of China's charm offensive, these are the notable characteristics that emerge on how China utilizes culture to advance its soft power: (a) China, like other countries, advances the utilization of tools or instruments of public and cultural diplomacy (e.g., international media, academic exchange programs, international cultural and art exhibitions, and cultural institutes abroad); (b) China emphasizes the 'significance' of culture in the concept of soft power as repeatedly manifested by the statements of the country's leaders; (c) China has more pragmatic rhetoric in using culture as an instrument of power – it capitalizes on controlling the narratives that will be disseminated abroad, and filter what goes into the country; (d) China has a very less distinction between public diplomacy and propaganda; and (e) the significant function of cultural diplomacy in ensuring cultural security and domestic coherence.

Engagement in Multilateral Institutions and Its Foreign Policy

China's soft power is also manifested by its increasing leadership in multilateral institutions which include the Asian Regional Forum, the Shanghai Cooperation Organization, the Association of Southeast Asian Nations (ASEAN) Plus Three, the Forum for East Asia–Latin America Cooperation (FEALAC) and the Forum on China-Africa Cooperation (FOCAC) (Jiang, 2007). These engagements significantly revealed that the engagements of China in multilateral diplomacy have not been limited to regional or cross-regional forums; it has also been global (Lee, 2009).

Furthermore, the United Nations community and non-members perceived China as a committed peacekeeping state because of the following reasons: (1) in 2015, China was declared as the second largest contributor to the peacekeeping budget; (2) committed a considerable number of troops for the UN standby peacekeeping force; (3) announce further financing for a new UN Peace and Development Fund; (4) provides a fund (amounting to US$100M) for African peacekeeping capacity training; (5) it revealed its Peacekeeping Affairs Center in 2018; and (6) co-host different UN trainings and workshops. Additionally, China led various expert working groups on peacekeeping intelligence and peacekeeper safety and security as well as deployed more UN peacekeeping troops than all the other UN Security Council permanent members combined[3] (Fung, 2023). In terms of its ongoing economic policy known as China's Belt and Road Initiative (BRI), a grand plan to connect the world to the 'Middle Kingdom' is presented to key partners as highly beneficial and furthered by economic initiatives and incentives thus supported by various countries (Carminati, 2020).

Since the assumption of office in 2012 by President Xi Jinping, China expressed its strategic interests in Asia militarily and economically as demonstrated by this BRI. Specifically, BRI aims to build infrastructure projects designed to better connect the country to Asia, Europe, Africa, and parts of South America (Zreik, 2024b). While it brings 'fear' to some countries, it is also viewed as a non-coercive means to get things done. This BRI or investment in infrastructure helps China in developing markets for its products in the long run, enhances the relevance and power of Chinese currency, alleviates excess industrial capacity in the short run, and generally brings itself in a position to continue its economic prosperity.

With these data, it can be asserted that the opportunities for trade and exchange that come with BRI allow the manifestation of soft power. The linkages or connections will eventually lead to multiple marketplaces where experiences, goods, ideas, knowledge, or culture can be spread to various parts of the world. Fundamentally, these things are not only economic, but also intellectual, spiritual, and emotional because they convey the manner, ideology, and identity of a country.

Domestic Policies and Values

China's soft power is also determined by its means and manner of implementing policies and values domestically. The consistent enhancement of its political and economic system transformed the country into now an economic powerhouse (Gill & Huang, 2006). This remarkable economic progress conjured up images of affluence and prosperity that other countries may wish to follow – China's economic miracle presents the developing world with another probable recipe for economic success. Further, the country has started promoting diplomatic ideas which include peaceful rise and development, a harmonious world, responsible power, a new security concept, and a "good neighbor policy" (Cho & Jeong, 2008).

Specifically, on October 25, 2021, President Xi Jinping highlighted these ideas in his speech at the Conference Marking the 50th Anniversary of the Restoration of the Lawful Seat of the People's Republic of China in the United Nations.

For these 50 years, the Chinese people have stood in solidarity and cooperation with people around the world and upheld international equity and justice, contributing significantly to world peace and development…We have unswervingly followed an independent foreign policy of peace, stood firm for fairness and justice, and resolutely opposed hegemony and power politics. The Chinese people are a strong supporter of other developing countries in their just struggle to safeguard sovereignty, security and development interests. The Chinese people are committed to achieving common development…. For these 50 years, the Chinese people have upheld the authority and sanctity of the United Nations and practiced multilateralism, and China's cooperation with the United Nations has deepened steadily. China has faithfully fulfilled its responsibility and mission as a permanent member of the UN Security Council, stayed true to the purposes and principles of the UN Charter, and upheld the central role of the United Nations in international affairs. (Xi Jinping, 2021 as mentioned in Ministry of Foreign Affairs of the People's Republic of China, 2021)

The statements of President Xi convey that the country is not a threat to the stability of the existing global power system; it is instead an effective and faithful partner that performs its best in realizing collective interests. In the same speech, President Xi furthered that the global community:

Should vigorously advocate peace, development, equity, justice, democracy and freedom, which are the common values of humanity, and work together to provide the right guiding philosophy for building a better world...jointly promote the building of a community with a shared future for mankind, and work together to build an open, inclusive, clean and beautiful world that enjoys lasting peace, universal security and common prosperity...stay committed to mutual benefit and win-win results, and work together to promote economic and social development for the greater benefit of our people...and step up cooperation, and work together to address the various challenges and global issues facing humanity. (Xi Jinping, 2021 as mentioned in Ministry of Foreign Affairs of the People's Republic of China, 2021)

China has, indeed, projected itself on the global stage as a benevolent and responsible power that aims to assist struggling countries as well as the international community in attaining globally valuable goals and objectives from which every country will benefit. This is opposed to China Threat theory, which claims that due to China's rise the world's future is determined by fear, anxiety, and uncertainty because this emergence will not be peaceful as it aims to subvert the West and the present global the present global order. Particularly, these statements want to convince the world that it is a peaceful and responsible partner.

Generally, based on the collected data from various scholarly works, China derives its 'charm offensive' in the following: (a) culture – China perceives its culture as a world culture; (b) engagement in multilateral institutions and its foreign policy; and, (c) domestic policies and values.

Limits of China's Charm Offensive

Limitations of this 'charm offensive' are reflected by (a) China's decision to use an aggressive approach (e.g., military coercion) in resolving territorial disputes (e.g., the West Philippine Sea issue); (b) the lack of necessary political reforms in China; and (c) foreign policy incoherence.

China's Use of Aggressive Approach

China utilizes an aggressive approach despite its deliberate intention of advancing 'diplomacy'. It has been accused of displaying 'geostrategic bullying' in the nearby regions (Pei, 2018). Specifically, in 2013, China unilaterally announced an air defense identification zone covering the East China Sea's disputed Senkaku/Diaoyu Islands which exacerbated its tensions with Japan. Then, a year later, China has started building large artificial islands in disputed areas of the South China Sea (Royandoyan, 2023).

In December 2023, an encounter between these two countries (China and the Philippines) occurred. Manila called out China's recent actions in the South China Sea and requested that it should stop to preserve the region's stability. In the same month and year, the Philippines shared that the "China Coast Guard shot water cannons at Philippine civilian vessels situated near Scarborough Shoal that were carrying oil and food meant for fisherfolk in the area." Then, a day later another encounter happened. China used water cannons and rammed Manila's vessels on the way to a resupply mission to Ayungin Shoal. This aggression caused one of the Philippine ships "severe engine damage" (Royandoyan, 2023). Meanwhile, China responded to these issues by urging Manila to "stop provocations" implying that the responsibility lies on the Philippines' side. It further argued that the incidents happened because the Philippine vessels ignored their warnings and intentionally rammed their vessels. These were countered by Manila claiming that "Beijing disrupted its routine resupply missions to its military outposts in the South China Sea, parts of which lay within the Philippines' exclusive economic zone" (Royandoyan, 2023). These direct and indirect confrontations between these two countries have been going on and off for years already and it has been affecting the stability and security of Southeast Asia (Zreik, 2023b).

Meanwhile, regarding the matter, the United States criticized China for undermining regional stability because China's actions reflect not only a complete disregard for the safety and livelihoods of Filipinos but also a sign of disrespect for international law. According to Zreik (2020), the United States may take these issues (e.g., South China Sea and Taiwan) as opportunities to pressure China therefore furthering the divide and shaping a new world order. Principally, the involvement of the United States is a double-edged sword that complicates matters for China. As a result, China is acting more aggressively in the South China Sea in order to defend its interests as expected to how other countries would react should there be an attempt to interfere in matters close to its borders.

Also, there were anti-Chinese riots in Vietnam following the positioning of a Chinese oil drilling rig in waters claimed by both countries. In March 2023, there was an encounter between a Vietnamese ship and a Chinese vessel within Vietnam's Exclusive Economic Zone (EEZ) in the South China Sea. The incident specifically took place as "Vietnam Fisheries Surveillance vessel KN-278 chased Chinese Coast Guard (CCG) vessel CCG-5205 because it interfered with Vietnam's EEZ (Strangio, 2023). In 2016, China imposed sanctions on South Korea because it allowed the United States to deploy a missile-defense system there.

These aggressions are viewed by the international community as a clear mismatch between China's words and actions. Its policy narratives champion democracy, collaboration, and diplomacy, however, its acts toward the South China Sea and other territorial boundaries imply otherwise. This mismatch fuels distrust and doubts about the real intention of China in advancing its soft power in the region.

Need for Political Reforms Within China

Another challenge to China's charm offensive was its domestic politics which is characterized by oppression, the government's harsh handling of critics (Lee, 2009), crackdowns on nongovernmental organizations, political repression, limits to the entry of foreign ideals and censorship of domestic and international media (Albert, 2018). These issues tainted the 'image' China is wishing to present to the world – benevolent, responsible, and powerful. As a result, there is constant doubt and hesitation about the sincerity of China to take part, if not shoulder the burden of an anarchic international environment to sustain a stable and peaceful de-centered and multipolar world (where power is not concentrated in a single country).

Moreover, the country is criticized because of issues involving the overcapacity of state-owned enterprises, Xi's exhaustive anticorruption campaign, food safety issues, and environmental pollution and degradation are among the issues that dissuade other countries from following China's model (Albert, 2018). These issues exposed a very unfavorable image of the country thereby limiting the extent and effectiveness of its soft power. In this specific case, China's soft power campaign is constrained by the conflict between the image it wishes to project to the world and its actions. If these shortcomings are not addressed, it would be very difficult for China to sell the idea that it is a purveyor of attractive ideals and values.

Foreign Policy Incoherence

China is argued to have some soft power problems. According to Linetsky (2023), a research fellow at the Eurasia Group Foundation, many people in South Korea, Singapore, and the Philippines provide unfavorable perceptions of China's soft power. For example, in the Philippines, China's soft power investment is demonstrated in the forms of promoting Chinese languages, pro-Chinese media, educational exchanges, and promises of Belt and Road Initiative (BRI) investment. The country's former President Rodrigo Duterte deliberately shifted the foreign policy alignment closer to China, but the Filipinos responded otherwise. The foreign policy shift was motivated by China's promise of $24 billion in BRI funding. As a response to this, Duterte's administration was mum or silent about the 2016 Permanent Court of Arbitration ruling invalidating Beijing's claims to the South China Sea. Despite this seemingly smooth and harmonious partnership between China's ruling regime and the Duterte administration, Filipinos have a generally unfavorable perspective about China – specifically, in terms of the latter's government system, influence on the Filipinos, and contradicting policy approaches as reflected by its consistent harassment of the Philippine Navy, Coast Guard, and fishermen. The aggressive foreign policy strategy of China outweighs its economic and cultural investment and Duterte's desire to align the country's foreign policy with China's foreign policy priorities.

Another instance is Singapore with which China does not have a direct conflict. China invests heavily in this country through family networks, business associations, think tanks, media, and grassroots organizations. However, these privileges seem to be insufficient to get the overwhelming support of Singaporeans. While older Singaporeans favorably view China because of their perceived good relations and like Chinese culture, the young the young Singaporeans believe that China's soft power resources often conflict with its military objectives. It failed to build a compelling popular culture and Chinese-language media, academia, and business association-funded scholarships received criticism as these Singaporeans defended their country's system (Linetsky, 2023). Hence, despite economic incentives, some countries in the region responded by taking a very cautious approach. This seemingly soft power deficit provides the United States an opportunity to rebuild its power assets in the region by building networks of cooperation on various issues that might include economic development, environmental concerns, and political instability.

Generally, the limits on China's charm offensive rest on its inconsistent behavior in terms of dealing with territorial issues with what it is trying to advance in the global community and also, the mismatch between its policy narratives and domestic political practices. In this case, if China sincerely wants to make reliable allies in the region, it must be ready to make far greater concessions on security issues, especially territorial disputes. But, with President Xi Jinping's pledge to 'make China great again', at present, there is no indication that the country is considering such concessions. If there is something that is apparent, it would be the fact that China takes a purely tactical or strategic approach which expects purely tactical gains.

Implications of China's Charm Offensive

China's intention to further its 'charm offensive' in Southeast Asia has considerable implications for the region's stability and growth and great power contest as well as overall [global] policy implications. Discussions in this section are significantly from the author's point of view after scrutinizing the collected data.

Region's Stability and Growth

Some Southeast Asian countries (e.g., Laos, Cambodia, and the Philippines during the Duterte Administration) regard China as a benign power to be emulated as opposed to how the United States wants China to be perceived by the global community. China, in this sense, is a balancing power to the current extent of influence and dominance of the United States in the region. It is evidently one of the most important emerging powers in the region (because there is Japan and India) while the United States struggles to maintain its sphere of influence. It has significantly shaped the economic landscape of Southeast Asia as a crucial engine of regional growth through a multi-layered export production network with dynamic foreign direct investment.

Particularly, China is one of the biggest investors, aid donors, buyers, and traders in the region, hence, the region can be perceived as slowly becoming Sino-centric. These Southeast Asian countries increasingly consider Beijing for regional leadership which contributes to China's diplomacy in becoming more confident, omnidirectional, and proactive (Shambaugh, 2005). Similarly, China has become the largest aid donor, investor, buyer, and trader in a number of geopolitically valuable African countries, replacing European, American, and Japanese diplomatic soft power (Mead, 2004). These mentioned economic involvements of China in different parts of the world have been more evident when the US-led global financial crisis in 2008 happened (Altman 2009). These considerable and valuable roles provided China with an important set of mechanisms and opportunities to wield its influence in bilateral relations as well as on multilateral level. However, despite these advantages of partnerships from various angles, the region is undeniably in the midst of a power tug-of-war between China and the United States.

Great Power Contest in the Region

Some scholars (e.g., Kivimäki, 2014; Kugler, 2006) asserted the stable and enduring 'peace' in Asia which defied expectations about [the possibility of] world war (Friedberg, 1994; Kaplan, 2014) and seemed likely to highlight further progress in the region. However, these arguments seem less assuring in today's geopolitical context because there has been a consistent debate and prediction that the United States and the People's Republic of China (PRC) are in an inevitable conflict that is likely to end in a war (Allison, 2017; Zreik, 2020) and the possible playground [of this great game politics] is Southeast Asia.

According to Sperling (2007), a considerable number of US pundits and policymakers perceived China as the US geostrategic competitor in Asia (particularly in East, Central, and Southeast Asia). China, on the other hand, is always mindful of the actions, behaviors, and policies of the United States in the region. This indicates that the Southeast Asia states are now completely caught amid the 'coalface' of great power politics.

For several years, the United States (US) has been widely viewed as a benign power in Southeast Asia but, recently, it has been criticized for the shortsightedness of its policy towards the region, particularly, the shaky and inconsistent attention American policymakers extend. Despite the United States' historical ties (important security, economic, political, and strategic ties) with the region, it has benignly neglected the area and its needs and growth potential. Specifically, under President Donald Trump, the US shifted away its strategic attention from the Southeast Asian region compared to the period of Obama's presidency. This situation led to discontentment in some Southeast Asian countries which forced them to consider strengthening their relations with China (Stepanov, 2022).

With this significant change in the regional landscape concerning the United States and some Asian countries, it is still worth noting that some of these countries still distrust the intentions of China for reasons of historical enmity and interference, geographical proximity, territorial disputes, and rising economic competition. Their leaders might have removed the idea of the "China threat" from their foreign policy considerations or rhetoric but, the "China challenge" remains. Southeast Asian leaders worry about the territorial issue in the West Philippine Sea, other border issues with Indonesia and Vietnam, and the possible confrontation between the United States and China over Taiwan (Goh, 2008).

Essentially, Southeast Asia's strategies involve engaging both China and the United States through a country-to-country effort and recognition of the relevance of multilateral institutions politically and economically. These efforts are aimed at facilitating closer economic ties, creating political and security dialogues, cooperation, and exchanges, and fostering military exchanges and relationships with the two major powers and other major regional players such as India, South Korea, and Japan. With these assertions, the Southeast Asian countries apparently adopted a broader and multidirectional strategy in dealing with both the United States and China (Goh, 2008). Yet despite available resources at disposal in dealing with the great power contest in the region, Southeast Asian countries are also wary about a potential transition of the current power bloc system toward an unstable multipolar global system with a number of major powers competing against one another. Particularly, Indonesia and Malaysia were worried about the dominance of China in the region as Singapore is more concerned about Japan.

Apparently, these countries differ on how they perceive China and the United States' role in the region but, they are all concerned about the destabilizing consequences of an awkward U.S.-Japan alliance and problematic U.S.-China relations. To hedge against the possibility of turmoil and other security concerns, Southeast Asian countries have decided neither to pick sides nor to become hostile against certain great powers, but rather to accommodate all different major powers in the strategic affairs of the region (Goh, 2008). Whether or not this approach brings more benefits than costs, Southeast Asian countries might believe that, at present, this is the most strategic and convenient option for them.

Policy Implications

Based on the collected data, China's charm offensive is a double-edged sword; it may contribute, as a positive force multiplier, to maintaining peace and stability in Southeast Asia while China strives to attain its foreign policy goals and purposes and, it may also jeopardize region's stability and peace as it continues to play the game of prestige politics and assert its narrow and self-interested national priorities with the goal of reducing the influence of the United States in the region.

In terms of President Xi's foreign policy projects, while these can be generally perceived as multiple opportunities for economic prosperity (tools for providing an economic alternative for countries that feel marginalized by the current global order), frustrations and disappointments are increasing due to China's aggressive political ambitions and unfulfilled promises. Hence, this 'charm offensive' may only work favorably in a short period of time due to China's inconsistent policies and behavior as well as contradicting actions domestically and internationally – simply, the charm may backfire.

At this point, it is essential to note that while there are Southeast Asian countries (e.g., Laos, Cambodia) endorsing China's geopolitical role and influence in the region, other countries remain uncertain and hesitant to consider China as an offensive front in the great power politics. They do not want to be caught in the crossfire of this geopolitical tug-of-war between China and the United States hence, they usually opt not to choose a side (hedging strategy) as much as possible. While they benefit economically from China and Western states, these countries prioritize diversified economic ties and further regional partnerships to avoid heavy reliance on any single country. Further, it must be noted that these countries are more likely to respond based on various factors which may include threat perceptions, historical accounts, geographical elements, and economic incentives hence, while most of them received economic advantages from various initiatives of China, the region, in general, might consider curtailing the influence of the BRI if China consistently exploits the region to further its political ambitions (e.g., West Philippine Sea and debt trap diplomacy). Taking these points into account, one undisputable truth remains - Southeast Asia is a very strategic playing field of future trade and geopolitical game which may facilitate different visions and realities. It is at the frontier of a new era of great power rivalry in the form of US-China strategic competition. Hence, this region remains a crucial and interesting subject of various discourses concerning power contest or game politics, security, and alliances.

On the other hand, given the trend and implications of China's charm offensive in the Southeast Asia region, the United States may revisit its soft power resources as well as existing economic and security architectures to discourage, if not counter the evident aggressive tendencies of China and compels it to embrace multilateralism instead. The United States may utilize its available power resources to encourage China to take on a responsible great-power role that champions regional expectations. Simply, it must offer a strategic response to China's charm offensive without overreacting to China's laudable initiatives.

These points crucially highlight that the international system is viewed as inherently competitive thus, Chinese and Western/US soft powers are always argued to be in a conflictual relationship with very little chance for cooperation or coexistence. However, this situation eventually forwards a reflective reminder that everyone must be taken into account - viewing the rise of China through its charm offensive as a zero-sum game, that is, a gain in Chinese soft power is interpreted as a loss of Western/US soft power might mislead the international community in making sense of the current global power dynamics. As such, it necessitates a comprehensive and holistic scrutinization of the entire issue instead of directly reducing the matter to a 'zero-sum game' politics.

Another crucial point that can be extracted is that soft power is a necessity in today's global game. Specifically, a world or dominant power must be a world cultural power also that can present big and valuable ideas, values, and beliefs that are attractive and appealing to the rest of the world. Because failure to attain this requirement will make the major power status vulnerable to various challenges hence, its power development is difficult to sustain. In this sense, soft power does not simply emerge out of material-based power, but must be purposefully cultivated and built up. Further, it must be taken into account that an effective projection of soft power is highly dependent on a state's economic and technical capabilities to portray a benevolent image and the country's economic, political, and military resources that make its claims of national success credible to other states. Significantly, soft power heavily relies on credibility.

FUTURE RESEARCH DIRECTIONS

Future studies may consider an in-depth assessment of the effectiveness of China's Charm offensive in terms of expanding its influence and countering negative perceptions or enhancing its global image since the scope of this paper is very limited. Further, researchers may also explore the regional variations as to China's utilization of its charm offensive, and countries in different regions may have responded differently to this soft power effort.

While this paper cited a very minimal discussion about public opinion towards China, future research works may conduct comparative surveys, media analysis, and qualitative research across countries to collect comprehensive data as to how the global public perceives the soft power resources of China or examine how China leverages digital platforms to shape narratives and engage with global audiences and how sustainable charm offensive is as an approach or strategy.

CONCLUSION

China's increasing economic dominance as well as recognition as another military and political power is often viewed as the decline of United States prestige and influence in Southeast Asia. It is furthered by the belief that China's charm offensive (China's soft power), if consistent as to its accomplishments, will eventually wear down the United States' strategic position in the region. If this happens, the capacity of the United States to deter Chinese aggressive actions in the Taiwan Strait, in the South/East China seas, and the Korean Peninsula will decline.

China initially invested resources (and still investing) in its hard power but, with the current geopolitical trends and realities in Asia, it is capitalizing on its 'soft power' resources known as the 'charm offensive'. This soft power is derived from its culture, engagement in multilateral institutions, [its] foreign policies, and domestic policies and values. However, limits are imposed by China's aggressive approach in some matters in the region, the need for political reforms within the country, and its foreign policy incoherence.

The increasing presence and involvement of China's charm offensive in the region imposes various consequences on the region's stability and growth, highlights great power contests, and provides policy implications. Significantly, the seemingly different extents of influence in the region are an offshoot of the asymmetrical power relations between the United States and China. However, China might enjoy certain advantages should it consistently and sincerely invest in cooperative diplomacy and multilateralism to limit the United States' influence in the region while simultaneously enhancing its military capabilities. This is primarily because, despite China promoting its 'charm offensive' it will still utilize hard power in the future, specifically, in desperate situations involving the Korean Peninsula, the South China Sea, East China Sea, or Taiwan Strait. These [inevitable] realities may force the United States to revisit the extent and effectiveness of its hard and soft power in the region. In China's charm offensive, US soft power is important in forming as well as maintaining a circle of democratic Asian states that can limit China's aggressiveness.

Ultimately, soft power is as valuable and influential as hard power in terms of realizing a country's strategic interests. Wielding this power may bring gains and, at the same time, costs – it is a double-edged sword where its usefulness lies in how the user utilizes this power.

ACKNOWLEDGMENT

This research received no specific grant from any funding agency in the public, commercial, or not-for-profit sectors.

REFERENCES

Albert, E. (2018). *China's Big Bet on Soft Power*. Council on Foreign Relations. Retrieved from: https://www.cfr.org/backgrounder/chinas-big-bet-soft-power

Allison, G. (2017). *Destined for war: Can America and China escape Thucydides's trap?* Houghton Mifflin Harcourt.

Altman, R. (2009, January/February). A Weakening of the West. *Foreign Affairs*, *88*(1), 2–14.

Carminati, D. (2020). *The State of China's Soft Power in 2020*. E-International Relations. Retrieved from: https://www.e-ir.info/2020/07/03/the-state-of-chinas-soft-power-in-2020/

Chang, E., & Kim, N. (2016*). The Myth of Soft Power in Asia*. E-International Relations. Retrieved from: https://www.e-ir.info/2016/05/24/the-myth-of-soft-power-in-asia/#_edn11

De Castro, R. (2007, December). The Limits of Twenty-First Century Chinese Soft-Power Statecraft in Southeast Asia: The Case of the Philippines*. *Issues & Studies*, *43*(4), 77–116.

Freeman, C. W. Jr. (1997). *Arts of Power: Statecraft and Diplomacy*. United States Institute of Peace.

Fung, C. J. (2023). *China's Small Steps into UN Peacekeeping Are Adding Up*. IPI Global Observatory. Retrieved from: https://theglobalobservatory.org/2023/05/chinas-small-steps-into-un-peacekeeping-are-adding-up/

Gill, B., & Huang, Y. (2006). Sources and Limits of Chinese "soft" power. *Survival*, *48*(2), 17–36. doi:10.1080/00396330600765377

Glaser, B. S., & Murphy, M. E. (2009). Soft power with Chinese characteristics. In C. McGiffert (Ed.), *Chinese soft power and its implications for the United States: competition and cooperation in the developing world: a report of the CSIS smart power initiative* (pp. 10–26). CSIS.

Goh, E. (2008). Great Powers and Hierarchical Order in Southeast Asia: Analyzing Regional Security Strategies. *International Security*, *32*(3), 113–157. doi:10.1162/isec.2008.32.3.113

Heng, Y. (2009). Mirror, mirror on the wall, who is the softest of them all? Evaluating Japanese and Chinese strategies in the 'soft' power competition era. *International Relations of the Asia-Pacific*, *10*, 275–304. doi:10.1093/irap/lcp023

Hoey, J. (2007). *The Global Reach of Chinese Soft Power China's Rise and America's Decline? Naval Postgraduate School, Monterey, California* (Unpublished Thesis).

Hwang, E. (2008). *China's Soft Power and Growing Influence in Southeast Asia. Naval Postgraduate School, Monterey, California* (Unpublished Thesis).

Jain, S., & Chakrabarti, S. (2023). The Yin and Yang of China's Power: How the Force of Chinese Hard Power Limits the Quest and Effect of Its Soft Power. *Asian Perspective*, *47*(1), 145–166. doi:10.1353/apr.2023.0006

Jia, Q. (2010). *Continuity and Change: China's Attitude tward Hard Power and Soft Power*. Brookings. Retrieved from: https://www.brookings.edu/articles/continuity-and-change-chinas-attitude-toward-hard-power-and-soft-power/

Jiang, W. (2007). Hu's Safari: China's Emerging Strategic Partnerships in Africa. *China Brief*, 7(4), 50–64.

Kaplan, R. D. (2014). *Asia's cauldron: The South China Sea and the end of a stable Pacific*. Random House.

Kivimäki, T. (2014). *The long peace of East Asia*. Ashgate.

Kong, D. (2015) *Imaging China: China's cultural diplomacy through loan exhibitions to British museums* (Thesis PhD). School of Museum Studies University of Leicester.

Kugler, J. (2006). The Asian Ascent: Opportunity for Peace or Precondition for War? *International Studies Perspectives*, 7(7), 36–42. doi:10.1111/j.1528-3577.2006.00228.x

Kurlantzick, J. (2007). *China's Charm Offensive in Southeast Asia*. Retrieved from: https://carnegieendowment.org/2007/04/24/charm-offensive-how-china-s-soft-power-is-transforming-world-pub-19126

Lai, H. (2012). China's cultural diplomacy: going for soft power. In L. Hongyi & L. Yiyi (Eds.), *China's soft power and international relations* (pp. 83–103). Routledge Taylor & Francis Group. doi:10.4324/9780203122099-11

Lane, J. E., & Ersson, S. (2016). *Culture and politics: A comparative approach*. Routledge. doi:10.4324/9781315575452

Lee, M., & Hao, Y. (2018). China's unsuccessful charm offensive: How South Koreans have viewed the rise of China over the past decade. *Journal of Contemporary China*, 27(114), 867–886. Advance online publication. doi:10.1080/10670564.2018.1488103

Lee, S. (2009). *China's Soft Power: Its Limits and Potentials*. Issue Briefing No. MASI 2009-07.

Linetsky, Z. (2023). *China Can't Catch a Break in Asian Public Opinion*. Foreign Policy. Retrieved from: https://foreignpolicy.com/2023/06/28/china-soft-power-asia-culture-influence-korea-singapore/

Liu, T.-T. T. (2018). *Public Diplomacy: China's Newest Charm Offensive*. E-international Relations. Retrieved from: https://www.e-ir.info/2018/12/30/public-diplomacy-chinas-newest-charm-offensive/

Lum, T., Morrison, W., & Vaughn, B. (2008). *China's "Soft Power" in Southeast Asia*. CRS Report for Congress.

Mead, W. R. (2004, March/April). America's Sticky Power. *Foreign Policy*, (141), 46–53. doi:10.2307/4147548

Ministry of Foreign Affairs of the People's Republic of China. (2021). *Speech by H.E. Xi Jinping President of the People's Republic of China at the Conference Marking the 50th Anniversary of the Restoration of the Lawful Seat of the People's Republic of China in the United Nations*. Retrieved from: https://www.fmprc.gov.cn/eng/zxxx_662805/202110/t20211025_9982254.html

Nye, J. (2004). *Soft Power: The Means to Success in World Politics*. Public Affairs.

Nye, J. (2005, Dec. 5). Soft power matters in Asia. *The Japan Times.*

Ørmen, J., Helles, R., & Bruhn Jensen, K. (2021). Converging cultures of communication: A comparative study of Internet use in China, Europe, and the United States. *New Media & Society, 23*(7), 1751–1772. doi:10.1177/14614448211015977

Pie, M. (2018). *The limits of China's charm offensive.* The Strategist. Retrieved from: https://www.aspistrategist.org.au/the-limits-of-chinas-charm-offensive/

Royandoyan, R. (2023). *Philippines urges restraint following South China Sea clash.* South China Sea. Retrieved from: https://asia.nikkei.com/Politics/International-relations/South-China-Sea/Philippines-urges-restraint-following-South-China-Sea-clash

Shambaugh, D. (2005). Return to the Middle Kingdom? China and Asia in the Twenty-First Century. In D. Shambaugh (Ed.), *Power Shift: China and Asia's New Dynamics* (pp. 23–47). University of California Press.

Shambaugh, D. (2015). China's Soft-Power Push: The Search for Respect. *Foreign Affairs, 94*(4), 99–107.

Sperling, J. (2007). The United States: The Unrelenting Search for an Existential Threat in the 21st Century. In Global Security Governance: Competing Perceptions of Security in the 21st Century. Routledge.

Statista. (2021). *Total number of Confucius Institutes and Confucius Classrooms worldwide from 2013 to 2018.* Retrieved from: https://www.statista.com/statistics/879340/china-confucius-institutes-and-confucius-classrooms-worldwide/

Stepanov, A. S. (2022). *US Policy towards Southeast Asia: from Barack Obama to Joe Biden.* doi:10.1134/S10193316222210183

Strangio, S. (2023). *Vietnamese, Chinese Vessels in Close South China Sea Encounter.* The Diplomat. Retrieved from: https://thediplomat.com/2023/03/vietnamese-chinese-vessels-in-close-south-china-sea-encounter/

Ullah, C. (2015). *China's Soft Power: Changing the World Perception. Naval Postgraduate School, Monterey, California* (Unpublished Thesis).

Wei, X. (2023). Xi's Thought on Culture put forward. *China Daily.* Retrieved from: https://www.china-daily.com.cn/a/202310/09/WS6522ef3ca310d2dce4bb96d5.html

Zheng, W. (2023). *Will culture be China's most important addition to Xi Jinping Thought?* China Politics. Retrieved from: https://www.scmp.com/news/china/politics/article/3237272/will-culture-be-chinas-most-important-addition-xi-jinping-thought

Zreik, M. (2023a). Digital Burnout in Second Language Acquisition: Exploring Challenges and Solutions in the Chinese Context. In A. Kurt (Ed.), *Perspectives on Digital Burnout in Second Language Acquisition* (pp. 169–194). IGI Global. doi:10.4018/978-1-6684-9246-8.ch008

Zreik, M. (2023b). Stirring Up Soft Power: The Role of Chinese Cuisine in China's Cultural Diplomacy. In K. Kankaew (Ed.), *Global Perspectives on Soft Power Management in Business* (pp. 292–306). IGI Global. doi:10.4018/979-8-3693-0250-7.ch015

Zreik, M. (2024a). Massive Chinese Investments in Latin America: What Is Taiwan's Diplomatic Fate in That Region? In C. R. Veney & S. O. Abidde (Eds.), *China and Taiwan in Latin America and the Caribbean. Studies of the Americas* (pp. 201–226). Palgrave Macmillan. doi:10.1007/978-3-031-45166-9_9

Zreik, M. (2024b). Assessing the Integration of Blockchain and Supply Chain Management: The Case of China. In M. Khan, N. Khan, & A. Ghouri (Eds.), *Achieving Secure and Transparent Supply Chains with Blockchain Technology* (pp. 38–56). IGI Global. doi:10.4018/979-8-3693-0482-2.ch003

ENDNOTES

[1] 'Charm Offensive' refers to the kind of soft power or growing attractiveness of China that is "conveyed through various means, including culture, diplomacy, participation in multinational organizations, businesses' actions abroad, and the gravitational pull of its economic strength" (Kurlantzick, 2007).

[2] By the end of 2018, a total of 548 Confucius Institutes and 1,193 Confucius Classrooms were established in the world based on the recent data of Statista. (2021). https://www.statista.com/statistics/879340/china-confucius-institutes-and-confucius-classrooms-worldwide/

[3] China deployed 2,227 troops (2.92 percent of overall troop deployment to UN peacekeeping); the United States: 36 troops (0.05 percent); the United Kingdom: 394 troops (0.52 percent); Russia: 87 troops (0.11 percent); France: 736 troops (0.97 percent) as of February 28, 2023. Source: (United Nations (UN) Data on Peacekeeping Contributions in Fung, 2023)

Chapter 13
Soft Power Competition:
A Comparative Analysis of China and the US in South Asia

Md. Obaidullah

https://orcid.org/0000-0003-2380-4557

Daffodil International University, Bangladesh

Md. Showkat Raihan

University of Barishal, Bangladesh

ABSTRACT

In the current multipolar world, China has emerged as a formidable competitor to the United States, employing soft power strategies to expand its influence, particularly in South Asia—a region of strategic importance for both nations. This study utilizes Joseph Nye's soft power theory to comparatively analyze the approaches of China and the US. Employing case study analysis, including document research and content analysis, the research reveals that China strategically utilizes soft power by promoting its culture in educational institutions and leveraging the Belt and Road Initiative (BRI) for trade infrastructure development in South Asia. Conversely, the US relies on its renowned education system, attracting students from the region, and implements soft power through foreign aid, trade, investment, and security cooperation. As the global order undergoes transformations, comprehending these soft power dynamics is crucial for deciphering the intricacies of contemporary international relations.

INTRODUCTION

Hegemony has dissipated, and the global landscape is no longer bipolar. Following the Soviet Union's collapse in the 1990s, multipolarity emerged. Presently, power is not confined to a single or dual nation; instead, numerous countries exhibit comparable power and capability (Ashford & Cooper, 2023; Dee, 2015; Varisco, 2013). Consequently, the dynamics of power in international relations have evolved into a more intricate and multifaceted paradigm. Power is no longer solely reliant on military strength or economic dominance (Bloor, 2022). In recent times, experts talk about two types of power: "hard" and

DOI: 10.4018/979-8-3693-2444-8.ch013

"soft." Hard power comes from military and economic strength, while soft power is about persuading others to share your values and goals for global order and security. The idea to distinguish between these concepts was first introduced by Nye (Nye, 2017).

As the global stage witnesses a paradigm shift towards nuanced diplomacy, the strategic deployment of soft power has become a paramount instrument in a nation's arsenal. Since the end of the Cold War, the ascent of China over the last three decades has been remarkable across economic, military, cultural, and political dimensions, alongside a notable presence in the international arena (Roland, 2021). The escalating influence of China is widely recognized as the "most geopolitically significant development of this century" for both Western and non-Western nations. Undoubtedly, China possesses the preeminent global hard power, exemplified by its formidable military. Nevertheless, it is actively seeking methods to transcend this hard power preeminence in order to execute a more remarkable "soft power" campaign (Islam, 2022).

Moreover, the United States has also been implementing a soft power strategy, even though it still relies significantly on its formidable hard power capabilities (deLisle, 2020). China has harbored enduring geopolitical, strategic, and economic interests in South Asia. Conversely, India and China have maintained a strained relationship, while the United States and India share overlapping vital national interests, including the promotion of peace and stability in South Asia, the combatting of international terrorism, and the prevention of the spread of weapons of mass destruction. The US desires strong allies in this area to impede China's elevation in the Indo-Pacific region. The region: South Asia, known for its geopolitical significance and cultural diversity, serves as a fertile ground for the exercise of soft power (Zreik, 2022). As China's Belt and Road Initiative extends its reach and the US recalibrates its foreign policy in the Indo-Pacific, the competition for influence in South Asia takes center stage. So, both China and the US have interests in South Asia to safeguard their influence and interests.

The rationale for this study lies in its potential to contribute to the understanding of contemporary global politics, with a specific focus on the strategic competition unfolding in South Asia. By dissecting the soft power strategies of China and the US, the study aims to offer valuable perspectives on the evolving geopolitical landscape, regional power dynamics, and the implications for both the countries involved and the broader international community.

This research aims to explore the soft power competition between two powerful competitors, China and the United States, within South Asia. It delves into their soft power strategies and conducts a comparative analysis.

LITERATURE REVIEW

The competition for soft power has become increasingly significant in the context of global geopolitics, with China and the US emerging as major contenders (Winkler & Nye, 2005). Soft power is defined as the ability to shape and influence others through political values, cultural elements, and legislation. Additionally, it refers to the capacity to impact and shape the opinions and behaviors of others by appealing to their interests and values, rather than resorting to force or financial incentives (Nye, 2019). Several previous studies indicate that the soft power of China and the United States has a significant impact on the South Asian region.

SOFT POWER COMPETITION BETWEEN CHINA AND US

China's Soft Power in South Asia

China's strategic pursuit of expanding influence in South Asia is intricately connected to the deployment of soft power (Berdiyev & Can, 2020). Chinese leaders consistently travel to Bangladesh, Nepal and Sri Lanka, affirming their ongoing commitment to actively engage in the affairs of South Asia (Malik, 2001). Importantly, the resurgence and revitalization of China in in this region are not linked to military tactics, but rather to a long-term commitment to cultural inclusivity (Chakrovorty, 2020). The country aims to build an optimal balance of power in South Asia and the surrounding waterways to limit the expansion of India (Mohan & Abraham, 2020). Also, China is looking to expand its influence in South Asia through the Belt and Road Initiative (BRI), particularly through projects such as the China-Pakistan Economic Corridor (CPEC) (Sharma & Khatri, 2019). The expanding influence of China in Pakistan, primarily through diplomatic initiatives and development aid, is an important aspect in this region (Hussain & Mehmood, 2018).

Apart from that, China seeks to expand its soft power in Bangladesh by highlighting its inclusive cultural strategy and promoting mutually beneficial relations (Chakrovorty, 2020). The extent of its cultural impact on Bangladesh is determined by factors such as the level of press freedom, the economic involvement, development initiatives, and the societal prosperity (Sparks, 2018). Besides, the "String of Pearl" strategy by China is one of the determinants of Bangladesh's present stance (Mannan, 2019). The primary reason for employing soft power is to facilitate the reshaping of Beijing's geopolitical alliances, thus expediting its ascent to a global power position (Huang & Ding, 2006).

United States' (US) Soft Power in South Asia

The use of Hollywood films, notably the Rocky tales, was a strategy for projecting U.S. soft power during the Cold War (Dautbašić, 2022). The provision of increased aid by the United States government elicits favorable reactions in terms of individual-level evaluations in seven Asian countries, namely China, Malaysia, Japan, Sri Lanka, India, Thailand, and South Korea (Kim, 2009).

The dissemination of the United States' soft power within each state has a notable impact on diminishing the perceived immediacy of the threat posed by China (Machida, 2010). The US utilizes a multifaceted approach in South Asia to exert its soft power, which encompasses cultural, economic, and military aspects. This strategy aims to oppose China's influence and uphold its own regional supremacy (Rashid & Ikram, 2023). Expressing significant apprehension at China's increasing influence through non-military means in the area, the US has been actively investigating strategies to counteract it (Yao, 2009). Moreover, it is capitalizing on Indian skepticism against Chinese policies to gain support against China in the South Asian region (Afridi et al., 2022).

Furthermore, the US grants duty-free tariff protection to specific components from designated developing nations as a way of exerting its soft power in trade (Blanchard & Hakobyan, 2015). This practice was previously implemented in several South Asian countries, including Bangladesh and India, suggesting a commitment by the U.S. to exert its soft power influence in this region (Kathuria, 2022).

On the contrary, our current understanding reveals a gap in scholarly exploration regarding the soft power strategies of the US in this region. Notably, recent observations indicate a growing U.S. involvement in the internal affairs of specific countries within South Asia. Moreover, the differences between the US and China's soft power approaches in this region is remained unexplored. Consequently, our paper aims to fill this void by scrutinizing and comparing the soft power strategies employed by China and the United States in the South Asian context.

THEORETICAL FRAMEWORK

The theoretical framework for this study is based on soft power. It serves as the foundation for understanding how states can influence others through attraction and persuasion rather than coercion (Nye, 2017; Nye, 1990). Nye asserts that *"Soft power relies on the capacity to influence the preferences of others."* He simplifies this notion by stating that, *"In practical terms, soft power equates to the power of attraction."* However, he deliberately excludes economics from the scope of soft power, regarding national economic strength as a coercive asset. He aligns it with hard power, contending that both economic sanctions and military might serve to intimidate defiant nations. Nye emphasizes culture, political values, and a nation's foreign policies as the primary components of soft power. Conversely, some analysts broaden the concept, incorporating the power of economic allure — termed as *"sticky"* power — within the realm of soft power. This perspective denotes influence that proves challenging to relinquish once drawn into its sphere (Mead, 2004).

Another scholar Joshua Kurlantzick offers a deeper exploration of the concept by highlighting the evolving nature of soft power. He explained that soft power has evolved beyond military realms, now encompassing popular culture, public diplomacy, and seemingly coercive tools in economic and diplomatic arenas, like aid, investment, and multilateral engagement (Kurlantzick, 2007).

According to (Nye, 2004) three fundamental components through which a nation can project its soft power: political values, especially when practiced both domestically and internationally; cultural values that resonate with other societies; and foreign policies, particularly effective when perceived as possessing moral authority and enjoying legitimacy. Indeed, Nye presents four tools for exerting soft power: values, culture, policies, and institutions.

The study's observations align with the framework: China strategically employs soft power by promoting its culture in educational institutions. This resonates with Nye's emphasis on cultural values as a component of soft power. Moreover, China's use of the BRI for infrastructure development aligns with the evolving debate on whether economic engagement, like the BRI, falls within the realm of soft power. This contrasts with Nye's exclusion of economics from soft power. But similar to the opinion of (Kurlantzick, 2007).

Our study also notes the U.S.'s emphasis on its education system and aid provisions. This corresponds with Nye's concept of attracting students through educational excellence and employing policies like foreign aid for soft power projection. However, China's focus on cultural education and infrastructure development differs from the U.S.'s emphasis on educational appeal, aid provisions, and broader strategic engagements. This illustrates the divergence in their soft power approaches. Both China and the U.S. leverage elements of Nye's soft power components: China emphasizing cultural values and infrastructure while the U.S. focuses on education, aid, and strategic engagements.

METHODOLOGY

This study outlines the case study analysis, which includes archival research and content analysis. Data triangulation and the case study method constitute the primary methodologies utilized in this book chapter. These methodologies are pivotal in assessing the validity and reliability of the research data, aligning with Berg et al.'s (2004) contention about the critical aspects of trustworthiness in case study research (Berg et al., 2004). This encompasses considerations of generalizability, reliability, and objectivity. In addition, research observations and a robust theoretical framework serve as indispensable tools in substantiating the credibility of the research (Bryman, 2008).

This study is qualitative in nature. Qualitative research method delves into real-world issues (Moser & Korstjens, 2017), offering in-depth insights by addressing the how's and whys rather than focusing on how many or how much (Aspers & Corte, 2019; Jackson et al., 2007). The qualitative research endeavors to comprehensively understand the soft power literature and conduct a comparative analysis of China and the US's soft power strategies. Additionally, it aims to identify and compare the strategies of China's soft power approach in contrast to that of the US in South Asia. The research uses a triangulating qualitative method to examine and assess issues and fundamental questions with the two methodological components: content analysis, document, and literature analysis.

Qualitative Content analysis "It is a research method for the subjective interpretation of the content of text data through the systematic classification process of coding and identifying themes or patterns" (Hsieh & Shannon, 2005). This type of analysis extends beyond word counting or extracting factual content from texts. Instead, it delves into uncovering meanings, themes, and patterns—both apparent and underlying—in specific texts. This approach enables researchers to grasp social realities in a subjective yet scientific manner. It is a method of analyzing written, verbal, or visual communication messages (Cole, 1988). Downe-Wamboldt (1992) provided an extensive definition, stating that "content analysis, as a research method, represents a systematic and objective approach for describing and quantifying phenomena (Downe-Wamboldt, 1992)." In order to find out the contents regarding the soft power strategy of China and the US in South Asia, the qualitative secondary data has been collected from the previous literature related to soft power, China and the US's soft power strategy, content analysis of documents, and media sources, interviews, focus groups, and case studies, document analysis, and observation.

Steps of Content Analysis

These steps are derived from a combination of two sources (Hurst, 2023; Zhang & Wildemuth, 2005) and the author's synthesis.

Document analysis served as a key methodology to investigate China and the US's soft power influence in the South Asian region. Stokes (2003) posited that *"document analysis is extensively utilized in the humanities, social sciences, as well as in media and cultural industries research. (Stokes, 2003)"* Within this chapter, this method played a pivotal role in acquiring primary and secondary data. It facilitated the identification of information concerning the regulatory environment, historical and present soft power strategies, and gaps within existing academic discourse. Various sources including policies, regulations, and reports related to the cultural, political, and economic engagements of China and the US with South Asia were accessed.

Three types of documents are focused on:

Figure 1. Steps of content analysis

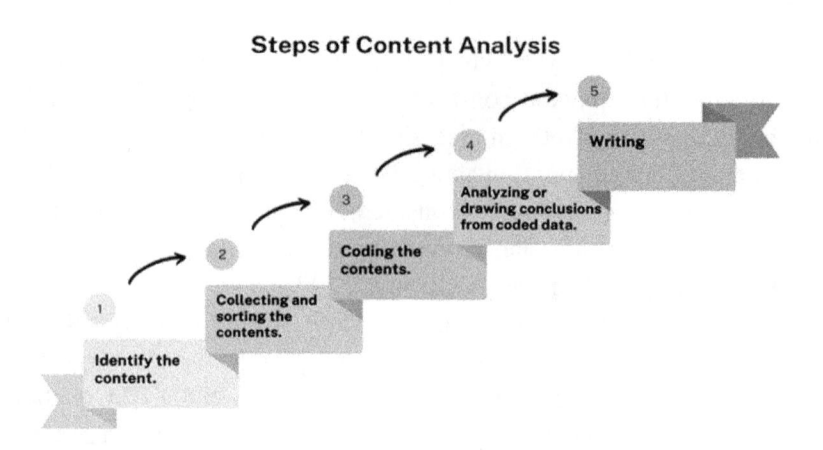

- Academic works and national reports.
- The policies, litigations, and regulations issued by governmental offices, notably those disseminated by state institutions like ministries and state press publications.
- Non-academic publications encompassing documents, assessments, reports, working papers, internet-based articles from journals, newspapers, magazines, and blog entries.

SOFT POWER STRATEGIES OF CHINA IN SOUTH ASIA

Overview of China's Soft Power Approach

Culture as a Soft Power Tool

Culture is indeed a vital tool for wielding soft power. China, too, harnesses this approach, utilizing cultural instruments like the Chinese language, traditional, and contemporary cultures to project its soft power. Cultural diplomacy is seen as an effective strategy not only to enhance understanding of China's ideals but also to reinforce its economic goals and fortify national security through subtle and lasting means (You, 2018; Zreik, 2024a). In recent years Chinese leaders are also emphasizing to push their culture as a soft power.

We must enhance culture as part of the soft power of our country to better guarantee the people's basic cultural rights and interests. The great rejuvenation of the Chinese nation will definitely be accompanied by the thriving of Chinese culture.

The statement was articulated by former Chinese President Hu Jintao during the 17th National Congress of the Chinese Communist Party in 2007. This marked the initial explicit declaration by China concerning its employment of soft power as a foreign policy instrument (China Today, 2007). At the outset, China commenced its emphasis on applying its culture as a form of soft power, primarily directed towards safeguarding the rights and interests of its populace.

In 2014, President Xi Jinping outlined China's ambition to enhance its soft power by spreading its culture and popularity, aiming to advance the idea of the "Chinese Dream" and the "China Model. (Islam, 2023)" He stated, *"We should increase China's soft power, give a good Chinese narrative, and better communicate China's message to the world."* Even, China's financial commitment to its soft power diplomacy was estimated at approximately $10 billion annually (Albert, 2018). Moreover, China's top leadership has advocated for significant reforms within its soft power framework. This strategy has led to the integration of additional platforms, including internet celebrities, into China's soft power toolkit (Jinping, 2017).

China perceives its culture as inherently a global heritage (Gill & Huang, 2006), rooted in a profound and ancient civilization spanning millennia. This heritage manifests in remarkable architectural wonders like the Great Wall and the Forbidden City, as well as in its diverse artistic expressions, spanning calligraphy, painting, Peking opera, and dragon dances.

Apart from that, an integral component of China's strategy for soft power lies in its cuisine, recognized globally as one of the most popular and influential (Zreik, 2023). Chinese culinary artistry, renowned for both its quality ingredients and health benefits, is celebrated for its rich and complex flavors. Elevating Chinese cuisine serves as a means to showcase the country's cultural diversity and richness. As part of its soft power initiatives, the Chinese government and affiliated organizations actively propagate the appreciation of Chinese cuisine worldwide. Notably, the China Cuisine Association plays a pivotal role by fostering international collaboration among chefs and actively promoting Chinese culinary traditions. Through its initiatives, this association has significantly contributed to disseminating knowledge and fostering enthusiasm for Chinese cuisine on a global scale (Demgenski, 2020).

Confucius Institute and Soft Power

China possesses a rich history of soft power epitomized by the legacy of Confucius. His philosophy, deeply rooted in the principles of soft power, advocates for the promotion of harmony, obedience, and benevolence. Confucius believed that leaders employing moral influence rather than physical force would garner the affection of the populace and wield a more significant long-term impact.

Aligned with this ideology, China has established Confucius Institutes (CIs) globally, commencing in 2004 (Chaziza, 2023). These educational entities serve as hubs for disseminating Chinese language and culture, thereby fostering multiculturalism, and playing a pivotal role in the cultivation of a harmonious global community. These Institutes, along with various Chinese nongovernmental organizations linked to the state through the Ministry of Education, offer an array of cultural courses. Such as: Mandarin language instruction, tutorials on traditional Chinese culinary arts, teaching Chinese calligraphy, and orchestrating celebrations for Chinese national holidays. Essentially, these Institutes mirror counterparts in cultural diplomacy, such as the British Councils (Britain), Alliance Française (France), Goethe Institutes (Germany), Yunus Emre Institutes (Turkey), and Cervantes Institutes (Spain). The Confucius Institute typically collaborates with universities, providing substantial annual support of at least $100,000 for programs, while Confucius Classrooms are predominantly established within primary and secondary educational institutions (Albert, 2018). Over 540 Confucius Institutes have been established in 160 countries (Ekstrom, 2021). According to another study, China has established more than 700 Confucius

Table 1. Number of Confucius Institutes worldwide

Region	Number of Institutes
Asia	132
Europe	189
Africa	71
America	130
Oceania	20
Total	542

Institutes and Confucius Classrooms worldwide, strategically aimed at promoting its language and culture (Hartig, 2012).

The Evolution of Chinese Educational Excellence and Soft Power

In conjunction with its swift economic advancement and expanding political influence globally, China is actively advancing its soft power capabilities through education, considering it a pivotal instrument to enhance its influence on the international stage. This has been achieved through the implementation of two primary strategies. Firstly, by establishing Chinese educational institutions across various nations worldwide. Secondly, by offering enticing programs and providing support through scholarships for students globally, encouraging their enrollment in Chinese universities (Markleku, 2019).

Over time, China has emerged as one of the foremost global destinations for a myriad of international students pursuing undergraduate, graduate, and postgraduate studies. Chinese universities are recognized for delivering high-quality higher education. As per the 2024 Times Higher Education ranking, China boasts seven universities within the top 100 globally. Many students finance their studies in China through self-funding or partial funding. However, the China Scholarship Council (CSC) extends full free scholarships to international students pursuing undergraduate or postgraduate studies in the country. Notably, in 2018, China accommodated an impressive count of 492,185 international students from 205 countries, marking a substantial increase from the figures in 2010 (Biney & Cheng, 2021). Please refer to the table below for detailed statistics.

The Belt and Road Initiative (BRI): A Catalyst for China's Soft Power

China has effectively utilized its economic prowess to extend its soft power influence. Among the most significant undertakings in the history of human civilization is the inception of the Belt and Road Initiative (BRI) by Chinese President Xi Jinping in 2013 (Clarke, 2017). This ambitious initiative seeks to enhance connectivity across continents, fostering partnerships among the 150 signatory nations of the BRI, particularly in Asia, Europe, and Africa. The primary objective of the BRI project is to bolster inter-regional and intercontinental connectivity through an interconnected network encompassing roads, railways, pipelines, and ports.

Indeed, the ambitious establishment of the BRI is recognized as an integral component of China's soft power foreign policy strategy, aimed at expanding its influence on the global political stage. Scholars perceive China's efforts as a modern revival of the ancient Silk Road (Garlick, 2020; Hobson &

Table 2. Number of international students in China

Year	International Students
2010	265090
2011	292611
2012	328330
2013	356499
2014	377054
2015	397635
2016	442773
2017	489200
2018	492185

Zhang, 2022; Ling, 2020; Mishra, 2020). Albert (2018) delineates the financial commitment to these international endeavors, noting that China allocated $50 billion to the Asian Infrastructure Investment Bank during its inception, constituting half of the bank's initial capital. Additionally, Beijing pledged $40 billion for its Silk Road Fund, $25 billion for the Maritime Silk Road, and an additional $41 billion to the New Development Bank established by BRICS states: Brazil, Russia, India, China, and South Africa (Albert, 2018).

The goal of the project is for China to forge new connections while reinforcing existing bilateral relationships. The BRI holds the potential to serve as a catalyst in enticing other nations to foster stronger bilateral connections with China. This capability lies in its capacity to cultivate trust among participating countries, recognized as a crucial element by scholars in defining China's "soft power. (Islam, 2023)"

Injecting "Soft Power", Vaccine Diplomacy, and COVID-19

While the emergence of the deadly COVID-19 pandemic was undoubtedly a curse, it inadvertently presented China with an opportunity to advance its soft power strategy through humanitarian aid, drawing significant attention from the international media. The Chinese government characterized its response as *"the most intensive and wide-ranging emergency humanitarian operation since the founding of the People's Republic of China in 1949"* (Fengyuan, 2020). Notably, this isn't the first instance; China has played pivotal humanitarian roles during previous crises, including the SARS outbreak in 2003, the 2004 Tsunami, the 2015 Nepal earthquake, and the Ebola outbreaks in 2014 and 2018.

By March 2020, China had furnished COVID-19 response equipment, including N95 respirators, ventilators, personal protective gear, and test kits, to 120 countries and 4 international organizations. Additionally, Chinese municipalities donated medical supplies to over 50 cities worldwide and dispatched medical staff to nations like Cambodia, Laos, Myanmar, the Philippines, and Pakistan to aid in the pandemic response (Xinhua, 2020a, 2020b). Chinese companies specializing in medical equipment manufacturing extended donations to over 100 countries (Hossain, 2021). Prominent Chinese philanthropists, including the Jack Ma and Alibaba foundations, played pivotal roles in COVID-19 responses by dispatching medical supplies to over 100 countries across Africa, Asia, and the Middle East. As well, they translated and distributed diagnostic manuals in eight languages through various internet platforms, including social media and Google (Sellen & Jaumont, 2020) China even supplied complimentary vaccines to the United States' close allies, shipping over 115 million vaccine doses to various nations. This action posed a significant challenge to the traditional perception of US exceptionalism. Consequently, countries started pivoting towards China instead of the US.

Hence, China has broadened its soft power diplomacy by leveraging existing platforms like the Belt and Road Initiative (BRI), including initiatives like the Health Silk Road, to extend COVID-19 aid to 120 states (Escobar, 2020). Thus, the pandemic outbreak has accelerated Chinese endeavors to assert a more prominent global leadership role (Guardian, 2020). This COVID-19-driven soft power initiative of China has notably surged in developing regions heavily indebted to Beijing, where China holds substantial investments (Hossain, 2021).

International Media

International Media significantly shapes the global narrative surrounding a country's image. Recognizing this, Beijing has made substantial investments in Chinese international media outlets, encompassing radio, television, and print media. The establishment of these affiliated outlets has granted China access to a wider global audience, allowing the country to highlight its positive yet often overlooked global initiatives in peace and development. For instance, the government-owned media agency, Xinhua, has experienced rapid expansion, boasting branches in 170 foreign bureaus, with plans to reach 200 by 2020 (Albert, 2018). Moreover, the launch of the China Global Television Network (CGTN) in December 2016 further augmented China's media reach. CGTN operates six channels, including two in English, as well as Spanish, Russian, Arabic, and French, with broadcasting teams spanning across more than 70 countries worldwide, covering all continents (Ye & Albornoz, 2018; Zreik, 2024b).

Soft Power Strategies of China in South Asia

China is extending its influence both towards the east and west. However, its focus lies in its neighboring regions including South Asia. This region encompasses eight countries: Afghanistan, Bangladesh, Bhutan, India, Maldives, Nepal, Pakistan, and Sri Lanka. The country also extends its influence over the Indian Ocean, especially its eastern parts, which have implications for the entire region. China's connections to this area have deep historical roots predating the establishment of the People's Republic in 1949 (USIP, 2020). But at the start of this century, China's connections with South Asia quickly intensified using soft power as part of its wider push to engage globally.

Chinese Culture and South Asia

China takes pride in its diverse and ancient cultural heritage. When a country celebrates a culture that promotes shared values and interests, it fosters appealing and obligational relationships, thereby enhancing the likelihood of achieving desired goals (Nye, 2004). Moreover, China's "cultural soft power" is thought to be appealing due to its distinctive nature, potentially mitigating adverse external perceptions that view China's rise as threatening (Lai & Lu, 2012).

China is advancing its cultural soft power in South Asia through three primary approaches. Firstly, it employs formal official programs directed at enhancing China's global image through policies and initiatives that facilitate the long-term development and export of cultural products. Secondly, it engages

Figure 2. Number of Confucious Institutes in South Asia

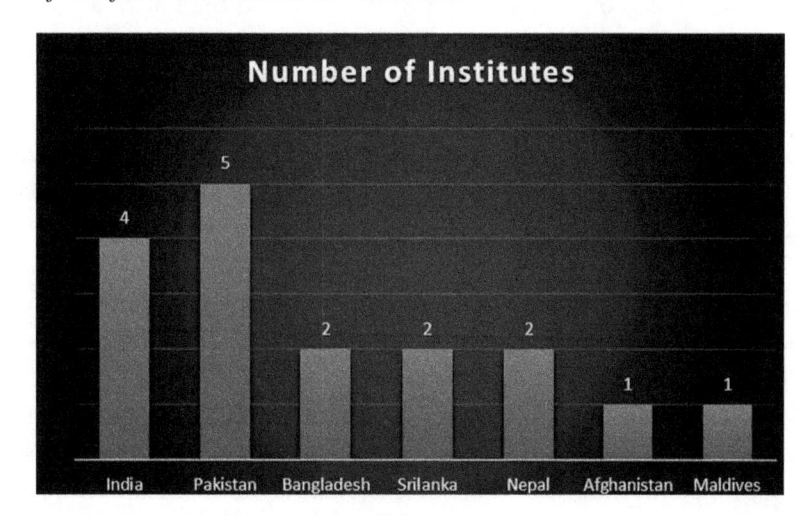

in international cultural exchange programs, promoting various forms of arts, entertainment (such as movies), cuisine, and more. Thirdly, it actively encourages the Chinese language and encourages the study of China.

China primarily disseminates its language and culture through the Confucius Institute, serving as a pivotal medium. This is evident in its efforts to engage smaller South Asian nations, with 17 institutes established across the region. For instance, Nepal welcomed first Confucius Institute in June 2007 (Chinese Embassy, 2007), complemented by a China Study Center in Jhapa (east Nepal) to support local entrepreneurs' interactions with China. Sri Lanka's University of Kelaniya integrates Chinese culture into its credit award system through the Confucius Institute. Similar institutes have been established in Afghanistan, Bangladesh (at the University of Dhaka and North South University), and other South Asian nations. Expanding its reach, China Radio International (CRI), the state-owned overseas broadcaster, launched on-air Confucius Institutes in the Maldives, Pakistan, Sri Lanka, Bangladesh, and Nepal, fostering deeper cultural and educational connections in South Asia (Pal, 2021).

Education as a Soft Power Tool

In the 21st century, alongside its growth in hard power, including military and economic prowess, China has strategically emphasized particularly in education as soft power (Duan & Qiu, 2023). Higher education stands as a crucial platform for propagating Chinese culture, language, and civilizational values not only within the South Asian region but also on a global scale.

Nepal, situated uniquely between India and China in South Asia, experiences influence from both nations. However, China has effectively utilized education as a soft power tool within Nepal. Several schools in Nepal have integrated mandatory Chinese-language courses, supported by the Chinese government covering teachers' salaries (The Times of India, 2019). By 2019, an estimated 6,400 Nepali students were pursuing studies in China, contributing to a continuous influx of technocrats and experts trained there into Nepal's professional circles, potentially shaping a generational pattern (Pal, 2021). A total of 71 Nepali students were awarded Chinese government scholarships for studies in Chinese universities in the 2023/2024 academic year (Xinhua, 2023).

China is implementing the geointellect model in Pakistan and Sri Lanka as part of its expanding educational and research endeavors catalyzed by The Belt and Road Initiative (Jain, 2022). The China Scholarship Council (CSC) has established a memorandum of understanding (MOU) with Pakistan's Higher Education Commission (HEC). This collaboration aims to identify approximately 1,000 college teachers or scientific researchers to pursue doctoral studies at Chinese higher education institutions. According to the Chinese Ministry of Education, there are over 28,000 students currently enrolled in China, positioning Pakistan as the third-largest source of international students in the country (The Express Tribune, 2019). This surge in Pakistani students can be attributed to preferential policies initiated by the Chinese government following the introduction of the China Pakistan Economic Corridor (CPEC). Additionally, 24 students from Sri Lanka were awarded scholarships by the Chinese government to study in China annually. By 2023, this number had increased to 40 (Ceylon Today, 2023). China actively engages with Bangladesh through scholarships and educational programs. Bangladeshi students are offered summer courses in China, visits to the Confucius Institute, and journalists receive funded fellowships. Newspapers collaborate with the Chinese embassy to discuss BRI benefits. Notably, 55 Bangladeshi students secured the Chinese Government Scholarship for the 2023-2024 academic year (The Business Standard, 2023). Also, an estimated 20,000-25,000 Indian students are studying in China currently (Venugopalan & Verma, 2020).

BRI: Economic Collaboration and Soft Influence

Economic engagement, perceived as facets of soft power, is the key tool employed by China through the Belt and Road Initiative (BRI). China's economic prowess notably surged following the global financial crisis of 2008, bolstering its appeal (Li et al., 2012). China's focus on promoting a stable regional environment is partly driven by its ambition for sustained economic growth.

Engaging with South Asia economically serves multiple purposes, particularly as several underdeveloped regions in Western China share proximities with South Asian nations. Xinjiang shares borders with Afghanistan and Pakistan, while Tibet borders Nepal, Bhutan, and the northeastern part of India. China's imperative to develop its western regions propels efforts to forge stronger economic ties with neighboring South Asian countries.

China-Bangladesh bilateral engagement started in early 1979s. Under the framework of the Asia-Pacific Trade Agreement (APTA), China removed tariff barriers on 84 types of commodities imported from Bangladesh, including jute and textiles (chief exports of Bangladesh). The landlocked Yunnan province of China has sought economic cooperation with Bangladesh to help gain access to the Bay of Bengal. The country has become a major investor in Bangladesh in sectors such as textiles, power generation, and construction, with investments made under the Belt and Road Initiative (BRI) (Baghernia & Meraji, 2020). According to data from The Observatory of Economic Complexity, China stood as the primary source of imports for Bangladesh in 2021, amounting to $24.1 billion. Recently, in the backdrop of strained relations between Bangladesh and the United States, where the U.S. has been exerting pressure on Bangladesh to ensure fair, credible, and human rights-centered elections (Kugelman, 2023), China has emerged as a supportive partner to Bangladesh in this context (Krishnan & Bhattacherjee, 2023).

The data from the William and Mary Global Research Institute illustrates a substantial increase in aid and credit commitments from Beijing to Dhaka. Specifically, the annual aid and credit disbursements, which amounted to $994 million from 2014 to 2017, witnessed a remarkable upsurge, reaching US$3.4 billion between 2018 and 2021 (Rahman, 2023). According to the data of Bangladesh Bank, Chinese loans in the nation's private sector amounting to slightly over $2.33 billion, with a significant portion allocated to the power and energy sector (Noyon, 2023).

In Nepal, China has extended concessional loans and provided economic as well as technical assistance. Chinese officials, leaders, journalists, and academics frequently visit Nepal as part of their public diplomacy initiatives. Moreover, China is actively involved in the development of rail networks, hospitals, polytechnic institutes, and communication infrastructure within Nepal. In 2011, both nations signed the Agreement on Economic and Technical Cooperation, and concurrently, the China-Nepal Youth Exchange Mechanism was officially inaugurated (Hazarika & Mishra, 2016).

The free trade agreement (FTA) between Pakistan and China was initially signed in 2006. Subsequently, Chinese corporations, such as China's Mobile, have made significant investments in Pakistan, an investment of US$1.7 billion, reportedly generating 41,700 employment opportunities. Presently, approximately 10,000 resident Chinese personnel are involved in various business ventures across Pakistan. Furthermore, The CPEC, valued at $62 billion in Chinese investments in Pakistan, is a pivotal initiative. Beijing continues to invest extensively to bolster China's soft power, aiming to foster a positive image among BRI partner nations, including Pakistan. Pakistan's English-language press actively promotes China's goodwill, emphasizing its cultural contributions, diplomatic support, and investments. This approach aligns with China's evolving stance on India-Pakistan disputes, increasingly favoring Pakistan to curb Indian influence in Asia rather than maintaining a neutral position (Ittefaq et al., 2023).

By the late 2000s, China became Sri Lanka's top donor, providing a consistent annual aid of over $1 billion since 2008, without imposing conditions tied to internal governance reforms. This robust economic relationship saw significant Chinese investments in various mega projects, including the Hambantota Port. By 2011, China became the largest source of Foreign Direct Investment (FDI) in Sri Lanka, surpassing Japan, and took the lead as the principal provider of development assistance (Singh, 2021). Notably, a concessional loan of $500 million was granted to support Sri Lanka's efforts in combating the pandemic. Additionally, the Chinese government and associated companies engaged in major projects in Sri Lanka contributed masks, Personal Protective Equipment (PPE), and test kits (Tewari, 2021). China's proactive involvement, in contrast to the absence of America and inaction from India, has significantly amplified its goodwill in Sri Lanka.

China and Afghanistan have shared a longstanding historical relationship, maintaining ties from ancient times to the present. During critical junctures like the Soviet and US invasions in Afghanistan, China remained remarkably supportive of Afghanistan. Post the US withdrawal and a devastating earthquake in Afghanistan, China extended substantial humanitarian aid, offering $7.5 million in assistance. Expressing gratitude, the Taliban acknowledged Chinese officials' support in a press conference during this period. In a significant move, China appointed Zhao Xing as its Ambassador in Afghanistan in September 2023, the first appointment after the Taliban's 2021 victory, although without formal recognition of the Taliban government, signaling China's interest in deepening relations. Diplomats serving as Ambassadors in Kabul were appointed before August 2021, distinguishing China's approach from other nations that designated individuals as charge d'affaires after their ambassadors' terms expired. China's recent $10 billion agreement with the Taliban, securing access to lithium deposits, aims to create 120,000 employment opportunities and support infrastructure development. Moreover, in May 2023, China, Pakistan, and Afghanistan agreed to extend the CPEC as part of the BRI into Afghanistan, an expansion plan initially proposed in 2017, illustrating ongoing efforts to integrate Afghanistan into regional economic initiatives (Obaidullah, 2023).

THE US'S SOFT POWER STRATEGY

Overview of the US's Soft Power Approach

Movies as a Soft Power Tool of the US

Numerous countries have invested in their film industries to build cultural soft power tool. Movies are the most viable means of communication by transmitting images, stories, culture, and values to worldwide audiences (Crane, 2014a; Vlassis, 2016). Therefore, American music, film, and television asserted significant sway, prevailing within local markets across a spectrum of nations, spanning from India to Indonesia (Kurlantzick & Minxin, 2006). The largest film industry in Hollywood in the US which is renowned worldwide for its captivating and dazzling movie to the world.

The Hollywood film industry serves as an archetype, effectively showcasing how the United States can propagate its societal norms and values on a global scale (Edelstein, 2022; Nye, 2008). These films serve to portray the US as a "universal nation," comprised of immigrants engaged in cultural exchange (Zoysa & Newman, 2002), while also suggesting that foreign social and political lifestyles can align with American values (Sun, 2008). So, Hollywood cinema portrays the American way of life as a form of global culture, emphasizing liberty as a universal value (Crane, 2014b). This depiction has contributed to heightened global recognition and receptivity toward American ideals.

When individuals watch Hollywood movies like *"Pearl Harbor," "The Pianist," "The Patriot," and "Saving Private Ryan,"* they often resonate with the narrative that implies America's neutrality during the Second World War. Similarly, in numerous American movies themed around World War II such as *"Operation Rogue" and "Tears of the Sun,"* there's a recurring use of storytelling strategies that portray Americans as global saviors, liberators, and rescuers of refugees from dictatorial regimes. This pattern underscores a prevalent theme of Americans depicted as those who save the world, champion freedom, and offer salvation to those oppressed by dictators (Barrech & Khan, 2023). Additionally, audiences may perceive Japan and Germany as aggressors during wartime, potentially leading to negative attitudes toward these nations and their people. In more extreme cases, such portrayals in movies could foster adverse sentiments among viewers towards Japan and Germany.

Similarly, during the Cold War, the US utilized its film industry to counter Communism led by the Soviet Union. The Hollywood movie "Ninotschka," became the most popular film promoting the US's official ideology of anti-communism. The US government enacted the "Smith-Mundt Act" and "Motion Picture Production Code" to utilize the film industry in disseminating American values against communist countries (Hussain, 2021).

Cultural Diplomacy

The US uses cultural diplomacy to promote American ideals of individuality, tolerance, and opportunity. The Bureau of Educational and Cultural Affairs uses cultural diplomacy to forge lasting connections between the US and other countries (The Bureau of Educational and Cultural Affairs, 2023). It achieves remarkable results with a budget of around $770 million, raising global connections by granting Americans exposure to international artists while sharing America's vibrant performing and visual arts culture worldwide (Hochberg, 2023). Government-sponsored cultural initiatives primarily aim to cultivate relationships beyond U.S. borders, ensuring open access to American culture encompassing movies, fashion, and ideas. Programs like the Fulbright exchange is pivotal in amplifying U.S. soft power through cultural exchanges (Bettie, 2015b). Additionally, the U.S. prioritizes media and the export of pop culture, which has transcended to become a significant component of global popular culture.

Education Is (Soft) Power

There are two educational avenues through which the US utilizes as tools of soft power. The first involves attracting talented students to study within the United States. The US is home to nearly 5000 universities, hosting a significant number of top-ranking institutions globally. As per the Times Higher Education World University Rankings 2024, 36 American universities are positioned within the top 100, with 7 of these universities securing spots among the top 10 worldwide (The Times Higher Education, 2023). The Pew Research Center conducted a survey in 16 advanced economies, revealing that a median of 59% of adults across these societies regards US universities as the best in the world (Silver, 2021). Despite the ongoing tensions between the US and China, Chinese students comprised roughly one-third of all international students enrolled at U.S. colleges and universities, totaling approximately 370,000 students, according to data gathered by IIE before 2020 (Nuwer, 2023).

Another method involves establishing branches of U.S. universities in various countries. The initiative to propagate American-style higher education stands as one of the enduring and longstanding elements of U.S. foreign policy. Currently, there are approximately 70 American-style universities situated in different countries, with the Middle East region hosting the highest number of such institutions. Universities shifted their focus and expanded their roles to engage in philanthropic endeavors, particularly in fields like health, education, and social development. This philanthropic effort aimed to bolster the soft power of the US within universities by delivering tangible benefits to students and their families (Gautam et al., 2023). Even, approximately 300 current and former heads of state were educated in the U.S., highlighting education as a service export that influences global leadership (Hochberg, 2023).

Media's Influence on Soft Power Dynamics

Media: radio, television, and social media, serves as a pivotal instrument for the United States to wield soft power, promoting its own ideology while impeding the dissemination of opposing ideologies such as those from Russia or China (Mavrodieva et al., 2019; Rugh, 2017). This strategic utilization of media traces its origins to World War II seen in initiatives like Voice of America, aimed at countering Nazi propaganda. Subsequently, this practice expanded during the Cold War era with the establishment of Radio Free Europe (RFE), an outlet geared towards combatting the proliferation of communism (Sowiński, 2023).

Initially supported by the CIA and denounced by the Soviet Union as U.S. propaganda, RFE played a significant role in disseminating information within Eastern European nations where local media was censored and dissent was suppressed. RFE's reporting spotlighted the contributions of exiled intellectuals and artists, along with news concerning pro-democracy movements and notable Soviet shortcomings like the Chernobyl nuclear disaster. These efforts strategically aligned with U.S. interests by discrediting the Soviet government and undermining communism as a viable political ideology.

Foreign Assistance

In pursuit of advancing their national interests and bolstering soft power internationally, governments frequently allocate resources, including financial aid, goods, and services, to other nations (Blair et al., 2022). The US exemplifies this practice, demonstrated in its post-World War II assistance to Europe through the Marshall Plan. This initiative aimed not only to aid in the reconstruction of Europe but also to curtail the spread of communism in the region (Grünbacher, 2012; McCourt & Mudge, 2023). The alignment of interests between the U.S. and Europe in reinforcing democratic principles and containing communism led to a convergence of goals, significantly enhancing America's soft power influence. Through U.S. support, nations like Germany and Japan successfully recuperated from the devastations of World War II, concurrently fostering strong economic ties and security alliances advantageous to the US. Notably, 11 out of the United States' current top 15 trading partners were once beneficiaries of U.S. foreign assistance (Runde, 2020).

Apart from that, the establishment of the U.S. Peace Corps in 1961 under President John F. Kennedy marked a pivotal step in deploying American humanitarian workers globally. Beyond its primary mission of aiding development initiatives, the Peace Corps was explicitly founded to cultivate a better understanding of American culture and values in the countries where its volunteers served. Over its history, more than 240,000 Americans have participated in the Peace Corps, contributing their services across 142 countries (US Embassy, 2023b).

Soft Power Strategies of the US in South Asia

Within the spectrum of US multilateral institutions, bilateral relationships have assumed a significance commensurate with that of ballistic missiles and aircraft carriers. This connotes the elevation of soft power to a level of importance akin to hard power within the US strategic purview. In the Indo-Pacific, the Biden administration has taken significant steps through soft-power initiatives: boosting ties with Vietnam, strengthening trilateral cooperation with the US, Japan, and South Korea, reinforcing the US-Philippines alliance, and expanding diplomatic presence throughout the Pacific (Krishnamoorthi, 2023). South Asia is vital for the US due to its strategic trade position, its role in fighting terrorism, supporting democracy, protecting human rights, and balancing power to counter China's influence in the broader Asian landscape (Smith, 2022).

Education and Cultural Exchange

Education stands as a tool through which the US leverages its soft power in the South Asian region. Given the prestige of the US education system as a global leader, students from India, Pakistan, and Bangladesh pursue various levels of higher education—ranging from bachelor's to doctoral degrees—both through fully funded scholarships and self-financed means. In line with the utilization of education as a tool of soft power, there has been a notable surge in the enrollment of international students from South Asian nations in the US. Specifically, the figures reveal a significant rise in the number of Indian students, marking a 35% increase, reaching a record high of 268,923 in 2022/23 (The Hindu Business Line, 2023). Moreover, Bangladesh has experienced a remarkable 300% increase in the number of students studying in the US over the past decade, solidifying its position as the 13th top sending country of origin for US students (Palma, 2023). Furthermore, there has been a substantial sixteen percent increase in the count of Pakistani students pursuing education in the United States in 2023 (Radio Pakistan, 2023).

Moreover, the Fulbright scholarship, a prominent initiative of the US, serves as a magnet for graduate students, budding professionals, and artists globally, inviting them to pursue studies and research there. Operating across over 160 countries, the program annually bestows approximately 8,000 Fulbright scholarships worldwide. Since its establishment, the Program has generously supported more than 400,000 students globally. In Bangladesh, about 650 scholars have availed themselves of this opportunity to study in the US, while in India, the program has benefited over 25,000 students and scholars. Additionally, 4,100 individuals from Pakistan have received Fulbright grants. The overarching aim of this program is to foster mutual understanding and cultivate amicable and peaceful relations between the people of the United States and those from other nations (Bettie, 2015a; Gallarotti, 2022).

Additionally, the US has set up 650 Spaces across 150 countries globally. These American Spaces serve as inviting hubs where visitors can engage and familiarize themselves with American culture through a variety of programs, lectures, and resources such as books, movies, and magazines (US Embassy, 2023a). These Spaces, hosted within embassies, schools, libraries, and other collaborating institutions worldwide, serve as essential platforms for disseminating information and encouraging active engagement through diverse activities. Moreover, alongside these initiatives, the burgeoning popularity of Hollywood movies in South Asia has significantly escalated, contributing to the cultural influence and outreach efforts in the region (Govil, 2021).

Assistance for South Asian Nations

Foreign assistance remains a fundamental soft power tool for the US, with USAID spearheading diverse projects across South Asia. These initiatives span health, education, infrastructure, and economic development, aiming to enhance lives and foster goodwill towards the US. Notably, the US stands as the fourth-largest official development assistance (ODA) donor in India, with a contribution of $132.3 million. In specific terms, the US Government through the USAID provided $64.59 million in 2021 and $10.28 million in 2022, while Johns Hopkins University allocated $12.41 million in the same period (US Government, 2023). Particularly during the pandemic, USAID has played a pivotal role, allocating over $200 million to support India's COVID-19 relief and response efforts (USAID, 2022).

In the landscape of Asian aid recipients, Bangladesh holds a pivotal position, having received over eight billion dollars from the US in the last five decades, aimed at enhancing the country's quality of life (US Department of State, 2022). The US has notably been a leading supporter in responding to the Rohingya refugee crisis, extending humanitarian aid to both the refugees and the host communities within Bangladesh. Furthermore, Bangladesh has emerged as a significant beneficiary of U.S.-donated COVID-19 vaccines via COVAX. Moreover, since the pandemic's onset in March 2020, the United States has contributed over $121 million in additional COVID-19-related assistance to Bangladesh (US Department of State, 2022). Alongside, while the US stands as the second-largest official development assistance (ODA) donor in Pakistan, providing a substantial $236.6 million, its contribution to Sri Lanka amounts to $54 million.

Trade and Investment Partnerships

Promoting trade and investment between the US and South Asian nations fosters economic interdependence and creates shared interests. Such as, the US stands as the largest importer of Bangladeshi products. In 2022, U.S. goods imports from Bangladesh totaled $11.2 billion, showcasing a notable increase from $8.3 billion in 2021 (US Department of State, 2022). Conversely, Bangladesh's imports in 2022 amounted to $3.0 billion, marking a significant surge of 26.0 percent ($612 million) from the figures recorded in 2021 (USTR, 2023a). In 2021, the US also stood as Bangladesh's primary export partner.

In 2022, the trade between the United States and India reached an estimated $191.8 billion, with exports valued at $73.0 billion and imports at $118.8 billion. Additionally, U.S. FDI in India amounted to $51.6 billion in 2022, marking a 15.1 percent increase from the previous year (USTR, 2023b). Conversely, the US has consistently served as Pakistan's largest export market, importing over $5 billion in Pakistani goods in 2021, surpassing imports from any other country. Besides, it has maintained a significant role as a leading investor in Pakistan for the last two decades. In the latest fiscal year, U.S. direct investment in Pakistan escalated by 50 percent, reaching its highest point in over ten years (US Department of State, 2022b).

Security Cooperation

Joint military exercises and training programs not only foster trust and cooperation but also bolster regional security. Over five decades, the US and Bangladesh have maintained amicable diplomatic ties and collaborated on various security matters, encompassing border and maritime security, counterterrorism efforts, peacekeeping, defense trade, and the development of defense institutions. Since 2014, the country has allocated $78.45 million in Foreign Military Financing (FMF) and $14.5 million in International Military Education and Training (IMET) aid to Bangladesh. Within the FMF assistance, $54.8 million has been directed to bilateral programs, while $23.6 million has supported the Bay of Bengal Initiative Regional FMF (US Department of State, 2023). Through the Department of State's Bay of Bengal Initiative, facilitated by FMF aid, efforts aim to enhance the capabilities of both civilian and military entities in detecting illicit activities within their borders and the wider region. This initiative focuses on fostering networks, promoting cooperation for information sharing, building prompt response capacities to counter illicit activities, and supporting partners in establishing a rules-based order within the Indian Ocean Region.

Continuing the strategic trajectory, the United States designated India as a Major Defense Partner in 2016. This designation led to India's elevation to Strategic Trade Authorization tier 1 status in 2018, granting the country license-free access to a broad spectrum of military and dual-use technologies regulated by the Department of Commerce. Over the years, the PM Bureau has actively supported the substantial growth of defense trade with India, escalating from negligible figures in 2008 to surpassing $20 billion in 2020. India's engagement in the International Military Education and Training (IMET) program has been consistent, with annual funding of at least $1 million since 2003 (US Department of State, 2021).

On the other hand, the enduring relationship between Pakistan and the US dates back to the 1950s. During the two-decade War on Terror, US military bases in Pakistan served as access points, primarily for logistics, relief operations, and as launching platforms for drone missions (Woods, 2011). Pakistan falls within the operational ambit of the United States Central Command (USCENTCOM), with the Afghanistan-Pakistan Center of Excellence operating under its purview, focusing on operational analysis within Pakistan and Afghanistan (formerly recognized as the AfPak theatre). Presently, there are no active US bases within Pakistan.

COMPARATIVE ANALYSIS BETWEEN SOFT POWER STRATEGIES OF THE US AND CHINA IN SOUTH ASIA

The rivalry for dominance in South Asia between China and the United States is an intricate and diverse matter (Afridi et al., 2022). Both countries emphasize the importance of higher education as a means to enhance their global influence, offering opportunities for foreign students (Thao, 2020; Yang, 2010). Higher education generates essential soft power in the linked global community, enabling negotiation in the face of new challenges (Li, 2018). Moreover, the US aimed to establish hegemony over China through the implementation of tariff and non-tariff measures, resulting in a conflict over trade (M. Hussain & Mehmood, 2018). The consequences of this competition have wide-ranging effects: influencing the stability of diplomatic affairs in South Asia (Tehseen, 2017). The rapid economic expansion and growing military power of China seem to be strategically directed at countering the US in the South Asian region (Khuhro, 2019). However, this competition for supremacy in South Asia poses a potential threat to triggering instability in the region (Tehseen, 2017).

In South Asia, China strategically employs soft power by leveraging its rich cultural heritage to cultivate a favorable perception. This approach involves establishing various language and cultural centers, notably exemplified by the Confucius Institutes. Additionally, higher education plays a pivotal role in disseminating Chinese culture, language, and civilizational principles. Annually, China offers scholarships to students from nations in this region—such as Pakistan, Bangladesh, India, and Sri Lanka—facilitating cultural exchange and promoting its values and language among the younger generation in these countries.

China's engagement in South Asia extends beyond cultural efforts through investments, aid, and infrastructure projects, positioning itself as a significant economic and diplomatic player in the region. At the heart of its influence lies the flagship program BRI, functioning as a pivotal economic tool and a widely discussed soft power mechanism employed by China. Through BRI, China strategically implements investments, aid, and infrastructure development, shaping the economic and diplomatic dynamics of South Asia.

Similarly, the US utilizes education as a soft power tool, leveraging its renowned education system and numerous top-ranked universities. Many students from India, Pakistan, and Bangladesh pursue fully funded scholarship opportunities in the US, which also offers extensive part-time job prospects. Moreover, the Fulbright scholarship, a prominent initiative, attracts graduate students, emerging professionals, and artists globally, aiming to foster mutual understanding and cultivate amicable relations between the US and other nations. Additionally, the US has established America Spaces, serving as inviting hubs for visitors to engage with American culture through diverse programs, lectures, and resources like books, movies, and magazines.

The US employs foreign assistance effectively as a soft power tool, providing aid in health, education, infrastructure, and economic development to enhance lives and foster goodwill. Notably, the US has been a leading supporter in responding to the Rohingya refugee crisis, extending humanitarian aid to both the refugees and host communities within Bangladesh, earning global acclaim. Promoting trade and investment between the US and South Asian nations enhances economic interdependence and fosters shared interests. The US maintains strong bilateral relations with India, Bangladesh, Pakistan, and Sri

Lanka. Finally, security cooperation, such as providing monetary assistance for military strengthening and training, contributes to enhancing US soft influence in the region.

CONCLUSION

In this chapter, we have delved into the intricate landscape of global power dynamics within the context of a multipolar world. The emergence of numerous influential powers has reshaped international relations, leading to a nuanced discussion surrounding the notions of hard power and the more recently introduced concept of soft power. While hard power remains a conventional approach, the inception of soft power gained prominence in the 1990s, despite its practical and theoretical existence before that period. The historical shift from the United States' hegemonic position to China's rising competition underscores the evolving global order. Amidst this transition, the region of South Asia has emerged as a pivotal arena for both these powerhouses due to its significance in trade, security, geopolitical positioning, and strategic interests.

Notably, both the United States and China have actively adopted soft power strategies within the South Asian context. This chapter aimed to comprehensively explore and analyze these strategies, offering a comparative understanding of their applications.

China strategically employs soft power tactics in South Asia through the promotion of Chinese culture in educational institutions and universities, attracting students from countries including Bangladesh, India, Pakistan, Sri Lanka, and Nepal. Additionally, China utilizes the Belt and Road Initiative (BRI) to expand trade infrastructure and bolster commercial activities across the region. In contrast, education serves as a pivotal tool through which the United States exerts its soft power in South Asia. Benefiting from the esteemed reputation of the US education system on the global stage, students from India, Pakistan, and Bangladesh pursue various levels of higher education in the United States. Moreover, the US significantly contributes foreign aid to this region, alongside employing strategies involving trade, investment, and security cooperation.

This dichotomy between China's emphasis on cultural education and infrastructure development and the US focus on educational appeal, substantial aid provisions, and strategic engagements underscores the divergent soft power approaches adopted by these nations in extending their influence and interests within the crucial South Asian landscape.

Through this exploration, we endeavor to contribute to the broader discourse on international relations, power dynamics, and the strategic maneuvering of key global actors in one of the world's most crucial regions. As the global order continues to evolve, understanding and analyzing these soft power strategies become increasingly vital in deciphering the complexities of contemporary international relations. This study acknowledges certain limitations concerning the evaluation of the comparative effectiveness of soft power strategies between countries in the South Asian region and the exploration of challenges faced by these nations. The examination of which country's soft power holds greater influence in the region and an in-depth analysis of the challenges encountered were not within the scope of this research.

REFERENCES

Afridi, M. K., Anjum, N., & Abbas, Z. (2022). Comparative Study of the US and China's Policies towards South Asia in the 21st Century: Implications for Pakistan. *Global Foreign Policies Review*, *V*(III), 14–22. doi:10.31703/gfpr.2022(V-III).02

Albert, E. (2018, February 9). *China's Big Bet Soft Power*. Council for Foreign Relations (CFR). https://www.cfr.org/backgrounder/chinas-big-bet-soft-power

Ashford, E., & Cooper, E. (2023, October 5). Yes, the World Is Multipolar. *Foreign Policy*. https://foreignpolicy.com/2023/10/05/usa-china-multipolar-bipolar-unipolar/

Aspers, P., & Corte, U. (2019). What is Qualitative in Qualitative Research. *Qualitative Sociology*, *42*(2), 139–160. doi:10.1007/s11133-019-9413-7 PMID:31105362

Baghernia, N., & Meraji, E. (2020). Understanding China's Relationship with Bangladesh. *CenRaPS Journal of Social Sciences*, *2*(3), 345–353. doi:10.46291/cenraps.v2i3.41

Barrech, D. M., & Khan, P. D. M. (2023). US-China Growing Competition in Soft Power. *Journal of Social Sciences Review*, *3*(2), 490–499. doi:10.54183/jssr.v3i2.288

Berdiyev, A., & Can, N. (2020). The importance of central Asia in China's foreign policy and Beijing's soft power instruments. *Central Asia and The Caucasus,* *21*(4), 15–24. doi:10.37178/ca-c.20.4.02

Berg, B. L., Lune, H., & Lune, H. (2004). Qualitative Research Methods for the Social Sciences. In *Teaching Sociology* (Vol. 18, p. 563). Pearson. doi:10.2307/1317652

Bettie, M. (2015a). Ambassadors unaware: The Fulbright Program and American public diplomacy. *The Journal of Transatlantic Studies*, *13*(4), 358–372. doi:10.1080/14794012.2015.1088326

Bettie, M. (2015b). The Scholar as Diplomat: The Fulbright Program and America's Cultural Engagement with the World. *Caliban*, *54*(54), 233–252. doi:10.4000/caliban.3066

Biney, P. A., & Cheng, M.-Y. (2021). International Students' Decision to Study in China: A Study of Some Selected International Students from Universities in China. *Open Journal of Social Sciences*, *09*(08), 305–325. doi:10.4236/jss.2021.98021

Blair, R. A., Marty, R., & Roessler, P. (2022). Foreign Aid and Soft Power: Great Power Competition in Africa in the Early Twenty-first Century. *British Journal of Political Science*, *52*(3), 1355–1376. doi:10.1017/S0007123421000193

Blanchard, E., & Hakobyan, S. (2015). The US Generalised System of Preferences in Principle and Practice. *World Economy*, *38*(3), 399–424. doi:10.1111/twec.12216

Bloor, K. (2022, May 21). Power and Development in Global Politics. *E-International Relations*. https://www.e-ir.info/2022/05/21/power-and-development-in-global-politics/

Bryman, A. (2008). Of methods and methodology. *Qualitative Research in Organizations and Management*, *3*(2), 159–168. doi:10.1108/17465640810900568

Chakrovorty, A. (2020). China's Soft Power in Bangladesh: A Comparative Studies. *American Journal of Social Sciences and Humanities*, *5*(1), 128–140. doi:10.20448/801.51.128.140

Chaziza, D. M. (2023). *China's Soft Power Projection Strategy: Confucius Institutes in the MENA Region.* https://besacenter.org/chinas-soft-power-projection-strategy-confucius-institutes-in-the-mena-region/

Clarke, M. (2017). The Belt and Road Initiative: China's New Grand Strategy? *Asia Policy*, *1*(1), 71–79. doi:10.1353/asp.2017.0023

Cole, F. L. (1988). Content Analysis. *Clinical Nurse Specialist CNS*, *2*(1), 53–57. doi:10.1097/00002800-198800210-00025 PMID:3349413

Crane, D. (2014a). Cultural globalization and the dominance of the American film industry: Cultural policies, national film industries, and transnational film. *International Journal of Cultural Policy*, *20*(4), 365–382. doi:10.1080/10286632.2013.832233

Crane, D. (2014b). Cultural globalization and the dominance of the American film industry: Cultural policies, national film industries, and transnational film. *International Journal of Cultural Policy*, *20*(4), 365–382. doi:10.1080/10286632.2013.832233

Dautbašić, L. (2022). US Soft Power through Hollywood during Cold War: Rocky IV. *MAP Education and Humanities*, *2*(1), 1–7. doi:10.53880/2744-2373.2022.2.1.1

De Zoysa, R., & Newman, O. (2002). Globalization, soft power and the challenge of Hollywood. *Contemporary Politics*, *8*(3), 185–202. doi:10.1080/1356977022000025678

Dee, M. (2015). The Emergence of a Multipolar World. In The European Union in a Multipolar World (pp. 1–20). Palgrave Macmillan UK. doi:10.1057/9781137434203_1

deLisle, J. (2020). Foreign Policy through Other Means: Hard Power, Soft Power, and China's Turn to Political Warfare to Influence the United States. *Orbis*, *64*(2), 174–206. doi:10.1016/j.orbis.2020.02.004 PMID:32292215

Demgenski, P. (2020). Culinary Tensions: Chinese Cuisine's Rocky Road toward International Intangible Cultural Heritage Status. *Asian Ethnology*, *79*(1).

Downe-Wamboldt, B. (1992). Content analysis: Method, applications, and issues. *Health Care for Women International*, *13*(3), 313–321. doi:10.1080/07399339209516006 PMID:1399871

Duan, S., & Qiu, F. (2023). China's soft power and higher education in South Asia:rationale, strategies and implications. *Asia Pacific Journal of Education*, *43*(3), 944–947. doi:10.1080/02188791.2022.2133474

Edelstein, D. M. (2022). Why Nations Rise: Narratives and the Path to Great Power. By Manjari Chatterjee Miller. New York: Oxford University Press, 2021. 208p. $99.00 cloth, $27.95 paper. *Perspectives on Politics*, *20*(1), 367–368. doi:10.1017/S1537592721003509

Embassy, U. S. (2023a). *American Spaces.* US Embassy in India. https://in.usembassy.gov/education-culture/american-spaces/

Embassy, U. S. (2023b, December 7). *Twenty-one new peace corps volunteers sworn-in to begin their service in Tanzania.* US Embassy in Tanzania. https://tz.usembassy.gov/twenty-one-new-peace-corps-volunteers-sworn-in-to-begin-their-service-in-tanzania/

Escobar, P. (2020, April 2). China Rolls Out the Health Silk Road. *Asia Times*. https://asiatimes.com/2020/04/china-rolls-out-the-health-silk-road/

Fengyuan, D. (2020, April 20). Three sayings to characterize China's role in the global pandemic fight. *CGTN*. https://news.cgtn.com/news/2020-04-20/Three-sayings-to-characterize-China-s-role-in-global-pandemic-fight-PGFh7IK5Ms/index.html

Gallarotti, G. M. (2022). Pedagogical offensives: Soft power, higher education and foreign policy. *Journal of Political Power*, *15*(3), 495–513. doi:10.1080/2158379X.2022.2127276

Garlick, J. (2020). The Regional Impacts of China's Belt and Road Initiative. *Journal of Current Chinese Affairs*, *49*(1), 3–13. doi:10.1177/1868102620968848

Gautam, P., Singh, B., Singh, S., Bika, S. L., & Tiwari, R. P. (2023). Education as a soft power resource: A systematic review. *Heliyon*, *23736*. Advance online publication. doi:10.1016/j.heliyon.2023.e23736

Gill, B., & Huang, Y. (2006). Sources and limits of Chinese 'soft power.'. *Survival*, *48*(2), 17–36. doi:10.1080/00396330600765377

Govil, N. (2021). Hollywood. *BioScope: South Asian Screen Studies*, *12*(1–2), 98–101. doi:10.1177/09749276211026070

Grünbacher, A. (2012). Cold-War Economics: The Use of Marshall Plan Counterpart Funds in Germany, 1948–1960. *Central European History*, *45*(4), 697–716. doi:10.1017/S0008938912000659

Guardian. (2020, April 7). China outraged after Brazil minister suggests Covid-19 is part of 'plan for world domination. *Guardian*. https:// www.theguardian.com/world/2020/apr/07/china-outraged-after-brazil-min ister-suggests-covid-19-is-part-of-plan-for-world-domination#maincontent

Hartig, F. (2012). Confucius Institutes and the Rise of China. *Journal of Chinese Political Science*, *17*(1), 53–76. doi:10.1007/s11366-011-9178-7

Hazarika, O. B., & Mishra, V. (2016). Soft Power Contestation between India and China in South Asia. *Indian Foreign Affairs Journal, 11*(2), 139–152. https://www.jstor.org/stable/45341093

Hobson, J., & Zhang, S. (2022). The Return of the Chinese Tribute System? Re-viewing the Belt and Road Initiative. *Global Studies Quarterly*, *2*(4), ksac074. Advance online publication. doi:10.1093/isagsq/ksac074

Hochberg, F. P. (2023, July 19). Cultural diplomacy is an essential US strategy. *The Hill*. https://thehill.com/opinion/international/4103124-cultural-diplomacy-is-an-essential-us-strategy/

Hossain, M. (2021). Coronavirus (COVID-19) pandemic: Pros and cons of China's soft power projection. *Asian Politics & Policy*, *13*(4), 597–620. doi:10.1111/aspp.12610

Hsieh, H.-F., & Shannon, S. E. (2005). Three Approaches to Qualitative Content Analysis. *Qualitative Health Research*, *15*(9), 1277–1288. doi:10.1177/1049732305276687 PMID:16204405

Huang, Y., & Ding, S. (2006). Dragon's underbelly: An analysis of China's soft power. *East Asia (Piscataway, N.J.)*, *23*(4), 22–44. doi:10.1007/BF03179658

Hurst, A. (2023). *Introduction to Qualitative Research Methods*. Oregon State University. https://open.oregonstate.education/qualresearchmethods/

Hussain, M., & Mehmood, S. (2018). Chinese Soft Power Approaches towards Pakistan: An Analysis of Socio, Economic and Political Impacts. *Malaysian Journal of International Relations*, 6(1), 47–66. doi:10.22452/mjir.vol6no1.5

Hussain, M. E. (2021, April 3). Hollywood movies: American soft power apparatus. *Daily Observer*. https://www.observerbd.com/news.php?id=306338

Islam, Md. N. (2023). China's Soft Power Strategy. In Power of Bonding and Non-Western Soft Power Strategy in Iran (pp. 69–104). Springer International Publishing. doi:10.1007/978-3-031-19867-0_3

Islam, M. N. (2022). Protecting China's interests overseas: Securitization and foreign policy. *International Affairs*, 98(4), 1486–1487. doi:10.1093/ia/iiac131

Ittefaq, M., Ahmed, Z. S., & Martínez Pantoja, Y. I. (2023). China's Belt and Road Initiative and soft power in Pakistan: An examination of the local English-language press. *Place Branding and Public Diplomacy*, 19(1), 1–14. doi:10.1057/s41254-021-00212-8

Jackson, R. L. II, Drummond, D. K., & Camara, S. (2007). What Is Qualitative Research? *Qualitative Research Reports in Communication*, 8(1), 21–28. doi:10.1080/17459430701617879

Jain, R. (2022). *China's Soft Power and Higher Education in South Asia Rationale, Strategies, and Implications* (1st ed.). Routledge. https://www.routledge.com/Chinas-Soft-Power-and-Higher-Education-in-South-Asia-Rationale-Strategies/Jain/p/book/9780367770389

Jinping, X. (2017, October 18). *Secure a Decisive Victory in Building a Moderately Prosperous Society in All Respects and Strive for the Great Success of Socialism with Chinese Characteristics for a New Era*. Delivered at the 19th National Congress of the Communist Party of China. http://www.xinhuanet.com/english/download/Xi_Jinping's_report_ at_19th_CPC_National_Congress.pdf

Kathuria, S. (2022, April 13). The U.S. Should Stop Nickel and Diming India and Bangladesh. *Foreign Policy*. https://foreignpolicy.com/2022/04/13/us-india-bangladesh-trade-gsp/

Khuhro, A. A. (2019). Rising geo-strategic competition between United States and China: A case study of South Asia in the emerging global order. *IJASOS-International E-Journal of Advances in Social Sciences*, 635–641. doi:10.18769/ijasos.476447

Kim, M. (2009). Evaluating US soft power in Asia: Military, economic and sociopolitical relationships between Asia and the United States. *Contemporary Politics*, 15(3), 337–353. doi:10.1080/13569770903132540

Krishnamoorthi, R. (2023, September 29). The U.S. Cannot Afford to Lose a Soft-Power Race With China. *Foreign Policy*. https://foreignpolicy.com/2023/09/29/congress-shutdown-us-china-ccp-soft-power-competition-biden-xi-jinping-beijing/

Krishnan, A., & Bhattacherjee, K. (2023, August 24). China says will back Bangladesh against 'external interference.' *The Hindu*. https://www.thehindu.com/news/international/china-says-will-back-bangladesh-against-external-interference/article67231493.ece

Kugelman, M. (2023, May 31). The U.S. Ups the Ante in Bangladesh. *Foreign Affairs*. https://foreign-policy.com/2023/05/31/us-bangladesh-visa-policy-election-democracy-promotion/

Kurlantzick, J. (2007). *Charm Offensive*. Yale University Press.

Kurlantzick, J., & Minxin, P. (2006, June 13). *China's Soft Power in Southeast Asia: What Does It Mean for the Region, and for the U.S.?* Carnegie Endowment for International Peace. https://carnegieendow-ment.org/events/?fa=eventDetail&id=892

Lai, H., & Lu, Y. (2012). *China's Soft Power and International Relations* (1st ed.). Routledge. doi:10.4324/9780203122099

Li, J. (2018). *Conceptualizing Soft Power Conversion Model of Higher Education*. doi:10.1007/978-981-13-0641-9

Li, L., Willett, T. D., & Zhang, N. (2012). The Effects of the Global Financial Crisis on China's Financial Market and Macroeconomy. *Economic Research International*, *2012*, 1–6. doi:10.1155/2012/961694

Ling, L. H. M. (2020). Squaring the Circle: China's "Belt and Road Initiative" (BRI) and the Ancient Silk Roads. In Critical Reflections on China's Belt & Road Initiative (pp. 23–40). Springer Nature Singapore. doi:10.1007/978-981-13-2098-9_2

Machida, S. (2010). U.S. Soft Power and the "China Threat": Multilevel Analyses. *Asian Politics & Policy*, *2*(3), 351–370. doi:10.1111/j.1943-0787.2010.01198.x

Malik, J. M. (2001). South Asia in China's Foreign Relations. *Pacifica Review*, *13*(1), 73–90. doi:10.1080/13239100120036054

Mannan, M. (2019). *"Shining" or "Suffering" South Asia?* China's South Asian Footprints., doi:10.1007/978-981-13-7240-7_3

Markleku, A. (2019). Education as an instrument for China's soft power. *TRT World*. https://www.trt-world.com/opinion/education-as-an-instrument-for-china-s-soft-power-25699

Mavrodieva, R., Rachman, Harahap, & Shaw. (2019). Role of Social Media as a Soft Power Tool in Raising Public Awareness and Engagement in Addressing Climate Change. *Climate (Basel)*, *7*(10), 122. doi:10.3390/cli7100122

McCourt, D. M., & Mudge, S. L. (2023). Anything but Inevitable: How the Marshall Plan Became Possible. *Politics & Society*, *51*(4), 463–492. doi:10.1177/00323292221094084

Mead, W. R. (2004). America's Sticky Power. *Foreign Policy*, *141*(141), 46. doi:10.2307/4147548

Mishra, V. (2020). The BRI and Strategic Revival of the Silk Road: Implications for Asia. *India Quarterly. Journal of International Affairs*, *76*(3), 479–484. doi:10.1177/0974928420936138

Mohan, S., & Abraham, J. C. (2020). Shaping the regional and maritime battlefield? The Sino-Indian strategic competition in South Asia and adjoining waters. *Maritime Affairs*, *16*(1), 82–97. doi:10.1080/09733159.2020.1781374

Moser, A., & Korstjens, I. (2017). Series: Practical guidance to qualitative research. Part 1: Introduction. *The European Journal of General Practice*, *23*(1), 271–273. doi:10.1080/13814788.2017.1375093 PMID:29185831

Noyon, A. U. (2023, October 1). How China's Belt and Road changing Bangladesh's economy and infrastructures. *The Business Standard*. https://www.tbsnews.net/economy/how-chinas-belt-and-road-changing-bangladeshs-infrastructures-709826

Nuwer, R. (2023). Chinese students stay local as favour falls with study abroad. *Nature*, *620*(7973), S11–S13. doi:10.1038/d41586-023-02162-y PMID:37558838

Nye, J. (2017). Soft power: The origins and political progress of a concept. *Palgrave Communications*, *3*(1), 17008. doi:10.1057/palcomms.2017.8

Nye, J. S. (1990). Soft Power. *Foreign Policy*, *80*(80), 153–171. doi:10.2307/1148580

Nye, J. S. Jr. (2004). Soft Power and American Foreign Policy. *Political Science Quarterly*, *119*(2), 255–270. doi:10.2307/20202345

Nye, J. S. Jr. (2008). Public Diplomacy and Soft Power. *The Annals of the American Academy of Political and Social Science*, *616*(1), 94–109. doi:10.1177/0002716207311699

Nye, J. S. (2019). Soft Power and Public Diplomacy Revisited. *The Hague Journal of Diplomacy*, *14*(1–2), 7–20. doi:10.1163/1871191X-14101013

Obaidullah, M. (2023, October 26). From Historical Bonds to Modern Alliances: Decoding China's Relations with Afghanistan. *The Geopolitics*. https://thegeopolitics.com/from-historical-bonds-to-modern-alliances-decoding-chinas-relations-with-afghanistan/

Pakistan, R. (2023, September 16). *Number of Pakistani students in US rises by 16 percen*. Radio Pakistan. https://www.radio.gov.pk/16-11-2023/number-of-pakistani-students-in-us-rises-by-16-percent

Pal, D. (2021). *China's Influence in South Asia: Vulnerabilities and Resilience in Four Countries*. https://carnegieendowment.org/2021/10/13/china-s-influence-in-south-asia-vulnerabilities-and-resilience-in-four-countries-pub-85552

Palma, P. (2023, September 15). Number of Bangladeshi students in US rose 300% in 10 years. *The Daily Star*. https://www.thedailystar.net/news/bangladesh/education/news/number-bangladeshi-students-us-rose-300-10-years-3470381

Rahman, M. M. (2023, November 8). How Chinese aid advances BD dev, gains soft power. *The Financial Express*. https://today.thefinancialexpress.com.bd/first-page/how-chinese-aid-advances-bd-dev-gains-soft-power-1699375363

Rashid, D., & Ikram, D. M. (2023). Power Struggle in South Asia Region: Hanging between Soft and Hard Balance Competition. *Praxis International Journal of Social Science and Literature*, *6*(5), 36–46. doi:10.51879/PIJSSL/060505

Roland, G. (2021). China's rise and its implications for International Relations and Northeast Asia. *Asia and the Global Economy*, *1*(2), 100016. doi:10.1016/j.aglobe.2021.100016

Rugh, W. (2017). American soft power and public diplomacy in the Arab world. *Palgrave Communications*, *3*(1), 16104. doi:10.1057/palcomms.2016.104

Runde, D. F. (2020). *U.S. Foreign Assistance in the Age of Strategic Competition*. https://www.csis.org/analysis/us-foreign-assistance-age-strategic-competition

Sellen, C., & Jaumont, F. (2020, April 7). China Billionaires a Force to be Reckoned With in Global COVID-19 Fight—and More. *Channel News Asia*. https://www.channelnewsasia.com/news/commentary/china-covid-19-coronavirus-alibaba-jack-ma-tencent-baidu-12614242

Sharma, B. P., & Khatri, R. S. (2019). The Politics of Soft Power: *Belt and Road Initiative (BRI) as Charm Influence in South Asia. China and the World*, *02*(01), 1950002. doi:10.1142/S2591729319500020

Silver, L. (2021). *Amid pandemic, international student enrollment at U.S. universities fell 15% in the 2020-21 school year*. https://www.pewresearch.org/short-reads/2021/12/06/amid-pandemic-international-student-enrollment-at-u-s-universities-fell-15-in-the-2020-21-school-year/

Singh, A. I. (2021, May 7). China's Port Investments in Sri Lanka Reflect Competition with India in the Indian Ocean. *The Jamestown Foundation*. https://jamestown.org/program/chinas-port-investments-in-sri-lanka-reflect-competition-with-india-in-the-indian-ocean/

Smith, J. (2022). *South Asia: A New Strategy*. https://www.heritage.org/asia/report/south-asia-new-strategy

Sowiński, P. (2023). Expression of Dissidence: NOW-a Publishing House as a Social Movement Campaign under an Authoritarian Regime. *East European Politics and Societies: And Cultures*. doi:10.1177/08883254231203333

Sparks, C. (2018). China's soft power from the BRICS to the BRI. *Global Media and China*, *3*(2), 92–99. doi:10.1177/2059436418778935

Stokes, J. (2003). *How to Do Media and Cultural Studies*. SAGE Publication.

Sun, H. H. (2008). International political marketing: A case study of United States soft power and public diplomacy. *Journal of Public Affairs*, *8*(3), 165–183. doi:10.1002/pa.301

Tehseen, M. (2017). Sino-US Competition: Implications for South Asia and the Asia-Pacific. *Strategic Studies*, *37*(4), 1–17. doi:10.53532/ss.038.01.00175

Tewari, S. (2021, May 7). Sri Lanka: Covid increases China influence in India's backyard. *BBC News*. https://www.bbc.com/news/world-asia-57167091

Thao, N. T. H. (2020). Higher education – the factor of soft power in U.S. foreign policy from the post-cold war to 2016. *Science & Technology Development Journal - Social Sciences & Humanities, 4*(3), 605–612. doi:10.32508/stdjssh.v4i3.578

The Bureau of Educational and Cultural Affairs. (2023). *Cultural Diplomacy*. The Bureau of Educational and Cultural Affairs. https://eca.state.gov/programs-and-initiatives/initiatives/cultural-diplomacy

The Business Standard. (2023, June 19). 55 Bangladeshi students get Chinese Government Scholarship this year. *The Business Standard*. https://www.tbsnews.net/bangladesh/education/55-bangladeshi-students-get-chinese-government-scholarship-year-652262

The Express Tribune. (2019, April 14). Over 28,000 Pakistanis studying in China. *The Express Tribune.* https://tribune.com.pk/story/1950783/28000-pakistanis-studying-china

The Hindu Business Line. (2023, September 13). Indian students to the US increase 35% in 2022-23. *The Hindu Business Line.* https://www.thehindubusinessline.com/news/education/indian-students-to-the-us-at-all-time-high-of-35/article67528835.ece

The Times Higher Education. (2023). *World University Rankings 2024.* https://www.timeshighereducation.com/world-university-rankings/2024/world-ranking#!/length/100/locations/USA/sort_by/rank/sort_order/asc/cols/stats

The Times of India. (2019, June 15). Nepal schools make Mandarin compulsory after China offers to pay teachers' salaries. *The Times of India.* https://timesofindia.indiatimes.com/world/south-asia/nepal-schools-make-mandarin-compulsory-after-china-offers-to-pay-teachers-salaries/articleshow/69799114.cms

Today, C. (2007). Hu Jintao Calls for Enhancing "Soft Power" of Chinese Culture. *China Today.* http://www.chinatoday.com.cn/17ct/17e/1017/17e1720.htm

Today, C. (2023, August 7). China announces full scholarships to 40 SL students. *Ceylon Today.* https://ceylontoday.lk/2023/08/07/china-announces-full-scholarships-to-40-sl-students/

US Department of State. (2021, January 20). *U.S. Security Cooperation With India.* US Department of State. https://www.state.gov/u-s-security-cooperation-with-india/

US Department of State. (2022a, July 19). *U.S. Relations With Bangladesh.* US Department of State. https://cutt.ly/KwSquA1j

US Department of State. (2022b, August 15). *U.S. Relations With Pakistan.* US Department of State. https://www.state.gov/u-s-relations-with-pakistan/

US Department of State. (2023, September 1). *U.S. Security Cooperation with Bangladesh.* US Department of State. https://www.state.gov/u-s-security-cooperation-with-bangladesh/#:~:text=For%2050%20years%2C%20the%20United,trade%2C%20and%20defense%20institution%20building

US Government. (2023). *US Foreign Assistance by country.* US Government. https://www.foreignassistance.gov/cd/india/2022/obligations/1

USAID. (2022). *U.S. Provides Additional Covid-19 Assistance to India.* USAID. https://www.usaid.gov/india/press-release/us-provides-additional-covid-19-assistance-india#:~:text=USAID%20has%20contributed%20more%20than,more%20than%2042%20million%20Indians

USIP. (2020). *China's Influence on Conflict Dynamics in South Asia.* https://www.usip.org/publications/2020/12/chinas-influence-conflict-dynamics-south-asia

USTR. (2023a). *Bangladesh Trade & Investment Summary.* Office of United States Trade Representative. https://ustr.gov/countries-regions/south-central-asia/bangladesh

USTR. (2023b). *India Trade & Investment Summary.* Office of United States Trade Representative. https://ustr.gov/countries-regions/south-central-asia/india

Varisco, A. E. (2013, June 3). Towards a Multi-Polar International System: Which Prospects for Global Peace? *E-International Relations*. https://www.e-ir.info/2013/06/03/towards-a-multi-polar-international-system-which-prospects-for-global-peace/#google_vignette

Venugopalan, A., & Verma, P. (2020, February 7). Indian students may reassess China option. *The Economic Times*. https://economictimes.indiatimes.com/news/politics-and-nation/indian-students-may-reassess-china-option/articleshow/73997547.cms

Vlassis, A. (2016). Soft power, global governance of cultural industries and rising powers: The case of China. *International Journal of Cultural Policy*, 22(4), 481–496. doi:10.1080/10286632.2014.1002487

Winkler, J. R., & Nye, J. S. (2005). Soft Power: The Means to Success in World Politics. *International Journal (Toronto, Ont.)*, 61(1), 268. doi:10.2307/40204149

Woods, C. (2011). *CIA drones quit one Pakistan site – but US keeps access to other airbases*. https://www.thebureauinvestigates.com/stories/2011-12-15/cia-drones-quit-one-pakistan-site-but-us-keeps-access-to-other-airbases

Xinhua. (2020, May 10). China donates more medical supplies to Philippines to help fight COVID-19. *Xinhua Net*. http://www.xinhuanet.com/english/2020-05/10/c_139045510.htm

Xinhua. (2023, August 15). 71 Nepali students granted Chinese scholarships. *Nepal News*. https://nepal-news.com/s/gallery/71-nepali-students-granted-chinese-scholarships

Yang, R. (2010). Soft power and higher education: An examination of China's Confucius Institutes. *Globalisation, Societies and Education*, 8(2), 235–245. doi:10.1080/14767721003779746

Yao, J. (2009). The United States' Cognition of China's Soft Power in Southeast Asia:An Analysis on Congressional Research Service Reports and Opinion Polls. *Journal of Xiamen University*. https://www.semanticscholar.org/paper/The-United-States'-Cognition-of-China's-Soft-Power-Yao/f88fe71115ff-78493befeee815c62074aee32ef2

Ye, P., & Albornoz, L. A. (2018). Chinese Media 'Going Out' in Spanish Speaking Countries: The Case of CGTN-Español. *Westminster Papers in Communication and Culture*, 13(1), 81–97. doi:10.16997/wpcc.277

You, W. U. (2018). The Rise of China with Cultural Soft Power in the Age of Globalization. *Journal of Literature and Art Studies*, 8(5). Advance online publication. doi:10.17265/2159-5836/2018.05.006

Zhang, Y., & Wildemuth, B. M. (2005). Qualitative Analysis of Content by. *Human Brain Mapping*, 30(7), 2197–2206. https://philpapers.org/rec/ZHAQAO

Zreik, M. (2022). The Chinese presence in the Arab region: Lebanon at the heart of the Belt and Road Initiative. *International Journal of Business and Systems Research*, 16(5-6), 644–662. doi:10.1504/IJBSR.2022.125477

Zreik, M. (2023). *Stirring Up Soft Power*. doi:10.4018/979-8-3693-0250-7.ch015

Zreik, M. (2024a). Harnessing the Dragon: The Intersection of Chinese Leadership, Sustainability, and Confucian Philosophy in Modern Management. In K. Kankaew, S. Chaudhary, & S. Widtayakornbundit (Eds.), *Contemporary Management and Global Leadership for Sustainability* (pp. 72–94). IGI Global. doi:10.4018/979-8-3693-1273-5.ch005

Zreik, M. (2024b). Soft Power and China-Taiwan Competition for Influence in Latin America. In C. R. Veney & S. O. Abidde (Eds.), *China and Taiwan in Latin America and the Caribbean. Studies of the Americas* (pp. 151–141). Palgrave Macmillan. doi:10.1007/978-3-031-45166-9_6

Chapter 14
Soft Power Diplomacy:
China's Influence in Asia and the Middle East

Habib Badawi

https://orcid.org/0000-0002-6452-8379
Lebanese University, Lebanon

Karim Wattar
Lebanese American University, Lebanon

ABSTRACT

In an epoch defined by China's staggering economic ascent, the global panorama witnesses an expansive sprawl of Beijing's interests, notably in regions as diverse as the Middle East and North Africa. Central to this burgeoning influence is China's deft and strategic employment of "soft power" strategies, fostering calculated and symbiotic "strategic partnerships" with Arab states. This diplomatic approach, characterized by nuanced elements such as non-interventionism, cultural dissemination, and collaborative economic ventures, stands as a linchpin in China's diplomatic toolkit. In the face of Western portrayals casting shadows of a "Chinese menace," Beijing finds itself compelled to vehemently defend its peaceful policy objectives. Beyond mere economic gains, China's motives are laced with geopolitical and geostrategic considerations, adding layers of depth to its engagements. This meticulously orchestrated outreach encapsulates a significant facet of China's broader recalibration towards the Western sphere. This chapter undertakes a comprehensive exploration of the intricate and manifold facets of China's soft power diplomacy, offering a panoramic view of its profound influence extending across the intricate landscapes of Asia and the Middle East. Through a nuanced lens, it illuminates the mosaic of strategies, motivations, and implications that underpin China's burgeoning presence in these pivotal regions, painting a vivid tapestry of its ever-evolving global entrenchment. Various sources are used as support for the chapter. Press conferences, readings, academic journals, and scholarly articles are just some of the references found in the chapter. Additionally, expert opinions from well-renowned scholars were taken into consideration about China's growing influence in Asia and the Middle East in the fields of trade, technology, and politics. Furthermore, visual representations, such as images and graphs, are placed to facilitate selected aspects for the readers.

DOI: 10.4018/979-8-3693-2444-8.ch014

I. INTRODUCTION: OVERVIEW OF CHINA'S GLOBAL ASCENDANCY

Chinese global presence spans thousands of years, encompassing cultural changes, dynastic rules, and modern economic and industrial evolutions. China's global superiority stands as one of the most substantial phenomena in the 21st century, modifying the international dynamics of global trade, international relations, and military spending. Over the past fifty years, China has undergone a remarkable journey that has shifted the country from a period of seclusion to a contemporary economic powerhouse enriched with technological advancements and economic prosperity. This introduction seeks to highlight the multifaceted and complex dimensions of China's rise by examining historical events and certain contemporary developments.

Chinese history validates the scope of relations that have developed throughout different caliphates and countries on the Asian and European continents through the years. A clear example of these deep-rooted relations is China's Silk Road Initiative. To summarize, the Silk Road was a series of trade routes that connected Mainland China with Central Asia, the Arabian Peninsula, and even parts of Eastern Europe. Not only were physical goods exchanged on this economic pathway, but also cultural norms, religious ideas, and technologies were traded among the diverse cultures. Despite the deterioration of the notion in the 14th century, the foundations of Chinese relations with their Asian counterparts were laid.

Moving on from an imperial political system, China faced major social and political changes at the start of the twentieth century. China was liberated after the fall of the Japanese imperial army after World War II. After this, a civil war broke out in 1949 in Mainland China between the Chinese National Party (KMT) and the Chinese Communist Party (CCP). The war ended with the victory of the CCP, which was led by Mao Zedong, and the banishment of the KMT to Taiwan. This incident prompted the establishment of the People's Republic of China, which followed communist ideas and was isolated from a large spectrum of Asian and Western countries.

Mao's isolationist strategy ended in the early 1970s with the formalization of U.S.-Chinese relationships. This step was a major development in China's global outreach, where it broadened its diplomatic and economic relations to include the nations of North America, South America, and Western Europe. This agreement paved the way for China's technological and economic development in the twenty-first century, whereas in 2024, China will become the second-largest economy in the world.

The main significance concerning China's economic and political growth is that it has been established with a non-combative military strategy. China's tactic for its current enhanced global influence can be traced back to a concept nicknamed "soft power." The concept was introduced by political scientist Joseph Nye in his book "Soft Power: The Means to Success in World Politics." According to Nye (2002), China is moving on an exponential trajectory of global influence, mainly due to its subtle approach to balancing its economic and military strengths with diplomatic and positive relations with other nations. The upcoming chapter will not only comprehensively explore China's soft power strategy in Asia in its various dimensions, but it will also offer an analysis of the implications of this method in the coming decades.

The concept of 'soft power' in international relations is simply the ability to achieve a series of goals by attraction rather than force. In his 2002 book, Joseph Nye explores in depth the various sources of soft power that can propel a country to the highest levels. Based on Nye (2002), cultural values, political ideals, foreign policy, and institutions are the main resources of soft power. To elaborate, these assets can help convey a positive image of a nation's main ideas and values, which attracts nations seeking worldwide cooperation.

Additionally, Nye (2002) illustrates the dynamics of soft power using historical and contemporary examples followed by various countries, most notably China. Regarding China's soft power approach, public diplomacy is the most critical target area. To explain, public diplomacy involves the communication of foreign governments to build influence, enhance cooperation, and influence opinions. The diplomatic reach of soft power can even help mediate conflicts between certain nations. For instance, China has offered insights and viable solutions to the long-standing Middle Eastern conflict between Israel and Palestine through a four-point peace plan (Associated Press, Times of Israel, 2017). This diplomatic strategy reappeared after the events of October 7 when China provided a concrete roadmap for peace between the conflicting parties, based on Lee & Wang's (2023) article. The concrete roadmap calls for a two-state solution and the establishment of a worldwide conference towards this goal.

However, the theoretical framework of Soft Power, which was formulated by political scientist Joseph Nye, has some limitations. In his 2002 book, Nye confesses that soft power is heavily circumstantial and dependent on global events and political stability. Political tension and rising instability are both factors that hinder a nation's soft power strategy. Additionally, Nye (2002) believes that soft power implementation needs to include some factors of hard power, and the best way to achieve global cooperation is the combination of both soft and hard power values. This process would later be nicknamed "Smart Power."

II. ANCIENT SILK ROAD: A HISTORICAL PRECEDENT FOR MODERN CHINESE DIPLOMACY

Modern Chinese diplomacy combines traditional diplomatic approaches with modern notions. The concepts of globalization and industrialization are evident in China's diplomatic plan through the modern-day Belt and Road Initiative. This economic development program, which spans multiple continents, promotes connectivity and economic global cooperation. This contemporary economic concept bears a resemblance to its predecessor, "The Ancient Silk Road."

The Ancient Silk Road, which first appeared during the Han dynasty's rule in 206 B.C.E., was the project that placed China on the international stage. In short, the Silk Road was a network of trade routes that connected the Far East with West Asia and even parts of Eastern Europe. It was nicknamed "The Silk Road" due to China's most famous commodity, silk. The trade routes contained overland and maritime pathways, and they facilitated the transfer of a wide range of goods, including textiles, precious gemstones, metals, and spices (Britannica, 2024).

This historic pathway paved the way for Chinese values, norms, and traditions to be heard and represented in several areas of the continent. Also, China benefited from the Silk Road by gaining knowledge of traditional values rooted in certain communities. The Silk Road contributed to the presence of several religious communities in Mainland China, most notably Buddhism, Christianity, and Islam. Although this principle ceased to exist after the 14th century, it laid down the framework for modern-day economic and diplomatic relations between China and one of Asia's most influential regions, the Middle East.

Current Chinese global engagements in the One Belt, One Road (OBOR) plan is correlated with the Ancient Silk Road. A clear example is the present-day economic projects between Egypt and China. Historically, Egypt was one of the many countries that were connected through the maritime Silk Road, which connected Southeast Asia, China, the Arabian Peninsula, Europe, and Africa via the oceans. Both parties benefited from this trade relationship where Chinese items, such as ironware and glazed pottery, were exchanged in the cities of Cairo and Alexandria, and Egyptian sugar and medical technologies were transmitted eastward (Kim, 2011).

Modern Chinese-Egyptian relations are based on three main characteristics. Connectivity through waterways, fluidity of good transportation, and complimentary are the three main pillars of Chinese-Egyptian relations, according to Xing et al.'s (2023) article. To elaborate, Egypt's geographical location, which overlooks both the Mediterranean and Red Seas, facilitated the transportation of rare Chinese items to Africa and even Europe. Also, Chinese-Egyptian relations were historically positive, and a clear historical example of this friendship was Queen Cleopatra VII's Chinese silk garments that were worn at banquets and gained the attention of the Egyptian upper class. This historical friendship transcended to modern history, where Egypt was the first Arab and African nation to declare diplomatic and formal relations with the People's Republic of China (PRC) in 1956, based on Chaziza's (2021) article. Presently, the characteristics of Chinese-Egyptian relations are evident in the 2021 Joint Agreement on Economic and Technology Cooperation and the TEDA SETZ project, where Chinese investments are being placed into the development of an industrial park in Egypt (Xing, Liu, Cooper, & Vrontis, 2023).

This soft power strategy raises concerns about the future relationship between the US and the Middle East (Eslami & Papageorgiou, 2023). In Almit's (2010) book, several examples can be described of the growing Chinese presence in the Middle East, especially after the events of World War II. The first level of this growing relationship can be found at the level of energy security. According to Almit (2010), as of 2010, 54% of China's energy needs are supplemented by Middle Eastern countries, and these requirements are expected to reach 70% by 2020. Another example of this growing relationship can also be observed on the economic level, where bilateral trade between both parties reached $220 billion in 2010 and $507.2 billion in 2022 (Almit, 2010; China Daily, 2023). Military development, arms sales, cultural exchange, and technological development are just a few illustrations of the impact that enhanced Sino-Middle East relations have brought to the Asian region.

To assess China's international imprint in the twenty-first century, the events that unfolded in this land in the twentieth century are key contributors. China's twentieth-century history shaped several events on the international platform and presented China as a main player. The first change in Chinese politics was the fall of the Qing dynasty, which was the final imperial household to rule mainland China, in 1912, according to Spence (1990). This central rule was followed by the rise of a feudalistic system where regional warlords emerged. However, these regional warlords would soon lose their grip on control of their territories against the United Front, which included the nationalist and communist parties of China (Fairbank & Goldman, 2006). This front was soon dismantled in 1927 after nationalists committed massacres against the communists in Shanghai (Fairbank & Goldman, 2006). The chaos continued in 1929 when the Chinese Civil War commenced between General Chiang-Kai Shek of the nationalist Kuomintang (KMT) party and Mao Zedong of the Chinese Communist Party (CCP).

From 1929 until 1932, the conflict was mainly contained between the previously mentioned parties. However, on September 18, 1932, the Empire of Japan invaded Manchuria in northern China, taking advantage of the conflict between CCP and KMT forces. From 1932 to 1937, three parties took control of Japan: the nationalist KMT party, which held governmental control in the Republic of China; the communist CCP faction, which held control in rural areas; and the Imperial Japanese forces, which controlled Northern China (Fenby, 2005).

The prevalence of Japanese forces in China prompted a ceasefire between the KMT and the CCP militaries, forming the Second United Front in 1937. This unification initiated the Second Sino-Japanese War, which lasted for eight years. At the end of the war in 1945, the Japanese imperial forces retreated from Northern China and were defeated by the Allied forces (Britannica, 2024). After approximately twenty-seven years since the war, Sino-Japanese relations were established. However, the effects of the war remain evident in present-day modern Chinese foreign policy, where China claims sovereignty over the Senkaku Islands/Diaoyutai Qundao, a collection of inhabited islands along the East China Sea. Although political tensions are periodic between both nations, Sino-Japanese economic ties remain strong and are witnessing an increase (Cheng, 2007).

Despite the Chinese victory over Japan and the formation of the Second United Front between the opposing factions, the Chinese Civil War resumed in 1945. The second phase of this bloody war lasted for four years, and it ended with the victory of Mao Zedong's CCP party in 1949. After this victory, General Chiang Kai-Shek, who was the leader of the nationalist KMT party, retreated from Mainland China to the island of Taiwan. On October 1, 1949, the People's Republic of China was formed, and it was led by the leader of the CCP Party, Mao Zedong. The Civil War ended with approximately five million deaths and ten million injuries.

III. EARLY ENGAGEMENTS ON THE WORLDWIDE STAGE

On a global scale, after World War II, a deeply divided world was formed. A bipolar political system emerged: one order called for the spread of capitalism, and the other called for the rise of Communist states. The main parties to these orders were the United States of America (USA) and the Soviet Union (U.S.S.R.), both of which were allies in the Second World War. The conflict between both parties was nicknamed "The Cold War," and it engulfed several countries and caused several wars. Mao's rise to power in China in 1949 was a clear victory for the U.S.S.R. in its quest for the spread of Communist rule around the world.

The political presence of China on an international scale started to appear in the early 1950s, specifically during the Korean War. The East Asian conflict laid the foundation for the emergence of China as a major player in geopolitical issues in East Asia. To elaborate, the Korean peninsula was divided into North Korea, which was influenced by communist ideas, and South Korea, which was persuaded by the economics of Western nations. In October 1950, the North Korean army launched an assault on the lands of South Korea to place the whole peninsula under the rule of Kim Il Sung, then leader of North Korea. After United Nations forces, which were led by US military generals, caused North Korean forces to retreat toward the Yalu River, Chinese military forces decided to intervene because of the strategic proximity of the Yalu River to the Chinese border based on Zheng (1995). Chinese forces aided North Korea in its efforts in the war and were able to turn the tide by causing UN forces to retreat beyond the 38th parallel line, which is currently the borderline that separates the Korean peninsula (Zhang, 1995).

China's actions in the Korean War affected its diplomatic relations on an international scale. Its intervention against UN forces caused a rift with the U.S.A., which prevented the establishment of formal foreign relations (Stueck, 1995). Furthermore, China did not establish relationships with several Western countries that followed the U.S. political and economic vision, and these countries include Canada, the United Kingdom, and France (Stueck, 1995).

Due to this isolation, China intensified its ties with the Soviet Union, where it formed the Sino-Soviet Alliance, and focused on building its relationships with Asian, Middle Eastern, and African countries. For example, concerning African and Asian nations, the 1955 Bandung Conference was a major diplomatic advantage for China because it built connections with over twenty-nine countries that broke from colonialism. Also, this conference accentuated the topics of peaceful coexistence, non-interference in internal affairs, and sovereignty, placing China as a top diplomatic country (Britannica, 2021; Zreik, 2022).

Despite the breakdown in Sino-US political relations during the reign of Mao Zedong, the administration changed its international relations priorities in the early 1970s. This was evident through the breakdown of the Sino-Soviet alliance in the late 1960s. The change in Chinese foreign relations was visible during President Nixon's visit to Beijing, where he held meetings with Mao Zedong to establish economic and political partnerships. In 1979, after approximately two decades, the U.S. officially rekindled its relationship with the Asian dragon, majorly shifting the dynamics of the Cold War (Council on Foreign Relations, 2023).

IV. BELT AND ROAD INITIATIVE (BRI): OBJECTIVES, AMBITIONS, AND IMPACT

The Belt and Road Initiative is the twenty-first-century modified version of the Ancient Silk Road. This economic pathway ties China with its Asian, Middle Eastern, and European partners through land and maritime trails. During state visits to Kazakhstan and Indonesia in 2013, President Xi Jinping announced his vision of the overland Silk Road Economic Belt and the Maritime Silk Road, which would later be referred to as the One Belt Initiative, as mentioned in McBride et al.'s (2023) article. This innovative program has a set of goals and ambitions that the Chinese state aims to achieve on the continental and global stages.

According to McBride et al. (2023), one of the main objectives of the BRI is political in nature. President Xi Jinping's vision aims to push back and limit the US political presence in Asia in the upcoming decades. In Lieberthal's (2011) commentary, the US, under the Obama administration, aimed to formulate a leadership role from the Indian subcontinent to Northeast Asia, especially after the death of the North Korean dictator Kim Jong Il, whose nuclear weaponry program posed a major threat to the USA and its allies. Other than political ambitions, the BRI was mainly driven by economic aspirations. China is driven to enhance Chinese incomes, develop new trade linkages, and export excess production to new markets (McBride, Berman, & Chatzky, 2023).

The economic ambitions of China for achieving the BRI have already started formulating on the physical level through its investments that amount to $1 trillion. After announcing the 21st-century Maritime Silk Road at the 2013 Association of Southeast Asian Nations (ASEAN), President Xi invested billions of dollars in the development of several ports that span from Southeast Asia to East Africa and parts of Europe, based on McBride et al.'s (2023) assessment. Furthermore, China has invested in physical infrastructure projects that include railways, energy pipelines, and highways that pass through the mountainous regions of the former Soviet republics, Pakistan, and India. Besides physical infrastructure, President Xi has invested in the construction of economic zones that offer high-tech services, such as the 5G telecommunications network powered by the Chinese company Huawei. Moreover, as of 2023, 147 countries, which comprise 40% of worldwide GDP, are interested in being part of the BRI (McBride, Berman, & Chatzky, 2023).

A crucial region for the BRI's success is the tumultuous Middle East. To elaborate, this region encompasses a wide array of religious communities that have caused tensions over the past few years. To navigate through the trenches of Middle Eastern troubles, President Xi developed a more proactive "Arab policy" because Middle Eastern oil supplies are crucial for Chinese economic development, as Castilla (2016) mentions in her policy brief entitled "China's Evolving Middle East Role." According to Castilla (2016), as of 2014, the Middle East supplied China with 51% of its crude oil imports. This energy cooperation is a central pillar of China's interaction with Middle Eastern countries, with infrastructure, investment, and trade also being essential elements. China has conducted several strategic economic projects to implement the Belt and Road Initiative. Examples of these strategic partnerships during President Xi's 2016 visit to the region include the Memorandums of Understanding (MOU) on 14 tech, research, energy, and trade projects with the Kingdom of Saudi Arabia (KSA), $15 billion financial investment agreements with Egypt, and infrastructure and trade deals with Iran (Castilla, 2016). Overall, the amount of trade between China and its Middle Eastern partners from 2017 to 2022 has increased from $262.5 billion to $507.2 billion in a span of five years, according to official Chinese Customs data. Also, the Middle East turned out to be China's fastest-growing trade partner in 2022, up by 27.1% year on year in comparison to the Association of Southeast Asian Nations (15%) and the European Union (5.6%) (Chinese Government, 2023).

Chinese relations are also developing with African nations. According to the Chinese Government (2023), trade volumes with Africa surged by 14.5% in 2022 to reach $266.3 billion. Chinese engagement with Africa encompasses not only North African nations but also sub-Saharan countries with minute economic capabilities. According to the IMF's (2023) report, the region's largest trading partner between 2000 and 2021 was China, where one-fifth of the region's total exports of goods were sent to China. Metals, mineral products, and fuel represent most Sub-Saharan exports, whereas China supplies the region with major funding deals for infrastructure and machinery projects. The economic partnerships with Sub-Saharan Africa generate high incomes from export revenues and highlight China's global engagements with diverse partners.

Chinese global ascension in different sectors was explained in detail. One of the aspects that was discussed was the Chinese economic system and its main characteristics. China's financial and monetary growth is primarily dependent on expert strategies that target specific economic sectors. These monetary approaches aim to promote economic growth and enhance collaboration domestically and internationally.

Domestically, economic collaboration can be achieved through regional partnerships between Chinese provinces. A 2012 study assessed the effect of growth spillover across all Chinese provinces by focusing on the impact of market potential on regional income growth. According to Bai et al. (2012), marketization and domestic market integration were key factors that played an essential role in China's real GDP growth rate, which was documented at 9% from the 1992–2004 period. Moreover, the paper tabulated provincial economic and demographic data like GDP per capita, labor force, and foreign direct investment (FDI) through certain regional economic indices to accurately show the importance of regional collaboration in promoting economic growth. Based on Bai et al.'s (2012) estimation, regional income growth is associated with not only capital and labor increases but also regional linkages and market potential.

Although China's global economic engagements seem to have provided positive results, the Belt and Road Initiative (BRI) has drawn criticism from several scholars. A main drawback of the BRI is the debt diplomacy trap, which burdens participating countries and negatively affects their ability to repay their loans. According to Hillman (2018), after Sri Lanka failed to pay a $1.3 billion loan for a new port, China took an undisclosed equity stake in the port. Environmental specialists also criticized the environmental concerns associated with the continuous BRI infrastructure projects. For instance, in Fang et al.'s (2021) research article, East Asian countries emit the largest carbon, phosphorus, and nitrogen footprints in the BRI. The study showed that China, India, Russia, Belarus, and Mongolia are significant countries that are the top net exporters of carbon.

V. REGIONAL DYNAMICS: CHINA'S NEIGHBORS IN EAST ASIA

East Asia has become the most dynamic economic region in the world over the past few decades. This area includes China and Tiger economies such as Japan, South Korea, Taiwan, and Indonesia. China's economic growth has transformed its role as a global economic powerhouse, which has certain implications for its neighbors in East Asia.

China has developed its relations with its East Asian neighbors in two ways: collectively and separately. Collectively, China has signed several monetary and fiscal agreements with the Association of Southeast Asian Nations (ASEAN) committee, which includes countries such as Indonesia, Singapore, and the Philippines. A clear example of this region's importance to China is the announcement of the Belt and Road Initiative (BRI) at the 2013 China-ASEAN meeting, according to McBride et al.'s (2023) paper. Additionally, China's economic rise has allowed its neighbors to become its major trading partners, which has enhanced economic integration and regional interconnectivity. Evidence of this relationship can be found in Flores's (2023) assessment, where bilateral trade amounts between China and Southeast Asian countries increased from $641 billion in 2019 to $975.3 billion in 2022, making the region its highest trade location.

Independently, China has built a diverse range of relations with East Asian countries, most notably Japan. Historically, Japan and China have engaged in two wars, most recently in World War II, when Japan annexed northern China. Politically, certain tensions are evident, specifically regarding territorial disputes over the Senkaku Islands/Diaoyutai Qingdao islands, which remained under Japanese rule after World War II (Zreik, 2024).

Although political tensions are evident, China and Japan are economically interdependent. Following Cheng (2007), Japanese investors spent $66.6 billion on the Chinese market between 1990 and 2004, making Japan China's number one foreign investor. According to the Observatory of Economic Complexity (OEC) (2021) numbers, over the past twenty-six years, Sino-Japanese trade has increased exponentially. In detail, Japanese exports to China increased at an annualized rate of 7.66%, from $22.5 billion in 1995 to $153 billion in 2021. On the other hand, Chinese exports to Japan have amplified at an annual rate of 6.54%, from $32.5 billion in 1995 to $168 billion in 2021 (Observatory of Economic Complexity, OEC, 2021).

China's soft power plan is an evolving notion that targets specific regions. The main regions that are affected by this approach are the Middle East and East Asia. Countries like North Korea, the Kingdom of Saudi Arabia, India, Iran, and Pakistan are just a few of the main Chinese target nations for soft power. The strategy of soft power has been implemented in the Middle East and East Asia, where certain cultural and political aspects have been taken into consideration.

Economic cooperation and financial investments are features of China's soft power plan in the Middle East and East Asia. The Belt and Road Initiative (BRI), which is a maritime and land project that emulates the Ancient Silk Road, is a common Chinese economic project in the Middle East and East Asia. According to Wang (2023), investments in BRI have increased to reach 48%, up from 29% in 2021, and BRI finance and investments span over 200 deals with a value of $67.8 billion in 2022. On the diplomatic level, numerous forums have been conducted on an annual basis in both regions with China to enhance its political and strategic influence. Examples of these meetings include the Asia-Pacific Economic Cooperation (APEC) and the China-Arab State Summits, which held their first meeting at the end of 2022, based on CGTN (2022). Other forms of soft power strategies in both regions include educational partnerships through Confucius Institutes, media, and communication programs such as CCTV, and energy and security arrangements, specifically in the Middle East.

VI. SOFT POWER EXPANSION: CHINA'S APPROACH IN THE MIDDLE EAST AND EAST ASIA

Internationally, China's economic partnerships transcend several regions and continents, most notably the Middle East and East Asia. As elaborated in Castilla's (2016) paper, the Middle East is an important region for Chinese economic growth and development, primarily because of China's rising crude oil needs for industrialization and trade. To maintain the availability of crude oil for its development as well as its rising status as an influential global power, China has constructed several economic agreements with Middle Eastern countries on the levels of trade, technology, and research. Furthermore, China has enhanced its cooperation with East Asian nations through the establishment of a free trade area with the Association of Southeast Asian Nations (ASEAN), where bilateral trade volume between both parties increased from $641 billion in 2019 to $975.3 billion in 2022 (Flores, 2023). Other cooperation deals include the China-Laos highway, the China-Thailand high-speed railway, and the current advancement of the Belt and Road Initiative (BRI) trade links that aim to boost connectivity, modify infrastructure, and enlarge economic potential (Flores, 2023).

Dating back to the Ancient Silk Road, religious ideas and practices were exchanged between the Chinese and their Asian neighbors. As of 2021, over 5,500 religious groups comprise the demographic fabric of Chinese society. According to the US State Department's 2022 report, folk and ethnic religions constitute 22% of the Chinese population. Other religions include Buddhism, Christianity, and Islam, which form 18.2%, 5.1%, and 1.8% of the Chinese population, respectively.

Religion has become a key tool used to shape foreign policy. In Brasnett's (2021) journal, he claimed that the Chinese Communist Party (CCP) recently increased its leverage on spiritual institutions to spread a positive narrative of its religious policies to enhance its relationship with countries that identify with those religions. This strategy started its implementation in 1978 when China liberalized its religious laws. After this, Buddhism and Christianity started to flourish in Chinese society, according to Hunter (2009). Examples of China's good religious practices that aim to strengthen its relationship with its neighbors are the World Buddhist Forum, which Beijing hosted in 2006, and the renovation of hundreds of historic monasteries, all of which strengthen Sino-Japanese relationships because many schools of Japanese Buddhism trace their origins to China (Hunter, 2009).

Although China is trying to appeal to certain nations through its religious diplomacy strategy, certain approaches concerning this plan seem alarming. As Bransett (2021) discussed in his paper, the Chinese Communist Party (CCP), which is the ruling party in China, is pursuing a path of information manipulation and censorship to control the narrative regarding certain religious communities in Chinese areas. Through their censorship methodology, the Chinese state can limit information reaching international societies where a positive narrative is conceptualized for Muslim-majority countries (Brasnett, 2021). Similarly, China implements a strategy of international coercion to control certain religious groups. A clear example of this approach is negotiating agreements with the Vatican to exert control and persuade Chinese Catholics (Brasnett, 2021).

Strategic partnerships are critical to the survival of any nation. These partnerships may vary and can be found on both the political and economic levels. To elaborate, according to Isoraite's (2009) article, a strategic partnership involves two or more groups that cooperate, share risks, and gain competitive advantages in their venture. As China builds up its influence and presence on the international stage, certain Chinese economic and political objectives need the help of certain strategic global partners to achieve success. Asian, Middle Eastern and European nations are needed as strategic partners for the accomplishment of Chinese strategic economic projects, most notably the Belt Road Initiative (BRI).

The BRI program's success in the Middle East is dependent on the de-escalation of tensions in the region. Iran and the Kingdom of Saudi Arabia have been at the center of Middle Eastern tensions for decades. After seven years of military and diplomatic strains, which were characterized by the closure of embassies and the support of anti-Saudi militias, China was able to broker an agreement that resumed diplomatic ties between Riyadh and Tehran on March 10, 2023, based on Farouk's (2023) assessment. This agreement came to fruition after five days of concentrated negotiations in Beijing, and it follows the set of principles agreed upon in the bilateral partnership deals of 1998 and 2001, as Farouk (2023) mentioned.

The deal not only highlights China's increasing role in the Middle East as a superpower, but it also highlights the extent of Chinese relations between both countries. Regarding Iran, Sino-Iranian, also nicknamed Sino-Persian, relations date back to the Ancient Silk Road, where religious, cultural, and physical elements were exchanged. The historical relationship has remained resilient throughout the years, and it has only grown stronger in the 21st century. A clear example of this resistant partnership is the 25-year cooperation agreement signed in 2021. This agreement provides China with copious amounts of discounted crude oil, allows Iran to gain from infrastructure and tech investments from China, and will allow 4G and 5G to be provided to the Iranian public, as Vaisi (2022) states in his article. However, this deal is not quite beneficial for the Iranian economy because Chinese goods that are flooding the Iranian consumer market are cheap, and they are putting local manufacturers and artisans out of business (Vaisi, 2022).

Similarly, the Sino-Saudi partnership has developed massively over the past thirty years. Numerous partnerships and agreements have been signed to strengthen the economic and diplomatic bond between both nations. According to Ali's (2022) article in the Gulf Research Center, as of 2022, Saudi Arabia exports $6.24 billion to China, which amounts to %17 of total Saudi exports. Additionally, Saudi Arabia will be China's main crude oil supplier, with approximately 85 million metric tons in 2021. Moreover, Chinese arms transfers to Saudi Arabia increased by 400% between 2016 and 2020, adding another dimension to their developing relationship (Ali, 2022).

VII. CONFUCIUS INSTITUTES: DISSEMINATING CHINESE CULTURE ON THE GLOBAL STAGE

Chinese influence on the international juncture has recently encompassed educational programs. Scholarships, academic partnerships, and exchange programs are just a few examples of educational collaborations that Chinese universities are conducting. As of 2019, China has focused on modernizing its educational system, and this is driven by the UN 2030 and Chinese national strategy. According to Zhu (2019), based on the Chinese Ministry of Education's data, China's educational development plan before 2019 was successful, where the tertiary education gross enrollment ratio increased from 2.7 to

45.7 between the years 1978 and 2017. On the global stage, Chinese educational systems have spread to several renowned institutions through Confucius organizations.

Named after the prominent Chinese philosopher Confucius, Confucius institutes are educational public organizations that help promote the Chinese language, culture, and history to foreign communities. Confucius Institutes (Hanban) are public organizations affiliated with the Chinese Ministry of Education, and their main headquarters are in the Chinese capital, Beijing. There are both positive and negative aspects associated with the dissemination of Chinese culture through educational organizations.

Chinese-oriented educational associations have provided a variety of services to highlight Chinese culture. A clear example of these services includes providing individuals with the chance to study Mandarin, which has increasingly become a primary language for business (Hanban, 2016). Other advantages of Confucius foundations include academic partnerships, joint research opportunities, and student exchanges between Chinese and foreign universities, all of which contribute to global educational collaboration. Additionally, Confucius institutes conduct cultural events, workshops, and programs that interject linguistic diversity and cross-cultural communication into person-to-person communication.

Although there are several advantages to these educational institutes, certain negatives hinder their further development. One of the main drawbacks of Confucius' institutions is the restrictions on certain academic topics, which limit scholarly freedom and expression, according to Knott (2023). Another potential downside is the spread of Chinese propaganda in international facilities. According to Jakhar (2019), Confucian institutes are extensions of the Chinese government that use hiring practices that consider political loyalty. Finally, security risks, primarily espionage, have led to the scrutiny of Confucius institutions and even the closure of some programs at Western universities, most notably at the University of New South Wales in 2019 (Jakhar, 2019).

China's global ascension transcends not only politics and education but also media, film, and pop culture. China's entertainment industry has witnessed an exponential rise over the past few years, thanks to the emergence of companies like Alibaba and Baidu, according to Davis & Frate (2020). Moreover, the restructuring of online streaming platforms such as iQiyi and Youku has helped increase the Video Sharing Market's activity in the Chinese market, where it is projected that revenues will reach $22.04 billion in 2024 based on the Statista Market insights (2024) report. Likewise, social media platforms like TikTok, Weibo, and WeChat have become an integral part of Chinese daily life, where these applications have been used for entertainment, advertising, and media purposes, based on Sweetman's assessment (2014). These applications help extend Chinese soft power influence through the exchange of traditions and cultural values and the promotion of Chinese businesses and innovations. However, content censorship, material disinformation, and privacy concerns are all challenges related to Chinese social media applications, according to Yang (2016). The 2023 US congressional hearing regarding TikTok data security supports negative ideas related to Chinese social media websites (Ayyub & Shepardson, 2023).

In the film industry, the Chinese market is a vital source of revenue and growth. In 2023, the Chinese box office rebounded from the COVID-19 pandemic, which generated 53 billion yuan ($7.7 billion). This high number highlights the future potential that this industry can generate in the Chinese market. Additionally, the top 10 earners in that year were all domestic films, which is a rare instance that only happened once in Chinese film history (Mengying, 2023).

VIII. DIGITAL DIPLOMACY: EXPORTING TECHNOLOGY AND INFRASTRUCTURE

China's economic plans, encapsulated within the Belt and Road vision, position technology and infrastructure as pivotal drivers for the nation's developmental trajectory. The genesis of China's technological prowess can be traced back to 1979, a watershed moment when the country transitioned from an isolationist state to a global economic powerhouse. Embracing the tenets of economic globalization and liberalization, China metamorphosed into a manufacturing behemoth, earning the moniker of the "world's factory" (Li & Worm, 2011). This transformation, propelled by advantageous tax policies, an abundance of labor capital, and a sprawling consumer market, laid the foundation for China's meteoric economic rise.

The astute economic management of Chinese resources has been instrumental in fueling the nation's rapid growth and development. The influx of various global industries into China has significantly enriched multiple economic sectors, with technology and infrastructure standing out prominently. In the realm of technology, China is actively pursuing a digital diplomacy program aimed at bolstering its contribution to the global telecommunications market.

Delving into the technological sphere, the BRI has emerged as a catalyst for China's global technological ambitions. The 5G telecom services network, pioneered by Huawei, not only exemplifies China's technological prowess but also aligns with the overarching goals of the BRI. This initiative seeks to fortify connectivity and communication channels between China and its international partners, fostering a more seamless exchange of goods, services, and ideas. As China solidifies its position in the global telecommunications market, the 5G network becomes a cornerstone of its digital diplomacy, facilitating enhanced collaboration and integration on the international stage.

In the intricate tapestry of China's economic landscape, infrastructure development occupies a vital role. The Belt and Road Initiative, a linchpin of China's economic outreach, encompasses a multitude of land infrastructure partnerships with nations such as Pakistan. These partnerships extend to the construction of highways, railways, and bridges, strategically positioned to facilitate the smooth transit of Chinese exports to global markets (McBride, Berman, & Chatzky, 2023). The infusion of Chinese capital into these infrastructure projects not only fosters economic development in partner nations but also cements China's influence in key geopolitical regions (Zreik, 2021).

The symbiotic relationship between technology and infrastructure within the broader framework of the BRI exemplifies China's multifaceted approach to economic expansion. The strategic integration of innovative technologies, such as 5G, with robust physical infrastructure underscores China's commitment to forging a comprehensive and interconnected global network. As the BRI unfolds, its impact on technology and infrastructure resonates far beyond the borders of China, shaping the contours of the international economic landscape.

Beyond the tangible manifestations of technology and infrastructure projects, the BRI represents a paradigm shift in China's approach to diplomacy and global economic engagement. It signifies a departure from unilateralism towards a more collaborative and interconnected world. By investing in the technological and infrastructural development of partner nations, China not only secures its economic interests but also cultivates diplomatic ties and influence. The reciprocation of benefits between China and its partners establishes a framework for sustained economic cooperation, fostering a shared vision of progress and prosperity.

Moreover, the BRI serves as a testament to China's ambition to shape the global narrative on technological innovation and infrastructure development. The initiative provides a platform for Chinese companies to display their expertise on the international stage, fostering a positive image of Chinese technological prowess. As nations collaborate on infrastructure projects, the ripple effects of Chinese innovation permeate global markets, setting new standards and benchmarks for technological excellence.

In the realm of technology, the BRI acts as a conduit for the dissemination of Chinese innovation and expertise. The construction of the 5G telecom services network by Huawei serves as a beacon of China's commitment to advancing global telecommunications. As the network spans across borders, it not only accelerates communication but also fosters technological collaboration between China and its partner nations. This collaborative approach contributes to the development of a global technological ecosystem where ideas, expertise, and innovations are shared, transcending geopolitical boundaries.

Simultaneously, infrastructure projects under the BRI reshape the physical and logistical landscape of partner nations. The construction of highways, railways, and bridges not only facilitates the movement of goods but also catalyzes economic development by creating employment opportunities and stimulating local industries. These infrastructural investments function as conduits for economic growth, enabling partner nations to leverage their strategic geographical positions within the BRI network.

However, the intertwining of technology and infrastructure within the BRI also raises pertinent questions about geopolitical influence and economic dependencies. The expansion of Chinese technological and infrastructure footprints globally has prompted concerns about the potential for asymmetric power dynamics. As China extends its economic reach, there is a need for vigilant scrutiny to ensure that collaborative ventures remain mutually beneficial and do not lead to undue economic or political dependencies.

Accordingly, China's economic ascent, as encapsulated by the Belt and Road vision, hinges on the strategic interplay between technology and infrastructure. The transformative journey from an isolationist state to a global economic powerhouse underscores the adaptability and resilience of China's economic policies. The symbiotic relationship between technological advancements and infrastructural development, exemplified by initiatives like the 5G telecom services network and the expansive Belt and Road Initiative, epitomizes China's multifaceted approach to global economic engagement. As China continues to shape the narrative of technological innovation and infrastructure development, the world watches with a mix of anticipation and scrutiny, cognizant of the profound impact these endeavors hold for the future of the global economy.

IX. ADAPTATION AND LEARNING: EVOLVING SOFT POWER STRATEGIES

Over the past few decades, political leadership in the Chinese political system has witnessed fresh faces in the top spots. With these new leaders, the Chinese Soft Power strategy evolved and is still even adapting under the Xi presidency. Major evolutions of President Xi's Soft Power strategy were evident at the level of foreign relations. In Glaser's (2014) paper, China has adopted a more avant-garde policy to defend its interests in the Asian region through the formation of regional security forums like the Shanghai Cooperation Organization (SCO). Moreover, President Xi emphasizes the concept of sovereignty without indulging in violence or threats to ensure that thought. As Glaser (2014) points out, China shows its mediating and peaceful nature by issuing criticism of North Korea's escalating behavior on the Korean peninsula and engaging in diplomatic and economic talks with the United States of America (USA) (Zreik, 2023).

The Soft Power policy has shaped China's stature on an international premise. With an evolving world marred with political, financial, and security conflicts, the Soft Power strategy may have worldwide implications for these issues. As mentioned in the previous sections, the Chinese state follows a notion of mediation and de-escalation in worldwide conflicts. However, regional engagements concerning sovereignty and security may pose a serious challenge to the Chinese Soft Power philosophy.

A distinct challenge to Chinese soft power is the island of Taiwan. As aforementioned, the KMT party and its leaders, who were the main rivals of the current ruling Communist Chinese Party (CCP), moved to the Chinese maritime island of Taiwan after their defeat in the Chinese Civil War in 1949. The island currently has its own currency, constitution, and armed forces that are independent of current Chinese rule. However, China, especially under President Xi's rule, has called for the One China policy, where Taiwan is considered a part of mainland China and not an independent state. This Chinese mindset was exacerbated by the elected presidents of Taiwan, who are continually calling for the consideration of Taiwan as a fully independent nation.

The USA and other Western nations are carefully following developments in Taiwan. The US has constantly supported the One China policy presented by the Republic of China but has always supported peace and stability across the Taiwan Strait. US-Chinese relations were threatened during the Biden administration, mainly due to the visit of House Speaker Nancy Pelosi to the island and the increase in defense agreements between both parties. Several experts fear that raising tensions between Taiwan and China might force the US into a large-scale conflict with China (Maizland, 2024).

Taiwan's constant calls for independence challenged the soft-power foreign policy mindset of China, where mediation is the key. This was evident on December 26, 2022, when China launched its largest air defense incursion over Taiwan. A total of seventy Chinese fighter planes flew over the Taiwanese skies, posing a message of warning for separation calls, as Lee (2022) reports.

The economic dimension of the Soft Power philosophy will shape China's monumental rise as an economic titan. As previously noted, the BRI's completion would facilitate trade between Asia, Africa, and Europe through linkages in the Middle East. This modified model of the Ancient Silk Road can contribute to the cultural, technological, and economic exchange of physical items and production advancement strategies.

X. CONCLUSION: NAVIGATING CHINESE SOFT POWER HORIZONS

In the dynamic landscape of Chinese political leadership, the evolution of soft power strategies has been a captivating journey, especially under President Xi's tenure. This metamorphosis is not a static phenomenon but a continuous adaptation to the complexities of global relations. Through the Belt and Road Initiative, China aims to strengthen its presence as an economic power around the world, particularly on the European and Asian continents. This is through its huge investments and the introduction of an alternative development model to the Western model, especially in Asian countries where China is making exceptionally large investments. As China navigates the intricacies of international dynamics, key findings emerge, revealing the nuanced facets of its Soft Power strategy.

1. Foreign Relations and Regional Security Forums:
   a. President Xi's Soft Power approach is marked by an avant-garde policy of defending Chinese interests, as evidenced by the formation of regional security forums like the Shanghai Cooperation Organization (SCO).
   b. The emphasis on sovereignty without resorting to violence or threats displays China's commitment to peaceful engagement in global affairs.
   c. Diplomatic efforts, such as engaging in talks with the United States and meditating on the North Korea issue, exemplify China's proactive and constructive role on the world stage.
2. Challenges and Mediation Philosophy:
   a. The Soft Power policy, rooted in mediation and de-escalation has positioned China as a diplomatic force in resolving worldwide conflicts.
   b. However, regional challenges, particularly those related to sovereignty and security, pose a formidable test to China's Soft Power philosophy.
3. Taiwan's Conundrum:
   a. Calls for independence from Taiwan clash with China's One China policy, leading to heightened tensions and even military posturing, as witnessed in the air defense incursion over Taiwan in December 2022.
   b. The island of Taiwan stands as a distinctive challenge to Chinese soft power, with historical and political complexities.
   c. USA's calls for security and peace in the East China Sea region despite the US administration's defense deals with Taiwan.
4. The Economic Dimension and the Belt and Road Initiative (BRI):
   a. Environmental and Financial drawbacks may hinder the progress of the BRI.
   b. The Belt and Road Initiative, with its ambitious goals of connecting Asia, Africa, and Europe, serves as a monumental pathway for cultural, technological, and economic exchange, reminiscent of the historical Silk Road.
   c. The economic dimension of China's Soft Power philosophy is integral to its rise as an economic titan.
   d. Transportation, Maritime, Technology, and Infrastructure sectors are the main targeted sectors of China's BRI plan.

The above literature tries to provide a detailed overview of China's global engagement on diverse levels. China's global outreach spreads to several social, political, and economic segments. This chapter might set the stage for future research studies concerning the development of China's global engagements and soft power stratagem under President Xi Jinping's third term.

In essence, the study illuminates the multidimensional nature of China's soft power strategy, highlighting its adaptability in the face of evolving global challenges. From diplomatic maneuvers and regional security initiatives to economic ambitions through the BRI, China's Soft Power narrative reflects a nation in constant flux, navigating the delicate balance between assertiveness and mediation on the international stage. The Taiwan issue emerges as a poignant example of the intricate challenges that evaluate China's Soft Power philosophy, hinting at the complexities inherent in the pursuit of global influence. As the world continues to witness China's diplomatic evolution, it is evident that the story of Chinese soft power is still unfolding, with each chapter revealing new dimensions of strategy, resilience, and adaptability.

REFERENCES

Ali, L. (2022, October 18). *Saudi Arabia Developing a Partnership with China*. Retrieved from Gulf Research Center: https://www.grc.net/single-commentary/66

Almit, M. S. (2010). *China and The Middle East: since World War II: Bilateral Approach*. Lexington Books.

Associated Press, Times of Israel. (2017, August 1). *China pushes four-point Israeli-Palestinian peace plan*. Retrieved from Times of Israel: https://www.timesofisrael.com/china-pushes-four-point-israeli-palestinian-peace-plan/

Ayyub, R., & Shepardson, D. (2023, March 24). *TikTok congressional hearing: CEO Shou Zi Chew grilled by US lawmakers*. Retrieved from Reuters: https://www.reuters.com/technology/tiktok-ceo-face-tough-questions-support-us-ban-grows-2023-03-23/

Bai, C., Ma, H., & Pan, W. (2012). *Spatial spillover and regional economic growth in China*. Tsinghua: School of Economics and Management, Tsinghua University.

Brasnett, J. (2021). Controlling Beliefs and Global Perceptions: Religion in Chinese Foreign Policy. *Sage Journals*, 41-58.

Britannica. (2021). *Bandung Conference*. Retrieved from Britannica: https://www.britannica.com/event/Bandung-Conference

Britannica. (2024, January 5). *Second Sino-Japanese War*. Retrieved from Britannica: https://www.britannica.com/event/Second-Sino-Japanese-War

Britannica. (2024, January 19). *Ancient Silk Road*. Retrieved from Britannica: https://www.britannica.com/money/topic/Silk-Road-trade-route

Castilla, C. (2016, March 18). China's Evolving Middle East Role. *Institute for Security and Development Policy. Policy Brief*, (193), 3. https://www.files.ethz.ch/isn/196849/2016-castilla-chinas-evolving-middle-east-role.pdf

CGTN. (2022, December 9). *Chart of the Day: First China-Arab States Summit, an epoch-making milestone*. Retrieved from CGTN: https://news.cgtn.com/news/2022-12-09/First-China-Arab-States-Summit-an-epoch-making-milestone-1fCWiaKTg1q/index.html

Chaziza, M. (2021). Egypt in China's Maritime Silk Road Initiative: Relations cannot surmount realities. In J.-M. F. Blanchard (Ed.), *China's Maritime Silk Road Initiative* (pp. 255–283). Africa, and the Middle East. doi:10.1007/978-981-33-4013-8_9

Cheng, C.-Y. (2007). Sino-Japanese Economic Relations: Interdependence and Conflict. In J. C. Hsiung (Ed.), *China and Japan at Odds* (pp. 81–94). Palgrave, Macmillan. doi:10.1057/9780230607118_5

China Daily. (2023, July 17). *Sino trade volumes soar with Middle East, Africa*. Retrieved from State Government: https://english.www.gov.cn/news/202307/17/content_WS64b49b48c6d0868f4e8ddd72.html

Chinese Government. (2023, July 17). *Sino trade volumes soar with Middle East, Africa.* Retrieved from the State Council the People's Republic of China Offcial Website: https://english.www.gov.cn/news/202307/17/content_WS64b49b48c6d0868f4e8ddd72.html#:~:text=Trade%20volume%20between%20China%20and,Emirates%2C%20Egypt%20and%20South%20Africa

Council on Foreign Relations. (2023, February 4). *U.S. China Relations.* Retrieved from Council on Foreign Relations: https://www.cfr.org/timeline/us-china-relations

Davis, R., & Frate, P. (2020, May 6). *How China's Tech Giants Charged Ahead When Coronavirus Shut Down Cinemas.* Retrieved from Variety: https://variety.com/2020/biz/features/china-entertainment-industry-internet-online-theaters-coronavirus-1234598816/

Eslami, M., & Papageorgiou, M. (2023, June 2). *China's Increasing Role in the Middle East: Implications for Regional and International Dynamics.* Retrieved from Georgetown Journal of International Affairs: https://gjia.georgetown.edu/2023/06/02/chinas-increasing-role-in-the-middle-east-implications-for-regional-and-international-dynamics/

Fairbank, J. K., & Goldman, M. (2006). China: A New History (2nd ed.). Belknap Press: An Imprint of Harvard University Press.

Fang, K., Wang, S., He, J., Song, J., Fang, C., & Jia, X. (2021). Mapping the environmental footprints of nations partnering the Belt and Road Initiative. *Resources, Conservation and Recycling, 164*, 12. doi:10.1016/j.resconrec.2020.105068

Farouk, Y. (2023, March 30). *Riyadh's Motivations Behind the Saudi-Iran Deal.* Retrieved from Carnegie Endowment for International Peace: https://carnegieendowment.org/2023/03/30/riyadh-s-motivations-behind-saudi-iran-deal-pub-89421

Fenby, J. (2005). *Chiang Kai Shek: China's Generalissimo and the Nation He Lost.* Da Capo Press.

Flores, W. L. (2023, September 20). *School of Economics and Management, Tsinghua University, China.* Retrieved from China Daily Global: https://regional.chinadaily.com.cn/en/2023-09/20/c_926787.htm#:~:text=In%202020%2C%20the%20economically%20rising,market%20of%202%20billion%20people

Glaser, B. (2014, December 3). *Chinese Foreign Policy under Xi Jinping: Continuity and Change.* Retrieved from Harvard: https://projects.iq.harvard.edu/files/asia-center/files/glaser_-_12-3-2014.pdf

Guobin, Y. (2016). The Power of the Internet in China: Citizen Activism Online. *International Journal of Communication, 4, 804-807.*

Hanban. (2016, November 6). *About Confucius Institutes & Hanban.* Retrieved from International Education Exchange Information Platform: http://www.ieeip.cn/bbx/1071727-1123792.html?id=27381&newsid=715399

Hillman, J. (2018, January 25). *China's Belt and Road Initiative: Five Years Later.* Retrieved from Center for Strategic International Studies: https://www.csis.org/analysis/chinas-belt-and-road-initiative-five-years-later

Hunter, A. (2009). Soft Power: China on the Global Stage. *The Chinese Journal of International Politics*, 2(3), 373–398. doi:10.1093/cjip/pop001

International Monetary Fund (IMF). (2023). *At a Crossroads: Sub-Saharan Africa's Economic Relations with China*. IMF.

Isoraite, M. (2009). Importance of strategic alliances. *Intellectual Economics*, 39-46.

Jakhar, P. (2019, September 19). *Confucius Institutes: The growth of China's controversial cultural branch*. Retrieved from BBC: https://www.bbc.com/news/world-asia-china-49511231

Kim, B. (2011). Trade and tribute along the Silk Road before the third century AD. *Journal of Central Eurasian Studies*, 1-24.

Knott, K. (2023, January 25). *Could Confucius Institutes Return to U.S. Colleges?* Retrieved from Inside Higher Ed: https://www.insidehighered.com/news/2023/01/26/report-proposes-waiver-criteria-confucius-institutes

Lee, L., & Wang, E. (2023, November 30). *China seeks 'concrete' roadmap for two-state solution to solve Gaza conflict*. Retrieved from Reuters: https://www.reuters.com/world/middle-east/china-calls-concrete-roadmap-two-state-solution-solve-gaza-conflict-2023-11-30/

Lee, Y. (2022, December 26). *Taiwan reports China's largest incursion yet to air defence zone*. Retrieved from Reuters: https://www.reuters.com/world/china/taiwan-says-43-chinese-air-force-planes-crossed-taiwan-strait-median-line-2022-12-26/

Li, X., & Worm, V. (2011, March). Building China's Soft power for a Peaceful Rise. *Journal of Chinese Political Science*, 16(1), 69–89. doi:10.1007/s11366-010-9130-2

Lieberthal, K. (2011, December 21). *The American Pivot to Asia*. Retrieved from Brookings: https://www.brookings.edu/articles/the-american-pivot-to-asia/

Maizland, L. (2024, February 8). *Why China-Taiwan Relations Are So Tense*. Retrieved from Council on Foreign Relations: https://www.cfr.org/backgrounder/china-taiwan-relations-tension-us-policy-biden#chapter-title-0-5

Mcrbride, J., Berman, N., & Chatzky, A. (2023, February 2). *China's Massive Belt and Road Initiative*. Retrieved from Council on Foreign Relations: https://www.cfr.org/backgrounder/chinas-massive-belt-and-road-initiative

Mengying, B. (2023, December 24). *2023: The year of resurgence and success in Chinese cinema*. Retrieved from Global Times: https://www.globaltimes.cn/page/202312/1304222.shtml

Nye, J. (2002). *Soft Power: the Means to Success in World Politics*. Public Affairs.

Observatory of Economic Complexity (OEC). (2021). *Japan-China*. Retrieved from OEC: https://oec.world/en/profile/bilateral-country/jpn/partner/chn

Regencia, T. (2021, June 8). *What you should know about China's minority Uighurs*. Retrieved from Al Jazera: https://www.aljazeera.com/news/2021/7/8/uighurs-timeline

Spence, J. D. (1990). *The Search for Modern China*. W Nortan & Company.

Statista. (2023, November). *Video Streaming (SVoD) - China*. Retrieved from Statista: https://www.statista.com/outlook/dmo/digital-media/video-on-demand/video-streaming-svod/china

Stueck, W. (1995). *The Korean War: An International History*. Princeton University Press.

Sweetman, M. (2014, September 23). *The Importance of Social Media in China*. Retrieved from South China Morning Post: https://www.scmp.com/article/1598699/importance-social-media-china?campaign=1598699&module=perpetual_scroll_0&pgtype=article

US Department of State. (2021). *2022 Report on International Religious Freedom: China (Includes Hong Kong, Macau, Tibet, and Xinjiang)*. US Department of State.

Vaisi, G. (2022, March 1). *The 25-year Iran-China agreement, endangering 2,500 years of heritage*. Retrieved from Middle east Institute: https://www.mei.edu/publications/25-year-iran-china-agreement-endangering-2500-years-heritage

Wang, C. (2023, February 3). *China Belt and Road Initiative (BRI) Investment Report 2022*. Retrieved from Green Finance and Development Center: https://greenfdc.org/china-belt-and-road-initiative-bri-investment-report-2022/

Xing, Y., Liu, Y., Cooper, S. C., & Vrontis, D. (2023). *Reviving China's global footprint along the Silk Roads and the 'Belt and Road Initiative': Chinese overseas industrial park in Egypt*. Buisness History. doi:10.1080/00076791.2023.2233426

Zhang, S. G. (1995). *Mao's Military Romanticism: China and the Korean War, 1950-1953*. University of Kansas.

Zhu, Y. (2019). New National Initiatives of Modernizing Education in China. *Sage Journals*, 353-362.

Zreik, M. (2021, September 1). The Potential of a Sino-Lebanese Partnership through the Belt and Road Initiative (BRI). *Contemporary Arab Affairs*, *14*(3), 125–145. doi:10.1525/caa.2021.14.3.125

Zreik, M. (2022). The Chinese presence in the Arab region: Lebanon at the heart of the Belt and Road Initiative. *International Journal of Business and Systems Research*, *16*(5-6), 644–662. doi:10.1504/IJBSR.2022.125477

Zreik, M. (2023). Navigating HRM Challenges in Post-Pandemic China: Multigenerational Workforce, Skill Gaps, and Emerging Strategies. In A. Even & B. Christiansen (Eds.), *Enhancing Employee Engagement and Productivity in the Post-Pandemic Multigenerational Workforce* (pp. 171–188). IGI Global. doi:10.4018/978-1-6684-9172-0.ch008

Zreik, M. (2024). China's Energy Conundrum: Navigating Through Crises, Policy Responses, and Global Impact. In M. Ozel Ozcan (Ed.), *Analyzing Energy Crises and the Impact of Country Policies on the World* (pp. 139–159). IGI Global. doi:10.4018/979-8-3693-0440-2.ch008

Chapter 15
Soft Power Dynamics:
Analyzing Chinese and American Influence in the Middle East

Mohamad Al Mokdad
https://orcid.org/0009-0002-9188-5272
CEDS, Paris, France

Weam Karkout
Lebanese University, Lebanon

ABSTRACT

This research deals with the study of the soft power and its effects on one of the most important regions in the world, which is the Middle East region, and it was found that through soft power, a country can penetrate other countries through a variety of tools without resorting to hard power. Three components of soft power were found—culture, political values, and foreign policy—as soft power does not mean concern for national interests only and ignoring the interests of others. By getting to know the components of American and Chinese soft power that have been identified in research and the continuous growth that is happening rapidly, both United States of America and China have been able to build soft power in areas that include political, economic, social, and technological. They have played the tools of soft power. Culture, foreign policy, and political values have an important role in establishing the principle of peace and international and regional cooperation. The study found that there are effects of the soft power of both countries in the Middle East, especially the Arab region, especially since the Chinese economic rise has made the Arab states the first supplier of oil, and that China's investments in the Arab Gulf region in various fields have contributed to the impact of its economic tools in the region. On the other hand, Chinese and American exports, including the military industries, increased to the Arab states, and they occupied advanced ranks in the import table. In addition, China and USA seek to find an important role for it in the future in protecting international shipping lines in the region to protect its growing economic interests. The study showed the difference regarding the way each of the two countries deal with soft power and its impact on the Middle East region.

DOI: 10.4018/979-8-3693-2444-8.ch015

INTRODUCTION

No society can live without relations with other societies, even if they differ from it in race, language, belief, and culture. Therefore, the major countries, through their research centers and thinkers, thought a lot about how to regain their position or face new challenges without resorting to the use of hard power and replacing it with soft power. First, we will define power in general, and then we will continue by talking about soft power.

The concept of power is considered one of the basic concepts in political science and political sociology, as it is the basic ruler of relations between countries. Power has several definitions, perhaps the most prominent one is for "Max Weber" who defined power as the capacity to influence, lead, dominate, or otherwise have an impact on the life and actions of others in society (Munro, 2023).

Based on this definition, force or the "threat of using it" has a significant impact on the international system, and may push weak dependent states and infiltrated societies to carry out actions against it, as well as to refrain from carrying out other practices in order to avoid being exposed to the consequences of the use of force against them. But the concept of power has evolved and taken on multiple forms and facets.

Traditional military power is hard power. This power has emerged since ancient times and was the main factor in resolving international conflict. Especially in the First and Second World Wars, in which hard power was used, and the arms race between the warring countries had priority to resolve the conflict, subjugate opponents, and impose pressure on the people.

After the collapse of the Soviet Union and the emergence of unipolarity, the influence of military power or the threat of its use diminished, and economic power emerged, which became the basic criterion for relations between countries, with the beginning of the era of globalization.

With the end of the Cold War between Russia and the United States of America, the USA became a unipolar center, so American experts and theorists began to propose new concepts of power, until the concept of soft power emerged. The term soft power appeared for the first time in an article published in 1990 by Joseph Nye, published in the American magazine Foreign Affairs, using the term "co-optive power."

After that, countries and research centers began to show a high interest in soft power, and sought to integrate it into international strategies and foreign policies. In 2007, Secretary-General of the Chinese Communist Party, Jintao, spoke about China's need to increase its soft power. In 2013, Russian Foreign Minister Sergei Lavrov considered that Russia had begun "to control the tools of soft power, but this came much later than its partners who invented those tools" (Lavrov, 2013).

Although the term soft power appeared in the 1990s, some thinkers considered that the concept appeared much earlier. This concept in general appeared in the writings of philosophers such as Socrates and Confucius. The writings of the Italian thinker Antonio Gramsci are the first nucleus for the gradual emergence of this concept through the theory of the cultural hegemony of capitalism through educational institutions, such as schools, universities, newspapers …

With the aim of controlling the minds of these people, ensuring that they do not leave, and preserving them in capitalist society" (Gramsci, 1971).

The thinker Joseph Nye defined soft power as "the ability to attract, not through coercion, military threats, or economic pressure, nor through paying bribes and offering money to buy support and loyalty, as was the case in traditional American strategies, but rather through attraction and making others want what you want (Nye J., 2007). This term is currently widely used in international affairs by researchers, analysts and politicians.

Nye considered that soft power is an effective weapon that achieves goals through attraction, rather than payment of money and coercion (Nye J., 2016). As for the thinker - Michel Foucault, he considered soft power as indirect coercion and obligation and a rational debate aimed at influencing public opinion inside and outside the country.

If we compare the two definitions, it becomes clear that Nye and Foucault agree that soft power is influencing public opinion and other countries, by direct non-violent means, in order to control minds. But Nye excluded economic means as part of soft power to influence, while Foucault thinks that economic means are necessary for influence.

Although soft power alone is not sufficient, its presence can be a power multiplier. It is important for the country to be able to define its political agendas in order to win the favor of other countries in the field of global politics, and not just force them to change through threats or the use of hard power.

Soft power, which pushes others to reach the outcomes it wants, makes the state gain people's sympathy instead of exposing them to coercion. A state that possesses soft power will be sparing in using the sticks and carrots it has.

So soft power is not considered relatively new, but its roots, as some see, began at the end of World War II, through the Fulbright student exchange program around the world in 1946 as a means of influencing cultures and dominating the minds of other societies.

The US Soft Power in the Middle East

The United States of America sought to employ the tools and means of its soft power to achieve the goals of its foreign policies in general and in the Middle East region in particular. America was able to invest these means in the field of its foreign political work to reach the goals that it wanted to achieve.

Based on the fact that foreign policy is a reflection of the interactions that take place within society, and that foreign policy is an extension of internal policy with all its pressures and components, cultural and social characteristics play a major role in the process of making foreign policy, such as the prevailing culture pattern, civilizational and intellectual traditions, the factor of historical experience, and religious and social values. The external political decision is an embodiment of the society's identity and the style of leadership thinking influenced by the social milieu (Fahmi, 2019).

Therefore, the influential relationship often appears between the foreign policy of decision makers and the national character of society, where the psychological characteristics of society are a factor that distinguishes it from other societies, and that the national character of any Middle Eastern country embodies the identity of this country in belonging to the ties and components that constitute it (Moukalled i. s., 2021). In this context, former US Secretary of State Colin Powell stated: "I cannot think of more valuable asset to our country than the friendship of future world leaders who received their education here" (Nye J., 2014).

This is because international students usually return home with a greater appreciation for American values and institutions. The millions of people who have studied in the United States over the years constitute a wonderful goodwill toward our country and many of these students reach positions where they can influence policy outcomes that are important to Americans.

The United States of America has sought to achieve goals of great importance to enhance its soft power. "Heeter Mahoney", the Counselor for Media and Cultural Affairs at the United States Embassy in Cairo, confirmed that American popular diplomacy seeks to achieve several goals, not just security and political ones. He added scientific and cultural goals, emphasizing the importance of the cultural axis of popular diplomacy in achieving cultural dialogue between peoples (Bouderdaben, 2019).

The biggest challenge facing the United States of America is trying to attract foreigners through the education strategy for the twenty-first century by using technology to teach education, as well as the strategy of the Ministry of education in the USA. The attractiveness of soft power, which grew through cultural relations between members of the elite in the targeted countries, made an important contribution to achieve the goals of American policy. It happened that many people in the Middle East, especially young people, accepted American lifestyles and popular culture, from fashion, fast food, to American music and movies. These aspects have become part of the globalization movement, reshaping the choices and tastes of millions of people, in addition to being a manifestation of the social and cultural transformations witnessed by the countries of the Middle East and the Arabian Gulf region during the last two decades in particular (Abdulsalam R., 2022).

One of the most prominent effects of American soft power has been evident through the use of the English language more than the mother tongue Arabic in the countries of the Middle East, not only in the field of business, but even more so in the field of public institutions and administration. English language has turned into a daily communication, especially in the Arabian Gulf region, which is inhabited by large non-Arab communities, witnessing a growing American-Anglo-Saxon presence. It has become a language that unites the world, as (60%) of foreign language learners in the world study the English language, which has entered as an essential part of all educational systems in the world (Bakir, 2018).

And also, through the widespread and rapid spread of universities and schools, in addition to American cultural and research centers in the Middle East region, as children of the middle and wealthy classes are moving more and more towards educating their children in Western schools and universities in general, and American ones in particular, after belonging to these foreign educational institutions has become a social prestige. Perhaps the most dangerous phenomenon is the almost complete isolation shown by American universities, especially in some Arab Gulf countries, from the cultural and linguistic environment in which they exist. The intellectual and political elite in the region tend to be American in culture and identity, with little connection to self-identity (Abdulsalam R., 2021).

Therefore, cultural tools and means are considered effective tools in spreading American culture in various countries of the world, as they try through these tools to form political elites or influence political elites, opinion leaders, youth, and university students in spreading American political thought, American culture, and American political values.

The propaganda carried out by the United States of America is a communication activity to spread its ideas and promote policies that it wants to implement, and to consolidate the convictions of the audience being addressed, which is intended to influence it with the aim of creating a public opinion supportive of it and its positions on the one hand, and then mobilizing this opinion on the other hand, against everyone who opposes this policy.

As "Harold Lasswell" says, the goal of this propaganda is determined to mobilize hatred against the enemy, preserve the friendship of allies, and preserve the friendship of neutral countries, and in return, destroy the morale of the enemy and create an internal public opinion that works against it. It requires propaganda, in order to be highly effective and influential to serve the goals of the state's foreign policy (Kaufmann, 2021).

American media institutions play a major role in achieving the goals and interests of the United States, as they are responsible for disseminating American concepts and values, in addition to their role in promoting information. According to "Helen Thomas", the dean of journalists at the White House, in 1990, the media has become an echo of what the White House declares (Latosh, 1992).

In another field, the United States, due to its great development in the field of information, media and communication technology, has begun to employ (propaganda) in implementing its strategy by influencing the minds of the masses and changing their attitudes and behavior in a way that serves its policy and achieves its interests and goals, or what (Nay and Awen) called soft power, which does not depends on the brutality of fleets and war cannons, but on capturing minds and hearts, and this is what Brzezinski emphasized: "The rapid spread of the Internet as a new tool for communication is one of the most important manifestations of America's great global influence as the social leader of the world."

On the same level, the USA employed propaganda with the film industry. During the era of President Roosevelt, coordination began at all levels between the Office of Military Intelligence, the US National Security Agency, and the main companies operating in the film industry in Hollywood, and the American government issued a directive to Hollywood including the types of topics that can honor the American national effort (Henry, 2015).

The media in the United States of America is considered an important force influencing the essence of its national policy. It has witnessed many profound changes in the field of international media through the way these media agencies and news organizations conduct their work at the international level. The American media has become a phenomenon that transcends national borders through its management, including the American CNN station and MTV channels, and it has established several of its channels, such as (Radio Sawa Radio and Al Hurra Channel) to improve its image in the Middle East (Garib, 2022).

Television also exerts a great influence in shaping the mentality and psychology of societies in the Middle East, as it is a primary source of political information, and creates immediate and simple impressions. It presents news and events without analysis, quickly, and indicates different points of view, in addition to its use with the film industry, given that the film industry is an instrument of American strategy.

Thus, we find that American foreign policy did not consider the media at the beginning of the forties of the twentieth century, due to secret diplomacy, and because the people were not interested in international affairs, they attached the utmost importance to the media to support their policy at the international level, and with regard to the various issues in which they were a party. The foreign political decision is linked to the extent of information available to foreign decision-makers about the trends of people in foreign countries related to this decision or targeted by it. Therefore, the state tries, through available and appropriate media, to influence foreign public opinion to gain its support for certain issues, and diplomacy searches for support in particular outside the national borders. In this way, the media is linked to diplomacy in implementing foreign policy. The great and continuous development of the media offices of various countries abroad clearly shows the importance of the media in serving the policies of foreign countries and serving their goals at the level of diplomatic work. US Minister "Dean Rusk" expressed the importance of the media's role in serving the goals of American foreign policy, saying: "The media is indispensable to the American foreign policy of the USA" (Hans, 2015).

In 2002, the United States of America launched Radio Sawa, which provides a news summary every half hour that includes the latest news about American politics and developments in the Middle East and the rest of the world. The summary does not take more than a few minutes, after which the radio returns to Western music, where it used to play the music segment (85%) of the total broadcast, while selected news that serves American politics occupies the remaining (15%) of the broadcast hours. Radio Sawa is one of the American international services supervised by the Board of Trustees of American International Broadcasting, which allocated $35 million. Although it began broadcasting under the auspices of Voice of America, Washington soon abandoned Voice of America in favor of the new Radio Sawa to penetrate the media in the Middle East and Arab youth under the age of 30. The goal of this is to try to influence the trends of public opinion in a direct way that allows the image to be conveyed at the level of internal public opinion and then at the external level. The only means to achieve this is the media. In this context, former President "Bill Clinton" said that the only foreign policy that can remain is the one supported by the public opinion are destined to survive, and this is done with the support of the media, which plays its role as a mechanism to direct this opinion (Lecoutre, 2020).

If we compare what "Joseph Nye" talked about soft power, and what happened in more than one country in the Middle East in terms of regime change movements, we will see that it applies very much to what "Nye" said, which is not to rely on direct and coercive military force, but rather to activate tools other than The military tool in the processes of change was such that this tool was effective, especially in a period in which the entire world was witnessing a technological boom that made the world very fast, and the average person could not distinguish between what harmed him and what benefited him from technological means. "Joseph Nye" emphasized in his talk about soft power that it is the ability of a particular nation to influence other nations, by making peoples influenced by other experiences in governance, exercising democracy and freedoms, and then directing their public choices, based on the attractiveness of its social cultural and its system of values, instead of relying on coercion or direct military threats. This attraction can be spread in various ways through making people take what they want and making them believe that they did it of their own free will, as well as soft power tools, international organizations, public diplomacy and all companies and institutions that work to get what they want through attraction rather than compulsion.

On the political level, the idea of spreading democracy is considered one of the most important soft power tools used by successive American administrations to confront or besiege countries they described as "axis of evil" countries (Nye J. S., 2003).

In December 2002, the democratic reform project was presented to the world under the title of the Middle East Partnership Mission. This project later developed into a partnership project for progress and a common future in the Middle East, a project that was officially approved at the G-8 summit in June of 2004 after "Bush" administration was forced to make amendments to it due to pressure from Europeans and Arab governments. Despite the political and media hype that accompanied this project, a careful reading of this document highlights that the issue of political reform was not the main focus of attention as much as attention focused on several major axes that are priorities for Americans before anything else, such as education, women, non-governmental organizations, business sector and new American institutions were sent to serve these major tasks, and to restructure and transform American institutions that support democracy and political reform in the Arab region (Nye J., 2014).

The American process to the issue of democracy was based from the beginning on a missionary perception, which assumed the existence of a kind of inevitable correlation between reform and democracy, and the promotion of American interests and options in the Middle East region. If the spread of tyranny, corruption, and one-party rule that dominated the Middle East region had contributed to the emergence of terrorism groups and hatred of the United States of America. Spreading freedom and democracy will contribute to eliminating terrorism, spreading liberal values, and consolidating American interests.

American policy is also based on winning the battle of minds and hearts by improving America's image in the middle eastern world, using the tools of soft diplomacy, public relations campaigns, building institutions, and pumping money. It is known that the increase in hatred towards the United States has become a major inconvenience to American decision-makers, as it results in the shrinkage of American influence in general and the decline of its interests at the levels of trade, culture and politics. In this context, the position of Assistant Secretary of State for Diplomacy and Public Affairs was created, and "Karen Hughes", who is close to President "Bush", was appointed to head it since 2005 in an attempt to improve America's public image in the world. However, Hughes did not last long in this difficult task. In 2007, she announced her resignation for special reasons. Observers attributed the reason for this resignation to the intensity of the conflicts between the centers of power in the American administration, in addition to her disappointment in the possibility of improving America's image in the countries of the Middle East in an atmosphere of expanding resentment and hatred for it is expanding and spreading day after day (Hehir, 2017).

In the context of political reform initiatives within the framework of democratic transformation, the United States of America put forward the Greater Middle East Initiative, which included three priorities: promoting democracy and good governance, building a knowledge society, and expanding economic opportunities, in an effort to impose democracy on all countries in the Middle East, Regardless of the circumstances of this country and its cultural specificity, the draft initiative that the USA was preparing to discuss at the summit of industrialized countries a few months later was leaked to the press, especially the London newspaper "Al-Hayat", which published a translation of the draft in its issue dated February 13, 2004, which made the United States allies who are close to the Americans in the Middle East, surprised by what is being proposed, especially since they were not consulted in advance about such initiatives. On the other hand, their fears have increased that the administration of President George Bush has decided that its ruling friends must be replaced with a new team, and many officials in these countries expressed positions that went beyond the threshold of lack of prior consultation to expressing dissatisfaction and astonishment (Buzan, 2022).

As for civil society organizations, they have a great role in contributing to the implementation of foreign policy in light of diplomatic practice, and this gives them the most important role in being a participating part in the process of implementing foreign policy alongside government agencies, through coordination between them and non-governmental organizations represented in all civil society.

In the last periods of the twentieth century, the term civil society has re-emerged to refer to the group of voluntary organizations that exist within modern societies, such as business federations, professional unions, farmers' unions, and civil society associations. Accordingly, new roles have emerged in civil society, especially with regard to foreign policy and diplomatic practice. Accordingly, the role of civil society institutions has grown in various fields of development, such as economic, social, educational, health, and environmental development, which has led to linking the activities of these institutions, whether at the local or international level, expanding globally, and enhancing their interaction and speed of response to developments.

The effective role that civil society organizations play in issues of conflict and disputes is through the efforts of informal diplomacy, which is represented in the roles of these organizations, in order to provide alternative ways to make peace, which occupies a good position as one of the informal bodies. Diplomacy and foreign policy, due to its deep presence in local communities, has the ability to create local infrastructure across different levels of society, which supports the resources of the reconciliation process and allows it to engage in negotiations at the international level that contribute to the implementation of foreign policy and thus resolve conflicts.

Thus, it played an effective role that paved the way for subsequent steps towards resolving the conflict. As happened in Somalia when the Institute for Peace and Life carried out an operation called Burma in 1992, which consisted of conducting several contacts at the sub-factional level, then contacts through the highest levels of society and then to the national and international level, which culminated in a meeting between the senior factions and resulted in the election of a government and president for Somalia (Lenczowski, 2019).

Therefore, it can be said that revitalizing the important and strategic role of civil society organizations in international affairs and achieving foreign policy goals is fundamentally linked to providing a climate of democracy, good governance, transparency, and respect for rights, public freedoms, and religious freedoms. If this climate is provided, it can allow for popular participation in confronting any external influence through these organizations, the role of which is increasing in a way that attracts official funding to implement the foreign policies of countries.

With the bombings of September 11, 2001, American foreign policy trends changed, and the beginning of these changes was a reconsideration of relations with its allies in the Middle East. The argument that was given in this context was the lack of a democratic climate in the countries of the region. This change in American policy was in line with its goals of launching retail projects on the ground, and this is what led to the inclusion of civil society organizations in middle eastern society to penetrate the Arab social fabric, and then the American administration at that time, headed by "Bush Jr.", moved towards changing the approach that had previously been adopted by other administrations of the White House, represented by a statement by then US Secretary of State "Condoleezza Rice" in Cairo in 2005 when she said that the United States had tried for sixty years to seek stability at the expense of democracy in the Middle East, and we had not achieved either (henri, 2018).

Traditional diplomacy is important and essential for the United States, but it has become insufficient. This is because global developments require reaching beyond governments, that is, direct communication with citizens, and expanding the scope of the Ministry of Foreign Affairs' files to include issues that were previously considered an internal matter, such as: environmental laws, drugs and organized crime, and what is related to the economy and hunger, given that the impact of these issues cross borders, and thus employees of the US State Department, the Civil Service, and the US Agency for International Development have become the backbone of the United States' partnership with other countries (Clinton, 2010).

Thus, it has become necessary for the United States to establish a global civil service to be at the same level of flexibility and efficiency enjoyed by the US Army, especially since interaction with governments has become insufficient in the information age, where public opinion is gaining increasing importance, Until non-governmental agencies became the most capable of influencing the course of events, and then the role of the American ambassador in any country became not limited to official relations with the government, but also with the people of the country in which he works. In this context, comes the Open Government Partnership (OGP) which revolves around dialogue between government and civil society, specifically the openness of governments to their citizens, through increasing transparency, accountability, and enhancing civic participation. This initiative works as a network of support for leaders and citizens working to achieve greater transparency and accountability for governments in the whole world, this solo effort may be dangerous, but through this partnership, there is hope to change that, according to Clinton.

Although the countries of the Middle East were able to achieve national independence through freedom from colonial control, the reality of this independence remained a formal and superficial independence that does not express the true political will to make decisions that may be described as historic.

This administration, which is supposed to express national independence, remained politically captive to external powers in one way or another, or it was an expression of a form of subordination to these powers. In this field, the intellectual cultural approach is considered one of the main approaches. The uniqueness of the United States in leading the world has led to the establishment of a cultural-intellectual strategy, where cultural dependency has turned into the process of consolidating the culture of penetration. American soft power, with its cultural, political and media shades, has contributed to a large extent to bringing about the required change without engaging in battles and military confrontations that could contribute to inflicting more material and moral losses on the United States of America. The most important characteristic of the amendment made by the United States of America to its strategy with the beginning of the events of the Arab Spring in the Middle East and the Arab countries in general, is the adoption of a new style of intervention as a means of directing the affairs of this region, the basic essence of which is replacing hard power with soft power. Therefore, through the United Nations, NATO, and many other mechanisms, it will demand that its European allies assume greater responsibilities in protecting American hegemony in the region. This is what US Secretary of State Hillary Clinton called the new pattern of intervention (Clement, 2022).

The amendment made by the United States of America to its strategy in the Middle East aims to avoid plunging again into a war similar to the Iraq war, while at the same time aiming to maintain its direction in the affairs of the Middle East.

The primary goal of the American strategy, through the comprehensive use of all diplomatic, economic and strategic means, is to reformulate American hegemony over the affairs of the Middle East. President Obama's strategy in the middle east, although it appears superficially harmful to American leadership, in fact, it suits American strategic interests.

Chinese Soft Power in the Middle East

China has been able to build its soft power in the areas of culture, political values, and model development, international institutions, international formation, and economic temptations which may be practiced through three diplomatic channels: official, economic, and public diplomacy (Worm, 2010).

China's soft power tools differed and distinguished themselves from other countries because of its political, economic and cultural specificity, as follows:

First: Culture

After the state adopted soft power, the intellectual opinion now prevailed that culture is the primary resource for the state's power. The Chinese leadership adopted this opinion, which led to the expansion of the scope of financing and development of cultural soft power resources inside China and its expansion abroad, as contemporary Chinese culture consists of its basic elements. The three are traditional culture, communist ideology, and more recently western values (Osman, 2017).

As for traditional cultural values, they are mainly derived from Confucianism, Taoism, and then Buddhism. Confucianism is considered the basic foundation of the Chinese cultural tradition, as it is without dispute the most influential doctrine and still constitutes a basic source of behavior of the Chinese in their relations with each other.

Chinese popular culture enjoys greater communication and ease of access to high culture, just like films and other forms of mass entertainment, and can spread more ideas than forms of high culture by expressing universal values that others desire and support, making the country more legitimate in the eyes of its audience (Ullah, 2015).

The role of Chinese arts, literature and cinema has been prominent, as many galleries and cinemas have been opened in order to highlight the most important elements of China's global success. These resources contribute to the cultural dimension of soft power and include many elements that may not be managed directly by the government but rather follow from broader forces within society. These elements include art, film, television, music, and sports, as well as writers, musicians, athletes, and artists that can contribute to the government's soft power when they achieve a significant and positive international reputation (Hussein, 2016).

Confucius Institutes were opened in Africa in Kenya, Nigeria, Zimbabwe, and South Africa, after the first institute at the University of Nairobi. The number of foreign students studying in Chinese universities with the support of the Chinese government also increased to 140,000 students in China until 2023 (Sayama, 2016).

Chinese culture has now entered the stage of what is called the China Dream. For a long time during the past century, the transformation of the American dream into a dream that humanity seeks was inevitable. Then, after the establishment of the European Union, the question of the European dream was raised: How could Europe achieve its dream? Here was the desire of the Europeans to achieve their dream in their own way, based on the strength of European unity. As for the dream of China, it is the dream of reviving culture. Therefore, our goal in all development is to show the world the reconstructed cultural image of China (all, 2014).

Second: Foreign Policy

China's view of international relations has been characterized by traditionalism, focusing on the principle of sovereignty of the nation-state, which must not be infringed upon or interfered in its internal affairs, even if this state commits a serious human rights violation or genocide on its territory. China also still emphasizes that Its rejection of the use of force outside the territorial borders of the state, and all of these principles have a background in Chinese culture, and in the ideas of ancient Chinese philosophers, most notably Confucius, which is a culture that calls for peace and stability and the rejection of what would be considered aggression (Manafih, 2014).

China's new strategy was built on important theoretical statements, the most prominent of which are: (Al-Badrani, 2015)

1- The rise of China was based on maximizing economic production, especially in the field of trade exchanges
2- China constantly declares that military solutions are considered to be rejected in the era of globalization.
3- Officially, China always reiterates the concepts of peaceful solution, internal stability, coexistence, world peace, sustainable human and economic development and mutual benefit.
4- China calls for joint international efforts to confront the challenges of globalization in light of global crises, in many areas, including environmental issues, global warming, development, desertification, food shortages, and confronting natural disasters.
5- China still considers itself a large developing country, with huge economic and military capabilities that qualifies it for a central role in the new world order.

China has now established a clear role for Nye's concept of public diplomacy, with its emphasis on communicating with populations rather than simply communicating with the governments of targeted countries. Public diplomacy is about establishing a logical, legitimate, and credible national position; that is, establishing specific agenda items as important and building relationships with specific individuals and groups in the targeted countries through conferences, research programs, and other activities (WANG, 2008).

This is the concept of China's soft power involves communicating Chinese attitudes and opinions, establishing a good international image for China, creating a favorable international environment, and promoting a peaceful, harmonious and cooperative world (Worm, 2010, p. 78).

The use of soft power has become an important aspect of China's foreign strategy, and this strategy not only helped Beijing dispel global anxiety about the Chinese threat theory, but also strengthened Beijing's image as a guardian of international peace, as adopting a soft power strategy in foreign policy is a necessary step to cast doubts surrounding its rise.

The soft power strategy may achieve two important goals for China: (WANG, 2008)

1- Reducing the impact of the Chinese threat theory and its challenges on national security.
2- Improving China's relations with neighboring countries.

China has also engaged in active and voluntary multilateral diplomacy since the 1990s. China hoped to expand its room for maneuver in the international arena through active participation in multilateral institutions, and as of 2008, China had become a member of more than 130 international organizations and had signed more than 250 multilateral treaties (all, 2014).

Third: Political Values

The world has not known a civilization that has preserved the purity of its identity like the Chinese civilization, and has influenced those around it through its religions that impart a state of alertness to possessing direct knowledge of things and the truth of the universe. The Chinese civilization is homogeneous and fused into a single unity by virtue of the isolation that nature imposed on China, an isolation that made all differences vanish. Although China is one of the oldest civilizations, its memory is still present and influential and effective so far (Nafi, 1999).

The civilization of ancient China and its moral values have been greatly reflected in the reality of China today, and what Chinese leaders say about the issue of soft power clearly affects how others define and discuss this issue, as there is a relatively common understanding among them about what soft power means, where it is considered as an attempt to promote what China is and stands for, including emphasizing its historical roots based on current thinking, designing identity and policy to correct misperceptions among the public across countries about Chinese motives and intentions, by bringing more people across the world into contact with Chinese understandings and preferences (Breslin, 2011).

Despite the criticism directed at China that it is not well recognized in terms of its political values, which often suffers from low freedom of expression, low religious freedom, and difficulty in granting its citizens and maintaining their political and other civil rights, some researchers argue that this is the weakness of China's soft power, as there are many problems in China today: corruption, censorship, unequal opportunities, privileged class, lack of transparency, etc. (Arif, 2017).

Many believe that China is still an authoritarian regime. Many see China increasing its influence in the global conscience, especially after the collapse of The Soviet Union and China's ability to avoid its collapse, despite the fact that it pursues the same central communist policy, but it remedied the matter and acted flexibly, responding to many of the sharp changes that prevailed in the world without losing its balance or its ideas (Nafi, 1999).

China found protection in its history and civilization from the political changes that changed the international community. Chinese morals also played a major role in China's social and political cohesion and its preservation of its independence for four thousand years (Raslan, 1998).

A Chinese researcher believes that the Chinese Communist Party must learn from its past, as it was learning and thinking about how to transform itself from a revolutionary party into a ruling party, and this is not an easy task (Worm, 2010).

THE EFFECTS OF CHINESE SOFT POWER IN THE MIDDLE EAST

The impact that has been made clear by Chinese soft power at the global level should have become clearer in the Arab countries for a set of geopolitical, economic, political and cultural justifications and factors. Researchers have emphasized that Arab-Chinese relations are historical and intertwined throughout the ages, and this is what facilitated these relations' ways of distinguishing them in the modern era (Al-Haddad, 2017).

The Arabs did not disagree on their relations with China, although the Arab countries differed among themselves on a number of regional and international issues, including international relations, the relationship with China is one of the few issues on which the Arab countries agree. When talking about the Middle East, at a time when Arab-Arab relations have declined or disappeared, the volume of Arab foreign relations has increased, especially with the United States of America, Western countries, and some Asian powers, especially Japan, the ASEAN countries, and China, being one of the important Asian economic powers in Asia, which has achieved high levels of high in the volume of economic relations with Arab countries, distributed into three sectors: oil, investments, and markets (Hamid, 2006).

Guo Zixing, head of the Institute for Research on Development in Asia and Africa of the Chinese State Council, explains the Chinese perspective on Arab-Chinese relations, as the philosophy on which Chinese economic policy towards Arab countries is based is to work to support sustainable cooperation between them and is based on the (win-win) rule. In addition to not interfering in its internal affairs, as the United States of America does with regard to its bargaining for investment in exchange for its direct intervention and imposing its oversight on the issues of democracy and human rights in Arab countries (Abdullah, 2018).

As for Chinese-Middle East relations, they have grown strongly, especially in economic aspects. China is currently the eighth largest trading partner of the Gulf Cooperation Council countries, which in turn is considered the backbone of Arab trade. It supplies China with about 50% of its oil imports, and the Kingdom of Saudi Arabia in particular is the first oil financier among these countries (Deifallah, 2016).

Highlighting the influence of China's soft power towards the Middle East through the economic and political tools of Chinese soft power, as follows:

First: Economic Tools

Researchers point out that Chinese interest in the Middle East is based on a number of considerations: This is because of the extreme geo-economic importance that the region occupies for China, given that these countries are rich in large reserves of petroleum, the main driver of the wheel of development and industrialization in China. Therefore, China has given special importance to its relations with the Arab oil-producing countries, and has worked to establish long-term economic partnerships with them in this vital sector, while presenting the best competing offers, European and American companies that have controlled the Arab oil markets for many decades (Deifallah, 2016).

China's relentless pursuit of the Arab region, within its new philosophy of soft power, with China's economic rise and a compatible pragmatic policy, was faced with a welcoming Arab economic reality, and this is what led China to view the Arab region as a broad economic field for Chinese investment and exports, as well as an important storehouse of energy. In managing and sustaining the wheel of Chinese economic development, East and Southeast Asia import 65% of their oil consumption from the Middle East Arab countries, and in the long run they will remain dependent on them (Hamid, 2006).

China has sought to enhance its security in the field of energy by investing significantly in resource-related sectors in Arab countries. It has also sought to diversify its sources of oil supply from Arab countries over the years, which has led it to develop its oil relationship with Iraq, and this has increased in importance since the invasion it led. The United States entered Iraq in 2003. Contrary to Beijing's fears that China would find the Iraqi oil market restricted for it, in October 2006, the Iraqi Oil Minister, Hussein al-Shahristani, embarked on a tour of the Asia-Pacific region to discuss the prospects for reviving the Ahdab field deal with Chinese energy officials and companies. Then-Iraqi President Jalal Talabani visited Beijing in 2007 to discuss new forms of cooperation (FULTON, 2017).

Thus, China became the largest investor in Iraq after the 2003 war, as the Chinese National Petroleum Company obtained the right to develop the Ahdab oil field, among other Iraqi oil fields, for a period of twenty-three years. Moreover, China is also involved in joint construction contracts with local companies (DORSEY, 2016).

In recent years, with the rapid development of the Chinese economy, China's oil consumption has risen, and dependence on foreign energy has risen, now rising to 57%. Among China's top ten sources of crude oil imports, four of them are Gulf Cooperation Council countries, as the Kingdom Saudi Arabia is China's largest source of crude oil imports. In 2009, China imported 41.86 million tons of crude oil from Saudi Arabia, representing 20.55% of China's total crude oil imports. In 2012, Chinese crude oil imported from the Kingdom of Saudi Arabia grew to 53,916 million tons, an increase of 7.24% (Meidan, 2015).

In general, the Middle East countries are turning to the Asian market after the decline in American demand; Saudi Arabia exported 16.1%, Oman 9.7%, Iraq 9.3%, the United Arab Emirates 3.8%, and Kuwait 3.4% of Chinese demand. On the other hand, the volume of Chinese trade with Arab countries in 2014 exceeded the volume of United States trade with them. The Middle East countries (Saudi Arabia, the United Arab Emirates, and Iraq) top the list of China's trading partners in the region (Osman, 2017).

The exports of Iraq's oil to China had increased with the decline in Chinese oil imports from Iran. The impact of sanctions on Iran's production capacity and part of the international complexity of importing from Iran through the sanctions network, as China confirmed its relations with Baghdad by forgiving 80 percent of Iraq's debt amounting to $8.5 billion. And the signing of commercial deals worth billions of dollars in the field of electricity production, transportation, infrastructure, and housing, and it is likely that Baghdad will be a future customer for China's industry and exports. In the long term, energy and defense cooperation could help define a new strategy between the two countries (Nehme, 2017).

Chinese national oil companies quickly established themselves in Iraq. In 2008, CNPC renegotiated a production-sharing contract to develop the Ahdab field, which it had previously concluded with the Iraqi government before 2003, and the new technical service agreement granted development rights to CNPC for 23 years (Meidan, 2015). In 2009, CNPC, in partnership with the British company BP in a consortium, won the right to develop the Rumaila field and increase its production from 985,000 barrels per day to 2,085 million barrels per day (Osman, 2017).

In May 2010, China National Offshore Oil Corporation (CNOOC) acquired a stake in the Maysan oil fields along the Iraq-Iran border. In Saudi Arabia, the Chinese company Sinopec, another national company, worked in cooperation with the giant oil company ARAMCO to build an oil refinery in the port of Yanbu, which resulted in a 37.5 percent stake in the factory. China continues to sign huge oil deals, which increases its influence in the region and it is hoped that in the future it will continue. China's sources of imports are developing, and Saudi Arabia remains an important exporter of oil to China, not least because Saudi Aramco has entered into a long-term contract to supply an additional refinery in Kunming, Yunnan Province (Hamid, 2006).

China had other economic interests that played a role in determining the nature of the direction of the Chinese decision towards it. The increase in Chinese industries and their technological and technical development, in addition to the intense competition between China and the rest of the Asian and Western powers, especially Japan, the United States of America and the Western countries, and the efforts of these powers to force China to open its markets to its goods. China pushed towards finding new directions for its exports and investments to get rid of European and American pressure and open larger markets for its products and money, especially since China aspires to build a new regional and global Asian position that is compatible with its rising economic capabilities. Therefore, it focused on the Arab and Gulf region in particular in the field of investment, as it represents an essential pillar for achieving its global ambition (Abdel-Reda, 2013).

The Middle East countries emphasize that China will be a trading partner for them, and that Chinese-Arab investments will be exchanged with each other. In addition to the intra-trade between the two parties, which is witnessing a continuous increase, investments between China and the Arabs have risen in an unprecedented manner, as direct Chinese investments reached in 2017.

During the visit of Chinese Foreign Minister Xi Jinping to the Kingdom of Saudi Arabia in 2017, the two governments signed nearly $70 billion in investment deals and joint projects between Chinese and Saudi companies in the sectors of energy, petrochemicals, renewable energy, and technology transfer. Thus, Chinese investment has produced about 88 projects in Kingdom of Saudi Arabia, and among these, 12 projects were of an industrial nature, where the Chinese side provided 44 percent of the capital, while in the other 76 non-industrial projects, the Chinese provided 77 percent of the total capital, and the value of direct investment for these projects was 256.56 million dollars (Abdullah, 2018).

China's commercial presence - mostly in the form of construction companies and joint ventures- has begun to flourish in the Kingdom, driven largely by the Saudi government's infrastructure development and manufacturing programs, valued at approximately $624 billion. Currently, there are about 90 to 100 companies. There are Chinese companies operating in the Kingdom of Saudi Arabia, the vast majority of which are engaged in construction work, and these companies employ approximately 19,000 to 20,000 people (Al-Sudairi, 2012).

Chinese Ambassador to the Kingdom of Saudi Arabia, Li Chengwen, says that in 2013, 140 Chinese companies participated in contracts worth 18 billion US dollars in the construction, communications and infrastructure sectors in the Kingdom of Saudi Arabia (DORSEY, 2016).

Second: Political Tools

On the political side, the emergence of Chinese soft power has had mixed repercussions between China and the Arab countries, according to the opinions of researchers. China is trying to restore balance to its internal, foreign and security policies so as not to lean too much in favor of the regions of East

China and East Asia, and increasing interest and participation with the Middle East countries appears through interest in resources. It is no secret that the Arab region in general has another importance, as it is among the third belt countries in China's field of soft power policy and partnership strategy in the Chinese geo-economic drawing, and with the growth of China's economy, this importance increases and takes on renewed images and trends. The Arab world, with its geographical location, attracts China to it, geo-economically, above all else (Nehme, 2017).

The policy pursued by China was described as wise, as it was a policy capable of reducing the gap of differences and building bridges for rapprochement and cooperation. This means that China, which is adopting this with various countries of the world, must take the initiative to do so with the Middle East countries, especially with which it has a long history of economic cooperation based on the Silk Road, which formed a lifeline for the region extending from the shore of the Mediterranean to the China Sea. It worked to bring cultures and civilizations closer to this Asian mainland, and made it a path to the global economy for more than a thousand years until now (Al-Haddad, 2017).

On the other hand, the Arab countries are trying to obtain a strong ally to form a parallel pole to the United States of America in the next stage, given that China is one of the major powers opposed to American hegemony. Despite the pattern of Chinese-American relations, it adopts political positions that are inconsistent with American interests, especially when it finds that its current and future interests require this, in addition to its rejection of American interference in internal affairs. In this regard, the Chinese Foreign Minister said: "The globe is made up of different peoples, and no country, no matter how large, can impose its opinion" (Abdel-Reda, 2013).

China's political role remains moderate, unlike Western countries, which try to impose their political policies on issues such as democracy and imposing values unilaterally. China does not deliberately interfere in the internal affairs of other countries out of respect for their sovereignty, independence, traditions, and ways of life, and this non-interference policy contributes to China's pragmatic position, towards the relations it fosters with all countries in the region, including regional competitors, because it believes that good relations contribute to improved economic opportunities, As for Saudi Arabia, for example, China may offer a partial solution to its troubled partnership with the United States (Osman, 2017).

China is a large country that enjoys a dynamic economy, ideological moderation, and political stability. It does not focus on human rights and does not impose significant restrictions on the types of weapons systems that Saudi Arabia may purchase. In addition, Beijing was seeking the gain of Riyadh's affection by increasing the number of visits by senior Chinese leaders since the mid-2000s (Nader, 2016).

Despite Chinese support for a historic settlement of the Arab-Israeli conflict, China was deliberately staying away from the details of this process, which it considered to be under the direct guardianship of the United States of America. China's dominant position was to support from afar everything related to the Arab-Israeli negotiations without direct interference in the negotiations. It continues to weave strong relationships with all parties to the conflict without siding with one person against the other (Al-Haddad, 2017).

The geostrategic factor plays an important role that contributed to the development of relations between the two parties, as the Middle East countries, occupy a strategic geographical position in the world and of great importance in the Arab and Islamic worlds, and cultural and civilizational starting points that differ radically from the values and starting points of Western culture and civilization, and this is what helps in giving priority to the idea of a dialogue of civilizations that is consistent with the concept of coexistence, and creating the peaceful international environment necessary for development and modernization (Al-Shaqaba, 2014).

China is trying to expand its soft power in the region based on several considerations, including maintaining its economic presence, enhancing its positive image, resisting attempts by Western powers to distort the Chinese presence in the region, and trying to establish a constructive Middle East characterized by the spirit of cooperation, peace and development.

The truth of the matter is - although Chinese soft power is in the process of expanding, and has not yet been able to compete with Western soft power, especially the United States - nevertheless, there are many indicators of an improvement in China's soft image in the region, and the establishment of an attractive force for China that stems primarily from its own model of development, which is compatible with the reality of the region and its culture. It has proven that there are other models of development far from Western models that have achieved remarkable degrees of progress and development while preserving the cultural specificity of peoples (Meidan, 2015).

The importance of this for China lies in strengthening its presence in the region and increasing the attractiveness of the peoples of the region to China. Thus, preparing the region for a prospective Chinese leadership that is officially and popularly acceptable, especially since it is not based on the priority of methods of coercion, militarization, and ideological bias.

Perhaps the recent Saudi-Iranian agreement on rapprochement of relations can be considered a direct reflection of Chinese soft power in the region. China has pushed for mediation between Tehran and Riyadh on a solid basis based on the inevitability of cooperation, rapprochement, and the primacy of common interests, without intimidation of either party (Hairon, 2016).

It cannot be denied that China's soft power still faces many challenges, including the fact that American soft power has gained a higher competitive advantage than Chinese soft power, in terms of the attractiveness of American cultural styles, such as films, the latest technological devices, music, and others. In addition, there are some fears of ideological dimensions regarding Chinese Confucian culture.

Therefore, China has to put in a lot of effort to expand its soft power in the region, innovate new ways to promote it, and increase China's educational missions.

But this also does not negate the fact that China's attractiveness is steadily increasing thanks to its peaceful, cooperative and developmental policies in the region, especially its complete abandonment of strengthening its military presence, which has distorted American attractiveness. Or he created the famous dilemma of loving America as a way of life and intensely hating it because of its arrogant foreign policy (Gallarotti, 2011).

In summary, Chinese soft power has contributed to strengthening China's presence in the region, protecting its interests, and improving its image among the peoples of the region, which will qualify it to take over the region in the future according to a leadership seeking development and cooperation and undermining the region's differences.

Comparison Between the American and the Chinese Soft Power Effects

China competes with the United States as a major soft power, as it has been able in recent years to benefit from the missteps of successive American administrations, and this was reflected in its adoption of soft power policies, its use of persuasion instead of coercion, and maximizing its ability to attract others through many cultural, diplomatic, and economic means.

Chinese scholar Min Honghua points out that Chinese soft power consists of culture, concepts, development model, international systems, and international image. Former Chinese President Hu Jintao launched the slogan of the Three Harmonies: peace in the world, reconciliation with Taiwan, and harmony within Chinese society. This led a number of Chinese officials and analysts to believe that China can exercise real soft power competing with American soft power in international politics (Sutter, 2005).

But there are a number of basic axes when comparing Chinese soft power with its American counterpart, which are as follows:

First: Scholarships: China has followed the American approach in increasing the number of scholarships for students from different countries of the world. But Chinese universities have not yet reached the level of American higher education institutions (Carl E. James, 2021, p. 102).

Second: Language institutes: such as Confucius Institutes; Now-a-days, there are more than 500 institutes and 1,000 classes in 140 countries around the world to spread the Chinese language and culture. The obstacle related to the Chinese language is considered a negative factor in the face of the English language, which is the most widespread and common language in the world (Gil, 2017).

Third: The media industry: China tried to build a major media empire. It launched a series of China Central Television channels and strengthened the power of the official news agency, Xinhua, with the aim of creating media that would parallel and compete with famous international and American media channels such as (CNN, BBC, Fox News), and international news agencies such as (Reuters, Associated Press, and Bloomberg). But the global audience for Chinese media constitutes only a small, almost insignificant percentage. The Chinese media and cultural industry do not have the power of the American media or the power of the American film industry in Hollywood (Hongyi Lai, 2012).

Fourth: Foreign investments: Direct Chinese investments abroad are attractive, especially for developing countries, because they are not linked to the conditions of respecting human rights, spreading democracy, etc. The only Chinese condition is "to recognize Taiwan as an integral part of Mother China, and not to establish any official diplomatic relations with it." China also provides low-interest loans to developing countries, on easy terms and without political conditions, as Western countries do. Many developing countries have begun to resort to borrowing from China, away from the influence and harsh and sometimes humiliating conditions on the part of international financial institutions such as the World Bank and the International Monetary Fund, which are controlled by the United States and its Western allies. China also launched the "Belt and Road" initiative, which aims to develop infrastructure in developing countries and in some European countries as well. It also established the "Asian Infrastructure Investment Bank" to be a competitor to the World Bank (Lampton, 2008).

Fifth: Exporting the model: The Chinese media focused on "China's economic success story" as an alternative to Western liberalism and democracy, in addition to the Chinese model with its corruption and lack of democracy. But it will not resonate strongly in the West, which is associated with the values of democracy, transparency, and integrity. The United States is still the truly dominant party in the international arena, with a democratic political system, a free market, and an excellent educational system (Honghua Men, 2016).

Sixth: Spreading culture: There are two main factors that limit China's soft power: The first is nationalism. The Communist Party based its legitimacy not only on the high rate of economic growth, but also on the temptations of nationalism. This was a reason for reducing the global appeal of what Chinese President Xi Jinping (the China Dream) was calling for. The second is to spread Chinese culture, but this culture is not currently in line with modernity, unlike American popular culture, which has almost imposed its presence on the world (Fei-Ling Wang, 2005).

The United States derives a large amount of its soft power not only from its administration, but also from its civil society, unlike China, which lacks non-governmental organizations that generate a large amount of America's soft power.

Therefore, Chinese soft power tools and the extent of the spread of Chinese culture do not qualify it to compete with American soft power at the present time. If China seeks to achieve the full potential of its soft power, it must reconsider its methods that do not suit the times, and unleash the full talents of its civil society. Otherwise, its soft power will remain limited in its impact and response.

CONCLUSION

Soft power is a weapon that countries use to adhere its goals, and to interact with other countries at the level of the international relations. Both the United States of America and People's Republic of China had gave the soft power a great concern, and had worked on spreading its relation all over the world.

This study had showed the soft power practiced in the Middle East countries from these two huge counties, and showed how each of them had taken a different way to spread its culture and ethics, and to enforce its morals, and rules, at some occasions, especially on the Arab countries, that are considered to be either poor dependant countries, or rich petroleum, but military dependant countries.

At the level of education for example, US soft power benefits from the image that the American educational institutions are elite and first-class. In contrast, Chinese universities use their relatively low tuition fees as well as the availability of state-funded scholarships as attractive qualities when accepting students from countries in the Middle East.

No matter how each country differ from the other in the way it tries to force soft power, it is stable that the United States of America and People's Republic of China have one of the greatest roles in the world, and both countries are working hard to improve their soft power effects, to ensure the ability to have the domination without the use of the military forces, which may lead to achieving goals, but destruction and harm to the human race. Can the soft power be the only way to be able to dominate? Or we will always see grand countries in continuous arms race?

REFERENCES

Abdel-Reda, S. N. (2013). *Arab-Chinese Relations*. Political and International Review.

Abdullah, Z. (2018). Chinese foreign policy towards the Arab Gulf states (Saudi Arabia as a model). *Journal of Political Trends, Arab Democratic Center,* (5), 51.

Abdulsalam, R. (2021). *The United States of America between hard power and soft power*. Arab Diffusion Foundation.

Abdulsalam, R. (2022). *The United States of America between hard power and soft power*. Arab Diffusion Foundation.

Al-Badrani, A. K. (2015). *The Impact of Continuity and Change on Chinese Foreign Policy Towards the Middle East Peace Process*. Mustansiriyya: Al-Mustansiriya Journal for Arab and International Studies.

Al-Haddad, M. (2017). A Reading in the History of Arab-Chinese Relations and Ways to Enhance them. *Conference on Prospects for Arab-African-Chinese Cooperation within the Framework of the Belt and Road Initiative* (p. 107). Khartoum: Global Africa University - Center for African Research and Studies and the Association of Arab-Chinese Friendship Societies.

Al-Shaqaba, A. M. (2014). The Political Dimension of Arab-Chinese Relations and Their Future Prospects. Dirasat Journal, 41, 381.

Al-Sudairi, M. T. (2012). *Sino-Saudi Relations: An Economic History*. GRC GULF PAPERS.

Arif, B. H. (2017). *The Role of Soft Power in China's Foreign Policy in the 21st Century*. International Journal of Social Sciences & Educational Studies.

Bakir, M. M. (2018). knowledge world. Kuwait: National Council for Culture, Arts and Letters.

Bouderdaben, M. (2019). *The role of informal diplomacy in implementing foreign policy*. Constantine University.

Breslin, S. (2011). The Soft Notion of China's "Soft Power." Asia Programme Paper: ASP. London: Chatam House.

Buzan, B. (2022). *Ole Waver, Regions and Powers*. Cambridge University.

Carl, E., & James, S. R. (2021). *Critical Approaches Toward a Cosmopolitan Education*. Taylor & Francis.

Clement, C. (2022). *Common Causes and Different Patterns*. Harva University.

Clinton, H. R. (2010). Redefining American Diplomacy and Development. Foreign Affairs.

Deifallah, B. B. (2016). *Report on the Seminar on China-Arab Relations: The Case of Algeria - Laboratory of Research and Studies in International Relations*. University of Algiers.

Dorsey, J. M. (2016). China and the Middle East: Venturing into the maelstrom. S. Rajaratnam School of International Studies.

Fulton, X. Q. (2017). China-Gulf Economic Relationship under the "Belt and Road" Initiative. *Asian Journal of Middle Eastern and Islamic Studies*, *11*(3), 678.

Gallarotti, G. M. (2011). Soft power: what it is, why it is important, and the conditions for, its effective use. Wesleyan University, Department of Government.

Garib, E. (2022). *American and Arab media*. Arab Future Magazine.

Gil, J. (2017). *Soft Power and the Worldwide Promotion of Chinese Language Learning, The Confucius Institute Project*. Channel View Publications.

Gramsci, A. (1971). Prison notebooks. Elec Book.

Hairon, C. T. (2016). Education Reform in China: Toward Classroom Communities. *Article*.

Hamid, H. K. (2006). Development of Arab-Chinese Relations. *Journal of Political Science*, (33), 160.

Hans, M. (2015). *Politics among nations*. McGraw-Hill.

Hehir, A. (2017). Building Theory and Practice. Routledge Taylor and Fransis Group.

Henry, F. A. (2015). *The Paradox of "Winning the War of Ideas" in the 21st Century*. U.S. Army War College.

Hussein, A. Q. (2016). *Smart Power Approaches as a Mechanism of International Change: The United States of.* Arab Center for Research and Policy Studies.

Kaufmann. (2021). *Open Government Partnership.* Brookings Institution.

Lai, H. Y. L. (2012). China's Soft Power and International Relations. Taylor & Francis.

Lampton, D. M. (2008). *The Three Faces of Chinese Power, Might, Money, and Minds.* University of California Press. doi:10.1525/9780520941502

Latosh, S. (1992). *Westernization of the world.* Cairo: House of the Third World.

Lecoutre, S. (2020). *the transatlantic security partnership.* EU International Relation and Diplomacy Studies.

Lenczowski. (2019). Dulyural Diplomacy, Political Influence. *Integrated Strategy*, 26.

Manafih, A. (2014). Determinants of China's Foreign Policy in the Middle East after the Arab Movement. *Research Journal - Publications of the Khaled Hassan Foundation - Studies and Research Center*, 22.

Meidan, Z. D. (2015). *China and the Middle East in a New Energy Landscape.* The Royal Institute of International Affairs, Chatham House.

Meidan, Z. D. (2015). China and the Middle East in a New Energy Landscape. The Royal Institute of International Affairs.

Men, S. T. (2016). *China in the Xi Jinping Era.* Springer International Publishing.

Munro, A. (2023). Power. *Britannica.*

Nader, A. S. (2016). *China in the Middle East.* The Rand Santa Monica Foundation.

Nafi, I. (1999). *China - The Miracle of the End of the Twentieth Century.* Cairo: Al-Ahram Center for Translation and Publishing.

Nehme, K. H. (2017). Chinese and Arab Soft Power. *Journal of Arab Studies, 26*, 41.

Nye, J. (2014). Soft power is the means to success in international politics. Conference Newspaper. 11.

Nye, J. (2016). Soft Power and Foreign Policy. *Foreign Policy Magazine*, 14.

Nye, J. S. (2003). *Limits of American Power.* USA. *Political Science Quarterly*, 9.

Osman, R. (2017). *China's soft power: An assessment of positive image building in the Middle East.* Leiden University.

Raslan, S. B. (1998). *Confucius, Pioneer of Human Thought.* Bibliotheca Alexandrina.

Sayama, O. (2016). *China's Approach to Soft Power Seeking a Balance between Nationalism.* Legitimacy and International Influence, Royal United Services Institute for Defence and Security Studies.

Sutter, R. G. (2005). China's Rise in Asia. Rowman & Littlefield Publishers.

Ullah, C. S. (2015). *China's soft power: Changing, the world perception.* Naval Postgraduate School.

Wang, Y. (2008). Public Diplomacy and the Rise of Chinese Soft Power. Wohan: The Annals of the American Academy.

Wang, F.-L. Y. D. (2005). China Rising, Power and Motivation in Chinese Foreign Policy. Wohan: Rowman & Littlefield Publishers.

Worm, X. L. (2010). *Building China's Soft Power for a Peaceful Rise.* Wohan: Journal of Chinese Political Science/Association of Chinese Political Studies.

Chapter 16
The Impact of China's Soft Power on the Educational Development of Young Mongolians

Enkhzul Buyandlai
Mandakh University, Mongolia

Ariunaa Lkhagvajav
University of Finance and Economics, Mongolia

Myadagmaa Bayartsogt
Dornod University, Mongolia

ABSTRACT

The study examines the effectiveness of investing in higher education, specifically providing scholarships for Mongolian students, in the context of China's soft power in higher education. A combination of quantitative and qualitative data analysis techniques was employed to identify China's influence on Mongolian education. The questionnaire was used for gathering quantitative data. The satisfaction survey included eight variables including reliability, correlation, regression, and crosstabulation. During the interview, participants were asked seven questions about their study experience in China. Additionally, the case study evaluated the advantages and disadvantages of studying in China based on the personal experiences of the participants. The study concluded with a SWOT and TOWS analysis. This level of satisfaction can be determined by various factors such as education outcomes, economic efficiency, cultural and social improvement, comparison of education quality with other countries, personal needs or development, and overall satisfaction with education in China.

DOI: 10.4018/979-8-3693-2444-8.ch016

INTRODUCTION

The objective of any government is to sustain favorable circumstances for long-term socioeconomic growth, utilizing various international policy tools, including hard and soft power. (Aidarbek Amirbek, 2014). Soft power strategy refers to a country's ability to influence other nations without using coercive methods such as military intervention, invasion or threat, as opposed to relying on financial investments. It is a process of influencing other nations to achieve their goals by attracting them through language, culture, education, politics, values, and foreign policy objectives (Diplomacy, 2019). Soft power techniques involve a number of factors such as international relations, diplomatic communication, belief, and social capital. These can be measured using both conventional and unconventional methods. Conventional measures include analyzing immigration, tourism, education, and culture. However, when it comes to soft power, the focus is on foreign students studying in the host country, rather than local students studying abroad (Wu). Spence defines human capital as a potential actor in the production process. As a result, it is necessary to continue studying China's soft power in tertiary education investment for Mongolian human capital. Since Mongolia was a component of the Qing Empire for nearly three centuries, there has been a great deal of cultural contact between China and Mongolia. (Tatiana Ponka L. P., 2019).

In recent times, education has been widely recognized as a means to advance the interests of nations worldwide. Therefore, several countries such as China, the United States, Russia, Germany, and other industrialized nations in Europe are emphasizing on providing high-quality education programs to the youth worldwide. From the start of diplomatic ties on October 16, 1949, China and Mongolia have followed a tumultuous road marked by mutual rejection, tight rapprochement based on communist doctrine, and subsequently diversified cooperation in political, economic, cultural, and other areas. (Tatiana Ponka L. P., 2019). China has invested in Mongolian human capital education, and as a result, there is a collaboration between Chinese and Mongolian ideas. The education modernization process is being accelerated by creating cultural and educational spaces that cater to the actual demands of foreign applicants at various levels of education, including bachelor's, master's, and doctoral degrees. China's Scholarship Committee has enabled many Mongolian students to pursue their academic degrees in Chinese universities. As of 2018, 258 Mongolian applicants received grants which included expenses for studying and living in a dormitory, as well as monthly scholarships ranging from 2 to 3 thousand yuan (Tatiana Ponka, January, 2019). t is important to examine the effectiveness of investing in education because people's attraction to another country can shift from short-term interest in movies and visits to long-term interest in education and emigration. According to statistical data from 2011, the majority of international students in China were from South Korea (Wu). Currently, more than 500,000 students from 196 countries are studying in China. Within this group, 290,000 students, or more than half, come from 64 nations that work under the "Belt and Road" framework. Mongolia is ranked tenth in the Asia-Pacific region, with 11,000 students studying in China, outnumbering top countries such as India, Japan, and Korea (Kucharčíková, 2011).

A combination of culture and education is the most effective means of soft power since domestic and socioeconomic progress with a range of ideals and models in competition can illuminate new trends in the era (Aidarbek Amirbek, 2014). The emergence of a knowledge-based economy has led to a shift in leadership towards human development progress. Many successful nations, including Brazil, Russia, India, and China, prioritize innovation through investment in their domestic educational systems at modern and global levels. This investment serves as a crucial soft power tool, attracting international students to their countries (Aidarbek Amirbek, 2014). Furthermore, foreign representatives achieve accomplishment in the host country's science and culture through their acquisition of the target language, since their learning experience abroad allows them to develop valuable social capital. Global citizens exhibit educational and linguistic maturity, enabling them to effectively transmit their target language and culture through private communication (Aidarbek Amirbek, 2014). When a country provides educational support to another nation, it helps the recipient country to showcase soft power of the host country to the world. This is more effective than relying on military force. Therefore, major powers focus on strengthening their domestic higher education systems as their graduates are considered to be an asset to their country. These graduates are often seen as a "Trojan horse" as they bring back their academic knowledge and qualifications from foreign countries to benefit their home nation (Aidarbek Amirbek, 2014).

Former Chinese leaders played an important part in establishing "peaceful raise" as "The Belt and Road Initiative" centered on scientific development, modernization, and internal improvement. In addition, "The Belt and Road Initiative" contributes to the realization of the "Chinese Dream" by expanding it both within and outside the country. Education is viewed as the development of soft power based on a country's culture, political values, and foreign and domestic policies.

The research focused on studying and affirming the theory on the positive influence of soft policy for the target country as China supports and invests education of the Mongolian young generation. The researchers focused on achieving the aim by scrutinizing the impression of the younger generation based on the results of quantitative and qualitative analysis, as China's soft power is built on educational investment.

RESEARCH METHOD

A mixed methodology of quantitative and qualitative data analysis enabled us to find out the influence of education on Mongolians. Firstly, the quantitative data questionnaire consists of three parts such as basic information, career development, and satisfaction of applicants. Factor analyses of the satisfaction survey covered 8 factors with 5 to 15 questions. SPSS and AMOS were used for working on the analysis of reliability, factor, correlation, and regression. Secondly, the interview covered 7 questions considering their studying experience in China. Structured interviews included open-ended questions that were asked to collect data for the interview. Finally, the SWOT and TOWS analysis focused on identifying the advantages and disadvantages of studying in China through their personal experience.

LIMITATION OF THE RESEARCH

As the sample size in this study was limited, it is imperative to conduct a more extensive study on a larger scale that encompasses all the young people in Mongolia. Moreover, if the results of the study are compared with another country's soft power program, it would yield more interesting findings.

Theoretical Framework of Soft Power Policy

In the field of political science and international relations, terms like hard power, soft power, and smart power are widely used. Professor Joseph Samuel Nye Jr. of Harvard University introduced the concept of soft power, which refers to a nation's ability to indirectly influence the interests and circumstances of another country through its policies. These policies are based on various factors such as a country's mindset, language, values, and culture (Diplomacy, 2019). David Baldwin was an advocate of using soft power policy to achieve international goals. This approach emphasizes cooperation, persuasion, and attraction rather than coercion. Soft power policy relies on tactics such as diplomacy, cultural exchange, and education to engage other countries in a social framework and convince them to align with certain objectives. In essence, it is a managerial technique that employs art, education, and similar resources to achieve its goals. (Diplomacy, 2019). As per the political foreign policy, soft policy is based on three main pillars.

1. Civilization (attraction and intrigue)
2. Political reputation (domestic and international reach)
3. Foreign policy (legal) (Diplomacy, 2019).

In this regard, China's soft policy creation might include the following:

The head symbolizes diplomacy, the body represents political values, and the arms and legs signify cultural policies.

It illustrates China is considered a main player in international platforms due to a combination of diplomacy, political values, and cultural policy. On the contrary, Joseph Samuel Nye Jr. mentioned that converting hard power (economy) as soft power is acceptable as a result of the current interdependent economy of the world and every nation's soft power policy is different because of its character in his research in 2013. Moreover, he emphasized that while US soft power relies on popular engagement, China and Russia's soft power is based on official authority (Uyanga. T).

In addition, three primary objections to soft power are outlined by Yukaruç (2017): its uniqueness, its immeasurable nature, and its overemphasis on the agent. While many lesser issues also exist and will be discussed below, these three seem to be the main ones in the argument as a whole. The reason Nye's concept lacks uniqueness is that it is similar to previous methods in the field of international relations (Yukaruç, 2017, 496). E.H. Carr categorizes power into three types: power over opinion, power over military, and power over economy. Since hegemony must be exercised through a combination of coercion and consent, the approach to international relations that is based on Gramsci's ideas also shares similarities. Furthermore, hegemony is present in various societal institutions and is perpetuated through media, religion, and educational systems, among others. In both systems, consensus and co-optation take precedence over the use of force for achieving one's objectives (Bush, 2021).

The nature of demonstrating whether one country's actions are altered by the soft power of another makes soft power impossible to quantify. It states that regrettably, this is not feasible. Even though measures are taken, soft power's impacts on other nations are impossible to accurately gauge or identify. Put another way, it is impossible to prove a true causal relationship between an action taken by one country and its response by another. Unlike its objectives and goals, soft power is more ethereal (Bush, 2021).

Scholars who study China and its soft power face three methodological problems that need to be resolved in order to define soft power in relation to China. Firstly, it is necessary to identify China's soft power objectives and the message that Beijing wishes to convey. Secondly, it is essential to evaluate the extent to which China's efforts at soft power have altered the global perception of the nation. Finally, it is important to ascertain whether the shifting perceptions have any bearing on policy (Bush, 2021).

The Belt and Road Initiative (BRI) is a means of spreading political principles throughout China. It helps to achieve the goals of the China Dream, which is to improve the living standards of people both within and outside the country. According to Rahman, this development is consistent with the China Dream's objectives. There is also the "peaceful rise" component, which past Chinese leaders used to gain international acceptance and credibility. The Belt and Road Initiative (BRI) fosters certain aspects of this ascent, such as scientific advancement, modernization, and domestic improvement. (Bush, 2021).

The formation of soft power depends on three vital factors - a country's culture, political principles, and foreign and domestic policies. When universal cultural ideals and foreign policies that promote shared interests and values are adopted, it is more probable to see an increase in soft power. This context requires willing interpreters and receivers to actualize the consequences of soft power. Soft power fails to propagate in the absence of willing translators and receivers (Bush, 2021).

As a result, modern great powers and industrialized or developed governments use soft power policies to safeguard their spheres of influence and national interests. Otherwise, soft power is a resource and an opportunity, but soft power strategy is regarded as a guarantee of power and security. Some Western researchers disputed Professor Nye's strategy restriction in soft power since soft power exposes only interaction with attraction, including resource and opportunity, rather than soft power implementation based on strategy (Uyanga. T).

Students' Satisfaction in Higher Education of China

According to Bateson and Hoffman (1999), consumer satisfaction is a short-term transaction with a specific measurement, while service quality, which includes customer satisfaction, is an attitude generated from the results of a long-term review. Elliot and Helay (2002) state that students' educational experiences allow them to evaluate results based on their short-term attitudes. Since students are consumers of education services as a result of marketing efforts, there is no difference in satisfaction with service quality and educational experience. Additionally, Bitner (1990) emphasized that quality of service provides happiness to customers since it matches consumer satisfaction. It is important to note that students' satisfaction levels vary depending on the range of available domestic programs (Abdul Ghaffar Mastoi, 2019). A study was conducted to measure student academic satisfaction in China's higher education institutions. The study measured Administrative Quality, Physical Environment Quality, Core Educational Quality, Support Facilities Quality, and Transformative Quality (Abdul Ghaffar Mastoi, 2019). The research modified the questionnaires to determine the impact of soft power on Mongolian students' education.

Mongolia is the recipient of 500 scholarships every year, out of which 200 are given by the Chinese Government, 100 are special grants from President Xi Jinping, and 200 awards are given by the People's Government of Inner Mongolia Autonomous Region. This clearly denotes that Mongolian human capital education receives ten times more assistance as compared to third-country investments like Australia, which only receives 50 grants per year. It is noteworthy that Presidnt Xi Jinping has expressed his willingness to grant 1,000 scholarships to Mongolian students over the next five years. This study shows that Mongolian higher education representatives benefit from universities in China, and their satisfaction with the quality of education will determine the value of their study experience.

In this article satisfaction construct is described as Mongolian students' feelings about the quality of different facilities and educational environment of Chinese universities based on five kinds of quality determinants such as Improvement in Personal Life of Students (6 questions), Improvement in Education of Home Country (5 questions), Improvement in Economy of Home Country (5 questions), Improvement in Culture and Society of Home Country (7 questions), Comparison of Chinese Education System with Other Country's Education System (questions), Academic Help for Students with Scholarships (9 questions), Ability to Cover Daily Expenses with the Received Scholarship and Satisfaction with Studying and Staying in China (15 questions) (Rashid Latief, 2018). The reliability and factor analysis of the questionnaire were sufficient to support further quantitative data analysis.

Literature review of Soft Power Policy

In 1993, Wang Huning (王沪宁), a professor at Fudan University and a member of the Standing Committee of the Political Bureau of the Central Committee, wrote the first paper on soft power. In his paper, he explained that the degree of soft power could be measured by its spread. Soft power can only be released when it is widely disseminated through culture. According to his basic concept of cultural power, when one type of culture is seen as not only a core value but also the universal culture of other nations and the global community, a large amount of soft power is accumulated in society (Maxim, 2023).

In 2014, China and Mongolia formed a comprehensive strategic partnership that included the signing of 30 agreements, including a currency swap. The agreement was signed by Chinese President Xi Jinping and Mongolian President Tsakhia Elvegdorj. As a result of this partnership, two major intergovernmental structures were established: the Intergovernmental Commission for Trade-Economic and Scientific-Technical Cooperation and the Commission for Cooperation in the Field of Mineral Resources, Energy, and Infrastructure. These organizations aim to strengthen the cooperation between China and Mongolia in various fields (Zhuravleva, 2018, March). Mongolia aims to join the One Belt One Road initiative and integrate with the national Steppe Road project as part of its diplomatic policy with China (Zhuravleva, 2018, March). China is currently investing $10 billion annually to establish its soft power, which is more than what the United States, England, France, Germany, and Japan spend combined. China offers several scholarships for Mongolian candidates each year, including the Government Scholarship, scholarships for "Belt and Road" nations, special grants from President Xi Jinping, and rewards for countries in Shanghai Cooperation Organizations (Zreik, 2024a). According to official records from 2012, 8.210.16 students were studying in China. However, this number decreased to 7,920 and 7,428 in 2014 and 2015, respectively. In recent years, more and more students have been learning Chinese as a foreign language. In recent years, more and more students have been learning Chinese as a foreign language. In 2002, 550 educational institutions were offering Chinese-taught programs, which increased to 1,760 by 2010. Of the students who chose to study Chinese, the majority (4,136) opted for private primary and secondary schools, while a minority (1,780) enrolled in public schools in 2010 (Zhuravleva, 2018, March). The host country's languages, religions, customs, education, national values, and foreign policy leadership allow for the execution of soft power programs, which are widely diffused and significant in modern international relations (Byambakhand. L, 2021).

In 2019, a poll conducted in Portland called "The Soft Power 30" ranked China as the 27th most successful country in executing soft power programs, and 4th out of 10 in Asia. Japan, South Korea, and Singapore were the only countries ranking higher than China. China's soft power is represented by symbols such as the Kungfu and Confucius institutes. Additionally, the "Asian Infrastructure Investment Bank" was established to build its financial leadership in the area. (Diplomacy, 2019). Due to the popularity of the entertainment and education sectors among Mongolia's youth, China and South Korea are perceived positively (Diplomacy, 2019). Young people in certain countries are more optimistic about investments compared to the older generations. This suggests that soft power has a greater influence on the youth. China and South Korea's soft power initiatives in Mongolia, which include language programs, educational exchanges, tourism, and entertainment, are the primary factors contributing to the positive perception among young people (Diplomacy, 2019). The research focused on soft power techniques employed by powerful states in small nations and made forecasts and suggestions for Mongolia's international soft power strategy (Diplomacy, 2019).

It has been observed that China's soft power deployment process has been evaluated worldwide. Results from empirical studies indicate that China's soft power policies in New Zealand have influenced New Zealanders' perceptions of Chinese investment positively. Moreover, seven out of ten Nigerians have viewed Chinese investment favorably, along with Lebanon, Mexico, Israel, South Africa, and Brazil. This demonstrates the successful implementation of China's soft power strategy in Africa, the Middle East, and Latin America. (Diplomacy, 2019). In this study, we aimed to evaluate China's soft power policy by investing in Mongolia's young population and assessing their attitude change towards China.

Belt and Road Initiatives in Asia

The "Belt and Road" initiative has two main components - the "XXI Century Maritime Silk Road" and the "New Silk Road Economic Zone." The Maritime Silk Road's primary objective is to connect Guangzhou, China, to India through a network of countries including Vietnam, Thailand, Malaysia, Singapore, and Indonesia. Preparations are currently underway globally to coordinate national development projects and participate in the "Belt and Road" program.

- Mongolia's "Road to Development,"
- Kazakhstan's "Bright Path,"
- Vietnam's "Two Corridors, One Circle,"
- Great Britain's "Northern Powerhouse,"
- Poland's "Amber Road," and
- Turkey's "Middle Corridor."

China's foreign and economic policy revolves around the Belt and Road Initiative, which was introduced by President Xi Jinping in 2013. The initiative aims to establish six economic corridors, including the Economic Corridor of Mongolia, Russia, and China, which is the most economical shortcut route linking the ports of Vladivostok in the east and Chita in the west, passing through three Chinese provinces. The three parties will collaborate in the fields of transportation, energy, and tourism to enhance economic development along the corridor (Zreik, 2023a).

China maintains good relations with Germany, Russia, Kazakhstan, Singapore, Malaysia, Mongolia, Thailand, Great Britain, New Zealand, Australia, and Indonesia, with Russia, Singapore, and Malaysia being ranked highly in recent times (Chandmani. S (M.A), 2020).

Therefore, as a nation that is a part of the "One Belt, One Road" economic corridor and situated close to the world's largest and fastest-growing economy, Mongolia finds it acceptable. (Batkhuyag Sodovyn, 2019).

Diplomacy of China and Mongolia in Development of Bilateral Cooperation and Education

China's border with Mongolia is easily accessible through level terrain, unlike its western and southern borders that are characterized by towering mountains and subtropical regions. This has caught the attention of large Chinese enterprises. In the past 20 years, China has developed a robust domestic railroad network, making it easier to expand it to Mongolia's mining resources. Not surprisingly, Chinese businesses have constructed mineral processing facilities in western and northeastern Chinese provinces, which are directly across the Sino-Mongolian border (Indra Bazarsad, 2021).

Caveats for the Mongolia-China Strategic Partnership

In 2011, China and Mongolia upgraded their bilateral relationship to a Strategic Partnership. China built the Great Wall partly due to its longstanding ties with Mongolia that date back thousands of years. More recently, both the People's Republic of China (China) in 1949 and the Republic of China (Taiwan) in 1945 recognized Mongolia's independence. After the Sino-Soviet split in the 1960s, relations between China and Mongolia were strained and remained so until the end of the Cold War in 1989. Both parties have different reasons for upgrading the bilateral relationship from the 2003 term of "good neighborly, mutually trusted partnership" to the current Strategic cooperation. However, all parties ultimately hope for a long-term and stable relationship. (JARGALSAIKHAN, 2014).

There are several reasons why China and Mongolia have developed good relations. Firstly, the two countries are close to each other geographically. Secondly, China has a large and growing market, as well as a strong economy. Mongolia has a lot of minerals, which complements China's industrial regions. Thirdly, China supports Mongolian businesses by offering loans and tax breaks. Finally, the populations of China's Inner Mongolia Autonomous Region and the Mongolian People's Republic have similar cultures and languages, which help to improve communication between the two countries (Tatiana Ponka L. P., 2019).

China and Mongolia have established strong ties due to their bilateral cooperation in social, political, and economic spheres. The two nations actively collaborate in education, engage in cultural exchanges, and host "Culture Days" to facilitate cultural and educational ties. These ties are crucial as China's economy depends on Mongolia's abundant natural resources. As a result, the improvement of cultural and educational ties is connected to the reality of direct participation from the peoples of both nations. It is impossible to have successful cooperation without considering the cultural, ethnic, and national traits of these people. Therefore, these efforts serve to strengthen ties in politics, economy, culture, and education between China and Mongolia. (Tatiana Ponka L. P., 2019).

The modernization of education systems in China and Mongolia is picking up pace due to the implementation of innovative educational practices. This highlights the significance of researching global experiences while developing multi-level education systems, including bachelor's and master's degree programs, within the framework of establishing cultural and educational spaces (Tatiana Ponka L. P., 2019).

In May 2017, a meeting was held to discuss the "One Belt, One Road" concept. At the meeting, the parties deliberated on interrelated development concerns and authorized a plan to establish economic corridors linking China, Russia, and Mongolia.

China and Mongolia have agreed to integrate their trade and economic cooperation efforts by synchronizing the "One Belt, One Road" and "Steppe Road" programs. This move is aimed at elevating relations between the two countries to the level of a comprehensive strategic partnership. (Tatiana Ponka L. P., 2019).

The China-Mongolia-Russia Economic Corridor holds immense potential for economic growth due to its favorable location, strong economic ties, and significant export opportunities. For Mongolia and the Baikal region, export diversification is crucial, particularly for high-value-added products. The development of new transit projects and improvements in transportation and cross-border infrastructure will significantly contribute to the continued socio-economic growth of these regions (Osodoev, 2021).

After conducting an empirical study, we attempted to examine the impact of investments on residents and their changing attitudes, as well as to determine the reasons behind these changes.

FINDINGS OF THE RESEARCH

I. Quantitative Data Analysis

To gain a better understanding of the responses we received from the questionnaire, we analyzed the quantitative data using SPSS 26 and AMOS. The first set of questions in the survey consisted of 13 demographic questions, which included information about age, gender, marital status, educational financial resources, years of study, the foreign language used in academic studies, topics of study, degree-seeking, and region of study. Additionally, respondents were asked to answer four yes or no questions related to their prior experience with learning Chinese, continuing their studies in China, and completing their studies there.

We collected demographic data from both current students and alumni to investigate the relationship between this general information and student happiness. This allows us to assess the effectiveness of soft power deployment through education investment. The questionnaire was divided into four sections.

The second section aimed to gather information about the previous and present careers of students and alumni. It also included questions about how their current positions compare to their previous careers. The purpose of this section was to support the study hypothesis that investing in education can lead to career advancement and contribute to China's soft power.

The third section contained eight categories of questions related to personal life improvements, home country education, economy, culture, and society, comparison of the Chinese education system, academic assistance, daily expenses with scholarship, and satisfaction with studies.

Finally, the fourth section focused on evaluating the correlation and regression analysis of student and alumni improvement through the results obtained from the questionnaire.

It is worth noting that Mongolians attach great importance to education and development opportunities for their girls, which is why the majority of the survey respondents are females (68%) rather than males (32%). The majority of responders are young people aged between 17 and 20, while there are also a few respondents aged 30 or more who have already reached maturity and got married. Figure 1 illustrates the evolving nature of soft power in Mongolia, where the Chinese soft power continues to gain ground among the younger generation, while the older generation still gives more weight to the fading Russian soft power (Byambakhand. L, 2021).

As mentioned earlier, only a small percentage (20%) of respondents are married. The majority of representatives (44%) are receiving support from the Scholarship Committee of China to pursue their studies, including university scholarships (24%). The remaining students are financing their education themselves. The conclusion drawn from this is that China's soft power is focused on economic growth and material well-being, rather than political values, which distinguishes it from soft power in the West (Byambakhand. L, 2021).

Table 1. Demographic information of respondents

Question	Sorts	Frequency	Percent	Cumulative Percent
Age	17-21	229	51.5	57.3
	22-27	74	16.6	75.8
	28-33	48	10.8	87.8
	34-40	49	11.0	100.0
	Total	400	89.9	
Gender	female	273	61.3	68.3
	male	127	28.5	100.0
Marital status	married	80	18.0	20.0
	single	320	71.9	100.0
Finance your education	China's Government	172	38.7	44.6
	Scholarship of Confuses	15	3.4	48.4
	University scholarship	92	20.7	72.3
	Self-funding	107	24.0	100.0
How many years have you been studying in China?	1-5 years	333	74.8	90.2
	5-10 years	30	6.7	98.4
	>10 years	6	1.3	100.0
Which foreign language was used to continue or complete your studies in China?	Chinese	234	52.6	59.7
	English	45	10.1	71.2
	Chinese and English	113	25.4	100.0
What is area of your studies?	Medical science	33	7.4	8.5
	Law and legislation	29	6.5	16.1
	Education studies	14	3.1	19.7
	Psychology	12	2.7	22.8
	Economy and business	110	24.7	51.3
	Chinese language and culture	25	5.6	57.8
	Engineering and technology	83	18.7	79.3
	Agriculture	2	0.4	79.8
	Other	78	17.5	100.0
Which degree are you pursuing or received from universities of China?	Bachelor	299	67.2	74.9
	Master	76	17.1	94.0
	Ph.D.	23	5.2	99.7
	Postdoctoral	1	0.2	100.0

continued on following page

Table 1. Continued

Question	Sorts	Frequency	Percent	Cumulative Percent
Which regions do/ did you study?	Beijing	69	15.5	17.3
	Shanghai	51	11.5	30.0
	Wuhan	32	7.2	38.0
	Tianjin	16	3.6	42.0
	Huhehot	53	11.9	55.3
	Xi An	5	1.1	56.5
	Dalian	13	2.9	59.8
	Qingdao	8	1.8	61.8
	Harbin	5	1.1	63.0
	Chongqing	1	0.2	63.3
	Nanjing	10	2.2	65.8
	Hangzhou	9	2.0	68.0
	Guangzhou	10	2.2	70.5
	Other	118	26.5	100.0

Based on a survey, it was found that 90% of students studying in China pursue their academic goals for a maximum of 5 years, as most of them already have a bachelor's degree. However, 10% of the respondents have been living in China for more than a decade, indicating that they are probably pursuing their highest degree with their families in the country. Among Mongolians, 60% of them enroll in Chinese-taught programs after completing a one-year Chinese language preparatory course. On the other hand, 29% of the respondents pursue degrees in both English and Chinese-taught programs, which could be due to language barriers. A group of applicants who had not been selected previously, attended an English-taught program in China. This means that Chinese soft power has been gaining ground through the teaching of Chinese language in academic studies among younger people in China. Meanwhile, the collective influence of third-party countries on Mongolia has also expanded considerably (Byambakhand. L, 2021).

Table 2. Studying experience of respondents

Questions	Answer	Frequency	Percent
Have you ever learned Chinese before keeping on your studies in China?	Yes	192	48.7
	No	202	51.3
Are you keen on pursuing your next academic journey in China?	Yes	287	79.1
	No	76	20.9
Are you planning to continue your studies in abroad?	Yes	220	61.6
	No	137	38.4
Have you already completed your studies in China?	Yes	133	36.5
	No	231	63.5

Figure 1. Experience of learning Chinese and continuing their studies

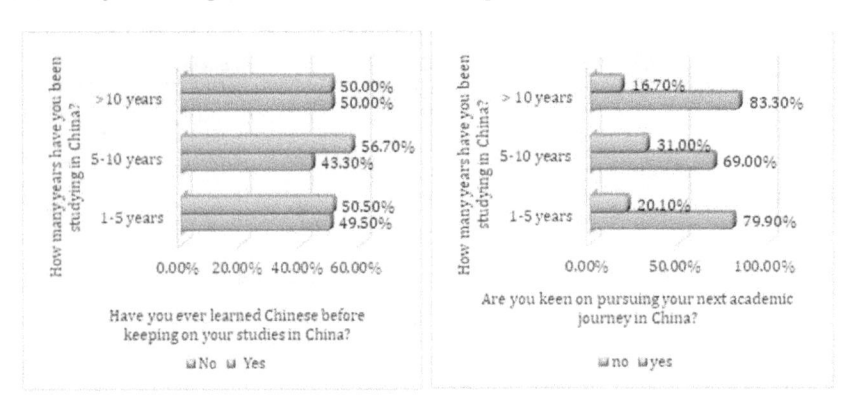

Table 1 indicates that the majority of responses came from individuals with a bachelor's degree (75%). This suggests that younger people are more attracted to soft power policies due to cultural and linguistic influences, in comparison to their older counterparts. Applicants for master's degrees account for 19%, while those for Ph.D. degrees are only 6%. This could be because the questionnaire was focused on bachelor's degree programs instead of higher levels of education. According to Figure 4, the use of public diplomacy as a tool works well in attracting overseas students or exchanging facilities, as younger people play a crucial role in advocating for the host country in the long run (Priya Gauttama, 2024).

The data shows that the highest number of students (28.5%) are pursuing degrees in economics and business, indicating that these fields are popular among students across Mongolia. Additionally, a significant percentage of applicants (21.5%) are in engineering and technology, which is not surprising given China's leading position in the industry. On the other hand, agriculture attracts the smallest number of students (0.5%). It has been found that 29.5% of surveyed respondents are currently pursuing their degrees in various regions of China, suggesting that the younger population of Mongolia is spread out throughout the country. During their education, students are being trained to represent diverse Chinese cultures. Additionally, 17.3% of the younger generation resides in Beijing, the capital city, for academic purposes in mainland China. This indicates that Beijing not only serves as a cultural hub but also as a historic metropolis for young foreign representatives (Zreik, 2024b).

According to Table 2, more than half of the applicants (51.3%) have no prior experience in learning the Chinese language in Mongolia. To promote their culture and language, China's Scholarship Committee encourages Mongolians to enroll in a year-long Chinese language preparation course with a full scholarship. This program serves as a form of soft power aimed at the target country. Moreover, the majority of applicants (79.1%) prefer to continue their studies in China upon completing their degree. However, a significant number of students (61.6%) choose to pursue their further studies outside of China. According to the survey, most respondents (63.5%) are currently pursuing further education, with 75% of students seeking a bachelor's degree in mainland China. Analyzing the experiences of these students shows that Nye (2004) considered education as a means to create soft power in the cultural sphere. The research supports this view by highlighting that higher education is a significant tool for soft power, as it stands on its own (Priya Gauttama, 2024).

Based on the data presented in Figure 1, it can be observed that 50% of the students had prior knowledge of the Chinese language before studying in China for 1-5 years. On the other hand, 43% of the students

Figure 2. Foreign language and current position of respondents

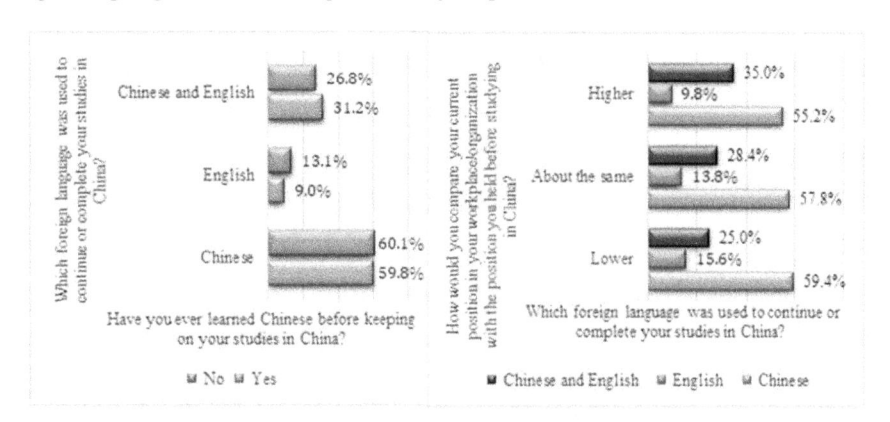

had studied Chinese before their 5-10-year studies. It was also found that among the students who had studied in China for more than 10 years, 50% of them did not have any prior knowledge of the language.

According to Figure 1, 80% of students who have been studying in China for 1-5 years have expressed their desire to continue their studies in the country. On the other hand, 69% of students with 5-10 years of experience also prefer to continue their education. Furthermore, the study found that 83% of students who have been studying in China for more than ten years are keen on continuing their education in the host nation. This indicates that the longer they stay in China, the more enthusiastic they become about pursuing their education there. The results of the study reveal that China is ranked fourth (9%) amongst the top host nations for foreign students in 2020, after the US (21%), all other countries (20%), and the UK (10%) for higher education in local universities (Priya Gauttama, 2024).

Figure 2 indicates that there is no significant difference in the Chinese learning experience of students before they begin their academic studies in China. However, after attending a year-long program of Chinese teaching, 60% of students tend to continue their studies. Additionally, there is hardly any difference between students pursuing their degrees through a bilingual program, except for their previous experience in learning Chinese, with only a minority of them attending academic programs in English. The second graph of Figure 2 shows that individuals with bilingual qualifications tend to have higher positions than those with only Chinese or English qualifications.

Figure 3. Academic degree and continuity of their studies

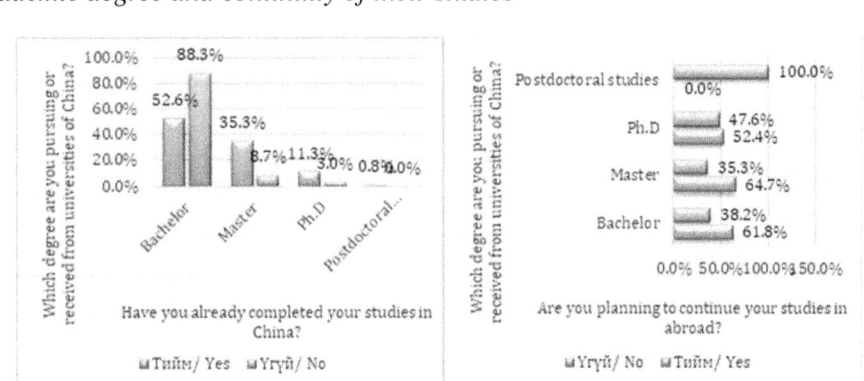

Table 3. Bartlett's test of sphericity

KMO=.923 Bartlett's Test of Sphericity=13145.933(p=.000)								
Cronbach alpha	**0.968**	**0.946**	**0.918**	**0.932**	**0.897**	**0.923**	**0.881**	**0.884**
N of items	15	10	9	7	6	5	6	5

Figure 3 illustrates that most undergraduate applicants have completed their studies, while only a small number of graduate and doctoral candidates are still pursuing their studies as the program progresses. The second graph in Figure 3 shows that 64.7% of graduates and 61.8% of undergraduates choose to continue their education abroad, while doctors are less likely to pursue post-doctoral courses. The above graph indicates that not only African students but also Mongolian students have long been benefiting from university program subsidies by completing a Chinese language preparatory course before pursuing their studies in various fields such as technology, medicine, or engineering (Hunter, 2009).

Checking Reliability of the Instruments

The Cronbach α, also known as reliability analysis, measures the correlation between variables. This indicates how well the questionnaire matches reality, or how effectively the sample represents the original population. A Cronbach's α value of 0.7 or higher suggests a well-defined sample and questionnaire (Alpha, 2016). In Attachment 1, Factor analysis you can see the reliability of the 63 questionnaires assessed based on their factor and one-by-one analysis. They all scored above 0.7, which indicates that the original population is suitable for future investigation. Table 3 presents eight factors along with the number of questions or variables related to each component, loadings, and Cronbach's alpha coefficient values. The reliability analysis shows that the questions meet the additional requirements of the analysis, as Cronbach's Alpha is greater than 0.900. Moreover, the KMO coefficient determines whether the sample size is sufficient for factor analysis. Typically, a value greater than 0.6 indicates that the sample is sufficient. On the other hand, Bartlett's test determines whether the variables or questions used in factor analysis represent a single object. If the test result is less than 0.05, it supports the alternative hypothesis, indicating that the variables or questions represent at least one factor.

Table 4. Average variance extracted

Construct	Number of Items	AVEs
Personal Improvement	6	0.6
Educational Improvement	5	0.6
Economic Improvement	5	0.4
Social Improvement	10	0.5
Educational Comparison	6	0.4
Academic Help	7	0.5
Scholarship & Expenses	9	0.5
Students' Satisfaction	15	0.6

Table 5. Discriminant validity

Indices	Chi-Square	Degree of Freedom	P	CMIN/DF	CFI	RMSEA
acceptable thresholds	>>	>0	≤0.05	≤3	>0.9	≤0.08
values	4957.937	1863	.000	2.661	1.000	0.061

The consistency of the survey questionnaire was assessed using factor analysis. According to Table 3, the Kaiser-Meyer-Olkin (KMO) measure of sample consistency is 0.923, which is greater than 0.9, and the significance value is 0.000, indicating that factor analysis is possible. Moreover, all variables, except 3.3.2, have factor loading values greater than 0.5, which implies that all variables are highly significant. The value of variable 3.3.2 is 0.464, which is greater than 0.4, suggesting that it is an important variable. Additionally, Bartlett's test (ChiSquare=13145.933, p=.000) indicates that there is a connection between the variables. The analysis reveals that the following factors are used to evaluate student satisfaction: Factor 1: Personal Improvement, Factor 2: Educational Improvement, Factor 3: Economic Improvement, Factor 4: Social Improvement, Factor 5: Educational Comparison, Factor 6: Academic Help, Factor 7: Scholarship & Expenses, and Factor 8: Questions.

Checking Validity of the Instruments

Validity is the ability of an instrument to measure what it is supposed to measure for a latent construct (Awang).

- Convergent validity

Convergent validity is a form of construct validity. Its indicator is the Average Variance Extracted (AVE).

Table 4 shows that six factors AVEs of more than 0.50, suggesting strong convergent validity. Other two factors- Economic Improvement, Educational Comparison AVEs (0.4) < 0.5.

- Discriminant Validity

In reality, the measurement model testing results demonstrate that the measurement model's factors (Attachment 2, Structure equation model) are associated with one another, and all factor loadings were more than the 0.5 limit. Furthermore, all fit indices are above the acceptable criteria we established.

As seen from table 4 the values of CFI, CMIN/DF and RMSEA are very close to the threshold values, thus representing an acceptable model fit.

Research Hypothesis

H1: Factor1- There is a difference in personal improvement when pupils compare their current position to their past position.

H2: Factor 2- There is a difference in educational improvement when comparing students' present positions to their past positions.

Table 6. Research hypothesis of position and eight factors

	Personal Improvement		Educational Improvement		Economic Improvement		Social Improvement		Educational Comparison		Student Satisfaction		Academic Help		Scholarship and Expenses	
	mean	SE	mean	SE	mean	SE	mean	SE	mean	SE	mean	SE	mean	SE	mean	SE
lower	3.402	0.941	3.219	0.898	3.253	0.755	3.417	0.838	3.469	0.727	3.353	0.858	3.08	0.915	3.582	0.896
about the same	3.583	0.739	3.538	0.709	3.437	0.638	3.717	0.614	3.845	0.67	3.819	0.707	3.334	0.77	3.904	0.776
higher	3.752	0.842	3.606	0.733	3.645	0.705	3.818	0.682	3.916	0.665	3.859	0.711	3.48	0.775	4.054	0.749

H3: Factor 3-For economic improvement, there is a disparity between students' current and prior positions.

H4: Factor4- In terms of social improvement, there is a difference between students' present and prior positions.

H5: Factor5- For educational comparison, there is a difference between comparing pupils' present positions to their former positions.

H6: Factor6- There is a difference in academic help when comparing students' present positions to their former positions.

H7: Factor7-There is a difference in scholarship and expenses when comparing students' present positions to their past positions.

H8: Factor8- There is a difference in student satisfaction when comparing their present job to their prior position.

According to the research hypothesis, students and alumni who received higher education degrees from Chinese institutions were able to advance in their careers after completing their studies.

Table 6 shows that H1 and factors are statistically significant, and there is a difference when comparing students' present positions to their former positions.

H2: China's soft power policy's effect assessments include personal improvement, educational improvement, economic improvement, social improvement, educational comparison, student satisfaction, academic help and scholarship, and expenses for alumni and students.

Table 7. Correlations between factors

		fac1	fac2	fac3	fac4	fac5	fac6	fac7	fac8
Personal Improvement	**Pearson Correlation**	1	.468**	.453**	.507**	.455**	.469**	.298**	.461**
Educational Improvement	Pearson Correlation		1	.584**	.578**	.466**	.400**	.320**	.395**
Economic Improvement	Pearson Correlation			1	.571**	.417**	.368**	.345**	.351**
Social Improvement	Pearson Correlation				1	.588**	.501**	.329**	.475**
Educational Comparison	Pearson Correlation					1	.607**	.362**	.612**
Academic Help	Pearson Correlation						1	.424**	.680**
Scholarship & Expenses	Pearson Correlation							1	.408**
Students' Satisfaction	Pearson Correlation								1

**. Correlation is significant at the 0.01 level (2-tailed).

Table 8. Regression analysis of student satisfaction as an independent variable

Model	Coefficients					R
	B	SE	Beta	t	Sig.	
(Constant)	0.295	0.109		2.716	0.007	
Personal Improvement	0.129	0.027	0.120	4.870	0.000	
Educational Improvement	0.011	0.029	0.011	0.392	0.695	
Economic Improvement	-0.018	0.033	-0.016	-0.538	0.591	0.536
Social Improvement	0.092	0.033	0.079	2.789	0.005	
Educational Comparison	0.249	0.030	0.222	8.245	0.000	
Academic Help	0.425	0.027	0.414	15.864	0.000	
Scholarship & Expenses	0.079	0.022	0.079	3.649	0.000	

Dependent Variable: Student Satisfaction

H3: China's soft power policy influences the degree of satisfaction among students and graduates. Attachment shows that the R-square coefficient of determination or coefficient of variation predictor factors account for 53% of the variance in student satisfaction. The model was also statistically significant when evaluated using ANOVA. (p=.000) indicates that this independent variable is associated with distant learning satisfaction.

There is a strong correlation at the 0.01 significance level. The probability Sig.=0.000 (2-tail) <0.01. Table 7 indicates that there is a positive relationship between all factors. Furthermore, the results indicate that all the factors are moderately correlated and very significant with one another. Table 7 divulges that there is a moderate and positive correlation between Personal Improvement and Social Improvement (.3<.507<0.7) while Educational Improvement and Economic Improvement (.3<.584<0.7) reveals moderate and positive correlation. In addition, Social Improvement and Educational Comparison (.3<.588<0.7) reveals correlation of moderate and strong whereas Educational Comparison and Academic Help demonstrates moderate and positive correlation. Moreover, correlation between Academic help and students' satisfaction (.3<.680<0.7) is moderate and positive. The correlation analysis discloses that students and alumni give weight to the above improvements due to investment of education from China through soft power policy.

Linear Regression

Table 7 releases that coefficient B shows how much change in the independent variable (satisfaction) occurs for one-unit change in the predictor variables. This analysis shows that Academic Help has a moderate correlation with student satisfaction. A one-unit change in Academic Help increases satisfaction by 0.425 units.

II. a. Qualitative Data Analysis for Interview

The interview questions are divided into two sections: general information (5 questions) and the main portion (7 questions from 23 interviewers). The researchers concentrated on iterating the interview findings by analyzing the key content and principles using coding, following Bernard's (2006) study approach of qualitative data analysis. The repetition rating of material was not only sorted but also structured, and the primary content was summarized in general using Saldana's data analysis approach (2006). The interview transcript was sorted using the 3-cycle approach, and the material was summarized.

During the first cycle, the information described in the interview notes was coded in detail without duplication; during the second cycle, the first cycle's content was merged and coded; and in the third cycle, the rated content from the second cycle was combined and individually examined. Individualized percentages of interview results were determined using duplicated values for each participant's replies. In describing the general information portion of survey participants:

1. In China, most students and alumni (70.8%) rely on government scholarships, while 16.6% rely on Confucius scholarships, 4.2% self-fund, and 4.2% rely on other funding sources.
2. Professional areas included 58.3% education, 8.3% medical, 4.2% agriculture, 4.2% construction and engineering, and 25% other.
3. When asked about their current and finished academic degrees, 33.3% had a PhD, 41.7% had a master's degree, and 25% had a bachelor's. According to the location of the their studying city, 62.5% are Changchun, 12.5% are Wuhan, 12.4% are Beijing, 4.2% are Dalian, and 4.2% are Chongqing.
4. When looking at the period of education of the participants in China, 8.3% chose from 2022, 25% from 2020-2023, 29.1% from 2017-2020, 12.5% from 2014-2017, and 25% chose other answers.

According to the above, the majority of Mongolian youngsters studying in China have finished their studies on government scholarships and are presently enrolled. In addition, many of them are pursuing (or have finished) master's or doctorate degrees in teaching. Between 2014 and 2020, a large proportion of the study's participants were young individuals studying in Shandong, China, or who had completed their studies.

Result of the interview reveals that the Mongolian government aims to develop strong ties with its neighbors, considering its strategic location between China and Russia. China considers Mongolia a crucial foreign policy ally (Tatiana Ponka L. P., 2019).

1. What five things are most important to you when choosing China to study in?

Within the scope of the preceding question, 16 categories were sorted and coded in the first cycle, 8 in the second cycle, and 4 in the third cycle (Figure 4). The respondents ranked the most significant reasons and criteria for studying in China as follows.

1. *Exploring Chinese history, culture, language, traveling, and socializing (Cat 1, 10, 13, 14).*
2. *Mongolia is a neighbouring nation with a fair cost of living, excellent weather and climate, a student-friendly atmosphere, and safety (Cat 5, 6, 8, 12).*
3. *The education system's quality, university rankings, and individual expertise can enhance one's education and profession (Cat 2, 3, 4, 16).*
4. *Applicants choose China as their study destination due to the Chinese Embassy's active participation, diversity of study possibilities, attractive development experience, and availability of scholarships (Cat 7, 9, 11, 15).*

Important factors and reasons for studying in China were defined as the following: learning culture and language, proximity to Mongolia, reasonable cost of living, favorable weather and climate, quality

Figure 4. Text coding of the first question

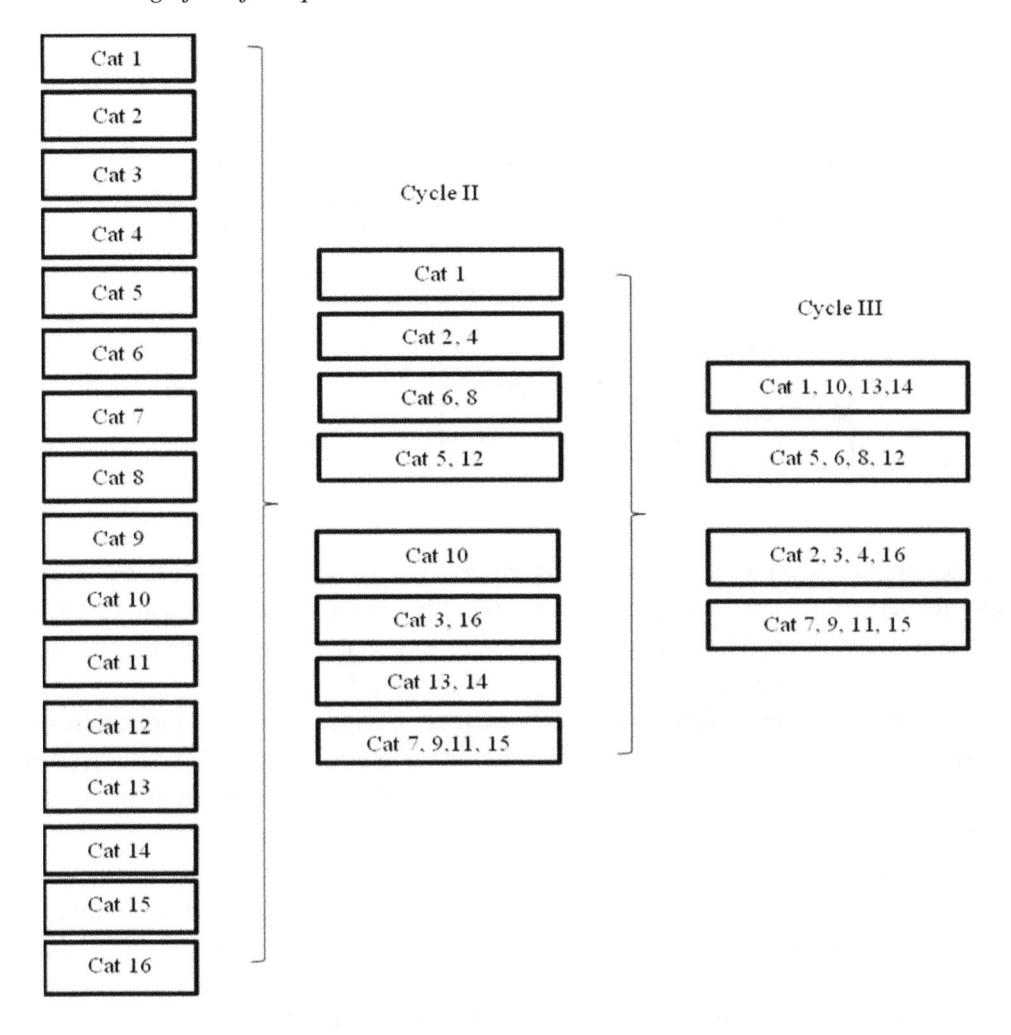

of education system, highly valued ranking and reputation of universities, active engagement of the Chinese Embassy, and scholarship availability for more applicants.

The most essential aspects of continuing their studies in China demonstrate that higher education institutions serve a critical role in national pride, technological advancement, and economic prosperity for Chinese citizens. Thus, the Chinese government implements educational diplomacy by disseminating Chinese language, culture, and official narratives. (Priya Gauttama, 2024).

2. In general, how environmentally friendly do you think universities are?

Within the scope of the preceding questions, six categories were sorted and coded in the first cycle, four in the second, and three in the third (Figure 5).

As shown in Figure 5, interview participants explained how environmentally friendly their colleges are in the following fashion.

The campus is well-kept with flowers and trees, mopeds and electric bikes are available for rent, the campus is quiet, everyone rides an electric bike or mini-moped, and the mini-buses that run on campus cost 2 yuan, the campus is fully regulated, the campus is clean with a lot of trees, everyone rides electric

Figure 5. Text coding of the second question

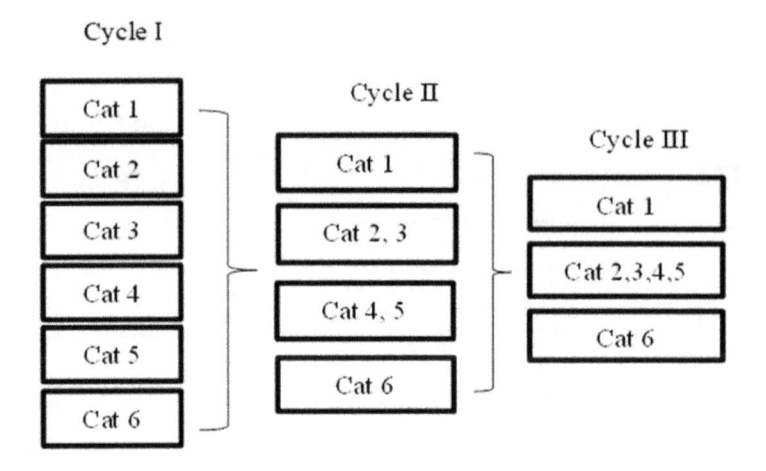

bikes, and the campus encourages the planting of various trees. Furthermore, waste management is effective; all rubbish is sorted, it is ecologically friendly, it has been able to establish a student-friendly atmosphere in which to study, it has been able to eradicate air pollution in recent years, and markets have been relocated to neighboring locations.

According to them, the campus and surrounding areas are planned in an environmentally responsible manner, resulting in a student-friendly atmosphere for individual learning and growth. However, a minority of individuals felt they produced chemical waste connected to the profession they were pursuing.

3. Do you expect to return to your home country after completing your course?

In the framework of the preceding questions, the interviewees completely stated their commitment to contribute to the development of their nation by using the academic information they had gained from the Chinese people. For example, they have been helping to disseminate their knowledge of languages and higher education.

4. What are their most important priorities when choosing a university?

Figure 6. Text coding of the fourth question

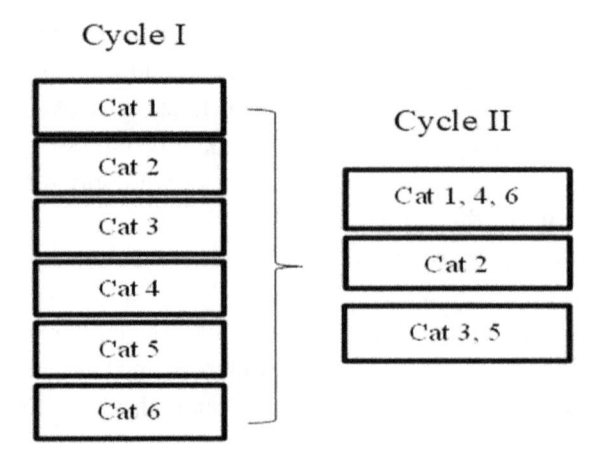

Figure 7. Text coding of the fifth question

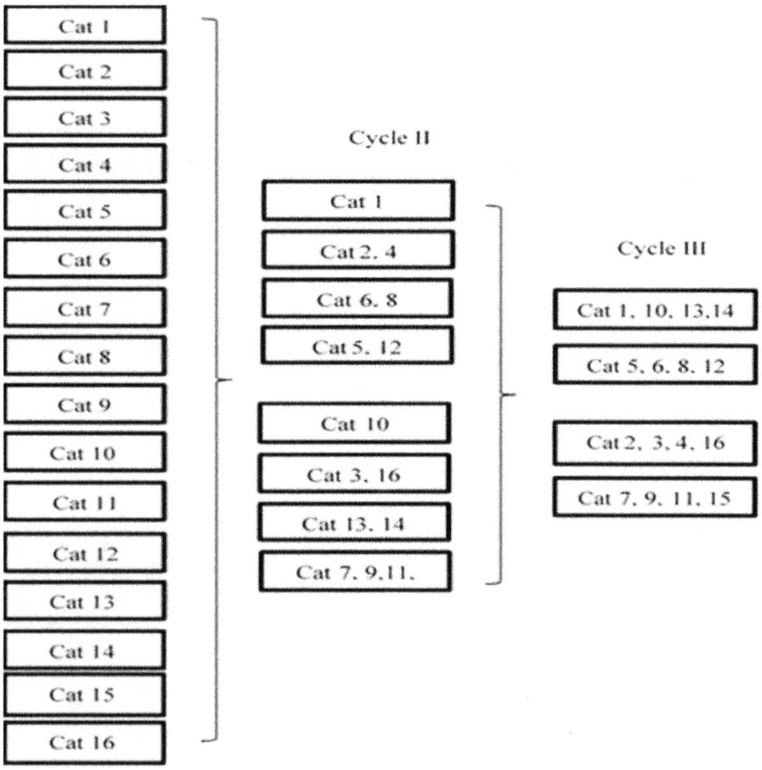

Within the context of the preceding question, 6 categories were sorted and classified into 6 categories in the first cycle and 3 categories in the second cycle (Figure 6).

Figure 6 depicts how and by what criteria the participants picked their institutions in response to the fourth question.

- *High-ranking universities, reputable education systems, experienced lecturers, and research organizations (Cat 1, 4, 6).*
- *Advantages of the site include ideal weather and climate, a student-friendly atmosphere, assured safety on university campuses, acceptance of urban areas, and proximity to Mongolia (Cat 2).*
- *Interviewees cited extensive experience in academic education, international student exchange, transnational cultural and communication programs, equal cooperation with other nations, and sharing experience with representatives from various countries (Cat 3, 5) as the most common responses.*

The results show that scholarship opportunities allow youths to benefit from competitive universities on an international and domestic level, domestically and globally accepted high ranking universities, a respectable reputation of higher education, a favorable location and weather, a broad range of foreign relations, extensive cooperation experience, and the opportunity to share experience with representatives from various nations while pursuing their academic degree in China.

5. Which of the following are most useful to you when making decisions about your studies?

Within the context of the preceding question, 18 categories were sorted and coded in the first cycle, 10 in the second cycle, and 5 in the third cycle (Figure 7).

According to Figure 7, the interviewees recognized the following advantages of studying in China. Within this,

- *Universities have a high demand for qualified and competitive instructors due to strict enrollment standards. Guest speakers from industrialized nations might visit on a regular basis to boost student participation at presentations and seminars lasting up to three days. It is worth noting that this is a unique opportunity to express one's thoughts on current events. Furthermore, scholarship opportunities motivate youngsters to continue their studies in a number of fields, including education, because students' academic achievements are recognized with a variety of scholarships, and the Chinese government scholarship quota is sufficient for applicants (Cat 1, 4).*
- *Sharing experience with foreign students, engaging with representatives from other countries, competing at an international level, receiving a degree at a fair cost, and advancing one's profession are all beneficial (Cat 2, 12, 15, 16).*
- *Interviewees cited benefits such as learning Chinese in a native language environment, improving Chinese and other foreign languages (也不是只有汉语水平,而是会学习到其他语言), accessing research sources in Chinese, comprehending Chinese books, and providing diverse research materials (Cat 3, 11, 13).*
- *Studying in China offers benefits such as fostering cultural knowledge, experiencing the development of a powerful nation, traveling around the country, enjoying affordable living costs, welcoming international students, ensuring student safety, and a peaceful environment (Cat 6, 7, 8, 10, 17).*
- *Strategic multifarious links with Mongolia, collaboration in numerous sectors, near geographical position, adjacent nation, and affordable cost of living (Cat 5, 9).*

As previously stated, interviewers emphasized the following strengths: Chinese government policy that works well for international applicants, a sufficient quota of scholarship availability for candidates, inspiration for sharing experience with global youths, encouragement for individual competitiveness, and support for research sources and materials for their studies in China. Furthermore, by cultivating cultural understanding, acquiring experience in the growth of a powerful nation, traveling around China, enjoying affordable living costs, ensuring student safety, and relying on a tranquil environment. As a result, they prioritize strategic multidimensional connections with Mongolia, collaboration in numerous sectors, close physical proximity, and Mongolia's neighboring nation (Zreik, 2023b).

The decision to study in China demonstrates that education investment allows China to reap a twofold gain by deploying soft power as a host country (Priya Gauttama, 2024).

6. Thinking about your parents, how important do you think they would consider each of the following aspects of your international study to be?

According to interviewees, when studying in China, their relatives and friends are concerned about health-related concerns such as health insurance, well-being, good diet, weather conditions, their studies, and safe travel.

7. What worries you most about studying in a different country?

According to the interview notes, students and graduates confront the following difficulties, which are summarized and ranked as follows. There are no barriers such as the Chinese language, but they do face challenges such as adjusting to spicy food, junk food, a ban on working hours for students, homesickness, no central heating system in the winter, expensive meat, limited Wi-Fi access for students, and cultural and mindset differences. It may be inferred that China's soft power has been gaining foothold in Mongolia, despite historic opposition to Chinese influence. Furthermore, China's influence is dominating in politics, economy, and culture, which is regarded not only a worldwide issue but also Mongolian wariness towards China's soft power (Byambakhand. L, 2021).

II. b. Qualitative Data Analysis of SWOT and TOWS

SWOT is an acronym of four letters: S (Strength), W (Weakness), O (Opportunity), and T (Threat), and the analysis is frequently employed at the organizational and corporate levels. It is a key way of analysis that managers in any organization may use to examine the firm's past and present position or to develop a strategy. However, the SWOT analysis was utilized to determine how soft power policies influence individuals through educational investment in the younger generation.

SWOT analysis was conducted on the three alumni instances listed below to study China's soft power influence in the sphere of education.

1. Undergraduate: She earned a Confucian scholarship and graduated as a Chinese language teacher from Zhejiang Normal University in Jinhua during the 2016-2020 academic year. During the Covid time, she completed her bachelor's degree while adhering to the university's rigorous quarantine policy. Furthermore, while studying, she was actively involved in undergraduate competitions and contests.
2. Master: She received her Master of Arts in Chinese from Central China Normal University during the 2017-2019 academic year; she excels at learning English and German but struggles with Chinese. During her education, she actively participated in a variety of activities, including editing, volunteering, and teaching Chinese.
3. Ph.D.: She graduated from Central China Normal University with a Ph.D. in Education during the 2017-2021 academic year. She resumed her academic education in an English-taught program after completing a year of Chinese preparatory. She graduated from university following an online defense of her dissertation due to the pandemic.

The preceding study demonstrates that graduates excel at sharing experiences with representatives from many nations and understanding Chinese culture. Furthermore, they are capable of pursuing their degree in Chinese due to their previous academic studies; they are active in participating in a variety of activities for them without any language barrier; however, they may face some weaknesses, such as a lack of fluency in Chinese or English to communicate with domestic or international students. It is worth noting that alumni with Chinese as their profession have the option of continuing their education or pursuing a job. However, employment is not permitted for students to complete their education, and a lack of internship opportunities owing to their position as international students in China is viewed as a big danger to them.

SWOT analysis suggests that China wrestles with increasing education quality by executing Projects 211 and 985 focused on nurturing roughly 100 higher education institutions (elite) to stimulate the application submission procedure of great students throughout the world. (Priya Gauttama, 2024)

Table 9. SWOT analysis

Strength	Weakness
Undergraduate: - Studied Chinese in a private school since elementary school - Received the Confucius Scholarship for academic achievement - No language barriers - Gained cultural experience - Satisfied with education quality - Actively participated in undergraduate activities and competitions.	**Undergraduate:** -English language barries in communicating with overseas students. - Occasional misunderstandings with international pupils due to cultural diversity
Master: - Studied Chinese at the undergraduate level in Mongolia. - Gained English skills to join the editorial team of a university magazine and volunteer in a Chinese language club. - Received monthly allowance to focus on studies. - Interacted with representatives from various countries. - Joined a volunteer organization and participated in various activities.	**Master:** -Distance relationship with family; undergraduate students prone to commit breaches such as alcohol consumption. -It is thought that the outcomes of the master's level education quality are significantly worse than those of Chinese students studying the same topic.
Ph.D: - Participated in an English academic program to exchange experiences with representatives from different countries. - Satisfied with attending lectures and workshops from experienced scholars from overseas. - Completed a year-long Chinese preparation course to learn from international students. - Learned Chinese for daily communication.	**Ph.D:** - Limited English communication skills - Requires advanced Chinese proficiency for weekly research discussions with supervisor's students
Opportunities	**Threat**
Undergraduate: - Acceptable to continue education and employment while also participating in cultural activities and contests. - Encourage foreign participation in trade fairs and business meetings. - Strengthen international commercial partnerships.	**Undergraduate:** - Foreign students have restricted internship opportunities. - Self-discipline is essential.
Master: - Pursuing a Ph.D. - Possibility of finding job after graduation.	**Master:** - Scholarship students are not permitted to work. - Opportunities for internships are restricted when compared to Chinese students in the same field.
Ph.D: - Concentrate on research thanks to a supportive learning atmosphere. - Use research papers from websites like CNK.	**Ph.D:** -Prefer to continue their education with scholarship opportunities.

TOWS Analysis

This analysis is performed following the SWOT analysis and determines the next actions based on the information received from the SWOT analysis. Here is a quick overview on how to accomplish it.

1. Strength - Opportunity: Maximizing opportunities based on strength.
2. Strength - Threat: Reducing dangers depending on strength
3. Weakness - Opportunity: Improving weakness via opportunity.
4. Weakness - Threat: Minimizing weaknesses to prevent potential threats.

Table 10. TOWS analysis

1. Strengths - Opportunities: Maximizing Opportunities Based on Strength	2. Strength - Threat: Reducing Dangers Depending on Strength
Undergraduate: International applicants with fluency in Chinese can get the same high-quality education as local students.	**Undergraduate:** Alumni of a disciplined private school in the Chinese education system are less likely to engage in immature conduct.
Master: Fluency in English and Chinese enhances alumni's competitiveness in the Chinese labor market.	**Master:** Foreign language expertise might be used as a tool to collaborate with foreign organizations rather than pursuing local internship opportunities.
Ph.D: Alumni of Ph.D. programs in China have been inspired to pursue academic studies and research.	**Ph.D:** Collaborative learning is available for both international and domestic students who can communicate in English.
3. Weakness - Opportunity: Improving weaknesses based on opportunities.	4. Weakness - Threat: Minimizing weaknesses to prevent potential threats.
Undergraduate: Gaining expertise through cooperation with domestic and international partners aimed at improving English.	**Undergraduate:** To foster collaboration with foreigners while aiming for English fluency.
Master: Applying for a job demands a foreign language and the same educational background as domestic applicants in a different area.	**Master:** Submit a request to share experiences with domestic students, including the same internship options.
Ph.D: Work on research requires English.	**Ph.D:** Encourage them to share their academic experiences with domestic pupils.

As previously said, China's soft power in education may be assessed by examining opportunities and threats to academic studies to strengthen them and decrease alumni weaknesses.

TOWS's strength-opportunity analysis reveals that graduates gain from academic studies in China via rigorous study and proficiency in both Chinese and English. According to the Strength - Threat analysis, alumni of undergraduate, master's, and doctoral programs have the opportunity to collaborate with local and foreign partners due to their intellectual maturity. Furthermore, the Weakness - Opportunity analysis shows that they are capable of working in China after successfully completing their degree. Weakness - Threat demonstrates that proficiency in both Chinese and English enables alumni to compete for home and international professional opportunities.

Since a consequence of TOWS analysis, an international community with connectivity may be built by traversing soft power, since higher education is the highest wheel of soft power (Priya Gauttama, 2024).

DISCUSSION

The nation's influence is exerted through non-coercive means, such as the education of persons at the higher education level. On the other hand, Nye's example of soft power is perfectly compatible with education because the target nations consent rather than coerce. According to the findings of a mixed methodological study, students and alumni benefit from higher education institutions in China since the host country invests in education. It is worth noting that the majority of responders are students, indicating that they are more interested in scholarship opportunities with substantial quotas than in accepting restricted scholarship opportunities from foreign nations.

According to the research findings, as an essential component of foreign policy, higher education in host countries is expanding from the domestic to the global level through educational investment. However, it is necessary to allow fair competition for young people to continue their studies abroad by improving their competency in a variety of abilities such as foreign language acquisition, both hard and soft skills, communication skills, and academic performance.

CONCLUSION

A variety of nations regard their domestic higher education institutions to be front-line soft power for the target countries since the area of international higher education is a dynamic force for globalization owing to its position in foreign policy goals.

Previous Chinese leaders were instrumental in constructing a "peaceful raise" oriented on scientific advancement, modernization, and internal betterment. Thus, "The Belt and Road Initiative" helps to realize the Chinese Dream by spreading it both within and outside of the country. As a result, education is regarded as the cultivation of soft power based on a country's culture, political beliefs, and foreign and domestic policy. It is important to highlight that soft power does not spread in the absence of willing interpreters and receivers.

The study examined the relationship between education and soft power using quantitative and qualitative data analysis.

- The correlation analysis result (.680) shows that the happiness of current students and graduates with academic support is higher than their other improvements. On the other side, China's efforts to foster competitive colleges succeed through soft power. Furthermore, a larger connection (.588) between social progress and educational comparison indicates that China's academic position is consistent with its global reputation. Thus, respondents prioritized educational and economic advancement (.584) while stressing social and personal development (.507).
- The analysis's linear regression result shows that their degree of satisfaction has altered as a result of academic assistance. In other words, their pleasure is contingent on academic assistance from the host nation, demonstrating that China's soft power is manifested through education.
- The research hypothesis was validated by the discovery that students and alumni benefited from higher education degrees at Chinese schools by earning higher positions after completing their studies.
- The interview results demonstrate that an adequate scholarship quota allows them to pursue their studies at internationally recognized Chinese higher education institutions with the Chinese government.
- The SWOT and TOWS analysis results show that China is growing soft power by recruiting competitive candidates and investing in their education in China.

As China's large power investment is greater than that of other nations, it is critical to research soft power via education for target countries that benefit from educational support. To analyze the educational returns of foreign representatives other than China, the study must be expanded with a larger sample size, including more master's and doctoral-level responses.

REFERENCES

Abdul Ghaffar Mastoi, L. X. (2019). Higher Education Service Quality based on Students' Satisfaction in People's Republic of China. *Journal of Education and Practice*, 112.

Aidarbek Amirbek, K. Y. (2014). Education as a Soft Power Instrument of Foreign Policy. *Procedia: Social and Behavioral Sciences*, 502.

Awang, Z. (n.d.). *A Handbook on SEM 2nd ediction*. Unviersity Sultan Zainal Abidin.

Batkhuyag Sodovyn, B. S. (2019). The China-Mongolia-Russia economic corridor and Mongolia's energy sector. *ESE Web of Conferences, 77*.

Bush, J. W. (2021). *China's Soft Power in the Context of the Belt and Road Initiative: Three Case Studies*. Academic Press.

Byambakhand, L. S. K. (2021). *Young Mongolians and the World in 2021 (National Opinion Poll Results)*. Friedrich-Ebert-Stiftung Mongolia & Mongolian Institute for Innovative Policies.

Chandmani, S. (2020). China's "Belt and Road Initiative Internationallly". Ulaanbaatar: People's Republic of China, Academy of Research and Institute for Strategic Studies.

Diplomacy, U. C. (2019). *The Soft Power 30, A Global Ranking of Soft Power 2019*. Portland: Designed by Portland's in-house Content & Brand team.

Hunter, A. (2009). Soft Power: China on the Global Stage. *Chinese Journal of International Politics, 2,* 373-398.

Indra Bazarsad, P. C. (2021). *Sino – Mongolian economic interconnectivity: Big talks, little progress*. Friedrich-Ebert-Stiftung Mongolia & Mongolian Institute for Innovative Policies.

Jargalsaikhan, M. (2014). Caveats for the Mongolia-China Strategic Partnership. *Asia Pacific Bulletin*.

Kucharčíková, A. (2011). Human Capital-Definitions and Accpoaches. *Human Resources Management & Ergonomics, 5,* 60.

Maxim, K. (2023). Character of PRC Soft Policy and Mongolia. Internationak Studies, 46(115), 65.

Osodoev, P. V. (2021). *Regional trade and economic cooperation along the China-Mongolia-Russia Economic Corridor*. doi:10.1088/1755-1315/885/1/012016

Priya Gauttama, B. S. (2024). Education as a soft power resource: A systematic review. *Heliyon*, 1–20. PMID:38268586

Rashid Latief, L. L. (2018). Analysis of Chinese Government Scholarship for International Students Using Analytical Hierarchy. *Sustainability*, 7.

Tatiana Ponka, A. B. (2019, January). Relations Between China and Mongolia: Cultural and Educational Dimensions. *Advances in Social Science, Education and Humanities Research, 356,* 1104.

Tatiana Ponka, L. P. (2019). Relations Between China and Mongolia: Cultural and Educational Dimensions. *Advances in Social Science, Education and Humanities Research, 356,* 1102–1105.

Uyanga, T. (n.d.). *Intensifying Soft Power Policy through diplomacy of economy*. Academic Press.

Wu, I. S. (n.d.). *Measuring Soft Power with Conventional and Unconventional Data*. Academic Press.

Zreik, M. (2023a). Harnessing Islamic Entrepreneurship for the Belt and Road Initiative: Opportunities, Challenges, and Future Directions. In A. Rafiki, A. Pananjung, & M. Nasution (Eds.), *Strategies and Applications of Islamic Entrepreneurship* (pp. 119–135). IGI Global. doi:10.4018/978-1-6684-7519-5.ch008

Zreik, M. (2023b). Navigating the Dragon: China's Ascent as a Global Power Through Public Diplomacy. In S. Kavoğlu & E. Köksoy (Eds.), *Global Perspectives on the Emerging Trends in Public Diplomacy* (pp. 50–74). IGI Global. doi:10.4018/978-1-6684-9161-4.ch003

Zreik, M. (2024a). Artificial Intelligence and the Future of Chinese Language Pedagogy: An In-Depth Analysis. In Z. Çetin Köroğlu & A. Çakır (Eds.), *Fostering Foreign Language Teaching and Learning Environments with Contemporary Technologies* (pp. 1–20). IGI Global. doi:10.4018/979-8-3693-0353-5.ch001

Zreik, M. (2024b). Soft Power and China-Taiwan Competition for Influence in Latin America. In C. R. Veney & S. O. Abidde (Eds.), *China and Taiwan in Latin America and the Caribbean. Studies of the Americas* (pp. 151–141). Palgrave Macmillan. doi:10.1007/978-3-031-45166-9_6

APPENDIX

Table 11. Factor analysis

	Factor8	Factor4	Factor7	Factor6	Factor1	Factor2	Factor5	Factor3
Confirmatory Factor Analysis								
variables	Students' Satisfaction	Social Improvement	Scholarship & Expenses	Educational Comparison	Personal Improvement	Educational Improvement	Educational Comparison	Economic Improvement
3.8.10	0.854	0.168	0.066	0.203	0.087	0.064	0.072	0.076
3.8.4	0.823	0.151	0.109	0.167	0.054	0.111	0.245	0.050
3.8.7	0.805	0.096	0.059	0.221	0.173	0.065	0.145	0.038
3.8.6	0.796	0.060	0.142	0.248	0.161	0.053	0.029	0.149
3.8.8	0.792	0.089	0.132	0.073	0.033	0.040	0.071	0.199
3.8.5	0.787	0.128	0.123	0.214	0.153	0.120	0.074	0.104
3.8.9	0.786	0.201	0.203	0.223	0.097	0.152	0.151	-0.021
3.8.3	0.773	0.123	0.090	0.289	0.137	0.058	0.152	0.067
3.8.11	0.766	0.188	0.114	0.132	0.092	0.012	0.151	-0.013
3.8.14	0.759	0.154	0.143	0.104	0.033	-0.048	0.136	0.082
3.8.2	0.755	0.173	0.117	0.132	0.122	0.234	0.245	-0.078
3.8.1	0.746	0.215	0.113	0.075	0.096	0.170	0.327	-0.069
3.8.15	0.741	0.168	0.190	0.107	0.178	0.012	0.112	0.077
3.8.12	0.734	0.272	0.153	0.217	0.127	0.072	0.182	-0.073
3.8.13	0.624	0.234	0.289	0.128	0.170	-0.068	-0.041	0.166
3.4.6	0.275	0.759	0.002	0.092	0.126	0.217	0.129	0.082
3.4.3	0.097	0.755	0.102	0.108	0.155	0.148	0.165	0.093
3.4. 2	0.161	0.748	0.168	0.169	0.057	0.106	0.124	0.126
3.4.7	0.167	0.711	0.076	0.145	0.198	0.123	0.208	0.150
3.4.9	0.178	0.693	-0.026	0.108	0.256	0.155	0.154	0.112
3.4.8	0.262	0.687	0.021	0.081	0.245	0.156	0.155	0.258
3.4.10	0.264	0.681	0.013	0.101	0.185	0.257	0.229	0.086
3.4.4	0.180	0.669	0.098	0.135	0.121	0.073	0.051	0.177
3.4.5	0.211	0.651	0.074	0.053	0.281	0.256	0.163	0.156
3.4. 1	0.259	0.593	0.207	0.100	0.008	0.094	0.154	0.236
3.7.3	0.077	0.023	0.833	0.061	0.075	0.054	0.101	0.085
3.7.4	0.135	0.108	0.821	0.141	0.089	0.051	-0.027	-0.019
3.7.9	0.109	0.175	0.776	0.138	0.037	0.139	-0.045	-0.074
3.7.5	0.189	0.047	0.776	0.055	0.043	0.178	0.079	-0.096
3.7.7	0.247	0.034	0.771	0.052	0.075	0.139	0.018	0.000
3.7.8	0.182	0.037	0.765	0.036	0.039	0.018	0.135	-0.059
3.7.6	0.124	-0.003	0.642	0.162	0.039	0.173	-0.018	0.102
3.7.1	0.078	0.054	0.622	0.059	0.068	-0.038	0.223	0.414
3.7.2	0.129	0.144	0.610	0.108	0.100	-0.084	0.210	0.265

continued on following page

Table 11. Continued

				Confirmatory Factor Analysis				
	Factor8	Factor4	Factor7	Factor6	Factor1	Factor2	Factor5	Factor3
3.6.5	0.273	0.109	0.217	0.776	0.161	0.160	0.087	0.041
3.6.4	0.357	0.087	0.105	0.770	0.084	0.074	-0.016	0.143
3.6.3	0.389	0.115	0.126	0.697	0.206	0.102	0.097	0.023
3.6.2	0.403	0.195	0.112	0.695	0.195	0.074	0.173	0.021
3.6.1	0.369	0.175	0.102	0.679	0.157	0.106	0.194	0.051
3.6.7	0.245	0.207	0.208	0.616	0.127	0.055	0.194	0.025
3.6.6	0.349	0.213	0.166	0.608	0.130	0.096	0.247	-0.012
3.1.5	0.146	0.156	0.133	0.167	0.785	0.062	0.067	0.123
3.1.4	0.180	0.219	0.101	0.173	0.765	0.167	0.078	0.115
3.1.3	0.201	0.115	0.026	0.108	0.761	0.129	0.132	0.061
3.1.1	0.146	0.174	0.071	0.169	0.746	0.186	0.121	0.122
3.1.6	0.173	0.340	0.188	0.057	0.724	-0.051	0.016	0.115
3.1.2	0.233	0.301	0.046	0.158	0.684	0.149	0.228	0.009
3.2.3	0.038	0.246	0.111	0.121	0.162	0.802	0.060	0.203
3.2.4	0.072	0.279	0.181	0.157	0.082	0.755	0.090	0.157
3.2.5	0.188	0.279	0.126	0.123	0.082	0.747	0.121	0.218
3.2.2	0.090	0.158	0.118	0.064	0.171	0.746	0.056	0.192
3.2.1	0.127	0.207	0.155	0.065	0.094	0.733	0.180	0.262
3.5.2	0.236	0.147	0.056	0.056	0.141	0.057	0.755	0.121
3.5.5	0.333	0.237	0.078	0.155	0.150	0.173	0.682	0.019
3.5.6	0.382	0.325	0.021	0.165	0.101	0.144	0.659	0.036
3.5.1	0.249	0.197	0.153	0.154	0.145	0.060	0.656	0.117
3.5.4	0.369	0.294	0.018	0.210	0.081	0.137	0.612	-0.028
3.5.3	0.116	0.235	0.249	0.118	0.064	0.068	0.558	0.104
3.3.5	0.058	0.289	0.007	0.062	0.187	0.260	0.077	0.728
3.3.3	0.109	0.303	0.058	0.058	0.161	0.271	0.024	0.723
3.3.4	0.187	0.342	0.018	0.044	0.143	0.305	0.130	0.698
3.3.1	0.019	0.240	0.061	0.054	0.038	0.367	0.047	0.648
3.3.2	0.138	0.406	0.155	0.014	0.150	0.317	0.114	0.464
хувийн утга	1.461	2.648	4.392	1.787	23.448	5.834	2.349	4.392
variance	5.075	7.016	9.231	5.957	17.883	11.165	6.942	9.231
cumulative	69.873	45.295	38.279	64.798	17.883	29.049	52.237	38.279
KMO=.923 Bartlett's Test of Sphericity=13145.933(p=.000)								
Cronbach alpha	0.968	0.946	0.918	0.932	0.897	0.923	0.881	0.884
N of items	15	10	9	7	6	5	6	5

Figure 8. Structure Equation Model

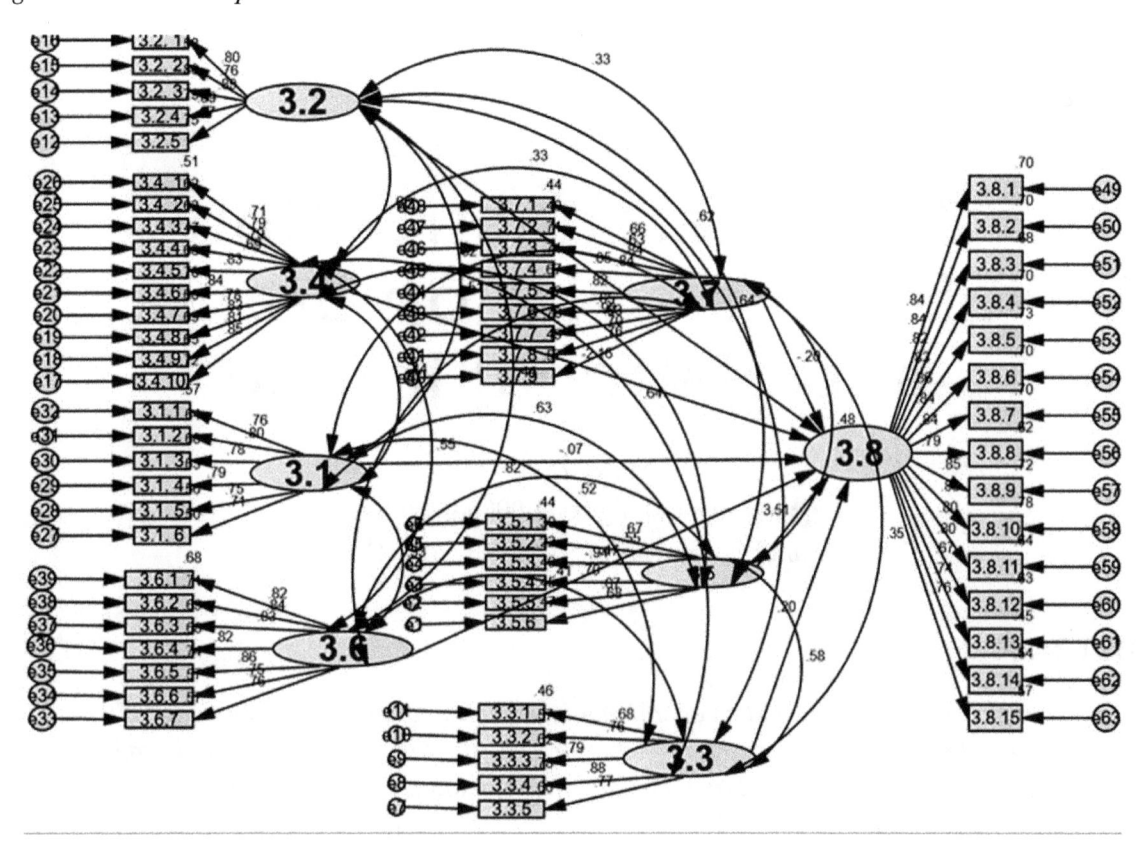

Chapter 17
The Interconstruction of China's Nation Brand and National Image

Jiaxi Zhou

🄳 https://orcid.org/0009-0006-0766-3917

Shanghai Academy of Social Sciences, China

ABSTRACT

In the era of globalization, the problem of national image becomes more prominent, and international brand marketing becomes one of the powerful ways for a country to enhance its national image. National branding is an active process aimed at enhancing the reputation of a country, while national image is something that exists in the perception of the audience. Since the reform and opening-up, China's comprehensive national strength has continuously increased, and the world's perception of China has become stronger. Chinese enterprises and brands have gradually overcome the stereotypical impression of being low-quality and cheap. However, in the increasingly fierce competition among major powers, it is urgent to construct China's national image through national brand marketing. China should implement a nation brand plan from a top-level design, involve the entire society, strengthen open communication with the international community, and further promote Chinese enterprises and brands to go global.

The formation of global village has led to an unprecedented level of interdependence between countries. In the era of globalization, nation brand holds tremendous economic value, as internationally recognized nation brand contributes to attracting foreign investment, increasing tourism revenue, and promoting the internationalization of products and services. Thus, national branding can enhance a country's global brand awareness and lead to substantial economic growth. From a national perspective, establishing a nation brand can effectively improve a country's national image. National image is crucial for a country's foreign relations and cross-cultural communication, influencing how other nations perceive and interact with it. Currently, all countries face competition in trade, investment, tourism, cultural exchanges, and so on. It is essential that nation brand and national image are built upon a country's comprehensive national strength. Currently, China ranks among the world's leaders in terms of comprehensive national strength.

DOI: 10.4018/979-8-3693-2444-8.ch017

However, there is a need to strengthen the brand effect during external communication. The creation of a more influential national branding should be considered an integral part of China's modernization and a practical requirement to enhance China's soft power on the global stage.

INTRODUCTION

The issue of nation brand has a long history dating back to ancient civilizations. Throughout the ages, various civilizations and nations have endeavored to shape their own images to showcase their economic and social development, cultural characteristics, and deepen their understanding and knowledge of other civilizations and countries.

Evolution of National Image and Nation Brand

British designer Olins (2002) pointed out that historically, nations have successfully crafted new images by emulating the marketing strategies employed by businesses. Literatures on national image can be broadly summarized as the impressions and perceptions of a country by foreign governments or citizens. Kunczik (1997, p. 46), in particular, defines national image as a cognitive representation, which refers to an individual's genuine perceptions of a country and its people. Li and Chitty (2009) define national image as private frameworks in individuals' minds and public frameworks visible in the media. Some scholars analyze national images from the perspective of communication management, dividing them into three fundamental and interconnected analytical dimensions: the identity of the nation, the international communication processes of the nation, and the perceptions and attitudes formed towards the nation during these processes. National image evolves into the subjective attitudes of stakeholders towards a nation and its people, encompassing specific beliefs and general sentiments on functional, normative, apathetic, and sympathetic dimensions (Buhmann & Ingenhoff, 2015, pp. 109–113). With the advent of globalization, informatization, and digitization, the connotation of a country's national image has become more enriched. As van Ham (2001, pp. 3–6) has mentioned, image and reputation are integral components of a nation's strategic interests. With traditional diplomacy fading away, politicians must find a branding position for their country and engage in competitive marketing.

Competition between nations has transcended the traditional military and economic domains, with the concept of comprehensive national strength becoming more diverse. Porter emphasized the industrial development and global economic competitiveness of a nation in his book *The Competitive Advantage of Nations*. Porter (1998) designed the Diamond Model theory, summarizing four key factors that influence a country's industrial development: factors of production, demand conditions, related and supporting industries, and firm strategy. In 1996, Anholt coined the term "nation brand," suggesting that countries can be marketed and branded as products. Subsequently, Anholt (2007, pp. 21–28) introduced the concept of "competitive identity," highlighting that governments can establish and maintain a competitive national identity both internally and externally. Compared to Porter, Anholt supplemented the "brand" as a soft concept in national development.

The American Marketing Association defines a brand as a name, term, sign, symbol, or design, or a combination of these, intended to identify the goods or services of one seller or group of sellers and to differentiate them from those of competitors (Kotler, 2000, p. 188). "Nation brand" refers to the brand constructed by a country. A country brand is a cross-disciplinary public domain (Fetscherin, 2010, p.

469). Kotler (1997) pointed out that the assessment of a country's wealth involves four factors: natural, tangible, human, and social capital. Nation brand involves the competitive management of both the tangible and intangible resources of a country, including natural resources, culture, history, and society (J. Rojas-Méndez, 2013, pp. 464–465).

Visualization of National Branding

Dinnie (2009, p. 15) believes that a nation brand is the provision of unique, multidimensional, culturally based mixed factors for its target audience, including three elements: identity, image, and positioning (Dinnie, 2009, p. 41). Nation brand can be seen as a result of economic globalization, reduced trade barriers, and the intersection of national identity and country of origin (Dinnie, 2009, p. 21). Soni (2019) held that nation brand is how a country or region positions and promotes itself as a place to visit and invest, building a good reputation based on the quality of its goods and services, as well as its talent. This goes beyond applying corporate marketing concepts and technologies to different countries. After analyzing 186 interdisciplinary studies, Kaneva (2011, pp. 117–118) summarized national branding as a compilation aimed at reconstructing the discourse and practices of nationality through marketing and branding paradigms.

To intuitively quantify the brand influence of different countries, in 2005, Anholt (2006) established the National Brands Index (NBI) to evaluate a country's performance based on six indicators. Compared to Porter, Anholt places greater emphasis on the country's image. Fetscherin constructed the Country Brand Strength Index (CBSI) with secondary data. In contrast to Anholt's National Brands Index, which relies on subjective survey data, the purpose of CBSI is to measure the actual strength of a country's brand (Fetscherin, 2010). There has been debate regarding national brand marketing. Olins believes that a nation's brand is crucial for economic development and wealth, while French scholar Michel Girard suggests that rebuilding France's national brand would be widely accepted because people perceive France as having a strong sense of national identity. Olins and Girard interpreted a nation brand from the perspectives of marketing significance and the history and culture of a nation, respectively (Girard, 1999; Olins, 2002).

Recently, scholars have delved into discussions beyond the traditional understanding of national branding. Stefan and others (2022, p. 200) found the majority of national branding research adopts the dyadic view of brand building, where the nation brand is an identity to be communicated to its target audience. Browning (2023, pp. 76–77) advocated the conceptualization of national branding as a practice built upon economic logic, globalization, and competitive national discourse. This approach considers the instrumentalization and commodification of national identity and culture as prerequisites. Alderman and Eggeling (2024) approached national branding as a sophisticated practice that has become part of the legitimation toolkit in non-democratic regimes. Many studies have associated national branding with national identity, elucidating the role of national branding practices in shaping national identity through concrete examples, such as Chile and Portugal (Lever et al., 2023; Miño, 2023; Miño & Austin, 2022; Nobre & Sousa, 2022).

Over the past two decades, one of the primary challenges facing national branding is the widespread terminology confusion in the field (Hao et al., 2019, p. 56). The lack of a clear definition of a nation brand has resulted in conceptual ambiguity, serving as a generative force that allows stakeholders to transform a nation brand into a practice according to their own agendas (Merkelsen & Rasmussen, 2016, p. 102). Overall, the concept of nation brand remains unclear, with both overlaps and distinctions from concepts such as national image and public diplomacy. From a national perspective, nation brand is a subset of national image. From a marketing standpoint, a national image is one of the marketing objectives of a nation brand. In other words, national branding is an active process aimed at enhancing the country's reputation, while national image is something that exists in the perception of the audience.

Relation With National Branding and National Image

Fan (2006, pp. 5–6) believes that "nation brand" has always existed, while "national branding" involves the application of branding and marketing communication techniques to enhance the national image. Fan defines nation brand as a process through which a country's image can be created, monitored, evaluated, and actively managed to improve or enhance the country's reputation among its target international audience. National branding is a complex polyhedron that depends on various factors such as other countries, specific events, or occasions (Fan, 2010). National branding is mainly conducted in five forms: country-of-origin effect, nation-state, sovereign state, region, and nation (Fan, 2005).

Nation brand is closely related to national image, a positive national image contributes to the cultivation of a recognizable nation brand. The success of national branding can enhance a country's international image. National branding is a conscious management process, whereas national image refers to how international consumers perceive a country (Montanari & Giraldi, 2018). National branding involves a systematic strategic process where both public and private sectors collaborate to design national branding strategies, communicate core national values and identity, and utilize brand strategies to enhance the country's image and reputation across different nations (J. I. Rojas-Méndez & Khoshnevis, 2022, p. 114). Ahmed and others (2022) illustrated that it is a recurrent idea that national branding is a core mean to empower a country on a world map, and the UAE's strides in sustainable development, environmental and infrastructure initiatives, fostering a competitive knowledge economy, building a cohesive society while preserving its identity, along with significant growth in tourism, have paved the way for global recognition and a robust national branding (Zreik, 2023a).

National branding and public diplomacy are intertwined, both being crucial components of a country's management of its international image and interaction with foreign audiences. In comparison to public diplomacy, national branding has higher visibility as it heavily relies on visuals and symbols, allowing the target audience to encounter another country's branding activities (Szondi, 2008, p. 16). In the field of public relations, branding can help a country or city shape a more positive and distinct image, fostering collaboration and communication with international organizations and other countries. Branding also plays a significant role in international relations, as countries can establish a clear and distinctive image through branding, thereby enhancing their international influence (van Ham, 2002).

LESSONS FROM OTHER COUNTRIES IN NATIONAL BRANDING

The term "marketing" originally referred to the promotion and sale of products by businesses. With the introduction of national branding, countries are also seen as needing marketing to establish a positive national image and reputation. In simple terms, while business marketing promotes products, national marketing enhances a country's quality. Traditionally, a country's brand identity system includes elements, such as the national flag, anthem, and national flowers. With the deepening of globalization, the significance of a country's brand image has gradually expanded, encompassing areas such as national brand identity design and creation of national slogans. Countries have engaged in various practical activities in the field of national branding, with some having developed globally recognized brand effects.

Country-of-Origin Effect and Place Branding

The country-of-origin effect refers to how a country's reputation influences people's perceptions of products and is commonly used to gauge consumer opinions and purchase intentions (White, 2012, p. 111). The country-of-origin effect is crucial for businesses to effectively position their products in the global market and cater to consumers' perceptions and preferences. For example, Swiss watches are highly regarded for their precision and craftsmanship; Italian fashion is known for its style and luxury, and German cars are favored for their reliable quality (Keegan & Schlegelmilch, 2001). The emotional and product images associated with different countries significantly influence consumers' purchasing decisions. Research has found that Chinese consumers generally perceive American products as having advanced technology, and this perception significantly affects their purchasing decisions for American cars and sportswear (D. Li et al., 2014). Shaping a product contributes to enhancing a country's image; conversely, an improved national image influences the acceptance of its products. Therefore, a country can strengthen the competitiveness of its products in the international market through a positive national image, and successful products can also help establish a positive image for the country (Zreik, 2024a). For example, Switzerland is the first country in the world to establish a National Brand Commission, closely overseeing "Swiss Made" and the national image (Roll, 2021).

Place branding aims to promote specific regions, cities, or destinations as part of a broader national branding. It serves as a complement to national branding, acknowledging that national identity is not uniform, but includes diverse geographic and cultural elements. Effective place branding involves creating unique identities for local cities and towns and highlighting their distinct features, culture, customs, and investment opportunities. In 1976, New York introduced the iconic "I Love New York" logo, widely regarded as one of the most successful examples of city branding. Through the combination of a red heart and the American Typewriter font, the logo quickly communicates the essence of New York (Bendel, 2011). Other successful place branding initiatives include Singapore's national branding development, which transformed the city-state into a global financial and business hub. Singapore's branding focuses on efficiency, innovation, and high-quality lifestyle, attracting numerous businesses and expatriates (Yee, 2009). Ireland initiated a large-scale tourism plan, developing a tourism product called the "Wild Atlantic Way" for the entire west coast region from Donegal to Cork. Each region promotes slightly different experiences, distinguished through iconic landmarks known as "Discovery Points." (TPBO, 2015)

National Branding as National Strategy

As part of an overall national strategy, international branding has become a primary means for a country to construct its national image. National branding strategy encompasses a country's cultural, economic, political, and diplomatic dimensions, presenting itself as an entity with a unique narrative, values, and vision. The goal of national branding strategy is to convey this narrative to international audiences, fostering positive perceptions and building meaningful relationships. As a comprehensive effort, national branding strategy is a complex and multi-dimensional undertaking aimed at enhancing a country's standing in the global community and influencing its image on the international stage.

Successful examples of national branding strategy include: In 2007, the Danish government officially launched the National Branding Initiative, which continued until 2012, with the clear goal of increasing the value of nation brand (Merkelsen & Rasmussen, 2016, p. 182). The initiative stemmed from the "cartoon crisis" in 2005 when Danish newspapers published cartoons depicting Prophet Muhammad, leading to strong opposition from Muslim countries and causing damage to Denmark's national image. In response to this crisis, the Danish government began researching ways to improve the country's image. Denmark emphasized its progressive, sustainable, and innovative national image, highlighting aspects such as being a leader in promoting sustainable development and green technology, gender equality, and hospitality. Simultaneously, the Danish government reassessed the national branding strategy targeting Muslim countries. Estonia and Costa Rica, on the other hand, established teams consisting of official, resilient, non-partisan, and independent individuals to promote Estonia's "world's most advanced digital society" and Costa Rica's "beyond nature" nation brand campaigns (City Nation Place, 2020).

South Korea, as an emerging economy, stands out as one of the most representative cases of East Asian national branding through the promotion of its popular culture, known as the "Korean Wave" or "Hallyu." In 2009, South Korea established the Cultural Industry Promotion Agency, a government-affiliated organization responsible for promoting and supporting the country's creative content industry, including animation, gaming, and character licensing. By 2010, South Korea's entertainment industry, encompassing pop music, Korean dramas, and online games, had gained tremendous global popularity. In 2021, the audio streaming platform Spotify launched the Global K-pop Center, with the global monthly average K-pop streaming exceeding 7.97 billion, and the hashtag #Kpop in Twitter breaking records with 7.8 billion global tweets (Redaktion, 2022). A study by the Korea Economic Research Institute found that from 2017 to 2021, the economic impact of the export growth of Hallyu projects (such as cosmetics, music, and performance) amounted to 37 trillion South Korean Won. The increase in consumer goods exports created 116,000 job opportunities, whereas an increase in cultural content exports contributed to 44,000 job opportunities (Dong-A Ilboi, 2023). The national government can leverage the Hallyu phenomenon to enhance a country's public diplomacy and strengthen relationships with other nations. Through the spread of Hallyu, South Korean culture has gained widespread recognition globally and has become a representative symbol of the country's national image (Jang & Paik, 2012). The success of Hallyu is the result of collaborative efforts between the government and private enterprises (Villabert, 2020).

Visual System in National Branding

Especially noteworthy is that the visual system within nation brand has begun to garner attention from some countries. Establishing a brand visual system goes beyond traditional symbols, such as flags and anthems, allowing symbols with national characteristics to find more extensive applications. Moreover, utilizing national identification as a brand facilitates marketing and promotions. One successful example of nation brand identification is Sweden's second-generation universal visual identity system, designed by the local branding agency Soderhavet. The Swedish second-generation visual system comprises comprehensive visual elements, primarily categorized into five aspects: brand trademarks, design principles, layout specifications, brand colors, and auxiliary elements (Zreik, 2023b). The design incorporates various forms of the Swedish national flag pattern, including single icons, avatars, primary symbols, other language symbols, and subsymbols. Specifically crafted for this visual system is the sans-serif "Sweden Sans" typeface, designed to support multiple languages. The overall expression of Sweden's second-generation identification system emphasizes its consistency and simplicity. The iconic blue and yellow colors of the Swedish flag convey the information of the nation brand (Shapiro, 2015).

In summary, successful national branding must encompass several elements. First, a country needs a well-established sense of identity, which is used as a foundation to communicate its traditions, culture, and values to the outside world. Second, as the primary audience for national branding is foreign populations, the storytelling content and approach must be carefully crafted to ensure that overseas audiences understand and accept it, thereby forming a positive perception of the country's image. Third, in the era of globalization, where interactions among nations are frequent, national branding must operate in open and global arenas, emphasizing engagement with other countries to successfully build a brand on a global scale and convey a nation's unique attributes and values to global society. Fourth, the progress of human society after World War II is inseparable from technological innovations and applications. National branding must keep pace with times, highlighting innovation and sustainability in the marketing process. Successful national branding is a dynamic and continuous process that requires deep understanding of a nation's identity and its ever-changing position in the world. Finally, the rising influence of non-state actors in international relations highlights the increasing importance of their roles. Therefore, national branding is inevitably a collaboration between the entire government and private sector, working together to build a robust media and content system.

NATIONAL BRANDING TO PROMOTE NATIONAL IMAGE

In recent years, the process of globalization has encountered obstacles, with many countries witnessing the rise of populism and protectionism. Domestically, the United States has become increasingly divided along political lines, several European countries have seen a shift towards right-wing politics, and the Russia-Ukraine war has heightened global awareness of crises. This has led to intensified competition among nations. Against this backdrop, maintaining a positive national image is crucial for a country's diplomacy, economic and trade relations, and cultural exchange. China is actively working to shape itself into a major power source. It has made significant contributions to global public domain governance and the promotion of economic globalization. However, as China's comprehensive national strength has grown, the policies of Western countries, led by the United States, towards China and the attitudes of their populations have undergone changes. The image of China as a nation has been significantly affected. Therefore, national branding is an urgent task that cannot be delayed.

China has made significant strides in shaping its national image through various channels, both domestically and internationally. One notable achievement is its effective utilization of media outlets to promote its global image. For example, studies found that Chinese media discourse consistently highlights China's intentions and achievements, fostering mutual understanding (X. Li & Lu, 2023; M. Yang & Wang, 2023). Moreover, China has strategically employed online media platforms to counter negative portrayals in Western media, thereby positively influencing public opinion. Through the use of metaphors and metonymy, China has successfully conveyed nuanced messages about its development and aspirations, shaping global perceptions. Efforts have also been made to bridge perceptual gaps between China and other nations regarding its achievements. By managing public perception, these initiatives indirectly contribute to enhancing China's national image (Zreik, 2024b).

Changes in China's Nation Brand and National Image

Over the years, with the growth in China's economic strength, the world's perception of China has become increasingly clear. Regardless of China's international image, its brand effect has become prominent. According to a survey by Morning Consult, which conducted July 10-12, 2023, as China's economic strength has grown, the Generation Z in the United States shows a preference for Chinese brands compared to older American consumers. The survey found that 37% of American Generation Z did not actively try to avoid purchasing products from Chinese brands. At the same time, 42% of Generation Z in the United States have a fairly accepting attitude towards Chinese brands entering the American market (Briggs, 2023). Another study found that the perception of Chinese products among American consumers is not significantly influenced by their political stance. While a negative image of China may impact consumer perceptions of Chinese products, consumers tend to prioritize factors such as quality over political considerations (C. Yang, 2020). On the other hand, China's development triggered negative impressions. A survey conducted by the Pew Research Center in 2023 found that in the 19 countries surveyed, many nations still hold negative views of China, especially in most high-income countries. For instance, approximately 83% of adults in the United States have negative opinions about China (Hui, 2023; Nadeem, 2022; Zhou, 2023). Another study also indicates that emerging Asian brands are perceived as less culturally authentic compared to established Asian brands, including Chinese brands (Southworth, 2019).

Since 2022, China's nation brand and global perception have undergone a multifaceted transformation influenced by diverse factors. As delineated in the report titled *China Country Performance, Brand Image, and Reputation Analysis*, China's nation brand epitomizes a dynamic amalgamation of time-honored heritage, economic prowess, and cutting-edge technological innovation (TPBO, 2023). Concurrently, persistently high levels of negative sentiments towards China persist across numerous nations (Silver et al., 2022).

Despite these challenges, Chinese government has displayed resilience by fortifying its endeavors in public diplomacy and nation branding, notably through extensive cultural, human, and technological exchanges on a global scale. This proactive stance seeks to counterbalance the prevailing negative narratives and augment China's positive global image. The unfolding narrative is further intertwined with the Beijing 2022 Winter Olympic Games, strategically positioned to solidify Beijing's status as an Olympic powerhouse (Dubinsky, 2022). In summary, China's nation brand and national image are intricate and multifaceted, intricately woven with threads of economic performance, human rights considerations, and strategic public diplomacy initiatives.

For many years, China has faced challenges in terms of recognizing and accepting its external communication efforts. As Hong Junhao and Yan Sanjiu have pointed out, in the process of Chinese culture "going outside," it has not truly "gone in." The core concepts and values have yet to be understood and recognized by people in other countries worldwide. Additionally, some individuals' negative behaviors have exceeded their positive influence (Hong & Yan, 2017, p. 302). The broad awareness of China in the international community stems from impressions of its ancient history and the enchanting civilization of the East. However, when it comes to some emerging aspects of China's modernization process, there is still a lack of sufficient understanding. History, geography, and language are listed as the three positive elements of China's national image, because the international community views China as a highly traditional nation with a long history and ancient civilization. This is evident in China's history, language, and tangible presence. Furthermore, China is a symbol of Eastern culture; hence, these elements are closely associated with Eastern or Asian culture (He et al., 2020).

Although many countries currently hold increasingly negative international perceptions of China, the nation still has the capacity to cultivate its nation brand and enhance its international image through multidimensional approaches. The first dimension involves leveraging traditional Chinese culture to further establish the impression of being an ancient civilization. However, it's crucial to note that shaping traditional cultural narratives in external communication must break free from foreign stereotypes of China, like Fu Manchu (Liu et al., 2023). Therefore, by showcasing millennia of traditional philosophical and artistic achievements, China can garner deeper admiration and respect globally.

The second dimension entails the integration of traditional elements with contemporary popular culture. Building a nation brand necessitates the incorporation of pop culture, intertwining ancient customs with modern innovations like film, music, and fashion. This approach allows China to craft a dynamic and engaging narrative, resonating with diverse audiences worldwide. Pop culture predominantly operates through a softer form of soft power strategy, executed through acquisitions of media outlets and investments in entertainment and gaming industries by Chinese enterprises (Eliküçük Yıldırım & Aslan, 2020).

Lastly, a critical strategy involves strategic positioning of China's national image and adopting a cautious, low-key approach to international communication to avoid "wolf warrior" style populism. By articulating its values, policies, and aspirations judiciously while avoiding unnecessary confrontations, China can cultivate more nuanced and receptive audiences on the global stage. Essentially, by tapping into its cultural heritage, embracing innovation, and adeptly managing international relations through wit and diplomacy, China can elevate its nation brand to new heights, fostering understanding, appreciation, and cooperation worldwide.

Pathways to Constructing China's National Branding

China's national branding not only requires showcasing its traditional culture but also integrating the innovative and global core of contemporary Chinese culture. American scholar Joshua Cooper Ramo, who proposed the Beijing Consensus, once suggested, "China must design a set of ideas, icons, brands, and information that fit the current reality and aspirations of China. This does not mean that China should abandon its traditional culture but rather that China needs to find ways to have the emerging knowledge, culture, and commercial products of new China complement and strengthen its traditional image." (Ramo, 2007, p. 18)

Brodsky points out that to make "Made in China" a more positive magnet for communication and maintain its influence, there is an urgent need to build Chinese brands that can give it new economic significance (Brodsky, 2020). Some scholars also suggest that, to enhance soft power, China may need to consider a more nuanced approach, integrating culture and governance to shape the world's perception of Chinese brands. A strategy focused solely on culture and avoiding political discussion seems to offer limited returns for China's investments in soft power (Dynon, 2014).

With the advent of globalization, the concept of national branding has evolved to include not only corporate brands but also the nation itself as a comprehensive brand system. In the context of China, both country branding and national branding are almost synonymous. China has consistently emphasized the concept of *guojia* (country or nation), making the concepts of nation brand and national image more complex. Chinese national branding requires not only top-level design but also extensive participation from various actors. Concepts such as the Community of Shared Future for Mankind, Belt and Road

Initiative, and Three Major Initiatives are more of a national concept or political concept. While they are part of national branding, they tend to focus on macro and political aspects. Therefore, there is a need to establish a comprehensive multilayered brand system.

First, a national branding program is planned at the national strategic level. Initially, government departments should lead and organize the establishment of the nation brand identification system, determining the goals, principles, and scope of the system. Conduct comprehensive market research and analysis to understand audience perceptions and expectations of the national brand image, thus providing a basis for the national branding plan. Form a professional design team composed of experts from various fields such as design, advertising, communication, business management, psychology, economics, international relations, etc., to provide professional opinions and suggestions for the national branding plan. Simultaneously, the government should establish a national branding plan management agency responsible for overseeing, managing, promoting, and endorsing the national brand. The most positive and affirmative image of China is "ancient civilization," (He et al., 2020) and national branding can enrich and strengthen the appeal of the national branding by incorporating elements from China's long history, cultural traditions, and values. The fusion of traditional and modern culture can not only enhance brand recognition but also strengthen international consumers' trust in Chinese brands.

Second, the primary audience for China's national branding is foreign populations, necessitating cross-border cooperation and cultural exchanges to promote the international development of the national branding. Traditional events like "Chinese Brand Day" mainly impact domestic audiences, so achieving genuine promotion of the Chinese national branding to the international community requires more in-depth international marketing. National branding institutions can promote China's brand image and values internationally by establishing international partnerships, engaging in cultural exchange activities, and implementing international marketing strategies in collaboration with governments, businesses, and cultural institutions of other countries. Successful international marketing strategies require a thorough understanding of each country's cultural background to ensure that brand communication and product promotion do not trigger cultural misunderstandings or conflicts under the premise of mutual respect. Furthermore, in the era of active global digital economy and the vibrant growth of young internet users, Chinese national brands should highlight characteristics of popular culture to break down communication barriers between nations, using popular culture to drive overseas audiences' conceptual understanding of the Chinese nation brand.

Third, the most straightforward national branding is the "going global" of Chinese corporate brands and products. In recent years, Chinese products have gradually shed labels such as cheap, poor quality, and low-end, transitioning to more positive labels such as cost-effectiveness, innovation, and design sense (Bezamat & Wu, 2022; Chen, 2021; Nast, 2024). Chinese enterprises are continuously promoting product localization, launching new products based on the characteristics and demands of the host country. Chinese companies need to consistently adhere to core concepts such as Made in China, Designed in China, and Created in China with an international perspective to build sustainable brands. When a country's image has strong emotional components, its direct impact on product evaluations is stronger than that of product beliefs. Conversely, when a country's image has strong cognitive components, its direct impact on product evaluations is smaller than that on product beliefs. Therefore, Chinese companies should emphasize and promote relevant information when the national image is positive and counteract negative influences by highlighting other product qualities when the national image is negative.

National branding is a long-term project that requires time and the participation of the entire society. China's national branding must embody national characteristics to create a unique brand image, enhancing China's international visibility and reputation. In this process, building international visibility and a positive image are key to the success of the national branding. Therefore, China needs to reevaluate national branding from a strategic perspective in the new environment.

CONCLUSION

The relationship between national branding and a country's image is closely intertwined, with the nation brand being a part of how a country showcases its image. As globalization continues to develop, the interdependence between nations deepens, and competition extends into the realm of soft power. By shaping and promoting its national branding, a country can enhance its soft power, attract international investments, facilitate international cultural exchanges, and increase its international political influence. Therefore, a national branding is not just a tool for image construction but also a reflection of a country's soft power.

Since 2013, with the enhancement of comprehensive national strength, China has adopted a more confident and proactive diplomatic policy, actively participating in international affairs and promoting initiatives like the Belt and Road, thereby increasing its influence in the international community. Simultaneously, Chinese enterprises and brands have widely ventured abroad, contributing to the internationalization and enhancement of China's image. With the intensifying environment of great power competition, issues related to national image have become a crucial field beyond hard power. Compared to Western countries like the United States, China still lacks in soft power. Therefore, a timely national branding plan is crucial for the next steps in China's style of modernization. Successful national branding not only requires the participation of the entire society but also demands innovation and sustainability that align with the times.

This chapter has underscored the pivotal role of national branding in shaping the national image. However, it is imperative to acknowledge certain limitations inherent in this focus. By primarily concentrating on national branding, the exploration may have inadvertently narrowed, potentially overlooking other influential factors such as national identity, regime type, and social dynamics. Moreover, the absence of a specific timeframe in the analysis raises questions about the temporal relevance of the findings. Despite the numerous successful cases of national branding cited in this chapter, it is essential to recognize that the practical application of these cases may not directly align with China's unique context. Addressing these nuances is paramount in refining future national branding strategies and optimizing the effectiveness of national image management.

REFERENCES

Ahmed, G., Abudaqa, A., Jayachandran, C., Limbu, Y., & Alzahmi, R. (2022). Nation Branding as a Strategic Approach for Emerging Economies: The Case of UAE. In O. Adeola, R. E. Hinson, & A. M. Sakkthivel (Eds.), Marketing Communications and Brand Development in Emerging Economies Volume I: Contemporary and Future Perspectives (pp. 41–57). Springer International Publishing. doi:10.1007/978-3-030-88678-3_3

Alderman, P., & Eggeling, K. A. (2024). Vision Documents, Nation Branding and the Legitimation of Non-Democratic Regimes. *Geopolitics*, *29*(1), 288–318. doi:10.1080/14650045.2023.2165441

Anholt, S. (2006). Anholt Nation Brands Index: How Does the World See America? *Journal of Advertising Research*, *45*(3), 296–304. doi:10.1017/S0021849905050336

Anholt, S. (2007). *Competitive Identity: The New Brand Management for Nations, Cities and Regions*. Palgrave Macmillan. doi:10.1057/9780230627727

Bendel, P. R. (2011). Branding New York City—The Saga of 'I Love New York. In K. Dinnie (Ed.), *City Branding: Theory and Cases* (pp. 179–183)., doi:10.1057/9780230294790_24

Bezamat, F., & Wu. (2022, May 23). *These Innovations from China Are Improving Resiliency and Sustainability*. World Economic Forum. https://www.weforum.org/agenda/2022/05/these-chinese-innovations-are-improving-resiliency-and-sustainability-in-2022/

Briggs, E. (2023, August 16). *America's Gen Z Favors Chinese Brands More Than Other Generations*. Morning Consult Pro. https://pro.morningconsult.com/analysis/gen-z-favors-chinese-brands

Brodsky, S. (2020, May 21). *Nation-Branding Soft Power: The Case of Brand China*. Brandingmag. https://www.brandingmag.com/2020/05/21/nation-branding-soft-power-the-case-of-brand-china/

Browning, C. S. (2023). *Nation Branding and International Politics*. McGill-Queen's University Press.

Buhmann, A., & Ingenhoff, D. (2015). The 4D Model of the Country Image: An Integrative Approach from the Perspective of Communication Management. *The International Communication Gazette*, *77*(1), 102–124. doi:10.1177/1748048514556986

Chen, P. (2021, February 9). *Improved Product Quality Populates Local Chinese Brands*. Intouch-Quality. https://www.intouch-quality.com/blog/improved-product-quality-populates-local-chinese-brands

City Nation Place. (2020, January 10). *Two Countries That Prove Nation Branding Works | Jose Torres, Bloom Consulting*. City Nation Place. https://www.citynationplace.com/two-countries-that-prove-nation-branding-works

Dinnie, K. (2009). Nation Branding: Concepts, Issues, Practice (Reprinted). Butterworth-Heinemann.

Dong-A Ilboi. (2023, July 11). *Hallyu's Economic Impact Reaches 37 Trillion Won*. The Dong-A Ilboi. https://www.donga.com/en/article/all/20230711/4281547/1

Dubinsky, Y. (2022, February 8). *Nation Branding, Public Diplomacy and the Dystopian Beijing 2022 Winter Olympic Games*. USC Center on Public Diplomacy. https://uscpublicdiplomacy.org/blog/nation-branding-public-diplomacy-and-dystopian-beijing-2022-winter-olympic-games

Dynon, N. (2014, January 11). *China and Nation Branding*. The Diplomat. https://thediplomat.com/2014/01/china-and-nation-branding/

Eliküçük Yıldırım, N., & Aslan, M. (2020). China's Charm Defensive: Image Protection by Acquiring Mass Entertainment. *Pacific Focus*, *35*(1), 141–171. doi:10.1111/pafo.12153

Fan, Y. (2005). Can Nations Do Brand Marketing Like a Product? *PKU Business Review*, *9*, 1–7.

Fan, Y. (2006). Branding the Nation: What Is Being Branded? *Journal of Vacation Marketing*, *12*(1), 5–14. doi:10.1177/1356766706056633

Fan, Y. (2010). Branding the Nation: Towards a Better Understanding. *Place Branding and Public Diplomacy*, *6*(2), 97–103. doi:10.1057/pb.2010.16

Fetscherin, M. (2010). The Determinants and Measurement of a Country Brand: The Country Brand Strength Index. *International Marketing Review*, *27*(4), 466–479. doi:10.1108/02651331011058617

Girard, M. (1999). *States, Diplomacy and Image Making: What Is New? Reflections on Current British and French Experiences*. A Conference on Image, State and International Relations, London School of Economics.

Hao, A. W., Paul, J., Trott, S., Guo, C., & Wu, H.-H. (2019). Two Decades of Research on Nation Branding: A Review and Future Research Agenda. *International Marketing Review*, *38*(1), 46–69. doi:10.1108/IMR-01-2019-0028

He, L., Wang, R., & Jiang, M. (2020). Evaluating the Effectiveness of China's Nation Branding with Data from Social Media. *Global Media and China*, *5*(1), 3–21. doi:10.1177/2059436419885539

Hong, J., & Yan, S. (2017). Image Management in Cross-Cultural Communication. In B. Shan & Y. Liu (Eds.), *National Image and Intercultural Communication* (pp. 295–417). Social Sciences Academic Press.

Hui, M. (2023, July 27). *China's Reputation as a Leading Economic Power Is Fast Eroding*. Quartz. https://qz.com/china-s-reputation-as-a-leading-economic-power-is-fast-1850676199

Jang, G., & Paik, W. K. (2012). Korean Wave as Tool for Korea's New Cultural Diplomacy. *Advances in Applied Sociology*, *2*(3), 196–202. doi:10.4236/aasoci.2012.23026

Kaneva, N. (2011). Nation Branding: Toward an Agenda for Critical Research. *International Journal of Communication*, *5*, 117–141.

Keegan, W. J., & Schlegelmilch, B. B. (2001). *Global Marketing Management: A European Perspective*. Financial Times Prentice Hall.

Kotler, P. (2000). Marketing Management (Millennium ed). Prentice Hall.

Kotler, P., Jatusripitak, S., & Maesincee, S. (1997). *The Marketing of Nations: A Strategic Approach to Building National Wealth*. Free Press.

Kunczik, M. (1997). *Images of Nations and International Public Relations*. Erlbaum.

Lever, M. W., Elliot, S., & Joppe, M. (2023). Pride and Promotion: Exploring Relationships Between National Identification, Destination Advocacy, Tourism Ethnocentrism and Destination Image. *Journal of Vacation Marketing*, *29*(4), 537–554. doi:10.1177/13567667221109270

Li, D., & Wang, C., Jiang, Y., R. Barnes, B., & Zhang, H. (2014). The Asymmetric Influence of Cognitive and Affective Country Image on Rational and Experiential Purchases. *European Journal of Marketing*, *48*(11/12), 2153–2175. doi:10.1108/EJM-09-2012-0505

Li, X., & Chitty, N. (2009). Reframing National Image: A Methodological Framework. *Conflict & Communication*, *8*(2), 1–11.

Li, X., & Lu, D. (2023). Conceptual Metaphors and Image Construction of China in the Space Probe Reports of China Daily: A Social Cognitive Approach. *Frontiers in Psychology, 14*. https://www.frontiersin.org/articles/10.3389/fpsyg.2023.1202988

Liu, Y., Liu, B., Lei, L., & Liu, T. (2023). *Deconstruction of the Images of Fu Manchu in American Popular Culture in the First Half of the Twentieth Century*. doi:10.2991/978-2-38476-130-2_3

Markovic, S., Gyrd-Jones, R., von Wallpach, S., & Lindgreen, A. (2022). *Research Handbook on Brand Co-Creation: Theory, Practice and Ethical Implications*. Edward Elgar Publishing. doi:10.4337/9781839105425

Merkelsen, H., & Rasmussen, R. K. (2016). Nation Branding as an Emerging Field – An Institutionalist Perspective. *Place Branding and Public Diplomacy*, *12*(2–3), 99–109. doi:10.1057/s41254-016-0018-6

Miño, P. (2023). Beyond Economic Dependency: Nation Branding in Latin America Subdued to Stereotypes and Neoliberal Globalization. *Public Relations Inquiry*. doi:10.1177/2046147X231224834

Miño, P., & Austin, L. (2022). A Cocreational Approach to Nation Branding: The Case of Chile. *Public Relations Inquiry*, *11*(2), 293–313. doi:10.1177/2046147X221081179

Montanari, M. G., & Giraldi, J. de M. E. (2018). A Theoretical Study on Country Brand and Its Management. *Revista Eletrônica de Negócios Internacionais (Internext)*, *13*(2), 14–29.

Nadeem, R. (2022, June 29). *Negative Views of China Tied to Critical Views of Its Policies on Human Rights*. Pew Research Center's Global Attitudes Project. https://www.pewresearch.org/global/2022/06/29/negative-views-of-china-tied-to-critical-views-of-its-policies-on-human-rights/

Nast, C. (2024, January 23). *A New Normal: The Levers to Success in China in 2024*. Vogue Business. https://www.voguebusiness.com/story/consumers/a-new-normal-the-levers-to-success-in-china-in-2024

Nobre, H., & Sousa, A. (2022). Cultural Heritage and Nation Branding – Multi Stakeholder Perspectives from Portugal. *Journal of Tourism and Cultural Change*, *20*(5), 699–717. doi:10.1080/14766825.2021.2025383

Olins, W. (2002). Branding the Nation—The Historical Context. *Journal of Brand Management*, *9*(4), 241–248. doi:10.1057/palgrave.bm.2540075

Porter, M. E. (1998). *The Competitive Advantage of Nations: With a New Introduction*. Free Press. doi:10.1007/978-1-349-14865-3

Ramo, J. C. (2007). *Brand China*. Foreign Policy Center.

Redaktion, A. F. M. (2022, May 28). *K-Pop Is Making Billions for South Korea*. AsiaFundManagers. Com. https://www.asiafundmanagers.com/gbr/kpop-and-economic-impact-on-south-korea/

Rojas-Méndez, J. (2013). The Nation Brand Molecule. *Journal of Product and Brand Management*, *22*(7), 462–472. doi:10.1108/JPBM-09-2013-0385

Rojas-Méndez, J. I., & Khoshnevis, M. (2022). Conceptualizing Nation Branding: The Systematic Literature Review. *Journal of Product and Brand Management, 32*(1), 107–123. doi:10.1108/JPBM-04-2021-3444

Roll, M. (2021, November 28). *How Nations and Brands Overcome Country of Origin*. Martin Roll. https://martinroll.com/resources/articles/branding/how-nations-and-brands-overcome-country-of-origin-challenges/

Shapiro, A. (2015, February 8). *Not Too Much, Not Too Little: Sweden, In A Font*. North Country Public Radio. https://www.northcountrypublicradio.org/news/npr/384346383/not-too-much-not-too-little-sweden-in-a-font

Silver, L., Huang, C., & Clancy, L. (2022, September 28). *How Global Public Opinion of China Has Shifted in the Xi Era*. Pew Research Center's Global Attitudes Project. https://www.pewresearch.org/global/2022/09/28/how-global-public-opinion-of-china-has-shifted-in-the-xi-era/

Soni, P. (2019, October 21). *Nation Branding: How to Build an Effective Location Brand Identity*. Brand Finance. https://brandfinance.com/insights/nation-branding

Southworth, S. S. (2019). U.S. Consumers' Perception of Asian Brands' Cultural Authenticity and Its Impact on Perceived Quality, Trust, and Patronage Intention. *Journal of International Consumer Marketing, 31*(4), 287–301. doi:10.1080/08961530.2018.1544528

Szondi, G. (2008). *Public Diplomacy and Nation Branding: Conceptual Similarities and Differences*. Clingendael Institute.

TPBO. (2015, May 12). *Vienna Destination Branding Case Study, Good Practice Example*. TPBO. https://placebrandobserver.com/case-study-city-destination-branding-vienna-austria/

TPBO. (2023, October 25). *China Country Performance, Brand Image and Reputation Analysis*. TPBO. https://placebrandobserver.com/china-country-performance-brand-image-reputation/

van Ham, P. (2001). The Rise of the Brand State: The Postmodern Politics of Image and Reputation. *Foreign Affairs, 80*(5), 2–6. doi:10.2307/20050245

van Ham, P. (2002). Branding Territory: Inside the Wonderful Worlds of PR and IR Theory. *Millennium, 31*(2), 249–269. doi:10.1177/03058298020310020101

Villabert, S. (2020, July 7). *To Hallyu and Beyond: Strengthening the Image of Korea the Brand*. Medium. https://medium.com/revolutionaries/to-hallyu-and-beyond-strengthening-the-image-of-korea-the-brand-75fe0aa285e4

White, C. L. (2012). Brands and National Image: An Exploration of Inverse Country-of-Origin Effect. *Place Branding and Public Diplomacy, 8*(2), 110–118. doi:10.1057/pb.2012.6

Yang, C. (2020). How China's Image Affects Chinese Products in a Partisan-Motivated US Market. *Global Media and China, 5*(2), 169–187. doi:10.1177/2059436420922702

Yang, M., & Wang, Z. (2023). A Corpus-Based Discourse Analysis of China's National Image Constructed by Environmental News in the New York Times. *Humanities and Social Sciences Communications, 10*(1), Article 1. doi:10.1057/s41599-023-02052-8

Yee, F. W. (2009). *Nation Branding: A Case Study of Singapore* [Master Dissertation]. University of Nevada, Las Vegas.

Zhou, M. (2023, April 13). *Over 80% of Americans Critical of China's Global Role: Survey*. Nikkei Asia. https://asia.nikkei.com/Politics/International-relations/US-China-tensions/Over-80-of-Americans-critical-of-China-s-global-role-survey

Zreik, M. (2023a). Managing Diversity: A Study of Multicultural Workplaces in Arab and Chinese Societies Post Pandemic. In R. Diab-Bahman & A. Al-Enzi (Eds.), *Global Citizenship and Its Impact on Multiculturalism in the Workplace* (pp. 250–273). IGI Global. doi:10.4018/978-1-6684-5436-7.ch011

Zreik, M. (2023b). Stirring Up Soft Power: The Role of Chinese Cuisine in China's Cultural Diplomacy. In K. Kankaew (Ed.), *Global Perspectives on Soft Power Management in Business* (pp. 292–306). IGI Global. doi:10.4018/979-8-3693-0250-7.ch015

Zreik, M. (2024a). Cultivating ILCs in China: A Pathway to Culturally Sustaining and Transformative Education. In S. Adams & A. Breidenstein (Eds.), *Exploring Meaningful and Sustainable Intentional Learning Communities for P-20 Educators* (pp. 120–140). IGI Global. doi:10.4018/978-1-6684-7270-5.ch006

Zreik, M. (2024b). Harnessing the Power of Digital Transformation and Sustainability: The Chinese Experience. In H. Nozari (Ed.), *Building Smart and Sustainable Businesses with Transformative Technologies* (pp. 247–266). IGI Global. doi:10.4018/979-8-3693-0210-1.ch014

Chapter 18
The Soft Power Impact of China in Strategic Competition With the United States in Vietnam

Kiet Le Hoang

https://orcid.org/0009-0002-9968-1952

Can Tho University, Vietnam

Hiep Xuan Tran

Dong A University, Vietnam

Minh Nguyen Anh

https://orcid.org/0009-0003-3501-6598

Can Tho University, Vietnam

Phúc Nguyễn

Hue University, Vietnam

ABSTRACT

In the context of increasing strategic competition between the United States (US) and China in the Indo-Pacific region, soft power has become an important tool in implementing foreign policy, enhancing the overall national power, especially for emerging superpowers like China. To achieve the goal of becoming a global superpower comparable to the US, China has focused on increasing its soft power in countries with important geopolitical positions on the regional and global map. Accordingly, Vietnam is China's neighboring country with a strategic position for China's process of expanding its power in Southeast Asia. Therefore, Vietnam is one of the countries most strongly affected by China's strategy to increase its soft power in strategic competition with the US. This chapter aims to analyze the opportunities and challenges that China's strategy to increase its soft power brings to Vietnam through political-diplomatic, economic-commercial, cultural educational fields.

DOI: 10.4018/979-8-3693-2444-8.ch018

INTRODUCTION

In the 21st century, scholars of realism argue that the state of an anarchic international system has become an important factor leading to power competition among great powers (Streeten, 2001). Thus, diplomatic relations between major powers are always evolving due to interactions and adjustments in foreign policy behavior, especially competitive relations between the US - a declining superpower that always wants to maintain global leadership, and China - an emerging superpower with ambitions to become the world's leading power. Therefore, since realizing the severe threat from the rise of China with the "Belt and Road Initiative" (BRI) and the "Chinese Dream" doctrine after President Xi Jinping took power in 2013, the US has taken decisive actions to curb China's power expansion strategies (Kiet and Tuyen, 2023). Of which, soft power competition is one of the most important strategies of both superpowers to shape the position of world superpower in the future. Currently, the Indo-Pacific region has officially become the center of power competition among world powers. Of which, the competitive relationship between the US and China is assessed to have the strongest impact on other countries in the region. Both superpowers have introduced competing initiatives to rally forces, establish new connectivity networks, and strengthen old cooperation mechanisms to enhance their power in this region (see Table 1).

Vietnam is China's neighboring country located on its southern border, with a very important geo-political position in the East Sea in particular and Southeast Asia in general. Therefore, Vietnam plays a very important role in China's policies and strategies deployed in Southeast Asia, especially the BRI. To curb China's ambition to expand its power, the US has adjusted its foreign strategy with Vietnam. In the new security policy of the US under President Joe Biden, Vietnam is seen as one of the top important partners in Southeast Asia (White House, 2022). Therefore, in recent times, Vietnam has been strongly affected by the strategic competition between China and the US in the region, in which the two superpowers' strategy to increase soft power has created many challenges and opportunities for Vietnam. As a neighboring country with thousands of years of historical relations, Vietnam is profoundly influenced by Chinese culture. The increase of China's soft power strategy in the region has strongly impacted Vietnam's political, economic and social situation. This has created challenges and opportunities for Vietnam to exploit similarities and interests towards prosperous and harmonious development in Vietnam-China relations.

Table 1. The competing cooperation initiatives between the US and China in the Indo-Pacific

US Initiatives (or US-Centric)	China's Initiatives (or China-Centric)
Indo-Pacific Economic Framework for Prosperity (IPEF)	Regional Comprehensive Economic Partnership (RCEP)
Quadrilateral Security Dialogue (QUAD) AUKUS trilateral security pact	Global Security Initiative (GSI)
Partnership for Global Infrastructure and Investment (PGII) CHIPS 4 alliance	Belt and Road Initiative (BRI)
Blue Pacific Initiative (BPI) Indo-Pacific Partnership for Maritime Domain Awareness (IPMDA) Pacific Strategic Partnership (PSP)	China-Solomon Islands Security Pact

Source: Hung, N.T. (2022). World Politics and Economy in 2022. National Political Publishing House Truth, Hanoi, pp. 83- 84.

LITERATURE REVIEW

Since scholar Joseph Nye introduced the concept of soft power in 1990 in his book "Bound to Lead: The Changing Nature of United States Power", it has stimulated research trend in this field. Accordingly, the soft power competition between the US and China has become one of the topics that scholars always pay attention to when analyzing and evaluating the strategic impact of competition between the two superpowers in the 21st century. Of which, scholar Barrech and Khan (2023) analyzed and compared China and the US's use of soft power, highlighting their respective soft power strategies. In addition, scholar Winkler (2023) analyzed the concept of strategic competition between China and the US, in which the research particularly emphasized the concept of soft power in the strategic competition between the two superpowers, assessing it as one of the important pillars in the strategy to compete for the position of number one world superpower in the future. When studying the soft power competition between the US and China, it is necessary to mention the research of scholar Joseph Nye (2023). His book "Soft Power and Great-Power Competition: Shifting Sands in the Balance of Power Between the US and China" is considered one of the most classic studies on soft power competition between the two superpowers. Through that, the research concluded that the US-China relationship is a "coopetition" rather than a mutually destructive competitive relationship. In which, there needs to be a "smart competition" strategy and cooperation to solve cross-national challenges such as climate change, pandemics, cyber terrorism and the proliferation of nuclear weapons, which will benefit not only China and the US, but the whole world in general. In addition, scholar Gupta (2013) highlighted and analyzed the diverse nature of soft power possessed by the US, China and India, while clarifying how they use their different soft power resources differently. And finally, an effort has been made to present a case in which each of these countries represents itself as a prototype - they can learn from each other's successes and mistakes in exercising soft power. The above research situation shows that the soft power competition between the US and China has attracted a lot of scholars' attention and has been exploited in detail on many aspects. However, there has not been any research that analyzes in detail the specific impact of China's soft power in strategic competition with the US in Vietnam. Therefore, this paper hopes to fill the gap in this research issue.

METHODOLOGY

This paper uses qualitative analysis methods, specifically international relations research methods, historical and logical methods, synthesis methods, and statistical methods through secondary data related to the research topic. The paper realizes that the soft power competition between China and the US in recent times has strongly affected Vietnam's political, economic and social situation. As an important neighboring country in China's ambition to expand its power in Southeast Asia, Vietnam is profoundly affected by China's strategy to increase soft power competition in the face of challenges from the US in the region. Therefore, the paper aims to clarify the impact of China's soft power on Vietnam. In part 1, the paper examines and analyzes the opportunities that Vietnam can exploit to cooperate with China in the context of increasing impact of this country's soft power in Vietnam. In part 2, the paper examines and points out the challenges that Vietnam will suffer negative impacts from China's strategy to increase soft power. Finally, the conclusion of the paper will summarize the opportunities and challenges facing Vietnam in the face of the increasing trend of China's soft power, focusing on 3 areas: politics - diplomacy, economy - trade, culture - education. From there, give basic recommendations for Vietnam's policy orientation in harmonious, balanced and stable cooperation with China.

RESEARCH RESULTS

The Impact of China's Soft Power: Opportunities for Vietnam

First, the Opportunity to Enhance Politics: Diplomacy

Since the 1990s, China has changed its perspective on Southeast Asia. China's policy towards this region has also changed significantly, regarding Southeast Asia as a key strategic region and actively deploying regional policies (Zha, 2022). In addition, under Xi Jinping, China has introduced many initiatives and strategies to realize the "Chinese Dream", emphasizing the strategic importance of Southeast Asia (Rubiolo et al., 2020). To do this, China needs to gain the support of countries in the region for its initiatives. Therefore, this is also an opportunity for Vietnam to enhance its position in China's multilateral initiatives and make a good impression with regional countries. Since the normalization of diplomatic relations in 1991, China has always been Vietnam's top partner; in politics, it is Vietnam's first Comprehensive Strategic Partner (since May 2008); in diplomacy, Vietnam has many ideological similarities with China. China's soft power strategy is reflected in the widespread centralized control system within the framework of the "Chinese path" development model which has enabled China to develop remarkably in over four decades. This also creates some similarities that Vietnam can study about national governance, although China's development model is considered difficult to replicate.

The most thorny and difficult issue between Vietnam and China is still the East Sea sovereignty dispute, but this is not the whole of bilateral relations. The mainstream of the relationship is still friendly cooperation for mutual development (Luong, 2022, p.369-370). Therefore, allowing the dispute to negatively affect the development of bilateral relations would be a major strategic mistake for Vietnam. In the current context of the East Sea, it is necessary to consider harmonious solutions that the parties can accept, aiming at common goals such as developing marine economy, modernizing the system of seaports connecting to international ports passing through the East Sea (Zreik, 2024a). The bilateral history between the two states and two political regimes spanning over seven decades has created a profound bond for Vietnam-China relations at many levels. Moreover, this relationship also has superior advantages over other countries thanks to the comrade relationship between the two Communist Parties. This is also an opportunity for Vietnam to be more proactive and creative in foreign affairs activities, while at the same time an important channel to minimize disagreements. Moreover, understanding the similarities between the two political systems will help Vietnam accurately grasp China's foreign policy formulation process. Overall, as a Comprehensive Strategic Partner, China plays an important role in supporting Vietnam's participation in multilateral mechanisms. As China's neighbor and being in China's strategic map such as BRI, Vietnam with its emerging economy and a population of about 100 million also has an important position with China in participating or supporting mechanisms led by China.

In return, Vietnam will also have the opportunity to receive China's support for its initiatives, strategies and mechanisms related to Vietnam. With the role of a key ASEAN member and at the same time China's largest trading partner in ASEAN, Vietnam has many opportunities to promote ASEAN-China relations, serving national interests (Quan, 2022, p.397). Therefore, Vietnam needs to pay more attention to strategic cooperation with China at forums, in responding to climate change, non-traditional security and within the Mekong sub-region cooperation framework. Some opinions argue that in the context of China's increasing strength, Vietnam's role has become blurred in China's global strategy, especially in the BRI (Luong, 2022, p.383). However, Vietnam's role has not yet been affirmed correctly with its rightful position, both from China and Vietnam. In the current context, China's need for strategic connectivity has not decreased but increased. In the future, China will adjust its strategy and increasingly need sharing from important partners, including ASEAN and Vietnam. Vietnam is fully capable of promoting an active and positive role to meet this need of China.

When China's power and position are increasingly enhanced, major powers are forced to adjust countermeasures to rebalance Beijing's growing influence (Dicicco and Onea, 2023). It can be said that it is the increase in soft power through China's centralized political system that has driven changes in the US foreign policy with Vietnam. The Washington administration realizes that if there is no strategy to strengthen relations with allies and partners, including Vietnam, then the regional balance of power will tilt towards China, which is not beneficial to the US leadership position in the Indo-Pacific. The soft power competition between the two superpowers is an opportunity for Vietnam to take advantage of its position and pursue the best policies for national interests. In the context of the formation of many alliances to contain China's influence, Vietnam needs to study and consider its relations with Beijing in the context of the regional and global balance of power in order to ensure a peaceful, stable and cooperative environment. Overall, China will become the first superpower with a socialist ideology in the mid 21st century. Therefore, identifying this trend to proactively respond is an urgent need for Vietnam today.

Second, the Opportunity to Promote Economic-Trade Cooperation

China is using economic diplomacy tools to expand its soft influence in Vietnam (Kiet and Tuyen, 2023). Through foreign direct investment (FDI), loans and official development assistance (ODA), Beijing creates direct economic opportunities for Hanoi. First of all, export credits help Vietnam maintain trade relations with China. Although not the only tool, trade and financial agreements are a key means for Beijing to expand its influence in developing countries. Specifically, Chinese-funded technology and infrastructure projects are the main focus for enhancing Beijing's presence and influence in the region. In Vietnam, FDI capital flows from China have continuously increased since 2015, especially surging in 2018-2019 when it ranked first among countries investing in Vietnam with 1.56 billion USD. In 2020, despite the impact of the Covid-19 pandemic, China's investment capital still ranked third. According to Figure 1, as of November 2020, China's total FDI capital in Vietnam reached 18 billion USD with 3,087 projects. In the next 3 years, by 2023, the number of projects increased by more than 1,000 projects, reaching 4,161 projects with a total investment capital of over 27 billion USD - bringing China to the sixth position among the 144 countries with the largest total FDI capital in Vietnam (Zreik, 2024b).

Geographically, China's FDI capital is concentrated mainly in coastal provinces, big cities with abundant human resources, convenient infrastructure for import-export activities as well as transportation connectivity with China. In the early stages, China's capital concentrated only on sectors such as hotels, restaurants and consumer goods production on a small scale. However, recently the investment structure from China has shifted to industrial sectors such as garment, footwear, fiber, thermal power plants, mining. Thanks to that, over 60% of FDI capital from China today focuses on processing and manufacturing industries, although it still relies heavily on labor-intensive activities (Vietnam's Ministry of Finance, 2023). As China moves up to higher rungs on the global value chain, the trend of Chinese

Figure 1. FDI capital flows from China to Vietnam in the period 2015 – 2023
Source: Authors' aggregation from Vietnam General Statistics Office

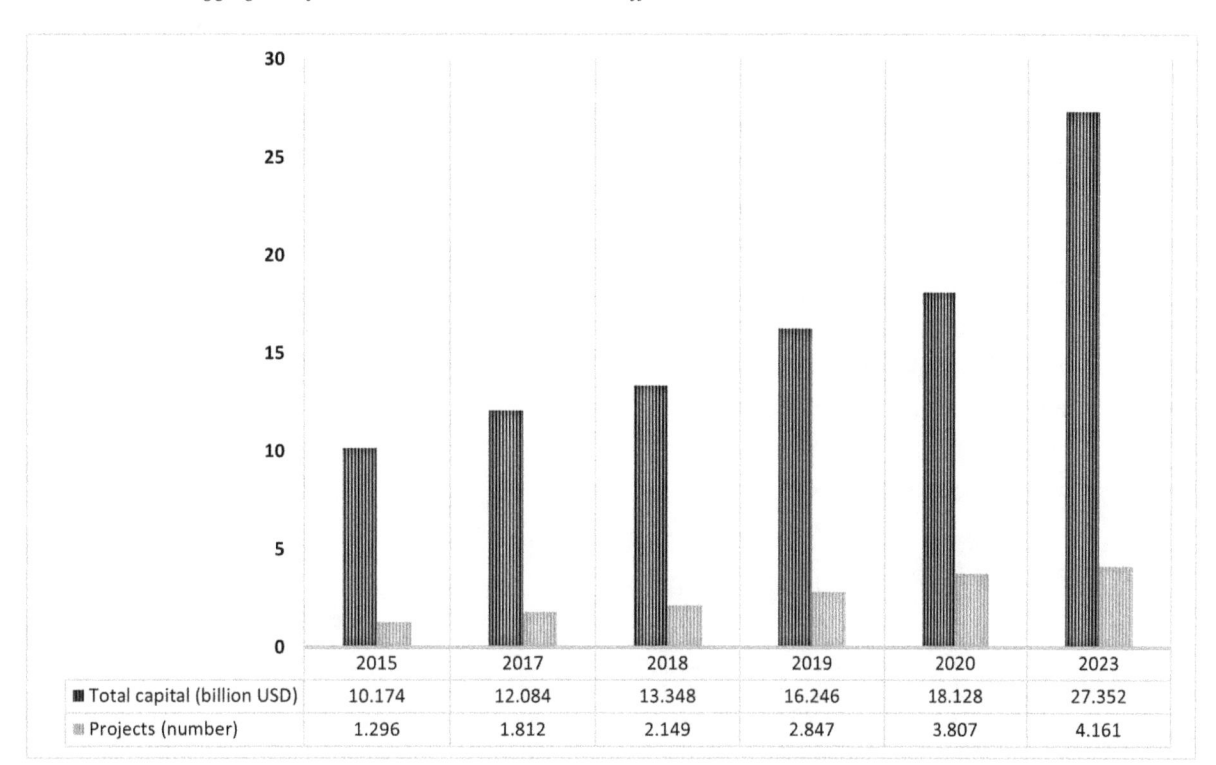

	2015	2017	2018	2019	2020	2023
■ Total capital (billion USD)	10.174	12.084	13.348	16.246	18.128	27.352
▨ Projects (number)	1.296	1.812	2.149	2.847	3.807	4.161

investors shifting to less developed industries in Vietnam and other developing countries is inevitable. Initially, capital was provided to countries to carry out key infrastructure projects. In essence, export credits are tools that China uses to strengthen relations with developing countries with high demands for markets and cheap goods. Vietnam is currently trying to diversify export markets to reduce excessive dependence on China. However, with a population of 1.4 billion people, China remains a very large and important market for Vietnam's economy.

In the context of increasingly extensive Vietnam-China trade relations, China is currently the largest trading partner and the largest supplier of goods, and the second largest export market of Vietnam, only after the US (Huan, 2023). In return, Vietnam is China's top trading partner within ASEAN (Huan, 2023). According to the data in Figure 2, Vietnam-China trade has increased rapidly every year. From 2011, the total bilateral trade turnover was only 36.48 billion USD, however by 2020, this figure reached 133.1 billion USD. In 2021, despite the impact of Covid-19, the bilateral trade turnover was 165.8 billion USD, up 24.6% over the previous year. By 2023, the total bilateral trade increased slightly to 171.2 billion USD. However, Vietnam's continuous trade deficit with China for 20 years has made its economy extremely dependent on China. Therefore, any impact from China could strongly affect the operation of Vietnam's economy.

In addition, China's ODA can also be exploited by Vietnam to improve infrastructure quality. Export credits play a key role in China's "going global" strategy, serving three objectives: (i) attracting diplomatic support for the "One China" policy; (ii) disseminating ideological values; (iii) expanding economic interests. In recent years, China's ODA to Vietnam, mostly in the form of preferential loans

Figure 2. Vietnam-China trade in the period 2011 - 2023
Source: Authors' aggregation from Vietnam Customs

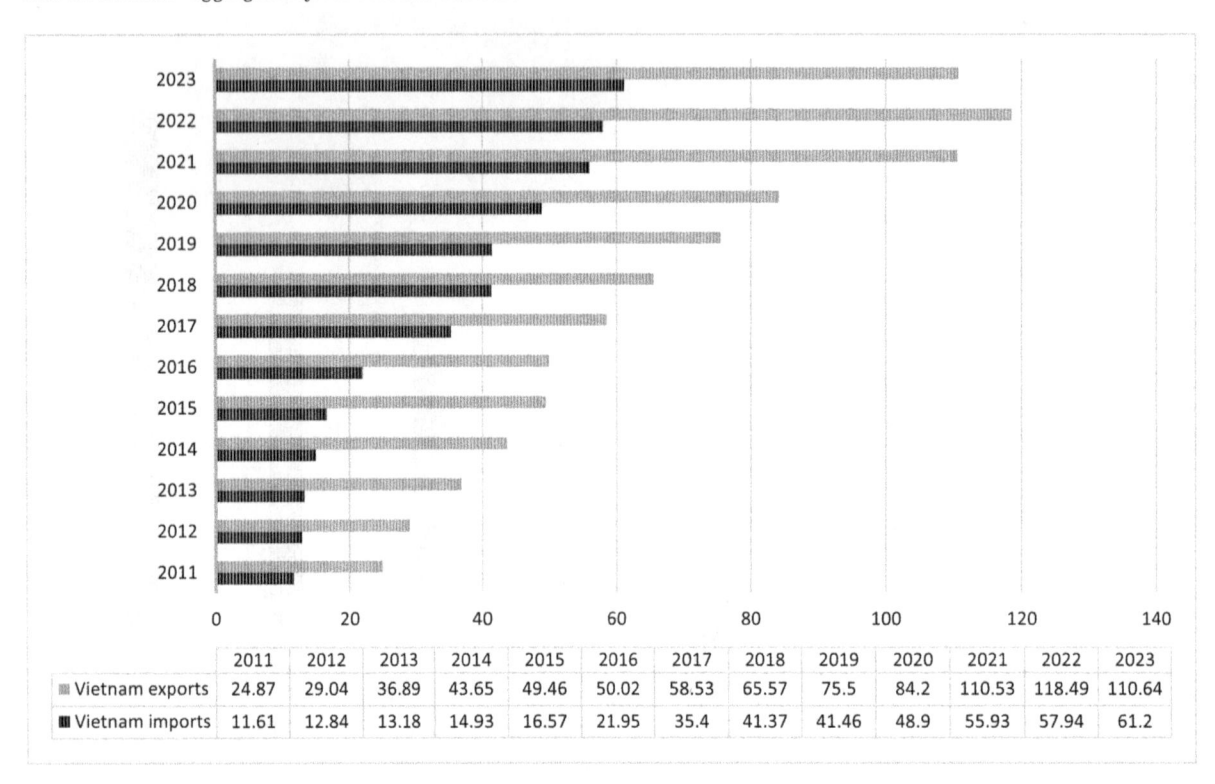

	2011	2012	2013	2014	2015	2016	2017	2018	2019	2020	2021	2022	2023
Vietnam exports	24.87	29.04	36.89	43.65	49.46	50.02	58.53	65.57	75.5	84.2	110.53	118.49	110.64
Vietnam imports	11.61	12.84	13.18	14.93	16.57	21.95	35.4	41.37	41.46	48.9	55.93	57.94	61.2

for infrastructure and energy development, has increased significantly. According to the International Institute for Sustainable Development (IISD), since 2008, China has spent billions of USD to support Chinese state-owned enterprises' hydropower projects in Laos, Cambodia and Vietnam (Global Energy Monitor, 2023). In the 2011-2015 period, China's ODA to Vietnam peaked in both scale and diversification (by then), with a total value of up to 2.2 billion USD, of which only 15,000 USD was humanitarian aid (Vietnam's Ministry of Finance, 2020). However, information on recent Chinese ODA projects has not been regularly updated, making it difficult to assess the impact of these projects. According to the Report of Vietnam's Ministry of Finance, the interest rate on Chinese ODA loans is up to 3% per annum plus fees, much higher than other ODA sources. Moreover, the preferential interest rate period is usually only the first 15 years while the projects are often prolonged (Vietnam's Ministry of Finance, 2020). Chinese investors currently dominate many of Vietnam's key energy, mineral infrastructure projects such as: Quang Ninh 1&2 Thermal Power Plants, Hai Phong 1&2 Thermal Power Plants, Ninh Binh Fertilizer Plant, Lam Dong Bauxite-Aluminum Complex, Vinh Tan 1&3 Thermal Power Plants, Vung Ang 2 Thermal Power Plant, Dak Nong Bauxite Project, Ca Mau Gas-Power-Fertilizer Complex, Duyen Hai Thermal Power Plant...

In addition to financial support, China also uses export credit tools to build and expand its economic models abroad. Over the past decade, Beijing has taken advantage of companies, economic zones (EZs), and special economic zones (SEZs) to promote "economic diplomacy". Specifically, China has invested in building two industrial and economic zones in northern and southern Vietnam, namely Long Giang (Tien Giang) and VCEP (Hai Phong). By the end of 2016, 70% of enterprises in Long Giang Industrial

Park were Chinese-owned and by 2023, 100% of enterprises in this industrial park belong to China (Tien Giang Provincial Portal, 2023). Simultaneous with the process of shifting production to Vietnam, China also mobilizes additional capital, experts and production models, technologies, and jobs for thousands of Vietnamese workers, mostly general laborers. Notably, Beijing still maintains the VCEP industrial park (renamed An Duong) invested and owned by Shenzhen in Hai Phong despite its slow growth rate and lack of transparency about efficiency. For managers and manufacturers here, profit is not the top priority but the key task is to promote the pioneering international economic cooperation model of the Chinese Government, serving the BRI (Luong, 2022, p.401). In addition, Vietnam can learn from and apply China's successful special economic zone model - one of the key factors that made China the "East Asian economic miracle". This is considered an attractive economic model that developing countries can learn from, although it is difficult to fully replicate.

Currently, Vietnam has many similarities with China 10-15 years ago: low labor wages, backward technology and export reliance on manufacturing. As China climbs higher on the value chain, Vietnam will replace and become an alternative choice for investors. In recent years, Vietnam has planned to build economic zones and special economic zones to boost its economy, with three highlights being Van Don, Bac Van Phong and Phu Quoc (Zreik, 2023a). Although not yet implemented, this plan still lays the foundation to attract investment and development. Among them, thanks to its favorable location in the Vietnam-China "Two Corridors, One Belt" Cooperation Zone, the gateway connecting ASEAN-China, and the South Nanning-Singapore Corridor, Van Don attracts great attention from Chinese investors. During the recent visit to China by General Secretary Nguyen Phu Trong at the invitation of President Xi Jinping, the two sides agreed to accelerate the exchange and signing of the Plan for Cooperation between the Governments of the two countries to promote the connectivity of the "Two Corridors, One Belt" with the BRI (Nhan Dan Newspaper, 2022). At the same time, Vietnam and China will also coordinate to soon implement cooperation projects on production capacity, infrastructure and transport, including evaluating the Feasibility Study on the Standard Gauge Railway Line Lao Cai - Hanoi - Hai Phong. Although there are still many concerns about China's investment capital flows into Vietnam, with skillful and prudent assessment and attraction, Vietnam can still take advantage of this capital for priority development sectors. The Vietnamese Government is currently introducing many measures and policies to promote the development of the domestic supporting industry, aiming to meet 70% of domestic demand by 2030 (Minh, 2023). Therefore, attracting experienced Chinese investors in supporting industries for multinational corporations is extremely urgent for Vietnam's industrialization and modernization goals.

China's influence on Vietnam-China economic, trade and investment relations can also be viewed from a multilateral perspective as China's rise has prompted major economies to recalculate the current economic order, especially cooperation mechanisms on economics, trade and investment. The adjustment of rules and the establishment of new rules towards liberalization and against protectionism by developed economies are beneficial for developing countries, including Vietnam. As an important link in China's infrastructure connectivity network with Southeast Asia, Vietnam is located on all three regional cooperation axes in China's BRI. Moreover, China sees Vietnam as a key country in this initiative with (i) its geographical location connecting both road and sea routes; (ii) China's largest trading partner in ASEAN; (iii) many political similarities and high international status. However, Vietnam's irreplaceable position is gradually declining as China becomes more powerful and has more options in the BRI. In fact, none of the 8 key ports in the Maritime Silk Road (MSR) belongs to Vietnam. Thus, Vietnam is gradually losing its indispensable "bridge" role, only maintaining a vague connectivity position in the sea route as well as the entire Indochina region with the Kunming - Singapore axis.

Third, the Opportunity to Expand Cultural and Educational Influence

Along with the strategy to create economic attractiveness, China also enhances the process of creating cultural influence to increase soft power. According to scholar Joseph S. Nye (2004), soft power is a form of national power based on the attractiveness of ideological and cultural ideas, which is intentionally or unintentionally used by subjects in international relations to achieve strategic orders. Facing the strong wave of attacks from Chinese soft power through cultural values, Vietnam will certainly be affected but the level of dependence depends on many factors. One point Vietnam can learn from China is to always value and promote the power of national culture, exploit the strengths in traditional culture to make breakthroughs in building modern soft power and expand international relations. China's BRI project is an example. Since emphasizing the importance of cultural soft power, China has promoted the establishment of Confucius Institutes worldwide to impress culturally. According to Xi Jinping, "Confucius Institutes are a symbol of China's unremitting efforts for world peace and international cooperation, and a bond connecting the Chinese people and people around the world" (Feng, 2014). After 20 years, there have been 498 Confucius Institutes and 773 Confucius classrooms in 160 countries (Yimeng, 2023).

In Southeast Asia, China has also established many Confucius Institutes to promote culture, with each country having more than one institute. Meanwhile, Western countries believe that Confucius Institutes are just political tools of Beijing, with the mission of disseminating a positive image of China even though the reality is not correct. The functions of these institutes are even more suspicious due to China's increasingly obvious hegemonic ambitions. The fact that Confucius Institutes are often located in universities raises concerns about the potential for interference with free speech and indirect political roles. In 2009, Vietnam allowed the first Confucius Institute in Hanoi on a trial basis, not officially operating until 2014 at the Hanoi University. This is the only Confucius Institute in Vietnam as of now. In addition to teaching and certifying Chinese language, the Institute also organizes cultural activities such as book exhibitions, calligraphy writing contests, Chinese culture weeks, Chinese translation and speaking contests, etc. As of late December 2022, the Institute had 52 teachers, including 02 contracted teachers, 36 Chinese teachers and 14 Lao teachers, with a total of 1,793 students (Lao Viet Magazine, 2022).

However, in reality there is almost no substantive support from China for academic cooperation or research on China. Recognizing the controversies surrounding the political role of Confucius Institutes, Chinese leaders have refrained from providing public guidance for the Institutes, including the Confucius Institute in Hanoi. Therefore, Vietnam still maintains caution in receiving Chinese cultural activities, including the Confucius Institute, to ensure national interests and security. Therefore, although being a close, intimate neighbor with China, the number of Confucius Institutes opened in Vietnam is only one school in Hanoi, very modest compared to other countries (see Table 2). This careful consideration is necessary in the face of the increasingly strong impact of Chinese soft power on the region. Although the number of students at the Confucius Institute in Hanoi is quite modest, only about 600 people per year, the Institute is very active in exchange activities. In the period 2018-2019, the Institute organized 8 delegations to attend summer camps in China, including 4 high school student delegations and 4 university student delegations, while receiving 15 delegations of Chinese teachers and students to Vietnam with more than 960 people (Luong, 2022, p.386). From 2014 up to now, the Institute has funded thousands of scholarships to study in China for Vietnamese students (Government Newspaper of Vietnam, 2024). Overall, the scholarship programs of the Confucius Institute are quite attractive with rich content.

Table 2. Comparison of the number of Chinese Confucius Institutes

No	Country Name	Number of Confucius Institutes
1	US	85
2	Canada	12
3	Brazil	11
4	Australia	14
5	France	18
6	Germany	19
7	Japan	15
8	Korean	23
9	Malaysia	5
10	Philippines	5
11	Russia	19
12	Vietnam	1

Source: Digmandarin. (2023). Confucius Institutes Around the World - 2023. https://www.digmandarin.com/confucius-institutes-around-the-world.html, accessed on 01/27/2024.

In addition, granting scholarships is also an exchange activity to expand China's soft power. Every year, China still provides many scholarships for Vietnamese students, contributing to promoting cultural exchanges and mutual understanding. Vietnamese provinces, cities and universities also offer many scholarships to study in China. Overall, the appeal of Chinese education to Vietnam is still relatively stable. According to the data in Table 3, in 2012 there were 12,500 official Vietnamese students in China, by 2020 this figure was 11,300. One reason why this number has not increased, even decreased, is due to the trend of globalization, Vietnamese international students now have more destination choices. Thus, China's position among the countries receiving Vietnamese students has dropped from 3rd place in 2011 to 5th place in 2020. This shows that although China has had many attractive policies, the effectiveness

Table 3. Number of Vietnamese students in China from 2006-2022

No	Time	Number (people)
1	2006	7.310
2	2008	10.000
3	2011	16.000
4	2012	12.500
5	2013	13.000
6	2018	11.299
7	2019	11.299
8	2020	11.300
9	2022	27.000

Sources: Authors' aggregation from Ministry of Education and Training of Vietnam

has not met expectations. However, by 2022, the number of Vietnamese students in China had risen sharply to 27,000, the direct cause stemming from the commitments and agreements between the two governments to enhance each other's exchanges and educational cooperation. In addition, the influence of the wave of Chinese culture on the status of Tsinghua University and Peking University is spreading more widely in Vietnam. During the visit of General Secretary Nguyen Phu Trong to China in October 2022, President Xi Jinping readily committed to provide no less than 1,000 government scholarships to Vietnam over 5 years, while facilitating Vietnam's easy access to Confucius scholarships (Zreik, 2023b). Thereby, the deployment of China's soft power has brought many opportunities for cultural and educational cooperation in bilateral relations.

The Impact of China's Soft Power: Challenges for Vietnam

First, the Challenge of Political and Diplomatic Pressure

With its geographical location bordering China, Vietnam can hardly avoid being affected by China's increasingly growing soft power policy in the region. In this context, along with the benefits that Vietnam can exploit, China's soft power policy also brings negative impacts on Vietnam's position in its relations with other countries. Politically, although Vietnam and China have many similarities, there are still unresolved sovereignty issues in the East Sea. As the East Sea is becoming an increasingly important hub of regional maritime activities, China's aggressive attitude will further increase instability, causing concerns for countries and disadvantageous to China's efforts to expand its influence. In fact, China has continuously delayed the renegotiation of the Code of Conduct in the East Sea (COC) to maintain a weak and incomplete set of rules, allowing China to easily continue threatening actions against other countries in the region. While Vietnam depends on China in many aspects, especially economically and recently Covid-19 vaccines, it still has to engage in peaceful struggles to protect its sovereignty. At the same time, the US is also increasing its presence in the region. Therefore, Vietnam needs to demonstrate flexibility and creativity in diplomacy to avoid dependence on any side.

The political and diplomatic challenge of China's soft power to Vietnam stems from the fact that the political systems of the two countries have many similarities. This is both an opportunity but also a challenge for Vietnam when China can take advantage of weaknesses and vulnerabilities in Vietnam's political system to influence economically, politically and in terms of soft power. The increased political and diplomatic influence of China in Vietnam often raises concerns about the decline in political and diplomatic influence from Western countries, as well as concerns about whether Vietnam will actively participate in Western-led multilateral institutions. In addition, China continues to promote propaganda and invest in the media to "tell good stories about China", which also disseminates distorted information about sovereignty on forums or even in international newspapers. This poses a considerable challenge to Vietnam's diplomatic struggle, which is how to make diplomacy more practically effective. What is more important is that soft power is formed based on the cognition and emotions of the public in the targeted country rather than on the scale of activities that enhance soft power, so the negative reaction of the Vietnamese public to China's soft power promotion activities also causes some sensitive issues for the two countries' diplomatic relations and poses many challenges for Vietnam.

Second, the Challenge of Ensuring Economic Security

Of all the resources that make up China's soft power, the economic sector is perhaps the most powerful factor and poses huge challenges for Vietnam. In other words, along with opportunities, China's soft power also brings endless trials and tribulations, and even disadvantages that outweigh the benefits. In fact, Vietnam still depends heavily on the Chinese economy. First, as a neighboring country, although Vietnam has the ability to access other potential markets, China is still seen as a major market for Vietnam. Moreover, the consumer needs of Vietnamese and Chinese people are quite similar, while China is the world's large manufacturing plant. Therefore, Vietnamese businesses have to face increasing competitive pressure from Chinese consumer brands such as Midea, Aqua, Xiaomi, Huawei, Oppo, as product quality has been significantly improved at competitive prices, gradually conquering Vietnam's market. In addition, Chinese corporations always focus on product marketing, making Vietnamese consumers increasingly aware of more and more Chinese brands. That is why Vietnam tends to import goods from China instead of spending more to access other faraway markets. Furthermore, with the limited level of industrial development, Vietnam needs time to be able to produce high-end products and access higher market segments. Therefore, the role of China as Vietnam's largest import and export market and major capital investment source cannot be denied. It is the over-dependence on the Chinese economy that is forcing Vietnam to face and choose solutions to resolve bottlenecks, especially issues of territorial sovereignty between the two neighboring countries.

Along with the positive impacts of China's export credit expansion to Vietnam, the limitations are also gradually emerging. First, Beijing's trade facilitation policy for Chinese imports only increases Vietnam's dependence on this market. According to the statistics from Figure 2, as of 2023, although it is no longer the largest export market, China still ranks first in Vietnam's imports and it is difficult for any other country to replace this position. Second, China's motivation to invest in Vietnam does not entirely stem from the goal of mutually beneficial cooperation within the bilateral framework. Instead, Beijing's bigger ambition is to create a certain bond between Vietnam and China, behind the guise of economic cooperation. Chinese companies invest in Vietnam, on the one hand, to alleviate trade competition domestically, on the other hand, to facilitate penetration and dominance in investing in Vietnam's market. Moreover, when China applies production models, the demand for Chinese machinery, equipment in Vietnam also increases accordingly, and even the Chinese workforce is also brought to Vietnam. At that time, those elements named "China" become more popular in Vietnam, which is also part of Beijing's desired soft power expansion efforts, negatively impacting Vietnam's social and economic situation.

Although Chinese capital and aid meet Vietnam's short-term capital needs, they also leave many consequences. Projects sponsored by China are often rated low in quality with stagnation, slow progress, cost overruns over initial investment along with low-quality equipment, leading to increased total investment or affecting project efficiency, of which Cat Linh - Ha Dong railway is a typical example (Hung and Son, 2021). Chinese-invested infrastructure projects in Vietnam are mainly thermal power plants, although they are not environmentally friendly and contrary to the world's sustainable development trend. Moreover, although China's loans do not require conditions on human rights, government and environment like Western countries, they also raise concerns about long-term adverse impacts such as the "debt trap" problem that some other countries have encountered. In addition, some Chinese companies come to Vietnam not only for economic development goals, but also to establish soft standards for Chinese projects and gradually universalize these standards. In Southeast Asia in general and Vietnam in particular, China has been trying to build economic zones and special economic zones both for investment, production and implementation of the Chinese Government's soft power policies. Of these, the VCEP Economic Zone (Shenzhen - Hai Phong), owned by the Shenzhen city government, was built and invested not for commercial purposes as very little growth data was recorded here. Instead, this economic zone has the mission of being "a showcase for China's BRI" in Vietnam (Quan, 2022, p.322).

Third, the Challenge of Cultural and Educational Harm

In the context of increasing competition between China and the US in the Indo-Pacific region, both in terms of level and scope, China has been deploying a comprehensive soft power policy in Vietnam, including economic, education, diplomacy, vaccine aid, sports, international films, investment, and cultural fields. China takes advantage of every edge to build a positive story about China's image, while striving to change how Vietnamese people view China as well as China's ambitions in the East Sea. China wants to spread a framework that includes norms, rules and thinking with Chinese characteristics to Vietnam as a norm and model. This is both an opportunity and a challenge for Vietnam to take advantage of and build ways to absorb the positive values of China and US's soft power. Compared to economic soft power, the cultural fields that China spreads to Vietnam are considered not very effective. However, once spiritual values have created influence, they are very difficult to erase. Therefore, the wave of infiltration of China's cultural soft power also poses potential challenges to Vietnam.

(i) The impact of Chinese films on Vietnam: Due to its geographical proximity to China, Vietnam is strongly influenced by China's strategies to popularize its cultural soft power across many fields. In 2003, former President Hu Jintao affirmed: "Chinese culture not only belongs to the Chinese but also to the whole world" (Leino, 2021). Under Xi Jinping, soft power is seen as a key component of the country's reconstruction process (Hagstrom and Nordin, 2020). The aggressive promotion of cultural soft power through entertainment helps China compensate for its economic and political value deficiencies. Currently, China has no shortage of financial resources to promote its soft power. The Beijing government invests heavily in the media, promoting a positive national image through the Great Wall, art, animals, martial arts, sports, cinema and leadership. In Vietnam, Chinese novels still account for about 60% of all foreign books in circulation (Luong, 2022, p.399). Chinese film, music and television attract many viewers, especially young people. In 2018, VTV channels led in terms of access but still aired many Chinese, Korean and even USn films, including prime time slots. From 2000-2010, the number and duration of Chinese films aired on VTV and local channels dominated in order to cater to audience tastes (En et al., 2022). Some Chinese films and TV series such as Journey to the West, The Romance of the Three Kingdoms, Princess Agents, Shanghai Bund... have left a deep impression on Vietnamese viewers and are regularly re-aired. For China, Hollywood films represent USn soft power and a competitive rival. Therefore, in addition to limiting Hollywood films domestically, the Chinese government also spends heavily to produce high-quality propaganda films, collaborates with Hollywood to produce blockbusters, in order to highlight Chinese values. At the same time, China also strives to export these cultural products abroad, with Vietnam being the main target. This is an opportunity for Vietnam to develop a film industry capable of competing, while selectively receiving cultural values.

(ii) The impact of Chinese social networking platforms on Vietnam: The increasingly strong penetration of Chinese social networks in Vietnam has posed significant challenges in information management. Some of China's social networking platforms have a very large number of users. In 2023, TikTok ranked first in global downloads with 3.5 billion downloads (Cleverads, 2023). According to statistics from We are Social and Meltwater on Digital 2023, at the beginning of 2023, Vietnam had about 70 million

Table 4. The most used social media platforms in Vietnam

No	Social Media Application Platforms	Percentage (%)
1	Facebook	96
2	Messenger	94
3	Zalo	93
4	Youtube	77
5	TikTok	69
6	Shopee	53
7	Momo	38
8	Gmail	35
9	Instagram	34
10	Grab	30

Source: We are Social and Meltwater on Digital. (2023). Anticipate TikTok market trends by industry. https://megadigital.ai/vi/blog/tong-quan-xu-huong-thi-truong
-tiktok/, accessed January 28, 2024.

Internet users, of which TikTok alone attracted 49.86 million people, accounting for 69% of frequent users in Vietnam. This shows that Chinese social networking applications are very popular with Vietnamese people (see Table 4).

In addition, other Chinese social networks such as Weibo, WeChat, Baidu have also seen a rapid increase in the number of users in Vietnam. Most of these platforms operate entirely in Chinese and are where some influential people on the Chinese internet interact. Therefore, if information is not strictly controlled and verified, content on Chinese social media can have negative consequences, especially for young people who do not have the ability to appropriately recognize bad and harmful information. Chinese online games are also an extremely dangerous soft power tool. According to recent statistics, about 85% of games legally released in Vietnam originate from abroad, of which China accounts for over 70% (Hoa, 2023, p.121). Mobile games released in Vietnam often use characters and content about Chinese history and culture. Some Sinicized Vietnamese games like Chronicles of the Clouds and Rivers, Storm of Proclamation, etc. have attracted a large number of young Vietnamese users. Moreover, Chinese game companies are increasingly easily launching directly into the Vietnamese market through app stores, even making Vietnamese versions for the convenience of players. The worrying issue is that Chinese games are often based on Chinese historical sources, resulting in most Vietnamese players having a better understanding of Chinese history than their own national history. This needs attention, especially when most of Vietnam's current game market share is still dominated by Chinese products, although the domestic market has seen remarkable development.

In recent years, although China's influence has spread across the world, perhaps no country has been more severely impacted by China's political ambitions and soft power than Vietnam. This stems from cultural, political similarities as well as close geographical, historical and economic ties between the two countries. Vietnam has always been at the center of China's strategy to spread its influence. At the same time, it also fully meets the conditions for Beijing to implement soft power policies. If successful in Southeast Asia, China's values and influence may be accepted by Vietnam and neighboring countries. This will enable Beijing to become a global power and realize President Xi Jinping's strategic goals. In summary, China has been implementing a comprehensive soft power policy in Vietnam, encompassing economic, investment, cultural, educational, diplomatic, vaccine aid, sports, film and music fields. Beijing takes advantage of all edges to change how Vietnamese people view China as well as its strategic ambitions. More importantly, Beijing wants to spread Chinese norms, rules and mindset to Vietnam as a norm and model. In the context of increasing US-China competition in the Indo-Pacific region, along with Vietnam's unique position, Beijing's soft power policy brings both opportunities and challenges for Hanoi to build ways to receive and absorb the positive values of China and US's soft power.

CONCLUSION

In the context of increasing strategic competition between the US and China in the Indo-Pacific region, with its strategic geographical position bordering southern China and straddling vital maritime routes in the East Sea, Vietnam plays a very important role in the competition policies and strategies between the US and China in Southeast Asia. Therefore, Vietnam is profoundly affected by China's soft power competition strategy as the US pays increasing attention to this country in its strategy to restrain China's ambitions to expand power in Southeast Asia. Thus, China's strategy to increase soft power competition has brought both opportunities and challenges to Vietnam.

Politically, Vietnam has the opportunity to enhance its position in China's multilateral initiatives like the BRI and China-led mechanisms. As a key ASEAN member and top Chinese trade partner in ASEAN, Vietnam can help steer China's regional strategy. In return, Vietnam can receive China's support for its own initiatives and strategies, consolidating its international integration. Moreover, some political system similarities allow Vietnam to predict and strategize around China's policies, especially regarding the East Sea. This helps Vietnam develop proactive foreign policies. Recently, Vietnam-China relations have improved with more high-level contacts and dialogues, driving further cooperation potential. However, unresolved East Sea disputes and China's aggression cause regional instability and distrust. China continues delaying the COC, increasing military activities, and threatening regional countries. With economic dependence on China, Vietnam faces Chinese political pressure leveraging "economic tools" in the East Sea disputes. This is a major challenge for Vietnam in balancing the relationship.

Economically, Vietnam can attract large Chinese FDI in manufacturing and local development. Vietnam can also utilize Chinese ODA for infrastructure serving its development goals. As China's top ASEAN trade partner, Vietnam can access the vast Chinese consumer market and grow exports like agriculture, seafood and textiles. Studying China's successful special economic zone model can also inform Vietnam's own industrialization and modernization. However, economic over-reliance on China poses challenges if used as political leverage over the East Sea. Fierce competition from Chinese firms with Vietnamese goods domestically also difficulties local companies. While offering low interest rates, China's investment often has more political than economic motives, creating dependence and competitive advantage for Chinese goods and services. The quality and efficiency of Chinese infrastructure cooperation is also rated as low. Vietnam must diversify markets and reduce China economic dependence while improving domestic competitiveness.

Culturally and educationally, scholarships allow thousands of Vietnamese students annually to access China's advanced university system, enhancing Vietnam's human capital amid severe skills shortages. Confucius Institutes also let thousands of Vietnamese access Chinese culture and language, despite controversies. With proactivity, Vietnam can open additional institutes and classes on Vietnamese culture and language worldwide, promoting its image internationally. Vietnam also has opportunities to organize cultural activities like exhibitions in China to showcase Vietnamese culture. However, close geographical proximity means Vietnam is severely impacted by China's cultural soft power expansion. Chinese cinema, TV, music and pop culture are increasingly popular in Vietnam, especially amongst youth. Chinese films take 60% of Vietnam's imported film market share. Chinese social networks and apps take 70% of Vietnam's market share, often rooted in Chinese history and culture. This risks eroding Vietnam's cultural identity. Preserving core national values while enhancing Vietnamese culture's attractiveness is key.

In general, in the context of increasing strategic competition between the US and China, Vietnam is facing both opportunities and challenges from the increase of China's soft power in the region. The opportunities focus on enhancing strategic position, attracting investment and expanding trade with China as well as accessing China's education and developed culture system. However, Vietnam needs to consider and overcome the challenges of political pressure, economic dependence, and the risk of losing cultural and national identity. Therefore, to promote healthy, balanced and stable long-term bilateral relations, Vietnam needs to proactively enhance its comprehensive power, diversify partners, promote internal strength, and preserve Vietnam's traditional cultural values. These are the basic orientations to help Vietnam overcome challenges and maximize opportunities from the increasing trend of strategic soft power competition between the US and China in the region.

REFERENCES

Barrech, D. M., & Khan, P. D. M. (2023). US-China Growing Competition in Soft Power. *Journal of Social Sciences Review*, *3*(2), 490–499. doi:10.54183/jssr.v3i2.288

Cleverads. (2023). *TikTok Statistics 2023: 27 key figures you need to know.* https://cleverads.vn/blog/tiktok-statistics-2023/

Dicicco, J., & Onea, T. (2023). *Great-Power Competition.* https://oxfordre.com/internationalstudies/view/10.1093/acrefore/9780190846626.001.0001/acrefore-9780190846626-e-756

En, L. B., Minh, V. N., & Cuc, N. T. K. (2022). Analyzing the influence of films on Chinese-learning students - Based on a survey of Nguyen Tat Thanh University students. *Van Hien University Scientific Journal, 8*(4), 143-150. https://vjol.info.vn/index.php/vhu/article/download/73193/62096/

Feng, D. (2014). *Xi Jinping: Confucius Institutes belong to China and the world.* http://www.xinhuanet.com//politics/2014-09/27/c_1112652079.htm

Global Energy Monitor. (2023). *International Chinese coal projects.* https://www.gem.wiki/International_Chinese_coal_projects

Government Portal of Vietnam. (2024). *Announcement of 2024 Chinese Government Scholarships.* https://baochinhphu.vn/thong-bao-hoc-bong-chinh-phu-du-hoc-trung-quoc-nam-2024-102231124161756527.htm

Gupta, A. K. (2013). Soft Power of the United States, China, and India: A Comparative Analysis. *Indian Journal of Asian Affairs*, *26*(2), 37–57. https://www.jstor.org/stable/43550355

Hagstrom, L., & Nordin, A. H. M. (2020). China's "Politics of Harmony" and the Quest for Soft Power in International Politics. *International Studies Review*, 22(3), 507–525. doi:10.1093/isr/viz023

Hoa, N. T. P. (2023). *China's neighborhood diplomacy under Xi Jinping through the case of Vietnam, Myanmar, Cambodia.* Social Sciences Publishing House.

Huan, D. V. (2023). *Vietnam - China investment, trade and tourism relations.* https://vneconomy.vn/quan-he-dau-tu-thuong-mai-du-lich-viet-nam-trung-quoc.htm

Hung, N. T. (2022). World *Economics and Politics.* National Political Publishing House Truth.

Hung, V., & Son, T. (2021). *Major projects with slow progress, huge capital of Chinese contractors in Vietnam.* https://cafef.vn/nhung-dai-du-an-cham-tien-do-doi-von-khung-cua-nha-thau-trung-quoc-o-viet-nam-20211114120443818.chn

Kiet, L. H., & Tuyen, N. V. (2023). Vietnam's geopolitical position for the United States in the strategy of containing China's hegemonic ambitions. *Science and Technology Journal - Da Nang University, 21*(8), 63-69. https://jst-ud.vn/jst-ud/article/view/8630

Lao Viet Magazine. (2022). *Confucius Institute receives great attention from those who want to learn Chinese in Laos.* https://tapchilaoviet.org/van-hoa-xa-hoi/vien-khong-tu-duoc-quan-tam-lon-cua-nguoi-co-nhu-cau-hoc-tieng-trung-quoc-tai-lao-52371.html#:~:text=Gi%C3%A1m%20%C4%91%E1%BB%91c%20H%E1%BB%8Dc%20vi%E1%BB%87n%20Kh%E1%BB%95ng%20t%E1%BB%AD%20cho%20bi%E1%BA%BFt%3A%20Ni%C3%AAn%20kh%C3%B3a,l%C6%B0%E1%BB%A3ng%20ho%E1%BA%A1t%20%C4%91%E1%BB%99ng%20gi%E1%BA%A3ng%20d%E1%BA%A1y

Leino, J. (2021). Battle of the hearts: China's aim to become a soft (super)power and Europe's response. *European View*, 20(2), 211–219. doi:10.1177/17816858211055553

Luong, D. T. H. (2022). *China's soft power: Impacts and implications for Vietnam.* National Political Publishing House Truth.

Minh, P. V. (2023). *Developing supporting industries in the context of integration.* https://kinhtevadubao.vn/phat-trien-nganh-cong-nghiep-ho-tro-trong-boi-canh-hoi-nhap-27278.html

Ministry of Finance of Vietnam. (2020). *Attracting and using Chinese ODA for infrastructure development in Vietnam and recommendations.* https://mof.gov.vn/webcenter/portal/vclvcstc/pages_r/l/chi-tiet-tin?dDocName=MOFUCM172887

Ministry of Finance of Vietnam. (2023). *Vietnam attracts over $13.4 billion in FDI in 6 months.* https://www.mof.gov.vn/webcenter/portal/ttpltc/pages_r/l/chi-tiet-tin-ttpltc?dDocName=MOFUCM279819

Nhan Dan Newspaper of Vietnam. (2022). *New momentum to enhance Vietnam-China friendship.* https://nhandan.vn/dong-luc-moi-tang-cuong-tinh-huu-nghi-nang-tam-quan-he-viet-nam-trung-quoc-post722793.html

Nye, J. P. (2004). *Soft Power: The Means to Success in World Politics.* PublicAffairs.

Nye, J. S. (2023). *Soft Power and Great-Power Competition: Shifting Sands in the Balance of Power Between the United States and China.* Spinger Publisher. doi:10.1007/978-981-99-0714-4

Quan, N. H. (2022). *China-US geopolitical competition: Impacts and implications for Vietnam's adaptive policies*. National Political Publishing House Truth.

Rubiolo, F., Busilli, V. S., & Escobar, M. E. (2020). Análisis de la política exterior de Xi Jinping hacia el Sudeste de Asia: Estrategias, intereses y dimensiones. *Revista Relaciones Internacionales*, *93*(2), 91–116. doi:10.15359/ri.93-2.4

Streeten, P. (2001). Interdependence and Globalization. *Finance & Development*, *38*(2), 1–10. doi:10.5089/9781451952858.022.A010

Tien Giang Portal. (2023). *Long Giang Industrial Park*. https://tiengiang.gov.vn/chi-tiet-tin?/khu-cong-nghiep-long-giang/11241528

White House. (2022). *Indo - Pacific Strategy*. https://www.whitehouse.gov/wpcontent/uploads/2022/02/U.S.-Indo%20PacificStrategy.pdf

Winkler, S. C. (2023). Strategic Competition and US-China Relations: A Conceptual Analysis. *The Chinese Journal of International Politics*, *16*(3), 333–356. doi:10.1093/cjip/poad008

Yimeng, Z. (2023). *Experts: Don't politicize work of Confucius Institutes*. https://www.chinadaily.com.cn/a/202312/09/WS6573a382a31040ac301a6f16.html

Zha, W. (2022). Great power rivalry and the agency of secondary states: A study based on China's relations with Southeast Asian countries. *International Relations of the Asia-Pacific*, *22*(1), 131–161. doi:10.1093/irap/lcaa018

Zreik, M. (2023a). Sustainable and Smart Supply Chains in China: A Multidimensional Approach. In B. Bentalha, A. Hmioui, & L. Alla (Eds.), *Integrating Intelligence and Sustainability in Supply Chains* (pp. 179–197). IGI Global. doi:10.4018/979-8-3693-0225-5.ch010

Zreik, M. (2023b). Navigating the Dragon: China's Ascent as a Global Power Through Public Diplomacy. In S. Kavoğlu & E. Köksoy (Eds.), *Global Perspectives on the Emerging Trends in Public Diplomacy* (pp. 50–74). IGI Global. doi:10.4018/978-1-6684-9161-4.ch003

Zreik, M. (2024a). Bridging the Digital Divide: The Role of China-Africa Cooperation in the Evolution of Higher Education Amidst COVID-19 and Beyond. In P. Mashau & T. Farisani (Eds.), *Accessibility of Digital Higher Education in the Global South* (pp. 232–246). IGI Global. doi:10.4018/978-1-6684-9179-9.ch012

Zreik, M. (2024b). Financial Misreporting and Corporate Governance Lapses: A Deep Dive Into the 1MDB Scandal in Malaysia. In R. Hasan (Ed.), *Cases on Uncovering Corporate Governance Challenges in Asian Markets* (pp. 178–201). IGI Global. doi:10.4018/978-1-6684-9867-5.ch009

Compilation of References

Abdel-Reda, S. N. (2013). *Arab-Chinese Relations*. Political and International Review.

Abdul Ghaffar Mastoi, L. X. (2019). Higher Education Service Quality based on Students' Satisfaction in People's Republic of China. *Journal of Education and Practice*, 112.

Abdullah, Z. (2018). Chinese foreign policy towards the Arab Gulf states (Saudi Arabia as a model). *Journal of Political Trends, Arab Democratic Center,* (5), 51.

Abdulsalam, R. (2021). *The United States of America between hard power and soft power*. Arab Diffusion Foundation.

Academicpositions. (2021). *American University of Iraq – Baghdad*. https://academicpositions.com/employer/american-university-of-iraq-baghdad

Acharya, A. (2003-2004). Will Asia's past be its future? *International Security*, *28*(3), 149–164. https://www.jstor.org/stable/4137480. doi:10.1162/016228803773100101

Adelman, L., & Riedel, S. L. (2012). *Handbook for evaluating knowledge-based systems: Conceptual framework and compendium of methods*. Springer Science & Business Media.

Afridi, M. K., Anjum, N., & Abbas, Z. (2022). Comparative Study of the US and China's Policies towards South Asia in the 21st Century: Implications for Pakistan. *Global Foreign Policies Review*, *V*(III), 14–22. doi:10.31703/gfpr.2022(V-III).02

Afzaal, M., Hu, K., Ilyas Chishti, M., & Khan, Z. (2019). Examining Pakistani news media discourses about China–Pakistan Economic Corridor: A corpus-based critical discourse analysis. *Cogent Social Sciences*, *5*(1), 1683940. doi:10.1080/23311886.2019.1683940

Ahmed, G., Abudaqa, A., Jayachandran, C., Limbu, Y., & Alzahmi, R. (2022). Nation Branding as a Strategic Approach for Emerging Economies: The Case of UAE. In O. Adeola, R. E. Hinson, & A. M. Sakkthivel (Eds.), Marketing Communications and Brand Development in Emerging Economies Volume I: Contemporary and Future Perspectives (pp. 41–57). Springer International Publishing. doi:10.1007/978-3-030-88678-3_3

Aidarbek Amirbek, K. Y. (2014). Education as a Soft Power Instrument of Foreign Policy. *Procedia: Social and Behavioral Sciences*, 502.

Aixin, L. (2023, December 23). Vietnam chooses justice and national interest that can prevent itself from becoming a pawn: Former Vietnamese official. *Global Times*. https://www.globaltimes.cn/page/202312/1303569.shtml

Al-Badrani, A. K. (2015). *The Impact of Continuity and Change on Chinese Foreign Policy Towards the Middle East Peace Process*. Mustansiriyya: Al-Mustansiriya Journal for Arab and International Studies.

Albert, E. (2018). *China's Big Bet on Soft Power*. Council on Foreign Relations. Retrieved from: https://www.cfr.org/backgrounder/chinas-big-bet-soft-power

Albert, E. (2018, February 9). *China's Big Bet Soft Power.* Council for Foreign Relations (CFR). https://www.cfr.org/backgrounder/chinas-big-bet-soft-power

Alderman, P., & Eggeling, K. A. (2024). Vision Documents, Nation Branding and the Legitimation of Non-Democratic Regimes. *Geopolitics, 29*(1), 288–318. doi:10.1080/14650045.2023.2165441

Alemany, A. B. (2006). Los frailes de Koxinga. In P. S. Aguilar (Ed.), *La Investigación sobre Asia Pacífico en España* (pp. 393–422). Universidad de Granada.

Alemi, A. (2021). Iran and China; Necessities and Realities of Mutual Cooperation in New Global Confrontations. *Iranian diplomacy.* http://irdiplomacy.ir/fa/news/2001428

Alfonso Mola, M. (2021). La ruta directa entre Cádiz y Manila (1765-1834): Tres alternativas al Galeón de Manila. *Andalucía en la Historia*, (73), 24–29.

Al-Haddad, M. (2017). A Reading in the History of Arab-Chinese Relations and Ways to Enhance them. *Conference on Prospects for Arab-African-Chinese Cooperation within the Framework of the Belt and Road Initiative* (p. 107). Khartoum: Global Africa University - Center for African Research and Studies and the Association of Arab-Chinese Friendship Societies.

Alhurra. (2018). *Iraqi and Mauritanian women among the 'bravest' women in the world.* https://www.alhurra.com/a/courage-award/426536.html

Ali, L. (2022, October 18). *Saudi Arabia Developing a Partnership with China.* Retrieved from Gulf Research Center: https://www.grc.net/single-commentary/66

Aljazeera. (2018). *Iraq elections final results: Sadr's bloc wins parliamentary poll.* https://www.aljazeera.com/news/2018/5/20/iraq-elections-final-results-sadrs-bloc-wins-parliamentary-poll

Allison, G. (2017). *Destined for war: Can America and China escape Thucydides's trap?* Houghton Mifflin Harcourt.

Almit, M. S. (2010). *China and The Middle East: since World War II: Bilateral Approach.* Lexington Books.

al-Qalam, S. M. (2010). The concept of power and the performance of foreign policy: comparing China and Iran. Foreign Relations Quarterly, 8(5).

Al-Shaqaba, A. M. (2014). The Political Dimension of Arab-Chinese Relations and Their Future Prospects. Dirasat Journal, 41, 381.

Al-Sudairi, M. T. (2012). *Sino-Saudi Relations: An Economic History.* GRC GULF PAPERS.

Alterman, J. B. (2009). China's Soft Power in the Middle East. In Chinese Soft Power and its implications for United States, Competition and Cooperation in the Developing World. Centre for Strategic and International Studies.

Altman, R. (2009, January/February). A Weakening of the West. *Foreign Affairs, 88*(1), 2–14.

Amanor, K. S., & Chichava, S. (2016). South–South Cooperation, Agribusiness, and African Agricultural Development: Brazil and China in Ghana and Mozambique. *World Development, 81*, 13–23. doi:10.1016/j.worlddev.2015.11.021

Amjadian, F., Sanai, A., & Jalali, R. (2022). Characteristics of Iran-US soft power in modern Iraq in the years (2016 to 2020). *Iranian Journal of Political Sociology, 5*(8), 2535–2554.

Andrés, A. (1952). *Historia de las Misiones Dominicanas en Amoy.* Unpublished manuscript, Archives of the Province of the Holy Rosary, Spain.

Anghie, A. (2004). Imperialism, Sovereignty and the Making of International Law. Cambridge University Press.

Anholt, S. (2006). Anholt Nation Brands Index: How Does the World See America? *Journal of Advertising Research, 45*(3), 296–304. doi:10.1017/S0021849905050336

Anholt, S. (2007). *Competitive Identity: The New Brand Management for Nations, Cities and Regions*. Palgrave Macmillan. doi:10.1057/9780230627727

Arif, B. H. (2017). *The Role of Soft Power in China's Foreign Policy in the 21st Century*. International Journal of Social Sciences & Educational Studies.

Arifon, O., Huang, Z. A., Zheng, Y., & Zyw Melo, A. (2019). Comparing Chinese and European Discourses regarding the "Belt and Road Initiative". *Revue française des sciences de l'information et de la communication*, (17).

Ashford, E., & Cooper, E. (2023, October 5). Yes, the World Is Multipolar. *Foreign Policy*. https://foreignpolicy.com/2023/10/05/usa-china-multipolar-bipolar-unipolar/

Aspers, P., & Corte, U. (2019). What is Qualitative in Qualitative Research. *Qualitative Sociology, 42*(2), 139–160. doi:10.1007/s11133-019-9413-7 PMID:31105362

Associated Press, Times of Israel. (2017, August 1). *China pushes four-point Israeli-Palestinian peace plan*. Retrieved from Times of Israel: https://www.timesofisrael.com/china-pushes-four-point-israeli-palestinian-peace-plan/

Atkinson, C. (2014). *Military soft power: Public diplomacy through military educational exchanges*. Rowman & Littlefield.

Awang, Z. (n.d.). *A Handbook on SEM 2nd ediction*. Unviersity Sultan Zainal Abidin.

Ayyub, R., & Shepardson, D. (2023, March 24). *TikTok congressional hearing: CEO Shou Zi Chew grilled by US lawmakers*. Retrieved from Reuters: https://www.reuters.com/technology/tiktok-ceo-face-tough-questions-support-us-ban-grows-2023-03-23/

Babones, S. (2017). Taking China Seriously: Relationality, Tianxia, and the 'Chinese School' of International Relations. Oxford Research Encyclopedia of Politics, 1. doi:10.1093/acrefore/9780190228637.013.602

Baghernia, N., & Meraji, E. (2020). Understanding China's Relationship with Bangladesh. *CenRaPS Journal of Social Sciences, 2*(3), 345–353. doi:10.46291/cenraps.v2i3.41

Bai, C., Ma, H., & Pan, W. (2012). *Spatial spillover and regional economic growth in China*. Tsinghua: School of Economics and Management, Tsinghua University.

Bakir, M. M. (2018). knowledge world. Kuwait: National Council for Culture, Arts and Letters.

Baldwin, D. A. (2013). Power and international relations. Handbook of International Relations, 2, 273-297.

Baldwin, D. A. (1978). Power and social exchange. *The American Political Science Review, 72*(4), 1229–1242. doi:10.2307/1954536

Baldwin, D. A. (2014). Neoliberalism, neorealism, and world politics. In *The Realism Reader* (pp. 313–319). Routledge.

Bardakci, M. (2023). *Iran and the Iraqi Shiites: A Cyclical Relationship*. https://www.uikpanorama.com/blog/2023/02/23/mb/

Barnett, M., & Duvall, R. (2005). Power in international politics. *International Organization, 59*(1), 39–75. doi:10.1017/S0020818305050010

Baron, X. (2019). *Histoire de la Syrie: de 1918 à nos jours*. Tallandier.

Barr, D. M. (2011). *Who's afraid of China? The challenge of Chinese soft power.* Bloomsbury Publishing. doi:10.5040/9781350223967

Barrech, D. M., & Khan, P. D. M. (2023). US-China Growing Competition in Soft Power. *Journal of Social Sciences Review*, *3*(2), 490–499. doi:10.54183/jssr.v3i2.288

Bartlett, K. (2022). *Survey: Africans See China as Positive Force.* VOA. https://www.voanews.com/a/survey-africans-see-china-as-positive-force/6813313.html

Bassan, M. (2021). VII China's Soft Power in Africa: Promoting Alternative Perspectives. In B. Baykurt & V. de Grazia (Eds.), *Soft-Power Internationalism: Competing for Cultural Influence in the 21st-Century Global Order* (pp. 181–207). Columbia University Press. doi:10.7312/bayk19544-009

Bastami, M. (2011). *American Public Diplomacy in the Middle East.* Imam Sadegh Publishing House.

Batkhuyag Sodovyn, B. S. (2019). The China-Mongolia-Russia economic corridor and Mongolia's energy sector. *ESE Web of Conferences, 77.*

Baumann, M.-O., Haug, S., & Weinlich, S. (2022). *China's expanding engagement with the United Nations development pillar: The selective long-term approach of a programme country superpower.* Friedrich-Ebert-Stifung.

Baylouny, A. M. (2006). Al-Manar and Alhurra: Competing satellite stations and ideologies. *European Center for Security Studies*, (2), 1–27.

Béja, J.-P. (2010). *The Impact of China's Tiananmen Massacre.* Taylor and Francis.

Bellamy, A. J. (2022). *Syria Betrayed: Atrocities, War, and the Failure of International Diplomacy.* Columbia University Press. doi:10.7312/bell19296

Belt and Road Initiative. (2022). *Belt and Road Initiative.* Retrieved from: https://www.beltroad-initiative.com/belt-and-road/

Belt and Road Portal - BRI Official Website. (2017, July 17). *Vinh Tan 1 power plant largest Chinese investment in Vietnam.* https://eng.yidaiyilu.gov.cn/p/20048.html

Bendel, P. R. (2011). Branding New York City—The Saga of 'I Love New York. In K. Dinnie (Ed.), *City Branding: Theory and Cases* (pp. 179–183)., doi:10.1057/9780230294790_24

Bennon, M., & Fukuyama, F. (2023, August 22). China's road to ruin: The real toll of Beijing's Belt and Road. *Foreign Affairs.* https://www.foreignaffairs.com/china/belt-road-initiative-xi-imf

Berdiyev, A., & Can, N. (2020). The importance of central Asia in China's foreign policy and Beijing's soft power instruments. *Central Asia and The Caucasus, 21*(4), 15–24. doi:10.37178/ca-c.20.4.02

Berg, B. L., Lune, H., & Lune, H. (2004). Qualitative Research Methods for the Social Sciences. In *Teaching Sociology* (Vol. 18, p. 563). Pearson. doi:10.2307/1317652

Besharati, N. A. (2019). *Measuring Effectiveness of South-South Cooperation* (52; Occasional Paper Series). Southern Voice. https://www.ssc-globalthinkers.org/sites/default/files/2019-10/191010-Ocassional-Paper-Series-No.-52_final-1.pdf

Bettie, M. (2015a). Ambassadors unaware: The Fulbright Program and American public diplomacy. *The Journal of Transatlantic Studies*, *13*(4), 358–372. doi:10.1080/14794012.2015.1088326

Bettie, M. (2015b). The Scholar as Diplomat: The Fulbright Program and America's Cultural Engagement with the World. *Caliban*, *54*(54), 233–252. doi:10.4000/caliban.3066

Bevir, M. (1999). Foucault, power, and institutions. *Political Studies*, *47*(2), 345–359. doi:10.1111/1467-9248.00204

Bezamat, F., & Wu. (2022, May 23). *These Innovations from China Are Improving Resiliency and Sustainability*. World Economic Forum. https://www.weforum.org/agenda/2022/05/these-chinese-innovations-are-improving-resiliency-and-sustainability-in-2022/

Biney, P. A., & Cheng, M.-Y. (2021). International Students' Decision to Study in China: A Study of Some Selected International Students from Universities in China. *Open Journal of Social Sciences*, *09*(08), 305–325. doi:10.4236/jss.2021.98021

Biran, M. (2017). Periods of Non-Han Rule. In M. Szonyim (Ed.), *A Companion to Chinese History*. Wiley Blackwell. doi:10.1002/9781118624593.ch11

Birn, A.-E., Muntaner, C., & Afzal, Z. (2017). South-South cooperation in health: Bringing in theory, politics, history, and social justice. *Cadernos de Saude Publica*, *33*(2, suppl 2). Advance online publication. doi:10.1590/0102-311x00194616 PMID:28977125

Blair, R. A., Marty, R., & Roessler, P. (2022). Foreign Aid and Soft Power: Great Power Competition in Africa in the Early Twenty-first Century. *British Journal of Political Science*, *52*(3), 1355–1376. doi:10.1017/S0007123421000193

Blanchard, E., & Hakobyan, S. (2015). The US Generalised System of Preferences in Principle and Practice. *World Economy*, *38*(3), 399–424. doi:10.1111/twec.12216

Blanchard, J. M. F. (2021). Belt and Road Initiative (BRI) blues: Powering BRI research back on track to avoid choppy seas. *Journal of Chinese Political Science*, *26*(1), 235–255. doi:10.1007/s11366-020-09717-0

Bloor, K. (2022, May 21). Power and Development in Global Politics. *E-International Relations*. https://www.e-ir.info/2022/05/21/power-and-development-in-global-politics/

Bohm, A. (2013). Responding to Crises: The Problematic Relationship between Security and Justice in The Responsibility to Protect. *Global Policy*, *4*(3), 247–257. doi:10.1111/1758-5899.12030

Bouderdaben, M. (2019). *The role of informal diplomacy in implementing foreign policy*. Constantine University.

Brasnett, J. (2021). Controlling Beliefs and Global Perceptions: Religion in Chinese Foreign Policy. *Sage Journals*, 41-58.

Brautigam, D. (2011). *The dragon's gift: the real story of China in Africa*. Oxford University Press.

Breslin, S. (2011). The Soft Notion of China's "Soft Power." Asia Programme Paper: ASP. London: Chatam House.

Briggs, E. (2023, August 16). *America's Gen Z Favors Chinese Brands More Than Other Generations*. Morning Consult Pro. https://pro.morningconsult.com/analysis/gen-z-favors-chinese-brands

Britannica. (2021). *Bandung Conference*. Retrieved from Britannica: https://www.britannica.com/event/Bandung-Conference

Britannica. (2024, January 19). *Ancient Silk Road*. Retrieved from Britannica: https://www.britannica.com/money/topic/Silk-Road-trade-route

Britannica. (2024, January 5). *Second Sino-Japanese War*. Retrieved from Britannica: https://www.britannica.com/event/Second-Sino-Japanese-War

Brodsky, S. (2020, May 21). *Nation-Branding Soft Power: The Case of Brand China*. Brandingmag. https://www.brandingmag.com/2020/05/21/nation-branding-soft-power-the-case-of-brand-china/

Brook, T. (2019). *Great state: China and the World*. Profile Books.

Brown, C. (2004). Do Great Powers have Great Responsibilties? Great Powers and Moral Agency. *Global Society*, *18*(1), 5–19. doi:10.1080/1360082032000173545

Browning, C. S. (2023). *Nation Branding and International Politics*. McGill-Queen's University Press.

Bruton, G. D., Ahlstrom, D., & Chen, J. (2021). China has emerged as an aspirant economy. *Asia Pacific Journal of Management*, *38*(1), 1–15. doi:10.1007/s10490-018-9638-0

Bryman, A. (2008). Of methods and methodology. *Qualitative Research in Organizations and Management*, *3*(2), 159–168. doi:10.1108/17465640810900568

Bry, S. (2017). Brazil's Soft-Power Strategy: The Political Aspirations of South–South Development Cooperation. *Foreign Policy Analysis*, *13*(2), 297–316. doi:10.1093/fpa/orw015

Buhmann, A., & Ingenhoff, D. (2015). The 4D Model of the Country Image: An Integrative Approach from the Perspective of Communication Management. *The International Communication Gazette*, *77*(1), 102–124. doi:10.1177/1748048514556986

Burns, J. S. (1996). Defining leadership: Can we see the forest for the trees? *The Journal of Leadership Studies*, *3*(2), 148–157. doi:10.1177/107179199600300212

Busbarat, P., & Camba, A. (2023, December 5). *How has China's Belt and Road Initiative impacted Southeast Asian countries?* https://carnegieendowment.org/2023/12/05/how-has-china-s-belt-and-road-initiative-impacted-southeast-asian-countries-pub-91170

Bush, J. W. (2021). *China's Soft Power in the Context of the Belt and Road Initiative: Three Case Studies*. Academic Press.

Buzan, B. (2022). *Ole Waver, Regions and Powers*. Cambridge University.

Buzan, B., & Lawson, G. (2014). Capitalism and the emergent world order. *International Affairs*, *90*(1), 71–91. doi:10.1111/1468-2346.12096

Byambakhand, L. S. K. (2021). *Young Mongolians and the World in 2021 (National Opinion Poll Results)*. Friedrich-Ebert-Stiftung Mongolia & Mongolian Institute for Innovative Policies.

Cai, C. (2013). New great powers and international law in the 21st century. *European Journal of International Law*, *24*(3), 755–795. doi:10.1093/ejil/cht050

Callahan, W. A. (2015). Identity and security in China: The negative soft power of the China dream. *Politics*, *35*(3-4), 216–229. doi:10.1111/1467-9256.12088

Carl, E., & James, S. R. (2021). *Critical Approaches Toward a Cosmopolitan Education*. Taylor & Francis.

Carminati, D. (2020). *The State of China's Soft Power in 2020*. E-International Relations. Retrieved from: https://www.e-ir.info/2020/07/03/the-state-of-chinas-soft-power-in-2020/

Carnegie. (2022, April 25). https://carnegieendowment.org/2022/04/25/denying-support-for-chinese-and-china-enabled-authoritarianism-and-repression-pub-86924

Castilla, C. (2016, March 18). China's Evolving Middle East Role. *Institute for Security and Development Policy. Policy Brief*, (193), 3. https://www.files.ethz.ch/isn/196849/2016-castilla-chinas-evolving-middle-east-role.pdf

Central Committee of the Communist Party of China. (2016). *13th Five-Year Plan for Economic and Social Development of the People's Republic of China, 2016-2020*. https://en.ndrc.gov.cn/policies/202105/P020210527785800103339.pdf

Cervera Jiménez, J. A. (2020). El Galeón de Manila: Mercancías, personas e ideas viajando a través del Pacífico (1565-1815). *México y la Cuenca del Pacífico*, *9*(26), 69–90. doi:10.32870/mycp.v9i26.677

CGTN. (2022, December 9). *Chart of the Day: First China-Arab States Summit, an epoch-making milestone*. Retrieved from CGTN: https://news.cgtn.com/news/2022-12-09/First-China-Arab-States-Summit-an-epoch-making-milestone-1fCWiaKTg1q/index.html

Chakraborti, T. (1985). *India and Kampuchea: A phase in their relations, 1978-1981*. Minerva Associates Pvt. Ltd.

Chakraborti, T., & Chakraborty, M. (2020). *India's strategy in the South Chia Sea*. Routledge.

Chakraborty, M. (2023, November). ASEAN's tryst with community-building: Towards comprehensive dispute settlement. In *Special Report: ASEAN's Critical Assessment and Practical Reforms*, (pp. 22-34). Asian Vision Institute & Konrad Adenauer Stiftung-Asian Vision Institute. https://www.kas.de/documents/264850/29101139/Special+Report+ASEAN%27s+Critical+Assessment+and+Practical+Reforms.pdf/

Chakrovorty, A. (2020). China's Soft Power in Bangladesh: A Comparative Studies. *American Journal of Social Sciences and Humanities*, *5*(1), 128–140. doi:10.20448/801.51.128.140

Chandmani, S. (2020). China's "Belt and Road Initiative Internationallly". Ulaanbaatar: People's Republic of China, Academy of Research and Institute for Strategic Studies.

Chang, E., & Kim, N. (2016). *The Myth of Soft Power in Asia*. E-International Relations. Retrieved from: https://www.e-ir.info/2016/05/24/the-myth-of-soft-power-in-asia/#_edn11

Chan, G. (2006). *China's Compliance in Global Affairs: Trade, Arms Control, Environmental ` Protection, Human Rights*. World Scientific Publishing Company.

Chanukvadze, S. (2024). *China: As an Emerging Superpower*. Georgian-American University.

Chatzky, A., & McBride, J. (2020). China's Massive Belt and Road Initiative. *Council on Foreign Relations*. https://www.cfr.org/backgrounder/chinas-massive-belt-androad-initiative

Chaziza, D. M. (2023). *China's Soft Power Projection Strategy: Confucius Institutes in the MENA Region*. https://besa-center.org/chinas-soft-power-projection-strategy-confucius-institutes-in-the-mena-region/

Chaziza, M. (2023). *China's Soft Power Projection Strategy: Confucius Institutes in the MENA Region*. BESA Centre Perspectives Paper No. 2,209.

Chaziza, M. (2021). Egypt in China's Maritime Silk Road Initiative: Relations cannot surmount realities. In J.-M. F. Blanchard (Ed.), *China's Maritime Silk Road Initiative* (pp. 255–283). Africa, and the Middle East. doi:10.1007/978-981-33-4013-8_9

Chebankova, E. (2017). Russia's idea of the multipolar world order: Origins and main dimensions. *Post-Soviet Affairs*, *33*(3), 217–234. doi:10.1080/1060586X.2017.1293394

Chen, P. (2021, February 9). *Improved Product Quality Populates Local Chinese Brands*. Intouch-Quality. https://www.intouch-quality.com/blog/improved-product-quality-populates-local-chinese-brands

Cheng, A. (2006). *Historia del Pensamiento Chino*. Bellaterra Edicions.

Cheng, C.-Y. (2007). Sino-Japanese Economic Relations: Interdependence and Conflict. In J. C. Hsiung (Ed.), *China and Japan at Odds* (pp. 81–94). Palgrave, Macmillan. doi:10.1057/9780230607118_5

Cheng, L. K. (2016). Three questions on China's "belt and road initiative". *China Economic Review*, *40*, 309–313. doi:10.1016/j.chieco.2016.07.008

Cheru, F. (2016). Emerging Southern powers and new forms of South–South cooperation: Ethiopia's strategic engagement with China and India. *Third World Quarterly*, *37*(4), 592–610. doi:10.1080/01436597.2015.1116368

Chimni, B. S. (2017). *International Law and World Order: A Critique of Contemporary Approaches* (2nd ed.). Cambridge University Press. doi:10.1017/9781107588196

China Daily. (2023, July 17). *Sino trade volumes soar with Middle East, Africa*. Retrieved from State Government: https://english.www.gov.cn/news/202307/17/content_WS64b49b48c6d0868f4e8ddd72.html

China, C. (2022). *Chronology of Chinese Dynasties*. Retrieved from: https://china.lu/en/our-history-26

Chinese Government. (2023, July 17). *Sino trade volumes soar with Middle East, Africa*. Retrieved from the State Council the People's Republic of China Offcial Website: https://english.www.gov.cn/news/202307/17/content_WS64b-49b48c6d0868f4e8ddd72.html#:~:text=Trade%20volume%20between%20China%20and,Emirates%2C%20Egypt%20and%20South%20Africa

Chitanava, N. (2021). *Global Challenges in the Unipolar World*. Iverioni.

Chunting, L. (2018, July 30). *Chinese-funded Vinh Tan Plant kicks off to boost power supply in Vietnam*. https://www.yicaiglobal.com/news/chinese-funded-vinh-tan-plant-kicks-off-to-boost-power-supply-in-vietnam

Chu, S. (2022). Whither Chinese IR? The Sinocentric Subject and the Paradox of Tianxia-Ism. *International Theory*, *14*(1), 19. doi:10.1017/S1752971920000214

City Nation Place. (2020, January 10). *Two Countries That Prove Nation Branding Works | Jose Torres, Bloom Consulting*. City Nation Place. https://www.citynationplace.com/two-countries-that-prove-nation-branding-works

Clarke, M. (2017). The Belt and Road Initiative: China's New Grand Strategy? *Asia Policy*, *1*(1), 71–79. doi:10.1353/asp.2017.0023

Clarke, M. T. (2022). Machiavelli's Virtuous Princes: Rhetoric, Power, and the Politics of Ironic Historiography. *The Journal of Politics*, *84*(1), 483–495. doi:10.1086/715596

Clement, C. (2022). *Common Causes and Different Patterns*. Harva University.

Cleverads. (2023). *TikTok Statistics 2023: 27 key figures you need to know*. https://cleverads.vn/blog/tiktok-statistics-2023/

Clinton, H. R. (2010). Redefining American Diplomacy and Development. Foreign Affairs.

Cloke, F. (2020). Soft Power Diplomacy on the African Continent: The Rise of China. *Journal of Social and Political Sciences, 3*(1). https://ssrn.com/abstract=3563515 doi:10.31014/aior.1991.03.01.165

Cohen, E. A. (2017). The big stick: the limits of soft power and the necessity of military force. Academic Press.

Coicaud, J.-M. (2016). The question of emotions and passions in mainstream international relations, and beyond. In Y. Ariffin, J.-M. Coicaud, & V. Popovski (Eds.), *Emotions in International Politics: Beyond Mainstream International Relations* (pp. 23–47). Cambridge University Press. doi:10.1017/CBO9781316286838.003

Cole, F. L. (1988). Content Analysis. *Clinical Nurse Specialist CNS*, *2*(1), 53–57. doi:10.1097/00002800-198800210-00025 PMID:3349413

Communication Theory. (n.d.). https://www.communicationtheory.org/authoritarian-theory/

Cook, H. (2013). *Performing Identity: Descriptive and Symbolic Representation in New Zealand and the United Kingdom* [Doctoral dissertation, University of Exeter]. University of Exeter Repository.

Cooke, J. G. (2009). China's Soft Power in Africa. In Chinese Soft Power and its implications for United States, Competition and Cooperation in the Developing World. Centre for Strategic and International Studies.

Copper, J. F. (2016). China's Foreign Aid and Investment Diplomacy in South Asia. In China's Foreign Aid and Investment Diplomacy, Volume II (pp. 49–91). Palgrave Macmillan US. doi:10.1057/9781137532725_2

Council on Foreign Relations in New York. (2023). *China's maritime disputes: 1895-2023*. https://www.cfr.org/timeline/chinas-maritime-disputes

Council on Foreign Relations. (2023, February 4). *U.S. China Relations*. Retrieved from Council on Foreign Relations: https://www.cfr.org/timeline/us-china-relations

Cox, R. W. (1983). Gramsci, Hegemony and International Relations: An Essay in Method. *Millennium*, *12*(2), 162–175. doi:10.1177/03058298830120020701

Crane, D. (2014a). Cultural globalization and the dominance of the American film industry: Cultural policies, national film industries, and transnational film. *International Journal of Cultural Policy*, *20*(4), 365–382. doi:10.1080/10286632.2013.832233

Cummings, M. C. (2003). *Cultural Diplomacy and the United States Government: A Survey*. Center for Arts and Culture.

Customs of the Islamic Republic of Iran. (2023). *Annual Statistics*. Available at: http://www.irica.ir/web-directiry/55335-html

D'Alessandro, C., & Zulu, L. C. (2017). From the Millennium Development Goals (MDGs) to the Sustainable Development Goals (SDGs): Africa in the post-2015 development agenda. A geographical perspective. *African Geographical Review*, *36*(1), 1–18. doi:10.1080/19376812.2016.1253490

Dagher, M. & Kaltenthaler, K. (2023). *The United States Is Rapidly Losing Arab Hearts and Minds Through Gaza War*. While Competitors Benefit. https://www.washingtoninstitute.org/policy-analysis/united-states-rapidly-losing-arab-hearts-and-minds-through-gaza-war-while

Dahl, R. A. (1957). The concept of power. *Behavioral Science*, *2*(3), 201–215. doi:10.1002/bs.3830020303

Daily Telegraph. (2014). *Iraq crisis: Iran pledges military help against ISIL as battle for Tikrit escalates*. https://www.telegraph.co.uk/news/worldnews/middleeast/iraq/10933934/Iraq-crisis-Iran-pledges-military-help-against-Isis-as-battle-for-Tikritescalates.ht

Dan, S., & Zhou, D. (2024, February 6). New productive forces need new industrialization. *China Daily*. https://global.chinadaily.com.cn/a/202402/06/WS65c17539a3104efcbdae9d5d.html#:~:text=Recently%2C%20%22new%20productive%20forces%22,advancing%20high%2Dquality%20economic%20development

DasK. N. (2022, March 23). https://www.reuters.com/world/chinese-foreign-minister-visit-india-friday-bloomberg-quint-2022-03-23/

Dautbašić, L. (2022). US Soft Power through Hollywood during Cold War: Rocky IV. *MAP Education and Humanities*, *2*(1), 1–7. doi:10.53880/2744-2373.2022.2.1.1

Davis, R., & Frate, P. (2020, May 6). *How China's Tech Giants Charged Ahead When Coronavirus Shut Down Cinemas*. Retrieved from Variety: https://variety.com/2020/biz/features/china-entertainment-industry-internet-online-theaters-coronavirus-1234598816/

De Castro, R. (2007, December). The Limits of Twenty-First Century Chinese Soft-Power Statecraft in Southeast Asia: The Case of the Philippines*. *Issues & Studies*, *43*(4), 77–116.

De Moraes Achcar, H. (2022). South-South cooperation and the re-politicization of development in health. *World Development, 149*, 105679. doi:10.1016/j.worlddev.2021.105679

De Zoysa, R., & Newman, O. (2002). Globalization, soft power and the challenge of Hollywood. *Contemporary Politics, 8*(3), 185–202. doi:10.1080/1356977022000025678

Dee, M. (2015). The Emergence of a Multipolar World. In The European Union in a Multipolar World (pp. 1–20). Palgrave Macmillan UK. doi:10.1057/9781137434203_1

DeHart, M. (2012). Remodelling the Global Development Landscape: The China Model and South–South cooperation in Latin America. *Third World Quarterly, 33*(7), 1359–1375. doi:10.1080/01436597.2012.691835

Deifallah, B. B. (2016). *Report on the Seminar on China-Arab Relations: The Case of Algeria - Laboratory of Research and Studies in International Relations*. University of Algiers.

deLisle, J. (2013). From economic development to what and why? China's evolving legal and political engagement between law and economic development. In *Rethinking Law and Development, Rethinking Law and Development: The Chinese Experience*. Taylor and Francis.

deLisle, J. (2020). Foreign Policy through Other Means: Hard Power, Soft Power, and China's Turn to Political Warfare to Influence the United States. *Orbis, 64*(2), 174–206. doi:10.1016/j.orbis.2020.02.004 PMID:32292215

Demgenski, P. (2020). Culinary Tensions: Chinese Cuisine's Rocky Road toward International Intangible Cultural Heritage Status. *Asian Ethnology, 79*(1).

Devonshire-Ellis, C. (2022, June 28). *silkroadbriefing*. https://www.silkroadbriefing.com/news/2022/06/28/china-has-urged-the-west-to-read-the-new-14th-brics-summit-declaration-carefully-this-is-what-it-says/

Di Cosmo, N. (2002). *Ancient China and Its Enemies: The Rise of Nomadic Power in East Asian History*. Cambridge University Press. doi:10.1017/CBO9780511511967

Dicicco, J., & Onea, T. (2023). *Great-Power Competition*. https://oxfordre.com/internationalstudies/view/10.1093/acrefore/9780190846626.001.0001/acrefore-9780190846626-e-756

Dijck, J. v. (2012). Tracing Twitter: The Rise of a Microblogging. *International Journal of Media and Cultural Politics*, 333–348.

Diko, N., & Sempijja, N. (2021). Does participation in BRICS foster South-South cooperation? Brazil, South Africa, and the Global South. *Journal of Contemporary African Studies, 39*(1), 151–167. doi:10.1080/02589001.2020.1837746

Dinnie, K. (2009). Nation Branding: Concepts, Issues, Practice (Reprinted). Butterworth-Heinemann.

Diplomacy, U. C. (2019). *The Soft Power 30, A Global Ranking of Soft Power 2019*. Portland: Designed by Portland's in-house Content & Brand team.

Dittmer, L., & Kim, S. (Eds.). (1993). *China's Quest for National Identity*. Cornell University Press. doi:10.7591/9781501723773

Dixon, J. M. (2017). Rhetorical adaptation and resistance to international norms. *Perspectives on Politics, 15*(1), 83–99. doi:10.1017/S153759271600414X

Dong, H. (2023a, September 17). *Chinese conglomerates eye railway expansion in Vietnam*. https://theinvestor.vn/chinese-conglomerates-eye-railway-expansion-in-vietnam-d6651.html#:~:text=He%20suggested%20that%20Power%20China,Hanoi%2DHai%20Phong%20rail%20lines

Dong, K. (2023, August 10). *China's infrastructure projects improving the Vietnamese life quality greatly*. https://www.ichongqing.info/2023/08/10/chinas-infrastructure-projects-improving-the-vietnamese-life-quality-greetly-insights/

Dong-A Ilboi. (2023, July 11). *Hallyu's Economic Impact Reaches 37 Trillion Won*. The Dong-A Ilboi. https://www.donga.com/en/article/all/20230711/4281547/1

Dongri, H. (2023, December 10). Enormous potential in economic and trade cooperation between China and Vietnam. *Global Times*. https://www.globaltimes.cn/page/202312/1303346.shtml

Dorj, H., & Shahidani, M. H. (2021). The Soft Impact of the Islamic Republic of Iran on Strengthening Shiite Power in the Iraqi Political Equation (2003-2020). *Soft Power*, *11*(25), 81–103.

Dorsey, J. M. (2016). China and the Middle East: Venturing into the maelstrom. S. Rajaratnam School of International Studies.

Do, T. H. (2019). *Vietnam and the South China Sea: Politics, security and legality*. Routledge.

Downe-Wamboldt, B. (1992). Content analysis: Method, applications, and issues. *Health Care for Women International*, *13*(3), 313–321. doi:10.1080/07399339209516006 PMID:1399871

Dreher, A., Fuchs, A., Parks, B., Strange, A. M., & Tierney, M. J. (2017). Aid, China, and Growth: Evidence from a New Global Development Finance Dataset. SSRN *Electronic Journal*. doi:10.2139/ssrn.3051044

Duan, S., & Qiu, F. (2023). China's soft power and higher education in South Asia:rationale, strategies and implications. *Asia Pacific Journal of Education*, *43*(3), 944–947. doi:10.1080/02188791.2022.2133474

Duara, P. (2019). The Chinese World Order in Historical Perspective. *China and the World*, *02*(04), 2019. doi:10.1142/S2591729319500238

Dubinsky, Y. (2022, February 8). *Nation Branding, Public Diplomacy and the Dystopian Beijing 2022 Winter Olympic Games*. USC Center on Public Diplomacy. https://uscpublicdiplomacy.org/blog/nation-branding-public-diplomacy-and-dystopian-beijing-2022-winter-olympic-games

Dunford, M., & Liu, W. (2019). Chinese perspectives on the Belt and Road Initiative. *Cambridge Journal of Regions, Economy and Society*, *12*(1), 145–167. doi:10.1093/cjres/rsy032

Dung, P. X., & Ho, B. T. E. (2022, September 13). How regime legitimation influences Vietnam's strategy toward US-China strategic rivalry. *International Journal of Asian Studies*, 1–20. doi:10.1017/S1479591422000286

Dunne, T. (2003). Society and Hierarchy in International Relations. *International Relations*, *17*(3), 303–320. doi:10.1177/00471178030173004

Dynon, N. (2014, January 11). *China and Nation Branding*. The Diplomat. https://thediplomat.com/2014/01/china-and-nation-branding/

Economic Times. (2022, January 14). conomictimes.indiatimes.com/news/economy/foreign-trade/india-china-trade-grows-to-record-125-billion-in-2021-despite-tensions-in-eastern-ladakh/articleshow/88900383.cms

Edelstein, D. M. (2022). Why Nations Rise: Narratives and the Path to Great Power. By Manjari Chatterjee Miller. New York: Oxford University Press, 2021. 208p. $99.00 cloth, $27.95 paper. *Perspectives on Politics*, *20*(1), 367–368. doi:10.1017/S1537592721003509

EinhornB. (2022). *Bloomberg*. https://www.bloomberg.com/news/features/2022-05-17/china-us-are-in-a-space-race-to-make-billions-from-mining-the-moon-s-minerals

Eliküçük Yıldırım, N., & Aslan, M. (2020). China's Charm Defensive: Image Protection by Acquiring Mass Entertainment. *Pacific Focus*, *35*(1), 141–171. doi:10.1111/pafo.12153

Elliott, J. H. (2002). *Imperial Spain, 1469-1716*. Penguin Books.

Embassy, U. S. (2023a). *American Spaces*. US Embassy in India. https://in.usembassy.gov/education-culture/american-spaces/

Embassy, U. S. (2023b, December 7). *Twenty-one new peace corps volunteers sworn-in to begin their service in Tanzania*. US Embassy in Tanzania. https://tz.usembassy.gov/twenty-one-new-peace-corps-volunteers-sworn-in-to-begin-their-service-in-tanzania/

En, L. B., Minh, V. N., & Cuc, N. T. K. (2022). Analyzing the influence of films on Chinese-learning students - Based on a survey of Nguyen Tat Thanh University students. *Van Hien University Scientific Journal, 8*(4), 143-150. https://vjol.info.vn/index.php/vhu/article/download/73193/62096/

Environment at Vinh Tan power complex under Scrutiny. (2018, February 26). *Vietnam Plus*. https://en.vietnamplus.vn/environment-at-vinh-tan-power-complex-under-scrutiny/126980.vnp#:~:text=Locals%20once%20blockaded%20the%20National,many%20perennial%20trees%20and%20crops

Escobar, P. (2020, April 2). China Rolls Out the Health Silk Road. *Asia Times*. https://asiatimes.com/2020/04/china-rolls-out-the-health-silk-road/

Eslami, M., & Papageorgiou, M. (2023). China's Increasing Role in the Middle East: Implications for Regional and International Dynamics. *Georgetown Journal of International Affairs, 24*(1).

Eslami, M., & Papageorgiou, M. (2023, June 2). *China's Increasing Role in the Middle East: Implications for Regional and International Dynamics*. Retrieved from Georgetown Journal of International Affairs: https://gjia.georgetown.edu/2023/06/02/chinas-increasing-role-in-the-middle-east-implications-for-regional-and-international-dynamics/

Evans, G., & Sahnoun, M. (2002). The Responsibility to Protect. *Foreign Affairs*, *81*(6), 99–110. doi:10.2307/20033347

Everycrsreport. (2010). *Iraq: Reconstruction Assistance*. https://www.everycrsreport.com/reports/RL31833.html

Fahmy, S. H., Wanta, W., & Nisbet, E. C. (2012). Mediated public diplomacy: Satellite TV in the Arab world and perception effects. *The International Communication Gazette*, *74*(8), 728–749. doi:10.1177/1748048512459144

Fairbank, J. K., & Goldman, M. (2006). China: A New History (2nd ed.). Belknap Press: An Imprint of Harvard University Press.

Fairclough, N. (2010). *Critical Discourse Analysis*. Routledge.

Fang, K., Wang, S., He, J., Song, J., Fang, C., & Jia, X. (2021). Mapping the environmental footprints of nations partnering the Belt and Road Initiative. *Resources, Conservation and Recycling*, *164*, 12. doi:10.1016/j.resconrec.2020.105068

Fan, Y. (2005). Can Nations Do Brand Marketing Like a Product? *PKU Business Review*, *9*, 1–7.

Fan, Y. (2006). Branding the Nation: What Is Being Branded? *Journal of Vacation Marketing*, *12*(1), 5–14. doi:10.1177/1356766706056633

Fan, Y. (2010). Branding the Nation: Towards a Better Understanding. *Place Branding and Public Diplomacy*, *6*(2), 97–103. doi:10.1057/pb.2010.16

Farouk, Y. (2023, March 30). *Riyadh's Motivations Behind the Saudi-Iran Deal*. Retrieved from Carnegie Endowment for International Peace: https://carnegieendowment.org/2023/03/30/riyadh-s-motivations-behind-saudi-iran-deal-pub-89421

Fenby, J. (2005). *Chiang Kai Shek: China's Generalissimo and the Nation He Lost*. Da Capo Press.

Feng, D. (2014). *Xi Jinping: Confucius Institutes belong to China and the world*. http://www.xinhuanet.com//politics/2014-09/27/c_1112652079.htm

Fengyuan, D. (2020, April 20). Three sayings to characterize China's role in the global pandemic fight. *CGTN*. https://news.cgtn.com/news/2020-04-20/Three-sayings-to-characterize-China-s-role-in-global-pandemic-fight-PGFh7IK5Ms/index.html

Ferrando, J., & Fonseca, J. (1871). *Historia de los PP. Dominicos en las islas Filipinas y en sus Misiones del Japón, China, Tung-king y Formosa, que comprende los sucesos principales de la historia general de este archipiélago, desde el descubrimiento y conquista de estas islas hasta el año de 1840* (Vol. III). Imprenta y Estereotipia de Manuel Rivadeneyra.

Fetscherin, M. (2010). The Determinants and Measurement of a Country Brand: The Country Brand Strength Index. *International Marketing Review, 27*(4), 466–479. doi:10.1108/02651331011058617

Figueroa, W. (2022). *China and Iran Since the 25-Year Agreement: The Limits of Cooperation*. Diplomat Media Inc. https://thediplomat.com

Financial Tribune. (2023). *Exports to Iraq Hit Record High of $10b in FY 2022-23*. https://financialtribune.com/articles/domestic-economy/117826/exports-to-iraq-hit-record-high-of-10b-in-fy-2022-23

Fletcher, T. (2016). The Naked Diplomat: Understanding Power and Politics in the Digital Age. HarperCollins UK.

Flores, W. L. (2023, September 20). *School of Economics and Management, Tsinghua University, China*. Retrieved from China Daily Global: https://regional.chinadaily.com.cn/en/2023-09/20/c_926787.htm#:~:text=In%202020%2C%20the%20economically%20rising,market%20of%202%20billion%20people

Folch Fornesa, D. (2008). Biografía de Fray Martín de Rada. *Revista Huarte de San Juan. Geografía e Historia, 15*, 33–63.

Foot, R. (2020). *China, the UN, and Human Protection: Beliefs, Power, Image*. Oxford University Press. doi:10.1093/oso/9780198843733.001.0001

Ford, C.A., (2015). *The mind of empire: China's History and Modern Foreign Relations*. Academic Press.

Forsberg, T., Heller, R., & Wolf, R. (2014). Introduction: Russia and the Quest for Status. *Communist and Post-Communist Studies, 47*(3–4), 261–268. doi:10.1016/j.postcomstud.2014.09.007

Foucault, M. (1995). *Discipline and Punish: The Birth of the Prison* (2nd ed.). Vintage Books.

Freeman, C. W. Jr. (1997). *Arts of Power: Statecraft and Diplomacy*. United States Institute of Peace.

Fulton, X. Q. (2017). China-Gulf Economic Relationship under the "Belt and Road" Initiative. *Asian Journal of Middle Eastern and Islamic Studies, 11*(3), 678.

Fung, C. J. (2023). *China's Small Steps into UN Peacekeeping Are Adding Up*. IPI Global Observatory. Retrieved from: https://theglobalobservatory.org/2023/05/chinas-small-steps-into-un-peacekeeping-are-adding-up/

Fung, C. (2019). *China and Intervention at the UN Security Council. Reconciling Status*. Oxford University Press. doi:10.1093/oso/9780198842743.001.0001

Gallarotti, G. M. (2011). Soft power: what it is, why it is important, and the conditions for, its effective use. Wesleyan University, Department of Government.

Gallarotti, G. M. (2015). Smart power: Definitions, importance, and effectiveness. *The Journal of Strategic Studies, 38*(3), 245–281. doi:10.1080/01402390.2014.1002912

Gallarotti, G. M. (2022). Pedagogical offensives: Soft power, higher education and foreign policy. *Journal of Political Power*, *15*(3), 495–513. doi:10.1080/2158379X.2022.2127276

GAO. (2005). *Information Technology Exchange Program*. Retrieved from: https://www.gao.gov/ products/GAO-07-216

Garib, E. (2022). *American and Arab media*. Arab Future Magazine.

Garishvili, M. (2019). *Introduction to the Philosophy of Law. Course of Lectures*. TSU.

Garlick, J. (2020). The Regional Impacts of China's Belt and Road Initiative. *Journal of Current Chinese Affairs*, *49*(1), 3–13. doi:10.1177/1868102620968848

Gautam, P., Singh, B., Singh, S., Bika, S. L., & Tiwari, R. P. (2023). Education as a soft power resource: A systematic review. *Heliyon*, *23736*. Advance online publication. doi:10.1016/j.heliyon.2023.e23736

Gedda, G. (2002). Radio Sawa: Music as a Tool. *Foreign Service Journal*, 53-56.

Gegout, C., & Suzuki, S. (2020). China, Responsibility to Protect, and the Case of Syria: From Sovereignty Protection to Pragmatism. *Global Governance*, *26*(3), 379–402. doi:10.1163/19426720-02603002

Geranmayeh, E. (2017). Iran's strategy against the Islamic State. *ECFR Council*. https://www.ecfr.eu/article/commentary_irans_strategy_against_the_islamic_state320

Gil, J. (2017). *Soft Power and the Worldwide Promotion of Chinese Language Learning, The Confucius Institute Project*. Channel View Publications.

Gill, S., & David, L. (1988). *The Global Economy: Perspectives, Problems and Policies*. Harwester Wheatsheaf.

Gill, B., & Huang, Y. (2006). Sources and Limits of Chinese "soft" power. *Survival*, *48*(2), 17–36. doi:10.1080/00396330600765377

Ginsburg, T. (2020). Authoritarian International Law? *The American Journal of International Law*, *114*(2), 221–260. doi:10.1017/ajil.2020.3

Girard, M. (1999). *States, Diplomacy and Image Making: What Is New? Reflections on Current British and French Experiences*. A Conference on Image, State and International Relations, London School of Economics.

Glaser, B. (2014, December 3). *Chinese Foreign Policy under Xi Jinping: Continuity and Change*. Retrieved from Harvard: https://projects.iq.harvard.edu/files/asia-center/files/glaser_-_12-3-2014.pdf

Glaser, B. S., & Murphy, M. E. (2009). Soft power with Chinese characteristics. In C. McGiffert (Ed.), *Chinese soft power and its implications for the United States: competition and cooperation in the developing world: a report of the CSIS smart power initiative* (pp. 10–26). CSIS.

Global Energy Monitor. (2023). *International Chinese coal projects*. https://www.gem.wiki/International_Chinese_coal_projects

Godwin, M., Talabany, S., Shelley, J., Verelst-Way, T., & El-Badawy. (2022). How to not lose friends and influence in the Middle East: The narratives advancing Russia and China's soft power. Tony Blair Institute of Global Change.

Goh, E. (2007-2008). Great powers and hierarchical order in Southeast Asia: Analyzing regional security strategies. *International Security*, *32*(3), 113–157. doi:10.1162/isec.2008.32.3.113

Goh, E. (2019). Contesting Hegemonic Order: China in East Asia. *Security Studies*, *28*(3), 614–644. doi:10.1080/09636412.2019.1604989

González de Mendoza, J. (2008). *Historia del Gran Reino de la China*. Editorial Miraguano.

González, J. M. (1955). *Un Misionero Diplomático. Vida del padre Victorio Riccio en el tercer centenario de su primera entrada en China (1655-1955)*. Studium.

Government Portal of Vietnam. (2024). *Announcement of 2024 Chinese Government Scholarships*. https://baochinhphu.vn/thong-bao-hoc-bong-chinh-phu-du-hoc-trung-quoc-nam-2024-102231124161756527.htm

Govil, N. (2021). Hollywood. *BioScope: South Asian Screen Studies, 12*(1–2), 98–101. doi:10.1177/09749276211026070

Graham, S., & Weiner, B. (1996). Theories and principles of motivation. Handbook of Educational Psychology, 4(1), 63-84.

Gramsci, A. (1971). Prison notebooks. Elec Book.

Gramsci, A. (2021). Cahiers de Prison: Anthologie. Gallimard.

Gray, C. (2015). *The Limits of Force. In RCADI* (Vol. 376). Brill.

Grieger, G. (2018). EPRS-European Parliamentary Research Service. *China's Arctic Policy*. European Union. Retrieved from: https://www.europarl.europa.eu/RegData/etudes/BRIE/2018/620231/EPRS_BRI(2018)620231_EN.pdf

Grünbacher, A. (2012). Cold-War Economics: The Use of Marshall Plan Counterpart Funds in Germany, 1948–1960. *Central European History, 45*(4), 697–716. doi:10.1017/S0008938912000659

Guardian. (2020, April 7). China outraged after Brazil minister suggests Covid-19 is part of 'plan for world domination. *Guardian*. https://www.theguardian.com/world/2020/apr/07/china-outraged-after-brazil-minister-suggests-covid-19-is-part-of-plan-for-world-domination#maincontent

Gülseven, Y. (2023). China's Belt and Road Initiative and South-South Cooperation. *Journal of Balkan & Near Eastern Studies, 25*(1), 102–117. doi:10.1080/19448953.2022.2129321

Guobin, Y. (2016). The Power of the Internet in China: Citizen Activism Online. *International Journal of Communication, 4*, 804-807.

Gupta, A. K. (2013). Soft Power of the United States, China, and India: A Comparative Analysis. *Indian Journal of Asian Affairs, 26*(2), 37–57. https://www.jstor.org/stable/43550355

Hagstrom, L., & Nordin, A. H. M. (2020). China's "Politics of Harmony" and the Quest for Soft Power in International Politics. *International Studies Review, 22*(3), 507–525. doi:10.1093/isr/viz023

Hai, D. T. (2021, May 26). Vietnam and China: Ideological bedfellows, strange dreamers. *Journal of Contemporary East Asia Studies, 10*(2), 162–182. doi:10.1080/24761028.2021.1932018

Hairon, C. T. (2016). Education Reform in China: Toward Classroom Communities. *Article*.

Halmstad, H. I. (2012). *Sino-Indian Relations:Complex Challenges in a Complex Relationship*. https://www.diva-portal.org/smash/get/diva2:543006/FULLTEXT01.pdf

Hamid, H. K. (2006). Development of Arab-Chinese Relations. *Journal of Political Science*, (33), 160.

Hanban. (2016, November 6). *About Confucius Institutes & Hanban*. Retrieved from International Education Exchange Information Platform: http://www.ieeip.cn/bbx/1071727-1123792.html?id=27381&newsid=715399

Hans, M. (2015). *Politics among nations*. McGraw-Hill.

Hao, A. W., Paul, J., Trott, S., Guo, C., & Wu, H.-H. (2019). Two Decades of Research on Nation Branding: A Review and Future Research Agenda. *International Marketing Review*, *38*(1), 46–69. doi:10.1108/IMR-01-2019-0028

Hartig, F. (2012). Confucius Institutes and the Rise of China. *Journal of Chinese Political Science*, *17*(1), 53–76. doi:10.1007/s11366-011-9178-7

Hatef, A., & Luqiu, L. R. (2018). Where does Afghanistan fit in China's grand project? A content analysis of Afghan and Chinese news coverage of the One Belt, One Road initiative. *The International Communication Gazette*, *80*(6), 551–569. doi:10.1177/1748048517747495

Haug, S., & Kamwengo, C. M. (2023). Africa beyond 'South-South cooperation': A frame with limited resonance. *Journal of International Development*, *35*(4), 549–565. doi:10.1002/jid.3690

Haynes, J. (Ed.). (2008). *Routledge Handbook of Religion and Politics*. Routledge. doi:10.4324/9780203890547

Hazarika, O. B., & Mishra, V. (2016). Soft Power Contestation between India and China in South Asia. *Indian Foreign Affairs Journal*, *11*(2), 139–152. https://www.jstor.org/stable/45341093

Hehir, A. (2017). Building Theory and Practice. Routledge Taylor and Fransis Group.

Heilman, S., & Schmidt, D. (2014). *China's Foreign Political and Economic Relations: An Unconventional Global Power*. Rowman & Littlefield Publishers.

He, L., Wang, R., & Jiang, M. (2020). Evaluating the Effectiveness of China's Nation Branding with Data from Social Media. *Global Media and China*, *5*(1), 3–21. doi:10.1177/2059436419885539

Heng, Y. (2009). Mirror, mirror on the wall, who is the softest of them all? Evaluating Japanese and Chinese strategies in the 'soft' power competition era. *International Relations of the Asia-Pacific*, *10*, 275–304. doi:10.1093/irap/lcp023

Henry, F. A. (2015). *The Paradox of "Winning the War of Ideas" in the 21st Century*. U.S. Army War College.

Heritage, A., & Lee, P. K. (2020). *Order, Contestation and Ontological Security-sSeeking in the South China Sea*. Palgrave Macmillan. doi:10.1007/978-3-030-34807-6

Hernández, B. (Ed.). (2019). Transocéanos. Viajes culturales en los mundos conocidos (siglos XVI-XVIII). Centro para la Edición de los Clásicos Españoles.

Herrera, R. (2005). Fifty years after the Bandung conference: Towards a revival of the solidarity between the peoples of the South? Interview with Samir Amin. *Inter-Asia Cultural Studies*, *6*(4), 546–556. doi:10.1080/14649370500316844

Herrero, A. G., & Xu, J. (2019). *Countries' perceptions of China's Belt and Road Initiative: A big data analysis* (No. 2019-59). HKUST IEMS Working Paper.

Hiep, L. H. (2013, December). Vietnam's hedging strategy against China since normalization. *Contemporary Southeast Asia*, *35*(3), 333–368. doi:10.1355/cs35-3b

Hillman, J. (2018, January 25). *China's Belt and Road Initiative: Five Years Later*. Retrieved from Center for Strategic International Studies: https://www.csis.org/analysis/chinas-belt-and-road-initiative-five-years-later

Hindustan Times. (2024, February 23). Jaishankar cautions against this 'mind game' by China: Raisina Dialogue 2024. https://www.hindustantimes.com/india-news/jaishankar-cautions-against-this-mind-game-by-china-i-dont-think-we-should-play-it-101708666270969.html

Hoa, N. T. P. (2023). *China's neighborhood diplomacy under Xi Jinping through the case of Vietnam, Myanmar, Cambodia*. Social Sciences Publishing House.

Hobson, J., & Zhang, S. (2022). The Return of the Chinese Tribute System? Re-viewing the Belt and Road Initiative. *Global Studies Quarterly*, *2*(4), ksac074. Advance online publication. doi:10.1093/isagsq/ksac074

Hochberg, F. P. (2023, July 19). Cultural diplomacy is an essential US strategy. *The Hill*. https://thehill.com/opinion/international/4103124-cultural-diplomacy-is-an-essential-us-strategy/

Hoey, J. (2007). *The Global Reach of Chinese Soft Power China's Rise and America's Decline? Naval Postgraduate School, Monterey, California* (Unpublished Thesis).

Hong, J., & Yan, S. (2017). Image Management in Cross-Cultural Communication. In B. Shan & Y. Liu (Eds.), *National Image and Intercultural Communication* (pp. 295–417). Social Sciences Academic Press.

Hossain, M. (2021). Coronavirus (COVID-19) pandemic: Pros and cons of China's soft power projection. *Asian Politics & Policy*, *13*(4), 597–620. doi:10.1111/aspp.12610

Hosseinpour, M. B. (2018). The public diplomacy of the United States of America in Iraq during the George D. Bush. *International Journal of Nations Research.*, *4*(40), 48–68.

Howarth, D. (2004). Towards a Heideggerian social science: Heidegger, Kisiel and Weiner on the limits of anthropological discourse. *Anthropological Theory*, *4*(2), 229–247. doi:10.1177/1463499604042817

Hsieh, H.-F., & Shannon, S. E. (2005). Three Approaches to Qualitative Content Analysis. *Qualitative Health Research*, *15*(9), 1277–1288. doi:10.1177/1049732305276687 PMID:16204405

Huan, D. V. (2023). *Vietnam - China investment, trade and tourism relations.* https://vneconomy.vn/quan-he-dau-tu-thuong-mai-du-lich-viet-nam-trung-quoc.htm

Huang, H. (2018). *China's image in the Belt and Road Initiative: case study of Pakistan and India.* Academic Press.

Huang, P. (2021). Beijing Consensus, or Chinese Experiences, or What? In *When China rules the world: the end of the western world and the birth of a new global order.* Penguin Books.

Huang, Y. (2016). Understanding China's Belt & Road initiative: Motivation, framework and assessment. *China Economic Review*, *40*, 314–321. doi:10.1016/j.chieco.2016.07.007

Huang, Y., & Ding, S. (2006). Dragon's underbelly: An analysis of China's soft power. *East Asia (Piscataway, N.J.)*, *23*(4), 22–44. doi:10.1007/BF03179658

Hui, M. (2023, July 27). *China's Reputation as a Leading Economic Power Is Fast Eroding.* Quartz. https://qz.com/china-s-reputation-as-a-leading-economic-power-is-fast-1850676199

Hui, V. (2010). *War and State Formation in Ancient China and Early Modern Europe.* Cambridge University Press. doi:10.1017/CBO9780511614545

Hu, L. (2019, October). External Communication Research of the Belt and Road Initiative——Comparative analysis of the relevant reports on the Belt and Road Initiative in China daily, CNN and CNBC. In *4th International Conference on Modern Management, Education Technology and Social Science (MMETSS 2019)* (pp. 615-623). Atlantis Press. 10.2991/mmetss-19.2019.125

Hung, V., & Son, T. (2021). *Major projects with slow progress, huge capital of Chinese contractors in Vietnam.* https://cafef.vn/nhung-dai-du-an-cham-tien-do-doi-von-khung-cua-nha-thau-trung-quoc-o-viet-nam-20211114120443818.chn

Hung, N. T. (2022). World *Economics and Politics.* National Political Publishing House Truth.

Hunter, A. (2009). Soft Power: China on the Global Stage. *Chinese Journal of International Politics, 2,* 373-398.

Hunter, A. (2009). Soft Power: China on the Global Stage. *The Chinese Journal of International Politics*, 2(3), 373–398. doi:10.1093/cjip/pop001

Huotari, M., Heilmann, S., Rudolf, M., & Buckow, J. (2014). China's Shadow. https://merics.org/en/report/chinas-shadow-foreign-policy

Hurd, I. (2019). *How to do Things with International Law*. Princeton University Press. doi:10.23943/princeton/9780691196503.001.0001

Hurst, A. (2023). *Introduction to Qualitative Research Methods*. Oregon State University. https://open.oregonstate.education/qualresearchmethods/

Hussain, M. E. (2021, April 3). Hollywood movies: American soft power apparatus. *Daily Observer*. https://www.observerbd.com/news.php?id=306338

Hussain, M., & Mehmood, S. (2018). Chinese Soft Power Approaches towards Pakistan: An Analysis of Socio, Economic and Political Impacts. *Malaysian Journal of International Relations*, 6(1), 47–66. doi:10.22452/mjir.vol6no1.5

Hussein, A. Q. (2016). *Smart Power Approaches as a Mechanism of International Change: The United States of*. Arab Center for Research and Policy Studies.

Hwang, E. (2008). *China's Soft Power and Growing Influence in Southeast Asia. Naval Postgraduate School, Monterey, California* (Unpublished Thesis).

IIACSS. (2019). *Iraq Recent Protests. Were they Unexpected*. https://iiacss.org/wpcontent/uploads/2019/10/October_protests_2019.pdf

IIE. (2023), Open Doors, at: https://www.iie.org/research-initiatives/open-doors/

Ikenberry, G. J., Wang, J. & Zhu, F. (2015). China, and the struggle for world order: ideas, traditions, historical legacies, and global visions. Palgrave Macmillan.

India Today. (2022, March 29). https://www.indiatoday.in/business/story/petrol-diesel-price-per-litre-hiked-century-delhi-fuel-rates-cities-1930720-2022-03-29

indiatoday.com. (2022, February 3). https://www.indiatoday.in/india/story/chinese-soldiers-drowned-river-galwan-clash-2020-austrialian-report-1908119-2022-02-03

Indra Bazarsad, P. C. (2021). *Sino – Mongolian economic interconnectivity: Big talks, little progress*. Friedrich-Ebert-Stiftung Mongolia & Mongolian Institute for Innovative Policies.

International Monetary Fund (IMF). (2023). *At a Crossroads: Sub-Saharan Africa's Economic Relations with China*. IMF.

Iran's Student Affairs Organization. (2023). *62 Iranian universities were recognized as accredited by the country of Iraq for the study of Iraqi students*. Available at: https://saorg.ir/portal/home/?news/235224/248672/285020/

IRIBNEWS. (2015). *Iran Series' popularity among Iraqi Kurdish people*. https://www.iribnews.ir/fa/news/2960040

IRNA. (2017). *Statistics of Iraqi Virtual users*. Available at: https://www.irna.ir/news/82786210/93

Islam, Md. N. (2023). China's Soft Power Strategy. In Power of Bonding and Non-Western Soft Power Strategy in Iran (pp. 69–104). Springer International Publishing. doi:10.1007/978-3-031-19867-0_3

Islam, M. N. (2022). Protecting China's interests overseas: Securitization and foreign policy. *International Affairs*, 98(4), 1486–1487. doi:10.1093/ia/iiac131

ISNA News Agency. (2009). *Al-Alam ranking among Arab news channels*. https://www.isna.ir/news/8806-00002.101886/%

Isoraite, M. (2009). Importance of strategic alliances. *Intellectual Economics*, 39-46.

Ittefaq, M., Ahmed, Z. S., & Martínez Pantoja, Y. I. (2023). China's Belt and Road Initiative and soft power in Pakistan: An examination of the local English-language press. *Place Branding and Public Diplomacy*, *19*(1), 1–14. doi:10.1057/s41254-021-00212-8

Jackson, R. L. II, Drummond, D. K., & Camara, S. (2007). What Is Qualitative Research? *Qualitative Research Reports in Communication*, *8*(1), 21–28. doi:10.1080/17459430701617879

Jacques, M. (2012). *When China rules the world: the end of the western world and the birth of a new global order*. Penguin Books.

Jadidi, A., Nasiri, S., & Barzin, S. (2022). Sources of soft power of the Islamic Republic of Iran in Iraq (2020-2010). Soft power. *Studies*, *11*(4), 29–54.

Jafari, A. A., & Nikravesh, M. (2015). Iran's cultural soft power resources in the Iraq. *Soft Power*, *5*(12), 29.

Jain, R. (2022). *China's Soft Power and Higher Education in South Asia Rationale, Strategies, and Implications* (1st ed.). Routledge. https://www.routledge.com/Chinas-Soft-Power-and-Higher-Education-in-South-Asia-Rationale-Strategies/Jain/p/book/9780367770389

Jain, S., & Chakrabarti, S. (2023). The Yin and Yang of China's Power: How the Force of Chinese Hard Power Limits the Quest and Effect of Its Soft Power. *Asian Perspective*, *47*(1), 145–166. doi:10.1353/apr.2023.0006

Jakhar, P. (2019, September 19). *Confucius Institutes: The growth of China's controversial cultural branch*. Retrieved from BBC: https://www.bbc.com/news/world-asia-china-49511231

Jang, G., & Paik, W. K. (2012). Korean Wave as Tool for Korea's New Cultural Diplomacy. *Advances in Applied Sociology*, *2*(3), 196–202. doi:10.4236/aasoci.2012.23026

Jargalsaikhan, M. (2014). Caveats for the Mongolia-China Strategic Partnership. *Asia Pacific Bulletin*.

Jervis, R. (1978, January). Cooperation under the security dilemma. *World Politics*, *30*(2), 167–214. doi:10.2307/2009958

Jia, Q. (2010). *Continuity and Change: China's Attitude tward Hard Power and Soft Power*. Brookings. Retrieved from: https://www.brookings.edu/articles/continuity-and-change-chinas-attitude-toward-hard-power-and-soft-power/

Jiang, W. (2007). Hu's Safari: China's Emerging Strategic Partnerships in Africa. *China Brief*, *7*(4), 50–64.

Jianming, Z. (2020). China and BRI: From Business to Geopolitics? In V. Talbot & U. Tramballi (Eds.), *Looking West*. Ledizioni. doi:10.14672/55262996

Jie, Y., & Wallace, J. (2021). What is China's Belt and Road Initiative (BRI)? *Chatham House*. https://www.chathamhouse.org

Jilin, X., & Ownby, D. (2018). *Rethinking China's Rise: A Liberal Critique*. Cambridge University Press.

Jinping, X. (2017, October 18). *Secure a Decisive Victory in Building a Moderately Prosperous Society in All Respects and Strive for the Great Success of Socialism with Chinese Characteristics for a New Era*. Delivered at the 19th National Congress of the Communist Party of China. http://www.xinhuanet.com/english/download/Xi_Jinping's_report_at_19th_CPC_National_Congress.pdf

Joint Statement between Vietnam and China. (2023, December 13). *VN Express*. https://www.vietnam.vn/en/tuyen-bo-chung-viet-nam-trung-quoc/

Jules, T. D., & Silva, M. M. de sá e. (2008). How Different Disciplines have Approached South-South Cooperation and Transfer. *Society for International Education Journal*, *5*(1), 45–64.

Jun, T., & Yanna, L. (2017, May 11). Interview: Vietnamese President looks forward to Belt and Road Forum in China. *Xinhua*. http://www.xinhuanet.com/english/2017-05/11/c_136273962.htm

Kagan, R. (2002). *Power and weakness* (Vol. 113). Hoover Institution.

Kamel, M. S. (2018). China's belt and road initiative: Implications for the Middle East. *Cambridge Review of International Affairs*, *31*(1), 76–95. doi:10.1080/09557571.2018.1480592

Kam-por, Y. (2010.) Confucian Views on War as Seen in the Gongyan Commentary on the Spring and Autumn Annals. *Dao, 9*, 97–111. https://doi.org/DOI 10.1007/s11712-009-9145

Kaneva, N. (2011). Nation Branding: Toward an Agenda for Critical Research. *International Journal of Communication, 5*, 117–141.

Kaplan, R. D. (2014). *Asia's cauldron: The South China Sea and the end of a stable Pacific*. Random House.

Karim, M., Kamal, R., & Haroon, O. (2019). China in Africa. In J. Syed & Y. H. Ying (Eds.), *China's Belt and Road Initiative in a Global Context*. Palgrave Macmillan Asian Business Series. Palgrave Macmillan. doi:10.1007/978-3-030-14722-8_10

Kathuria, S. (2022, April 13). The U.S. Should Stop Nickel and Diming India and Bangladesh. *Foreign Policy*. https://foreignpolicy.com/2022/04/13/us-india-bangladesh-trade-gsp/

Katzman, K. (2008). *Iran's Activities and Influence in Iraq*. https://www.files.ethz.ch/isn/118352/2007-12-26_Iran-Influence-Iraq.pdf

Kaufmann. (2021). *Open Government Partnership*. Brookings Institution.

Keating, V. C., & Kaczmarska, K. (2019). Conservative soft power: Liberal soft power bias and the 'hidden' attraction of Russia. *Journal of International Relations and Development*, *22*(1), 1–27. doi:10.1057/s41268-017-0100-6

Keegan, W. J., & Schlegelmilch, B. B. (2001). *Global Marketing Management: A European Perspective*. Financial Times Prentice Hall.

Keohane & Nye, Jr. (1987). Power and interdependence revisited. *International Organisation, 41*(4).

Khuhro, A. A. (2019). Rising geo-strategic competition between United States and China: A case study of South Asia in the emerging global order. *IJASOS-International E-Journal of Advances in Social Sciences*, 635–641. doi:10.18769/ijasos.476447

Kiet, A. (2022, January 19). Vietnam's largest waste-to-power plant to begin operation from January 20. *Hanoi Times*. https://hanoitimes.vn/vietnams-largest-waste-to-power-plant-goes-into-operation-from-jan-20-319806.html

Kiet, L. H., & Tuyen, N. V. (2023). Vietnam's geopolitical position for the United States in the strategy of containing China's hegemonic ambitions. *Science and Technology Journal - Da Nang University, 21*(8), 63-69. https://jst-ud.vn/jst-ud/article/view/8630

Kim, B. (2011). Trade and tribute along the Silk Road before the third century AD. *Journal of Central Eurasian Studies*, 1-24.

Kim, M. (2009). Evaluating US soft power in Asia: Military, economic and sociopolitical relationships between Asia and the United States. *Contemporary Politics*, *15*(3), 337–353. doi:10.1080/13569770903132540

Kivimäki, T. (2014). *The long peace of East Asia*. Ashgate.

Klotz, A., & Prakash, D. (Eds.). (2008). *Qualitative Methods in International Relations: 1 Pluralist Guide*. Palgrave Macmillan. doi:10.1057/9780230584129

Knippa, M. (2016). Features of Human Anatomy: Marshall McLuhan on Technology in the Global Village. *Lutheran Mission Matters, 24*(3), 371–384.

Knott, K. (2023, January 25). *Could Confucius Institutes Return to U.S. Colleges?* Retrieved from Inside Higher Ed: https://www.insidehighered.com/news/2023/01/26/report-proposes-waiver-criteria-confucius-institutes

Kohlenberg, P. J., & Godehardt, N. (2021). Locating the 'South' in China's connectivity politics. *Third World Quarterly, 42*(9), 1963–1981. doi:10.1080/01436597.2020.1780909

Kolb, A. (2018). *The UN Security Council Members' Responsibility to Protect. A Legal Analysis*. Springer. doi:10.1007/978-3-662-55644-3

Kong, D. (2015) *Imaging China: China's cultural diplomacy through loan exhibitions to British museums* (Thesis PhD). School of Museum Studies University of Leicester.

Koskenniemi, M. (2004). International law and hegemony: A reconfiguration. *Cambridge Review of International Affairs, 17*(2), 197–218. doi:10.1080/0955757042000245852

Kothari, M. (2018). Rereading the Media War Case in Iraq: America and the Rapid Media Response Team. *Middle East Studies Quarterly, 16*(1), 33-54.

Kotler, P. (2000). Marketing Management (Millennium ed). Prentice Hall.

Kotler, P., Jatusripitak, S., & Maesincee, S. (1997). *The Marketing of Nations: A Strategic Approach to Building National Wealth*. Free Press.

Krishnamoorthi, R. (2023, September 29). The U.S. Cannot Afford to Lose a Soft-Power Race With China. *Foreign Policy*. https://foreignpolicy.com/2023/09/29/congress-shutdown-us-china-ccp-soft-power-competition-biden-xi-jinping-beijing/

Krishnan, A. (2021, December 22). *The Hindu*. https://www.thehindu.com/

Krishnan, A., & Bhattacherjee, K. (2023, August 24). China says will back Bangladesh against 'external interference.' *The Hindu*. https://www.thehindu.com/news/international/china-says-will-back-bangladesh-against-external-interference/article67231493.ece

Kucharčíková, A. (2011). Human Capital-Definitions and Accpoaches. *Human Resources Management & Ergonomics, 5*, 60.

Kugelman, M. (2023, May 31). The U.S. Ups the Ante in Bangladesh. *Foreign Affairs*. https://foreignpolicy.com/2023/05/31/us-bangladesh-visa-policy-election-democracy-promotion/

Kugler, J. (2006). The Asian Ascent: Opportunity for Peace or Precondition for War? *International Studies Perspectives, 7*(7), 36–42. doi:10.1111/j.1528-3577.2006.00228.x

Kunczik, M. (1997). *Images of Nations and International Public Relations*. Erlbaum.

Kurlantzick, J. (2007). *China's Charm Offensive in Southeast Asia*. Retrieved from: https://carnegieendowment.org/2007/04/24/charm-offensive-how-china-s-soft-power-is-transforming-world-pub-19126

Kurlantzick, J., & Minxin, P. (2006, June 13). *China's Soft Power in Southeast Asia: What Does It Mean for the Region, and for the U.S.?* Carnegie Endowment for International Peace. https://carnegieendowment.org/events/?fa=eventDetail&id=892

Kurlantzick, J. (2007). *Charm Offensive*. Yale University Press.

Kurlantzick, J. (2007). *Charm offensive: How China's soft power is transforming the world*. Yale University Press.

Kwak, J.-H. (2021). Global justice without self-centrism: Tianxia in dialogue on mount Uisan. *Dao, 20*(2), 289–307. doi:10.1007/s11712-021-09777-w

Lai, H. Y. L. (2012). China's Soft Power and International Relations. Taylor & Francis.

Lai, H. (2012). China's cultural diplomacy: going for soft power. In L. Hongyi & L. Yiyi (Eds.), *China's soft power and international relations* (pp. 83–103). Routledge Taylor & Francis Group. doi:10.4324/9780203122099-11

Lai, H., & Lu, Y. (2012). *China's Soft Power and International Relations* (1st ed.). Routledge. doi:10.4324/9780203122099

Laksmana, E. A. (2017). Pragmatic equidistance – how Indonesia manages its great power relations. In D. B. H. Denoon (Ed.), *The United States and the future of Southeast Asia* (pp. 113–135). New York University Press.

Lampton, D. M. (2008). *The Three Faces of Chinese Power, Might, Money, and Minds*. University of California Press. doi:10.1525/9780520941502

Lane, J. E., & Ersson, S. (2016). *Culture and politics: A comparative approach*. Routledge. doi:10.4324/9781315575452

Lao Viet Magazine. (2022). *Confucius Institute receives great attention from those who want to learn Chinese in Laos.* https://tapchilaoviet.org/van-hoa-xa-hoi/vien-khong-tu-duoc-quan-tam-lon-cua-nguoi-co-nhu-cau-hoc-tieng-trung-quoc-tai-lao-52371.html#:~:text=Gi%C3%A1m%20%C4%91%E1%BB%91c%20H%E1%BB%8Dc%20 vi%E1%BB%87n%20Kh%E1%BB%95ng%20t%E1%BB%AD%20cho%20bi%E1%BA%BFt%3A%20Ni%C3%AAn%20 kh%C3%B3a,l%C6%B0%E1%BB%A3ng%20ho%E1%BA%A1t%20%C4%91%E1%BB%99ng%20gi%E1%BA%A3ng%20 d%E1%BA%A1y

Laskar, R. H. (2020, June 13). *India: Hidustan Times*. https://www.hindustantimes.com/india-news/chinese-diplomat-links-ladakh-standoff-to-scrapped-art-370-creates-a-flutter/story-Jn0zkpbBFql6pcsdfKe82K.html

Lasswell, H. (1927). *Propaganda technique in the world war/Harold D. Lasswell*. Kegan Paul, Trench, Trubner & Co.

Latosh, S. (1992). *Westernization of the world*. Cairo: House of the Third World.

Le, H. (2023, August 31). Vietnam opposes China's new national map. *VN Express*. https://e.vnexpress.net/news/news/vietnam-opposes-china-s-new-national-map-4648426.html

Lecoutre, S. (2020). *the transatlantic security partnership*. EU International Relation and Diplomacy Studies.

Lee, L., & Wang, E. (2023, November 30). *China seeks 'concrete' roadmap for two-state solution to solve Gaza conflict*. Retrieved from Reuters: https://www.reuters.com/world/middle-east/china-calls-concrete-roadmap-two-state-solution-solve-gaza-conflict-2023-11-30/

Lee, S. (2009). *China's Soft Power: Its Limits and Potentials*. Issue Briefing No. MASI 2009-07.

Lee, Y. (2022, December 26). *Taiwan reports China's largest incursion yet to air defence zone*. Retrieved from Reuters: https://www.reuters.com/world/china/taiwan-says-43-chinese-air-force-planes-crossed-taiwan-strait-median-line-2022-12-26/

Lee, M., & Hao, Y. (2018). China's unsuccessful charm offensive: How South Koreans have viewed the rise of China over the past decade. *Journal of Contemporary China, 27*(114), 867–886. Advance online publication. doi:10.1080/10 670564.2018.1488103

Leino, J. (2021). Battle of the hearts: China's aim to become a soft (super)power and Europe's response. *European View, 20*(2), 211–219. doi:10.1177/17816858211055553

Lenczowski. (2019). Dulyural Diplomacy, Political Influence. *Integrated Strategy*, 26.

Leonard, M., Stead, C., & Smewing, C. (2002). *Public diplomacy*. Foreign Policy Centre.

Levenson, R. J. (1958). *Confucian China and Its Modern Fate: the problem of intellectual continuity*. Routledge.

Leverett, F., & Bader, J. (2005). Managing China-U.S. energy competition in the Middle East. *The Washington Quarterly*, *29*(1), 187–201. doi:10.1162/016366005774859643

Lever, M. W., Elliot, S., & Joppe, M. (2023). Pride and Promotion: Exploring Relationships Between National Identification, Destination Advocacy, Tourism Ethnocentrism and Destination Image. *Journal of Vacation Marketing*, *29*(4), 537–554. doi:10.1177/13567667221109270

Lewis, M. E., & Hsieh, M. (2017). Tianxia and the Invention of Empire in East Asia. In *Wang Bang Chinese Visions of World Order: Tianxia, Culture, and World Politics*. Duke University Press. doi:10.1215/9780822372448-002

Li, X. (2010). *Civil Liberties in China*. ABC-CLIO.

Li, X., & Lu, D. (2023). Conceptual Metaphors and Image Construction of China in the Space Probe Reports of China Daily: A Social Cognitive Approach. *Frontiers in Psychology, 14*. https://www.frontiersin.org/articles/10.3389/fpsyg.2023.1202988

Lian, H. (2006). *Taiwan Tongshi* [General History of Taiwan]. Huadong Shifan Daxue Chubanshe.

Library, China-US Focus. (2022). *Xi Jinping's Speech in Commemoration of the 2,565th Anniversary of Confucius' Birth - Library CHINA US Focus*. Retrieved from: http://library.chinausfocus.com/article-1534.html

Li, D., & Wang, C., Jiang, Y., R. Barnes, B., & Zhang, H. (2014). The Asymmetric Influence of Cognitive and Affective Country Image on Rational and Experiential Purchases. *European Journal of Marketing*, *48*(11/12), 2153–2175. doi:10.1108/EJM-09-2012-0505

Lieberthal, K. (2011, December 21). *The American Pivot to Asia*. Retrieved from Brookings: https://www.brookings.edu/articles/the-american-pivot-to-asia/

Lien, D., Oh, C. H., & Selmier, W. T. (2012). Confucius institute effects on China's trade and FDI: Isn't it delightful when folks afar study Hanyu? *International Review of Economics & Finance*, *21*(1), 147–155. doi:10.1016/j.iref.2011.05.010

Li, J. (2018). *Conceptualizing Soft Power Conversion Model of Higher Education*. doi:10.1007/978-981-13-0641-9

Li, J., & Xiaohong, T. (2016). A global experiment in the internationalization of Chinese universities: Models, experiences, policies, and prospects of the Confucius Institutes' first decade. *Chinese Education & Society*, *49*(6), 411–424. doi:10.1080/10611932.2016.1262682

Li, L., Willett, T. D., & Zhang, N. (2012). The Effects of the Global Financial Crisis on China's Financial Market and Macroeconomy. *Economic Research International*, *2012*, 1–6. doi:10.1155/2012/961694

Lim, L., & Bergin, J. (2020). *The China Story: Reshaping the World's Media*. International Federation of Journalists. https://findanexpert.unimelb.edu.au/scholarlywork/1460412-the-china-story--reshaping-the-world's-media

Linetsky, Z. (2023). *China Can't Catch a Break in Asian Public Opinion*. Foreign Policy. Retrieved from: https://foreignpolicy.com/2023/06/28/china-soft-power-asia-culture-influence-korea-singapore/

Ling, L. H. M. (2020). Squaring the Circle: China's "Belt and Road Initiative" (BRI) and the Ancient Silk Roads. In Critical Reflections on China's Belt & Road Initiative (pp. 23–40). Springer Nature Singapore. doi:10.1007/978-981-13-2098-9_2

Lin, J. Y., & Wang, Y. (2017). Development beyond aid: Utilizing comparative advantage in the belt and road initiative to achieve win-win. *Journal of Infrastructure. Policy and Development*, *1*(2), 149. doi:10.24294/jipd.v1i2.68

Li, Q., Han, Y., Li, Z., Wei, D., & Zhang, F. (2021). The influence of cultural exchange on international trade: An empirical test of Confucius Institutes based on China and the 'Belt and Road' areas. *Ekonomska Istrazivanja*, *34*(1), 1033–1059. doi:10.1080/1331677X.2020.1819849

Liu, T. (2018). *Public Diplomacy: China's Newest Charm Offensive*. https://www.e-ir.info/2018/12/30/public-diplomacy-chinas-newest-charm-offensive/

Liu, T.-T. T. (2018). *Public Diplomacy: China's Newest Charm Offensive*. E-international Relations. Retrieved from: https://www.e-ir.info/2018/12/30/public-diplomacy-chinas-newest-charm-offensive/

Liu, Y., Liu, B., Lei, L., & Liu, T. (2023). *Deconstruction of the Images of Fu Manchu in American Popular Culture in the First Half of the Twentieth Century*. doi:10.2991/978-2-38476-130-2_3

Liu, F. (2020). The recalibration of Chinese assertiveness: China's responses to the Indo-Pacific challenge. *International Affairs*, *96*(1), 9–27. doi:10.1093/ia/iiz226

Liu, J. (2006). The Evolution of Tianxia Cosmology and Its Philosophical Implications. *Frontiers of Philosophy in China*, *1*(4), 517–538. Advance online publication. doi:10.1007/s11466-006-0023-6

Livemint. (2021, December 17). https://www.livemint.com

Li, X., & Chitty, N. (2009). Reframing National Image: A Methodological Framework. *Conflict & Communication*, *8*(2), 1–11.

Li, X., & Worm, V. (2011, March). Building China's Soft power for a Peaceful Rise. *Journal of Chinese Political Science*, *16*(1), 69–89. doi:10.1007/s11366-010-9130-2

Lowenheim, O., & Heimann, G. (2008). Revenge in international politics. *Security Studies*, *17*(4), 685–724. doi:10.1080/09636410802508055

Lukes, S. (2004). *Power: A Radical View* (2nd ed.). Palgrave Macmillan.

Lum, T., Morrison, W., & Vaughn, B. (2008). *China's "Soft Power" in Southeast Asia*. CRS Report for Congress.

Luong, D. T. H. (2022). *China's soft power: Impacts and implications for Vietnam*. National Political Publishing House Truth.

Machida, S. (2010). U.S. Soft Power and the "China Threat": Multilevel Analyses. *Asian Politics & Policy*, *2*(3), 351–370. doi:10.1111/j.1943-0787.2010.01198.x

Mai, N. (2023, October 27). "Grey zone" activities cast a shadow over cooperation and peaceful prospects in East Sea. *Hanoi Times*. https://hanoitimes.vn/grey-zone-activities-cast-a-shadow-over-cooperation-and-peaceful-prospects-in-east-sea-325164.html

Maizland, L. (2024, February 8). *Why China-Taiwan Relations Are So Tense*. Retrieved from Council on Foreign Relations: https://www.cfr.org/backgrounder/china-taiwan-relations-tension-us-policy-biden#chapter-title-0-5

Malik, J. M. (2001). South Asia in China's Foreign Relations. *Pacifica Review*, *13*(1), 73–90. doi:10.1080/13239100120036054

Manafih, A. (2014). Determinants of China's Foreign Policy in the Middle East after the Arab Movement. *Research Journal - Publications of the Khaled Hassan Foundation - Studies and Research Center*, 22.

Mancall, M. (2013). The Ch'ing Tribute System: An Interpretive Essay. In J. K. Fairbank (Ed.), *The Chinese World Order: Traditional China's Foreign Relations*. Harvard University Press.

Mannan, M. (2019). *"Shining" or "Suffering" South Asia?* China's South Asian Footprints., doi:10.1007/978-981-13-7240-7_3

Markleku, A. (2019). Education as an instrument for China's soft power. *TRT World.* https://www.trtworld.com/opinion/education-as-an-instrument-for-china-s-soft-power-25699

Markovic, S., Gyrd-Jones, R., von Wallpach, S., & Lindgreen, A. (2022). *Research Handbook on Brand Co-Creation: Theory, Practice and Ethical Implications*. Edward Elgar Publishing. doi:10.4337/9781839105425

Marques, A. C. (2023). *Women's economic empowerment in Iraq: a double-edged sword?* https://cfri-irak.com/en/article/womens-economic-empowerment-in-iraq-a-double-edged-sword-2023-11-08

Marsh, V., Madrid-Morales, D., & Paterson, C. (2023). Global Chinese media and a decade of change. *The International Communication Gazette*, *85*(1), 3–14. doi:10.1177/17480485221139459

Martínez-Sicluna y Sepúlveda, C. (Ed.). (2020). *Autoridad, Poder y Jurisdicción en la Monarquía Hispánica*. Dykinson. doi:10.2307/j.ctv153k3z8

Maslow, A., & Lewis, K. J. (1987). Maslow's hierarchy of needs. *Salenger Incorporated*, *14*(17), 987–990.

Masoudi, H., & Nourian, A. (2023). Arbaeen March and Its Effect on Iran's Soft Power in Iraq:Practice Theory. *Contemporary Researches on Islamic Revolution*, *5*(15), 1–18.

Mathebula, N. C., & Sekgololo, M. J. (2023). Africa-China Relations: A Case of Foreign Direct Investment and the Democratic Republic of Congo's Mining Sector. *African Review (Dar Es Salaam, Tanzania)*, (Special Issue), 1–15. doi:10.1163/1821889x-bja10083

Mattingly, D. C., & Sundquist, J. (2023). When does public diplomacy work? Evidence from China's "wolf warrior" diplomats. *Political Science Research and Methods*, *11*(4), 921–929. doi:10.1017/psrm.2022.41

Mavrodieva, R., Rachman, Harahap, & Shaw. (2019). Role of Social Media as a Soft Power Tool in Raising Public Awareness and Engagement in Addressing Climate Change. *Climate (Basel)*, *7*(10), 122. doi:10.3390/cli7100122

Mawdsley, E. (2012a). *From recipients to donors: Emerging powers and the changing development landscape*. Zed Books. doi:10.5040/9781350220270

Mawdsley, E. (2012b). The changing geographies of foreign aid and development cooperation: Contributions from gift theory. *Transactions of the Institute of British Geographers*, *37*(2), 256–272. doi:10.1111/j.1475-5661.2011.00467.x

Mawdsley, E. (2019). South–South Cooperation 3.0? Managing the consequences of success in the decade ahead. *Oxford Development Studies*, *47*(3), 259–274. doi:10.1080/13600818.2019.1585792

Maxim, K. (2023). Character of PRC Soft Policy and Mongolia. Internationak Studies, 46(115), 65.

McCourt, D. M., & Mudge, S. L. (2023). Anything but Inevitable: How the Marshall Plan Became Possible. *Politics & Society*, *51*(4), 463–492. doi:10.1177/00323292221094084

Mcrbride, J., Berman, N., & Chatzky, A. (2023, February 2). *China's Massive Belt and Road Initiative*. Retrieved from Council on Foreign Relations: https://www.cfr.org/backgrounder/chinas-massive-belt-and-road-initiative

Mead, W. R. (2004, March/April). America's Sticky Power. *Foreign Policy*, (141), 46–53. doi:10.2307/4147548

Medeiros, E. S. (2016). *Chinese Foreign Policy: The Africa Dimension*. ChinaAfrica.

Mehr news agency. (2023). *More than 50 thousand Iraqi students study in Iran.* Available at: https://www.mehrnews.com/news/5900848

Meidan, Z. D. (2015). China and the Middle East in a New Energy Landscape. The Royal Institute of International Affairs.

Meidan, Z. D. (2015). *China and the Middle East in a New Energy Landscape.* The Royal Institute of International Affairs, Chatham House.

Melissen, J. (2005). *The New Public Diplomacy.* Palgrave Macmillan.

Men, S. T. (2016). *China in the Xi Jinping Era.* Springer International Publishing.

Mengying, B. (2023, December 24). *2023: The year of resurgence and success in Chinese cinema.* Retrieved from Global Times: https://www.globaltimes.cn/page/202312/1304222.shtml

Merkelsen, H., & Rasmussen, R. K. (2016). Nation Branding as an Emerging Field – An Institutionalist Perspective. *Place Branding and Public Diplomacy, 12*(2–3), 99–109. doi:10.1057/s41254-016-0018-6

MFA of China. (2022). *Harmonious World: China's Ancient Philosophy for New International Order.* Retrieved from: https://www.mfa.gov.cn/ce/cena//eng/xwdt/t410254.htm

Minh, P. V. (2023). *Developing supporting industries in the context of integration.* https://kinhtevadubao.vn/phat-trien-nganh-cong-nghiep-ho-tro-trong-boi-canh-hoi-nhap-27278.html

Ministry of Finance of Vietnam. (2020). *Attracting and using Chinese ODA for infrastructure development in Vietnam and recommendations.* https://mof.gov.vn/webcenter/portal/vclvcstc/pages_r/l/chi-tiet-tin?dDocName=MOFUCM172887

Ministry of Finance of Vietnam. (2023). *Vietnam attracts over $13.4 billion in FDI in 6 months.* https://www.mof.gov.vn/webcenter/portal/ttpltc/pages_r/l/chi-tiet-tin-ttpltc?dDocName=MOFUCM279819

Ministry of Foreign Affairs of the People's Republic of China (FMPRC). (2015, March 28). *Vision and actions on jointly building Silk Road Economic Belt and 21st-Century Maritime Silk Road.* https://en.ndrc.gov.cn/newsrelease/201503/t20150330_669367.html

Ministry of Foreign Affairs of the People's Republic of China (FMPRC). (2022, October 20). *Foreign Ministry Spokesperson Wang Wenbin's Regular Press Conference.* https://www.fmprc.gov.cn/mfa_eng/xwfw_665399/s2510_665401/2511_665403/202210/t20221020_10788936.html

Ministry of Foreign Affairs of the People's Republic of China (FMPRC). (2022a, October 25). *Full Text of the Report to the 20th National Congress of the Communist Party of China.* https://www.fmprc.gov.cn/eng/zxxx_662805/202210/t20221025_10791908.html

Ministry of Foreign Affairs of the People's Republic of China (FMPRC). (2023, October 18). *Building an open, inclusive and interconnected world for common development.* Keynote Speech by H. E. Xi Jinping, President of the People's Republic of China at the opening ceremony of the Third Belt and Road Forum for International Cooperation. http://www.beltandroadforum.org/english/n101/2023/1018/c124-1175.html

Ministry of Foreign Affairs of the People's Republic of China (FMPRC). (2023a, October 26). *The 21st Senior Officials' Meeting on the Implementation of the Declaration on the Conduct of Parties in the South China Sea Held in Beijing.* https://www.mfa.gov.cn/mfa_eng/wjbxw/202310/t20231027_11169603.html

Ministry of Foreign Affairs of the People's Republic of China. (2021). *Speech by H.E. Xi Jinping President of the People's Republic of China at the Conference Marking the 50th Anniversary of the Restoration of the Lawful Seat of the People's Republic of China in the United Nations.* Retrieved from: https://www.fmprc.gov.cn/eng/zxxx_662805/202110/t20211025_9982254.html

Ministry of Planning and Investment of the Socialist Republic of Vietnam. (2023, November 13). *Vietnam, China enjoy stronger partnership.* https://www.mpi.gov.vn/en/Pages/2023-11-23/Vietnam-China-enjoy-stronger-partnershiptnvm4e.aspx

Miño, P. (2023). Beyond Economic Dependency: Nation Branding in Latin America Subdued to Stereotypes and Neo-liberal Globalization. *Public Relations Inquiry.* doi:10.1177/2046147X231224834

Miño, P., & Austin, L. (2022). A Cocreational Approach to Nation Branding: The Case of Chile. *Public Relations Inquiry, 11*(2), 293–313. doi:10.1177/2046147X221081179

Mishra, V. (2020). The BRI and Strategic Revival of the Silk Road: Implications for Asia. *India Quarterly. Journal of International Affairs, 76*(3), 479–484. doi:10.1177/0974928420936138

Mitić, A. (2023). China's New Initiatives and the Shaping of Eurasia's Strategic Environment. In D. Proroković & E. Entina (Eds.), Eurasian Security After NATO (pp. 113–139). Institute of International Politics; Economics; Institute of Europe of the Russian Academy of Sciences. doi:10.18485/iipe_easnato.2023.ch6

Mogensen, K. (2015). International trust and public diplomacy. *The International Communication Gazette, 77*(4), 315–336. doi:10.1177/1748048514568764

Mohan, G., & Power, M. (2008). New African choices? The politics of Chinese engagement. *Review of African Political Economy, 35*(115), 23–42. doi:10.1080/03056240802011394

Mohan, S., & Abraham, J. C. (2020). Shaping the regional and maritime battlefield? The Sino-Indian strategic competition in South Asia and adjoining waters. *Maritime Affairs, 16*(1), 82–97. doi:10.1080/09733159.2020.1781374

Montanari, M. G., & Giraldi, J. de M. E. (2018). A Theoretical Study on Country Brand and Its Management. *Revista Eletrônica de Negócios Internacionais (Internext), 13*(2), 14–29.

Morris, J. (2011). "How Great is Britain?" Powers, Responsibility and Britain Future Global Role. *British Journal of Politics and International Relations, 13*(3), 326–347. doi:10.1111/j.1467-856X.2011.00450.x

Morton, K. (2016). China's ambition in the South China Sea: Is a legitimate maritime order possible? *International Affairs, 92*(4), 909–940. doi:10.1111/1468-2346.12658

Moser, A., & Korstjens, I. (2017). Series: Practical guidance to qualitative research. Part 1: Introduction. *The European Journal of General Practice, 23*(1), 271–273. doi:10.1080/13814788.2017.1375093 PMID:29185831

Mucha, J. (2007). The concept of "social relations" in classic analytical interpretative sociology: Weber and Znaniecki. In Essays in Logic and Ontology (pp. 119-142). Brill.

Mulder, N. (2022). *The Economic Weapon: The Rise of Sanctions as a Tool of Modern War.* Yale University Press.

Munro, A. (2023). Power. *Britannica.*

Murphy, D. C. (2022). *China's rise in the Global South: The Middle East, Africa, and Beijing's alternative world order.* Stanford University Press.

Murphy, D. C. (2022). *China's Rise in the Global South: The Middle East, Africa, and Beijing's Alternative World Order.* Stanford University Press.

Nadeem, R. (2022, June 29). *Negative Views of China Tied to Critical Views of Its Policies on Human Rights*. Pew Research Center's Global Attitudes Project. https://www.pewresearch.org/global/2022/06/29/negative-views-of-china-tied-to-critical-views-of-its-policies-on-human-rights/

Nader, A. S. (2016). *China in the Middle East*. The Rand Santa Monica Foundation.

Nafi, I. (1999). *China - The Miracle of the End of the Twentieth Century*. Cairo: Al-Ahram Center for Translation and Publishing.

Nantulya, P. (2018). Grand Strategy and China's Soft Power Push in Africa. *Africa Centre for Strategic Studies*. https://africacenter.org/spotlight/grand-strategy-and-chinas-soft-power-push-in-africa/

Narasimhan, S. L. (2024, February 20). India must be wary of China's global security plan. *The Tribune*. https://www.tribuneindia.com/news/comment/india-must-be-wary-of-chinas-global-security-plan-592477

Nast, C. (2024, January 23). *A New Normal: The Levers to Success in China in 2024*. Vogue Business. https://www.voguebusiness.com/story/consumers/a-new-normal-the-levers-to-success-in-china-in-2024

Nathan, A. J., & Scobell, A. (2015). *China's Search for Security*. Columbia University Press.

National Ethnic Affairs Commission. (2012, November 29). *Achieving rejuvenation is the dream of the Chinese people*. https://www.neac.gov.cn/seac/c103372/202201/1156514.shtml

Nedopil, C. (2024). *China Belt and Road Initiative investment report 2023*. Griffith Asia Institute, Griffith University & Green Finance & Development Center. https://greenfdc.org/china-belt-and-road-initiative-bri-investment-report-2023/#:~:text=Of%20the%202023%20engagement%2C%20about,the%20onset%20of%20COVID%2D19

Nehme, K. H. (2017). Chinese and Arab Soft Power. *Journal of Arab Studies, 26*, 41.

Newton, T. (1999). Power, subjectivity and British industrial and organisational sociology: The relevance of the work of Norbert Elias. *Sociology, 33*(2), 411–440. doi:10.1177/S0038038599000243

Nguyen, H. (2023a, December 28). Vietnam wary of China's swift, large-scale investment. *Voice of America*. https://www.voanews.com/a/vietnam-wary-of-china-s-swift-large-Scale-investment/7416324.html

Nguyen, M. (2023b, December 12). Vietnam, China sign 36 agreements in Xi's visit. *Hanoi Times*. https://hanoitimes.vn/vietnam-china-sign-36-agreements-in-xis-visit-325615.html

Nguyen, S., & Wu, Y. (2023, June 15). Cat Linh-Ha Dong urban rail becomes popular means of transport. *Hanoi Times*. https://hanoitimes.vn/cat-linh-ha-dong-urban-rail-becomes-popular-means-of-transport-323957.html#:~:text=The%20Cat%20Linh%2DHa%20Dong%20elevated%20railway%20has%20brought%20great,urban%20railway%20line%20in%20Hanoi

Nguyen, S. T., & Wu, Y. (2023, April 26). Vietnam's bilateral trade intensity: The role of China. *Journal of Chinese Economic and Business Studies*, 1–22. doi:10.1080/14765284.2023.2206785

Nhan Dan Newspaper of Vietnam. (2022). *New momentum to enhance Vietnam-China friendship*. https://nhandan.vn/dong-luc-moi-tang-cuong-tinh-huu-nghi-nang-tam-quan-he-viet-nam-trung-quoc-post722793.html

Nobre, H., & Sousa, A. (2022). Cultural Heritage and Nation Branding – Multi Stakeholder Perspectives from Portugal. *Journal of Tourism and Cultural Change, 20*(5), 699–717. doi:10.1080/14766825.2021.2025383

Noyon, A. U. (2023, October 1). How China's Belt and Road changing Bangladesh's economy and infrastructures. *The Business Standard*. https://www.tbsnews.net/economy/how-chinas-belt-and-road-changing-bangladeshs-infrastructures-709826

Núñez Fernández, A. (2010). Jesuitas. *Inforsi*, *106*, 4.

Nuwer, R. (2023). Chinese students stay local as favour falls with study abroad. *Nature*, *620*(7973), S11–S13. doi:10.1038/d41586-023-02162-y PMID:37558838

Nye, J. (2005, Dec. 5). Soft power matters in Asia. *The Japan Times*.

Nye, J. (2014). Soft power is the means to success in international politics. Conference Newspaper. 11.

Nye, J. (2016). Soft Power and Foreign Policy. *Foreign Policy Magazine*, 14.

Nye, J. S. (2004). *Can America Regain Its Soft Power After Abu Ghraib?* https://archive-yaleglobal.yale.edu/content/can-america-regain-its-soft-power-after-abu-ghraib

Nye, J. S. (2004*). Soft power: The means to success in world politics*. Public Affairs.

Nye, J. (2002). *Soft Power: the Means to Success in World Politics*. Public Affairs.

Nye, J. (2017). Soft power: The origins and political progress of a concept. *Palgrave Communications*, *3*(1), 17008. doi:10.1057/palcomms.2017.8

Nye, J. S. (1990). Soft power. *Foreign Policy*, (80), 153–171. doi:10.2307/1148580

Nye, J. S. (1991). *Bound to lead: the changing nature of American power*. Basic books.

Nye, J. S. (2003). *Limits of American Power*. USA. *Political Science Quarterly*, 9.

Nye, J. S. (2004). *Soft Power: The Means to Success in World Politics*. Public Affairs.

Nye, J. S. (2010). The Future of Soft Power in US Foreign Policy. In I. Parmar & M. Cox (Eds.), *Soft Power and US Foreign Policy: Theoretical, Historical and Contemporary Perspectives*. Routledge.

Nye, J. S. (2011). *The Future of Power* (1st ed.). Public Affairs.

Nye, J. S. (2019). Soft power and public diplomacy revisited. *The Hague Journal of Diplomacy*, *14*(1-2), 7–20. doi:10.1163/1871191X-14101013

Nye, J. S. (2023). *Soft Power and Great-Power Competition: Shifting Sands in the Balance of Power Between the United States and China*. Spinger Publisher. doi:10.1007/978-981-99-0714-4

Nye, J. S. Jr. (1990). The changing nature of world power. *Political Science Quarterly*, *105*(2), 177–192. doi:10.2307/2151022

Nye, J. S. Jr. (2004). Soft power and American foreign policy. *Political Science Quarterly*, *119*(2), 255–270. doi:10.2307/20202345

Nye, J. S. Jr. (2008). Public diplomacy and soft power. *The Annals of the American Academy of Political and Social Science*, *616*(1), 94–109. doi:10.1177/0002716207311699

Nye, J. S. Jr. (2016). Limits of American power. *Political Science Quarterly*, *131*(2), 267–283. doi:10.1002/polq.12478

Obaidullah, M. (2023, October 26). From Historical Bonds to Modern Alliances: Decoding China's Relations with Afghanistan. *The Geopolitics*. https://thegeopolitics.com/from-historical-bonds-to-modern-alliances-decoding-chinas-relations-with-afghanistan/

Observatory of Economic Complexity (OEC). (2021). *Japan-China*. Retrieved from OEC: https://oec.world/en/profile/bilateral-country/jpn/partner/chn

Odgaard, L. (2020). Responsibility to Protect goes to China: An interpretivist analysis of how China's coexistence policy made it a Responsibility to Protect insider. *Journal of International Political Theory*, *16*(2), 231–248. doi:10.1177/1755088219899416

Ohnesorge, H. W., & Owen, J. M. (2023). Mnemonic Soft Power: The Role of Memory in China's Quest for Global Power. *Journal of Current Chinese Affairs*, *52*(2), 287–310. doi:10.1177/18681026231193035

Oh, Y. A., & No, S. (2020). The patterns of state-firm coordination in China's private sector internationalization: China's mergers and acquisitions in Southeast Asia. *The Pacific Review*, *33*(6), 873–899. doi:10.1080/09512748.2019.1599410

Okano-Heijmans, M., & Asano, T. (2018). Economic diplomacy. In *Routledge Handbook of Japanese Foreign Policy* (pp. 251–266). Routledge. doi:10.4324/9781315643076-17

Oktav, O. Z. (2018). Understanding Iran's Approach to Violent Non-state Actors: The ISIS and YPG Cases. *Violent Non-state Actors and the Syrian Civil War*, *16*(2), 193–210. doi:10.1007/978-3-319-67528-2_10

Olimat, M. S. (2023). China and the Middle East: An Overview. *Routledge Companion to China and the Middle East and North Africa*, 9-24.

Olins, W. (2002). Branding the Nation—The Historical Context. *Journal of Brand Management*, *9*(4), 241–248. doi:10.1057/palgrave.bm.2540075

Ollé, M. (2002). *La Empresa de China. De la Armada Invencible al Galeón de Manila*. Acantilado.

Oppermann, K. (2014, January). Delineating the scope conditions of the poliheuristic theory of decision making: The noncompensatory principle and the domestic salience of Foreign Policy. *Foreign Policy Analysis*, *10*(1), 23–41. doi:10.1111/j.1743-8594.2012.00182.x

Ørmen, J., Helles, R., & Bruhn Jensen, K. (2021). Converging cultures of communication: A comparative study of Internet use in China, Europe, and the United States. *New Media & Society*, *23*(7), 1751–1772. doi:10.1177/14614448211015977

Osborne, E. W. (2004). *Britain's Economic Blockade of Germany: 1914 - 1919*. Cass. doi:10.4324/9780203495230

Osman, R. (2017). *China's soft power: An assessment of positive image building in the Middle East*. Leiden University.

Osman, R. (2017). *China's soft power: An assessment of positive image building in the Middle East*. Masters Dissertation.

Osodoev, P. V. (2021). *Regional trade and economic cooperation along the China-Mongolia-Russia Economic Corridor*. doi:10.1088/1755-1315/885/1/012016

Owen, D. (2017). The new media's role in politics. In The age of perplexity: Rethink the world we knew. Penguin Random House Grupo Editorial.

Ozturk, A. E. (2023). Religious Soft Power: Definition(s), Limits and Usage. *Religions*, *14*(2), 135. doi:10.3390/rel14020135

Pakistan, R. (2023, September 16). *Number of Pakistani students in US rises by 16 percen*. Radio Pakistan. https://www.radio.gov.pk/16-11-2023/number-of-pakistani-students-in-us-rises-by-16-percent

Pal, D. (2021). *China's Influence in South Asia: Vulnerabilities and Resilience in Four Countries*. https://carnegieendowment.org/2021/10/13/china-s-influence-in-south-asia-vulnerabilities-and-resilience-in-four-countries-pub-85552

Palit, P. S. (2018). *India's Use of social media in public diplomacy. Rising Power Quarterly, 3*.

Palma, P. (2023, September 15). Number of Bangladeshi students in US rose 300% in 10 years. *The Daily Star*. https://www.thedailystar.net/news/bangladesh/education/news/number-bangladeshi-students-us-rose-300-10-years-3470381

Parepa, L.-A. (2020). The Belt and Road Initiative as continuity in Chinese foreign policy. *Journal of Contemporary East Asia Studies*, *9*(2), 175–201. doi:10.1080/24761028.2020.1848370

Parlar Dal, E., Dipama, S., Çaytaş, Ş., & Sezgin, A. (2021). Assessing the Development–Foreign Policy Nexus of the Asian Rising Powers: South Korea, China, Japan and Indonesia. *Global Policy*, *12*(5), 653–662. doi:10.1111/1758-5899.13008

Peerenboom, R. (2005). Assessing human rights in China: Why the double standard. *Cornell International Law Journal*, *38*(1), 71–172.

Peña-Araya, V., Quezada, M., Poblete, B., & Parra, D. (2017). Gaining Historical and International Relations Insights from Social Media: Spatio-Temporal Real-World News Analysis using Twitter. *EPJ Data Science*.

Penta, L. J. (1996). Hannah Arendt: On power. *The Journal of Speculative Philosophy*, 210–229.

Perelomov, L. (2017). *Yang Shang: Book of the Ruler of the Shang Region Librarium*. Ripol-Classic.

Permanent Mission of China to the UN. (2013). *China's Position Paper on the Development Agenda beyond 2015* (Meetings and Statements). http://un.china-mission.gov.cn/eng/hyyfy/201309/t20130925_8399922.htm

Phillips, C. R. (2007). The Organization of Oceanic Empires: The Iberian World in the Habsburg Period. In J. H. Bentley, R. Bridenthal, & K. Wigen (Eds.), *Seascapes: Maritime Histories, Littoral Cultures, and Transoceanic Exchanges* (pp. 71–86). University of Hawaii Press. doi:10.2307/j.ctt6wr35q.8

PIB. (2022, June 24). https://pib.gov.in/PressReleaseIframePage.aspx?PRID=1836853

Pie, M. (2018). *The limits of China's charm offensive*. The Strategist. Retrieved from: https://www.aspistrategist.org.au/the-limits-of-chinas-charm-offensive/

Pietrzak, P. (2022). How Did Bashar Al-Assad Get Away With the Ghouta Chemical Attack? The Promise of Relinquishing Syria's Chemical Weapons Arsenal That Was Never Fully Fulfilled. In Regulating Human Rights, Social Security, and Socio-Economic Structures in a Global Perspective (pp. 125-141). IGI Global.

Pietrzak, P. (2022b). Introducing the idea of Ontology in statu nascendi to the broader International Relations Theory. In *International Conference Proceeding Series-International Conference on Economics and Social Sciences in Serik* (pp. 570-585). Academic Press.

Pietrzak, P. W. (2009). American "Soft Power" after George W. Bush's Presidency. In A. Mania & Ł. Wordliczek (Eds.), The United States and the World: From Imitation to Challenge (pp. 187–194). Jagiellonian University Press.

Pietrzak, P., & Grębowiec, M. (2023). Building trust on social media as part of higher education institutions' marketing strategy. In Privacy, Trust and Social Media (pp. 242-252). Routledge.

Pietrzak, P. (2021). Immanuel Kant and Niccolò Machiavelli's Traditions and the Limits of Approaching Contemporary Conflicts—The Case Study of the Syrian Conflict (2011–Present). *Statu Nascendi Journal of Political Philosophy and International Relations*, *2*, 53–84.

Pietrzak, P. (2023). Approaching Regional Conflicts through the Prism of Ontology in statu nascendi—The New Compartmentalization of the IR Theory. *Statu Nascendi*, *6*(1), 97–154.

Pines, Y. (2009). *Envisioning Eternal Empire: Chinese Political Thought of the Warring States Era*. University of Hawaii.

Pollack, J. D. (2003). *China and the United States Post-9/11*. Foreign Policy Research Institute.

Por, S. S. (2020). *Tianxia: China's Concept of International Order*. Global Asia. Retrieved from: https://www.globalasia.org/v15no2/cover/tianxia-chinas-concept-of-international-order_shiu-sin-por

Porter, M. E. (1998). *The Competitive Advantage of Nations: With a New Introduction*. Free Press. doi:10.1007/978-1-349-14865-3

Press Release on opening session of 13th National Party Congress. (2021, January 26). *Vietnam Plus* https://en.vietnamplus.vn/press-release-on-opening-session-of-13th-national-party-congress/195396.vnp

Qi, J. J., & Dauvergne, P. (2022). China's rising influence on climate governance: Forging a path for the global South. *Global Environmental Change*, *73*, 102484. doi:10.1016/j.gloenvcha.2022.102484

Quan, N. H. (2022). *China-US geopolitical competition: Impacts and implications for Vietnam's adaptive policies*. National Political Publishing House Truth.

Quansheng, Z. (2018). *The influence of Confucianism on Chinese politics and foreign policy*. Asian Education and Development Studies.

Rafizadeh, M. 2023 (23 July). How China became an ideal partner in the Middle East. *Arad News*. https://arab.news/9peht

Rahman, M. M. (2023, November 8). How Chinese aid advances BD dev, gains soft power. *The Financial Express*. https://today.thefinancialexpress.com.bd/first-page/how-chinese-aid-advances-bd-dev-gains-soft-power-1699375363

Ramo, J. C. (2007). *Brand China*. Foreign Policy Center.

RaoN. (2020, July 7). https://thewire.in/diplomacy/india-china-70-years-diplomatic-relations

Rashid Latief, L. L. (2018). Analysis of Chinese Government Scholarship for International Students Using Analytical Hierarchy. *Sustainability*, 7.

Rashid, D., & Ikram, D. M. (2023). Power Struggle in South Asia Region: Hanging between Soft and Hard Balance Competition. *Praxis International Journal of Social Science and Literature*, *6*(5), 36–46. doi:10.51879/PIJSSL/060505

Raslan, S. B. (1998). *Confucius, Pioneer of Human Thought*. Bibliotheca Alexandrina.

Ratha, K. C., & Mahapatra, S. K. (2014). *India-China Bilateral Relations: Confrontation and Conciliation. In Vision 2020: Sustainable Growth*. Economic Development, and Global Competitiveness.

Ravitsky, M. (2018). Jumping onto the train? How Russian media cover China's Belt and Road Initiative. *Asian Politics & Policy*, *10*(3), 564–570. doi:10.1111/aspp.12403

Redaktion, A. F. M. (2022, May 28). *K-Pop Is Making Billions for South Korea*. AsiaFundManagers.Com. https://www.asiafundmanagers.com/gbr/kpop-and-economic-impact-on-south-korea/

Regencia, T. (2021, June 8). *What you should know about China's minority Uighurs*. Retrieved from Al Jazera: https://www.aljazeera.com/news/2021/7/8/uighurs-timeline

Riccio, V. (1667). Hechos de la orden de Predicadores en el imperio de China [Unpublished manuscripts]. Archives of the Province of the Holy Rosary, Section 34 China, Volume 31, Books I, II, III.

Roach, S. (2014). Unbalanced: The Codependency of America and China. Yale University Press.

Roberts, A. (2017). *Is International Law International?* Oxford University Press. doi:10.1093/oso/9780190696412.001.0001

Roger, T. A., & Rosemont, H. (1998). *The Analects of Confucius: A Philosophical Translation, trans*. Ballantine Books.

Rojas-Méndez, J. (2013). The Nation Brand Molecule. *Journal of Product and Brand Management*, *22*(7), 462–472. doi:10.1108/JPBM-09-2013-0385

Rojas-Méndez, J. I., & Khoshnevis, M. (2022). Conceptualizing Nation Branding: The Systematic Literature Review. *Journal of Product and Brand Management*, *32*(1), 107–123. doi:10.1108/JPBM-04-2021-3444

Roland, G. (2021). China's rise and its implications for International Relations and Northeast Asia. *Asia and the Global Economy*, *1*(2), 100016. doi:10.1016/j.aglobe.2021.100016

Roll, M. (2021, November 28). *How Nations and Brands Overcome Country of Origin*. Martin Roll. https://martinroll.com/resources/articles/branding/how-nations-and-brands-overcome-country-of-origin-challenges/

Roman, M., Roman, M., Grzegorzewska, E., Pietrzak, P., & Roman, K. (2022). Influence of the COVID-19 Pandemic on Tourism in European Countries: Cluster Analysis Findings. *Sustainability (Basel)*, *14*(3), 1602. doi:10.3390/su14031602

Rønning, H. (2016). How Much Soft Power Does China Have in Africa? In X. Zhang, H. Wasserman, & W. Mano (Eds.), *China's Media and Soft Power in Africa*. Palgrave Series in Asia and Pacific Studies. doi:10.1057/9781137539670_5

Ronzitti, N. (2016). *Coercive Diplomacy. Sanctions and International Law*. Brill. doi:10.1163/9789004299894

Roy ChaudhuryD. (2021, October 29). https://economictimes.indiatimes.com/news/defence/chinas-aggression-in-south-china-sea-faces-strong-global-pushback/articleshow/87351835.cms?from=mdr

Royandoyan, R. (2023). *Philippines urges restraint following South China Sea clash*. South China Sea. Retrieved from: https://asia.nikkei.com/Politics/International-relations/South-China-Sea/Philippines-urges-restraint-following-South-China-Sea-clash

Rubiolo, F., Busilli, V. S., & Escobar, M. E. (2020). Análisis de la política exterior de Xi Jinping hacia el Sudeste de Asia: Estrategias, intereses y dimensiones. *Revista Relaciones Internacionales*, *93*(2), 91–116. doi:10.15359/ri.93-2.4

Ruggie, J. G. (1982). International regimes, transactions, and change: Embedded liberalism in the postwar economic order. *International Organization*, *36*(2), 379–415. doi:10.1017/S0020818300018993

Rugh, W. (2017). American soft power and public diplomacy in the Arab world. *Palgrave Communications*, *3*(1), 16104. doi:10.1057/palcomms.2016.104

Rühlig, T. (2018). *How China Approaches International Law: Implications for Europe*. Jorgensen.

Ruiz Ortiz, M. Á. (2012). La monarquía española de los Austrias en los siglos XVI y XVII. *Revista de Claseshistoria*, (336), 1–12.

Runde, D. F. (2020). *U.S. Foreign Assistance in the Age of Strategic Competition*. https://www.csis.org/analysis/us-foreign-assistance-age-strategic-competition

Ruwitch, J. (2021, March 5). What China's 'Total Victory' Over Extreme Poverty Looks Like in Actuality. *NPR*. https://www.npr.org/2021/03/05/974173482/what-chinas-total-victory-over-extreme-poverty-looks-like-in-actuality

Sarvjeet, S. (2016). *Digital Diplomacy in India: Virtual networks, Real gains*. Communication des Institutions Publiques.

Sasongkojati, R. M. H. D., & Subono, N. I. (2023). Strategic Culture, South-South Cooperation, and Soft Power Politics: Explaining Brazilian Foreign Aid. *Jurnal Ilmu Sosial Dan Ilmu Politik*, *27*(2), 176. doi:10.22146/jsp.81267

Sayama, O. (2016). *China's Approach to Soft Power Seeking a Balance between Nationalism*. Legitimacy and International Influence, Royal United Services Institute for Defence and Security Studies.

Schweller, R. L., & Pu, X. (2011). After Unipolarity: China's Visions of International Order in an Era of U.S. Decline. *International Security*, *36*(1), 41–72. doi:10.1162/ISEC_a_00044

Scobell, A., & Nader, A. (2016). *China in the Middle East: the wary dragon*. RAND Corporation.

Sellen, C., & Jaumont, F. (2020, April 7). China Billionaires a Force to be Reckoned With in Global COVID-19 Fight—and More. *Channel News Asia*. https://www.channelnewsasia.com/news/commen tary/china-covid-19-coronavirus-alibaba-jack-ma-tencent-baidu-12614242

Serna Arnaiz, M. (2019). Modos y modas. Primeros retratos occidentales de los reinos de China y de los indios de América. In B. Hernández (Ed.), Transocéanos. Viajes culturales en los mundos conocidos (siglos XVI-XVIII) (pp. 249-264). Centro para la Edición de los Clásicos Españoles.

Shambaugh, D. (2005). Return to the Middle Kingdom? China and Asia in the Twenty-First Century. In D. Shambaugh (Ed.), *Power Shift: China and Asia's New Dynamics* (pp. 23–47). University of California Press.

Shambaugh, D. (2013). Assessing the US "pivot" to Asia. *Strategic Studies Quarterly*, 7(2), 10–19.

Shambaugh, D. (2015). China's Soft-Power Push: The Search for Respect. *Foreign Affairs*, 94(4), 99–107.

Shapiro, A. (2015, February 8). *Not Too Much, Not Too Little: Sweden, In A Font*. North Country Public Radio. https://www.northcountrypublicradio.org/news/npr/384346383/not-too-much-not-too-little-sweden-in-a-font

Sharma, A. (2023). China's Soft Power in the Middle East. In China's Engagement with the Islamic Nations. Understanding China. Springer. doi:10.1007/978-3-031-31042-3_2

Sharma, B. P., & Khatri, R. S. (2019). The Politics of Soft Power: *Belt and Road Initiative (BRI) as Charm Influence in South Asia. China and the World*, 02(01), 1950002. doi:10.1142/S2591729319500020

Shih, G. (2022, March 22). *World: The Washington Post*. https://www.washingtonpost.com/world/2022/03/17/india-russia-oil/

Shipton, L., & Dauvergne, P. (2021). The Politics of Transnational Advocacy Against Chinese, Indian, and Brazilian Extractive Projects in the Global South. *Journal of Environment & Development*, 30(3), 240–264. doi:10.1177/10704965211019083 PMID:34393471

Siddiqui, H. (2022, March 25). *Financial Express*. https://www.financialexpress.com/defence/why-did-chinese-foreign-minister-wang-yi-come-unannounced-here-is-what-experts-say/2472016/

Silver, L. (2021). *Amid pandemic, international student enrollment at U.S. universities fell 15% in the 2020-21 school year*. https://www.pewresearch.org/short-reads/2021/12/06/amid-pandemic-international-student-enrollment-at-u-s-universities-fell-15-in-the-2020-21-school-year/

Silver, L., Huang, C., & Clancy, L. (2022, September 28). *How Global Public Opinion of China Has Shifted in the Xi Era*. Pew Research Center's Global Attitudes Project. https://www.pewresearch.org/global/2022/09/28/how-global-public-opinion-of-china-has-shifted-in-the-xi-era/

Singh, A. I. (2021, May 7). China's Port Investments in Sri Lanka Reflect Competition with India in the Indian Ocean. *The Jamestown Foundation*. https://jamestown.org/program/chinas-port-investments-in-sri-lanka-reflect-competition-with-india-in-the-indian-ocean/

Smith, J. (2022). *South Asia: A New Strategy*. https://www.heritage.org/asia/report/south-asia-new-strategy

Smith, S. N. (2021). China's 'Major Country Diplomacy': Legitimation and Foreign Policy Change. *Foreign Policy Analysis*, 17(2), orab002. Advance online publication. doi:10.1093/fpa/orab002

Snell, G. (2023, June 17). Tensions high as Chinese vessels shadow Vietnam's oil, gas operations. *Voice of America*. https://www.voanews.com/a/tensions-high-as-chinese-vessels-shadow-vietnam-s-oil-and-gas-operations-/7141273.html

Snow, D. M. (2016). *The Middle East, Oil, and the US National Security Policy: Intractable Conflicts, Impossible Solutions*. Rowman & Littlefield.

Snow, N. (2020). Rethinking public diplomacy in the 2020s. In *Routledge handbook of public diplomacy* (pp. 3–12). Routledge. doi:10.4324/9780429465543-2

Son, N., & Phong, V. (2023, December 12). New stature in Vietnam-China relations. *Nhandan*. https://special.nhandan.vn/vietnam-trungquoc_en/index.html

Song, L. (2021). Deepening Cooperation in Running Schools Between China and Southeast Asia to Promote the Development of "the Belt and Road Initiative". *2nd International Conference on Management, Economy and Law (ICMEL 2021)*, 291–296. 10.2991/aebmr.k.210909.043

Soni, P. (2019, October 21). *Nation Branding: How to Build an Effective Location Brand Identity*. Brand Finance. https://brandfinance.com/insights/nation-branding

Southworth, S. S. (2019). U.S. Consumers' Perception of Asian Brands' Cultural Authenticity and Its Impact on Perceived Quality, Trust, and Patronage Intention. *Journal of International Consumer Marketing*, *31*(4), 287–301. doi:10.1080/08961530.2018.1544528

Sowiński, P. (2023). Expression of Dissidence: NOW-a Publishing House as a Social Movement Campaign under an Authoritarian Regime. *East European Politics and Societies: And Cultures*. doi:10.1177/08883254231203333

Sparks, C. (2018). China's soft power from the BRICS to the BRI. *Global Media and China*, *3*(2), 92–99. doi:10.1177/2059436418778935

Spence, J. D. (1990). *The Search for Modern China*. W Nortan & Company.

Sperling, J. (2007). The United States: The Unrelenting Search for an Existential Threat in the 21st Century. In Global Security Governance: Competing Perceptions of Security in the 21st Century. Routledge.

State Council of the People's Republic of China. (2023, October 18). *Xi announces major steps to support high-quality Belt and Road cooperation*. https://english.www.gov.cn/news/202310/18/content_WS652f65e6c6d0868f4e8e05bd.html

State Council. (2009, Jan. 12). *China White paper on National Defence 2008*. Retrieved 12 01, 2009, from www.china.org.cn

Statista. (2021). *Total number of Confucius Institutes and Confucius Classrooms worldwide from 2013 to 2018*. Retrieved from: https://www.statista.com/statistics/879340/china-confucius-institutes-and-confucius-classrooms-worldwide/

Statista. (2023). *Languages most frequently used for web content as of January 2023, by share of websites*. https://www.statista.com/statistics/262946/most-common-languages-on-the-internet/

Statista. (2023, November). *Video Streaming (SVoD) - China*. Retrieved from Statista: https://www.statista.com/outlook/dmo/digital-media/video-on-demand/video-streaming-svod/china

Stepanov, A. S. (2022). *US Policy towards Southeast Asia: from Barack Obama to Joe Biden*. doi:10.1134/S1019331622210183

Stokes, J. (2003). *How to Do Media and Cultural Studies*. SAGE Publication.

Storey, I. (2024, February 16). Vietnam and the Russia-Ukraine War: Hanoi's 'bamboo diplomacy' pays off but challenges remain. *ISEAS Perspective, 2024*(13), 1-9. https://www.iseas.edu.sg/articles-commentaries/iseas-perspective/2024-13-vietnam-and-the-russia-ukraine-war-hanois-bamboo-diplomacy-pays-off-but-challenges-remain-in-ian-storey/

Strangio, S. (2023). *Vietnamese, Chinese Vessels in Close South China Sea Encounter*. The Diplomat. Retrieved from: https://thediplomat.com/2023/03/vietnamese-chinese-vessels-in-close-south-china-sea-encounter/

Streeten, P. (2001). Interdependence and Globalization. *Finance & Development, 38*(2), 1–10. doi:10.5089/9781451952858.022. A010

Stueck, W. (1995). *The Korean War: An International History*. Princeton University Press.

Subramanian, N. (2020, June 16). *indianexpress.com.* https://indianexpress.com/article/explained/lac-stand-off-india-china-darbuk-shyok-daulat-beg-oldie-dsdbo-road-6452997/

Suisheng, Z. (2015). Rethinking the Chinese World Order: The imperial cycle and the rise of China. *Journal of Contemporary China*, 2–22.

Sun, H. H. (2008). International political marketing: A case study of United States soft power and public diplomacy. *Journal of Public Affairs, 8*(3), 165–183. doi:10.1002/pa.301

Sutter, R. G. (2005). China's Rise in Asia. Rowman & Littlefield Publishers.

Swaine, M. D. (2010). Beijing's Tightrope Walk on Iran. *China Leadership Monitor*, 3.

Sweetman, M. (2014, September 23). *The Importance of Social Media in China*. Retrieved from South China Morning Post: https://www.scmp.com/article/1598699/importance-social-media-china?campaign=1598699&module=perpetual_scroll_0&pgtype=article

Szekely, O. (2023). *Syria Divided: Patterns of Violence in a Complex Civil War*. Columbia University Press. doi:10.7312/szek20538

Szondi, G. (2008). *Public Diplomacy and Nation Branding: Conceptual Similarities and Differences*. Clingendael Institute.

TanW. (2022, March 27). *CNBC*. https://www.cnbc.com/2022/03/28/russia-india-india-buys-cheap-russian-oil-china-could-be-next.html

Tatiana Ponka, A. B. (2019, January). Relations Between China and Mongolia: Cultural and Educational Dimensions. *Advances in Social Science, Education and Humanities Research, 356*, 1104.

Taylor, W. A. (2018). *Contemporary security issues in Africa*. Bloomsbury Publishing USA. doi:10.5040/9798400631450

Tehseen, M. (2017). Sino-US Competition: Implications for South Asia and the Asia-Pacific. *Strategic Studies, 37*(4), 1–17. doi:10.53532/ss.038.01.00175

Tewari, S. (2021, May 7). Sri Lanka: Covid increases China influence in India's backyard. *BBC News*. https://www.bbc.com/news/world-asia-57167091

Textor, C. (2023, November 11). *Annual FDI flows from China to Vietnam, 2012-2022*. https://www.statista.com/statistics/720408/china-outward-fdi-flows-to-vietnam/

Thao, N. T. H. (2020). Higher education – the factor of soft power in U.S. foreign policy from the post-cold war to 2016. *Science & Technology Development Journal - Social Sciences & Humanities, 4*(3), 605–612. doi:10.32508/stdjssh.v4i3.578

The Bureau of Educational and Cultural Affairs. (2023). *Cultural Diplomacy*. The Bureau of Educational and Cultural Affairs. https://eca.state.gov/programs-and-initiatives/initiatives/cultural-diplomacy

The Business Standard. (2023, June 19). 55 Bangladeshi students get Chinese Government Scholarship this year. *The Business Standard*. https://www.tbsnews.net/bangladesh/education/55-bangladeshi-students-get-chinese-government-scholarship-year-652262

The Cradel. (2024). *Iraq mulls suspension of border security deal with Iran.* https://thecradle.co/articles-id/19283

The Economic Times. (2017, December 17). https://economictimes.indiatimes.com

The Express Tribune. (2019, April 14). Over 28,000 Pakistanis studying in China. *The Express Tribune.* https://tribune.com.pk/story/1950783/28000-pakistanis-studying-china

The Guardian. (2015). *What do Iraqis think of Iran?* Retrieved from: https://www.theguardian.com/world/iran-blog/2015/mor/17/iran-viewed-from-iraq-fight-against-isis

The Hindu Business Line. (2023, September 13). Indian students to the US increase 35% in 2022-23. *The Hindu Business Line.* https://www.thehindubusinessline.com/news/education/indian-students-to-the-us-at-all-time-high-of-35/article67528835.ece

The State Council Information Office of the People's Republic of China. (2023, December 13). *Bilateral trade between China, Vietnam hits monthly record high.* http://english.scio.gov.cn/pressroom/2023-12/13/content_116876643.htm#:~:text=Vietnam%20has%20since%202016%20remained,first%2011%20months%20of%202023

The State Council Information Office of the People's Republic of China. (2023a, March 19). *Global Civilization Initiative injects fresh energy into human development.* http://english.scio.gov.cn/topnews/2023-03/19/content_85177312.htm

The Times Higher Education. (2023). *World University Rankings 2024.* https://www.timeshighereducation.com/world-university-rankings/2024/world-ranking#!/length/100/locations/USA/sort_by/rank/sort_order/asc/cols/stats

The Times of India. (2019, June 15). Nepal schools make Mandarin compulsory after China offers to pay teachers' salaries. *The Times of India.* https://timesofindia.indiatimes.com/world/south-asia/nepal-schools-make-mandarin-compulsory-after-china-offers-to-pay-teachers-salaries/articleshow/69799114.cms

Thomas, N. (2021, July 28). *Far more world leaders visit China than America.* Lowy Institute. https://www.lowyinstitute.org/the-interpreter/far-more-world-leaders-visit-china-america

Tiboris, M. (2019). *Addressing China's Rising Influence in Africa.* Chicago Council on Global Affairs.

Tien Giang Portal. (2023). *Long Giang Industrial Park.* https://tiengiang.gov.vn/chi-tiet-tin?/khu-cong-nghiep-long-giang/11241528

Tobin, L. (2018). Underway-Beijing's strategy to build China into a maritime great power. *Naval War College Review, 71*(2), 1–32. https://digital-commons.usnwc.edu/nwc-review/vol71/iss2/5/

Today, C. (2007). Hu Jintao Calls for Enhancing "Soft Power" of Chinese Culture. *China Today.* http://www.chinatoday.com.cn/17ct/17e/1017/17e1720.htm

Today, C. (2023, August 7). China announces full scholarships to 40 SL students. *Ceylon Today.* https://ceylontoday.lk/2023/08/07/china-announces-full-scholarships-to-40-sl-students/

TomarR. (2002, June 25). https://www.aph.gov.au/About_Parliament/Parliamentary_Departments/Parliamentary_Library/pubs/rp/rp0102/02RP20

TPBO. (2015, May 12). *Vienna Destination Branding Case Study, Good Practice Example.* TPBO. https://placebrandobserver.com/case-study-city-destination-branding-vienna-austria/

TPBO. (2023, October 25). *China Country Performance, Brand Image and Reputation Analysis.* TPBO. https://placebrandobserver.com/china-country-performance-brand-image-reputation/

Tremml-Werner, B. (2015). Spain, China and Japan in Manila, 1571-1644: Local Comparisons and Global Connections. Amsterdam University Press.

Tully, J. (Ed.). (1988). *Meaning and context: Quentin Skinner and his critics*. Princeton University Press.

Ullah, C. (2015). *China's Soft Power: Changing the World Perception. Naval Postgraduate School, Monterey, California* (Unpublished Thesis).

Ullah, C. S. (2015). *China's soft power: Changing, the world perception.* Naval Postgraduate School.

UNCTAD. (2019). *Energizing South-South trade: The global system of trade preferences among developing countries* (Policy Brief 74). https://unctad.org/system/files/official-document/presspb2019d3_en.pdf

UNDESA. (n.d.). *Partnering for a better future.* https://www.un.org/sites/un2.un.org/files/progress_report_bri-sdgs_english-final.pdf

United Nations Economic and Social Commission for Asia and the Pacific. (2017, September 15). *Infrastructure financing strategies for sustainable development in Vietnam.* https://www.unescap.org/sites/default/files/20170915%20National%20Study%20-%20Infrastructure%20Financing%20-%20Viet%20%20Nam.pdf

UNOSSC. (2023). *Belt and Road Forum Seeks to Strengthen South-South Cooperation.* https://unsouthsouth.org/2023/10/22/belt-and-road-forum-seeks-to-strengthen-south-south-cooperation/

UNOSSC. (n.d.). *About South-South and Triangular Cooperation.* https://unsouthsouth.org/about/about-sstc/

US Department of State. (2004). *U.S. Commitment to Women in Iraq.* https://2001-2009.state.gov/g/wi/rls/36751.htm

US Department of State. (2019). *The Fulbright Program.* Retrieved from: https://www.stste.gov/fulbright-program-univeils-updated-indentity

US Department of State. (2021). *2022 Report on International Religious Freedom: China (Includes Hong Kong, Macau, Tibet, and Xinjiang).* US Department of State.

US Department of State. (2021, January 20). *U.S. Security Cooperation With India.* US Department of State. https://www.state.gov/u-s-security-cooperation-with-india/

US Department of State. (2022a, July 19). *U.S. Relations With Bangladesh.* US Department of State. https://cutt.ly/KwSquA1j

US Department of State. (2022b, August 15). *U.S. Relations With Pakistan.* US Department of State. https://www.state.gov/u-s-relations-with-pakistan/

US Department of State. (2023, September 1). *U.S. Security Cooperation with Bangladesh.* US Department of State. https://www.state.gov/u-s-security-cooperation-with-bangladesh/#:~:text=For%2050%20years%2C%20the%20United,trade%2C%20and%20defense%20institution%20building

US Government. (2023). *US Foreign Assistance by country.* US Government. https://www.foreignassistance.gov/cd/india/2022/obligations/1

USAID. (2018). *Iraq: Sophisticated emergency,* Retrieved from: https://www.usaid.gov/sites/default/files/documents/1866/iraq_arabic_fs05_03-09-2018.pdf

USAID. (2022). *U.S. Provides Additional Covid-19 Assistance to India.* USAID. https://www.usaid.gov/india/press-release/us-provides-additional-covid-19-assistance-india#:~:text=USAID%20has%20contributed%20more%20than,more%20than%2042%20million%20Indians

USIP. (2020). *China's Influence on Conflict Dynamics in South Asia*. https://www.usip.org/publications/2020/12/chinas-influence-conflict-dynamics-south-asia

USTR. (2023a). *Bangladesh Trade & Investment Summary*. Office of United States Trade Representative. https://ustr.gov/countries-regions/south-central-asia/bangladesh

USTR. (2023b). *India Trade & Investment Summary*. Office of United States Trade Representative. https://ustr.gov/countries-regions/south-central-asia/india

Uyanga, T. (n.d.). *Intensifying Soft Power Policy through diplomacy of economy*. Academic Press.

Vaisi, G. (2022, March 1). *The 25-year Iran-China agreement, endangering 2,500 years of heritage*. Retrieved from Middle east Institute: https://www.mei.edu/publications/25-year-iran-china-agreement-endangering-2500-years-heritage

van Ham, P. (2001). The Rise of the Brand State: The Postmodern Politics of Image and Reputation. *Foreign Affairs*, *80*(5), 2–6. doi:10.2307/20050245

van Ham, P. (2002). Branding Territory: Inside the Wonderful Worlds of PR and IR Theory. *Millennium*, *31*(2), 249–269. doi:10.1177/03058298020310020101

van Ness, P. (2018). China and the Third World: Patterns of Engagement and Indifference. In S. S. Kim (Ed.), *China and the World: Chinese Foreign Policy Faces the New Millennium* (4th ed.). Routledge. doi:10.4324/9780429501708-7

Varisco, A. E. (2013, June 3). Towards a Multi-Polar International System: Which Prospects for Global Peace? *E-International Relations*. https://www.e-ir.info/2013/06/03/towards-a-multi-polar-international-system-which-prospects-for-global-peace/#google_vignette

Vatanka, A. (2021). Making Sense of the Iran-China Strategic Agreement. *Middle East Institute*. https://www.mei.edu

Venugopalan, A., & Verma, P. (2020, February 7). Indian students may reassess China option. *The Economic Times*. https://economictimes.indiatimes.com/news/politics-and-nation/indian-students-may-reassess-china-option/articleshow/73997547.cms

Verdinejad, D. (2020). *The Importance of Iran for China, Donya-e-Eqtesad newspaper*. Retrieved on 1 Bahman 1400, No. 3748878. https://donya-e-eqtesad.com

Vietnam Chamber of Commerce and Industry- Center for WTO and International Trade. (2023, July 5). *China – Vietnam's largest trading partner*. https://wtocenter.vn/chuyen-de/22257-china--vietnams-largest-trading-partner

Vietnam Plus. (2023, June 28). PM calls for more Chinese investments. https://en.vietnamplus.vn/pm-calls-for-more-chinese-investments/255398.vnp

Vila Seoane, M. F. (2023). China's digital diplomacy on Twitter: The multiple reactions to the Belt and Road Initiative. *Global Media and Communication*, *19*(2), 161–183. doi:10.1177/17427665231185697

Villabert, S. (2020, July 7). *To Hallyu and Beyond: Strengthening the Image of Korea the Brand*. Medium. https://medium.com/revolutionaries/to-hallyu-and-beyond-strengthening-the-image-of-korea-the-brand-75fe0aa285e4

Vlassis, A. (2016). Soft power, global governance of cultural industries and rising powers: The case of China. *International Journal of Cultural Policy*, *22*(4), 481–496. doi:10.1080/10286632.2014.1002487

Vostlit. (2022). *Treaty of Nerchinsk August 28, 1689*. Retrieved from: https://www.vostlit.info/Texts/Dokumenty/China/XVII/1680-1700/Russ_kit_otn_17_v_II/pril1.htm

Vuving, A. (2009). How Soft Power Works. SSRN *Electronic Journal*. doi:10.2139/ssrn.1466220

Walder, A. M. (2015). A theoretical model for pedagogical innovation: A tripartite construction of pedagogical innovation focusing on reasons for and means of innovating. *Journal of Studies in Social Sciences*, *12*(1).

Wallace, W. (1999). The sharing of sovereignty: The European paradox. *Political Studies*, *47*(3), 503–521. doi:10.1111/1467-9248.00214

Waltz, K. N. (1997). Evaluating theories. *The American Political Science Review*, *91*(4), 913–917. doi:10.2307/2952173

Wang, C. (2023, February 3). *China Belt and Road Initiative (BRI) Investment Report 2022*. Retrieved from Green Finance and Development Center: https://greenfdc.org/china-belt-and-road-initiative-bri-investment-report-2022/

Wang, F.-L. Y. D. (2005). China Rising, Power and Motivation in Chinese Foreign Policy. Wohan: Rowman & Littlefield Publishers.

Wang, Y. (2008). Public Diplomacy and the Rise of Chinese Soft Power. Wohan: The Annals of the American Academy.

Wang, B. (2017). *Chinese Visions of World Order: Tianxia, Culture, and World Politics*. Duke University Press. doi:10.1515/9780822372448

Wang, J. (Ed.). (2011). *Soft power in China: Public diplomacy through communication*. Springer. doi:10.1057/9780230116375

Wang, J., & Cheng, H. (2022). China's approach to international law: From traditional westphalianism to aggressive instrumentalization in the Xi Jinping Era. *Chinese Journal of Comparative Law*, *10*(1), 140–153. doi:10.1093/cjcl/cxac020

Wang, Q., & Guo, G. (2015). Yu Keping and Chinese Intellectual Discourse on Good Governance. *The China Quarterly*, *224*, 985–1005. doi:10.1017/S0305741015000855

Watkins, J. (2020). *Iran in Iraq: The limits of 'smart power' amidst public protest*. http://eprints.lse.ac.uk/105768/

Wei, X. (2023). Xi's Thought on Culture put forward. *China Daily*. Retrieved from: https://www.chinadaily.com.cn/a/202310/09/WS6522ef3ca310d2dce4bb96d5.html

Weiwei, Z. (2012). *The China Wave: Rise of a Civilizational State*. World Century Publishing Corporation.

Westfall, J. (2009). Ironic midwives: Socratic maieutics in Nietzsche and Kierkegaard. *Philosophy and Social Criticism*, *35*(6), 627–648. doi:10.1177/0191453709104450

White House. (2022). *Indo - Pacific Strategy*. https://www.whitehouse.gov/wpcontent/uploads/2022/02/U.S.-Indo%20PacificStrategy.pdf

White, C. L. (2012). Brands and National Image: An Exploration of Inverse Country-of-Origin Effect. *Place Branding and Public Diplomacy*, *8*(2), 110–118. doi:10.1057/pb.2012.6

Wilhelm, K. (1991, November 6). China and Vietnam normalize relations. *The Washington Post*. https://www.washingtonpost.com/archive/politics/1991/11/06/china-and-vietnam-normalize-relations/8b90e568-cb51-44a3-9a84-90a515e29129/

Winkler, J. R., & Nye, J. S. (2005). Soft Power: The Means to Success in World Politics. *International Journal (Toronto, Ont.)*, *61*(1), 268. doi:10.2307/40204149

Winkler, S. C. (2023). Strategic Competition and US-China Relations: A Conceptual Analysis. *The Chinese Journal of International Politics*, *16*(3), 333–356. doi:10.1093/cjip/poad008

Wodak, R., & Meyer, M. (Eds.). (2016). *Methods of Critical Discourse Studies* (3rd ed.). Sage.

Wong, E. (2007). *Iran Is Playing a Growing Role in Iraq Economy*. https://www.nytimes.com/2007/03/17/world/middleeast/17iran.html

Wood, C. (2015). *Iran-Iraq Relations Cooling*. Available at: https:// www.thetrumpet.com/article/13106.2.0.0/middle-east/iran/iran-iraq-relations-cooling

Woodberry, R. D. (2012). The Missionary Roots of Liberal Democracy. *The American Political Science Review, 106*(2), 244–274. doi:10.1017/S0003055412000093

Woods, C. (2011). *CIA drones quit one Pakistan site – but US keeps access to other airbases*. https://www.thebureauin-vestigates.com/stories/2011-12-15/cia-drones-quit-one-pakistan-site-but-us-keeps-access-to-other-airbases

World Bank. (2023, April 14). *The World Bank in Vietnam*. https://www.worldbank.org/en/country/vietnam/overview

World Bank. (n.d.). *GDP, PPP Data*. World Bank Open Data. Retrieved 5 February 2024, from https://data.worldbank.org

World Learning. (2019). *Iraqi Young Leaders Exchange Program*. Retrieved from: https://www.worldlearning.org/program/iraqi-young-leaders-exchange-program

Worm, X. L. (2010). *Building China's Soft Power for a Peaceful Rise*. Wohan: Journal of Chinese Political Science/ Association of Chinese Political Studies.

Wu, I. S. (n.d.). *Measuring Soft Power with Conventional and Unconventional Data*. Academic Press.

Wu, S. (2016). *Maritime security in the South China Sea: regional implications and international cooperation*. Routledge.

Xiamen Chorography Compilation Committee. (1993). *Xiamen Gangshi* [History of Xiamen Port]. Renmin Jiaotong Chubanshe.

Xiantang, P., & Nascimento, A. (2020). Research on the Selecting Model of Confucius Institute Scholarships. *Boletim Do Tempo Presente, 9*(1), 2–12.

Xiaojing. (1999). *Selections from the Classic of Filiality (Xiaojing), Asia for Educators*. Columbia University.

Xiao, Y., Li, Y., & Hu, J. (2019). Construction of the Belt and Road Initiative in Chinese and American media: A critical discourse analysis based on self-built corpora. *International Journal of English Linguistics, 9*(3), 68–77. doi:10.5539/ijel.v9n3p68

Xiaoyang, S. (2012). *China in UN Security Council Decision-Making on Iraq: Conflicting Understandings, Competing Preferences*. Taylor & Francis. doi:10.4324/9780203113615

Xi, J., & Primiano, C. (2020). China's Influence in Asia: How Do Individual Perceptions Matter? *East Asia (Piscataway, N.J.), 37*(3), 181–202. doi:10.1007/s12140-020-09334-x PMID:32837181

Xing, Y., Liu, Y., Cooper, S. C., & Vrontis, D. (2023). *Reviving China's global footprint along the Silk Roads and the 'Belt and Road Initiative': Chinese overseas industrial park in Egypt*. Buisness History. doi:10.1080/00076791.2023.2233426

Xinhua. (2020, May 10). China donates more medical supplies to Philippines to help fight COVID-19. *Xinhua Net*. http://www.xinhuanet.com/english/2020-05/10/c_139045510.htm

Xinhua. (2023, August 15). 71 Nepali students granted Chinese scholarships. *Nepal News*. https://nepalnews.com/s/gallery/71-nepali-students-granted-chinese-scholarships

Xinhua. (2023, December 12). Xi Kicks off Vietnam visit, calling for China-Vietnam community with a shared future. https://english.news.cn/20231213/c6bb337d3a454a468ad426793ea4f0cb/c.html

Xin, J., & Matheson, D. (2018). One Belt, competing metaphors: The struggle over strategic narrative in English-language news media. *International Journal of Communication, 12*, 21.

Xuetong, Y. (2013). *Ancient Chinese thought, modern Chinese power*. Princeton University Press. doi:10.1515/9781400848959

Xuetong, Y. (2019). *Leadership and the Rise of Great Powers*. Princeton University Press. doi:10.2307/j.ctvc77dc8

Xu, H., Wang, K., & Song, Y. M. (2020). Chinese outbound tourism and soft power. *Journal of Policy Research in Tourism, Leisure & Events, 12*(1), 34–49. doi:10.1080/19407963.2018.1505105

Xuming, Q. I. A. N. (2018). "One Belt One Road" Initiative and China and the Middle East Media Exchanges. *Journalism, 8*(5), 239–245.

Yağcı, M. (2016). *A Beijing Consensus in the Making: The Rise of Chinese Initiatives in the International Political Economy and Implications for Developing Countries* (SSRN Scholarly Paper 2910831). https://papers.ssrn.com/abstract=2910831

Yan, L. (2023, November 22). China aids Hanoi with waste to power plant. *China News*. http://www.ecns.cn/business/2023-11-22/detail-ihcvcsuf3225468.shtml

Yang, L. (2023, December 12). China-Vietnam trade soars amid complementary economic cooperation. *Global Times*. https://www.globaltimes.cn/page/202312/1303497.shtml

Yang, M., & Wang, Z. (2023). A Corpus-Based Discourse Analysis of China's National Image Constructed by Environmental News in the New York Times. *Humanities and Social Sciences Communications, 10*(1), Article 1. doi:10.1057/s41599-023-02052-8

Yang, C. (2020). How China's Image Affects Chinese Products in a Partisan-Motivated US Market. *Global Media and China, 5*(2), 169–187. doi:10.1177/2059436420922702

Yang, H., & Van Gorp, B. (2021). A frame analysis of political-media discourse on the Belt and Road Initiative: Evidence from China, Australia, India, Japan, the United Kingdom, and the United States. *Cambridge Review of International Affairs*, 1–27.

Yang, R. (2010). Soft power and higher education: An examination of China's Confucius Institutes. *Globalisation, Societies and Education, 8*(2), 235–245. doi:10.1080/14767721003779746

Yao, J. (2009). The United States' Cognition of China's Soft Power in Southeast Asia: An Analysis on Congressional Research Service Reports and Opinion Polls. *Journal of Xiamen University*. https://www.semanticscholar.org/paper/The-United-States'-Cognition-of-China's-Soft-Power-Yao/f88fe71115ff78493befeee815c62074aee32ef2

Yao, W., Hu, S., Chu, Z., & Zhang, B. (2020). The Status of University-Industry Collaboration Participating in the People-to-People and Cultural Exchanges in Engineering Technology Among the Belt and Road Initiative Participants. *2020 ASEE Virtual Annual Conference Content Access Proceedings*, 35375. 10.18260/1-2--35375

Yee, F. W. (2009). *Nation Branding: A Case Study of Singapore* [Master Dissertation]. University of Nevada, Las Vegas.

Ye, P., & Albornoz, L. A. (2018). Chinese Media 'Going Out' in Spanish Speaking Countries: The Case of CGTN-Español. *Westminster Papers in Communication and Culture, 13*(1), 81–97. doi:10.16997/wpcc.277

Yiğit, S. (2021). Trump vs China. *The Trade Wars of the USA, China, and the EU: The Global Economy in the Age of Populism*, 67.

Yiğit, S. (2022). "Cicero and the Art of Rhetoric", 5. Media Literacy Forum, Social Sciences in the Age of Digital Transformation Proceedings Book, Eds: ADILBEKOVA, OZEL, TURKER, COSAN & SAHIN, Iksad Publications 25 December 2022, ISBN: 978-625-8254-04-4, pp. 557-574.

Yigit, S. (2022a). European Union's Strategy in the Far North: Arctic Rivalry. In Global Agenda in Social Sciences (vol. 9). IJOPEC Publication.

Yigit, S. (2022b). Digital Transformation: The Challenges Facing SMEs. In Digital Transformation and New Approaches in Trade, Economics, Finance and Banking. Rowman & Littlefield.

Yildirimcakar, E., & Han, Z. (2022). China's soft power strategy in the Middle East. *Israel Affairs*, *28*(2), 199–207. doi:10.1080/13537121.2022.2041309

Yimeng, Z. (2023). *Experts: Don't politicize work of Confucius Institutes.* https://www.chinadaily.com.cn/a/202312/09/WS6573a382a31040ac301a6f16.html

You, W. U. (2018). The Rise of China with Cultural Soft Power in the Age of Globalization. *Journal of Literature and Art Studies*, *8*(5). Advance online publication. doi:10.17265/2159-5836/2018.05.006

Yu, M. (2021). *Iran in China's Grand Strategy*. Stanford University Hoover Institution. https://www.hoover.org

Yu, G. (2013). *Rethinking Law and Development: The Chinese Experience*. Taylor and Francis. doi:10.4324/9780203583104

Yuhan, P. S., Zakharova, S., & Fedorova, G. (2022). China's strategy to strengthen soft power in the Asia-Pacific region: 016. *Dela Press Conference Series: Economics, Business and Management, 1*.

Yusheng Goa, H.E. (2008). *China, India and the United States Competition for Energy Resources*. The Emirates Center for Strategic Studies and Research (ECSSR).

Yu, X. (2008). *The Role of Soft Power in China's Foreign Strategy. In China International Studies: Guoji Wenti* (Vol. 11). Yanjiu.

Zakaria, F. (2009). *The Post American World*. Allen Lane.

Zarakol, A. (2022). *Before the West: The Rise and Fall of Eastern World Orders*. Cambridge University Press. doi:10.1017/9781108975377

Zhang, D. (2021). *China's Third White Paper on Foreign Aid—A Comparative Analysis* (2021/3; Brief). Department of Pacific Affairs, Australian National University.

Zhang, S. G. (1995). *Mao's Military Romanticism: China and the Korean War, 1950-1953*. University of Kansas.

Zhang, F. (2015). Confucian Foreign Policy Traditions in Chinese History. *The Chinese Journal of International Politics*, *8*(2), 197–218. doi:10.1093/cjip/pov004

Zhang, F., & Buzan, B. (2022). The Relevance of Deep Pluralism for China's Foreign Policy. *The Chinese Journal of International Politics*, *15*(3), 246–271. doi:10.1093/cjip/poac014

Zhang, L., & Wu, D. (2017). Media representations of China: A comparison of China daily and financial times in reporting on the belt and road initiative. *Critical Arts*, *31*(6), 29–43. doi:10.1080/02560046.2017.1408132

Zhang, L., & Zhengrong, H. (2017). Empire, Tianxia and Great Unity: A Historical Examination and Future Vision of China's International Communication. *Global Media and China*, *2*(2), 202. doi:10.1177/2059436417725213

Zhang, X., Wasserman, H., & Mano, W. (Eds.). (2016). *China's media and soft power in Africa: promotion and perceptions*. Springer.

Zhang, Y., & Wildemuth, B. M. (2005). Qualitative Analysis of Content by. *Human Brain Mapping*, *30*(7), 2197–2206. https://philpapers.org/rec/ZHAQAO

Zhao, G. (2016). Reinventing China: Imperial Qing Ideology and the Rise of Modern Chinese National Identity in the Early Twentieth Century. *Modern China*, *32*(1), 6. https://www.jstor.org/stable/20062627

Zhao, S. (2023). Culture and trade: Chinese practices and perspectives. *International Journal of Cultural Policy*, *29*(2), 135–151. doi:10.1080/10286632.2021.2009820

Zha, W. (2022). Great power rivalry and the agency of secondary states: A study based on China's relations with Southeast Asian countries. *International Relations of the Asia-Pacific*, *22*(1), 131–161. doi:10.1093/irap/lcaa018

Zheng, W. (2023). *Will culture be China's most important addition to Xi Jinping Thought?* China Politics. Retrieved from: https://www.scmp.com/news/china/politics/article/3237272/will-culture-be-chinas-most-important-addition-xi-jinping-thought

Zheng, C. (2016). China debates the non-interference principle. *The Chinese Journal of International Politics*, *9*(3), 349–374. doi:10.1093/cjip/pow010

Zheng, C., Zheng, J., & Zheng, H. (2012). *Yanping Erwang Yiji* [The collection of works of the two Yanping sovereigns]. Shanghai Cishu Chubanshe.

Zhenqiu, G. (2017, May 11). UN to help Belt and Road countries improve National Policy Capacity: Senior official. *Xinhua*. http://www.xinhuanet.com//english/2017-05/11/c_136272667.htm

Zhongguo Junshishi Bianxiezu. (2015). *The Compilation Team of 'China's Military History'. Zhongguolidai zhanzheng nianbiao* (Vol. I). II A Chronology of Wars in Chinese History.

Zhou, M. (2023, April 13). *Over 80% of Americans Critical of China's Global Role: Survey*. Nikkei Asia. https://asia.nikkei.com/Politics/International-relations/US-China-tensions/Over-80-of-Americans-critical-of-China-s-global-role-survey

Zhouxiang, L. (2020). *Introduction: Constructing and Negotiating Chineseness in the Age of Globalisation. In Chinese National Identity in the Age of Globalisation*. Palgrave Macmillan.

Zhu, Y. (2019). New National Initiatives of Modernizing Education in China. *Sage Journals*, 353-362.

Ziabari, K. (2021). Iran's New Asia-Focused Foreign Policy Is a Fantasy. *Foreign Policy*. https://foreignpolicy.com

Zreik, M. (2021). China and Europe in Africa: Competition or Cooperation? *Malaysian Journal of International Relations, 9*, 51-67. no1.3 doi:10.22452/ mjir.vol.9

Zreik, M. (2021c). China and Europe in Africa: Competition or Cooperation? *Malaysian Journal of International Relations, 9*(1), 51-67.

Zreik, M. (2023). USA–Myanmar relations: democratization and beyond. *Southeast Asia: A Multidisciplinary Journal, 23*(3), 162-174. doi:10.1108/SEAMJ-02-2023-0018

Zreik, M., Iqbal, B., & Rahman, M. N. (2022). Outward FDI: Determinants and Flows in Emerging Economies: Evidence from China. *China and WTO Review, 8*(2), 385-402. doi:10.14330/cwr.2022.8.2.07

Zreik, M. (2021a). Academic Exchange Programs between China and the Arab Region: A Means of Cultural Harmony or Indirect Chinese Influence? *Arab Studies Quarterly, 43*(2), 172–188. doi:10.13169/arabstudquar.43.2.0172

Zreik, M. (2021b). The Potential of a Sino-Lebanese Partnership through the Belt and Road Initiative (BRI). *Contemporary Arab Affairs, 14*(3), 125–145. doi:10.1525/caa.2021.14.3.125

Zreik, M. (2022). Chinese Soft Power: A Case Study of Panda Diplomacy. *Global Politics and Current Diplomacy, 10*(1), 19–37.

Zreik, M. (2022). The Chinese presence in the Arab region: Lebanon at the heart of the Belt and Road Initiative. *International Journal of Business and Systems Research*, *16*(5-6), 644–662. doi:10.1504/IJBSR.2022.125477

Zreik, M. (2023). Governance in Post-COVID-19 China: Challenges, Responses, and Opportunities. In C. Negrão, I. Maia, & J. Brito (Eds.), *Multidisciplinary Approaches to Organizational Governance During Health Crises* (pp. 214–235). IGI Global. doi:10.4018/978-1-7998-9213-7.ch011

Zreik, M. (2023). Navigating HRM Challenges in Post-Pandemic China: Multigenerational Workforce, Skill Gaps, and Emerging Strategies. In A. Even & B. Christiansen (Eds.), *Enhancing Employee Engagement and Productivity in the Post-Pandemic Multigenerational Workforce* (pp. 171–188). IGI Global. doi:10.4018/978-1-6684-9172-0.ch008

Zreik, M. (2023a). Digital Burnout in Second Language Acquisition: Exploring Challenges and Solutions in the Chinese Context. In A. Kurt (Ed.), *Perspectives on Digital Burnout in Second Language Acquisition* (pp. 169–194). IGI Global. doi:10.4018/978-1-6684-9246-8.ch008

Zreik, M. (2023a). Harnessing Islamic Entrepreneurship for the Belt and Road Initiative: Opportunities, Challenges, and Future Directions. In A. Rafiki, A. Pananjung, & M. Nasution (Eds.), *Strategies and Applications of Islamic Entrepreneurship* (pp. 119–135). IGI Global. doi:10.4018/978-1-6684-7519-5.ch008

Zreik, M. (2023a). Stirring Up Soft Power: The Role of Chinese Cuisine in China's Cultural Diplomacy. In K. Kankaew (Ed.), *Global Perspectives on Soft Power Management in Business* (pp. 292–306). IGI Global. doi:10.4018/979-8-3693-0250-7.ch015

Zreik, M. (2023a). The Sacred Paths: A Case Study of Pilgrimage Routes in Southeast Asia With a Special Focus on Thailand. In V. Martinho, J. Nunes, M. Pato, & L. Castilho (Eds.), *Experiences, Advantages, and Economic Dimensions of Pilgrimage Routes* (pp. 226–240). IGI Global. doi:10.4018/978-1-6684-9923-8.ch011

Zreik, M. (2023b). Managing Diversity: A Study of Multicultural Workplaces in Arab and Chinese Societies Post Pandemic. In R. Diab-Bahman & A. Al-Enzi (Eds.), *Global Citizenship and Its Impact on Multiculturalism in the Workplace* (pp. 250–273). IGI Global. doi:10.4018/978-1-6684-5436-7.ch011

Zreik, M. (2023b). Navigating the Dragon: China's Ascent as a Global Power Through Public Diplomacy. In S. Kavoğlu & E. Köksoy (Eds.), *Global Perspectives on the Emerging Trends in Public Diplomacy* (pp. 50–74). IGI Global. doi:10.4018/978-1-6684-9161-4.ch003

Zreik, M. (2023b). Sustainable and Smart Supply Chains in China: A Multidimensional Approach. In B. Bentalha, A. Hmioui, & L. Alla (Eds.), *Integrating Intelligence and Sustainability in Supply Chains* (pp. 179–197). IGI Global.

Zreik, M. (2023b). Uncovering the Methods of Operation and Funding of Armed Groups in the MENA Region: A Special Focus on Libya and Yemen. *Asian Journal of Political Science*, *1*(1), 100–119.

Zreik, M. (2024). Soft Power and China-Taiwan Competition for Influence in Latin America. In *China and Taiwan in Latin America and the Caribbean: History, Power Rivalry, and Regional Implications* (pp. 115–141). Springer Nature Switzerland. doi:10.1007/978-3-031-45166-9_6

Zreik, M. (2024a). Artificial Intelligence and the Future of Chinese Language Pedagogy: An In-Depth Analysis. In Z. Çetin Köroğlu & A. Çakır (Eds.), *Fostering Foreign Language Teaching and Learning Environments with Contemporary Technologies* (pp. 1–20). IGI Global. doi:10.4018/979-8-3693-0353-5.ch001

Zreik, M. (2024a). Bridging the Digital Divide: The Role of China-Africa Cooperation in the Evolution of Higher Education Amidst COVID-19 and Beyond. In P. Mashau & T. Farisani (Eds.), *Accessibility of Digital Higher Education in the Global South* (pp. 232–246). IGI Global. doi:10.4018/978-1-6684-9179-9.ch012

Zreik, M. (2024a). China's Energy Conundrum: Navigating Through Crises, Policy Responses, and Global Impact. In M. Ozel Ozcan (Ed.), *Analyzing Energy Crises and the Impact of Country Policies on the World* (pp. 139–159). IGI Global. doi:10.4018/979-8-3693-0440-2.ch008

Zreik, M. (2024a). Cultivating ILCs in China: A Pathway to Culturally Sustaining and Transformative Education. In S. Adams & A. Breidenstein (Eds.), *Exploring Meaningful and Sustainable Intentional Learning Communities for P-20 Educators* (pp. 120–140). IGI Global. doi:10.4018/978-1-6684-7270-5.ch006

Zreik, M. (2024a). Harnessing the Dragon: The Intersection of Chinese Leadership, Sustainability, and Confucian Philosophy in Modern Management. In K. Kankaew, S. Chaudhary, & S. Widtayakornbundit (Eds.), *Contemporary Management and Global Leadership for Sustainability* (pp. 72–94). IGI Global. doi:10.4018/979-8-3693-1273-5.ch005

Zreik, M. (2024a). Massive Chinese Investments in Latin America: What Is Taiwan's Diplomatic Fate in That Region? In C. R. Veney & S. O. Abidde (Eds.), *China and Taiwan in Latin America and the Caribbean. Studies of the Americas* (pp. 201–226). Palgrave Macmillan. doi:10.1007/978-3-031-45166-9_9

Zreik, M. (2024b). Assessing the Integration of Blockchain and Supply Chain Management: The Case of China. In M. Khan, N. Khan, & A. Ghouri (Eds.), *Achieving Secure and Transparent Supply Chains with Blockchain Technology* (pp. 38–56). IGI Global. doi:10.4018/979-8-3693-0482-2.ch003

Zreik, M. (2024b). Financial Misreporting and Corporate Governance Lapses: A Deep Dive Into the 1MDB Scandal in Malaysia. In R. Hasan (Ed.), *Cases on Uncovering Corporate Governance Challenges in Asian Markets* (pp. 178–201). IGI Global. doi:10.4018/978-1-6684-9867-5.ch009

Zreik, M. (2024b). Harnessing the Power of Digital Transformation and Sustainability: The Chinese Experience. In H. Nozari (Ed.), *Building Smart and Sustainable Businesses with Transformative Technologies* (pp. 247–266). IGI Global. doi:10.4018/979-8-3693-0210-1.ch014

Zreik, M., & Zhu, R. (2024b). Riding the Dragon: The Emergence and Impact of Over-the-Top Media in China. In N. Kalorth (Ed.), *Exploring the Impact of OTT Media on Global Societies* (pp. 75–90). IGI Global. doi:10.4018/979-8-3693-3526-0.ch005

About the Contributors

Mohamad Zreik, a Postdoctoral Fellow at Sun Yat-sen University, is a recognized scholar in International Relations, specializing in China's Arab-region foreign policy. His recent work in soft power diplomacy compares China's methods in the Middle East and East Asia. His extensive knowledge spans Middle Eastern Studies, China-Arab relations, East Asian and Asian Affairs, Eurasian geopolitics, and Political Economy, providing him a unique viewpoint in his field. Dr. Zreik is a proud recipient of a PhD from Central China Normal University (Wuhan). He's written numerous acclaimed papers, many focusing on China's Belt and Road Initiative and its Arab-region impact. His groundbreaking research has established him as a leading expert in his field. Presently, he furthers his research on China's soft power diplomacy tactics at Sun Yat-sen University. His significant contributions make him a crucial figure in understanding contemporary international relations.

* * *

Mohamad Al Mokdad holds a double PhD in International Relations and Geopolitics. He is an expert in international security, specialized in the MENA region.

Habib Al Badawi has been a scholar of Japanese studies since 2005. His M.A. thesis and Ph.D. dissertation covered the modern history of Japan (Meiji-tenno, Taisho-tenno, and Showa-tenno). Dr. Badawi is currently a professor at Lebanese University and a freelance researcher in international relations. In 2016, he became the coordinator of the "United States of America - History and Civilization" course at the History Department for the university's five branches. Dr. Badawi earned the "Academic Excellence Award in the Arab World" in the category of "Academic Personality of the Year 2018" for his role in introducing "Japanese studies" to the Arab world as a stand-alone academic field of "Human Sciences." https://www.ul.edu.lb/common/news.aspx?newsId=1683&lang=2.156b0163-ad95-47a8-a914-4e969cfe00c6

Myadagmaa Bayartsogt is a senior lecturer who is pursuing her Ph.D. in Management of Education at Central China Normal University.

Enkhzul Buyandlai received her Ph.D. in principles of education form Central China Normal University.

Mohor Chakraborty is Assistant Professor in Political Science at South Calcutta Girls' College (aff. To University of Calcutta), Kolkata, India. She studies International Relations & Area Studies, with particular focus on South Asia, Southeast Asia and the Indo-Pacific regions and Conflict Resolution &

Peace Studies. She has three co-authored books to her credit (two published by Routledge, London & New York, 2020 and 2023; and one by Knowledge World Publishers, New Delhi in 2018), in addition to articles in refereed journals and edited books by Routledge, Wiley, Palgrave Macmillan, and other Indian publishers like ICWA, Pentagon, Gyan and Readers' Service. Her contribution to the Special Report, ASEAN's Critical Assessment and Practical Reforms, has been published by Asian Vision Institute-Konrad Adenauer Stiftung in November 2023. She has presented papers at Indian and international conferences pertaining to her research areas, thus adding to her research interests and motivation, such as at SOAS (London), United States Naval Academy (Maryland), Vietnam Academy of Social Sciences (Hanoi), International Society of Military Sciences (Copenhagen) and Universities in Germany, Italy, South Korea (online) and the United States.

Moumita Chatterjee is currently associated with Aliah University, Kolkata as an Assistant Professor in the Department of Computer Science & Engineering. She did her M.Sc, MTech and PhD in CSE from Calcutta University.

Asma Emami is PhD student of International Relations at the University of Isfahan-Iran. Her dissertation is on Iranian Foreign Policy.

Matthieu Grandpierron is head of the Political Science department and associate professor at ICES. His research looks at the impact emotions, virile understanding of status and history have on foreign policy decision-making processes. His research has also focused on great power conflict and geo-politics as well as area studies concerning EU security including China, Russia. He lectures at Ecole Polytechnique and Shanghai University of Political Science and Law. He is co-conveners of BISA's 'International Relations as Social Sciences' working group. He was an invited Research Fellow at the University of Ottawa and at Columbia University.

Zhicang Huang is currently a postdoctoral fellow at Sun Yat-sen University and a researcher at the Institute for Area Studies. She is also a member of the Centre for the Study of Colonial America, Spain.

Asad Hyatt is a graduate student at COMSATS University, Islamabad, Pakistan.

Inayat Kalim is a tenured Associate Professor at COMSATS University, Islamabad, Pakistan.

Weam Karkout is an ambitious thinker, looking forward for a better future. Influenced by Law and continuing further more than masters degree in law. Up to date with different technological sectors and network and software development; already had a degree in MIS and continuing my masters degree. Moreover, I've finished two years in the Lebanese University in computer communication and network engineering.

Piyush Kumar has completed his MCA from Amity University Kolkata and currently working with Accenture, Kolkata.

Ariunaa Lkhagvajav holds a Ph.D. in Teaching Methods and Curriculum from Central China University.

Ndzalama C. Mathebula is an assistant lecturer at the University of Johannesburg, Department of Politics and International Relations. She lectures international law and her research interests range from international relations, political risk, African intellectualism, Energy security, and the political economy.

Minh Nguyen Anh is a social scientist in the Department of Sociology, School of Social Sciences and Humanities at Can Tho University. She has experience collaborating on internationally projects. Her research focusses on gender equality, equity and empowerment, sustainable development in the agriculture, migration under impacts changes, human rights (i.e., women, disability people, and children), and rural development. She has conducted international research projects in different fields in the Vietnamese Mekong Delta including gender and migration.

Phúc Nguyễn Hữu was born in 1993 and graduated from Hue University of Education, majoring in History Education. He is currently a Scientific Member of the History Association of Thua Thien Hue province. He has also published articles in prestigious scientific journals and proceedings of national and international conferences. Mr Nguyen Huu Phuc has participated in reporting at conferences related to Vietnamese and world history. His research interests are modern international relations regarding the foreign policies of the US, China, and India.

Md. Obaidullah presently serves as a lecturer at the Department of Development Studies, Daffodil International University, located in Dhaka-1216, Bangladesh. Prior to this position, he held roles as a researcher in various organizations across Bangladesh. His primary research interests lie within Asian Politics, Public Policy, and International Relations.

Ali Omidi is an Associate Professor of International Relations and Senior Lecturer of Public International Law at the Department of Political Science, University of Isfahan, Isfahan, Iran. He has an extensive background in academia and research, having published numerous articles, books, and analyses on topics such as Iranian foreign policy, International Law, and International Relations. Ali Omidi's expertise has been recognized through prestigious fellowships awarded to him by institutions like SIPRI in Stockholm and UNITAR in The Hague. He has actively participated in various international conferences and events, further contributing to the academic discourse in his field. Ali Omidi's areas of teaching and research encompass Middle East Politics, Iranian Foreign Policy, Comparative Foreign Policy, and International Law, with a particular emphasis on self-determination cases. Due to his expertise, he is often sought after for interviews and consultations on Iranian foreign policy by local, national, and international media outlets. For more detailed information regarding Ali Omidi's background, including his CV and list of publications, please refer to the available resources: and https://scholar.google.com/citations?hl=en&user=F70iCB0AAAAJ&view_op=list_works&sortby=pubdate.5b0f6796-59b1-4d39-8e0a-caed9d799445

Aileen Joy Adion Pactao is a political science instructor under the Social Science Department, College of Arts and Humanities at Palawan State University, Palawan, Philippines. She is particularly interested in conducting research works about foreign policy, political economy, security issues, local politics, and international relations.

Eric Pomès is associate professor in international law and head of the law faculty of ICES-Catholic Institute of Vendée (France). He is also a former officer in the French army and member of the Research Centre of French military Academy of Saint-Cyr and the Center for Studies and defense and security research (CERDES) of GEREDIC, from the University of Nice Sophia Antipolis. His research focuses on military robotics and the international law of the use of force applied to cyberspace. Eric Pomès also researches on the evolution of international law and practices following Chinese rise and Russian resurgence.

Tianzhe Qi is a lecturer of School of Journalism and Communication, Northwest Minzu University, research interest: intercultural communication, international communication.

Md. Raihan has earned both his BSS and MSS degrees in Public Administration from the University of Barishal, Bangladesh. Currently, he is engaged as an independent researcher, with a focus on international relations, climate policy, and governance.

Reema Roy is currently working as an Assistant Professor and Head, Department of Journalism and Mass Communication at Asutosh College under the University of Calcutta. She has more than 18 years of teaching and research experience.

Dhrubasish Sarkar is currently working with Supreme Knowledge Foundation, Mankundu, Hooghly, West Bengal as a Professor of Computer Science and Information Technology at Supreme Institute of Management and Technology. He has more than 26 years of experience in teaching, corporate training, academic administration, and institutional development. He holds PGCACS, MCA, M.Tech (IT) and PhD (CSE). He has more than 40 publications including reputed international journals, conference proceedings and book chapters to his credit. Currently he is serving as editorial review board member for few reputed international journals. His research interest includes social network analysis, recommendation system and data mining. He is a professional member of ACM and IEEE.

Hiep Tran Xuan, Associate Professor, PhD, is a member of the Faculty International Relations and a researcher at the Institute of Social Research, Dong A University, Danang City, Vietnam. General political and international relations issues, the Southeast Asian region, and Vietnam's international integration are among his main research interests. He has published many papers on above theme such as, India Quarterly: A Journal of International Affairs, International Journal of China Studies, Journal of Educational and Social Research, Contemporary Chinese Political Economy and Strategic Relations, Academic Journal of Interdisciplinary Studies, Journal of Asian Finance, Economics and Business, Cogent Arts and Humanities, Vestnik of Saint Petersburg University. Asian and African Studies, AUSTRAL: Brazilian Journal of Strategy and International Relations.

Sureyya Yigit is a professor of Politics and International Relations School of Politics and Diplomacy New Vision University Tbilisi, Georgia. He is an Editorial Board member of the IGI Book Series Conflict Management - 3 Volumes, an International Academic Board member of RIPEA - Journal of Argentine Foreign Policy Research, an Associate Editor on the Editorial Board of the International Journal of Green Business, a member of the Editorial Board of AcademCraft - Open access journal of education research and case studies. He is also the senior consultant to ZDS – Women's Democracy Network Public Fund, a non-governmental organisation based in Bishkek, Kyrgyz Republic, and a consultant to Aeropodium, a London-based business. Professor Yigit recently published a book entitled India-Mongolia Relations:

Beyond Greater Central Asia in 2023, and his newest book entitled Africa at Crossroads; Society, Security and Geopolitics will be published in April 2024. His research interests include Nonquantitative Research: A Modern Primer, Village Institutes: A Turkish Contribution to Modern Education and Development, Can the European Union's Global Gateway Challenge China's Belt and Road Initiative?, Miscalculated Cause-and-Effect Russian Invasion of Ukraine and Finland's Accession to NATO, and States, Sustainable Development and Multilateral Environmental Agreements, all published as book chapters in 2024.

Jiaxi Zhou is an Assistant Research Fellow at Institute of International Relations, Shanghai Academy of Social Sciences. He received his Ph.D. in international relations from Nanjing University in 2022. He has published several research articles in Chinese journals. His research interest includes China-US relations, especially the information warfare and public opinion, international communication and international relations, African studies with perspective of comparative politics.

Index

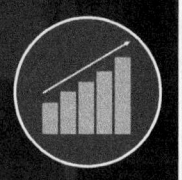

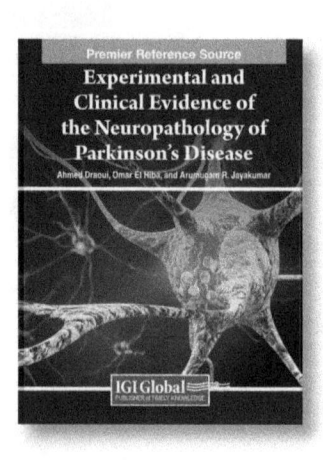

Printed in the USA
CPSIA information can be obtained
at www.ICGtesting.com
LVHW060546170924
791293LV00006B/607